MARTIN LUTHER'S
COMMENTARY ON SAINT PAUL'S EPISTLE
TO THE GALATIANS (1535)

MARTIN LUTHER'S
COMMENTARY ON SAINT PAUL'S EPISTLE
TO THE GALATIANS (1535)

LECTURE NOTES TRANSCRIBED
BY STUDENTS *&* PRESENTED
IN TODAY'S ENGLISH

TRANSLATED BY HAROLDO CAMACHO

Commentary on Saint Paul's Epistle to the Galatians (1535): Lecture Notes
Transcribed by Students & Presented in Today's English
© 2018 Haroldo S. Camacho

Published by:
1517 Publishing
PO Box 54032
Irvine, CA 92619-4032

978-1-945978-24-1 | | Commentary on Galatians (SC)
978-1-945978-25-8 | 1-945978-25-2 | Commentary on Galatians (HC)
978-1-945978-27-2 | 1-945978-27-9 | Commentary on Galatians (EB)

Printed in the United States of America

Cover design by Brenton Clarke Little.

Publisher's Cataloging-In-Publication Data
(Prepared by The Donohue Group, Inc.)

Names: Luther, Martin, 1483–1546. | Camacho, Haroldo S., translator.
Title: Martin Luther's Commentary on Saint Paul's epistle to the Galatians
    (1535) : lecture notes transcribed by students & presented in today's English /
    translated by Haroldo S. Camacho.
Other Titles: In epistolam S. Pauli ad Galatas commentarius (1535). English. |
    Commentary on Saint Paul's epistle to the Galatians (1535)
Description: Irvine, CA : 1517 / Fifteen-Seventeen Publishing, [2018] | "In
    Modern English (2017)." | Includes bibliographical references.
Identifiers: ISBN 9781945978241 (softcover) | ISBN 9781945978258 (hardcover)
    | ISBN 1945978252 (hardcover) | ISBN 9781945978272 (ebook) | ISBN
    1945978279 (ebook)
Subjects: LCSH: Bible. Galatians—Commentaries.
Classification: LCC BS2685 .L88 2018 (print) | LCC BS2685 (ebook) | DDC
    227/.407—dc23

From the translator
To Solarians and Non Solarians

It's impossible to list all in my family who, through the years, have formed a circle of support throughout the undertaking of this translation. I am also including my family in the Gospel. In particular, I thank my wife, Mercedes. Her patient persistence eventually led to my starting this endeavor. And there are several others: My dear friend in the Gospel Carlos Pérez, who was always willing to offer timely suggestions. My mother who at ninety-seven years old still provides encouragement. She instilled in me an insatiable curiosity for translation both as an art and a science. My father unknowingly sowed in me a love for the Gospel through his vibrant preaching of the cross. Then there are my children and grandchildren, whose growth in grace provided the initial vision for the translation of this commentary into modern English. Orlando Samuel; Kristina and Tyler, and Jaylee Jill, Alan and Esther, Noah and Violet; Leslie and Laura, Sophia, Alana and Ethan; this translation is specially dedicated to you. A special appreciation to 1517 The Legacy Project, who from the outset believed in this project and provided gentle but indispensable guidance in bringing it to fruition. Among them is my new friend and brother in the Gospel, Steve Byrnes. I must also thank the "Schwärmerei" of the law, among whom I walked for many years. Their relentless hammering on the law drove me to Christ, to Paul, to Luther, and to this commentary on Galatians. *Soli Deo gloria*.

VIRTUS MEA PER INFIRMITATEM PERFICITUR

This subtitle from the 1538 Latin edition quotes 2 Corinthians 12:9: "My power is made perfect in weakness." The 1535 edition (the first Latin edition) had this subtitle: "Ecce, His pofitus est in ruinam & in resurrectionem multorum in Israel, & in fignum cui contradicitur." The quote is from Luke 2:34: "Behold, this child is set for the fall and rising of many in Israel, and for a sign that is spoken against." The 1538 edition does not give a reason for the change in the title page Latin quote. Please see the appendix "About the Latin Text."

Content by Lecture, Date, and Galatians Texts

July 3–December 12, 1531

CONTENT

CONTENT

CONTENT

Foreword

Everyone thinks "Romans" when the Reformation—and Luther in particular—comes to mind. But actually, it was Galatians that really consolidated things for the German Reformer. Luther worked hard to understand Romans. His earliest lectures were not that far from what a usual Augustinian would have said in his day. Later, he came to see more light from Romans: especially what Paul meant by "the righteousness *from* God." But it was Paul's letter to the church in Galatia that really gave Luther new categories for understanding the Word of God. By 1531, when these lectures were given to seminarians in Wittenberg, Luther was "Luther": The indefatigable leader of the magisterial Reformation who stood guard at the golden door of the gospel.

As the Reformer says in the introduction, Satan does not have to labor to keep "fornicators, thieves, assassins, perjurers, heathens, blasphemers and unbelievers" in his service. "No, rather he leaves them alone in peace and quiet; he keeps them in his court, lavishes them with all kinds of pleasures and delights, and gives them whatever they wish." Instead, he focuses all of his energies on toppling the church from within: "to persecute Christ, who without any work of our own, is our righteousness." This was always the devil's aim: to bruise Christ's heel even as his own head was crushed by the triumphant Messiah (Gen 3:15–16). As Luther points out, the Anabaptists and Rome formed a common flank against this gospel of an imputed righteousness: the justification of the ungodly.

But, sadly, it is no different today. Nobody ever drifts toward the gospel. On the contrary, self-trust is the religion of the fallen heart. It is exhibited in every religion, every self-help program, and in the daily lives of all who work feverishly to climb ladders to make it to the top. Instead, God has come to the bottom, to a manger and to a cross. That is where we find God—not in the majesty of human works, but in the humility of the Suffering Servant. But we do not like this God. If we will have a god at all, he will be no more than a source of inner empowerment, or a facilitator of our personal growth.

Survey after survey indicates that even those who profess to be evangelicals—the name by which Luther's followers were called—have little knowledge of this doctrine. Worse, these studies show that evangelicals are as likely as non-Christians to say that human beings are basically good and that, with a little encouragement and instruction, they can gain sufficient righteousness to appear before God on the last day. Jesus has become for many a mascot for whatever political, social, moral or financial cause that people have in mind. He is there to help us achieve "our best life now" or to "become a better you." This meager—indeed, poisoned—diet leaves disillusionment and despair in its wake, as the majority raised in evangelical backgrounds are unchurched by their sophomore year in college.

It is definitely time for a new Reformation—the proclamation that our salvation comes to us from outside of ourselves, by the incarnation, life, death and resurrection of Christ our Savior. Pastors, parents, grandparents—everybody—needs to be roused from dogmatic or moralistic slumbers, for their sake and for the sake of the younger generations.

It is also time for a new translation of these epoch-changing lectures. Luther wrote for the masses, not for academic specialists. Few preachers in church history have combined integrity of doctrine—faithful to the biblical text—with an ability to explain it to a child. However, translations are often stilted and the Reformer's popular prose is sometimes lost. Just as Luther was confident that his students rendered his lectures faithfully, he would, I'm sure, be just as delighted at the appearance of this translation. Luther often expressed pride in speaking plain German and in this volume you have Luther in plain English.

So please, read this new translation. Tell a friend. Pass it along, dog-ears and underlined sentences and all, to anyone who is doubting whether Christ is enough.

Michael Horton
J. Gresham Machen Professor of Systematic Theology and
Apologetics, Westminster Seminary California, co-host of the
White Horse Inn, and author of *Core Christianity*.

Translator's Introduction[1]

At times, I seemed to be caught in a time warp. Often, as I repeated out loud the Latin text, its meaning came alive and I had to take my hands off the keyboard. The echo of the words and the power of their meaning transported me back in time and place. Suddenly, I was one of the seminarians seated at the Wittenberg seminary's lecture hall, enthralled, listening to Doctor Luther raising hell over the article of justification! Better yet, bringing sinners into the kingdom of God through this "principal article of the Christian faith." But then, my eyes would refocus back on the screen. There was the Latin text staring at me. However, the moment would be relived many times over as Luther painted word pictures of Paul in word-to-word conflict with the false apostles to the Galatians. Then, Luther would relate that same conflict to his own struggle with the papacy and the "fanatical spirits" of his day who dared taint the article of justification with the false righteousness of works!

In fact, this Commentary at times reads like a historical novel. Although you already know the outcome, you hope against hope that, somewhere near the end, Luther would tell of the final knock-down of the false doctrine of works among the Galatians and the victory of the righteousness of Christ alone through faith alone. One also hopes against hope that Luther's own word-and-pen conflict against the false righteousness of works would be declared the winner at ringside. But the end, as in a good novel, is left open. Frustrating, yes; but the challenge is given to the Christian confessional and evangelical churches today: "*justificatio est articulus stantis et cadentis ecclesiae*" ("justification is the article on which the church stands or falls"). Yet, it is not just to pick up the fight where Luther left off. True, that is one of his stated goals: "to incite all my brothers in Christ to counter the trickery and evil crookedness of Satan." However, his second goal is both pastoral and confessional: "I formulated my commentaries . . . only for those to whom the apostle wrote this epistle—the perturbed, afflicted, and tempted (the only ones who can understand these things), the Galatians who are despondent in their faith."

This commentary records a stand-alone historical event. From July 3 through December 12, 1531, Luther addressed 41 lectures on Galatians to his seminarians at the Wittenberg seminary. Three of his students, led by Georg Rörer, took

---

[1]   Please see appendix "Translator's Notes," for helpful tips as you read this translation. For instance, why are certain sections in *italics*?

careful notes in a Latin shorthand of their own invention.[2] Later, Luther edited and approved the entire text for publication.

Having worked for the California courts as a certified Spanish/English interpreter, I have transcribed and translated hundreds of hours of audio/video recordings from Spanish into English for numerous criminal and civil law hearings. The audio originals were full of pauses, stammering, incomplete sentences, repetitions, changes in tone and mood, among other nuances of speech. As I read the Latin text of Luther's lectures on Galatians, the transcript nature of the text was immediately apparent to me. Throughout my many years of experience working with judicial transcripts, I developed a unique appreciation for how they should be translated. The task is not to produce a well-written literary work of the interview from the recorded statements. The goal is to make the interview and narrative come alive to the reader. It is a formidable task, for one must put into the written word what was once said in spoken speech, with all of its various nuances of tone, speed, facial gestures, meaning of pauses, and other variables. The translator may neither change the register of the speaker's words, nor attempt to soften the harshness of the words, nor attempt to use synonyms that will add a nuance or meaning not intended by the speaker. The written word of the transcript must attempt to provide as accurate a record of the entirety of the event. If there are feeling-shaded or emotionally coded words, the translator must use words that will convey those feelings as well. The entire transcript must speak on behalf of the interlocutor's entire spoken record. That is what I have attempted to do with Luther's Commentary on Galatians. I began with the assumption that Rörer provided, as accurately as possible, a written transcript of Luther's lectures.[3] Then, I translated using Luther's own norm for translating: The original language is translated into the target language as if one were speaking or writing originally in the target language. Thus, I have attempted to have Luther speak "Today's English" throughout this translation.

However, my overriding motive in providing this twenty-first-century English version of Luther's Commentary on Galatians is to bring the readers into

---

[2] Rörer's notes are available for perusal in the Weimar Edition WA 40. Do not expect to see characters representing phonetic speech, as in modern shorthand. Rather, they are key Latin words (some are in German) which seem to represent entire sentences, words, or specific arguments.

[3] Inasmuch as I do make a case for the Latin text to be considered a transcript of Luther's lectures, I do beg the reader's leniency in not judging the translation as an actual modern transcript of a series of lectures. It is of course a request beyond the obvious, for which I beg for further clemency, since my assumption is only based on "circumstantial evidence" (which nonetheless carries probative value in a court of law). I completely understand that there is no "direct evidence" for my assumption and no way to test my hypothesis except for the circumstantial evidence presented throughout the translation.

that lecture hall in Wittenberg. Hopefully, once there, you, too, will be held spell-bound by hearing Luther's masterful and persuasive exposition on the article of justification, the principal teaching of the Christian faith. You will hear Luther, the Reformer: uncouth, brash, unyielding, persuasive, and uncompromising. I think my translation of the commentary reads best if read out loud. In fact, if there is a sentence or a paragraph that seems too complex, reread it out loud and its meaning will come alive.

Ergo, I invite you to take a seat beside me in that great lecture hall at Wittenberg. Doctor Luther, that great man of God, is stepping up to the podium. Let's listen as he calls today's church to attention and bring us back to the article of justification.

Haroldo S. Camacho, PhD (Claremont School of Theology, 1991)
Certified Court Interpreter, Judicial Council of California
Cathedral City, CA
November 16, 2017

Soli Deo gloria

Martin Luther's Preface to the Epistle to the Galatians (1535)[1]

I can hardly believe I was so wordy[2] when I gave these public lectures on Paul's Epistle to the Galatians, except for this little exhibit.[3] However, I feel that all these thoughts[4] are mine. The brothers[5] so diligently sealed them into this written work that I must confess all of them are mine, if not more, as they appear in this publication attributed to me, for my heart is governed by only this one fundamental truth—namely, faith in Christ.[6] He is from whom, by whom, and toward whom all my theological studies revolve, continually, day and night. And even so, I realize that I cannot even come anywhere near the height, width, and depth of such great and priceless wisdom; you will only see some rickety and tattered signposts strewn along the way.

I am ashamed that my comments, so barren and cold, are placed next to the apostle's, a chosen vessel of God. But shame on my shame, I must be forceful and bold. There is an infinite and horribly profane abomination that has always raged against God's church. To this day, it continues to rage without letup against the solid rock. That rock is the unique place of our justification.[7] With all confidence, we can say that we are justified not by our own works (which are less than we are) but through relief provided outside of us.[8] That relief is none other than God's only Son. He has redeemed us from sin, death, and the devil and has given to us the gift of eternal life.

Satan certainly rammed against this rock in paradise when he persuaded our first parents that they could be like God through their own wisdom and power. They turned their backs on faith in God, who had given them life and the promise to

---

[1]   In 1516, while Luther was still an Augustinian monk, he gave his first lecture on Galatians. The 1531 lectures manifest a much deeper understanding of Paul's teaching on justification.

[2]   *verbosum fuisse me.*

[3]   *Libellus exhibet.*

[4]   *cogitationes.*

[5]   Luther is referring to his students Georg Rörer, Veit Dietrich, and Caspar Cruciger. Led by Rörer, they took *ver vatim* notes of Luther's lectures in a Latin shorthand of their own invention.

[6]   *Nam in corde meo iste unus regnat articulus, scilicet, fides Christi.*

[7]   *justificationis locum.*

[8]   *alienum auxilium.*

prolong it. Soon after, this liar and assassin (but always true to himself) incited Cain to turn against his brother and take his life. There was no other reason but that his pious brother, by faith, offered a more excellent sacrifice. But Cain offered his own works, without faith, and did not please God. Thereafter followed the most intolerable persecution of this same faith, from Satan through the children of Cain, until God was moved to purify the earth by means of the flood and defend Noah, a preacher of righteousness. Notwithstanding Satan extended his seed in Ham, Noah's third son, and in others far too many to mention. After these things, the whole world went insane against this faith. It created an infinite number of idols and strange religions. As a result (as Paul said), each one went his own way, trusting in his own works. Some hoped to pacify and please a certain god, others a goddess, others many gods, and yet others many goddesses—that is, without the relief brought by Christ[9]—and through their own works, they hoped to redeem themselves from all their ills and sins, as the deeds and writings of all nations abundantly testify.

However, these works are nothing when compared to the works God performed for His people, Israel, or the synagogue. They had been blessed over all the rest, not only with the sure promise given to the fathers and by the law given by God Himself through His angels, but also through the constant witness of the words, miracles, and examples of the prophets. Yet even among them, Satan (the essence of self-righteousness in all its fury) prevailed to the point where they killed all the prophets and even Christ Himself, the Son of God, their promised Messiah. There was no other reason for their death except their doctrine—that men and women are accepted and received into God's favor by grace alone and not by their own righteousness. However, this is the entire sum of the devil's doctrine—and the world's—from the beginning: "We will not give the appearance of doing something wrong, but in all that we do, God must consent to it, and all His prophets as well, for if they refuse, they will perish. Abel will die, and Cain will live. This is our law." And so it is.

Nevertheless, things have not gone much better in the church of the Gentiles. Rather, things have gone from bad to worse. By comparison, the fury of the synagogue has only seemed like child's play, for they (as Paul put it) "did not know their anointed and thus crucified the Lord of glory." True, the church of the Gentiles has accepted Christ and confessed that He is the Son of God and that He has been made our righteousness. That is how the church publicly sings, reads, and teaches. Yet those who make this confession are the same ones who get rid of it. Although they allege they are the church, they persecute and rage against those who preach in word and deed nothing else but Christ. The persecutors are obliged to confess Him, but they are only pretending, for today, by taking over the name of Christ, they have consolidated their power. If they could retain their power without His name, they would openly declare just what they think of Him in their hearts. They esteem Him less than the Jews, who at least take Him as a *thola*—in effect, a thief

---

[9]   *alieno auxilio Christi.*

paying what he deserves, hanging from a cross. But these other men take Him as a fable and think that He is a god invented by the Gentiles, which is obvious in Rome, in the papal curia, and almost throughout all Italy.

Thus since Christ becomes a mockery among His Christians (because Christians they will be called) and because Cain continually kills Abel and Satan's abomination now reigns supreme, it is necessary that we diligently pay attention to this pivotal doctrine[10] and turn it around against Satan, no matter whether we are rude or eloquent, educated or uncouth, for if everyone else should keep quiet, this massive boulder should be proclaimed by the rocks and stones themselves.

That is why I am more than willing to hereby fulfill my duty and allow the publication of this commentary, so full of words, to incite all my brothers in Christ to counter the trickery and evil crookedness of Satan. In these last days, he has greatly raged against this plain knowledge of Christ—so much so that even today, those who seemed to be possessed by furious demons without respite seem to be possessed by worse devils and rage with greater fury than the ones before! All this is an immensely powerful argument that the enemy of truth and life knows that the Day of Judgment is near, which is the day of his destruction, but for us, it is the day of our redemption and the end of his tyranny over us. His anger is not without reason because his members and powers are under assault, as when a thief or an adulterer, when morning comes and his wickedness is exposed, is caught red-handed.

For who would have imagined (without considering the abominations of the Pope) so many monsters bursting into the world at once as we see today just with the Anabaptists? Certainly, through them Satan is huffing and puffing, as it were, bringing in the latest outbreak of his kingdom through horrible disturbances. He deploys them everywhere with such fury as if through them he would destroy the entire world not only with uprisings but also with countless sects he pretends to swallow in one gulp all of Christ together with His church. He does not lord it over those who have other beliefs and live in evil—namely, fornicators, thieves, assassins, perjurers, heathens, blasphemers, and unbelievers. No, rather he leaves them alone in peace and quiet; he keeps them in his court, lavishes them with all kinds of pleasures and delights, and gives them whatever they wish. This is what he did soon after the inception of the church; he not only left alone all the idolatries and false world religions, granting them peace without disturbance, but also sustained them powerfully. Everywhere he harassed the church and the faith of Christ. Even to this day, he is committed just to this one task (which has always been his alone), to persecute Christ, who without any work of our own, is our righteousness.[11] But this was written about him: "You will bruise His heel" (Genesis 3:15).

---

[10] *articulum.* The article or pivotal doctrine of justification by faith in Christ. "Articulus" in Latin means "pivotal point or fulcrum."

[11] *Christum qui est justitia nostra sine operibus nostris.*

However, I don't publish my thoughts on this epistle against these people but for our own people, who will either thank me for my labor or forgive my weakness and foolishness. Certainly, I have no illusions about getting a favorable review from the unbelievers, but rather these thoughts will rattle them and their god. I formulated my commentaries (with great effort) only for those to whom the apostle wrote this epistle—the perturbed, afflicted, and tempted (the only ones who can understand these things), the Galatians who are despondent in their faith. Those who cannot identify with them might as well listen to the Papists, the monks, the Anabaptists, and all other teachers of great wisdom and religion, who with all their hearts scorn what we do and say without taking on the task to understand it.

Because even today the Papists and the Anabaptists conspire against God's church in this world on this point (even though they disguise their words), claiming and affirming that God's work depends on the virtue of the individual. Such is the teaching of the Anabaptists—baptism is worthless unless the person is able to believe. This is their starting principle (or so they call it) and from there it follows that all God's works are worthless unless a person is good. If baptism, which is a work of God, is no longer a work of God when a person is evil, then it follows that marriage,[12] the courts,[13] the ministry,[14] which are works of God, are no longer works of God because people are evil. The wicked have the sun, the moon, the earth, water, air, and everything that is subject to man, but since they are not godly, then it follows that the sun is not the sun nor the moon, the earth, water, and air what they are. The Anabaptists themselves had bodies and souls before being rebaptized, but since they were not godly, their bodies and souls were not really real! By the same token, their parents were not truly married—for so they claim—because they had not been rebaptized. Therefore, the Anabaptists themselves, all of them, are illegitimate and their parents were adulterers and fornicators. Nonetheless, they inherit properties from their parents, even though they themselves admit they were illegitimate and without rights of inheritance. Who can't catch on that the Anabaptists are not possessed by demons but rather demons themselves possessed by worse demons?

In the same way, the Papists until today insist on works that assume the virtue of the human being, contrary to grace, and thus (at least in word) vigorously come to the rescue of their brothers, the Anabaptists. These foxes are all tied together at the tail, even though their heads point in opposite directions. To all appearances, they pretend to be great enemies, but on the inside, they all think, teach, and defend the same things against Christ, who is our only righteousness. Therefore, everyone who is able, let him hang on to this one principle; and the rest who've already shipwrecked, let the wind and the waves wash them away,

---

[12] *Coniugium.*
[13] *Magistratus.*
[14] *Servitus.*

until they come back to ship or can swim to shore. But we will have more to say about the Anabaptists later, if the Lord Jesus Christ allows it. Amen.

The previous appeared in the first edition (1535). In the second (1538) and subsequent editions, the following paragraphs were added after "swim to shore."

The sum and the end of this dispute is that it's not worth it to wait for calm or for the dispute to end as long as Christ and Belial are not in agreement. "One generation goes, and another generation comes." If one heresy dies, not much later another one springs up, for the devil neither slumbers nor sleeps. I, myself (although I am nothing), already have twenty years in the ministry of Christ. I attest to have been pestered by over twenty sects, some of which have already perished. Others (like parts of a dismembered insect) are still twitching.

However, Satan, the god of all sectarians, daily stirs up new sects, and the last one is the one that I would have least suspected or expected. I speak of those who teach that the Ten Commandments should be banned from the church and that people should not fear the law but should be kindly exhorted by the preaching of the grace of Christ, to fulfill what was said by the prophet Hosea, "Let no man bring a charge, neither let any man accuse," and by the prophet Micah, "Don't prophesy!" (Micah 2:6), as if we were ignoramuses or had never been instructed that the afflicted and brokenhearted spirit must be comforted by Christ. But the hard-hearted pharaohs, to whom the grace of Christ is preached in vain, must feel the fear of the law. And they see themselves pressured to invent new revelations of the wrath of God against the wicked and ungodly, as if the law were something other than a revelation of the wrath of God. Such is the blindness and presumption of these folk who dictate their own αὐτοκατακριτῶν (sentence of condemnation).

Therefore, the ministers of the word of God are compelled to be fully convinced (if they are to be counted among the faithful and wise in the day of Christ) that it was not just a whim when Paul spoke the word nor that he prophesied as if it were a matter of small consequence when he said, "For there also must be factions among you, that those who are approved may be revealed among you." Yes, and I say so, let the minister of Christ know that as long as he teaches Christ with purity, there will never be a lack of perverse spirits, yes and even of our own and among our own, who will commit themselves to harass the church of Christ. And let him be comforted with the thought that "there is no peace between Christ and Belial, and between the Seed of the serpent and the seed of the woman." Yes, let him rejoice in the anguish caused by these sects and the constant succession of seditious spirits, for our glory is this, "the testimony of our conscience," that we may be found firm and fighting on behalf of the Seed of the woman against the seed of the serpent. Let it bite our heel all it wants. On our part, we will not cease to crush its head through Christ, the first one to crush it, may He be blessed forever and ever. Amen.

Let's Hear It for Self-Righteousness and Its Fifty Select Virtues Resulting from Works! As Penned by the Apostle Paul to the Galatians[1]

Chapter 1

1. It calls people away from grace.
2. It embraces another gospel.
3. It perturbs the minds of the faithful.
4. It flips the Gospel of Christ upside down.
5. It is damned.
6. It seeks human approval.
7. It pleases men.
8. It does not serve Christ.
9. It is from men and does not proceed from revelation.
10. The most outstanding righteousness of the law is nothing.
11. It devastates God's church.

---

[1] *Quinquaginta praeconia et virtutes justitiae propriae ex operibus quaesitae, auctore Apostolo Paulo ad Galatas.* The facetious nature of the title is of course obvious. Luther paints the following picture in the listener's mind. The town crier (the *praeconium*) rides into the plaza. He blows a horn calling people to attention. A crowd surrounds him. He unscrolls a parchment and proclaims this *praeconia*, which may be loosely but accurately translated into today's English as "Let's hear it for" self-righteousness, and so on. Luther was a master of sarcasm, and you will see numerous examples throughout this Commentary. If you are not careful you may be fooled by them. He seems to have spoken them with a straight face, but very tongue in cheek. These *praeconia* first appeared in the 1538 edition, with the annotation at the end: *Mense Augusto, Anni M.D.XXXVIII.* Given their stated satirical title and nature, it is a question of interest, what was the original intended purpose of these questions, and why did they appear in the 1538 edition rather than in the 1535? Were these questions originally prepared as a kind of syllabus for the Galatians lectures, but not printed until 1538? The question of course remains unanswered, but I have included the 50 questions here for their historical value and of course relevance to the Galatians text and subject matter.

Chapter 2

12. It is impossible for its works to justify.
13. It makes sinners out of those who are righteous in Christ.
14. It makes Christ a minister of sin.
15. It rebuilds sin previously destroyed.
16. It produces transgressors.
17. It rejects God's grace.
18. "Christ died in vain" is its conclusion.

Chapter 3

19. It produces idiots like the Galatians.
20. It casts a spell.
21. It does not obey the truth.
22. It crucifies Christ.
23. It insists that the Spirit is received by works.
24. It drives away the Spirit and ends up in the flesh.
25. It is under a curse.
26. It replaces God's covenant with its own.
27. It makes sin abound.
28. It locks you up under sin.
29. It serves rudimentary principles.

Chapter 4

30. It nullifies the preaching of the Gospel.
31. It undoes all good things done before.
32. It is born from the slave woman and lives in slavery.
33. Its followers are sent away with the slave woman and lose their inheritance.
34. It makes Christ of no avail.
35. It makes debtors to the entire Law.

Chapter 5

36. Nothing of Christ is left in its followers.
37. It knocks people away from grace.
38. It gets in the way of producing good fruit.
39. Its persuasiveness does not come from God.
40. It is leaven of corruption.
41. Everything it teaches is under judgment.

42. It leads people to bite and devour one another.
43. It is listed among the works of the flesh.

Chapter 6

44. It makes you think you are something when you are nothing.
45. It boasts in others rather than in God.
46. From the flesh, it seeks to please the flesh.
47. It hates being persecuted for the cross.
48. It does not even keep the law.
49. It glories in the teachings of the flesh.
50. It profits nothing, and neither are its works worth anything at all.

Martin Luther's Introduction

I have once again taken up the task, in the name of the Lord, to expound on this Epistle of Saint Paul to the Galatians, not because I want to teach new things, or such as I have never heard before, since by the grace of Christ, Paul had already made them fully known. But (as I warned you often) we must fear as the greatest and nearest danger that the devil will shake us off from the purity of this doctrine and faith and bring once again on the church the doctrine of works and human traditions. That is why it is of the utmost importance that this doctrine be proclaimed always in public as well as put into practice, in its reading as well as by its hearers. And although it may never be fully known, never learned with exact precision, even so, let us be ever mindful that our adversary the devil, who is continually stalking, wanting to devour us, hasn't died yet. It is also true that our flesh and our old man still live. Further, we are confounded and oppressed by all types of temptations from all sides; therefore, this doctrine can never be taught, urged, or repeated often enough. If this doctrine should be lost, then also the doctrine of truth, life, and salvation will have been lost and disappeared. If this doctrine should flourish, then everything good will also flourish: religion, true service to God, glory to God, and the correct understanding of all that is necessary for a Christian in all aspects of his life. Therefore, let us stay busy and not get lazy; we will begin at the conclusion, according to the proverb of the son of Sirach: "When a man thinks he is done, he has barely just begun"[1] (Sirach 18:7).

---

[1] Translator's own rendition of the Sirach text.

Saint Paul's Argument in the Epistle to the Galatians

By Dr. Martin Luther

First, we are compelled to state the main argument of this epistle. What did Paul intend to do with this epistle?

His purpose is the following.

Saint Paul proposes to establish the doctrine of faith, grace, the forgiveness of sin, or Christian righteousness so that we may perfectly understand the difference between Christian righteousness and all other types of righteousness. There is a political or civil righteousness. Emperors, the princes of this world, philosophers, and attorneys must deal with this one. There is also a righteousness of social behavior, according to human traditions. Parents as well as tutors may teach this type of righteousness without fear, since they do not attribute to these types of actions any satisfaction for sin to please God or to merit grace. They teach that these types of behaviors are only necessary to correct bad habits and certain observances regarding social life. Parallel to these there is another righteousness, called the righteousness of the law, or the Ten Commandments, taught by Moses. According to the doctrine of faith, we also teach this one.

However, there is another above all others—namely, "the righteousness of faith, or Christian righteousness." We must diligently tell this one apart from the others. This last one opposes the others a great deal. The first types of righteousness flow from the laws of the emperors, the traditions of the Pope, and the commandments of God. They also consist in our good works and can be done by us through our sheer natural effort (as the Papists say) or even as a gift from God. All these types of righteousness are gifts of God, as well as other good things that we enjoy.

But this more excellent righteousness that I say is of faith is this: God through Christ, apart from any work of our own, puts it freely to our account.[1] It is not political or behavioral.[2] It is not the righteousness of the law of God.[3] It does not concern our works but exists on a different level. It is a simple passive righteousness, since all the previous ones are active. To obtain this one, we don't do any work at all, nor do we offer anything to God. Rather, we only receive and allow Another to work in our behalf, none other than God Himself. Therefore,

---

[1] *nobis absque operibus imputat.*

[2] *ceremonialis.*

[3] *nec legis divinae justitia.*

it has seemed right to me to call this passive righteousness, the righteousness of faith, or Christian righteousness.

This righteousness is a hidden mystery, the world is not aware of it. What's more, Christians themselves don't understand it fully, and they can hardly take hold of it in their temptations. Therefore, it is necessary to teach it and practice it continually, without any letup. And whoever can't understand it or is unable to hold on to this righteousness will be hounded by the constant fears of his conscience and will certainly be defeated. There is no other comfort as firm and sure for the conscience as is offered by this passive righteousness.

But human nature is so pathetic and miserable[4] that when our conscience panics with fear or death is near, we can't see anything but our works, our merit, and the law. The law uncovers our sins, and in an instant, our memory recalls our old life of sin. It is then when the sinner moans in great anguish of spirit and thinks to himself, "How I regret it! I have lived such a crazy life! If God would only have mercy on me and give me the chance to live a little longer, then I would change my life!" Human reason can't stop from fixating on the active righteousness[5] or in the development of its own righteousness![6] Neither can it lift its gaze to look upon the passive righteousness, or Christian righteousness, but seeks refuge in its own active righteousness, so deeply ingrained is this evil within us.

On the other hand, Satan takes advantage of the weakness of our nature and certainly increases and exacerbates this worrisome brooding within us. It should not come as a shock to us that the poor conscience is then stressed out, horrified, and befuddled, for it is impossible for the human mind by itself to conceive any comfort or to look only upon grace when it feels the horror of sin; neither can it constantly reject all the arguments in favor of its own works. This is way beyond human strength and ability, as well as over and above what God's law can give. It is true that with regards to all in this world the law is of utmost excellence, but it cannot quiet down a mortified conscience. Rather, it increases its crushing sorrow, dragging it to desperation. "That sin might be shown to be sin, and through the commandment might become sinful beyond measure" (Romans 7).

There is no medication for the mortified and perturbed conscience when it is under condemnation of eternal death. It must take hold of the promise of grace offered in Christ Jesus[7]—that is, unless it takes hold of this "passive righteousness, or Christian righteousness." If it's able to grasp it, then the conscience will find rest. It will trustingly say, "I don't seek this active righteousness or the righteousness of works, even though I know I must also have it and fulfill it. But even if I had it and fulfilled it without a doubt, even so, I could not trust it; neither

---

[4] *imbecillitas et miseria.*

[5] *spectro justitiae activae.*

[6] *propriae evolvere.*

[7] *promissionem gratiae oblatae in Christo.*

could I bring it as a defense against God's judgment. Therefore, I will strip myself of all active righteousness, mine as well as that of God's law, and embrace only the passive righteousness, the righteousness of grace, based on God's mercy and His forgiveness of sins. In summary, I find rest only on this righteousness that is the righteousness of Christ and the Holy Spirit; *we don't produce it, but we submit to bear it; it is not found within us, but we receive it as a gift from God the Father through Jesus Christ.*"[8]

A parched land cannot through its efforts bring on itself the joyful satisfaction of a long torrential rain. Neither can it produce rain through its own splendor and strength. Instead, it receives the rain as a gift from God. In the same way, God gives us this heavenly righteousness without our merits or our works. So just as much as the earth is unable to bring on itself rain showers to make its fruit grow, we are unable through our works and strength to bring on ourselves this heavenly and eternal righteousness. We would never obtain it except that God freely imputes[9] it to us; we acquire it only as a gift from God. Words fail us to describe its worth! Therefore, the totality of a Christian's wisdom is to be unacquainted with the law, ignore all the works of active righteousness, especially when the conscience struggles against God's judgments. However, the highest wisdom and knowledge of those who do not belong to God's people is to fathom the depths of the law and urge its works and active righteousness.

However, it's something quite odd and unheard of in the world to teach Christians to want nothing to do with the law and to live like that before God as if the law didn't exist. But you cannot be saved unless you want nothing to do with the law and are confidently persuaded in your heart that God's law and wrath no longer exist but only His grace and mercy through the gift of Christ. That is because through the law comes only the knowledge of sin (Romans 3:20). Still, on the other hand, the world should be pressured to produce works and to keep the law, as if there were no promise or grace. This is because of the stubborn, proud, and hard-hearted. Their eyes should see nothing but the law so that they will be scared to death and humbled. Because the law is given to frighten them to death and knock them down and to harass the old man. Therefore, the word of grace and the word of wrath should be rightly handled according to the apostle Paul (2 Timothy 2).

Here is where someone wise and faithful is needed to accurately handle the word of God, someone who is capable of restraining and keeping the law within its limits. Those who teach that people are justified before God by the keeping of the law trespass the limits of the law; they confuse the two types of righteousness, the active and the passive. They mistakenly end up trying to come up with

---

8   *quam non facimus, se patimur, non habemus, sed accipimus, donate eam nobis Deo Patre per Iesum Christum.*

9   *gratuitam imputare,* literally "freely, or graciously, imputes it to us, credits it to our account."

logical explanations because they do not teach them correctly. But on the other hand, those who lay out the law and works to the old man and the promise and forgiveness of sins as well as God's mercy to the new man represent the word correctly. The flesh or the old man should be tied to the law and works, and the spirit or the new man should be joined to the promise of God and His mercy. Therefore, when I see someone who has been bruised and battered by the law, more than enough bullied by sin and thirsts for assurance, then it is time to change his focus from the law and active righteousness and let him see a full display of the Gospel, the Christian, and passive righteousness. This one excludes Moses and his law and offers him the promise made in Christ, who came for sinners and the distressed. Man is able to get back up on his feet with this, and the good hope is born within him, since he is no longer under law but under grace (Romans 6:14). But how is it that he is no longer under law? According to the new man, it is because the law no longer has anything to do with him. That is because the law reaches its boundary when it meets up with Christ; as Paul would say later, "the law takes us to Christ" (Galatians 3:24).[10] Once He came, He put an end to Moses and his law, circumcision, sacrifices, Sabbaths, yes, and even all the prophets.

This is where our theology is rooted: we teach how to spot the difference between these two types of righteousness, the active and the passive. The result is that socially acceptable behavior and faith, works and grace, politics and theology should not be mixed up or confused one with the other. Both are necessary, but both should be restrained within their own proper boundaries. Christian righteousness is binding on the new man, but the righteousness of the law is binding on the old man who has been born of flesh and blood. On this old man, as you would with an old mule, you should put such a heavy load that it will wear him out, and he should not enjoy the freedom of the spirit given by grace. First he needs to put on the new man, through faith in Christ, although he will always come up short in this life. Only then will he be able to enjoy the kingdom and the priceless gift of grace.

I say all this so that no one will end up thinking that we reject or ban good works, as the followers of the Pope allege. They slander us with lies, but they understand neither what they are saying nor what we teach. The only thing they know is the righteousness of the law. Yet they consider themselves capable of judging a teaching that goes beyond the law, outside of what the carnal person can judge. Therefore, it's totally predictable that they will feel offended because they cannot fix their gaze above the law. For them, everything that is above the law is greatly offensive.

We'd rather imagine, putting it simply, two worlds, one belonging to the heavens and the other belonging to the earth. In each, we place one of these two types

---

[10] This is an example of Luther paraphrasing Scripture. Here he paraphrases the Vulgate on Galatians 3:24: "lex usque ad Christum." The Vulgate reads, "itaque lex pedagogus noster fuit in Christo."

of righteousness, far apart from each other. The righteousness of the law belongs to the earth, and it has to do with earthly matters, and on its behalf, we do good works. The earth cannot produce any fruit unless it is watered from above, and it yields fruit due to what comes from above (*for the earth cannot decree over the sky, nor renew it, nor govern over it; on the contrary, it is the sky that judges, renews, and brings fruit to the earth so that it will fulfill God's decree*). It is the same with the righteousness of the law: even after having done many things, we've accomplished nothing. But when we think we have fulfilled the law, we haven't fulfilled it at all, unless first, without any merit or work of our own, we are justified by this Christian righteousness,[11] which has nothing to do with the righteousness of the law, that earthly and active righteousness. However, we do not have in us this heavenly and passive righteousness, as it is often called. Rather, we receive it from above. We don't work toward it; instead, it already has worked on our behalf, and we cling to it by faith. That is why we are able to soar way above all law and works. Therefore, just as we carry the image of the earthly Adam (as Paul said), "let us carry the image of the heavenly, which is the new man in a new world" (1 Corinthians 15:49).[12] Here, there is no law, no sin, no remorse, no guilty conscience, no death, but rather perfect joy, righteousness, grace, peace, salvation, and glory.

What then? So don't we have to do anything? Don't we have to work at all to obtain this righteousness? My answer is simple: Absolutely not, for this is perfect righteousness: "To do nothing, to hear nothing, to know nothing about the law, or works." We are to know only this: that Christ has gone to the Father, so we cannot see Him and that He is seated in heavenly places at the right hand of His Father, not as a judge, but rather as God on our behalf. He has been made for us wisdom, righteousness, holiness, and redemption. In brief, He is our High Priest interceding for us and, by grace, reigns over us and in us. In this heavenly righteousness, there is no place for sin, since there is no law, and where there is no law, there cannot be any transgression.

Here, then, there is no place at all for sin, nor a horror-struck conscience, nor fear, nor despair. That is why John said (1 John 5:18), "Any one born of God does not sin." But if there is any fear at all, or a conscience full of remorse, it is a sign that this righteousness has departed, that grace has gone into hiding, and that Christ has been obscured and has gone from our sight. But where Christ truly shines, inevitably there will be full and perfect joy in the Lord. The conscience will be at peace. With total conviction, it will think like this: "Even though according to the law I am a sinner, and I am under the condemnation of the law, I don't punish myself and I don't die because Christ lives, who is my righteousness as well as my

---

[11] *justificati simus per justitiam christianam.*

[12] *novus homo in novo mundo.* Staying with Paul's (and thus Luther's) juxtaposing of the earthly Adam with the one man (Romans 5), the *novus homo* is indeed the "one man Jesus Christ." Luther would not be pointing to us but to Christ (trans.).

eternal life." In that righteousness and life, I don't have sin, I have no fear, and my conscience has neither remorse nor anxiety about death. With regards to this life and its righteousness and as a son of Adam, I am sure that I am a sinner. With this earthly righteousness, the law would accuse me; death would reign over me and at last would swallow me. But I have another righteousness and life over and above this life, which is Christ the Son of God, who knows neither sin nor death but only righteousness and eternal life, and because of Him, this my body, having been dead and in the dust of the earth, will rise again, freed from the slavery of the law and sin, and will be sanctified together with the spirit.

So these two live side by side while we are here. The flesh is accused, it struggles against temptations, oppressed by despair and grief, hurt by this active righteousness of the law, but the spirit reigns, it rejoices, and it is saved through this passive and Christian righteousness. The spirit knows that it has a Lord in the heavens, at the right hand of His Father, who has abolished the law, sin, death and has crushed all evil under His feet—He has taken them captive and He Himself has triumphed over them (Colossians 2:15).

Therefore, in this epistle, Paul takes on the task of diligently teaching, comforting, and perfecting us in the knowledge of this most excellent Christian righteousness, for if we should lose the article of justification,[13] then all true Christian doctrine will be lost. And everyone in the world who does not hold on to this doctrine is either a Jew, a Muslim, a follower of the Pope, or a heretic. Because between the "righteousness of the law" and "Christian righteousness," there is no halfway point. Whoever strays from this "Christian righteousness" inevitably falls into the "righteousness of the law." In short, once he loses Christ, he must by default fall into the confidence of his own works.

We can see this today in the fanatical spirits and authors of sects.[14] They hardly teach anything about grace. And when they do, they don't teach anything reliable about the righteousness of grace.[15] True, they have taken the words out of our mouth and our writings, and that is all they talk about and write. But when it comes to the topic itself, they cannot state it or preach it clearly, since they can't understand it or assimilate it, because they only hang on to the righteousness of the law. Therefore, they are and keep on practicing as attorneys for the law, lacking every faculty that could make them soar above that active righteousness. Therefore, they stay the same as they were under the Pope only that now they invent for themselves new names and new works. But even so, they don't change the subject; it is always the same, just as the Muslims do different works than the followers of the Pope, and the latter different from the Jews, etc. But even though some will perform the most splendid works, so

---

[13] *articulo justificationis.* The pivotal doctrine of justification.

[14] The reader should remember that italics indicate content left out in the first and subsequent English translations.

[15] *justitiam gratiae.*

grandiose and difficult that no one else could do them, the substance is still the same. The only difference is in the quality. To put it another way, the works only differ in appearances and names but not in the deeds, since after all, they are only works, and those who perform them are not, nor ever will be, Christians. Rather, they do them for the salary, no matter if they are called Jews, Muslims, or followers of the Pope, etc.

That is why we vigorously repeat this teaching of "faith" or "Christian righteousness," so we may constantly take refuge in it and that we may clearly see that it exists far apart from the "active righteousness of the law." Otherwise, we could never uphold the true doctrine, since the church came into existence from this doctrine alone.[16] *If not, we immediately turn it into dung.*[17] We become nothing but experts of church law, keepers of ceremonies, lawyers for the law, and Papists. In consequence, Christ becomes so obscured that no one in the church is properly taught and established. Therefore, if we are going to be teachers and leaders, it is binding on us to be extremely careful in these matters and be able to draw a clear line between the righteousness of the law and the righteousness of Christ. And this distinction is easy to come out of the mouth but very difficult to use and know it personally. When death approaches, or in other moments when the conscience suffers beyond pain, these two types of righteousness approach each other more than you would expect or want. Therefore, I urge upon you, especially those who will instruct and guide in matters of the conscience, as well as everyone else. You need to exercise all the time reading and studying, meditating on the word, and in prayer so that when temptation comes you will be able to teach and comfort your own consciences as well as those of others. Take people from the law over to grace and from the active righteousness and its works to the passive righteousness and have them receive it. In conclusion, lead them from Moses to Christ.

When we suffer affliction and when our conscience is deeply troubled, the devil sets out, law in hand, to frighten us and put to our account our guilt and sin, our horrible past, the wrath and the judgment of God, hell, and eternal death. This way, he intends to throw us into desperation, make us his slaves, and snatch us away from Christ. Moreover, he aims at us those texts in the Gospel where Christ Himself requires good works from us and with plain words threatens to condemn those who won't do them. If we cannot now judge between these two types of righteousness, if by faith, we cannot cling to Christ seated at the right hand of God, who intercedes before the Father on our behalf, miserable sinners though we may be, then we are under the law and not under grace. Christ ceases to be our Savior, and we turn Him into a Legislator so that there is no longer any salvation but rather the assurance of desperation and eternal death, unless we proceed to repentance.

Then let us diligently learn to judge between these two types of righteousness so that we will know up to which point we must obey the law. We have said

---

[16] *sola doctrina fit et consistit ecclesia.*
[17] *sed fimus statim.* Both Middleton and Watson omitted this phrase.

this before, the law in a Christian must not overstep its limits but have control only over the flesh, which is subject to it and remains under it. As long as this is so, the law remains within its limits. But if it presumes to slither up to your conscience wanting to command you from there, you'd better play the part of an astute expert in logic and wisely pull them apart. Don't give over to the law more than what is proper. Rather, say to the law, "Law, you pretend to climb up to the kingdom of my conscience and from there govern and rebuke it of sin; rip the joy out of my heart, which is mine by faith in Christ; and throw me over the ditch into desperation so that I will lose all hope, bringing me to ruin until I perish. But you are overstepping your role. Stay within your boundaries, apply your power over my flesh, but don't even touch my conscience. I have been baptized, and through the Gospel, I am called to share in righteousness and eternal life, in the kingdom of Christ, where my conscience finds its rest, where there is no law, but only the complete forgiveness of sins, peace, calm, joy, health, and eternal life. Don't annoy me anymore with these matters, for I will not tolerate such an oppressive despot and cruel taskmaster to rule over my conscience, for it is the throne and temple of Christ, the Son of God. He is the King of righteousness and peace and my sweetest Savior and Mediator. He will keep my conscience with joy and peace in the sound doctrine of the Gospel and in the knowledge of this passive righteousness."

When this righteousness reigns in my heart, I come down from heaven as the rain makes the earth to sprout. In other words, I enter another kingdom, and I do "good works," according to whatever the occasion may require. If I am a minister of the word, I preach, I bring comfort to the depressed in heart, and I administer the Sacraments. If I am the head of a household, I govern my home and my family, bringing up my children in the knowledge and the fear of the Lord. If I am a judge, a mandate that is given me from above, I practice it with diligence. If I am a servant, I faithfully carry out the business of my lord. In summary, everyone who is confidently persuaded that Christ is his righteousness not only carries on the functions of his vocation with joy and happiness but also, in love, submits to the judges, their laws, even though they may be severe, sharp, and cruel. If the need arises, Christians will carry all types of burdens and face all kinds of dangers in this life because they know this is the will of God and that this obedience pleases Him.

LECTURE 2: Saturday, July 4

As far as the argument of this epistle, Paul exhorts the Galatians because the false teachers had obscured this righteousness of faith among them. At the same time, Paul opposes them, even as he defends and upholds his authority and office.

COMMENTARY ON SAINT PAUL'S EPISTLE TO THE GALATIANS (1535)[1]

By Martin Luther, DD

Translator/Editor: Haroldo S. Camacho[2] (2017)

Galatians 1

LECTURE 2 - CONTINUED.

VERSE 1. Paul, an apostle—sent not from men nor by a man, but by Jesus Christ and God the Father, who raised him from the dead.[1]

Now that we have brought out and shown the argument of the epistle to the Galatians, before going forward to its subject matter, it would be well to point out the occasion that moved Paul to write it. He had sown the pure doctrine of the Gospel[2] and the righteousness of faith among the Galatians. But as soon as he left, certain false teachers moved in. Working behind the scenes, they uprooted everything his teachings had sown among the Galatians. The devil can do nothing else but furiously discredit this doctrine with all strength and stealth. Neither can he rest but attacks without letup through the viciousness of tyrants and certain crooked fanatics. He will use very wicked people camouflaged with the garb of great religious devotion to squash the gospel as someone would try to extinguish sparks with an ax. For this one single reason—our delivery of the doctrine of the Gospel in all its purity—today we face the hostility of the devil. He unites the world and the heretics by stirring up bitter hatred against us.

However, the Gospel is a unique doctrine—higher than the wisdom, righteousness, and religions of the world by far—for it teaches nothing but the free forgiveness of sins through Christ.[3] It leaves everything else in its place and endorses all good things created by God. But the world prefers these works of creation over their Creator. To make matters worse, through them, it eagerly tries to take away its own sin, shake itself free from death, and merit eternal life. The Gospel damns all that.[4] In turn, the world can't tolerate anyone damning and taking away the things it cherishes the most.

Therefore, the world takes note and indicts the Gospel. It alleges that the Gospel is a subversive, erroneous doctrine. It claims that the Gospel overthrows

---

[1]   Unless otherwise noted, all quotes are from the Revised Standard Version.

[2]   I have capitalized *Gospel* due to its divine origin and to differentiate it from any other gospel.

[3]   *Remissionem peccatorum gratuitam per Christum.*

[4]   *hoc damnat evangelium.* Luther did not mince words; do not wince. This is the way his students heard him. There is a lot more coming.

official authority, countries, dominions, kingdoms, and empires, thus it sins against God as well as Caesar.[5] It charges that because of the Gospel, laws are abolished, good manners are corrupted, and people feel free to do whatever they please. Therefore, the world uses the pretext of having a holy zeal and rendering great service to God (or so it would seem) to persecute this doctrine, detest its teachers and professors, and attempt to destroy it as if it were the worst plague over all the earth.

What's more, through the teaching of the Gospel, the devil is crushed and his kingdom overthrown. He has taken hold of the law, sin, and death and uses them as if they were the strongest and most invincible tyrants, and through them he holds the entire world subject to himself. But the Gospel snatches away his prisoners and transports them from the kingdom of darkness and slavery to the kingdom of light and liberty. Do you think the devil is going to put up with that? Is there any chance that the father of lies is not going to take advantage of all his strength and craftiness to obscure, corrupt, and altogether uproot this doctrine of salvation and eternal life? Indeed, the apostle Paul weeps over this situation in this and all the other epistles, for in his time, the devil had already exposed himself to the apostles as still very much alive.

In the same way, today we protest and grieve that Satan has caused greater damage to our Gospel through his ministers, the fanatical spirits, than through all the persecutions of the tyrants, kings, princes, and bishops. Today, they are still the same persecutors. If in Wittenberg we hadn't attentively and carefully watched and labored in planting this doctrine of faith, we would not have remained to this day of one accord. However, even before we came, the sects were already there. But because we have not moved away from this doctrine, and we constantly promote it, we remain in the greatest unity and peace. Others who neglect it or think they have some other more sublime doctrine rush to various harmful errors and sects (these are endless) and will come to ruin.[6]

We think it well to stress here that the Gospel is a unique teaching, since it condemns all types of righteousness and preaches only the righteousness of Christ.[7] All who take shelter in it receive a conscience at rest and everything that is good. Even so, the world hates it and viciously persecutes it.

As I said before, what moved the apostle Paul to write this epistle was that as soon as he left, false teachers destroyed among the Galatians what he had built with great and exacting labor. But these false apostles were from the

---

[5] *Deum et Caesarem,* "God and the emperor."

[6] The reader is reminded that when the text appears in *italics,* it represents the sections that were omitted from the first English translation in 1575. Those translators did not want to offend Zwingli's followers. In those passages, Luther not only rejects Zwingli's doctrine of the Sacraments; more importantly, in those passages Luther categorically rejects all human contribution to justification, including one's love to God and neighbor since love is the fulfillment of the law.

[7] *solam Christi praedicet.* In the tradition of the earliest English translations, I have kept "righteousness."

circumcision and the sect of the Pharisees. These were men held in high regard and authority. They boasted among the people that they were that holy and chosen lineage of the Jews. They said they were Israelites, of the seed of Abraham, and that they had all the promises of the fathers. Finally, they said that they were ministers of Christ and scholars taught by the apostles. They claimed to have fellowshipped with them, that they had seen their miracles, and perhaps that they themselves had worked some signs and miracles (since Christ himself testifies in Matthew 7 that the wicked also perform miracles). Further, these false teachers, using all the craftiness they could imagine, disfigured the authority of Paul, saying, "Why do you value him so much? Why do you respect him so much? Among those who were converted to Christ, he was the very last. But we are disciples of the apostles, and we fellowshipped together with them. We saw Christ performing miracles and heard Him preach. Paul came after us, and he is not quite up to our level. It isn't possible for us to be in error, since we are His holy people, the ministers of Christ, and we have received the Holy Spirit. Further, we are many, but Paul is just one, and he is all by himself. He's not even acquainted with the apostles, neither has he seen Christ. And he even persecuted the church of Christ for quite some time. Do you think God is going to allow so many churches to be deceived just so that Paul can be proven right?"

When characters with such authority arrive at some country or city, they soon win over the admiration of the people. Under the guise of this piety and religiosity, they bamboozle not only the simple minded but also the well-educated. They're able to even fool those who seemed to be well established in the faith. These characters boast (that's how the false apostles did it) that they were in the bloodline of the patriarchs, the ministers of Christ, the scholars of the apostles, etc. Even the Pope today, although he has no biblical authority to support him, keeps on promoting this argument against us: "The church, the church. Do you think God is so offended that because of a few heretics like Luther's dissidents, He's going to reject His entire church? Would you think that God would allow His church to remain in error for so many centuries?" And with this he obstinately keeps his footing: "The church will never be conquered!" Just as today this argument convinces many, so in the time of the apostle Paul, these false apostles, appealing to their boasts, singing their own praises, blinded the eyes of the Galatians. The upshot was that Paul lost his authority among them, and people began to question his doctrine.

Against all this boastful insolence of the false apostles, Paul with great persistence and boldness[8] establishes his authority as an apostle. He defends his ministry and highly recommends his own vocation. There is no text at all where there

---

[8] Luther inserted the Greek παρρησία as he lectured in Latin. This is the word for "boldness" used in Acts 4:13: "Now when they saw the boldness of Peter and John." It literally means "freely speaking one's convictions."

is the smallest hint that Paul yielded his own position, not even before the apostles themselves.

And to knock them off their pedestal of pharisaic pride and shamelessness, he brings up the incident at Antioch, where he, himself, confronted Peter face-to-face. Further, without considering the scandal that would have resulted, according to the text, he had the courage to accuse and rebuke Peter himself, the chief of the apostles, the one who had seen Christ and had been one of His closest followers. Paul said, "I am an apostle and of such sort that I did not overlook the faults of the other apostles. What's more, fear did not stop me from rebuking the pillar himself of all the other apostles." In this manner, Paul does nothing more in the first two chapters than to establish his vocation, his office, and his Gospel. He affirms that he did not receive his Gospel from men but from a revelation of Jesus Christ. And if he or even an angel from heaven would bring a different Gospel from what he had already preached, then he should be accursed.

The Certainty of the Calling

But what could Paul be getting at with this kind of boasting? I answer that what seems so natural has the following purpose: that every minister of the word of God should be sure of his calling. Whoever has this certainty may glory before God and man without his conscience bothering him, since he preaches the Gospel as he has been called and sent. In the same way, an ambassador of a king glories and boasts that he comes not as an ordinary citizen but as a royal ambassador. Due to the dignity of his title as royal ambassador, he receives the highest honor; he is given the greatest respect. If he came as an ordinary citizen, he would not receive any of these honors. Therefore, let every preacher of the Gospel be sure that his calling is from God. It is beneficial, according to Paul's example, to magnify his calling and to obtain the proper trust and authority among the people. Accordingly, it isn't bragging but a certain type of dignifying, since you are glorying not in yourself but in the king who has sent you, whose glory you yourself honor and exalt. *And when in the king's name, he announces the will of the king, he doesn't say, "We plead with you," but says, "We command you," "Our will is that you do this or that," etc. As an ordinary citizen, he says, "We plead with you" etc.*

Likewise, when Paul so highly recommends his ministry, it is not to seek his own praises. He exalts his ministry due to a holy and necessary pride. In Romans 11:13[9], he says, "Inasmuch then as I am the apostle to the Gentiles, I take pride in my ministry."[10] That is to say, "I want you to receive me, not as Paul of Tarsus, but as Paul the apostle or ambassador of Jesus Christ." He puts it that way because it was

---

[9] There seems to be a typo in the Latin text, for it cites the reference as Romans 1:13. The reference has been corrected in the text above.

[10] English MOUNCE version.

necessary to claim his authority so that when people listened to him, they would listen more closely and pay more attention, since they not only hear Paul but in Paul listen to Christ Himself and God the Father, who sends him with His message. In the same manner that men should religiously honor the divine authority and majesty, they should also listen to God's messengers who bring His word and message.

This is no ordinary matter, since Paul boasts and glories in his calling as if he would spurn all others. Anyone who according to the ways of the world values himself and despises all others, claiming that he's above all others, only shows himself off as a fool and offends others. But Paul's way of boasting is necessary, since it's not about Paul's glory but God's, to whom we offer sacrifices of thanks and praise. It is through this kind of boasting that God's name, grace, and mercy are made known to the world. And it is with this that he begins his epistle.

VERSE 1. Paul, an apostle—sent not from men nor by a man.

Here, at the beginning, Paul points to the false teachers.[11] They boasted to be disciples of the apostles and sent by them. Yet they despised Paul, saying that he was neither a scholar of the apostles nor sent by any one of them to preach the Gospel. They claimed that Paul by his own hand had given himself that calling. Paul defends his calling, saying, "To you my calling does not seem to be of divine origin. But those who have suddenly appeared among you have been sent by men or by some man. If they have arrived on their own, it's because they have not been called. Otherwise, others have sent them. But my calling is neither of men nor of man. My calling is superior to any calling after the apostles, for it is 'of Jesus Christ and of God the Father.'"

Where he says "of men," he talks about those who call themselves and then push their way in when neither God nor man has called or sent them. They run by themselves and speak for themselves. It is the same today. There are certain fanatical minds that lie in wait at the corners looking where to pour their venom. They come to certain public places or to congregations where the Gospel has already been established. Of these, I say that they have been sent by men. But when he says "of man," I understand that to say that someone receives a divine calling, but it reaches him through human means. God calls them in both ways, using some human means or a call directly from Him. Today God calls them to the ministry of His word, not directly from Himself, but using other means—that is, through other human beings. But the apostles were called directly by Christ Himself, just as the prophets of old were called by God Himself.

The apostles thereafter called their disciples, as Paul called Timothy, Titus, etc. They then called the next in line, the bishops (as in Titus 1), and the bishops called their successors. This calling has continued until our days and will continue until the

---

[11] *falsos . . . doctores.*

end of the world and through the intervening times, although these callings come through human mediators, since they are from men but are divine.

So when a prince, magistrate, or I call any one man, he has his calling through a man. This has been the way callings generally have been made around the globe of the earth since the time of the apostles. They should not be changed but expanded due to the fanatics because they scorn the callings. They boast of a new and improved[12] calling; they say it's the Spirit that moves them to teach. But they are liars and impostors, for it is not a good spirit that calls them but an evil spirit. I am not allowed to leave the place fallen to me by lot, to go to another city to which I was not called as a minister of the word. I cannot preach there (although as a doctor [in theology] I could go preach throughout the entire papacy, if they would put up with me[13]). [I should not go], even if I heard they were souls seduced and damned through the teaching of falsehoods, and I could deliver them from error and condemnation through my sound doctrine. Rather, I should submit the entire matter to God, who in His due time will find the occasion to legitimately call ministers and those devoted to the word, for He is the Lord of the harvest and will send workers to gather in the fruit. Our part is to pray (Matthew 9:38).

Therefore, we should not slip into another's harvest, for the devil incites his ministers to do just that. So they run without being called and profess great zeal and pain that people are being so pitifully seduced. They pretend to teach them the truth and snatch them from the devil's snare. Therefore, even if someone with a pious fervor and good intentions attempts through his own sound doctrine to rescue them from error, they are nonetheless giving a bad example. They only give an excuse for teachers of the devil to work their way in. Thereafter, Satan occupies the bishop's chair, causing maximum damage.

But when I am called by a prince, or by another authority,[14] then I can go with certainty and assurance boasting against the devil and the enemies of the Gospel that I am called by God's mandate given through the voice of man. In that instance, God's calling is delivered through the prince; and those are true divine callings. We are also called by divine authority, not directly by Christ as were the apostles, but "by man."

This passage with respect to the certainty of the calling is indispensable due to those pestilent and satanic spirits. They go beside and beyond the way of the Spirit and the heavenly calling; with their particular spin,[15] they deceive many, but yet they are nothing but brazen liars. Because we are certain of our calling, we can glory with John the Baptist: "The word of God has come over me." Therefore, when I teach the word, baptize, and administer the Sacraments, I accomplish what I was ordered and called to do, for the voice of the Lord has in fact been over me. It has not been done

---

12   *alimam meliorem.*

13   *modo me tolerent.*

14   *alius magistratus.*

15   *et hoc fuco,* literally "and with this coloring."

in a corner, as the fanatics boast, but through the voice of a man who is legitimately authorized. But if one or two individuals would ask me to preach, I should not pay attention to such a private calling, since I will be opening a window of opportunity for Satan's ministers to follow that example and bring harm, as I said before. But when those who already bear a public office plead with me, then I should meet the need.

Therefore, when Paul says, "Not by men, nor by man," he belittles the false apostles. It's as if he had said, "No matter how much those vipers brag, they have nothing else to brag about than they were sent by men. In other words, they sent themselves or went sent by other men, wanting to say others sent them. I don't pay attention to those things, and neither should you. With respect to me, I am not sent by men or by man. I am sent without a middleman; I am sent by Jesus Christ Himself. My calling is on par with all the other apostles, since with all certainty, I am an apostle." Therefore, Paul effectively confronts the issue of the apostolic calling. In another text, he places the apostleship in a category all its own, apart from all others, as in 1 Corinthians 12:28 and in Ephesians 4:11, where he says, "And God has placed in the church first of all apostles, second prophets, and third teachers." Here, he places apostles in the first place so that they may duly be called apostles, "sent directly by God Himself" without any middle entity in common. That's how Matthias was called only by God. When the apostles designated two, they didn't dare to choose between them. They drew lots and prayed for God to show His appointment. Since the chosen one would be an apostle, it was necessary to receive the calling from God. That is how Paul was called to be the apostle to the Gentiles. That is why the apostles are also called saints, since they are sure of their calling and doctrine, having remained faithful to their office. None were rejected, only Judas, since the apostolic calling is sacred.

This was Paul's first offensive against the false apostles, who ran where no one had sent them. The calling must not be despised. Sound doctrine and word are not enough. It is also imperative to be sure of the calling. If anyone comes in without this confidence, he comes in only to kill and destroy. God never prospers the work of those who have not been called. Although they teach some good and useful things, they don't edify. It is the same with today's fanatics. They have the words of faith in their mouths but yield no fruit at all. Their main objective is to attract people to their false and perverse opinions. Those who have a sure and holy calling will go through many and great conflicts. Those who hold a sound and pure doctrine must remain faithful to their proper calling. They will have to face infinite and unending conflicts from the devil and the fury of the world. In view of this, is there any hope for those who are not sure of their calling and their doctrine is impure?

Therefore, those of us who are in the ministry of the word are comforted in that we have a holy and heavenly calling. And those of us who have been duly called triumph against all the gates of hell. On the other hand, it is a horrendous experience when the conscience says, "What is this you've done without a proper calling?" It is then when a mental horror shakes those who haven't been called. They wish that they had never heard the word they now teach. Due to this disobedience, all their works turn into evil, so much so that even their greatest works and labor become their greatest sins.

We then see how good and necessary it is to boast in the glory of our ministry. Some time back when I was still a brand-new theologian with a doctorate, I thought that Paul was not too wise in glorying so often of his calling throughout his epistles. But I did not understand his purpose. I didn't even know that there was such a thing as the ministry of the word. I didn't know anything about the doctrine of faith and a sure conscience. Neither the seminaries nor the churches taught anything with any certainty, but everything was full of the subtle sophisticated arguments of the scholars. Therefore, no one could understand the dignity and the power of this holy and spiritual boasting based on a proper and certain calling, for this calling first renders honor to the glory of God and then to the uplifting of our office, then above all to our salvation and the salvation of others. Due to our boasting, we don't seek the esteem of the world or the praises of men or money or pleasures or favors of the world. Ours is a divine calling, and the work is of God. It is necessary for the people to trust our calling so that they will know that our words are the word of God. Therefore, with pride, we boast and glory in our ministry. It is not a vain conceit but a pride in every way holy against the devil and the world but one we carry with humility before God.

VERSE 1. By God the Father, who raised him from the dead.

Paul is so fired up with zeal that he can't wait to get to the topic. Right away, in the title itself, he breaks through and states what's in his heart. His intention in this epistle is to expound about the righteousness that comes through faith and defend it. Putting it another way, his purpose is to knock the law off its pedestal and the righteousness that comes through works. He is full of thoughts. Therefore, out of the abundance of his heart, his mouth speaks overflowing with the marvelous and abounding excellence of the wisdom and knowledge of Christ.

This flame, this great fire that burns in his heart, cannot be quenched. It won't allow him to keep his mouth shut. Therefore, it's not enough for him to say that he is "an apostle sent by Jesus Christ." He must also add, "By God the Father, who raised Him from the dead."

However, it would seem unnecessary to add the words "and by God the Father." But as I said before, Paul speaks out of the abundance of his heart, his mind burns with the desire to show, from the beginning of his epistle, the unsearchable riches of Christ and to preach the righteousness of God, which carries the name of "the resurrection from the dead." The living Christ speaks through Paul and moves him to express himself in those terms. Therefore, there is a reason for him to add that he is an apostle by "God the Father who has resurrected Jesus Christ from the dead." It's as if he had said, "I have to struggle with Satan and with those vipers, the instruments of Satan who pretend to strip away from me of the righteousness of Christ, who was raised from the dead by God the Father. We are justified through Him, and He will also raise us from the dead at the last day, to eternal life. But those who commit themselves to overthrow the righteousness of Christ resist the Father and the Son as well as the work of both."

Thus Paul from the outset breaks through with his epistle's plea. That is why (as I said), he immediately fixes his sight on the resurrection of Christ, who was raised from the dead as our righteousness (Romans 4:25).[16] With His resurrection, He has overcome the law, sin, death, hell, and all evil. The victory of Christ is the victory that overcomes the law, sin, our flesh, the world, the devil, death, hell, and every evil. And this victory He has given to us. Then when these tyrants, who are our enemies, accuse and terrorize us, they can't push us into desperation, neither can they condemn us. Why not? Because God the Father has raised Christ from the dead who "is our righteousness and our victory." Therefore, "thanks be to God who has given us the victory through our Lord Jesus Christ." Amen.

Note how precise and to the point Paul's declaration is. He does not say, "Because God who made the heavens and the earth, the Lord of the angels, who commanded Abraham to leave his land, who sent Moses to pharaoh the king, who led Israel out of Egypt." Neither did Paul boast of the God of his fathers (like the false apostles) as Creator and Sustainer, who maintains all things and works marvels among His people. It's that Paul had something else in his heart. It was nothing but "the righteousness of Christ." Therefore, he doesn't mince words to say, "I am an apostle, not by men, nor by man, but by Jesus Christ and God the Father who raised Him from the dead." You can see then that Paul is guided with great zeal of spirit in this matter. He sets out to establish and sustain this teaching against all the kingdom of hell, the power and wisdom of the world, and against the devil and his apostles.

VERSE 2. And all the brothers who are with me.

This should suffice to stop the mouths of those false apostles. All Paul's arguments are designed to promote and magnify his ministry while discrediting theirs. It's as if he had said, "It should suffice that I, through a divine calling, should be sent as an apostle of Jesus Christ and God the Father who resurrected Him from the dead. But so that I will not be alone, I add to make it abundantly clear (which is

---

[16] *qui propter nostram justitiam resurrexit.* Luther adds this footnote: *Victoria Christi Nostra est,* "Christ's victory is ours." The Biblical reference is probably another typo or Luther's slip of the tongue misciting the reference and taken down by Rörer and then left uncorrected as part of the record. However, I have corrected the reference here in the text. Originally, the Latin text had Romans 4:15.

more than what's necessary) all the brothers, who are not apostles, but who are with me in the trenches. They write this epistle together with me. They testify that my doctrine is true and pious. Therefore, we are sure that Christ is with us and that He teaches and speaks among us and in our church. The false apostles, if they are anything, are only sent by men or by man. But I am sent by God the Father and by Jesus Christ, who is our resurrection and our life (John 11:25). My other brothers are sent by God, although through man—that is, by me. Thus don't let anyone say that I am bragging standing all by myself against so many. I have my brothers with me. They all share in the same thought, as faithful witnesses, who think, write, and teach as I do."

VERSE 2. To the churches in Galatia.

Paul had preached the Gospel throughout all Galatia. Although the entire region had not converted to Christ, he had established many churches. But the ministers of Satan, the false apostles, invaded them stealthily. In the same way, the Anabaptist fanatics don't go to places where the adversaries of the Gospel are in charge. They go to places where there are already Christians and men of good faith who love the Gospel. Even in areas where tyrants and persecutors of the Gospel govern, they creep into the homes of the believers. Under false pretenses, they pour out their venom deceiving many. Why won't they rather go to the cities, countries, and dominions of the followers of the Pope? Why won't they rather profess and uphold their doctrine in the presence of wicked princes, bishops, and scholars of the universities as we have done with God's help? These delicate martyrs don't take any risks at all. Their only security measure is to go to places where the Gospel has already found port. There they live in peace and quiet. Similarly, the false apostles didn't risk their lives going to Jerusalem before Caiaphas, nor to Rome before the emperor, nor to any place where no one had yet preached, as did Paul and the other apostles. They came to Galatia, which had already been won to Christ by the work of Paul's journeys. They also went to Asia, Corinth, and other places where there were already people of good faith, who professed the name of Christ, who didn't bother anyone but suffered everything in silence. There the enemies of the cross lived in great security, without suffering any persecution.

By this, we can learn what's in store for every pious teacher. On top of the persecution they suffer from an evil and ungrateful world and the great effort to establish new churches, they must suffer even more. Having taught the truth for a long time, soon the truth is overthrown by the fanatical spirits, who then take control and lord it over them. This causes great pain to those faithful teachers, more so than the persecution of the tyrants. Thus there should not be a minister of the Gospel who cannot take joy in such scorn and who would not want to take that suffering. But if there is one, let him hand his ministry over to another. Today we also suffer the same in our own flesh and blood. From the outside, we are condemned without mercy and harassed by dictators. From the inside, we are denounced by those who at one time we restored to the freedom of the Gospel as well as by false brothers. But our comfort and glory is that in having been called by God, we have the promise of eternal life. We set our eyes in that reward that eye has not seen, nor ear heard, nor entered into the heart of man. "And when the Chief Shepherd appears, you will receive the crown of glory that will never fade away,"[17] and while we are here in this world, He will not allow us to starve to death.

Here, Jerome poses a question: "Why does Paul call churches those that were not churches?" Jerome goes on that "Paul was writing to the churches that had become perverted and turned their backs to Christ, to grace, following after Moses and the law." But I respond that Paul calls them the churches of Galatia using the principle that a part represents the whole, something common in the Scriptures, for he writes in the same way to the Corinthians, he rejoices in them: "For the grace of God was given to them in Christ, having been made rich through Him in all word and knowledge" (1 Corinthians 1:5). Nonetheless, many of them were led astray by the false apostles and did not believe in the resurrection of the dead. *In the same way, we call the Roman church holy. Similarly we call all their bishops holy, although they are rebellious and their ministers are wicked. But it is God who "rules in the midst of his enemies"; likewise, the "antichrist sits in the temple of God," and Satan is present among the children of God. Even if the church is "among a crooked and perverse generation" (as Paul said to the Philippians[18]), even if it is found in the middle of wolves and assailants, in other words, spiritual dictators, the church is still the church! Although the city of Rome exists as Sodom and Gomorrah, yet it retains baptism, the sacrament, the voice and the text of the Gospel, the Holy Scriptures, the ministries, the name of Christ, and the name of God. Those who have these things, have them! Those who don't have them are without excuse, for the treasure is there. Therefore, the church of Rome is holy because it has the holy name of God, the Gospel, baptism, and the like. If these things are found among the people, they are called holy. In the same way, the citizens of Wittenberg are holy, and we are truly holy because we have been baptized, we have been divinely taught and called, we partake at the Lord's table, and we have God's works among us—that is, the word and the Sacraments; these designate us as holy.*

I say these things in such a way so that we may diligently distinguish between Christian holiness and the others. Monks call their orders holy (although they themselves dare not call themselves holy), but they themselves are not holy. This is because as we have said before, Christian holiness is not an active holiness but a passive holiness.[19] Therefore, no one should consider himself holy based on his way of living or his works or if he fasts or

---

[17] This is one of many instances where Luther quotes a Biblical passage but does not give the reference. This is a practice still followed by many preachers and teachers.

[18] Luther's footnote: *Ecclesia est in medio luporum etc.,* "the church exists among wolves."

[19] *christiana sanctitas non est active, sed passive sanctitas.*

prays or punishes his body or gives generous donations to the poor or such works. If it were so, the Pharisee in Luke would also be holy. Although these works are divinely mandated and God strictly requires them from us, they most certainly do not sanctify us before God. Instead, you and I, the church, the city, and the people are holy, not in ourselves, but due to a holiness outside of us.[20] *It is because we possess divine and sacred things, such as the calling to the ministry, the Gospel, baptism, and others, that we are holy.*

Thus the Galatians retained baptism, the word, and the name of Christ; notwithstanding they had strayed away from Paul's doctrine. There were also a few of good faith who had not turned against him. They had a proper understanding of the word and the Sacraments and administered them correctly. Further, these things cannot be profaned by the renegades. Baptism, the Gospel, and other things do not become impure even though people are tainted and impure and have a wrong concept of them. They continue to be holy things regardless if found among the pious or the wicked, since they cannot be contaminated or sanctified. Through our good or bad words, although our life be good or bad, notwithstanding our lifestyle, they could be profaned or sanctified before the pagan world but not before God. *Therefore, the church is holy even where the fanatic spirits rule, as long as they don't deny the word and the Sacraments. But if these are denied, it's not possible for the church to exist.* That is why wherever the substance of the word and the Sacraments remain, there is the holy church and although the Antichrist may govern there, for Scripture says he rules not in a stable of devils, nor in a pigsty, nor in the company of unbelievers, but in the highest and holiest place, the temple of God (2 Thessalonians 2:4). Therefore, although the spiritual tyrants reign there, even so, there would be a temple of God, and the temple itself would be preserved under them. That is my brief answer to that issue—the church is universal throughout the whole world, wherever the Gospel of God and the Sacraments may be found. The Jews, Muslims, and other empty spirits are not the church, since they struggle against these things and deny them. Up to this point, I have expounded on the title and the inscription of this epistle. Now I go on to Paul's greeting.

LECTURE 3: Thursday, July 9

VERSE 3. Grace and peace to you from God our Father and the Lord Jesus Christ.

I hope that you are not unfamiliar with the meaning of *grace* and *peace*. These are words that Paul uses frequently, and today they are no longer dark or

---

[20] *aliena sanctitate.* Luther is saying that we are holy due to a holiness or righteousness that resides "outside of us" and not "in us."

unknown. We propose to comment on this epistle not because it is an obliga-tion, or because I might say some harsh things. We take on this task to confirm our consciences against the heresies that will come. Don't think it tedious if we repeat things that we have taught, preached, sung, and written elsewhere. Consequently, if we neglect the article of justification,[21] we will have lost all. Therefore, it is most necessary that we place it above everything else and contin-ually drive home and insist on[22] this article,[23] as Moses said of the law, because it cannot resound often enough in our ears, nor can we hear it in excess. Although we may learn it and understand it well, there is no one who can master it or perfectly believe it in his heart. Our flesh is way too slippery[24] and our spirit much too disobedient.

The apostle's greeting is new and unknown to the world. Before the Gospel was preached, this greeting had never been heard. These two words, "grace" and "peace," encompass all that belongs to Christianity. Grace loosens the bonds of sin, and peace soothes the conscience. The two demons that tor-ment us are sin and the conscience. But Christ has overcome these two mon-sters and has crushed them underfoot, in this world as well as the next. The world is unaware of this. That is why it cannot teach with any certainty that sin and death have been defeated and the conscience pacified. Christians are the only ones who have this teaching and have experience in using this weapon in defeating sin, despair, and eternal death. This doctrine does not come from the use of free will; neither is it an invention of reason or human wisdom, but it has been given from above.

Further, these two words, "grace" and "peace," envelop the total sum of Christianity. Grace grants the remission of sins. Peace provides for a quiet and joyful conscience. Nonetheless, the conscience can never be at peace unless it first knows that sin has been forgiven. But sin is not forgiven by fulfilling the law, since no one is able to satisfy the law. Rather, the law denounces sin, declares the wrath of God, accuses and harasses the conscience, and throws it over the cliff into despair. Sin is removed even less through works and the ingenious devices of men, such as wicked rituals, strange religions, vows, pil-grimages, and such.[25]

---

[21] *articulo justificationis*, the pivotal doctrine of Christianity (remember *articulus* in Latin means "pivotal point or fulcrum").

[22] *perpetuo inculcemus et acuamus*. Middleton translates "teach and repeat."

[23] Luther adds this footnote: *Articulus justificationis perpetuo inculcandus*, "we must perpetually inculcate (drive home) the article of justification."

[24] *lubrica*.

[25] Luther's footnote: *Peccatum per solam gratiam remittitur*, "Remission of sins is by grace alone."

In brief, there is no work at all that can remove sin. On the contrary, works increase sin. But the arrogant legalists, as they struggle and sweat to get rid of sin, only make it worse. There is only one way to get rid of sin, and it is by grace alone.[26] There is simply no other way.[27] Therefore, Paul, even in the greetings of his epistle, confronts sin and a wicked conscience with grace and peace. This must be emphasized. It is easy to say it with words. But in the hour of temptation, there is nothing more difficult than to be fully convinced that *by grace alone*,[28] excluding all other means on heaven and earth, we have remission of sins and peace with God.[29]

The world doesn't understand this doctrine. Therefore, it can't tolerate it today or tomorrow. It condemns it as evil. The world brags about free will, the light of reason, the integrity of nature with its powers and qualities. It also boasts of good works as the means to discern and achieve grace and peace—that is, to obtain the forgiveness of sin and a conscience at peace. But it is impossible for the conscience to have joy and peace unless it is through grace. What that means is the forgiveness of sins promised in Christ. Many have tried tirelessly to find various religious orders with their practices looking to obtain peace and quiet for the conscience. But in all this, the only thing they have found is to sink ever deeper into horrendous misery. All these devices are only means to increase doubt and desperation. Therefore, there won't be any rest for their weary bones nor mine until we hear the word of grace and then hang on to it with perseverance and faithfulness. Then, without doubt, we will find grace and peace for our conscience.

The apostle correctly tells the difference between this grace and peace and any other type of grace and peace. He wishes that the Galatians may have grace and peace. However, these do not come from the emperor or kings or princes, for their common task is to persecute the faithful and to rise up against the Lord and Christ His Anointed (Psalm 2:2). Neither does he wish them the peace given by the world (because in John 16:33 Christ said, "In the world . . . you will have tribulation"). The peace he wishes for them is from God our Father. It is the same as wishing them a heavenly peace. That is why Christ said, "My peace I leave with you, my peace I give to you; not as the world gives it, I give it to you" (John 14:27). The peace given by the world is nothing more than the peace found in goods and material things. The grace or favor of the world allows us to enjoy our goods and does not strip us of our possessions. But when affliction comes, in the hour of death, the grace and favor of the world are useless to us, for they cannot free us from trial, anguish, and death itself. But when the grace and peace from God are in the heart, then there is strength to be found. Adversity cannot knock us off our feet, nor can prosperity ruin us with pride. Rather, we walk straight ahead,

---

26 *Sola gratia.*

27 *et simpliciter nullo alio modo.*

28 *Solam gratiam.*

29 *habeamus remissionem peccatorum et pacem cum Deo.*

not straying from the path. We gather strength and courage in the victory found through the death of Christ. Confidence over sin and death will begin to rule our conscience, since through Christ we have assurance of the forgiveness of his sins. Once that confidence is ours, then there is rest for our conscience, and our breath returns by the word of grace. Therefore, those who have been encouraged and strengthened by the grace of God (forgiveness of sins and a peaceful conscience) with courage can deal with and overcome all heartache, even death itself. This peace of God is not given to the world, since the world neither craves it nor understands it but is given only to those who believe. And there is no way at all this can happen but only by the grace of God.

A Guiding Principle: Abstain from Speculating about the Nature of God

But why does he add, "And from our Lord Jesus Christ"? Wasn't it enough to say, "And from God our Father"? Why does he join[30] Jesus Christ to the Father? We've often said that it's a norm and principle in the Scriptures that we should carefully abstain from inventing theories about the greatness of God just out of curiosity, for the human body can't take it and the mind even less. "No one can see me (says the Lord), and live" (Exodus 33:20). The Pope, the Muslims, and all those who trust in their own merits neglect to stick to this norm. Thus they push aside Christ their Mediator from view. They speak only of God, pray only to God, and do all that they do.

For instance, the monk ponders in his imagination, "My works are pleasing to God; God will take into account my vows and for all that will grant me salvation." The Muslim says, "If I keep all the precepts of the Koran, God will accept me and give me eternal life." The Jew thinks, "If I observe the things that the law commands, I will find God's mercy; therefore, I will be saved." In the same way, today we see some heads covered with mud, boasting in the Spirit of revelations, visions, and many other monstrosities—how many there are, I've lost count, who have their heads up in the clouds way above their feet. These new monks have invented a new cross and new works, dreaming that by doing them they can please God. In short, all who ignore the article of justification[31] push Christ right out of the mercy seat. However, they insist on understanding God's majesty through the judgment of human reason and desire to appease Him through their works.

However, true Christian theology (as I have cautioned you often) does not present God to us in His majesty, as did the doctrine of Moses and others. It does not command us to investigate the nature of God. It commands us to know His will toward us in Christ, whom He put forward to become flesh in our behalf, to be born and to die for our sins, and this should be preached to all the nations. "For since the world did not know God through wisdom, God decided, through

---

[30] *annectit.*
[31] *Quotquot ignorant articulum justificationis.*

the foolishness of our proclamation, to save those who believe." Therefore, when your conscience is full of conflict, struggling against the law, sin, and death, before the presence of God, there is nothing more dangerous than detouring into curious speculations regarding heavenly things. No doubt you'll be able to marvel at God's incomprehensible power, His wisdom, His majesty, His creation of the world, and His governance. However, if you attempt to understand God like that, will you then also attempt to pacify Him without Christ the Mediator, making of your works the bridge between you and God? If so, you will also fall like Lucifer, losing God altogether in horrible agony. God in His own nature cannot be measured or understood. He is infinite; human nature wouldn't be able to endure such knowledge.

Therefore, if you wish to be out of danger, to put your conscience in a safe place, rein in that brash and haughty spirit. Then you'll be able to search for God as Paul teaches it. He says, "But we preach Christ crucified; a stumbling block to Jews, and foolishness to Greeks, but to those who are called, both Jews and Greeks, Christ is the power of God and the wisdom of God" (1 Corinthians 1:23, 24). Therefore, begin at the same place where Christ began, in the womb of a virgin, in the manger, at His mother's breast, for it was for that purpose that He descended, lived among men, suffered, was crucified, and died. Utilizing all these ways, He clearly showed Himself to us so that the eyes of our heart would see nothing but Him. In that way, He prevents us from climbing up to heaven and getting all curious, speculating about God's divine nature.

When you deal with the topic of justification and begin to argue with yourself about how to find the God that justifies and accepts sinners, where and how to look for Him, understand that there is no other God but this one man Jesus Christ. Embrace Him and hang on to Him with all your heart, putting aside all speculations about what God is like, for everyone who searches for the greatness of God will be overcome by His glory. I say this by experience. But these fanatics want to find God by excluding the Mediator. However, don't take my word for it. Christ Himself said, "I am the way, the truth, and the life; no one comes to the Father except by me" (John 14:6). Therefore, apart from this way, Christ, you will find no other way to the Father; rather you will walk around all lost. You will find no assurance but hypocrisy and lies. You will not find life but eternal death. Therefore, with respect to justification, keep it clear that whenever any one of us must fight against the law, sin, death, and all other evils, there is no other God that can be known except this God in human flesh.

However, when the topic is not justification, when you must argue with Jews, Muslims, the followers of the Pope, heretics, and others with respect to the power, wisdom, and majesty of God, then put all your ingenuity and effort to that end. You will have to dig deep into this matter as sharp witted as you can get, for then you will be dealing with another topic. But when the topic turns to conscience, righteousness and life, and how to overcome the law, sin, death, and the devil, you must point out the difference. When the topic is how to satisfy divine justice, forgiveness of sin, reconciliation, and eternal life, you must put aside all pondering from your mind and quit speculating about the nature of God. You must look at only this one man Jesus Christ. He shows Himself before us as the Mediator. He tells us, "Come to me all you who are weary and heavy burdened, and I will give you rest" (Matthew 11:28). If you do this, you will realize the love, kindness, and sweetness of God. You will see His wisdom, power, and majesty properly sweetened and prepared to your capacity to understand. You will find in this pleasant contemplation the truth Paul gave to the Colossians: "Christ, in whom are hidden all the treasures of the wisdom and knowledge" (Colossians 2:3). Also, "For all the fullness of God resides bodily in Him" (Colossians 2:9). The world doesn't pay attention to this but instead searches into the will of God putting aside the promise of Christ, thus destroying itself. "No one knows the Father except the Son, and no one knows the Father except the Son and anyone to whom the Son chooses to reveal him" (Matthew 11:27).

This is the reason Paul frequently joins Jesus with the Father. He intends to teach us which is the true Christian faith, for this faith doesn't start way out in the most unreachable place but in the lowest. It asks us to climb up Jacob's ladder, where God Himself holds onto the ladder, and whose feet touch the ground, and on whom Jacob laid his head.

Therefore, when you are thinking about your own salvation, put aside all speculations about the unsearchable majesty of God. Don't stray into musing about works, traditions, and philosophies, not even about God's law. Rather, run to the manger without losing your way, embrace that newborn, and take that infant from the virgin into your own arms. Gaze on him such as He was born, feeding from the breast, growing, talking among men, teaching, dying, resurrecting, ascending to the highest heavens, and working His power over all things. That's how you will shake off all terror and error, as the sun burns away the fog. Contemplating Him will keep you in the straight and narrow way so that you may follow Christ along His way. Therefore, when Paul wishes grace and peace not only from the Father but also from Jesus Christ, he is teaching primarily that we should abstain from speculating about the divine nature, for no man has known God. Listen to Christ. He is at the bosom of the Father, and He declares His will to us, for the Father has appointed Him as our teacher so that in all things we may hear His voice.

Christ Is God by Nature

Another topic that Paul teaches here for the confirmation of our faith is that "Christ is God of very God." Phrases such as these, about the Deity, should be multiplied and emphasized repeatedly. They should be used not only against the Arians and other heretics who have been or will be but also to confirm us in the faith, for Satan will not quit casting doubt on all the articles of our faith until we're dead! He is the most relentless and mortal enemy of our faith, for he knows that this is the victory that overcomes the world. Therefore, the task before us is to secure the foundation our faith and further to strengthen and diligently increase it by constant exercise in fervent word and prayer so that we may be able to resist Satan.

That Christ Himself is God is expressly stated, since Paul attributes to Him the same things that he attributes to the Father—namely, to execute divine power, to grant grace, to forgive sins, to deliver peace to the conscience, to bring life, and to have victory over sin, death, the devil, and hell. None of these things could be legitimately said about Him. In fact, it would be a sacrilege if Christ had claimed to do them and yet was not in Himself God of very God. This is according to what has been said, "I will not give my glory to another" (Isaiah 42:8). Once again, no one can give others what is not His to give. But seeing that Christ grants grace, peace, the Holy Spirit and gives freedom from the power of the devil, sin, and death, He certainly has infinite and divine power, equal in every respect as the Father's power.

Nor is it that Christ grants grace and peace in the same way as the apostles. They granted these gifts through the preaching of the Gospel. But Christ grants grace and peace as the Author and Creator of these gifts. The Father creates and gives life, grace, peace, and every good gift. They are the same things that the Son creates and gives. To give grace, peace, eternal life, forgiveness of sins and to declare righteous,[32] vivify, free from death and the devil are not the works of any creature but only come from the Divine Majesty. Angels can neither create nor give these things. Therefore, these works belong only to the glory of the sovereign Majesty, the Creator of all things. Seeing that Paul attributes equally the same power to create and give these things to Christ and the Father, it follows that Christ is God of very God by nature.

John details many similar arguments where he proves and concludes by the works attributed to the Son as well as the Father that the divinity of the Father and the Son is one and the same. Therefore, the gifts that we receive from the Father and those we receive from the Son are joined together in one and the same whole. Otherwise, Paul would have said "grace from God the Father and peace from our Lord Jesus Christ." But since he weaves them together, he attributes them equally as given by the Son as well as by the Father. I admonish you to be diligent in this matter, for there is a danger. So many errors arise, and there is such a great variety of confusion among the sects, that Arians, Eunomians, Macedonians, and other heresies could harm the church with so much hair splitting.

In fact, the Arians were quite clever characters. They conceded that Christ had two natures. They acquiesced that Christ would also be called "God of very God," but only as a nominal title. Christ is a creature (they said), the most noble and perfect and superior to the angels, by whom God proceeded to create heaven and earth and all things. Mohammed similarly honors Christ with his words. But all this is nothing more than an impressive imagination.[33] They are pleasant and

---

[32] *iustificare*. Middleton (and Watson) incorrectly translates this term as "make righteous."

[33] *speciosae coginationes*.

plausible words that appeal to human reason. Thus the fanatical spirits deceive men and women, unless they are on alert. However, Paul speaks of Christ in another way: "You (he said) are rooted and established in this doctrine, that Christ not only is a perfect creature but is in Himself God, who does the same things as God the Father." He does the divine works not of a creature but of the Creator, for He gives grace and peace. To have the power to give them is to condemn sin, vanquish death, and stomp the devil underfoot. No angel can do these things. But seeing that they are attributed to Christ, it follows that He is God in His own nature.

VERSE 4. Who gave himself for our sins.

Paul uses almost every single word to promote the theme of his epistle. The only thing you can hear coming out of his mouth is Christ. Thus there is passion of spirit and life in every single word. Listen carefully[34] to how well he states his purpose. Paul doesn't say, "He, Himself, received our works from our hands." Neither did He receive the sacrifice of the law of Moses, nor ritualistic worship, nor religions, nor recitations of the mass, nor vows, nor pilgrimages. Instead, Paul says, "He gave." Gave what? It was not gold, nor silver, nor cattle, nor Passover lambs, nor an angel, but Himself. For what? Not for a crown, or a kingdom, or for our holiness or righteousness, but "for our sins." These words ring out from heaven as thunders of protest against all kinds of righteousness. John similarly says, "Behold the Lamb of God that takes away the sin of the world" (John 1:29). Therefore, we should pay careful attention to every single word, not just a cold glance or cursory reading. That's because to the panic-stricken, they are astonishingly comforting and reassuring.

But the question remains, how is it possible for us to obtain remission of sins, for others and ourselves?[35] Paul answers, "The man called Jesus Christ, the Son of God gave Himself for them." These words are huge in the comfort they bring.[36] They are the same promises as given by the ancient law—our sins are not taken away by any other consideration other than the Son of God surrendered Himself over to death. With such gunpowder and battering rams, the papacy is

---

[34] *attende autem.* A reminder that Luther is giving a live lecture and that the reader is reading its transcript.

[35] *Quaestio est, quomodo consequi possimus remissionem peccatorum, aliorum et nostrorum?* The awkward repetition is in the original. If we understand the Latin text as a transcript of Paul's lecture, we can hear him repeating the question for maximum effect—he wants to draw all his listeners in. We can almost hear a long pause at the end of this question.

[36] *magnifica et consolatoria.* This is an instance where the emotional tone of the transcript dictates the actual words used in the English translation. "Magnificent and consoling" would not be used in modern English to convey the feeling of these Latin words. "Huge in the comfort they bring" would be an equivalent in modern English. The reader might think of similar equivalents.

being demolished. It is also the downfall of all pagan religions, every kind of worship, and all works and merits, for if our own works, painful exercises of regret,[37] and merits could get rid of our sins, then why should the Son of God have given Himself for them? But seeing that indeed He was given for our sins, it follows that they will not be deleted[38] by our own works.

Once again, this statement exposes the truth that our sins are so great, so infinite and invincible, that it is impossible for any human being to provide satisfaction for even one of them. Certainly, the great value of the price for our ransom, Christ the Son of God who gave Himself for our sins, shows that it is way beyond ourselves to provide ransom for sin or even claim to subdue it. The strength and the power of sin are amplified with these words: "Who gave Himself for our sins." Therefore, let it be known that the price paid for our sins was infinitely great. There was no way to take sin away but that the very Son of God would have to give Himself "for our sins." Paul probes these things to their very depths and understands that this word *sin* encompasses all God's eternal wrath and Satan's entire kingdom. Certainly, it should make us tremble with fear. But we are careless, and we take sin very lightly, as if it were just a "whatever." But in itself, it has a stinger and stirs up a remorseful conscience. However, we think that it weighs so little that with just a tiny work or some merit we can take it away.

However, the following statement testifies "that every human being is slave and servant of sin" and, as Paul said elsewhere, "sold under sin" (Romans 7:14). Sin is the cruelest and most powerful tyrant over every human being. No creature, angelic or human, could ever conquer it. It has only been conquered by the sovereign and infinite power of Jesus Christ, who gave Himself for sin.

What's more, this statement announces a unique comfort to every conscience horrified by the greatness of its sins. Although sin is an invincible tyrant, now that Christ has conquered it through His death, everyone who believes in Him cannot be broken. Further, if we take this faith as our weapon and with all our heart we take hold of this man Jesus Christ, a light comes on, and we are granted a sound judgment that we may judge with all certainty and freedom the many ways people live, for when we hear that sin is such an invincible and uncontrollable tyrant, we can then infer the consequence of all other doctrines. As it works out then, all the followers of the Pope, monks, nuns, priests, Muslims, Anabaptists, and all who trust in their own works, resolving to abolish and conquer sin through their own traditions, preparatory works, satisfactions, and so on are wicked and

---

[37] *satisfactiones.* In Roman Catholic theology, these "satisfactions" are punishments to satisfy God's wrath. They conform to the sacrament of Penance, leading to the translation "painful exercises of regret."

[38] "Deleted." A word from the digital age that immediately conveys the meaning of *abolebimus* to the twenty-first-century reader.

cruel sects. They disfigure and altogether obscure the glory of God, but consequently our cause advances and is even more established.

Every word of Paul must be weighed carefully and in particular the pronoun "our" should be emphasized. There is a great effect that consists in rightly relating the pronouns, which is used powerfully in the Scriptures to plead with great intensity. You would find it easy to say and believe that Christ the Son of God was given for the sins of Peter, Paul, and other saints. We consider them worthy of that grace. But it is very difficult to personalize it and believe that it's for you, since you consider yourself unworthy of that grace. "What?" you will ask, "Christ was given for my incorrigible, infinite, and horrible sins?" Thus it is common practice to use it without the pronoun that He was given for the sins of others who deserved it. But when it comes to putting the pronoun "our," our feeble human nature and reason steps back and dares not take one more step toward God. Human nature cannot believe the promise that such great treasure would be freely given for it, and thus it wants nothing to do with God, unless first it purifies itself from all sin. That is why when people read or listen to this decree, "that He gave Himself for our sins," etc., they do not relate it to themselves but believe it relates to others, thinking that others deserve it due to their apparent holiness. But insofar as they are personally concerned, they'll wait until they think themselves worthy based on their works.

This is nothing more than reason's empty wish. Oh, reason would want nothing more than to take sin head on and put it within the reach of its imagination! These hypocrites ignore Christ. Yet because they still feel remorse for their sins, they think they can get rid of them through their good works and merits. They silently pray wishing that the words "which gave himself for our sins" were said merely as a show of humility. They hope that their sins are not really serious and true but empty and fictitious. Summing it up, human reason dares to present to God a fake and false sinner, who is not afraid of sin and who doesn't even feel it. They would present to God healthy sinners who have no need of a doctor; when they no longer feel sin, that's when they are going to believe that Christ was given "for our sins."

The whole world has been taken in by this—especially those who would like to pose as more righteous and holy than others, such as the monks and the religious vigilantes. These confess with their mouths that they are sinners and that they sin daily but that their sins are neither so many nor so huge that they can't take them away through their own works. As if that were not enough, they will dare bring their own righteousness and meritorious works to the judgment seat of God demanding the reward of eternal life from the Judge's hand. Meanwhile, since they presume great humility (for they are not so conceited as to consider themselves entirely free of sin), they fake certain sins. They claim to obtain forgiveness by mimicking the devotion of the publican's prayer: "God, have mercy on me, a sinner!" (Luke 18:13). For them, these words of Saint Paul, "for our sins," seem few and small. Therefore, they don't understand them or are unable to use them in temptation when they become aware of their sin; neither can they find comfort in Paul's words but rather sink deeper into hopelessness.

Thus what stands at the forefront of the Christian's knowledge and true wisdom is this: "That Christ was given over to death not for our righteousness or holiness, but for our sins." These sins are altogether true, they are huge and many, infinite and invincible. They are real, potent, and of great consequence. Therefore, don't think they are mere trifles and as such can be canceled out by good works. Neither give in to hopelessness when you feel overwhelmed by them, in life or in death. Rather, learn here from Paul to believe that Christ was given, not for made-up sins, or for water-color sins,[39] or for petty sins, but for immense and enormous sins. Not for one or two but for all. Not for sins that you have overcome (for neither man nor angel can overcome the slightest sin) but for sins that you cannot overcome. And unless you count yourself among those who say, "Our sins," meaning those who hold this doctrine of faith and teach it, learn it, love it, and believe it, there is no salvation for you.

Therefore, make a diligent effort so that not only when you are away from temptation but when you are being tempted and in the struggles of death you will also have this faith and also when your conscience is smitten, remembering your past sins. When the devil blasts against you with great violence, when he tries to drown you with surging swells, floods, and entire seas of sins to drown you in fear, to pull you away from Christ, and to sink you into despair, that is when I say that you can declare with all confidence, "Christ, the Son of God was given not for the righteous and holy but for the unrighteous and sinful. If I were righteous and had no sin, it would not be necessary for Christ to be my Reconciler. Why then Satan, you faker of holiness,[40] do you try to get me to look for holiness within myself, when in reality, I have nothing in me but the most disgusting sins?"

These are not make-believe sins; neither are they just tidbits of sin. They are sins against the first table: great skepticism, doubts, hopelessness, despising God, hate, ignorance, blaspheming God, thanklessness, abusing the name of God, negligence, despising one's own self, despising God's word, and others. That's not all; there are the sins of the flesh in the second table: dishonoring one's parents, disobeying the law, and coveting your neighbor's goods, his wife, and such. However, these are slight compared to the first. I know that I have not murdered, nor fornicated, nor robbed, nor committed other sins of the second table. But in fact, I have done them in my heart. Therefore, I am a violator of all the commandments of God. The multitude of my sins is such that it is countless: "My sins are more in number than the sands of the sea."[41]

---

[39] *fictis aut pictis.*

[40] *in modum sancte Satan.*

[41] Luther does not provide a reference for this quote, but it's from the Prayer of Manasses 9.

What's more, Satan is such a fanciful magician that he changes my right living and doing into my greatest sins.[42] He perpetrates this damage to such an extent that my sins become so heavy, infinite, horrible, and invincible that what I thought was my righteousness only gets in the way between God and me. That is why "Christ, the Son of God, gave Himself to die for them, to take them away, and thus save all those who believe." That is how eternal salvation takes place. Let these words be taken as effective, true, and of great importance. I'm not just saying that. I've experienced on my own how difficult it is to believe every day (when the conscience is full of conflict, especially) "that Christ gave Himself," not for the saints, the righteous, and the seemingly worthy, as if they were His friends. Rather, He was given for perverse sinners, for the unworthy, and for His enemies, who are worthy of nothing but God's wrath and eternal death.

Therefore, armed with these and similar statements of the Holy Scriptures, we can respond to the devil when he accuses us: "You are a sinner; that is why you are condemned." Let us respond like this: "You say I am a sinner and that is why I am justified and saved." "No," says the devil, "you will be lost." "No," I respond, "because I take refuge in Christ, who gave Himself for my sins. Therefore, Satan, you won't be able to defeat me, for you intend to crush me, to depress me with the greatness of my sins, and to oppress me with grief, mistrust, hopelessness, hate, contempt, and blasphemy against God. I want you to know that when you say that I am a great sinner, you have actually given me an armor plate and weapons against you. With your own sword, I'll cut your throat and will trample you because Christ died for sinners. What's more, you in fact preach to me the glory of God because you remind me of God's fatherly love toward me, a poor and miserable sinner. 'For God so loved the world that He gave His only Son, that whoever believes in Him should not perish, but have eternal life' (John 3:16). And every time you argue back that I am a sinner, you still remind me of the benefit that is mine in Christ, my Redeemer, for it was His shoulders and not mine that took the load of all my sins, for the Lord 'laid on him the sins of us all' and 'he was struck down for the rebellion of my people' (Isaiah 53:5–8). Therefore, when you say that I am a sinner, you don't stress me out,[43] but rather comfort me without measure."

Whoever can put this cunning to use will easily avoid all the ploys and tricks of the devil, for he pushes people over the brink of desperation reminding them of their sins. In this way, he tries to destroy them, unless he is resisted by a heavenly wisdom and cunning. This is the only way to overcome sin, death, and the devil. But whoever can't get his sin out of his mind but keeps on tormenting himself with a million thoughts will soon think he can come to his own rescue through his own strength and strategies. Otherwise, he will wait it out until his conscience is once

---

[42] *justitia mea possit facere maximum peccatum.* Luther in a footnote adds, *Satan justitiam vertere in peccatum solet,* "Satan habitually turns my righteousness into sin."

[43] *non terres,* "you don't terrify me."

again at ease. But at last, he will fall victim to the snares of Satan, become miserably distressed, and eventually will be overwhelmed by relentless temptation, since the devil will never stop accusing him through his conscience.

Against this temptation, we should use these words of Paul, which truthfully and precisely define who Christ is: "Christ is the Son of God, and of the Virgin, delivered and put to death for our sins." If the devil alleges any other definition of Christ, tell him, "Your definition and what you define is false. Therefore, I do not accept it." I know what I am talking about, for I know what moves me to ardently say that we must learn to define Christ with the words of Paul. Christ is no debt collector[44] but He who by His sacrifice has paid the penalty for the sins of the entire world.[45] If you are a sinner (as we certainly all are), don't picture Christ as a judge on his bench over a rainbow. Otherwise, you will be terribly distraught and lose all hope in His mercy. Rather, hang on to His true definition, that Christ the Son of God and of the Virgin is not someone that threatens, oppresses, and condemns us over our sin. Neither does He require for us to render an account over our past life. Rather, He gave Himself for our sins and with only one sacrifice has taken away the "sins of the whole world." He has hung them on the cross and all by Himself has completely extinguished them.

Learn this definition diligently. In particular, make use of this pronoun "ours." Have full confidence that these syllables devour all your sins. You may know with all confidence that Christ has taken away not just the sins of certain people but also yours and those of the whole world. Then let those sins be not just sins but also your sins. You can believe that Christ was given not just for the sins of others but also for yours. Take hold of this and don't let it go. Don't let yourself wander away from this sweetest definition of Christ in which the very angels in heaven rejoice. According to the proper and true definition of Christ, He is no Moses, no oppressor, no butcher.[46] Rather, he is merciful toward you; He is the giver of grace, righteousness, and life. He gave Himself, not for our merits, holiness, right doing, and Spirit-led life.[47] He gave Himself for our sins. Indeed Christ interpreted the law but that was not the main mission assigned to Him.

Since we know these things to quite an extent, we can talk about them, particularly about the words and their meaning. But in real life, and in the conflict, when the devil goes around stalking and disfiguring Christ, snatching away from our heart the word *grace*, we don't quite understand them as well as we should. When that hour comes, he who is able to define Christ as he should, he who can praise him and gaze on Him as his sweetest Savior and High Priest (not as a demanding judge), has conquered every evil and already lives in the kingdom of

---

[44] *exactor.*

[45] *sed propitiator peccati totius mundi.*

[46] *carnifex.*

[47] *sancta vita nostra,* literally, "our life of holiness." *Spirit-led life* is the equivalent term used in popular Christianity today.

heaven. But it is most difficult to achieve this in the middle of the conflict. I speak from my own experience. I know the trickery of the devil. When in conflict, he comes out to inject[48] us with the terrors of the law. Just as you get much lumber from a tiny seed, from something that is not even sin, he makes it out to be a real burning hell. He is a real magician at making sin appear enormous. He even puffs up in our conscience the good things we do. But he also takes delight in frightening us with the very person of the Mediator, for he puts on that disguise. He expounds before us a certain text of Scriptures or the very words of Christ. With these, he stabs our hearts. He shows up as Christ Himself, leaving us paralyzed pondering about what we think we are seeing. Our conscience could even swear that it has heard Christ Himself speaking the words used by the devil to accuse us. Such is the cunning of the enemy that he does not present Christ to us in His fullness. He just presents some aspect of Christ. It could even be that He is the Son of God born of a virgin. But from there, he stitches something else, some saying of Christ that sows panic among unrepentant sinners, such as Luke 13:3: "You will perish, too, unless you repent of your sins." This is how he alters the true definition of Christ with his poison. Even though we believe that Christ is the true Mediator, the devil afflicts our conscience making us feel and believe that Christ is a tyrant and a judge. Therefore, once the devil has deceived us, we lose Christ from our sight, our sweet High Priest and Savior. Once we have lost our way like this, we shun Him as if He were the very devil.

This is the reason I plead with you, with all my heart, that you learn the true definition of Christ beginning with these words of Paul: "That He gave Himself for our sins." If He gave Himself for our sins, then without doubt He's no tyrant or judge that will then turn around and condemn us for them. He does not crush the distressed but rather picks up the fallen. He is a merciful encourager and comforter of all whose hearts are tired and heavy burdened. Otherwise, Paul would be lying when he says, "He gave Himself for our sins." If I so define Christ with this correct definition, then I hold on to the true Christ, and I can fully trust that He belongs to me. And at this point, I let go of all curious speculations about God's divine nature. I only keep Christ's humanity, and thus I truly learn the will of God. Here, I have no fears but only sweetness and joy, a conscience at peace, and similar things. Here shines a light that illumines the true knowledge of God, of my own self, and of every creature, and of all evil in the kingdom of the devil. We don't teach new things but repeat what has been established from old, the teachings of the apostles and all pious people before us. Oh, that we would teach and establish them in such a way that they are found not only in our mouths but also in the very depths of our heart, fully established. Thus we will be able to use them in suffering and in the final struggle with death.

---

[48] Luther says in Latin *inflare*, "he comes out to inflate us." I use the more common English term *inject*.

VERSE 4. To deliver us from the present evil age.

With these words, Paul more effectively presses the argument of this epistle. He labels the entire history of this passing world—what has been, what is, and what will be—"the present evil age." In this way, he places a difference between this world and the eternal world to come. Further, he calls it "evil" because it is subject to the perversity of the devil who reigns over the whole world. This is the reason this world is the devil's kingdom. It is because the world ignores, despises, blasphemes, and hates God; it disobeys all God's words and works. We are in and under this temporary world.

Once again you can see that no one is able, neither by his works nor by his own strength, to remove his own sin because this present age is evil; as Saint John said, "The whole world lies in the power of the evil one" (1 John 5:19, NASB). Therefore, all who are in the world are slaves of the devil, under obligation to serve him and to do everything that pleases him.

Why then establish so many religious orders with the sole purpose of abolishing sin? Why invent so many great works that are extremely painful? Why dress in sackcloth and flog yourself until you see blood run red? Why the pilgrimages to Santiago all harnessed up like horses and such things? Even though you may do all these things, and no one doubts they are done, you are in this present evil age and not in the kingdom of Christ. And if you are not in the kingdom of Christ, then most certainly you belong to the kingdom of Satan, which is this present evil age. Thus whatever talents you may have, of the body or the mind, such as wisdom, righteousness, holiness, eloquence, power, beauty, and wealth, are only instruments and weapons at the service of his hellish tyranny. With these, you are required to promote and increase his kingdom.

First, with your knowledge, you obscure the wisdom and knowledge of Christ. With your wicked doctrine, you throw them off the path so that they cannot arrive at grace and the knowledge of Christ. You display and praise your own righteousness and holiness. But the righteousness of Christ, the only one by which we are justified and brought to life, you hate and condemn as wicked and diabolic. In brief, with your power, you destroy the kingdom of Christ, and with your own might you abuse and uproot the Gospel, persecuting and killing the ministers of Christ and all who pay attention to them. Therefore, if you don't have Christ, your wisdom is counted as double nonsense. Your righteousness is counted as double sin and wickedness because it ignores the wisdom and the righteousness of Christ. What's more, it obscures, hinders, blasphemes, and persecutes this righteousness. Thus Paul is right on when he calls it "this evil or wicked age." Because when this world is experiencing its best moment, that is when it is at its worst. As far as its high-profile religious people, the wise and highly educated, the world counts them as the best it has. However, just because of that, it is counted against the world as wickedness times two. I am not even talking here about the gross vices condemned by the second table of the law. These are disobedience to one's parents, judges, adulteries, fornications, greed, theft, murder, and all kinds of violence. The world is drowning in these things. However, these are slight faults when compared to the wisdom and righteousness of the world because these are at war against the first table. This white devil pressures men to commit spiritual sins that they then sell off as religion.[49] This white devil is more dangerous than the black devil, which only pressures men to commit sins of the flesh, which even the world itself recognizes as sins.

Using these words, "to deliver us," Paul points to the argument of his epistle: we need the grace of Christ. No other creature, human or angelic, can deliver the human being from this present evil world. That is because these works only belong to the divine majesty and are not under the power of anyone else, human or angelic. Christ has taken away sin and has delivered us from the tyranny and the kingdom of the devil—that is, He has delivered us from this present evil age, which is by its own choice, an obedient servant of the devil, its god. Everything that assassin and father of lies does or says the world follows and obeys down to the smallest detail as its most faithful and obedient child. Therefore, it is famous for putting God aside for its hate, lies, errors, blasphemies, and despising of God. Further, its cup runs over with gross sins such as murders, adulteries, fornications, thefts, assaults, and such because it knows its father the devil and that he is a liar and a murderer. However, the wiser, holier, and more pious that people can be without Christ, to that same extent they offend the Gospel. Before we were also religious folk, but twice as wicked because we were in the papacy. We lived disguised by what looked like true piety and holiness until we were illumined by the knowledge of the Gospel of Christ.

Then let Paul's words remain forever, since they are indeed true and effective: "this present evil age." He doesn't nuance them or give them a certain spin. Don't let it bother you that there are countless people who display excellent virtues and that hypocrites put on a great theater of holiness. Rather, pay attention to what Paul says. Take his words and with great boldness and freedom pronounce sentence against the whole world, for the entire world with all its wisdom, power, and ethical living is only the kingdom of the devil and only God can deliver us from it through His only Son.

Therefore, let us praise God the Father, giving Him thanks for His infinite grace without measure, in that He has delivered us from the kingdom of the devil. He delivered us through His Son while we were still captives and it was impossible for us to free ourselves through our own efforts. Let us recognize with Paul that "all our works and righteousness" are nothing but "waste and dung" (and won't make the devil hang his head in shame by even a hair). Also let us stomp all over and detest altogether the power of those who put free will on the highest pedestal,

---

[49] *pro justitia.*

as well as the holy living and wisdom of the hypocrites,[50] orders, masses, religions, sects, ceremonies, vows, fasts, dressing up in sackcloth, and similar things as the foulest smelling menstrual rags,[51] for it is the devil's most pestilent and pervasive poison. But rather, let us exalt and enlarge the glory of Christ, who not only rescued us but with His death also saved us from this evil world.

LECTURE 4: Friday, July 10

By using this degrading label, "evil," Paul is indicating what the kingdom of this world looks like. It is nothing else but the devil's kingdom of wickedness, ignorance, errors, sins, death, blasphemies, desperation, and eternal damnation. Christ's kingdom on the other hand is the complete opposite. It is the kingdom of equity, light, grace, forgiveness of sins, peace, consolation, salvation, and eternal life to where we have been translated by our Lord Jesus Christ, to whom be the glory for evermore, Amen.

VERSE 4. According to the will of our God and Father.

Here, Paul arranges each word so that all of them without exception will engage in battle against the false apostles in defense of the article of justification.[52] Christ, he says, has delivered us from the devil's wicked kingdom and this world. He has accomplished it "according to the will, the good pleasure, and the order given by the Father." Therefore, we are not delivered using our wit or will. It is God who has had mercy on us. He has loved us, as it is written: "In this is love: not that we loved God, but that He loved us and sent His Son to be the atoning sacrifice for our sins" (1 John 4:10). That we are delivered from this present evil age is absolutely by sheer grace and not because we deserve it. Paul is so abundant, so passionate in magnifying and exalting the grace of God, that he sharpens each word and launches it against the false apostles.

There is also another reason here why Paul mentions the will of the Father. John in his Gospel, when he exalts the work of Christ, shows that Christ Himself refers us to the will of the Father. Christ lets us know that when we listen to His words and admire His works we are actually seeing the Father. The reason Christ came to the world taking on human nature is to offer Himself as a sacrifice for the sins of the entire world and thus we are reconciled with God the Father. In this manner, Christ assures us that all was done from the Father's good pleasure. Thus when we fix our eyes on Christ, we are attracted and taken directly to the Father.

---

[50] *justitiam pharisaicam* (pharisaical righteousness).

[51] *foedissimum menstruateae pannum.*

[52] *articulo justificationis.*

We cannot get into a frame of mind (as we've warned you before) that through conjectures about God's greatness we can understand how God provides for our salvation. Instead, we must take hold of Christ, who, according to the Father's will, gave Himself over to die for our sins. You must recognize that that is precisely God's will for you in Christ, for only then God's wrath comes to an end, and your fear and trembling will vanish as the morning mist. At that moment, God will appear altogether merciful, because through His unchanging will, He determined that His Son should die for us and that we should live through Him. To know this brings joy to your heart. You will grow in understanding that God is not angry with us. You will realize that His love is so generous toward us poor and miserable sinners that He gave His only Son for us. It's not just on a whim that Paul repeats and hammers into our brains that Christ was given for our sins for no other reason than the Father's goodwill toward us. On the contrary, to surmise about God's greatness or the reason for His dreadful judgments as to why He destroyed the entire world with a flood or why God destroyed Sodom and such questions is extremely dangerous. These thoughts bring people to the edge of desperation and can in fact push them over the border into self-destruction. Elsewhere I have talked about this.

VERSE 4. Our God and Father.

This word *our* is related to both so that the meaning is this: "of our God and of our Father." Then the Father of Christ and our Father is one and the same. John 20:17 puts it the same way. Christ says to Mary Magdalene, "I am ascending to my Father and your Father, to my God and your God." Therefore, God is our Father and our God but only through Christ. This is an apostolic phrase, and it is unique to Paul. Even though he doesn't speak with pompous and pretentious words, these go right to the matter boiling over with burning zeal.

VERSE 5. To whom be glory forever and ever! Amen.

The Hebrews would scatter throughout their writings expressions of praise and gratitude. This uniqueness belongs both to the Hebrews and to the apostles. Frequently we see this in Paul. The name of the Lord is to be valued with great reverence and never should it be mentioned without praise and gratitude. When we do this, we render nothing but praise and worship to God. For example, when it comes to matters of this world, and we mention the name of kings or princes, we are in the habit of doing some gesture of reverence, such as bending the knee. How much more should we do this when we speak of God; we should bend the knee of our heart and speak God's name with gratitude and great reverence!

VERSE 6. I am astonished.

You can see how creatively and ingeniously Paul deals with his wayward Galatians when he realizes that the false apostles have seduced them. At the beginning, he does not charge against them with harsh and coarse words. Rather, as a father, he not only tolerates their going off course but also, in some way, excuses them. Moreover, he shows them a certain maternal affection, since he speaks gently to them while reproving them at the same time. Nevertheless, he does it with very appropriate words, wisely chosen according to the need. On the other hand, he expresses his burning indignation against the false apostles who had seduced them, and he pours all the blame on them. Therefore, at the beginning of his epistle, he explodes with unmistakable thunder and lightning against them. "If anyone," he says, "is preaching to you a gospel contrary to what you received, let him be damned!" (Galatians 1:9). Then in chapter 5, he threatens the false apostles with condemnation. "He who is troubling you shall bear his judgment, whoever he is" (Galatians 5:10). He pronounces them under a curse with terrible words, saying, "I wish that those who are troubling you would castrate themselves!" (Galatians 5:12). These are resounding thunderbolts against the righteousness of the flesh or of the law.

He could have dealt more harshly with the Galatians. He could have cuttingly insulted them: "I am ashamed of you for having left the truth. It hurts me that you have been so ungrateful with me. I am disgusted with you." Or he could have tongue lashed them as in a [Greek][53] tragedy: "You are a sign of the times!"[54] But since his purpose is to lift up the fallen and with fatherly affection turn them back from their error to the purity of the Gospel, he puts aside the stern and coarse words, especially at the beginning. Here, he deals gently and uses restraint with them. Seeing that his work was to heal the wounded, it was not beneficial to reinjure their wounds by putting a rough and irritating bandage, hurting them even more. Therefore, of all the gentle and measured words at his command, he chooses the phrase most appropriate to their need: "I am astonished." These words mean "I am hurt and displeased that you failed me."

Here, Paul remembers his command in Galatians 6:1, where he says, "Brothers, if a person is caught doing something wrong, those of you who are spiritual should restore that person gently. Watch out for yourself so that you are not tempted as well" (ISV). We should follow this example showing affection to those who go astray, like parents toward their children. That way they will be aware of our fatherly and motherly affection toward them and will see that we don't wish

---

[53] Added for clarity. Obviously, Luther had read some Greek tragedies!

[54] *o secula, o mores.* This is a Latin idiomatic expression (usually *O tempore, o mores*) to express dismay over the bad times: literally "O the times! O the customs!," intending to mean that they are really bad. Luther ups the ante and says, "O secula (ages), O mores (O unending ages)."

their ruin but rather their wellbeing. On the other hand, against the devil and his ministers and against the authors of false doctrine and the sects, we should also follow the other example of the apostle. With them, we should show ourselves impatient, proud, cutting, bitter, detesting, and condemning of their trickery and double-talk with all possible zeal and severity. This is what parents do when a dog bites their son and hurts him, they chase the dog, but with the sweetest words comfort and speak gently to the child.

Therefore, Paul's spirit is marvelously cunning when dealing with the afflicted conscience of the fallen. On the contrary, the Pope (for he is led by an evil spirit) explodes with violence as a tyrant and issues his thunder and curses against the anguished and distressed conscience. This attitude is seen in his infamous bulls and particularly in his bull regarding the Lord's Supper. The bishops, not even in the least, try to mend themselves in the discharge of their duty. They do not teach the Gospel, they do nothing for the salvation of the souls under their care. They only look to see how they can exercise power and control over them. Therefore, their works and double-talk have no other purpose but to uphold and support their tyranny. Their arrogant scholars and spokespersons are equally affected.

VERSE 6. You are turning away so soon.

Paul complains about how easy it is to abandon the faith. In this regard, in another text, he warns, "Let him who thinks he stands take heed, lest he fall" (1 Corinthians 10:12). Every day we see this proven by minds hardly able to conceive and retain a healthy and persevering faith. It is also very difficult to gather together a congregation perfected for the Lord. Someone can diligently labor for ten years until planting a small church, duly organized according to its doctrine. And when he has it assembled in such good order, some deranged nut infiltrates it, let's say an illiterate idiot, and all he does is stir up slander and disdain against the sincere preachers of the truth. In a moment, he's able to tear down everything. Who is not going to feel resentful at such evil and insolent foul play?

We, by the grace of God, here in Wittenberg, have accomplished the formation of a Christian church. The truth is taught with purity, the Sacraments are administered properly, and we pray for the rulers and exhort them. In brief, everything is going forward and prospering. This happiness would soon be over if a lunatic crept in. In an instant, he would tear down everything that we have built over the course of many years. Paul, God's chosen vessel, didn't fare any better. He had won the churches of Galatia with great effort and dedication. But soon after his departure, the false apostles arrived and knocked down his work, as is attested in this and other epistles. So great is the weakness and contempt of this present age. We walk in the middle of Satan's traps. Just one fanatic's head can destroy and, in a short time, totally overthrow everything that many true ministers, working day and night, have raised up after many years of labor. This is our experience today, which leaves us in great pain. Even so, we cannot remedy this enormous offense.

Seeing then that the church is such a delicate and fragile object and so easily overthrown, we must in good faith keep a vigilant eye over these fanatical spirits, for they listen to a couple of sermons or read a few pages of Holy Scriptures and think they are already lords and masters over all those who are well educated and properly instructed, turning upside down everyone's authority. You will find such characters today, faking it and bragging insolently all in one. They don't know what temptation is, nor have they learned to fear God, nor have they ever tasted and felt the gift of grace. Since these characters don't have the Holy Spirit, they teach what feels right to them and what is most appealing and pleasing to common people because they think those teachings are within their reach. The masses lack expertise[55] and then, eager to hear new things, gather all around them. There are also many who are held in high esteem within the doctrine of faith, but when exposed to this temptation, they fall prey to its seduction.

Paul, from his own experience, teaches us that congregations that have been established with great effort can be overthrown rather quickly. Likewise, we should watch diligently and carefully against the devil, since he is going from here to there, and if we sleep, he will come and sow weeds among the wheat. Even when the pastors are alert and vigilant, the Christian flock will always be in danger of Satan. Paul, with great care and diligence, had planted the churches in Galatia, but as soon as he stepped out the door (so to speak), the false apostles came in, deceiving some, and great was the fall of the Galatian churches. For Paul, this sudden and great loss brought more grief than death itself. Therefore, we should be on high alert. First, each one should be watching out for himself. Then let all the teachers be vigilant, not just for themselves, but also for the entire church so that we do not enter into temptation.

VERSE 6. I am astonished that you are so quickly deserting him.

Once again, he doesn't use a harsh word but a most delicate expression. He doesn't say, "I am astonished that you have so quickly gone astray, that you are so disobedient, frivolous, inconsistent, and ungrateful that you have moved away." It's as if he had said, "You, yourselves, didn't cause the harm; you were just trying to be tolerant. Yet you have suffered and have been victimized." His intention is to call them back from their detour. That is why he accuses the troublemakers rather than those who've gone astray. However, quite gently, he also accuses them, for he complains that they have abandoned the way. It's as if he had said, "Although I embrace you with a fatherly hug, I know you have been deceived, it's not your fault, but rather it's the false apostles' fault. Even so, I would have liked for you to mature even more in the strength of sound doctrine. You didn't grasp the word firmly enough; you didn't sufficiently stand firm on your roots. That's why with

---

[55] *vulgus imperitum.*

the slightest flurry, the wind blew you away." Jerome wonders if Paul wanted to interpret "Galatians" by relating it to the Hebrew word *Galath*,[56] as if saying, "You are right in calling yourselves Galatians, which means, moving away."

Some think that the German folk are descendants from the Galatians, and they would not be far from the truth. The Germans are rather similar. I would also like for my countrymen to be more consistent and perseverant. In everything we do, we go full gallop from the start, but when the fire of our affection begins to diminish, we ease up. Then with the same momentum we began our tasks, we let them go, and at the end, we reject them altogether.

At the beginning, when the light of the Gospel shone, after great darkness due to the traditions of men, many turned to the truth with burning zeal. They were hungry and listened to the sermons and had great respect for the ministers of the Gospel. But now, when a reformation has taken place and the word of God has greatly increased, many who began as zealous disciples have turned their backs, uttering condemnations. They abandoned not only the study and zeal for the word of God but also their ministers. They also hate proper teaching, becoming nothing but lazy pigs, whose god is their belly, worthy (no doubt) of being compared with the foolish[57] and frivolous Galatians.

VERSE 6. From Him who called you in the grace of Christ.[58]

The meaning of the original is somewhat uncertain, and that is why there are two ways to understand the phrase. The first is "that Christ has called you in grace." The other is "from Him, meaning 'from God,' who has called you in the grace of Christ." The former attracts my preference because it corresponds to Paul's arguments. First, because a few texts before, Paul had spoken of Christ as the Redeemer, who through His death had delivered us from this evil world. Further, he had also declared Christ as the giver of grace and peace equally and together with the Father. So here, he declares that Christ is the One who gives the call to grace. In these various ways, Paul shows that his specific purpose is to drive into our brains the benefit of Christ by whom we have come to the Father.

In these words, "who called you in grace," there is also great passion. A relationship of opposites is uncovered. It's as if he had said, "Incredible! How is it that you've allowed yourselves to be drawn away from Christ! He is the one who has called you, not as Moses called you to the law, to works, to sin, to wrath, to

---

[56] Luther refers to Jerome's understanding of the Hebrew name גָּלָה. One of its root meanings is simply "rolling away." The Hebrew characters are found in the text of the Latin originals.

[57] During this lecture, Luther used the Greek term ἀνόητοι that is found in Galatians 3:1.

[58] Translated from the Latin text *Abe o, qui vocavit vos in gratia Christi.*

condemnation. Rather, He has called you to the fullness of grace!" In the same way, we, together with Paul, protest against the blindness and perversity of men. It is horrible, for no one receives the doctrine of grace and salvation. Or if anyone receives it, how soon he falls away and abandons it! However, it is grace that brings with it every good gift, to our spirit as well as to our body. These are forgiveness of sins, true righteousness, peaceful conscience, and eternal life. Further, grace brings light and a norm from which to judge correctly in all kinds of disciplines and tasks of life. It approves and establishes the civil government, discipline in the home, and all lifestyles ordained and approved by God. It uproots all doctrinal error, rabble-rousing, confusion, and such. It vanishes away the fear of sin and death. In summary, it uncovers all the devil's schemes and works, opening the benefits of God's love toward us. Because the world hates this word, it harms everyone who embraces this good news of eternal comfort, grace, salvation, and eternal life. Does it surprise you that the Gospel is persecuted with such spite and hellish fury?

Previously, Paul had called this present age wicked and evil, "the kingdom of the devil." Otherwise, this present age would recognize the benefit and the mercy of God. But since it is under the dominion of the devil, it hates and viciously persecutes the kindness of God. The world loves darkness, error, the kingdom of the world more than light, truth, and the kingdom of the Christ. And it is not due to ignorance or hate but due to the perversity of the devil. This is perfectly clear because Christ the Son of God, when He gave Himself over to death for the sins of every human being, has not gotten anything out of this perverse and accursed world. In exchange for His priceless benefit, He has been blasphemed and His word persecuted, which is the only word of salvation. And if the world could, once again, it would nail and hang Him to the cross. Thus it's not just that the world lives in darkness but that it is darkness itself, such as it is written in John 1:5.

Therefore, Paul stands on these words: "From Christ, who has called you in grace." It's as if he had said, "My preaching was not about Moses' strict laws. Neither did I teach that you should be slaves under that yoke. I only preached the doctrine of grace and freedom from the law, sin, wrath, and condemnation." He was saying to them, "Christ has mercifully called you to grace so that you may be free in Christ and not serve as slaves under Moses. But once again, you have gone back into slavery thanks to the false apostles. Because they, through the law of Moses, have not called you to grace but to God's wrath, God's hatred, sin, and death. But Christ calls you to His grace and it saves you completely. He calls you so that He may lead you to the good news of the Gospel instead of leading you to the law, where you will only suffer mental anguish." Through Christ, we are transferred from God's wrath to God's favor. Christ removes us from sin and places us inside righteousness. He has brought us out of death and taken us into life. But are you going to allow the false apostles to take you away so easily and so quickly send you on another path, far from the abundant fountain of life and the fullness of grace? Now, if Moses calls men to God's wrath and to sin through God's law, where then do we think the Pope leads men and women through his traditions? The other meaning that "the Father calls them in the grace of Christ" is also appropriate. But the first meaning with respect to Christ brings greater comfort to any conscience in distress.

VERSE 6. Turning to another gospel.

Here, we learn how to spy on the illusions and deviousness of the devil. You will not find a single heretic in the *Index of Errors and Satanic Delusions*.[59] Neither does the devil appear as the devil, especially that white devil we talked about. Even the black devil that forces people to uncover their own evil, first gives them a cape to cover the sin they commit or the motive for their crime. The assassin in his fury can't see how immense and horrible his sin is because he covers up with a disguise. Prostitutes, thieves, the greedy, drunkards—these brag about their mischief, and with their boldness, they cover up their sins. In the same way, the black devil puts on a disguise and conceals all his works and strategies. But in the spiritual realm, Satan doesn't go out decked in black but in white. Dressed in the craftiest disguise, he pretends to be an angel, or even God Himself, posing as the real thing with all his performances and charades. He reserves his deadliest venom for the doctrine of grace, for the word of God, for the Gospel of Christ. For this reason, Paul calls the doctrine of the false apostles, the ministers of Satan, "another gospel." But he derides them, as if saying, "Oh Galatians, so now, you have other evangelists and another gospel. But I feel sorry for you now, since you no longer have anything worthwhile."

By this, we understand that these false apostles had condemned Paul's Gospel among the Galatians. They had said, "Paul began rather well. But a good start is not enough. There are still higher and loftier themes. As he says in Acts 15:1, 'It is not enough just to believe in Christ, or to be baptized.' But now it is necessary for you to be circumcised, for 'unless you are circumcised after the custom of Moses, you can't be saved.'" This is the same thing as saying, "Christ was a good craftsman, and in fact, He got the building started. But He didn't finish it. We have to leave that to Moses' hands."

In the same way today, the sectarian fanatics, the Anabaptists, and others, openly condemn us. They say, "These Lutherans are too tentative, they don't dare to profess the truth freely and honestly to the very end." They keep saying that we have laid a good foundation. They say that we have taught faith in Christ, but that the beginning, the middle, and the end, should all be tied together. Then they say that God has called them to accomplish all that. They claim that is not our

---

[59] *sub titulo erroris et Satanae.*

task. In such a way, those perverse and diabolic spirits exalt and magnify their accursed doctrine, calling it the word of God. Thus taking the name of God in vain, they deceive many. The devil is not going to show his ugly face, neither is he going to dress his ministers in black. Instead, they look rather handsome dressed in white. Further, to disguise his doctrine in goodness, he decorates all his words and works with a varnish of truth and God's name. There's a German proverb that has its roots in that kind of thinking: "God's name covers up every misfortune."

Therefore, let us learn that the Gospel is a special target of the devil's craftiness. If he cannot wreak havoc with persecution and destruction, he does it under the guise of correcting and building upon it. That is why today he persecutes us with the power of the sword. Once he has gotten rid of us, he will not only disfigure the Gospel but also reduce it to rubble altogether. But up until today, he has not prevailed. Even though he has destroyed many who persevered in our holy and heavenly doctrine, the shedding of their blood has watered rather than destroyed God's church.

However, since he was not able at all to destroy the church in that manner, he now raises up depraved spirits in wicked teachers.[60] At first, they tolerate our doctrine, they teach it with us in mutual consent. But soon after, they say that it is our task just to deliver the basic principles of the Christian faith.[61] However, they continue and say the mysteries of the Scriptures have been revealed to them from on high, by God Himself, and they have been called to make those things known to the world. Thus the devil puts obstacles before the Gospel on the left and on the right, but more on the right, as I said before. He pretends to build and correct, instead of going to the left persecuting and destroying. That is why we are compelled to be constant in prayer, to read the Holy Scriptures, and to take a firm hold of Christ and His holy word. In this way, we will be able to overcome the cunning of the devil, with which he attacks us left and right. "For our wrestling is not against flesh and blood, but against the principalities, against the powers, against the world's rulers of the darkness of this age, and against the spiritual forces of wickedness in the heavenly places" (Ephesians 6:12).

VERSE 7. It's not really another gospel, but certain people are confusing you [CEB].

Once again, the apostle excuses the Galatians but bitterly rebukes the false apostles. It's as if he had said, "You Galatians have been fooled into thinking that the Gospel you received from me is not the true and genuine Gospel. Is this is why you think you are doing the right thing in receiving that new gospel that the false apostles teach and that appears to be better than mine? I can't blame you for this

---

[60]   *suscitat nequam spiritus impios doctores.*
[61]   *traderemus prima rudimenta doctrinae christianae.*

fault as much as I blame those agitators that trouble your consciences and pull you out of my hand." Do you see the intensity of his feelings against these impostors? His harsh and rough words uncover their disguise. They are the ones who perturb the churches. They do nothing else than seduce and swindle countless suffering consciences. They cause terrible harm and grief in the congregations. Today, we see this enormous evil with great heartache. But we are as helpless in correcting the situation as Paul was in his day.

This text means that the false apostles had given a report that Paul was an imperfect apostle as well as a weak and misguided preacher. Thus he uncovers what they do, saying they perturb the church and demolish the Gospel of Christ. Here, there is mutual condemnation. The false apostles condemned Paul, and Paul condemned the false apostles. These same disputes and mutual condemnations have always existed in the church, especially when the doctrine of the Gospel is in full bloom. Wicked teachers persecute, condemn, and oppress the faithful. On their part, the faithful rebuke and condemn the wicked.

Today, the followers of the Pope and the sectarian fanatics hate us and condemn our doctrine as wicked and mistaken. On our part, we detest and condemn their accursed and blasphemous doctrine with perfect hatred. Meanwhile, the people continue in their misery with no relief in sight, wavering and doubting whether they can find support in their faith, or which of the two they are going to follow, for not everyone is able to use sound judgment in these matters of such great weight. But at the end, it will be seen who teaches the truth and who is in the right when one condemns the other. Indeed, we don't persecute anyone or oppress anyone, and we don't put anyone to death. Neither do we harass the consciences of anyone. Instead, we deliver them from countless errors and snares of the devil. What is true is that we have the testimony of many good men who thank God for our doctrine, since they have received comfort and assurance for their consciences. Just as Paul was not at fault for the false apostles who perturbed the churches, neither are we at fault today. Rather, it is the Anabaptists and such frenzied sectarian spirits that create many and great problems within the churches.

Pay close attention. All those who teach works and the righteousness of the law are perturbing the churches and the consciences of men and women. Who would have imagined that the Pope, cardinals, bishops, monks, and the entire synagogue of Satan would be "troublers" of people's consciences? Especially the founders of the religious orders, although there may still be some who God will save miraculously! Yes, frankly they are even worse than those false apostles. The false apostles believed that in addition to faith in Christ, the works of God's law were necessary for salvation. But the followers of the Pope get rid of faith and teach the traditions of men and works that God has never ordered. They themselves have invented them without the support of the word of God and against it. Not only have they given tradition an equal place with the word of God, but they have exalted tradition way above the word. With regards to the heretic sectarians, notwithstanding their great theatrical performances, they cause an equal amount of harm, for if the false apostles had not been gifted with outstanding talents, great authority, and an appearance of holiness, boasting to be ministers of Christ, disciples of the apostles, and sincere preachers of the Gospel, they would not have been able to so quickly disfigure Paul's authority and send the Galatians astray on another path.

The reason the apostle became so severely upset at them, calling them "troublers" of the churches, is because besides faith in Christ, they also taught that circumcision and the keeping of the law were necessary for salvation. Paul testifies about this further on, in chapter 5. Luke, writing in Acts chapter 15, also quotes them saying the same words: "Unless you are circumcised according to the custom we've received from Moses, you can't be saved" (Acts 15:1). Therefore, the false apostles heatedly and stubbornly argued for the keeping of the law. The Jews who were already stiff necked joined in, making it easier to persuade those who were not well established in the faith. They argued that Paul was not an honest teacher because he did not take the law into account but rather preached a doctrine that abolished and put an end to the law. It seemed very strange to them that the law of God had been altogether removed and that the Jews who up to now had always been counted as God's only people and the people of the promise had also been rejected. Further, it seemed even stranger to them that the Gentiles, being wicked idolaters, now obtained the glory and dignity of being God's people, without circumcision and without the works of the law but only through grace and faith in Christ.

The false apostles had exaggerated these things to the extreme with the purpose of generating greater hatred toward Paul among the Galatians. With a view to turn them even more against him, they said that through his preaching Paul taught the Gentiles freedom from the law. The consequence, they said, was that God's law would be despised and finally abolished together with the entire Jewish nation. In short, Paul's preaching was contrary to apostles' own example. Therefore, he had to be stopped because he was blaspheming openly against God, and had rebelled against the entire Jewish nation. They added that they instead (the false apostles) deserved the attention of the Galatians because besides preaching the Gospel properly, they were disciples of the very apostles. Instead, Paul had never taken the time to get acquainted with them. Through this strategy, they defamed and denigrated Paul to the Galatians. It was because of this perverse treatment that Paul was obligated to counter these false apostles, saying that they were troublers of the churches and that they were abolishing the Gospel of Christ, as you will see in what follows.

VERSE 7. And want to distort the gospel of Christ.

In other words, this is saying, "These false apostles not only perturb you, but they pretend to abolish and turn into rubble the Gospel of Christ."

The devil is committed to two things without respite. One, through the false apostles, he perturbs and deceives many. What's more, he takes advantage of them, attempting to tear down the Gospel altogether. He manipulates them without letup until he achieves his objective. However, nothing perturbs those apostles more than to be called apostles of the devil. On the contrary, they glory more than others in the name of Christ and boast to be the sincerest preachers of the Gospel. But since they mingle together the law and the Gospel, they are in fact, destroyers of the Gospel. Consequently, take note. It's one of the two: either Christ stands firm and the law perishes or the law stands firm and Christ perishes. Where the righteousness of the law reigns, the righteousness of grace cannot reign. Where the righteousness of grace reigns, the righteousness of the law cannot reign. One of the two must bow to the other.

If you can't believe that God forgives your sins on account of Christ, who He sent to the world as our High Priest, how then are you going to believe that He will forgive your sins on account of your works of the law, which you'll never be able to fulfill? Is it that perhaps you think that your own works will be able to neutralize God's judgment? (You will have to confess that's what you think.)

Therefore, the doctrine of the law cannot remain standing together with the doctrine of grace. One must be rejected and abolished, and the other confirmed and established.

But just as the Jews abhorred this doctrine of faith and of grace, we also shrink back from it. I, myself, would be more than willing serve the righteousness of grace that justifies and the other one of the law by which God should take me into consideration. But as Paul explains here, to combine the one with the other is to pervert the Gospel of Christ.

However, if it's about a debate that receives appearances as evidence, be on the alert. The best evidence will not win out. Instead, it's the greater show of appearances that wins the day. Christ on his part is meek and mild,[62] and the preaching of the Gospel is considered foolishness. But on the other hand, the kingdom of the world and the devil, its prince, seem strong, for they present appearances without end. The wisdom and the righteousness of the flesh are known for putting great shows! Using the measure of appearances, the righteousness of grace and faith lose out, but the other righteousness of law and works make headway and consolidate their ground. However, our comfort is that the devil with all his members cannot achieve what they set out to. They may perturb many, but it cannot overthrow the Gospel of Christ. The truth can be hemmed in on every side but it cannot be overcome because the word of the Lord remains forever.

LECTURE 5: Friday, July 17

It would seem like a small thing to intermingle the law and the Gospel, faith and works, but the result is the biggest chaos the human mind could ever conceive. To

---

[62] *infirmus.*

mix the law and the Gospel together not only blurs the knowledge of grace but totally leaves out Christ with all His benefits. Our own flesh is the cause of this evil. When it sees itself drowning in its countless sins, it cannot see any other way out except through works. The flesh commits to live in the works of the law and without rest seeks to find rest and assurance in its own works. That is why the flesh lives in total ignorance of the doctrine of faith and grace. However, without this doctrine, the conscience cannot find peace and rest.

The words of Paul, "they want to pervert the Gospel of Christ," also points to the excessive pride and shamelessness of these false apostles. But Paul only magnifies his ministry and Gospel with the following words.

VERSE 8. But even though we, or an angel from heaven, should preach to you any "good news" other than that which we preached to you, let him be cursed.

Here, Paul ignites flames with his words, and his zeal burns so intensely that he almost curses the angels themselves. He says, "Even if we ourselves, my brothers Timothy, Titus, and I, and all who preach Christ in His purity together with me (I am not talking about those who seduce the conscience) or an angel from heaven announces another good news, then let all of us, beginning with me, my colleagues, and even the heavenly angels, be cursed by God! Let all of us be under God's curse, but let not my good news be overthrown!" Paul burns with zeal, since he dares to pronounce such a powerful curse. He invokes condemnation not only on himself and his brothers but on an angel from heaven! The Greek word Ἀνάθημα (anathema), the Hebrew חֵרֶם (herem), and the Latin maledictum mean something accursed, abhorrent, and despicable and which has no relationship, participation, or communion at all with God. Joshua says it this way: "Cursed before the Lord is the man who rises up and builds this city" (Joshua 6:26). At the end of Leviticus, it is written, "Anyone put under a curse cannot be bought back, he must be put to death" (Leviticus 27:29). That is what God stated with respect to Amalek and other cities. God's curse decreed that they should be totally leveled and wiped out! Paul then has this in mind: "I prefer that I, myself, together with my other brothers, even an angel in heaven, should be put under God's curse rather than we or others should preach a good news different to what we have already preached." This way Paul puts himself first under a curse, for those who are skilled in persuasion first find fault in themselves in order to rebuke others with greater freedom and severity.

Therefore, Paul concludes that there is no other good news but the one he, himself, had preached. But he had not preached a good news of his own invention, but the very same one that God had promised before through his prophets in the Holy Scriptures (Romans 1). Thus he includes himself and others, and even an angel from heaven, who would certainly be cursed, had he taught anything contrary to the previous good news. That is because the voice of the Gospel, once it is issued, cannot be taken back until the final day.

VERSE 9. As we said before, I will say it again. If any man is preaching another good news to you which is not the one you have received, let him be cursed.[63]

Paul repeats the curse, directing it now toward other persons. Before, he had cursed himself, his colleagues, and an angel from heaven. "Now," he says, "if there are others who preach a different Gospel than what you received from us, let them also be under God's curse." With this, Paul excommunicates and curses all the false teachers including his adversaries. Here, he displays a great and passionate spirit. He dares to curse all the teachers throughout the world and in the heavens above who pervert his Gospel and teach any other. All should believe in the Gospel that Paul had preached, otherwise, they are under a curse and condemnation. Oh, that this horrible decree from the apostle Paul would strike fear in the hearts of those who seek to pervert the Gospel of Paul! But sadly, the world is saturated with these perversions.

Here, we should note a change in the people Paul addresses. In the first curse, Paul speaks differently than in the second. In the first, he says, "But if even we, or an angel from heaven should announce another good news contrary to what we have announced." In the second, he states, "Contrary to what you received." He says this on purpose, to prevent the Galatians from saying, "Paul, we did not pervert the good news you preached. It's just that we didn't understand it well. But the teachers who have come after you, they have told us what it really means." "This," he says, "I will not accept. You should not add anything to it nor correct it. What you heard from me is the straight word of God; leave it alone. I don't wish that I had been a different teacher when I was with you, nor do I wish that you had been different disciples. Therefore, if you hear any other man who brings another good news different from what you already heard from me or boasting that he will deliver better things than what you received from me, then let him be his disciple and be cursed by God!"

However, such is the nature of Satan's ministers that with this hoax they know how to creep into people's minds and work their way in. They confess that those who came before and taught the Gospel started well but that it was not enough. However, it is they who announce the most reliable truth. Thus in order to produce the greatest number of disciples possible, everyone must surrender to them.[64] Even

---

[63] The New Life Version best translates Luther's understanding of this verse as found in the Latin text.

[64] *se vero certissima afferre, quae ita velint tradere, ut auditores magnum fructum inde ferre possint etc.* This is a difficult phrase. I offer this translation because its

today the fanatic sectarians grant us this praise, that we began well this matter of the Gospel. But because we detest and condemn their blasphemous doctrine, they say that we are out just for the glory[65] and call us the new Papists, twice worse than the old. With this planned hoax, the sectarians, like robbers and assailants, infiltrate the fold of the Lord to steal, kill, and destroy. First, they confirm our teaching. But then they claim to correct us and expound more clearly what we have not sufficiently or not quite correctly understood.[66] It was just like this how the false apostles gained entrance to the Galatians. "Paul," they said, "certainly has laid the foundation of the Christian doctrine. However, he does not have the proper understanding of justification because he teaches the people to stray away from the law. Therefore, take from our hands what he was unable to give you." However, Paul will not tolerate anyone else teaching any other doctrine; neither will he tolerate the Galatians to hear or receive some other teaching.[67] He will only allow what he, himself, had taught them before and what they had heard and received from him. Then he says, "All others who teach and receive something else, let them be damned!"

The first two chapters contain only the defense of his doctrine and the refutation of errors. Thus he does not deal with the central theme of this epistle until the end of the second chapter. That theme is the place of justification.[68] Even so, this particular statement from Paul should be a warning to us. All who think the Pope is the judge of the Scriptures are under a curse. The papal scholars have wickedly taught the following false argument. The church has only permitted four Gospels; therefore, there are only four. If it had allowed others, there would be more. Therefore, the church has the power to receive and allow as many Gospels as it can, since the church is over the Gospel. What a great argument! I approve the Scriptures, *ergo* (therefore), I am above the Scriptures! John the Baptist recognized and confessed Christ and pointed him out; therefore, he is above Christ! The church approves of faith and Christian doctrine; therefore, the church has authority over these! To overthrow this wicked and blasphemous doctrine, there is no better text than this one, which resounds like a clap of thunder. Here, Paul submits himself and an angel from heaven, together with all the scholars on the earth and all teachers and professors everywhere under the authority of the sacred Scriptures. This queen must reign and all must be subject to her. The teachers, judges, and arbiters should not reign; they should be only simple witnesses, disciples, and confessors.

---

difficulty is resolved by the context. Luther's argument is that the harvest of a greater *fructus* or "great number of disciples" is the reason for false teachers to oppose the Gospel, both in Paul's time and in Luther's time. Obviously, we cannot omit in our reflection whether the same is true today as well.

[65] *adulatores et novos papistas.*

[66] *minus recte intellexerimus.*

[67] Pelikan summarizes this sentence.

[68] *locum justificationis.*

It doesn't matter if it's the Pope, Luther, Augustine, Paul, or an angel from heaven. Neither should any other doctrine be taught in the church, nor should anything else be heard that is not the pure word of God, which is the Holy Scriptures. Otherwise, let teachers, hearers, and the doctrine itself be damned!

VERSE 10. For am I now seeking the recommendation of men, or of God?[69]

These words are stated with the same fiery spirit as those before. It's as if he had said, "After having preached so openly in your churches, don't you remember what I, Paul, have been through? How could you still be unaware of my bitter conflicts and sharp battles with the Jews? It seems to me (or so I think) that after all my preaching and all the great afflictions I have suffered everywhere, it would be enough for you to realize whether I serve men or God, for all can see that through my preaching, I have not only stirred up persecution against me everywhere but also gained the cruel hate of my own nation and everyone else. Therefore, it's obvious that I do not want the compliments or the applause of men, but what I want is for the benefit and the glory of God."

Neither do we seek to be complimented by men through my doctrine, since we teach that every human being is wicked by nature and a child of wrath. We condemn in all human beings their free will, capability, wisdom, righteousness; we denounce all religions of human invention. In brief, we say that there is nothing in us that will equip us to merit the grace and forgiveness of sins. We preach that we obtain this grace only through the gracious mercy of God on account of Christ. Therefore, the heavens are telling the glory of God and His works, which condemn everyone in general with all their works. This preaching attracts neither people's goodwill nor the world's. Neither can the world tolerate the voice that condemns its wisdom, righteousness, religion, and might. To speak against those powerful and glorious gifts of the world is not to receive commendations but rather to reap the hate and the indignation of the world, for if we speak against men, or any other thing that relates to their glory, the only result is persecutions, excommunications, assassinations, and condemnations.

"If then," says Paul, "they have insight into other matters, why can't they see this, that I teach the things of God and not of men? Can't they see that through my doctrine I don't seek the considerations of anyone, but rather display God's mercy offered to us in Christ? For if I sought out to be accepted by others, I would not condemn their works. But it's true; I condemn human works. By that I mean that I declare God's judgment against every human being, according to His word (of which I am a minister and apostle). I announce that all are sinners, unjust, wicked, children of wrath, slaves of the devil, and under condemnation. Further, I

---

[69] *Nunc enim homines suadeo an Deum?*

announce that they are not declared righteous because of their works[70] or circumcision but only through grace and faith in Christ. For doing all this, I win the mortal hatred of men, for they can't tolerate to hear that they are just the way they are, it's as plain as that! No! They would rather have me praise them for their wisdom, righteousness, and holiness. Therefore, this is more than enough evidence that I don't teach the doctrine of any man at all."

Christ states the same in John 7: "The world can't hate you, but it hates me, because I testify about it, that its works are evil" (John 7:7). The same is stated in John chapter 3: "And this is the judgment, that the light has come into the world, and men loved darkness rather than light, because their deeds were evil" (John 3:19).

"Well, then, let it go on the record that I teach the things of God," says the apostle, "since I preach only God's grace, mercy, kindness, and glory. Further, just as Christ said, the one who declares the things that his Lord and Master has commanded and doesn't glorify himself but the one who sent him is the one who brings and teaches the true word of God. But I only teach those things that have been given to me from on high. I do not glorify myself but the one who sent me. Further, I incite against me the fury and indignation of Jews as well as Gentiles. Therefore, my doctrine is true, sincere, undeniable, and of God. It is not that there could be another or even one better than my doctrine. Therefore, any other doctrine that does not teach as mine does, that every human being is a sinner and that they are justified by faith alone in Christ,[71] is by default false, wicked, blasphemous, accursed, and diabolic, as well as all those who teach it and receive it."

So together with Paul we declare boldly that all doctrine that does not correspond with ours is under a curse. The reason is that we don't seek the praises of men through our preaching or the good graces of princes or bishops. We only seek God's favor, preaching only His grace and mercy, despising and treading under foot everything that belongs to ourselves. Therefore, everyone who teaches any other good news or good news that is contrary to what ours, we are bold enough to say that he has been sent by the devil, and let him be damned!

VERSE 10. Or am I striving to please men?

In other words, "Am I at the service of men or of God?" He's always looking out of the corner of his eye to the false apostles. These, he says, are always looking to flatter and please men. They want people to give glory to them in the flesh. Further, they cannot bear the burden of hate and persecution from men; that is why they

---

[70] *iustificentur non operibus*; Middleton and Watson incorrectly translate this as "made righteous."

[71] *et sola fide in Christus justificari.*

teach circumcision, just to avoid persecution for the sake of the cross of Christ, as it says in Galatians 5:11.

In the same way, today we find many that seek to please men so that they can live in the peace and safety of the flesh. They teach the things of men, wicked things. They tolerate the blasphemies and unjust judgments of the adversaries, which is contrary to the word of God. They do this contrary to their own conscience to retain the favor of the princes and the bishops and have them keep their own gods. But we, since we are committed to please only God and not men, we stir against us the wickedness of the devil and of hell itself. We suffer the censure and slander of the world, death, and all the evils that could ever be invented against us.

That is what Paul says here. I do not strive to please men just so that they will praise my doctrine and give reports that I am such an excellent teacher, but I just want to please God. For this reason, I end up making mortal enemies. I know from my own experience how true this is. The reward they give me is dishonor, slander, prison, the sword, etc. On the contrary, the false apostles teach the things of men, the things that are well within the possible according to human reason. That way, they live comfortably and buy the good graces, the goodwill and compliments of the people. And they find what they are looking for, since they receive the commendations and adulations of men. That is what Christ said (Matthew 6:2), that the hypocrites do everything to receive the praises of men. And the Gospel of John rebukes them severely: "How can you believe since you accept glory from one another but do not seek the glory that comes from the only God?" (John 5:44, NIV). The things that Paul has taught up to this point are only examples. Elsewhere, he has taught fervently that his doctrine is pure and sound. Therefore, he exhorts the Galatians not to abandon it in favor of some other doctrine.

VERSE 10. For if I were still pleasing men, I wouldn't be a servant of Christ.

These words embrace Paul's entire designation and ministry. They show the contrast between what his life had been before under Jewish law and his life now according to the Gospel. It's as if he had said, "Do you think that I am still looking to see how I can please men as I did in the past?" He talks like this in chapter 5: "If I am still preaching circumcision, why am I still being persecuted?" (Galatians 5:11). It's as if he had said, "Can't you see and hear that every day I suffer conflict, great persecution, and affliction? After my conversion, I was called to the office of apostle; that is why I have never taught the doctrine of men, nor do I seek to please men but God alone."

Once again, we see how Paul points to the shrewd and evil intent of the false apostles, setting up the Galatians to harbor hate against him. They combed the sermons and writings of Paul to find certain contradictions (just as our opponents set out to do with our books today). They could have even convinced him that he had contradicted himself. Therefore, they said, they shouldn't pay him any attention. However, they did have the obligation to circumcise and keep the law. They alleged that Paul himself had allowed it with his example, since he had circumcised Timothy according to the law. Together with four other men, he had purified himself in the temple of Jerusalem and had shaved his head in Cenchrea. Subtly they alleged that Paul had seen himself obligated to fulfill these rites as commanded by the apostles and mandated through their authority. But Paul had observed these things in freedom as a gift to the weaker brothers; he did not want to upset them, since they did not yet understand what it meant to be free in Christ.

To all these smears he answered, "What's certain is that the truth speaks for itself. There's no doubt that what the false apostles forge against me is the plan to overthrow my Gospel, raising up once again the law and circumcision, for if I preached the law and circumcision and praised the capacity, the strength, and the free will of man, they would not despise me as much, rather they would be quite pleased with me."

VERSE 11–12. I want you to know, brothers and sisters, that the gospel I preached is not of human origin. I did not receive it from any man, nor was I taught it; rather, I received it by revelation from Jesus Christ.

The main objective of this passage is dedicated to refuting his adversaries and defending his doctrine until the end of the second chapter. *Paul always recites this story. Jerome takes many turns trying to harmonize it. But he doesn't get to the heart of the subject, for he doesn't consider Paul's purpose or what Paul considers important. Further, the stories in the Scriptures often are told just briefly and out of order.*[72] *Thus they cannot be harmonized easily; for example, Peter's denials, the story of the passion of Christ, etc. In the same way, Paul doesn't tell the whole story here. Therefore, I don't stress out,*[73] *nor do I worry a great deal to harmonize it. What I consider is what Paul had in mind and what he takes into consideration.*

The main point here is this: "My Gospel is not according to man, nor did I receive it from man, but by revelation of Jesus Christ." He takes this stand and confirms it with an oath. The Galatians' unbelief prompted him to take the oath, hoping his oath would convince them to stop paying attention to the false apostles. Thus he rebukes them because they had said that he had learned and received his Gospel from the apostles.

With regards to what he says, that his Gospel is not according to man, he doesn't mean that his Gospel is not human.[74] This is obvious all by itself. Further,

---

[72] *concisae et confusae.*

[73] *non laboro.*

[74] *humanum.*

the false apostles boasted that their doctrine was not human but divine.[75] What he means is that he learned his Gospel not through the ministry of men nor by any human means[76] like we all learned it through the ministry of men or received it through some other means,[77] such as listening, reading, writing, or painting.[78] However, he received it only through a revelation from Jesus Christ. If others receive it differently, that's fine with me. By the way, here the apostle shows that Christ is not only a man but also both true God and man in the flesh when he says that he did not receive his Gospel through human means.

Paul received his Gospel on the way to Damascus, where Christ appeared and spoke to him. Thereafter, He also talked with him in the temple of Jerusalem. But he received his Gospel as he went along the way, as Luke narrates the story in Acts 9:6. "Get up," Christ said, "and you will be told what you must do." He doesn't say go to the city to learn the Gospel from Ananias. Rather, Ananias was sent to go and baptize him, lay hands on him, and recommend him to the church. Ananias did not receive the order to teach him the Gospel, for Paul had already received it—as he himself boasts—"only by revelation from Jesus Christ." Ananias confesses the same, saying, "Brother Saul, the Lord who appeared to you on the way has sent me so that you may receive your sight." Therefore, he did not receive his doctrine from Ananias. Rather, he had already been called, illumined, and taught of Christ along the way. His contact with Ananias was so that he would also receive the testimony of men, giving evidence that Paul had been called of God to preach the Gospel of Christ.

Paul recited this narrative because he felt compelled to undo the slander of the false apostles, who constantly plotted how to incriminate him before the Galatians, saying that Paul was inferior to the rest of the scholars who came from the apostles. Also, the false apostles claimed that they had received their teaching and ceremonies from the apostles themselves and further that they had accompanied the apostles for a long time and that Paul himself had received their very same doctrine from the same apostles, although now he denied it. Why then should the Galatians obey someone inferior and despise the authority of the apostles themselves, since they were the elders who for some time had already been teaching the Galatians as well as the churches all over the world?

This argument, that the false apostles supported their doctrine on the authority of the apostles, was presented vigorously and powerfully. Therefore, the Galatians' fall was sudden, particularly due to this matter. I, myself, would have never believed (had it not been for the example of the churches in Galatia and Corinth and others)

---

[75] *divinum.*

[76] *humano medio.*

[77] *humano medio.*

[78] *Pingendo*—"painting": Middleton and Watson both omitted it from the list of ways in which the Gospel may be learned.

that those who receive God's word at the beginning with great joy, among whom there were many personalities of renown, could have fallen so suddenly. Good Lord![79] How easy it is to cause horrible and infinite loss through one single argument! One single argument that removes God's grace can pierce and demoralize someone's conscience. In an instant, people can lose all the peace they ever had. The false apostles easily deceived them with their slander, since the Galatians were not firmly established and rooted but were still weak in the faith.

Further, the article of justification is a slippery doctrine.[80] This is true not due to its own nature because it's sure and true; but it is slippery within us. I know from personal experience. I've become acquainted with this problem in the long nights of struggle when darkness emerges and meets me face-to-face. I know how often and quickly I am separated from the soft winds of the Gospel and grace; it's as if a shadow falls that overwhelms me in dark and gloomy clouds. I know all too well the slippery[81] slopes that meet even those who are experienced and seem to be standing firm in the faith. We have plenty of experience in this matter. We are able to teach others, and this is a sign that we understand the faith. But when in the middle of the conflict, we need to use the Gospel, which is the word of grace, comfort, and life; at that moment, the law shows up, the word of wrath, gloom, and death. It hinders the Gospel with its thunders and terrors that resound throughout the conscience, no less than the display at Mount Sinai. With just one text from Scripture that contains some threat from the law, it overwhelms and drowns out all comfort and shakes all inner strength. The result is that we forget about justification, grace, Christ, the Gospel, and all that these embrace.

Therefore, as far as we are concerned, the Gospel is very slippery[82] because we are slippery.[83] We have against us half of what we are, which is our reason, with all its powers. On top of this, the flesh resists the spirit so that we cannot fully believe and trust that the promises of God are sure and true. The flesh resists the spirit. As Paul said, it "holds the spirit captive" so that the spirit cannot be consistent in believing, as it wishes it could. That is why we teach that to know Christ and believe in Him doesn't come as a human achievement. It is simply the gift of God, who similarly creates faith, and sustains it within us. Just as He first grants us faith through the word, He also exercises, increases, strengthens, and perfects it in us through the word. Thus the highest worship, the Sabbath of all Sabbaths, is the pious exercise of properly understanding and listening to the word. On the contrary, there is nothing as dangerous as getting bored with the word.[84] Thus

---

[79] *Bone Deus.*

[80] *lubrica.*

[81] *lubrico.*

[82] *lubrica.*

[83] *lubrici.*

[84] *fastidium verbi.*

whoever thinks he already knows enough gets colder and colder, until little by little, he begins to detest the word. Such a person has let go of Christ and the Gospel. Whoever thinks he already knows it all is only gazing at clouds of his own imagination. James says that such a one "is like a man looking at his face in a mirror. After he sees himself and goes away, he forgets what he looks like." These are the ones that eventually end up as fanatics and counterfeits.

Therefore, let all with great effort and diligence learn and observe this teaching. Humbly and with heartfelt prayer, let us study it consistently and meditate on it. When it seems to us that we have done too much, it still won't be enough to keep us firmly in the doctrine, for our enemies are not small but strong and powerful. They're continually at war against us. I mean our own flesh, all the dangers of the world, the law, sin, death, the wrath and the judgment of God, and the devil himself, for this last one never ceases to tempt us from within with his fiery darts and on the outside through his false prophets with the goal of taking everything away from us, and if he can't take all, he takes the best part of what we have.

Therefore, this argument of the false apostles made for a good presentation and seemed quite convincing. This same argument convinces many today: that what the church thinks and believes today is what the apostles, the holy fathers, and their successors have thought and believed. But there's more. They argue that it is impossible for Christ to have permitted His church to remain in error for such a long time. They say, "So it just happens that only you are the wisest among the holy men? Wiser than the entire church?" In this way, they change the devil into an angel of light, and today, they stalk us with these subtleties. There are certain pestilent hypocrites who say, "We won't even forgive the Pope, we detest the hypocrisy of the monks" and things like that. "But don't touch the authority of the church. This is what the church has believed and taught for such a long time. All the scholars of the early church were pious men, with better pedigree and education than you. Who do you think you are daring to dissent from all of them and bring us a contrary doctrine?" When Satan reasons with you in this way, taking advantage of reason and the flesh as accomplices, your conscience becomes intimidated, and you will lose hope, unless you come to your senses, saying, "It doesn't matter if Cyprian, Ambrose, Augustine, Saint Peter, Paul, or John, or even an angel from heaven teaches something else, this I know with all confidence: that I do not teach the doctrines of men but of God. In other words, I give all the credit to God for everything, man gets nothing."

When I first took on the task of defending the Gospel, I remember Doctor Staupitz, a noble man, said to me, "I like this so much, that this doctrine you preach gives glory and everything else only to God and nothing to man. One can never render enough glory, kindness, and mercy to God." These words comforted and confirmed me beyond measure. And it is true that the doctrine of the Gospel takes away from man all the glory, wisdom, righteousness, and so on and offers it only to the Creator who made everything from nothing. There is greater safety in attributing too much to God than to man. That is why in this case I can boldly state, "So be it, that the church, Augustine, and all other scholars, as well as Peter and Apollos, if even an angel from heaven should teach a contrary doctrine, my doctrine is such that it will only teach God's grace and glory alone! However, let all human wisdom and righteousness (offered for salvation) be damned! In this, there is no possible sin because I render to God as well as to man what belongs to each."

But you say, "The church is holy, the fathers are holy." That's true. But even so, regardless how holy the church is, it still has the obligation to pray, "And forgive us our sins." Thus no matter how holy the fathers are, even they are saved through the forgiveness of sins. Neither should they believe me, nor the church, nor the fathers, nor the apostles, nor even an angel from heaven, if we teach anything contrary to the word of God. Let the word of God remain forever. Had it been otherwise, this argument of the false apostles would have prevailed powerfully against Paul's doctrine. Certainly, it was a great thing, a great argument, I say, to expound before the entire church of Galatia, alleging the support of the apostles, "that Paul was alone, that he was only a latecomer, and with very little authority." Therefore, it was a powerful argument with powerful conclusions, for not just anyone is willing to say, "The church is in error." Nonetheless, it is necessary to say that, "yes, it is mistaken" if it teaches things that are not in the word of God or that contradict it.

Peter, foremost among the apostles, was teaching with his life as well as with his doctrine something more that was not in the word of God. Therefore, he was mistaken and thus deceived. Paul did not cover up his error, although it seemed like only just a small fault. Paul saw that it would be to the detriment of the entire church. Therefore, "I rebuked him to his face, because he was not walking in the truth of the Gospel"[85] (see below in chapter 2). For that reason, one must not listen to the church, or Peter, or the apostles, not even the angels from heaven, unless they bring and teach the word of God in its purity.

This argument[86] still wreaks havoc against our cause today. If we are not going to believe the Pope, or the fathers, or Luther, or anyone else unless they teach the pure word of God, then who are we going to believe? Who, in the meantime, is going to certify to our consciences? Which of the two parties teaches the word of God in its purity? Do we teach it correctly or do our adversaries? They brag that they also have the pure word of God and that they teach it. But again, we do not believe the followers of the Pope because they don't teach the word of God, nor could they even teach it. On the contrary, they hate us bitterly and persecute us as if we were the most detestable heretics who seduce the people. What should be done in this case? Is it legitimate that each fanatical sectarian spirit teaches what it seems right considering that the world won't even hear and even less remain in

---

[85] Luther joins Galatians 2:11 and 2:14 in this sentence.

[86] The "Gospel plus something else" argument.

our doctrine? We glory with Paul that we teach the pure Gospel of Christ.[87] *And to this Gospel, the emperor, the Pope, and the entire world should surrender, receive it with open hands, embrace it with affection, and diligently care for it so that it will be taught everywhere. But if others teach their own varieties of the gospel,[88] whether it's the Pope, Saint Augustine, an apostle, or an angel from heaven, let them be accursed together with their gospel.* There's nothing we can do as we move forward. At the same time, we are forced to listen so that what we teach and cherish as our glory is not only vain, harsh, and conceited but also diabolic and full of blasphemy. But if we lower our chin, giving in to the fury of our adversaries, then the followers of the Pope and the fanatics will be fired up with pride! The latter will boast that they bring and teach a certain peculiar thing that the world has never heard. The former will champion their teachings and reestablish themselves and their abominations. They will all feel revindicated. Therefore, let everyone stay alert, certain of their calling and their doctrine so that with Paul they can boldly say with all confidence, "But even though we, or an angel from heaven . . ."[89]

Up to this point, he has proposed the argument in this passage: that he did not receive the Gospel from any one person but through the revelation of Jesus Christ. He now proceeds to tell a number of stories to prove his argument.[90]

VERSES 13 and 14. You have heard, no doubt, of my earlier life in Judaism. I was violently persecuting the church of God and was trying to destroy it. I advanced in Judaism beyond many among my people of the same age, for I was far more zealous for the traditions of my ancestors.[91]

This passage does not contain any particular doctrine. However, Paul cites his own example. He says, "I have defended the traditions of the Pharisees, and of the Jewish religion, more than any of you and all your false teachers. If the righteousness of the law had something worthwhile, I would not have left it behind. But when I kept it, before I came to know Christ, I made such a great effort to profit from it that I outdid many of my own compatriots. What's more, I was so zealous to defend it that I persecuted the church to the extreme and sought to destroy it altogether. Since I had received authority from the high priests, I sent many to

---

[87] *nos purum Christi evangelium docere.*

[88] *diversum doceat.*

[89] This is one of many instances where Luther cuts off a verse with an "etc." Most likely this was a pause intended for his students to finish Galatians 1:8: "should preach to you any Gospel other than that which we preached to you, let him be accursed." One can almost hear the chorus of voices in the lecture hall repeating the verse.

[90] Watson omits this brief paragraph.

[91] NRSV.

prison. When the time came to send them to death, I pronounced the sentence. I punished them throughout the synagogues. I forced them to blaspheme, and in my fury, I persecuted them as far as unknown cities."

VERSE 14. I was far more zealous for the traditions of my ancestors.

Here, he doesn't say whether the traditions of the fathers are either pharisaic or human, as Jerome correctly points out. The subject is not the traditions of the Pharisees, but a topic of much greater importance. The topic here is that he lumps together even the holy law of Moses with the traditions of the forefathers. He considered both as one and the same inheritance. His zeal did not make any distinctions; for him, they were both the same: "When I was in the Jewish religion, I was very zealous." He tells the Philippians the same thing (3:5–6): "As to zeal, a persecutor of the church; as to righteousness under the law, blameless." It's as if he had said, "I could glory in this and compare myself with the entire Jewish nation, even with the best and holiest of the entire circumcision! Show me if you can, someone who defended the law of Moses with greater zeal and passion than I. I was the standard bearer, much better than the others in showing zeal for the traditions of the fathers, totally devoted to the righteousness of the law. This, oh Galatians, should have persuaded you not to believe in those impostors who puff up the righteousness of the law as the topic of greatest importance. Well, if there were a good reason to glory in the righteousness of the law, I would have it much more than anyone else!"

I could say the same thing about my experience. Before I was enlightened by the knowledge of the Gospel, I was equally zealous for the papal laws and the traditions of the fathers. I could match up with anyone, promoting and defending them with intense passion as holy and necessary for salvation. Even more, I, myself, sought to observe and keep them in every way possible. I punished my body with fasts, vigils, prayers, and other exercises. I did it more than all who today hate me and persecute me relentlessly because I have taken away all their glory of justifying themselves through their works and merits. I was so diligent and superstitious in observing these things that I forced my body beyond what it could tolerate, even putting my health at risk. As a matter of conscience, I honored the Pope. I obeyed without pretenses and without seeking perks, promotions, or housing benefits. Everything I did was from the heart, with loyalty, and for the glory of God. But all these things that I considered valuable, now with Paul, I count them as loss for the excellence of knowing Jesus Christ, my Lord. But our adversaries, well fed and lazy, who've never been put to the test, don't believe that I, and others with me, have endured such things. I talk about these experiences because I looked to find in them great peace and rest for my conscience. However, it was impossible to find these in that great darkness.

VERSES 15, 16, and 17. But when God, who separated me from my mother's womb, and called me through his grace, was pleased to reveal his Son to me, so that I might proclaim him among the Gentiles, I did not confer with any human being, nor did I go up to Jerusalem to those who were already apostles before me, but I went away at once into Arabia, and afterwards I returned to Damascus.

This is Paul's first trip. *Here, Jerome works overtime,*[92] *saying that in Acts Luke doesn't say anything about Paul's trip to Arabia. But was it really necessary to explain all the events and happenings of every single day? That would have been impossible! Let it suffice that we have certain particulars and a number of narratives that we can use as instructive examples.* Here, he testifies that once he had been called by the grace of God to preach Christ among the Gentiles, immediately, he went to Arabia without consulting with anyone regarding the work to which he had been called. Here, he testified about who taught him and the way he came to know the Gospel and about his apostleship. "And when God was pleased," he says. As if saying, "I did not merit it because I was so zealous for God's law that I didn't fear the judgment. Instead, this foolish and wicked zeal moved so intensely within me that God in His patience permitted my headlong fall into the most abominable and shameless sins. I persecuted the church of God, I was an enemy of Christ, I blasphemed His Gospel, and to top it all, I was the author of shedding much innocent blood. That was my merit.[93] In the middle of such cruel fury, I was called to such immeasurable grace. What? Was it perhaps because of my merciless cruelty? Not at all! Instead, it was because of the abundant grace of God, who calls and shows mercy to whom He wills, He forgave me and freed me from all those blasphemies. For these horrible sins of mine, which I then thought were perfect righteousness and pleasing service to God, He granted me His grace, the knowledge of His truth and called me to be an apostle."

We also have arrived to the knowledge of grace due to the same merits. Daily, I crucified Christ with my life as a monk. I blasphemed God with my false faith, in which I lived continually. To all appearances, I was not like other men, deceiver, pernicious. Instead, I practiced celibacy, poverty, and obedience. I was also free from all the stresses of daily life. I gave myself over to fasts, vigils, prayers, saying mass, and such things. Meanwhile, under that mantle of presumed holiness, I nurtured confidence in my own righteousness, which I constantly doubted, fearing, hating, and blaspheming God. And with this, my righteousness, I was nothing more than a cesspool, the kingdom of the devil himself, for Satan

---

[92] *sudat*, literally "sweats." I have used a comparable modern English expression, "works overtime."

[93] *hoc meum meritum.*

loves such saints, spoils them as his favorite children, those who destroy their bodies and souls and deny themselves all God's gifts. Meanwhile and notwithstanding, wickedness, blindness, scorn for God, despising the Gospel, profaning the Sacraments, blaspheming Christ, stepping all over Him, and abusing all the benefits and the gifts of God, these reigned without measure. In brief, such saints are slaves of Satan. Therefore, they are moved to talk, think, and do all that he wants. But to all appearances, they seem to be way above all others in good works, holiness, and self-controlled lifestyle.

That is how we were in the papacy. Certainly, we were no less but more stubborn and blasphemers against Christ and His Gospel than Paul himself. I was particularly like that. I had such a high esteem for papal authority that I thought dissenting from the Pope was a sin worthy of eternal death. That wicked opinion led me to think that John Huss had been a cursed heretic. I took it as a despicable crime. When I thought about him, it occurred to me that to defend the authority of the Pope I, myself, would have provided the fire and the sword to burn and destroy that heretic, thinking that in doing that I would have rendered a great service to God. Therefore, if one compares the publicans and the prostitutes with these hypocritical Holy Joes, the former are not that bad. When these sinners offend, their consciences bother them, and they don't justify their bad works. However, the latter are so far from recognizing that their abominations, idolatries, wicked ceremonies, and their idolatry of free will and the capacity to choose are nothing else but sin. They think that they themselves are an acceptable sacrifice unto God, and they worship them as if they were validation of unique holiness. Through these, they promise salvation to others; there are still others that sell them for money, as capital available for salvation.

That is the extent of our high-quality righteousness, as well as that of our great merit that brings us to the knowledge of grace. It's this: that we have persecuted to death and diabolically blasphemed, stomped on, and condemned God, the Gospel, faith, the Sacraments, every good person, and the true worship to God. In fact, we have taught and established things totally the opposite. And the more "holier-than-thou" we were, the worse our blindness, worshipping the devil even more. But there was not even one among us who was not a leech, if not in deed, then in the very heart.

VERSE 15. But when God was pleased.

"I was forgiven only by God's boundless grace, even though I was so wicked and accursed, such a blasphemer, persecutor, and extremely rebellious! And as if that was not enough, He wasn't satisfied with just forgiving me. On top of that, God granted me the knowledge of His salvation, His Spirit, Christ His Son, the office of apostle, and eternal life." When God fixes His gaze on our guilt due to similar sins, through His pure mercy and because of Christ, He not only forgives our wickedness and blasphemies but also overwhelms us with great spiritual benefits and gifts. But many who have shared this knowledge with us have been ungrateful with God for His immeasurable grace. However, it's also written about them, "Forgetting that they were cleansed from their past sins" (2 Peter 1:9). Further, some have once again opened the window to the devil and, despising the word, have perverted and corrupted it, becoming the authors of new errors. "That person is worse off at the end than at the beginning."

VERSE 15. God, who separated me from my mother's womb.

This is a Hebrew phrase. It's as if he had said, "God sanctified, ordained, and prepared me. God had already predestined me,[94] even while I was still in my mother's womb, that I would lunge at His church, and thereafter, He would call me by His pure grace to turn to Him in the middle of my cruelty and blasphemy, through His sheer grace, to the path of truth and salvation. In brief, even before I was born I was already an apostle in God's sight, and when the time was right, I was declared an apostle before the entire world."

In this way, Paul cuts out all merit and gives glory only to God but as to himself, only shame and confusion. It's as if he had said, "All the gifts, small and great, spiritual and bodily; all that God set out to give me; everything good that I would ever do in my life, God Himself had already ordained when I was still in my mother's womb. There I could not wish, think, or do any good work. Therefore, this gift came to me through God's predestination[95] and freely given mercy before I was born. But there's more. After I was born, He sustained me, for I was overburdened with incalculable wickedness and the most detestable evil for Him to declare even more clearly the inexpressible and immeasurable greatness of His mercy toward me through His pure grace forgave my infinite and abominable sins. What's more, he supplied me with such great abundance of His grace that He not only gave me understanding of the things He has given us in Christ but that I would preach them to others. Without this, we get what every human being rightly deserves and especially those useless old fools, who have exercised in the dung of human righteousness longer than the others."[96]

VERSE 15. And called me through his grace.

Look at how diligently the apostle beckons. He says, "He called me. How? Was it because I practiced my religion as a devout Pharisee? Was it perhaps due to my impeccable and virtuous life? No. Was it perhaps due to my prayers, fasts,

---

[94] *predestinaverat.*
[95] *predestinaverat.*
[96] *qui sese in stercoribus justitiae humanae prae ceteris exercuerunt.*

and works? No. Then it was even less due to my blasphemies, persecutions, and oppressions. Then why did He call me? Out of pure grace."[97]

VERSE 16. To reveal His son in me.

Now we hear the type of doctrine entrusted to Paul: the doctrine of the Gospel, which is the revelation of the Son of God. This is a doctrine quite contrary to the law. The doctrine of the law does not reveal the Son of God but only puts the spotlight on sin; mortifies the conscience; reveals the certainty of death, wrath and the judgment of God, and hell. The Gospel is so unique a doctrine that it doesn't admit any law. It should be separated as far from the law as the distance that separates heaven and earth. By itself, this difference exists easily and clearly. However, for us, it is difficult and replete with difficulties, for it is easy to say that the Gospel is nothing else but the revelation of the Son of God or the knowledge of Jesus Christ and that it is not the revelation of the law. However, when the conscience is agonizing and deeply stressed, to grasp this and put it into practice, it is difficult even for those who are experienced in this exercise.

Well then, if the Gospel is the revelation of the Son of God, as Paul defines it here, then it certainly does not accuse, terrify with consequences, threaten with death, nor bring on despair, as does the law, for the Gospel is a doctrine referring to Christ. And He is not a law, or a work, but rather our righteousness, wisdom, sanctification, and redemption (1 Corinthians 1:30). Even though this is clearer than daylight, nonetheless the madness and blindness of the followers of the Pope has been so great that they have turned the Gospel into a law of love and transformed Christ into a legislator more demanding and strict than Moses himself. But the Gospel teaches that Christ did not come to establish a new law or to give commandments that regulate behaviors. The Gospel teaches that He came with this purpose: to give His life as an offering for the sins of the entire world, for the forgiveness of our sins so that eternal life will be granted to us for His sake and not for our works of the law or our own righteousness. This is that priceless treasure that the Gospel rightly proclaims to us. Therefore, this doctrine is not learned, nor received through diligent study or the wisdom of man, nor even by the law of God. God Himself reveals the Gospel, as Paul says here: first by means of the external word and then by the work of the Holy Spirit working internally. The Gospel is the divine word that descends from heaven and is revealed by means of the Holy Spirit, who was sent with the same purpose. However, the external word comes first. Paul himself did not receive an internal revelation until after he heard the external word from heaven, saying, "Saul, Saul, why do you persecute me?" (Acts 9:4). First then, he heard the external word and then came the revelations, the knowledge of the word of faith, and the gifts of the Holy Spirit.

---

[97] *per meram gratiam.*

VERSE 16. To proclaim him among the Gentiles.

"God was pleased," says the apostle, "to reveal His son to me." To what purpose? Not only that I, myself, would believe in the Son of God but that I could preach Him among the Gentiles. And why not among the Jews? Here, we see that Paul is chiefly the apostle to the Gentiles, although he also preached Christ among the Jews.

Here, in just a few words, Paul outlines his entire theology (as is his custom), which is to preach Christ among the Gentiles. It's as if he had said, "I am not going to impose the burden of the law on the Gentiles because I am the apostle and evangelist to the Gentiles, but I am not their law giver." In this way, he directed all his words against the false apostles. It's as if he had said, "Oh Galatians, you have heard me teach neither about the righteousness of the law nor about works. That task belongs to Moses and not to me, Paul, for I am the apostle to the Gentiles. My function and ministry is to deliver the Gospel to them and teach them the same revelation that I received. Therefore, you should not listen to any teacher that promotes the law. The reason is that the law should not be preached among the Gentiles but rather the Gospel. Not Moses but the Son of God. Not the righteousness of works but the righteousness of faith. This is the preaching that rightly belongs to the Gentiles."

VERSE 16. I did not confer with flesh and blood.

On this point, Jerome has nothing good to say about Porphyrius and Julian. They accuse Paul of arrogance, since he did not consult with the apostles to see if his Gospel was the same they were teaching. Further, Paul calls the apostles just "flesh and blood." But here, when Paul mentions flesh and blood, he is not talking about the apostles, since he adds, "Nor did I go up to Jerusalem to those who were already apostles before me." What Paul wants to say is that once he received the revelation of the Gospel of Christ he didn't consult with anyone in Damascus. Further, he didn't ask anyone to teach him the Gospel. Thus he didn't go to Jerusalem, to Peter and the other apostles, to learn the Gospel from them. Rather, he immediately preached Christ in Damascus, where he received baptism from Ananias, as well as the laying on of hands. It was necessary for him to obtain the sign and the external testimony of his calling. Luke also writes the same in Acts 9.

VERSE 17. Nor did I go up to Jerusalem to those who were already apostles before me, but I went away at once into Arabia, and afterwards I returned to Damascus.

He says, "I went to Arabia before I saw the apostles or consulted with them. I immediately took on the task of preaching to the Gentiles." That was my calling, and I also had received a revelation from God. *Therefore, Jerome in vain questions what Paul was doing in Arabia. What else was he doing but preaching Christ? For this reason, he says, the Son of God was revealed to him, to preach Him among the Gentiles. Therefore, he immediately travels from Damascus, a city of the Gentiles, to Arabia, also among the Gentiles, and there he powerfully exercises his commission.* Therefore, he did not receive his Gospel from any human being, nor from the apostles themselves, but rejoiced only in his heavenly calling and with the revelation of Jesus Christ.

LECTURE 6: Saturday, July 18

Therefore, this entire passage is a refutation of the false apostles' argument that they used against Paul, saying that he was only self-taught; that he had only heard about the apostles who lived according to the law and further that Paul himself had lived according to the law. Therefore, it was also necessary for the Gentiles to keep the law and to be circumcised. Thus to shut the mouths of these pretenders, he repeats this long story. Before my conversion, he says, I did not learn the Gospel from the apostles nor from any of the other believers (for I had relentlessly persecuted not only this doctrine but also the church of God, striking it down). Neither did I learn from them after my conversion, for immediately, I preached in Damascus, not Moses with his law but Christ. I did not confer with anyone because I had not seen any of the apostles.

In the same way, it's impossible for us to boast that we learned our doctrine from the Pope. From him, we have received the Scriptures and the external symbols[98] *but not the doctrine, which we have received solely as a gift from God. To that we have added our study, reading, and research. Thus the argument of our adversaries is but a trifle, for today, they tell us, "Oh Lutherans, who is ever going to believe your doctrine, since you have never been publicly appointed? You owe your doctrine to the Pope and learned it from the bishops, since they have been duly ordained and serve legitimately, and such."*

VERSES 18–19. Then after three years I went up to Jerusalem to visit Peter, and stayed with him fifteen days. But of the other apostles I saw no one, except James, the Lord's brother.

Paul admits that he was with the apostles, but not with all. However, he makes it clear that he went to Jerusalem, not because they ordered him to appear, but of his own free will, and not to learn anything from them, but to see Peter. Luke narrates the same thing in Acts 9:27, that Barnabas had taken Paul to see the apostles. He

---

[98] *externa symbola*, in other words, the sacraments.

58

declared before them how he had seen the Lord on the way and that he had spoken with Him and also that he had preached boldly in Damascus in the name of Jesus (Barnabas testified about this). All his words are within that context and serve to prove that his Gospel was not from man. It is true that he admits to having seen Peter and James the brother of our Lord but none of the other apostles aside from these two and that he learned nothing from them.

Therefore, he admits to having been in Jerusalem with the apostles. This is all contained in the report of the false apostles. Further, he recognizes that he had lived according to the custom of the Jews but always only among the Jews. Paul restricted himself to this rule: "When in Rome do as the Romans." This is what he says in 1 Corinthians 9:19–22: "Though I am free from all, I have made myself a slave to all, that I might win the more. To the Jews, I became as a Jew, in order to win Jews; to those under the law, I became as one under the law . . . I have become all things to all men, that I might by all means save some."[99] He acknowledges that he was in Jerusalem with the apostles but denies having learned his Gospel from them. He also denies that he was required to teach the Gospel in a manner prescribed by the apostles. The force of all this issue is contained in the phrase "I went," as he says, "to see Peter, not to learn from him. Therefore, neither Peter nor James taught me." Insofar as the other apostles, he altogether denies that he met with any of them.

But why does Paul repeatedly state that he learned his Gospel neither from men nor from the apostles themselves? His purpose is this: to persuade the Galatian churches, now under the leadership of the false apostles, that the Gospel he taught was the true word of God. This is the reason for his repeated assertions. If he had not prevailed on this issue, he would not have been able to shut the mouths of the false apostles. Otherwise, they would have protested against him: "We are as good as Paul; we are disciples of the apostles, just like him. Further, he stands all by himself, whereas we are many. Therefore, we surpass him in authority as well as in the number of believers."

Here, Paul was compelled to glory, affirm, and vow that he had neither learned his Gospel from any man nor received it from the apostles themselves. *For him, it was a must to glory in this manner, and it wasn't just empty boasting, as Porphyrius and Julian falsely allege, for they couldn't see (neither could Jerome) Paul's intent.* Paul's ministry on this issue was in great danger, as well as all the churches, since he had been their pastor and main teacher. Therefore, his ministry and all the churches called for him to boast of his vocation with a holy pride and of the knowledge of the Gospel that Christ had revealed to Him so that their consciences would be totally persuaded that his doctrine was the true word of God. Here, Paul struggled with a matter of the highest magnitude: that all the churches in Galatia should be preserved in the sound doctrine. The controversy was no less a matter of

---

[99] CEB.

eternal life and death, for if the word of God should disappear, there would no lon-ger be abundant comfort, life, or salvation. This is the reason he chooses to recite these issues, to keep the churches in the true and upright doctrine. He perseveres in this struggle not to defend his own glory as Porphyrius slanders. His will is to show through this narrative that he had not received his Gospel from any man. Again, he preached the same Gospel taught by the apostles. He first received it by revelation from God and then preached it for three or four years in Damascus and Arabia before meeting with any of the apostles.

Here, Jerome is rather flippant about the mystery of the fifteen days. He also says that in those fifteen days Peter instructed Paul in the mysteries of Ogdoad and Hebdoad. But these things have nothing to do with the facts. Paul clearly says that he came to Jerusalem to see Peter and he stayed with him for fifteen days. Had his purpose been to learn the Gospel from Peter, it would have taken him several years. In fifteen days, he could not have become the great apostle and teacher[100] of the Gentiles—not to mention that in those fifteen days (as Luke testifies in Acts 9:27), he spoke boldly in the name of Jesus and debated with the Greeks.

VERSE 20. Before God, I'm not lying about the things that I'm writing to you!

Was it necessary for Paul to swear this oath? It was because he had narrated a his-torical event. Thus he had the obligation to swear the truth, so that the churches would believe him and also so that the false apostles would not say, "Who knows if Paul is really telling the truth?" Thus you can already see how the Galatians already had very little esteem left for Paul, a vessel chosen by God. Even though he had already preached Christ to them, he saw it necessary to swear that he was telling the truth. If the apostles already had to deal with such powerful opponents, does it surprise us at all that we suffer the same things? And by no means do we consider ourselves worthy to be compared to the apostles. Therefore, he swears an oath, due to something that to us seems like a trifle. But he speaks the truth, that he did not delay his stay with Peter as if to learn something from him but only to see him. But if we weigh this matter carefully, we see it's of great consequence and importance, as can be understood from what he says before. In the same way, we swear as Paul did on this matter: God knows we are not lying.

VERSE 21. Then I went into the regions of Syria and Cilicia.

Syria and Cilicia are border countries. By saying this, he still wants to persuade the Galatians that he always taught the same Gospel, both before and after meeting

---

[100] *doctor gentium.*

the apostles. Paul insists that he had received the Gospel by revelation from Christ and not from the apostles for he had never been their disciple.

VERSES 22, 23, and 24. But I wasn't known personally by the Christian churches in Judea. They only heard a report about me: "The man who used to harass us now preaches the faith that he once tried to destroy." So they were glorifying God because of me.

He adds this to continue the story. After seeing Peter, he went to Syria and Cilicia preaching there with such power that he gained the good testimony of all the churches of Judea. It's as if he had said, "I appeal to the testimony of all the churches, even those in Judea, for the churches give witness that not only in Damascus, Arabia, Syria, and Cilicia but also in Judea, I have preached the same faith that I refuted and persecuted in times past. They glorified God in me. Not because I taught circumcision and the keeping of the law of Moses but due to my preaching of faith, and for the building up of the churches through my ministry in the Gospel. Therefore, you have the testimony not only of the entire people of Damascus and Arabia but also of the entire catholic, or universal, church of Judea."

Galatians 2

VERSE 1. Then after fourteen years I went up to Jerusalem.

Paul taught that the Gentiles are declared righteous through faith alone, without the works of the law.[1] This was the doctrine that he had proclaimed among the Gentiles. When he arrived at Antioch, he declared to the apostles what he had done. Those who had grown up under the old traditions of the law got upset at Paul, since he preached to the Gentiles freedom from the yoke of the law. What followed was a huge disagreement that brought up new problems. Paul and Barnabas remained in the truth. They testified, "Everywhere we preached to the Gentiles, *the Holy Spirit smote[2] those who received the word in all the churches of the Gentiles. We didn't preach circumcision; we did not place on them the requirement of observing the law. We preached over and over again faith alone in Jesus Christ.[3] Through our preaching of faith, God gave the Holy Spirit to those who listened.*" Therefore, the Holy Spirit approved of the Gentiles' faith without the law and circumcision. If the word of the Gospel and the Gentiles' faith in Christ had not pleased the Holy Spirit, He would not have descended in visible form on the uncircumcised who heard the word. Just by hearing the word of faith alone,[4] the Holy Spirit fell upon them. This was a sure sign that the Holy Spirit approved the Gentiles' faith, since it had never been heard before that such a thing happened at the preaching of the law. Such was the argument of Paul and Barnabas.

Many of the Jews and Pharisees had believed. Yet they still defended the glory of the law and zealously fought and opposed Paul very forcefully. Yet Paul kept on sowing the truth that the Gentiles are justified by faith alone without the works of the law.[5] The Jews insisted that the Gentiles should keep the law and be circumcised; otherwise, they could not be saved. This argument always has its impact, since the very name "the law of God" is holy and foreboding. The pagan, who has never heard anything about God, just as soon as he hears about the law of God becomes troubled. How can a Jew then not be an even greater advocate for the law of God and be moved by it, seeing that he was nurtured and formed by the law ever since he was a tiny infant?

Today, we see the stubbornness of the followers of the Pope as they defend their traditions and devilish doctrines. Thus it's not surprising that the Jews

---

[1] *sola fide justificari, sine operibus legis.*

[2] *venit Spiritus sanctus et cecidit super eos.*

[3] *sed tantum fidem in Christum praedicationem.*

[4] *Per solum auditum fidei.*

[5] *gentes sola fide sine operibus legis justificarentur.*

showed so much passion and zeal in trying to retain the law they had received from God. The keeping of the law is such a strong habit that over time its strength is redoubled. Thus it was impossible for the Jews recently converted to Christ to abandon the law from one moment to the other. Notwithstanding that they had received faith in Christ, they nonetheless thought it necessary to continue observing the law. The Lord tolerated this weakness for some time, until the doctrine of the Gospel could clearly be distinguished from the law. During the time of King Ahab, the Lord had tolerated the weakness of Israel when the people hesitated between two religions. He also tolerated our weakness when we were under the blindness of the Pope, for "He is slow to anger and abundant in loving kindness." But we should not abuse this kindness and leniency of the Lord nor follow in our weakness and error, since the truth has now been revealed through the clear light of the Gospel.

What's more, they opposed Paul under the pretense that the Gentiles should also be circumcised. Further, first, they had to pay attention to the law and the traditions of the nation and then follow the example of the apostles. Finally, they argued that Paul himself had given the example of circumcising Timothy. Therefore, if Paul in his defense had said that he did not do it out of obligation but out of love and the Christian's liberty and to avoid offending the weaker in the faith, who would have believed him? In fact, all would have told him, "It is obvious that you circumcised Timothy, and say what you will, you did it." This matter overwhelmed their capacity to understand Paul's teaching. Further, there is no defense that will help you when the people have already impeached you, becoming a victim of their disdain and mortal hate. Thus Paul, seeing that this dispute grew day by day and having been warned in a revelation from God, after fourteen years (in addition to those he had already worked in Damascus and Arabia), goes up once again to Jerusalem. His wish is to compare his Gospel with the other apostles—not to defend himself but to defend the Gospel among the Gentiles.[6]

This argument with respect to the keeping of the law annoyed Paul for a great while to the point of almost wearing him out. But I think this is not the same dispute mentioned by Luke in Acts 15, which seems to have come up as soon as the preaching of the Gospel began. The story that Paul mentions here seems to have taken place some time later, when Paul had already been preaching the Gospel for almost eighteen years.

VERSE 1. With Barnabas, taking Titus also with me.

He took two witnesses with him, Barnabas and Titus. Barnabas had accompanied Paul preaching freedom from the bondage of the law to the Gentiles. He had witnessed everything that Paul did and had seen the Holy Spirit poured out among

---

[6] *populi causa.*

the uncircumcised Gentiles, free from the law of Moses, just by preaching to them faith in Christ.[7] That is why he faithfully backed up Paul in this matter, that it was not necessary to impose the law on the Gentiles but that belief in Christ was sufficient.[8] Through his own experience, Barnabas would give witness together with Paul that the Gentiles became God's children saved by faith alone in Jesus Christ,[9] without the law of the circumcision.

Titus was not only a Christian but also the main overseer[10] in Crete, since Paul had charged him with administering those churches (Titus 1). This Titus was a Gentile.

VERSE 2. I went in response to a revelation.

Paul would not have gone had he not received a revelation that he should go to Jerusalem. But God advised[11] him through a special revelation and ordered him to go. Paul obeyed. His intention was to rein in the Jews or at least to calm down those who had believed and yet at the same time obstinately adhered to the law. With his trip, Paul sought to advance and confirm the truth of the Gospel.

VERSE 2. I presented to them the gospel that I preach.

Here, we hear that at long last, after eighteen years, Paul consults with the apostles in Jerusalem regarding the Gospel.

VERSE 2. That I preach among the Gentiles.

For a time, Paul tolerated the law and circumcision among the Jews, as did the other apostles: "I have become all things to all" (1 Corinthians 9:22). However, he always upheld the true doctrine of the Gospel, putting it above the law, circumcision, the apostles, and even the angels of heaven, for to the Jews, he said, "Through this Christ is announced forgiveness of sins." And then he adds with all clarity, "From which you could not be justified by the law of Moses" (Acts 13:38). For this cause, Paul taught and defended the Gospel everywhere, always safeguarding it from danger. Even so, at the beginning, he did not leave anyone behind, but always had in mind those who were weak. So that they would not take offense, he spoke to the Jews in these terms: "If the useless service to the law of Moses, which gets you nowhere, so pleases you, do it on my behalf, on the condition that you will not

---

[7] *praedicationem fidei in Christum.*

[8] *sed sufficiere, quod credant in Christum.*

[9] *per solam fidem in Christum.*

[10] *Archiepiscopus,* "Archbishop."

[11] *admonitus fuisset Paulus pero revelationem.*

subject the Gentiles to this law to which they are not bound and that it will not be imposed on them as a burden."

Therefore, Paul confesses that he communicated to the apostles the Gospel that he preached. But he added, "They did not contribute anything, they didn't teach me anything. On the contrary, because I defended the freedom of the Gospel in the presence of the apostles, I constantly resisted those who would impose the keeping of the law on the Gentiles, and I overcame them. Thus their false apostles lie, saying that I circumcised Timothy, that I shaved my head in Chencrea, and that I went up to Jerusalem by order of the apostles. No! Instead, I glory that I went to Jerusalem by revelation from God and not by order of the apostles. Having communicated my Gospel to them, I accomplished the opposite: the apostles gave me their approval instead of approving my adversaries."

The topic of this animated[12] consultation with the apostles was this: Is it possible to be justified without the law?[13] Paul answered, "I have preached to the Gentiles according to my Gospel that I received from God, faith in Christ, not the law.[14] When I preached faith, they received the Holy Spirit of which Barnabas gives witness. Thus I conclude that neither the burden of the law nor circumcision should be imposed on the Gentiles. However, I do not impose any prohibition on the Jews here, that if they need to keep the law and be circumcised, I won't oppose it, as long as they do it with a free conscience. For thus I have taught among the Jews, 'to the Jews as a Jew,' but always holding higher the truth of the Gospel."

VERSE 2. I met privately with those who were of reputation.

In other words, I consulted not only with the fellowship but also with their leaders.

VERSE 2. I wanted to be sure I was not running and had not been running my race in vain.

It's not that Paul had any doubts that he had run in vain, since he had already preached the Gospel for eighteen years. The text faithfully states that during that entire time he had not only been consistent but had also persevered in the Gospel. However, many thought that Paul had preached the Gospel in vain for many years since he had freed the Gentiles from the keeping of the law. This opinion grew daily, that the law was necessary for justification. Therefore, when he went to Jerusalem directed by divine revelation, Paul wanted to correct that evil. In meeting with them, it was clear that his Gospel was in no way contrary to that of the other apostles. By showing they were in agreement, Paul intended to shut the mouth of

---

[12] *agitata.*

[13] *ultrum homines possint sine lege justificari?*

[14] *fidem in Christus, non legem.*

his adversaries so that they would not say that he ran or had run in vain. Here, it should be understood that those who teach the virtue of self-righteousness, or the righteousness of the law, are those who run and live in vain.

VERSE 3. Yet not even Titus, who was with me, was compelled to be circumcised.

This word, "compelled," states the conclusion of the entire conference: "The Gentiles were not compelled to be circumcised!"

Out of respect for the fathers, circumcision would be tolerated for a time until they were strengthened in the faith but not as conditional for receiving righteousness and also out of love for the weak, so as not to offend them, until they grew in faith and matured. It would have seemed something very rare and improper to so suddenly abandon the law and the traditions of the fathers, which had been given to this people by God with such great glory.

Therefore, Paul didn't reject circumcision as a practice to be condemned, and neither by word nor by deed did he require the Jews to abandon it. In chapter 7 of his first letter to the Corinthians, he said, "Was a man already circumcised when he was called? He should not become uncircumcised" (1 Corinthians 7:18). However, he rejected circumcision as something necessary for righteousness. He showed that the fathers were not justified because of their circumcision (Romans 4:11). For them, it was only a sign, a seal of righteousness, by which they testified that they had expressed their faith. Even so, those believing Jews who were still weak and retained a zeal for the law, when they heard that circumcision was not necessary for righteousness, could not accept it no matter how it was presented. They could only understand that Paul said that it didn't profit them anything and that it was reproachable. The Jews weak in the faith had a great deal of affection for the doctrine of the law, so the false apostles sang its praises. As a consequence, they were able to turn the people against Paul in order to discredit his doctrine, if possible in all its totality. Similarly, today we do not reject the fasts and other religious exercises as reproachable. However, we teach that by these things we do not obtain the remission of sins. But when people hear this, they accuse us of speaking against good works. The followers of the Pope confirm this opinion and enlarge it in their sermons and writings. However, for many years now, there hasn't been a more sound and spiritual doctrine regarding good works as the one we teach until this very day.

Thus Paul did not condemn circumcision as if it were a sin to receive it or retain it, since the Jews would have been greatly offended. But at this council, the decision was taken that it was not necessary for justification and thus should not be imposed on the Gentiles. They agreed on this ἐπιείκεια:[15] out of respect for the

---

[15] Remember, Luther is lecturing seminarians. Here, he uses a Greek term that he assumes his students will recognize and understand. It is from the New Testament

fathers and love for those who were still the weak in the faith, the Jews for some time would retain the law and circumcision. However, they would have to remember that those practices would not serve them for justification. Further, they would not be imposed on the Gentiles because it would be something very strange and an intolerable burden (Acts 15). In brief, no one should feel compelled to circumcise or prohibited from circumcision.

The bitter dispute between Jerome and Augustine regarding Paul's authority is well known. The argument that Augustine defends is based on the term compelled.[16] *Jerome does not understand this term. The argument here is not what Peter or Paul did regarding circumcising or not circumcising, as Jerome thinks. Jerome asks, "Why did Paul dare to reproach Peter?" It is obvious in what is written that Paul circumcised Timothy. When he was with the Gentiles, he lived as a Gentile, and with the Jews, he lived as a Jew. Jerome thinks that what happened in this instance is not so critical that either one of them should have been at fault. He tends to downplay their faults, saying that they both pretended and told a little white lie.[17] But in reality, all their arguments were and are of great weight and importance. Therefore, they weren't just putting on a show.[18]*

But here, this is the main question posed by the text: "Is the law necessary for justification or not?"

This theme is the center and the sum of all Christian doctrine and the reason for the dispute between Paul and Peter. Paul was a man far too honorable as to confront Peter and correct him with something made up in the presence of the entire church of Antioch! He confronted him due to the centrality of the Christian doctrine.[19] In the absence of the Jews, Peter ate with the Gentiles. But when the Jews came, he did the opposite. Thus Paul rebukes him. His hypocrisy would have compelled both Gentiles and Jews [to include the law and circumcision as requirements for justification].[20] The strength of this entire argument is found in the phrase "you compel." But Jerome never saw it.

Greek, which means "consideration, forbearance."

[16] *coactus est*, literally "forced."

[17] *officioso mendacio*, a "white lie."

[18] The reader is reminded that wherever the text is found in italics, it represents sections omitted by the first English translators in 1575. They didn't want to offend the followers of Zwingli since in those sections Luther categorically rejected every human contribution to justification, including love since love is also the fulfillment of the law. Those sections also represent differences between Luther and Zwingli regarding the sacraments. Although these sections were originally rescued by Watson (1953), the translation of those segments of the Latin text is my own.

[19] *propter praecipuum locum doctrinae christianae*. "Christian doctrine" is Luther's abbreviation for the doctrine of justification.

[20] Note that Luther did not finish the sentence. Remember that we are reading a transcript of Luther's lecture. As Luther concludes his thought, he pauses and lets his

Therefore, Paul neither forced anyone to circumcise nor forced anyone to remain uncircumcised. His intention was to make it clear that circumcision was not necessary for justification. Paul did lift that requirement. Therefore, he tolerated the Jews in the keeping of the law, as long as they did it with a free conscience, for he had always taught Jews and Gentiles that the conscience should feel free from the law and circumcision. All the patriarchs and faithful of the Old Testament had freedom of conscience and were justified by faith and not by the law or circumcision. It is true that Paul would have tolerated the circumcision of Titus, but since he realized that their intention was to require it from him, he did not allow it. If they had won out, they would have soon concluded that circumcision was necessary for justification and that would have been the reigning principle.

Thus we leave at liberty those who wish to put on a cowl,[21] enter or leave a monastery, or eat meat or vegetables. However, let it be done freely without offending the conscience or to please a brother as an example of love. But faith does not consist in these things, and they should know that these things are worthless as satisfaction for our sins or to merit grace.

But just as in that time the false apostles didn't leave alone the topic of circumcision and the keeping of the law but imposed it as necessary for salvation, in the same way today, our adversaries are equally hardheaded. They persist in saying that the traditions of men cannot be omitted without putting salvation at risk. Thus as an example of faith, they come up with love as an example. But they cannot see that there is only one example of faith: to believe in Jesus Christ.[22] This faith, being the only thing necessary for salvation, is equally binding on all men and women. However, our adversaries, instead of worshipping God, would rather fall to their knees a thousand times before the devil in order to block such faith. Therefore, every day they become more hardened and strive to establish their evil deeds and blasphemies against God. They defend them by force of tyranny and aren't able to reach an agreement or endorsement of our position. Well, what then? Let us go forward with courage in the name of the Lord of hosts. In all this, let's not quit placing before us the glory of Jesus Christ. Let us fight courageously against the kingdom of the Antichrist using the word and prayer so that the "name of the Lord be sanctified, His kingdom come, and His will be done." Our desire is for all this to happen soon; it is the deepest desire of our hearts; thus let us say, "Amen and amen."

This was a glorious victory for Paul. Titus, a Gentile, had been in the middle of this heated debate in front of the apostles and all the faithful. Yet he was not required to be circumcised. Paul took this victory with him, saying that in this meeting, per agreement of all the apostles, it was decided with the approval of the

---

students finish the paragraph. In brackets, I've suggested the conclusion Luther may have intended for his students.

[21] A hood that is part of a monk's habit.

[22] *credere in Iesum Christum.*

entire church that Titus should not be circumcised. This is a powerful argument against the false apostles. With this argument, Titus was not forced to be circumcised, and Paul was able to persuade and bridle all his adversaries. It was as if he had said, "Why do these fake apostles give false testimony against me, saying that by order of the apostles I am obligated to practice circumcision, seeing that I have the testimony of all the faithful in Jerusalem and, what's more, of all the apostles themselves? Can't they see that because of my trip, the decision was against what they allege? That I not only prevailed, since Titus was not circumcised, but all the apostles confirmed and ratified my ministry? Therefore, their false apostles are shameless liars and they slander me in the name of the apostles, deceiving you with falsehoods! I have the apostles and all the faithful not against me but in my favor. My evidence is Titus's experience!"

Nonetheless, Paul (as I have often said) did not rebuke circumcision as something useless, nor did he make it mandatory, for it is neither a sin nor righteousness to circumcise or not to circumcise, in the same way that it is neither a sin nor righteousness to eat or drink. "We are no worse if we do not eat and no better if we do" (1 Corinthians 8:8). But if someone adds sin or righteousness, saying, "If you eat, you sin; if you abstain, you are righteous," that person is foolish and wicked. Thus to tie the ceremonies with sin or righteousness is great wickedness. This is the same thing done by the Pope, for in his way of excommunicating, he threatens all who do not obey the law of the Roman pontiff, saying that God's indignation and curse falls on them, and in this way they establish that their laws are necessary for salvation.[23] This is why the devil himself speaks in the person of the Pope and in all the papal decrees, for if salvation consists in keeping the decrees of the Pope, what need would there be for Christ to be our Justifier and Savior?

VERSES 4 and 5. This matter arose because some false believers had infiltrated our ranks to spy on the freedom we have in Christ Jesus and to make us slaves. We did not give in to them for a moment, so that the truth of the gospel might be preserved for you.

Here, Paul shows the reason he went to Jerusalem and compared his Gospel with the other apostles, and his argument for not circumcising Titus. It was not to be more certain or to be confirmed in the Gospel by the other apostles, for he had no doubts at all. It was so that the truth of the Gospel would remain throughout the churches of Galatia and all the churches of the Gentiles. We see that Paul's mission was no slight matter. When he talks about the truth of the Gospel, it is to point out that there are two Gospels: one true and another false. In itself, the Gospel is

---

[23] In Latin, Luther adds this footnote: "On the contrary, in his tradition, the Pope puts righteousness at his disposal."

simple, true, and sincere. But due to the perversity of Satan's ministry, it has been corrupted and undermined. Thus when he talks about "the truth of the Gospel," I also want us to understand the opposite. It's as if he had said, "The false apostles also preach a faith and a Gospel, but both are false.[24] That is why I have persisted in confronting them. Because I did not give in to them one bit but instead held my ground, the truth of the Gospel remains among you." In the same way, the Pope and the fanatical spirits boast today that they also teach the Gospel and faith in Christ. It is true but with the same fruit as the false apostles who Paul in chapter 1 calls those who perturb the church and are subversive against the Gospel of Christ. On the contrary, he says that he teaches "the truth of the Gospel." It's as if he had said, "The things taught by the false apostles, no matter how much they boast that they are teaching the truth, are nothing more than pure lies." In the same way, all the heretics today disguise themselves with the name of God, of Christ, and of the church. In the same way, they insist that they don't teach lies or errors. Rather, they testify that they teach the truth and nothing but the truth as well as the purest Gospel.

However, the truth of the Gospel is that our righteousness comes by faith alone, without the works of the law.[25] To pervert or falsify the Gospel is to affirm that we are justified by faith but not unless we provide the works of the law.[26] The false apostles preached the Gospel adding that condition. Today, the intellectual moralists and the followers of the Pope make the same claim.[27] They allege that we must believe in Christ, that such is the foundation of our faith, but that it doesn't justify unless it is surrounded by love. That is not the truth of the Gospel but a forgery and a sham. The true Gospel is that the works of love are not the trimmings or the perfection of faith but that faith itself is the gift of God and the divine work of love in the heart, which justifies, for it has us take hold of Christ as our Savior.[28] Human reason takes hold of the law as its point of reference,[29] thinking within, "I've already fulfilled this, but I still lack the other." But faith in its true function does not have any other point of reference[30] but Jesus Christ the Son of God, given

---

[24] Luther adds in this footnote: *Evangelium papae et haereticorum*, "the gospel of the Pope and of the heretics."

[25] *Est autem veritas evangelii, quod justitia nostra est ex sola fide, sine operibus legis.*

[26] *sed non sine operibus legis*, "but not without the works of the law."

[27] Luther's footnote: *Doctrina papistarum de fide*, "the Pope's doctrine of faith."

[28] *opus divinum in corde, quod ideo justificat, quia apprehendit ipsum Christum salvatorem.* Note that Luther uses the phrase "the divine work of love in the heart" in a completely different way than in Trentian theology. The work of love in the heart according to Luther is not to make the heart justifiable, or worthy of justification. Rather, the work of love in the heart is so that the heart "will take hold of Christ as our savior."

[29] *objectum habet legem.*

[30] *objectum habet quam Iesum Christum filim Dei.*

over to death for the sins of the entire world. Faith does not measure itself by love.[31] Faith does not say, "What have I already accomplished? How did I sin? What is it that I deserve?" Instead, faith says, "What is it that Christ has already done? What does He deserve?" Here, the truth of the Gospel responds, "He has redeemed you from sin, the devil, and eternal death." Thus faith recognizes that in this one unique person, Jesus Christ, it has forgiveness of sins and eternal life. Whoever turns away from that point of reference does not have true faith but only a fantasy and an empty opinion. Such a person's gaze has turned away from the promises of Christ and is fixated on the law, which only frightens and stirs up a sense of hopelessness.

The imaginative scholars[32] of the Pope have taught that justifying faith has to be dressed up in love, but this is only an empty illusion. Because the faith that takes a hold of Christ takes a hold of Christ the Son of God and dresses up in Him. This is the very faith that justifies and not the faith that includes love. True and lasting faith needs to take hold of Christ alone and nothing else. When the conscience is tormented by all its feelings and horrors, it has no other support but only this one diamond, Jesus Christ. Whenever we feel intimidated by the law and oppressed by the weight of our sins, we nonetheless hold on to Christ by faith alone, we may at the same time boldly boast that we are righteous. How so? How could that happen? Through this precious pearl, Jesus Christ, who belongs to us by faith. Our adversaries do not understand this and turn Christ down, the pearl of great price. They replace Him with love. This love, they say, is their precious diamond. But since they can't even say what faith is, it is even more impossible for them to have love! Even less are they able to teach others how to obtain faith. What they seem to have is nothing more than what comes from raw reason, which is only opinions, empty thinking. There is no faith at all in that.

I say all this so that you will see that with the words "the truth of the Gospel," Paul with great vigor rejects everything to the contrary. He rebukes the false apostles who had taught a false gospel, imposing circumcision and the keeping of the law as necessary for salvation. Further, they set a trap for Paul. They watched him closely to see if he was going to circumcise Titus. They also wanted to see if he would dare contradict them in the presence of the apostles. He rebukes them harshly for this reason. He says they set out "to spy on the freedom we have in Christ Jesus and to make us slaves." The false apostles armed themselves with whatever they could to persuade and confuse the congregation. Further, they willingly abused the authority of the apostles, accusing him in their presence. They said, "Paul has brought Titus, who is uncircumcised to the company of all the faithful. He denies and condemns the law in your presence. If Paul so dares to act like that in front of you, can you imagine what he dares to do when he's away from you, mingling with the Gentiles?"

---

[31] *[fides] non respicit caritatem.*
[32] *Sophistae.*

Therefore, when he realized that they were stalking him stealthily, he denounced them forcefully, saying, "We are not going to allow our freedom in Christ to be put at risk, no matter all the efforts of the false brothers to ensnare us and cause us problems. We defeated them on the apostles' own ruling, and we didn't yield not even for an hour." They would have wanted to put the bridle on Paul for at least a time since Paul realized they wanted to add the keeping of the law as binding for salvation. But if they had wanted from Paul nothing more than to bear lovingly with the weakness of the new believers, Paul would surely have accommodated them. However, they wanted something else: to enslave Paul together with his entire doctrine. Therefore, he didn't yield, not even for a second.

In the same way, we offer the Papists everything we have and even more than that. Only that we reserve the freedom of conscience that we have in Jesus Christ. We will not tolerate our conscience to be bound to any work. We will not tolerate anything that will tell us if we do this or that, we are righteous or if we don't do this or that, we are damned. We will be more than happy to eat the same meats they eat; we will keep the same feast and fasting days, just as long as they will allow us the freedom of our conscience. Let them withdraw their threatening words. They have used them to intimidate and subject the entire world. With these, they declare, "We mandate, order, decree, decree once again, excommunicate, etc." However, we cannot obtain this freedom, just as Paul was unable to obtain it in his day. Thus we will do the same as he did, for when he saw they he could not obtain that freedom, he did not give the false apostles the time of day, no, not even for an hour!

In the same way that our adversaries do not allow us this freedom, that only faith in Christ justifies,[33] neither shall we accept their pretentious claim that faith dressed up in love is what justifies. At this point, we will not compromise, but we will be rebellious and stubborn against them. Otherwise, we will lose the truth of the Gospel. We would lose the freedom that we have, not in the emperor, nor in kings or princes, nor in the Pope, the flesh, blood, reason, and so on, but the freedom we have in Christ. As I have said, we would lose faith in Christ unless we grasp on to Jesus alone, the pearl of great price. By this faith, by which we are reborn, we are justified and grafted into Christ; and if our adversaries leave it alone whole and pure, we will willingly do anything as long as it is not contrary to faith. But since they do not place that faith in our hands, on our part, we will not yield not even by a hair. This matter we have in our hands is of great weight and importance, since it has to do with the death of the Son of God. He, by the will and mandate of the Father, was made flesh, crucified, and died for the sins of the world. But if faith succumbs, then this death and resurrection of the Son of God was in vain. That Christ is the Savior of the world would be nothing but a fable. God would be a liar for He has not kept His promise. Therefore, in this persistence, we are holy and pious. Let us seek then to preserve our freedom in Jesus Christ and retain the

---

[33] *quod sola fides in Christum justificet.*

truth of the Gospel, for if we lose it, we will also lose God, Christ, all the promises, faith, righteousness, and eternal life.

However, here some will say, "The law is divine and holy." Well, let the law have its glory. Although no law, no matter how divine and holy, should teach that by its keeping I will be justified, that by it I will live. I grant that it can teach me that I should love God and my neighbor, that I should be pure, patient, and the like. But it cannot teach me how I should be saved from sin, the devil, death, and hell. Here, I should take counsel listening to the Gospel. The Gospel teaches me not what I should do (for that is the proper function of the law) but rather what Jesus Christ the Son of God has already done for me: He suffered and died to free me from sin and death. The Gospel greets me with this news and leads me to grasp and believe it. This is the truth of the Gospel. It is also the principal teaching of all Christian doctrine,[34] which contains the knowledge of all holy living. Thus there is an urgent need to know this central teaching thoroughly, and to teach it to others, and to instill it continually, for once it is found within us, it is easily damaged. This was the experience of Paul, as well as everyone who is truly devout.

LECTURE 7: Friday, July 24

In summary, Paul was not going to circumcise Titus under any circumstance and just as he said, especially because certain false brothers crept in to spy on his freedom, trying to force him to circumcise the young Greek. Paul, seeing that they were pressuring him, did not give them the time of day, not even for a second, but resisted them. He said, "Yet not even Titus, who was with me, was compelled to be circumcised, even though he was a Greek." If they had made this petition as a concession to love, no doubt he would not have denied their request. But seeing that they considered it as something necessary, and they requested it as an obligation, giving others a bad example, in order to defeat the Gospel and enslave their conscience, Paul opposed them forcefully and prevailed. Titus was not circumcised.

It seems quite insignificant, to be circumcised or not. But when someone finds their security in such a trifle and is afraid if he doesn't do it, then he denies God, rejects Christ, and despises grace and all the promises of God. But if circumcision is observed without this condition, there is no danger at all. If the Pope in the same way would ask us to keep his traditions as simple ceremonies, it would not be so grievous to observe them. *But what value is there in displaying the cowl? Marching to show off the tonsure?*[35] *They throw everything together in their use of ceremonies! On top of this great evil, they claim that on trifles such as these are found*

---

[34] *principalis est doctrinae christianae articulus.*

[35] A small shaved circle on the crown of the head, as was the custom of the monks during Luther's time.

life and salvation, death and damnation. This is nothing but a satanic blasphemy! In regard to this, whoever doesn't protest, let him be damned![36] *With respect to food, drink, dress, cowls, I would comply with everything the Pope prescribes as long as we would be given freedom in all things. But he requires these things as if they were necessary for salvation. Thus he enslaves the conscience to these trivialities, as if these things were acceptable worship to God! At that point, I repudiate them altogether. There is no harm in a sculpture of wood, stone, or a statue. The harm is when these are used to render worship to God, and divinity is attributed to wood, to stone, to this or that image, and worship is rendered to an idol rather than to God.*

Therefore, consider Paul's behavior. It was not as Jerome explained it foolishly, supposing the issue and dispute were about trifles. In this, Jerome is mistaken. In fact, the argument is not about this or that piece of wood, this or that stone. Instead, the issue and dispute is about adding meaning to the object itself. The debate is whether this piece of wood is God or whether divinity dwells in this or that stone. To this we answer: wood is wood, and the same with the others. Thus Paul says, "Circumcision is nothing, and a prepuce is worthless."[37] *But to deposit righteousness, awe, assurance of salvation, and fear of death to these things is to attribute divinity to ceremonies. Thus we should not concede anything to the adversaries; no, not even something unimportant, just as Paul not even in the least gave in to the false apostles because righteousness has nothing to do with circumcision or the prepuce or tonsures*[38] *or cowls but only with grace and grace alone. This is the truth of the Gospel.*[39]

VERSE 6. But from those who were reputed to be important (whatever they were, it makes no difference to me . . . [what they were in times past doesn't matter to me][40]) [WEB].

This is a rhetorical device called an eclipsis.[41] *The words omitted are "I didn't receive anything." Absolution is granted! Paul is speaking in the Spirit, even if he sins occasionally with his grammar. He's speaking with great passion. In fact, he speaks with such intensity that he cannot keep himself within the exact limits of all the rules of grammar and rhetoric.*

This is also a passionate and superb refutation. Paul does not confer on the apostles any glorious title. Rather, it's as if he were underrating their dignity when

---

[36] Cursed by God.

[37] Remember that Luther was speaking to a group of male seminarians.

[38] A circle shaved in the head to signify devotion to a religious order.

[39] *sed sola et mera gratia. Haec est evangelii veritas.* Middleton omits the last two paragraphs.

[40] Luther added the text in the brackets.

[41] A device sometimes used even by skilled modern speakers in which they omit essential parts of grammar in order to emphasize what is obviously missing.

he says "those who were reputed to be important." He refers to those who were in authority, who judged over all matters. The authority of the apostles certainly had been greatly established throughout the churches. Paul's intention was not to minimize in the least the apostles' authority. However, with his words, he spurns the arguments of the false apostles who sought ways to undermine Paul's authority throughout the churches by contrasting the authority and dignity of the apostles with Paul's. This way, Paul's authority would be weakened and his entire ministry would fall into disdain. Paul was not going to tolerate that attitude. He responds forcefully; otherwise, the truth of the Gospel, which includes freedom of the conscience, would not be preserved among the Galatians and throughout the Gentile churches. Thus he declares that he was not impressed with the greatness of the apostles or what they had been in the past. Even though they alleged the authority of the apostles against him, he didn't let that impress him. He declared that indeed the apostles were something and that their authority needed to be recognized. However, Paul's Gospel and ministry were not going to be defeated by the name nor the title of anyone, be it an apostle or an angel from heaven!

This was the greatest argument that the false apostles used against Paul: "The apostles lived with Christ for a span of three years. They heard and saw all his sermons and miracles. Further, they themselves preached and performed miracles while Christ was still on earth. Paul never saw Jesus in the flesh. As far as his conversion, it happened long after Christ's glorification. Now, think things over, who are you going to believe more: Paul who shows up all by himself, just one mere disciple and the last of them all? Or are you going to believe the greater and more excellent apostles who were sent and confirmed by Christ Himself long before Paul arrived on the scene?"

Paul answered, "And what conclusion do you want to reach with all this? This argument goes nowhere. No matter how great the apostles were, even if they were angels from heaven, that does not impress me at all. The issue is not over the excellence of the apostles. What is at stake is the word of God and the truth of the Gospel. This must be kept pure and undefiled and preferred over all things. Therefore, all Peter's and the apostles' miracles don't matter at all. That has nothing to do with me. The goal of my struggle is that the truth of the Gospel be preserved among you." This would seem like a weightless argument with which he rejected or minimized the authority of the apostles because the false apostles challenged him appealing to that authority. However, Paul resolves their powerful argument only with this: "It doesn't matter to me." Nonetheless, he goes on and adds a reason to refute them.

VERSE 6. God does not show favoritism.

Here, Paul refers to the words of Moses: "You shall not be partial in judgment to the rich or poor"[42] (Deuteronomy 1:17). This is a theological γνώμη:[43] "God is not partial to anyone." Paul used this proverb to block the false apostles. It's as if he had said to them, "You judge me against those who seem to be something, but God is not impressed by appearances. He does not see which apostle ranks higher nor what is the dignity or authority of anyone. As evidence, He tolerated Judas, one of the chief apostles. He was more than patient with Saul, one of the most outstanding kings, even though he was the first to fall into disgrace and condemnation. He also rejected Ishmael and Esau, who were both firstborn. Throughout the entire Scriptures, one can find people who appeared to be good and holy. In these examples, it would seem that God is cruel, but it was necessary for these examples to be written down."

We have as this evil graft implanted in us that we value people and the external appearance of people as even more valuable than God's own word. But God wants us to fix our sight on the word itself. God does not order us to reverence and worship Peter and Paul but the Christ that spoke through them and the word they brought and preached to us.

However, man as a mere animal[44] has a veil over his eyes and cannot see the word. The spiritual man is the only one who can discern between the person and the word, between the veiled God and the person of God Himself. God is veiled[45] from every creature.[46] In this life, God does not come to us face-to-face but veiled as if wearing a mask. As Paul said, "What we see now is like a dim image in a mirror; then we shall see face-to-face" (1 Corinthians 13:12, GNT). We cannot do away with the mask. Discernment is needed to distinguish the person of God from the mask, but the world does not have this ability. The materialistic person hears that "man does not live on bread alone but on every word that comes from the mouth of the Lord." So he eats the bread but cannot discern God in the bread. This man can only see the veil and the dim images. Thus he can only trust in the gold and in other creatures, trusting in them only as long as he has them. But when these abandon him, he gets desperate. He does not see the Creator but the creatures. He does not worship God but his own belly.

---

[42]   Although in the Latin text Luther cites Deuteronomy 1:17, the quote is actually a summary of various biblical texts: 2 Chronicles 19:7; Romans 2:11; Acts 10:34; Ephesians 6:9; Colossians 3:25. The Vulgate rendering of Deuteronomy 1:17 is quite different.

[43]   Luther is lecturing seminarians who he assumes are acquainted with the Greek. Here, he uses the term γνώμη, which means a judgment or decree.

[44]   *animales homo.*

[45]   *larva*—"veil" or "mask."

[46]   *tota* (first edition: *universa*) *creatura.*

I say all this so that no one thinks that Paul totally condemns these external veils or persons. He doesn't say that there shouldn't be persons at all but that God does not show partiality among them. People exist with the veils God has given them, and they are God's good creatures. But we shouldn't put our trust in them. What matters is their proper use and not the things themselves. There is no fault in circumcision or uncircumcision but in the meaning attributed to them. "Circumcision is nothing and uncircumcision is nothing." However, to worship, reverence, and establish circumcision as righteousness but condemn the foreskin as sin is damnable! These meanings must be lifted, and once removed, circumcision and the foreskin are good things in themselves.

Thus the judge, the emperor, the king, the prince, the governor, the scholar, the preacher, the tutor, the disciple, the father, the mother, the free, the owner, and the servant are all persons with their veil. They are creatures that exist for God and should be recognized and respected as necessary to this life. However, so that we will not exalt people because of their appearance, or trust in them, God leaves important people with offensive faults and sins, sometimes shocking faults, in order to show us the great difference there is between any one person and God. David was a good king. Yet so that he would not have the appearance of someone to be trusted, he fell into horrible sins, adultery and murder. Peter, excellent apostle, denied Christ. The Scriptures are full of such examples. They warn us that we should not fix our trust in anyone or in their appearances with their display of shadows and shows. In the papacy, appearances count above everything. Indeed, everything in the papacy is nothing less than showing partiality to men.[47] God has willed that all His creatures will have a useful purpose, but not as idols for us to worship them. Then let us use the bread, the wine, our dress, goods, gold, silver, and anything else. But let us not put our confidence in them. We are to put our trust and glory in God alone.[48] Our love should be only for Him, and He alone must we reverence and honor.

In this verse, Paul calls the apostolate and the work of the apostles (who performed many and great miracles, taught and converted many to the faith, and who were also with Christ) nothing more than "persons." In brief, this word *persons* includes the apostles' entire lives of holy living and great authority. Nonetheless, before God, such lives are neither a small nor a great matter. As far as the truth of justification, whether they are great or glorious persons, God does not take that into account. It is necessary for us to draw this distinction between theology and matters of human politics. Insofar as civil matters, God wishes that we honor and respect the human instruments through which He governs and preserves the world. But when it comes to matters such as faith, the conscience, reverence, assurance, and

---

[47] Here, Luther uses the Greek word προσωποληψία, which means to pretend reverence before persons of greater rank with a view to obtaining favors.

[48] *In solo enim Deo gloriandum.*

worship, we should not fear the appearances of these persons, nor place our confidence in them, nor hope they will save us in body or soul. That is why God shows no partiality to anyone, since the judgment is His. My confidence should depend only in God, the true judge. I should respect and honor the judge or magistrate, for they serve on God's behalf.[49] But my conscience should neither rest nor trust in the minister's sound or just judgment nor fear him for his tyranny or injustice. If so, I would fall into the temptation of offending God with false witness, lying, denying the truth, etc. Otherwise, I will honor the decrees of the civilian authorities.

On my part, I would honor the Pope and show due respect to his person if he would leave my conscience alone and would not compel me to sin against God. But the Pope wishes to be feared and worshiped to the extent that if we would not, we would offend God's majesty. Since we need to let go of one or the other, let us lose the one with the mask and hold on to God. I would willingly tolerate the Pope's dominion, but since he abuses his authority with such tyranny against us and compels us to deny and blaspheme against God, imposing on us to recognizing him as our only lord and master, blinding our consciences, robbing us of the fear and trust we should place in God, I will obey God and resist the Pope. This is God's command, as it is written: "We should obey God rather than men" (Acts 5:29). Therefore, without a guilty conscience, by which we are comforted, we condemn the Pope's authority.

Müntzer and other frenzied individuals would like to extinguish the Pope, but they resorted to weapons and not to the word. They confronted his person but not based on God's word. As for us, we would render our respects even to Behemoth[50] and his entire posse, with all their dignitaries and personalities at their command, if they would only leave us alone with Christ. But since for them this is impossible, we condemn their persons and confidently say with Paul, "God does not show favoritism" (Romans 2:11).

There is a certain fervor in the word *God*. In issues having to do with God's word, we will not show favoritism. But as far as religion and its policies, other than God, we should honor the person. Otherwise, all authority and order would be despised. In this world, God wants to see order, respect, and honor between one person and the other. Otherwise, the child, the servant, and the laborer would say, "If I am also a Christian as my father, teacher, employer, governor, why should I respect them?" Therefore, before God, we make no distinction between persons. There is neither Greek nor Jew, but we are all one in Christ. But it is not so before the world.   .

We have seen how Paul was able to refute the argument of the false apostles regarding the authority of the apostles. The issue is not about showing partiality to one class of people over others. There is something of greater importance. Are we going to respect God and His word or are we going to respect the apostolate? To

---

49 *larvam.*
50 In the Latin text, Luther inserts the Hebrew word בֶּהֵמוֹת.

which Paul responds: For the Gospel to go forward, for the word of God and the righteousness of faith to be preserved pure and without corruption, let all perish! Let it not matter if they are apostles, an angel from heaven, even Peter, or Paul.

VERSE 6. As for those who were held in high esteem . . . they added nothing to my message [NIV].

It's as if he had said, "I didn't consult with the apostles, so they didn't teach me anything at all. What else could they teach me if Christ through His revelation had already taught me everything? I already have eighteen years preaching the Gospel among the Gentiles. Christ has confirmed my doctrine with miracles. The consultation was but a conversation and there was no argument at all. I didn't learn anything. I didn't have to renounce anything, nor did I have to defend my position. I only declared what I had already accomplished, that I had preached faith in Christ among the Gentiles, without the law, and that in response to my preaching the Holy Spirit was poured on the Gentiles, since immediately they spoke in different languages. When the apostles heard this, they also witnessed that I had taught the truth. Therefore, the false apostles cause me great harm and pervert what is already clear."

Neither is Paul's pride spiteful when he says the apostles didn't teach him anything. Rather, it is extremely necessary. Had he yielded, the truth of the Gospel would have perished. Paul didn't yield to the false apostles, even less should we yield before our adversaries. They do nothing more than boast of their idol, the Pope. I know that a Christian should be humble, but against the Pope, I am going to have a holy pride and tell him, "I will not submit myself to you, Pope; neither will you order me around, because I am sure that my doctrine is from heaven." But the Pope does not accept this doctrine. What's more, he would force us to obey his laws and decree under the threat of excommunication with curses, condemning us as heretics. Such pride against the Pope is imperative. If we do not forcefully condemn him as well as his entire doctrine together with the devil (the father of lies who speaks through him), we will never succeed in preserving the central teaching of the righteousness of faith.[51] We do not pretend to be lords over the Pope, nor do we exalt ourselves above all supreme authority. It is obvious that we strive for every man with all humility to be subject to the authorities established by God. But we only insist on giving glory to God alone and preserving the righteousness of faith safe and sound.

If the Pope would concede that God alone, out of sheer grace, through Christ, declares sinners righteous,[52] then we would carry him on our shoulders, and we would kiss his feet. But since we cannot obtain this concession, by God, we will

---

[51] *nulle modo retinere possemus articulum justitiae fidei.*

[52] *Si igitur papa nobis concesserit, quod solus Deus ex mera gratia per Christum justificet peccatores.*

vigorously uplift ourselves against the Pope. We will not yield to anyone, not even before all the angels in heaven, nor Peter, nor Paul, nor before a hundred emperors, nor a thousand Popes, nor before the entire world. If we would humbly submit on this matter, they would take God away from us (our Creator) and Jesus Christ, who has redeemed us with His blood. We are committed to this, to suffer the loss of everything, the loss of our good name, of life itself, but we are not going to allow anyone to take the Gospel away from us or our faith in Jesus Christ. Further, let all humility be cursed that on this matter would lower its head and submit. Instead, let all Christians stand indomitable without letup, lest they deny Christ.

Therefore, and with God's help, I will be more stubborn than anyone else. And let them give me that title according to the proverb: *cedo nulli*, "I will not yield to anyone." Yes, I rejoice with all my heart that in this point I will seem rebellious and defiant. Here, I confess that I am and will always be forceful and rigid; I will not yield an inch before any creature. Love yields, since love "bears all things, believes all things, hopes all things, endures all things" (1 Corinthians 13:7). But faith makes no concessions; faith tolerates nothing. According to the ancient saying, *Non patiter ludum fama, fides, oculus* ("Don't play with my reputation, faith, or stick your finger in my eye"). Thus the Christian, regarding his faith, can never be too proud or energetic; neither should he yield or relax his grip, not even by a hair. In this matter, faith turns man godlike, because God neither tolerates nor makes any concession, since God changes not. In the same way faith is unchangeable and thus cannot tolerate any change nor yield its place to anyone. But with regards to love, let the Christian suffer and yield in everything because in this he is nothing but a mere mortal.

VERSES 7 and 8. But to the contrary, when they saw that I had been entrusted with the Gospel for the uncircumcision, even as Peter with the Gospel for the circumcision (for he who appointed Peter to the apostleship of the circumcision appointed me also to the Gentiles).

With these words, the apostle refutes the false apostles, since he claims for himself the same authority granted to the original apostles. He uses a figure of speech called inversion,[53] since he turns around the argument they had used against him: "The false apostles allege against me the authority of the great apostles and with this argument they pretend to achieve success in their objective. But in turn, I allege the same against them and defend myself, since the apostles are with me. Therefore, my Galatians, don't believe these counterfeit apostles who boast so much about the authority of the apostles over me. When the apostles saw that the uncircumcision had been entrusted to me, and they became aware of the grace given to me; they welcomed me and Barnabas with their handshakes. With this

---

[53] *inversione rhetorica.*

gesture, they gave my ministry their approval, giving thanks for the gift given to me." In this way, he turned the argument around against his adversaries. In these words, there is a fervent intensity, and the topic contains much more than words can express. *It just so happened that Paul forgot his grammar and thus turned the meaning around.*[54] *But when he says they "who were reputed to be pillars," he doesn't say it vain, since they were truly considered as pillars. The apostles were reverenced and honored by the entire church. They had the authority to approve and proclaim the doctrine of truth and condemn everything else to the contrary.*

This is a very outstanding text, since Paul had said that the uncircumcision had been commended to him and to Peter, the circumcision. Nonetheless, Paul also preached to the Jews in their synagogues and Peter to the Gentiles. Both instances are found in Acts. Peter converted the centurion with his entire family, who were Gentiles (Acts 10). He also wrote to the Gentiles as attested by his first epistle. Paul preached Christ in the synagogues of the Jews (Acts 9). In Mark 16:15 and then in Matthew 28:19, Christ commands all the apostles to preach to every creature throughout the entire world. Similarly, Paul says that the Gospel "is preached to every creature under heaven" (Colossians 1:6). Why then is he called the apostle to the Gentiles and Peter and the other apostles to the circumcision?

Paul notes that the apostles waited in Jerusalem until God called them to other regions. Things didn't change as long as the Jews' political situation remained the same. The apostles stayed in Jerusalem. But as the destruction of Jerusalem approached, they were scattered throughout the world. According to the book of Acts, Paul was the apostle chosen to the Gentiles, and departing from Judea, he traveled throughout their countries (Acts 13). In his trips among the Gentiles, Paul found the Jews in their synagogues, and since they were the children of the kingdom, he announced to them the good news that the promises made to the fathers had been fulfilled in Jesus Christ. When they didn't want to listen, he turned to the Gentiles, as Luke testifies in Acts 13:46. There Luke introduces Paul's vigorous warning about the Jews' zeal for the law that he issued because they were contradicting him. On that basis, Paul says, "It was necessary for us to preach first to you the word of God. However, since you have rebuffed it, you have judged yourselves unworthy of eternal life. Thus we turn to the Gentiles." And in Acts 28:28, he says, "Therefore I want you to know that God's salvation has been sent to the Gentiles, and they will listen!" (NIV).

Therefore, Paul was sent particularly to the Gentiles; however, since he was a debtor to all becoming all things for all, every time the occasion presented itself, he would enter the synagogue of the Jews. There, Jews as well as Gentiles would hear him preaching Christ. Otherwise, he would preach publicly in the market places, in homes, and at the riverside. And as he was the apostle to the Gentiles, so Peter was to the Jews, although he also preached Christ to the Gentiles when the occasion presented itself.

---

[54] *perturbaverit constructionem.*

Here, Paul calls the Gentiles "the uncircumcision," and the Jews "the circumcision" by way of a synecdoche. This figure of speech is used frequently in sacred literature, where one part represents the whole.[55] The Gospel to the uncircumcision refers or designates the Gentiles. This Gospel, he says, was commissioned to him, just as the Gospel to the circumcision was commissioned to Peter. In the same way that Peter preached the Gospel among the Jews, Paul preached among the Gentiles.

By the way, it should be noted here that the Hebrew people take the genitive mode sometimes as an active voice and other times as passive. On occasion, this obscures the meaning. There are examples in all Paul's writings and throughout the Scriptures. For example, the phrase "the glory of God" is somewhat ambiguous, since it can be interpreted as both active and passive. Actively, it is that glory that is God's own. Passively, it is the glory with which we glorify God. The same is true of "fides Christi," or "the faith of Christ." We almost always interpret such phrases passively, as in "the faith of Christ" we understand as that faith by which we believe in Christ. Similarly, "the Gospel of God" is understood actively as that which God can only give and send to humanity. But the Gospel of the circumcision and the uncircumcision is understood passively as that which is sent to the Gentiles and Jews and received by them.

Paul repeats frequently that Peter, James, and John, although they were seen as pillars of the church, didn't teach him anything. Neither did they commission him to preach the Gospel as if they had authority and mandate over him.[56] They themselves, he says, saw that he had been commissioned with the Gospel. He had not received his authority from Peter, since he didn't receive or learn the Gospel from any man. Neither did he receive from anyone the mandate to preach it among the Gentiles. God commissioned him immediately, just as God had commissioned Peter to preach among the Jews.

This text clearly testifies that the apostles held in common only one calling, one commission, and just one Gospel. Peter didn't preach a Gospel different from the other apostles, nor did he confer a function and office to another. Among them there was equality,[57] since all were taught of God. Their vocation and commission were given entirely and immediately by God. Therefore, there was no one greater than another. So when the Pope boasts that Peter was the chief of the apostles in order to confirm the primacy he has usurped, he is nothing but a shameless liar.

VERSE 8. For God, who was at work effectually in Peter.

With this, he refutes another argument of the false apostles. Paul questions why they boast of Peter's Gospel that he was powerful, converted many, worked great and many miracles, raised people from the dead, and even with his shadow he

---

[55] Synecdoche: a figure of speech where one part represents the whole.
[56] *ut maiores et ordinatores.*
[57] *aequalitas.*

healed the sick? Given, all these things are true, but Peter received this power from on high. God granted such virtue to his word so that many believed through him, and God worked great miracles through him. "But I also received the same power, and it was not from Peter. The same God that worked powerfully in Peter worked powerfully in me. I obtained the same grace. I taught many. I worked many miracles and the sick were also healed at the passing of my shadow." Luke testifies, "God did extraordinary miracles through Paul so that even handkerchiefs and aprons that had touched him were taken to the sick and their illnesses were cured and the evil spirits left them" (Acts 19:11,12 [NIV]; read further in Acts 13, 16, 20, 28).

The conclusion is that Paul does not at all think that he is inferior to the rest of the apostles and here he glories with a pious and holy pride. As the need arose, he was moved to oppose Peter, moved by the fiery zeal he felt for the glory of God. Certain profane spirits such as Julian and Porphyrius don't see it this way, saying that Paul was displaying pride in the flesh. We see the same today in the Pope and his generation. But Paul was moved by the doctrine of faith and not by any self-interest. When it comes to faith, we should be invincible and as hard as diamonds. Insofar as our dealing with each other, in love, we should be gentle and more flexible than the reed shaken by the wind, willing to yield in all things. But the issue here was not regarding Paul's glory but the glory of God, the word of God, worship of the true God, true religion, and the righteousness of faith so that these things would be preserved pure and unpolluted.

VERSE 9. And when they perceived the grace that was given to me, James and Peter and John, they who were reputed to be pillars, gave to me and Barnabas the right hand of fellowship, that we should go to the Gentiles, and they to the circumcision [NIV].

(i.e., to preach the Gospel)[58]

In other words, they heard that I had received my calling and commission from God. I told them that I had been commissioned to preach the Gospel among the Gentiles and further that God had worked many miracles by my hand and also that a great number of the Gentiles had come to the knowledge of Christ through my ministry. The Gentiles had received the Holy Spirit, only through the preaching of faith. They had not received it through the preaching of the law and circumcision. Seeing all this, the apostles glorified God for the grace that had been given to me.

The grace that he talks about here is about everything he had received from God. In brief, although he persecuted and demolished the church, he was made an apostle, taught by Jesus Christ, and was enriched with spiritual gifts. By this, he

---

[58] Subtitle found in the Latin text, also in lower case.

shows that Peter gave witness to him, that he was a true apostle, sent and taught not by Peter but by God alone. Peter recognized Paul's authority and that he had spiritual gifts. He also approved and confirmed them, not as if he were his superior and emissary[59] but as a brother and a witness. James and John did the same. Thus "the apostles who are the pillars are for me, they do not stand against me."

VERSE 9. The right hand of fellowship.

In other words, they shook hands as a gesture of belonging to the same community. They said, "We are of the same mind Paul, we preach the same Gospel together with you. We are allies in the same doctrine; we are now in one fellowship. We share the same doctrine because we preach the same Gospel, the same baptism, the same Christ, and the same faith. Therefore, we can neither dictate nor impress anything on you, since we are in mutual agreement in all things. We do not teach anything different or more excellent than your doctrine. You have the same gifts that we have, only that you have been commissioned the Gospel to the uncircumcision and we to the circumcision. So right here, we conclude that neither uncircumcision nor circumcision should get in the way of our fellowship. No matter who it is, we all preach the same Gospel."

Here, we are admonished that it is the same Gospel for Gentiles, Jews, monks, nuns, laypeople, young and old, men and women.[60] There is no partiality to anyone, since the same word and doctrine is for all. Everyone who hears it and believes is saved, no matter if he is uncircumcised or circumcised.

LECTURE 8: Friday, July 31

All this is evidence that the apostle has proven through many witnesses not only from God but also from man and through the apostles, that he had preached the Gospel in all its truth and faithfulness. With this, he shows that everything the false apostles had said to diminish his authority was nothing but hypocrisy and falsehood. But since he was alone and without witnesses, Paul adds an oath, calling upon God to put on the record that his words were true.

VERSE 10. All they asked was that we should continue to remember the poor, the very thing I had been eager to do all along.

Once the Gospel is preached, the task and obligation of a true and faithful pastor is to care for the poor. Wherever there's a church, you will find the poor. By far, the

---

[59] *auctor.*

[60] Luther's footnote: *Idem ese evangelium omnium,* "it's the same Gospel for all."

only true disciples of Christ are the poor. About them Christ said, "And the poor have the good news announced to them" (Matthew 11:5). The world and the devil persecute the church and then leave many in poverty. Then they are abandoned and discarded by the world. The world offends even more, since it neglects and does not preserve the Gospel, the true religion, and true service to God. Those who care for the ministers of the church and build schools are gone. The only ones left are those who build and establish false worship as well as superstition and idolatry. No expense has been spared. Instead, all are more than willing to contribute freely and generously. No wonder there are so many monasteries, so many churches turned into cathedrals, so many bishoprics in the papal church, where wickedness reigns with great income for its provisions. When the Pope was king with all his wickedness, there was more than enough to sustain numberless monasteries, friars, nuns, and hives of priests. Now there is hardly enough to maintain one or two poor ministers of the Gospel. In brief, true religion is always suffering due to its needs. Christ bemoans that he "is hungry, thirsty, homeless, naked, and sick." On the contrary, false religion and wickedness is always in bloom and abounds with all worldly pomp and wealth. Therefore, a true and faithful pastor[61] needs to care for the poor. Paul confesses that he has that same caring.

VERSE 11. But when Peter came to Antioch, I resisted him to his face, because he stood condemned [WEB].

Paul continues his rebuttal, saying that in his defense he not only brings the testimony of Peter and the other apostles who were in Jerusalem but also opposed Peter in the presence of the entire church at Antioch. This incident did not take place in the dark where no one could see it, but it was in the presence of the entire church at Antioch. *And this is a marvelous story. It has been the cause for many to falsely accuse him, such as Porphyrius, Celcius, Julian, and others. They accuse Paul of pride because he confronted the chief of the apostles and in front of the entire church. They say he overstepped the boundaries of Christian discretion and humility. But this is no surprise from those who think and talk like that, wanting to sweep away Paul's dispute. Onis non vident.*[62]

As I have said before, for Paul the issue was neither about goats' wool nor the price of bread in order to get some cash![63] It entailed the principal teaching[64]

---

[61] *episcopus.*

[62] *onis non vident,* "no one saw it." I have left the short Latin phrase in the text. It is a powerful summary of Luther's understanding of how others tried to brush away the dispute. Obviously, the Latin phrase is a rhetorical device Luther used in his teaching. The question he seemed to be posing to his seminarians was "would you have seen it?"

[63] *de lana caprina nec de pane lucrando.*

[64] *sed de praecipuo articulo christianae doctrinae.*

of the Christian faith. Whoever values that which in itself is useful and majestic, everything else seems vile and despicable. Who is Peter? Who is Paul? Who is an angel from heaven? Of what value are all other creatures when compared to the central teaching of justification?[65] If we indeed understand it, we will see that nothing else could be clearer. But if we pretend not to see it, we will be walking in the thickest and darkest fog. Therefore, if it is discredited or endangered, let's not fear to resist Peter or an angel from heaven, *for it cannot be exalted sufficiently. But Porphyrius and others are fixed on Peter's great dignity; they admire his person and forget the majesty of the central teaching.*[66] *Paul goes to the contrary: he does nothing injurious toward Peter but rather treats him with enough respect.* But seeing that the majesty of this central teaching of justification[67] would be forgotten if he favored Peter's dignity, he didn't take him into account in order to preserve and defend this teaching safe and sound, for it is written, "Anyone who loves their father and mother more than me is not worthy of me; anyone who loves their son or daughter more than me is not worthy of me" (Matthew 10:37).

That is why we are not ashamed to defend the truth of the Gospel. We are called and counted among the hypocrites, proud, and stubborn, that we boast to have the corner on wisdom, that we don't listen to anyone, and that we do not show respect to anyone. It's precisely on this matter that we need to be stubborn and inflexible. Regardless how we may offend, it's because we demean the dignity of the world or people's fame. Thus we are judged as the vilest sinners, but in God's heart that is our greatest virtue.[68] We are admonished: "If we love our parents, honor the authorities, show reverences to Peter and the other ministers of the word, we do well." But the issue at hand is not to sing the praises of Peter or the fathers or the magistrates or the world or the other creatures, but rather, we exalt the praises of God Himself. In this regard, if I don't give preference to my parents or the civil authorities or even to an angel from heaven, "I do well." Because how big is a creature if it tries to measure up to its Creator? And what are all the creatures if they compare themselves to Him? They are as a drop in all the oceans. Why then should I reverence Peter so greatly, if he is only a drop, and despise God, who is greater than all the oceans put together? Let the drop yield its place to the ocean and Peter yield his place to God.

I say all this that we may weigh and ponder Paul's appeal, since he appeals to the word of God, which cannot be sufficiently exalted. *Augustine has pondered this issue with Paul better than Jerome, since the latter gives priority to Peter's dignity and authority. Jerome reasons like this: Peter was chief among the apostles. Thus he should not have rebuked Paul. But if Paul rebuked him, he was only pretending.*

---

[65] *articulum justificationis.*
[66] *obliviscuntur majestatis hujus articuli.*
[67] *majestatem articuli de justificatione.*
[68] *summae virtutes coram Dei.*

Therefore, Jerome claims that Paul was pretending, that Paul was only making believe that Peter should have been rebuked. In that way, Paul could promote his own apostolate by defending the Gentiles. But he makes all kinds of excuses to justify Peter, granting him nothing but the truth. However, this is turning the text totally around, since it explicitly declares plainly that Peter was to be rebuked, because Peter had strayed from the truth. [Jerome also suggests] that the other Jews together with Peter also were pretending so that even Barnabas strayed with them taking part in playing pretend. Jerome cannot see these words clearly, since he can only grasp this: Peter was an apostle; thus he was above rebuke and could not sin. Augustine responds to this conclusion, saying, "You can't say that Paul was pretending, since he had to swear by an oath that he was saying nothing but the truth."

Therefore, both Jerome and Erasmus aggrieve Paul. They interpret these words, "to his face,"[69] as "superficially,"[70] meaning that Paul's actions were not from the heart but only to give an appearance. They allege that Paul resisted Peter but not from the heart, since he was only pretending to be resisting; otherwise, the Gentiles would have been offended if Paul had kept quiet about it all. But "in his face" means nothing but "in plain public view." Thus Paul resisted Peter openly and not off in a corner. Peter himself had been present and the entire church had been on its feet!

He directs the phrase "to his face" especially against those poisonous snakes and apostles of Satan. They slandered him behind his back, but they didn't dare open their mouths to his face. Paul was saying, "Thus I did not speak offensively to Peter, but honestly and openly, I confronted him. I did not pretend that I had brotherly affection for him, but his behavior merited blame and sharp reproach."

Others can debate whether an apostle can sin or not. As I see it, we cannot overlook Peter's fault making it seem less than what it was. The prophets themselves sometimes erred and were deceived. Nathan, moved by his own spirit, told David to build a house for the Lord. But this prophecy had to be corrected through a special revelation from God. "It would not be David but Solomon who would build the house of the Lord, since David had been a man of war and spilled too much blood." The apostles also made mistakes, since they imagined Christ's kingdom would be of the flesh and of this earth. In Acts 1, they asked Christ, "Lord, would you restore the kingdom now to Israel?" (Acts 1:6). Peter—even though he heard Christ's mandate, "go into all the world" (Matthew 28:19)—would not have gone to Cornelius's house unless God had urged him in a vision. And with regards to the issue we are considering here, he not only erred but also committed a great sin. If Paul had not resisted him, all the Gentile believers would have been obligated to circumcise and keep the law. The Jewish believers would have felt confirmed in their opinion, that it was necessary to keep these things for their salvation. Through Peter, they would have received the law one more time instead of the Gospel; they would have received

---

[69] *secundum faciem.*

[70] *in speciem.*

Moses instead of Christ. And Peter, because of his two-faced behavior, would have been the only cause of this enormous and egregious sin. Thus we should not claim so much perfection for the saints, as if they could not have sinned.

Luke relates that between Paul and Barnabas "arose a sharp contention, so that they separated from each other" (Acts 15:39). However, both had been set apart for the ministry among the Gentiles, traveling together, preaching the Gospel throughout many regions. But it is obvious that one of the two had a fault. Neither was the dispute for just a trifle, because their union in holy fellowship notwithstanding, they separated. These examples were written to comfort us. It is a great comfort to realize that even the saints sin, even though they have God's Spirit. But when they say that the saints don't sin, it's because they wish to strip us of that comfort.

Samson, David, and many others of great fame, full of the Holy Spirit, fell into shameful sins. Job and Jeremiah cursed the day they were born. Elijah and Jonah wearied of life and in prayer wished for death. Such faults and offenses of the saints are shown in Scriptures in order to comfort those who feel afflicted and oppressed by desperation. By the same token, they frighten the proud. No one, at any moment, has ever fallen so low that they cannot get back up. On the other hand, no one stands so firm that they cannot fall. If Peter fell, so can I. If he got back up, so can I. The weak of heart and fragile conscience may take a great deal of comfort from these examples. They will help them when they pray so that they will understand the reason for the words "and forgive us our trespasses" and "I believe in the forgiveness of sins."

We have the same spirit of grace and prayer available to the apostles and the saints, since they had no advantage at all over us. We have the same gifts they had, the same Christ, the same baptism, word, and forgiveness of sins. In this, their need was never any less than ours. Thus they were sanctified and saved in the same way as we are.

I say this against the hugely embellished praise and worship with which the foolish sophists and monks have adorned the saints. They say, "The church is holy and totally without sin." Indeed, the church is holy, as in the confession of our faith: "I believe in the holy church" etc. Notwithstanding, it is sinful. That is why it believes in the remission of sins, for it prays, "And forgive us our trespasses." Thus the church is not holy by nature, such as one would say of a wall, that it is white due to its inherent whiteness. However, [before God] that holiness does not satisfy. Instead, it is Christ in His perfect and total holiness. All those other inherent things never satisfy; it is Christ who satisfies.

VERSE 12. For before certain men came from James, he used to eat with the Gentiles.

The Gentiles who had been converted to faith in Christ ate foods prohibited by the law. Peter, while fellowshipping with these Gentile converts, ate meat and drank wine with them, knowing those things were prohibited. Thus he did well in boldly breaking the law among the Gentiles. Paul declared that he had done the same, that he had become a Jew with the Jews and to those who had no law as if he had no law. He ate and drank with the Gentiles unconcerned about keeping any law. But when he was with the Jews, he abstained from everything prohibited by the law, for his task was to serve and please all so that "I might gain the more" (1 Corinthians 9:20, 21). Therefore, when Peter ate and drank with the Gentiles he certainly didn't sin. Instead, he did well, knowing that it was right for him to do so. With this transgression, he showed that the law was not necessary to obtain righteousness as well as freeing the Gentiles from keeping the law, for if it was right for Peter to break the law in just one thing, then it was right for him to break the law in all things. But Paul does not rebuke Peter for his transgression but for putting on airs, as he was about to do.

VERSE 12. But when they arrived, he began to draw back and separate himself from the Gentiles because he was afraid of those who belonged to the circumcision group [NIV].

Paul clearly exposes Peter's fault. He does not accuse him of any wickedness or ignorance but of being a phony and two faced. Peter abstained from meats prohibited by the law because he was afraid of offending the Jews that had been sent by James. Therefore, he showed greater respect to the Jews than to the Gentiles. By his actions, he gave occasion to overthrow Christian liberty and the truth of the Gospel. By withdrawing and separating himself altogether, he abstained from eating meats prohibited by the law, even though he had eaten them before! By doing this, he became a minister of scruples for the conscience of the faithful who would follow his example. They would think like this: "Peter abstains from meats prohibited by the law. Therefore, whoever eats meats prohibited by the law sins and transgresses the law. But whoever abstains is righteous and keeps the law; otherwise, Peter would not have abstained. By refusing the meats that he ate before, the conclusion is that those who eat what the law forbids indeed are sinners. But those who abstain from meats prohibited by the law are keepers of the law and thus they are justified."

Do take note that Paul rebukes the result of what Peter did, not the act in itself. The evil was not in eating. Eating and drinking or not eating and drinking is worth nothing. But if from there you figure that "if you eat, you sin; if you abstain, you are righteous," that is wicked. Circumcision in itself is good, but this conclusion is wicked: "If you do not circumcise according to the law of Moses, you cannot be saved." Similarly, there's no evil in eating the meats forbidden by the law. But it was evil for Peter to withhold his fellowship and put on a different face, which was evil. From there, one could easily conclude the following: Peter abstains from meats prohibited by the law; therefore, if you do not abstain, you cannot be saved. Paul could not merely wink his eye at this fault because the truth of the Gospel was at risk. Paul resisted Peter face-to-face so that the truth of the Gospel would remain unaltered.

Here, we must distinguish between two matters. There are two reasons why you can refuse to eat meats. The first is due to Christian brotherly love. In this, there is no danger at all. To carry the burden of my brother's weakness is a good thing. Paul taught and urged the same thing (1 Corinthians 9:19–22). The second is to abstain in order to achieve righteousness and avoid falling into sin. That reason is damnable. In this regard, let that love be damned, together with all the service and works of love that could be performed in this regard. To abstain for this reason is to deny Christ, tread upon His body, blaspheme the Holy Spirit, and despise everything sacred. Therefore, if we are going to lose a friend or a brother, let us then lose that person. But if we lose God, our Father, we will also lose the friend and the brother.

Jerome, not understanding this passage or the entire epistle, thinks that Paul was just pretending to be rebuking Peter, and he excuses Peter's fall, saying, "He did it from ignorance." But Peter offended due to his two-facedness, since by pretending to follow the prohibitions of the law, he was establishing the need for the law. At the same time, his example compelled both Gentiles and Jews to rebel against the truth of the Gospel. He had given them a wonderful occasion to abandon Christ, despise grace, and return to the Jewish religion. If Paul had not rebuked him, they would have had to carry all the burdens of the law. This example of Peter would have revoked among Gentiles and Jews the freedom to be found in Christ as well as the truth of the Gospel. Peter's fault was serious, and if someone would care to enlarge it, the result would be huge. However, Peter's fault was not because he had bad intentions or was ignorant of his actions. His fault was due to his fear given the occasion. We must be watchful of all the great harm done by the fault and the fall of just one man, if it isn't corrected in time. Therefore, we cannot play with this article of justification.[71] Neither are we without good reason for bringing it to mind so frequently and diligently.

It is surprising that Peter, an apostle par excellence, did what he did. Previously, at a Council in Jerusalem, he was practically the only one who defended this central teaching. He prevailed arguing that through faith we believe that we are righteous without the law.[72] He who previously with such perseverance had defended the truth and liberty of the Gospel now, due to his fall by abstaining from meats forbidden by the law, not only offends greatly but also offends against his own decree. "Therefore let him who thinks he stands be careful that he doesn't fall." Who would have thought there would be any risk in traditions and ceremonies? What could be more necessary than the law with its ceremonies? However, there is a great

---

[71]   *jocandum cum articulo justificationis.*

[72]   *per fidem contingere credentibus justitiam sine lege.*

risk, since the very same men who teach these are the ones who deny Christ. With the keeping of the law comes a certain confidence and trust in its works. Wherever that exists, there cannot exist confidence in Christ. Therefore, Christ is denied in an instant, as we saw in Peter, who knew this central article of justification better than we do.[73] But this teaching would have crumbled easily if Paul had not rebuked him. All the Gentiles would have departed from Paul's preaching, casting away the Gospel and Christ Himself. All this would have occurred due to a very pious pretext. The Gentiles would have said, "Paul, up till now you have taught that we must be justified by grace without the law.[74] But can't you see that Peter does the opposite? He abstains from the meats prohibited by the law. With that, he teaches that we cannot be saved unless we receive circumcision and keep the law."

VERSE 13. And the rest of the Jews joined him in his hypocrisy; so that even Barnabas was carried away with their hypocrisy.

Here, we can clearly see that Paul attributes hypocrisy to Peter. But on the contrary, Jerome attributes it to Paul. If Peter was pretending, it's because he certainly knew what the truth was and what it wasn't. He who pretends does not sin due to ignorance but because he paints things with a color he knows all too well is false. "And the rest," he says, "joined Peter in his hypocrisy so that even Barnabas (Paul's companion and for a long time a preacher of the Gospel among the Gentiles, faith in Christ without the law[75]) also fell into their same pretense." Here, Peter's fault is clearly defined as hypocrisy. If Paul had not rebuked him, then the end of the Gospel would have come soon after its arrival.

It is amazing how God preserved the church in its infancy, and the Gospel itself, through just one person. Only Paul remained firm in the truth, for he lost Barnabas his companion and Peter was against him. Sometimes, just one person can achieve more in one assembly than the entire assembly itself. The followers of the Pope know this only too well. Paphnutius prevailed against the entire Council of Nicea (the best of all councils since the Jerusalem Council with the apostles).

I say this so that we will most diligently learn the central teaching of justification[76] and be able to see clearly the difference between the law and the Gospel.[77] In this matter, we need to do away with double-talk or give preference to one man over another. In this way, we will retain the truth of the Gospel and preserve the faith sound and without pollution. Otherwise, as I have said before, these are easily damaged. Thus in this matter, send reason away, since it is an enemy of faith. The

---

[73] *qui melius novit articulum justificationis quam nos.*

[74] *oportere nos sola gratia sine lege justificare.*

[75] *fidem in Christum sine lege.*

[76] *ut summa diligentia articulum justificationis discamus.*

[77] *purissime discernamus evangelium a lege.*

temptations to sin and those found in death do not lean toward the righteousness of faith. They even ignore it altogether. They lean to their own righteousness or at least the righteousness of the law. As soon as the law is joined with reason, faith immediately loses its virginity.[78] The most powerful adversaries of faith are the law and reason joined together. These two enemies cannot be overcome except with great effort and difficulty. However, if we are to be safe, they must be conquered.

Therefore, when the conscience is extremely stressed by the law and struggles against the judgment of God, do not seek advice from either reason or the law. Rest only on grace as the word of comfort. Stay and hold your ground there, as if you had never heard at all from the law. Rise up to the crystal of faith, where neither the law nor reason is able to shine. Only the flickering light of faith shines there, which gives us the confidence that we are saved outside and beyond the law, in Christ alone.[79] Thus the Gospel leads us way beyond and above the light of the law and reason. It takes us to the uttermost secret places of faith, where the law and reason have nothing to say at all. However, we must also listen to the law but in its proper place and time. When Moses was on the summit of the mountain talking to God face-to-face, he didn't have any law, he didn't write any law, nor was he a minister of the law. But when he came down from the mountain, he was a legislator governing the people by the law. That's how the conscience should be free from the law, but on the other hand, the body needs to be obedient to the law.[80]

Paul then rebuked Peter for no small matter. The rebuke was on behalf of the principal teaching of the Christian faith.[81] This teaching, due to Peter's hypocrisy, had fallen into great danger. Barnabas as well as other Jews also joined with him in his hypocrisy. In the end, all of them offended, not due to ignorance or bad intentions but because they feared the Jews. They were so blind they could not see their own sin. Indeed, it is astonishing that men of renown, such as Peter, Barnabas, and others, could fall so easily and quickly. They knew their duty quite well; they had even taught others what to do. That is why it's so dangerous to trust in our own strength (as Dr. Staupitz would so frequently warn us). Never should we think that we are so holy, so well instructed, and confident that we have learned it all. Because the more confident we are, just as much, we can err and fall, placing ourselves and others at great danger and risk. Therefore, let us diligently seek with all humility to exercise ourselves in the study of the Scriptures and let us pray from the depths of our heart that we will never lose the truth of the Gospel.

We see then that, notwithstanding all our gifts and how great they might be, we are nothing without God's help. When He leaves us alone to our own devices,

---

[78] *Quam primum autem lex et ratio conjunguntur, statim virginitas fidei violata est.*

[79] *salvari extra et ultra legem, in Christo.* I have added "alone" because clarity in the English requires it, whereas in the Latin it is understood.

[80] *sic conscientia libera sit a lege, corpus autem obediat legi.*

[81] *sed propter praecipuum articulum doctrinae christianae.*

our own knowledge and wisdom are worthless. *Unless He sustains us, not even the highest educational degree, no, not even theology[82] itself, is worth anything to us,* for in the hour of temptation, it so happens that the devil with his snares shuts our eyes to the Scriptures that comfort us. We cannot see anything else but threats before our eyes. In such moments, we are oppressed and totally confused. Let us learn that if God withdrew His hand we would be defeated. Let no one glory in his own righteousness, wisdom, or other gifts. With humility, let us pray with the apostles, "Lord, increase our faith" (Luke 17:5).

VERSE 14. But when I saw that they were not acting consistently with the truth of the gospel [NRSV].

This is a marvelous example of those who are considered pillars of the church. Only Paul had kept his eyes opened. Only he saw the fault of Peter, Barnabas, and the other Jews who together with Peter were playing pretend. But they themselves didn't see their own fault, not at all. Instead, they thought they had done right in carrying the weakness of the weaker Jews. That is why it was so necessary that Paul should rebuke his fault and not wink his eye at it. For this reason, he accuses Peter, Barnabas, and others that they did not walk in accordance with the truth of the Gospel. In other words, they strayed from the truth of the Gospel. It is a serious matter that Paul should accuse Peter for having fallen from the truth of the Gospel. His rebuke could not have been any harsher. However, Peter took it patiently. No doubt that with a glad heart he recognized his fault. As I have said, many have the Gospel but not the truth of the Gospel. That is why Paul says that Peter, Barnabas, and other Jews "did not walk consistently with the truth of the Gospel." They had the Gospel but did not walk properly in accordance with the Gospel. Although they had preached the Gospel, because they had been pretending (hypocrisy does not have any place alongside the truth of the Gospel), they were actually establishing the law. But to establish the law is to abolish and overturn the Gospel.

Everyone who is able to rightly judge between the law and the Gospel can give thanks to God and know that he is a theologian.[83] When temptation comes, I, myself, confess that I am not able to separate them as I should. The way to separate them is to place the Gospel in the heavens and the law on earth. The righteousness of the Gospel is to be called heavenly. The righteousness of the law is to be called earthly. There must be placed as much separation between the righteousness of the Gospel and the righteousness of the law as God placed between daylight and nighttime. And would to God that we could even place them further apart!

Therefore, if the issue has to do with faith or the conscience, let's exclude the law altogether. Let's leave it on earth. If it has to do with works, let there be light

---

[82] *Theologia.*

[83] *et sciat se esse theologum.*

from the beam of works and the righteousness of the law. But when it is day, let the sunlight and the priceless light of the Gospel and grace light the way. When it is night, let the light come from the beam of the law.

Therefore, if your conscience trembles with panic due to the feelings and emotions of sin, you have to think like this: "You are, as it were, like a mule on this earth. This is the place for the mules to roam and work. Let the mule remain there serving and carrying the load it was meant to carry. In other words, let it stay there with its members subject to the law. But when you rise up to heaven, leave the mule on earth with its burden. The conscience has nothing to do with the law, or works, or with the earthly righteousness. Let the mule remain in the valley, but let the conscience climb up with Isaac to the mountaintop. Let it not carry any of the law or its works. Let it climb looking only at the remission of sins and the purity of the righteousness that Christ freely offers us."

On the other hand, in our daily life on earth, a rigorous obedience to the law should be required. In this area, the Gospel doesn't exist, nor the conscience, grace, remission of sins, heavenly righteousness, even Christ Himself. Only Moses should appear, with his law and its works. If we mark well this difference, neither one nor the other should exceed its limits. The law ignores there's a heaven; it has neither a heart nor a conscience. In contrast, the freedom of the Gospel will exist away from this earth, without the body or its members. Therefore, as soon as the law and sin show up in heaven (meaning the conscience), they should be thrown out as soon as possible. The conscience, which always responds in fearful panic when it hears about God's wrath and judgment, should not take the law and sin into account. Instead, it should fix itself on Christ alone. On the other hand, when grace and freedom land on earth (i.e., on the body), you should say, "You have no business here among the scum and dung of this bodily life; the place where you belong is in heaven."

With his pretenses, Peter blurred this distinction between the law and the Gospel. He persuaded the believing Jews that they needed to be justified by the Gospel together with the law. Paul could not tolerate this and thus rebuked Peter. He didn't do it to shame him but to once again mark a clear difference between these two: That the Gospel justifies in heaven and the law on earth. The Pope not only combines the law with the Gospel but has also turned the Gospel into mere laws that are only ceremonial. He has also combined and confused politics with religion, which is also a Satanic and infernal confusion.

It is extremely necessary to know the difference between what is law and what is Gospel, since it is the sum of the Christian doctrine. Everyone who loves and fears God, let him learn diligently to discern between one and the other, not only in words but to practice it and live it out in deeds. What I mean is to know it in the heart and in the conscience. As far as expressing the difference with words, it's easy to see. But when temptation comes, you will see that the Gospel is not your frequent visitor. Instead, it is the law who will not only come to see you but will want to stay and live with you, since reason carries with it the knowledge of the law.

That is why when the conscience is terribly stressed out by sin, by the unceasing verbiage of the law that always shouts ever louder, respond like this: "There is a time to die and a time to live. There's a time to listen to the law and a time to show indifference to the law. There's a time to listen to the Gospel and a time to ignore it. Well then, the time has come for the law to retreat and give way to the Gospel. Now it is no longer the time to hear the law but the Gospel. That's because I haven't done anything good at all. In fact, I have behaved like a criminal and have sinned shamefully. Nonetheless, I confess that I have remission of all my sins through Jesus Christ, *and by Him, all my sins have been forgiven.*"

But when you are free from the conflict with your conscience, when you have to do your duty every day, *then, it doesn't matter if you are a minister of the word, a judge, husband, scholar, disciple, and so on*, it is not the time to hear the Gospel. *You must listen to the law and fulfill the obligations of your profession.*[84]

VERSE 14. I said to Peter before them all, "If you, being a Jew, live as the Gentiles do, and not as the Jews do, why do you compel the Gentiles to live as the Jews do?" [WEB].

He says, "You are a Jew and have the obligation to live as a Jew, such as abstaining from the meats prohibited by the law. Even so, you live like a Gentile, since you do what is against the law. You break the law by the way you live. In fact, you eat your fill (as you well should) of common and unclean meats, just as all other Gentiles who are free from the law. But in the presence of your Jewish converted brothers, you now abstain from meats prohibited by the law and thus are doing nothing else but serving the law. What you are doing is making Jews out of Gentiles—that is, you are telling them that it is necessary to serve the law! When you abstain from unclean meats, you give occasion for the Gentiles to think like this: 'Peter abstains from meats that the Gentiles are used to eating, and he, himself, ate before. So in the same way, we should avoid them and live like the Jews. Otherwise, we cannot be saved.'" Thus we see that Paul did not reproach Peter for his ignorance (for Peter knew full well he could eat freely whatever he wanted with the Gentiles). However, Paul reproached Peter for his hypocrisy, which actually imposed on the Gentiles the obligation to live like the Jews.

I repeat the admonition that there's nothing wrong in living like a Jew. To eat or not to eat pork and other meats, what does it matter? But to play the part of a Jew so that as a matter of conscience you have to abstain from certain meats, that's to deny Christ and abolish the Gospel. Therefore, when Paul saw that Peter's deceptiveness had that purpose, he opposed him. He told him, "You know that

---

[84] *ibi servito vocationi.*

the keeping of the law is not necessary for righteousness; instead, we must only take hold of Christ.[85] That is why you don't keep the law. Instead, you break it and eat all kinds of meats. But due to your example, you are putting pressure on the Gentiles to despise Christ and have them go back to the law. Because you give them the chance to think, 'Faith alone does not justify; instead, law and works are simultaneous requirements. Thus with his example, Peter is teaching us that the keeping of the law is to be tied to faith in Christ, if we are to be truly justified.'" Thus Peter's actions pollute not only the purity of the doctrine but also the truth of faith and Christian righteousness. What the Gentiles received from Peter was that the keeping of the law was necessary for righteousness. If this error had been allowed, then Christ would have been altogether worthless.

Then it is obvious what this disagreement and dispute between Paul and Peter is all about. Paul does not play pretend about anything. He rebukes from a sincere heart. Instead, it is Peter who pretends, *as the text clearly says, and Paul rebukes his hypocrisy. Paul does not pretend about anything. Instead, his Christianity is pure and uncompromising; he has a holy pride. Paul would have been at fault if Peter had only committed a small fault and had not sinned against the principal article of the Christian doctrine.[86] But since the truth of the Gospel would have been perverted by Peter's actions, Paul cannot relinquish his obligation to defend it. He is committed to preserving its integrity, and he is totally unconcerned whether Peter, Barnabas, or anyone else exists at all!*

Therefore, Porphyrius and Julian malign Paul when they allege that he rebuked Peter just out of sheer arrogance. That could not be! Reason itself, if it's able to figure out the subject that Paul was pressing, would be compelled to confess that it was better for Peter to be neglected, than to put at risk the place that belongs to the majesty of God. That's because the subject matter at issue here is this: Or Peter deserves a strong rebuke or you have to remove Christ altogether. Here, it would be best if Peter perished and goes to hell if there were no other alternative[87] than for Christ to disappear. Porphyrius and the rest should agree with this sentence. No one can deny that in this instance Paul's actions were right and pious. If this had been an issue of no consequence (compare with the disagreement between Paul and Barnabas in Acts 15:39, which is clearly a trifle), then Paul would have yielded. However, this was the greatest of all issues, and he should not have yielded in the least. Paul's example should make every Christian proud. Love tolerates all things, believes all things, hopes all things (1 Corinthians 13:7); but it is faith that mandates, governs, triumphs, and does not yield.[88] For all things must be subject to faith and yield their place to faith—peoples,

---

[85] *Tu nosti observationem legis non esse necessariam ad justitiam, sed eam nobis per solum Christum contingere.*

[86] *et non contra praecipuum articulum christianae doctrinae peccasset.*

[87] *Hic potius pereat Petrus, et ad infernum abeat, si aliter fieri non potest.*

[88] *nulli cedat.*

nations, kings, and judges of the earth—as stated in Psalm 2:10, 11: "Therefore, you kings, be wise; be warned, you rulers of the earth. Praise the Lord with reverence and so on, lest you perish along the way."[89] Thus the effects, the functions, and the virtues of love and faith are clearly contrary among themselves.

Therefore, all the emphasis is centered on this phrase: "You compel the Gentiles to live like Jews." In other words, from grace and faith you are pushing them to fall into law and works, denying Christ as if He had suffered and died in vain. This word compel contains all those dangers and sins, which Paul warns against and amplifies throughout this entire epistle. If such compulsion or need is allowed, then faith is made null and void. And where faith perishes, all God's promises are canceled out. All the gifts of the Holy Spirit are stepped on, and it necessarily follows that every human being should be condemned and perish. Throughout this entire epistle, Paul attributes to the righteousness of the law many of these characteristics.

LECTURE 9: Saturday, August 1

Then, since it is so dreadful to fall into the hands of the law and such fall can occur so suddenly and to such great depths, as if falling from the highest heaven into hell itself, every Christian should diligently learn to discern between the law and the Gospel. Let the law govern over their bodies and its members but not over the conscience because she is like the queen and the wife and cannot be spoiled. She should be preserved without spot or wrinkle for her one and only husband, Christ. That's how Paul puts it: "I married you to one husband" (2 Corinthians 11:2, WEB). Let the conscience reside in its honeymoon suite, not in the valley below but on the mountaintop. Let Christ live, reign, and govern from there, not terrorizing and distressing sinners but comforting, forgiving, and saving them! Therefore, wherever there's a distressed conscience, let it not think about anything else and let it not offer anything to repel God's judgment but only the word of Christ. This is the word of grace, remission of sins, salvation, and eternal life. But this is difficult to achieve. Reason and human nature do not have the power to persevere in holding on to Christ. Sometimes they go astray perturbed by the law and sin. They are always looking for the freedom of the flesh, but bondage and slavery for the conscience.

In front of Peter, Paul summarizes the scope of the article of justification by saying to him, "If you being a Jew," and continuing until the words "because by the works of the law," where he begins talking to the Galatians once again. But the words he spoke to Peter were not to teach him the Gospel but to strengthen him while the entire church was listening and standing on tiptoe. That is why he continued speaking to Peter in the verses that follow.

---

[89] Luther combines Psalm 2:10–12 in his quote.

VERSE 15. We, being Jews by nature, and not Gentile sinners [WEB].

In other words, we are Jews by nature, we were born in the righteousness of the law, in Moses, in circumcision; we are even born with the law under our arm.[90] By nature we have the righteousness of the law. Paul said as much of himself in chapter 1: "I was far more zealous for the traditions of my fathers" than all the rest. Therefore, if we compare ourselves to the Gentiles, we are not sinners. We are not without the law, without works, as the Gentiles. We are naturally born Jews, we are born in that righteousness, and we are brought up in that righteousness. Our righteousness begins right from birth, since the Jewish religion is ours by nature because God commanded Abraham to circumcise all male children on the eighth day (Genesis 17:10–14). Afterward, Moses confirmed the law of the circumcision received from the ancestors. This is enormous, that we are naturally born Jews. We have this uniqueness, in which we are righteous by nature, born to the law and its works. We are not even sinners like the Gentiles, and yet, given all this, we are not righteous before God.[91]

Even though you could show me the most morally impeccable Jew,[92] lawfully conceived, and since the day he was born has kept the law to perfection, even so, he is not righteous before God.[93] Certainly, we are circumcised, but that does not justify us. Circumcision is only a "seal of righteousness" (Romans 4:11). Neither are the children circumcised in Abraham's faith saved through circumcision but by their faith. It doesn't matter that we are 100 percent Jews[94] and could never be holier and that we can glory against the Gentiles that we have the law as our justifier,[95] the true worship of God, the promises, and the patriarchs (truly a great glory)—even with all that, we are not righteous before God,[96] nor do we have any advantage over the Gentiles.

From all this, it is obvious that Paul was not urging ceremonies, as Origen and Jerome suppose. After Christ, these are nothing but destructive. But Paul is talking about a weightier matter: that having been born Jews, he refuses to designate them as righteous even though they had been born holy, were circumcised, kept the law, and had the adoption, the glory, the covenant, the patriarchs, the worship, God, Christ, and the promises. They glory in those things, as they say, "We are the seed of Abraham" (John 8:33); "We have one Father, even God" (John 8:41); and "You call yourself a Jew" (Romans 2:17). Therefore, even though Peter,

---

[90] *et cum nativitate ipsam legem afferimus*, literally "and we even bring the law with us when we are born."

[91] *non sumus justi coram Deo*. Luther adds the footnote, "Lex non justificat."

[92] *Iudaeum optimum.*

[93] *tamen ideo coram Deo non est justus.*

[94] *Ut maxime igitur simus Iudaei nati et sancti.*

[95] *quod habemus justificationem legis.*

[96] *non sumus justi coram Deo.*

Paul, and the other apostles were children of God, righteous according to the law, *and even the apostles of Christ, notwithstanding all that, they were not righteous before God.*[97] *You may have all these things bunched together—the totality of the law,* its works, and its righteousness, circumcision, the adoption, the covenants, the promises, the apostolate, and so on; however, none of that is faith in Christ, and according to the following text, that is what justifies and not the law.[98] It's not that the law must be condemned as something evil. The law, circumcision, and such cannot be condemned because they don't justify. But Paul strips away from them the power to declare anyone righteous because the false apostles insisted that by doing those things without faith, people were justified and saved just by performing the work.[99] Paul would not tolerate such teaching because without faith all things deserve death: the law, circumcision, the adoption, the temple, and the worship of God. Yes, the promises, and even God and Christ Himself, without faith, serve no purpose at all! Thus Paul categorically opposes everything that is repugnant to faith and not just the mockery of ceremonies.[100]

VERSE 16. Yet we know that a person is justified not by the works of the law but through faith in Jesus Christ [NRSV].

This phrase, "the works of the law," covers a lot of ground and should be emphasized. *I say this due to the indolent religious philosophers and monks. They take words like these from Paul, then with their foolish and wicked glosses blur and corrupt his entire argument dealing with justification. But they have no idea of what they are talking about!* Therefore, we must learn that simply stated, the works of the law are in antithesis [contrary] to grace.[101] Everything and anything that is contrary to grace belongs to the law.[102] It doesn't matter if it's judicial, ceremonial, or the Ten Commandments. Supposing that you could really do the works of the law according to this commandment, "You shall love your God with all your heart" (Matthew 22:37) and so on (which no one has ever done or ever will), even so, you won't be justified before God, since there is no human being that could ever be justified by the works of the law.[103] Later on, we will have much more to say about this.

---

[97] *non tamen ideo eran justi doram Deo.*

[98] *quia non sunt fides in Christum, quae sola . . . justificat.* Here, Luther adds this footnote: *Fides justificat, praeterea nihil,* "faith justifies, in addition, there is nothing else."

[99] *ex opere operato.*

[100] *quae fidei repugnant, non solum ceremonias cavillatur.*

[101] *Opus ergo legis accipe simpliciter per antithesis, contra gratiam.*

[102] *Quid quid non est gratia, lex est,* literally "everything and anything that is not grace is law."

[103] *quia ex operibus legis non justificatur homo.*

According to Paul, then, the phrase "works of the law" refers to the entire work of the law, whether it is ceremonial or the Decalogue.[104] By way of contrast then, if the works of the Ten Commandments do not justify,[105] much less does circumcision justify, which is a work of the ceremonial law. Thus when Paul says (as he did frequently) "that man is not justified by the law, or by the works of the law" (for Paul, both are the same), he simply is talking about the entire law.[106] By way of antithesis, Paul opposes the righteousness of faith over against the righteousness of the entire law,[107] whether furnished through divine power or human effort, according to the law.[108] On account of the righteousness of the law, he says, nobody shall be declared righteous before God.[109] But the true righteousness of faith is imputed by God's grace, by sheer mercy, on account of Christ.[110] Thus the emphasis is on the phrase "from the works of the law." There is no doubt that the law is holy, just, and good. There is no doubt that the works of the law are also holy, just, and good. And yet, through these, no human being is justified before God.[111]

Therefore, we must reject Jerome and others' opinions, for they imagine that Paul here is not talking about the works of the Ten Commandments but about the ceremonial law.[112] However, they are also compelled to admit that the ceremonial law was also good and just. Certainly, circumcision and other laws concerning the rituals of the temple were good and just, since God's command had issued both ceremonial and moral laws. But here they say, "The ceremonial laws concluded after Christ." But they make this up in their own heads! Here, Paul is not talking about the Gentiles; for them, the ceremonial laws would be nonexistent. But here, Paul is talking about the Jews, and such laws were good for them, even Paul himself observed them. Thus not even in that time when the ceremonial laws were good and just, they still could not justify!

Thus Paul is talking not just about one part of the law (which was also good and just) but about the law as a whole,[113] saying that a work done according to the entire law cannot justify. Neither does he talk about sinning against the law nor about a work of the flesh but about "the works of the law," meaning works done according to the law. Thus not murdering, not committing adultery, and so on, whether you do

---

[104] *legis sive ceremonialis sive decalogi,* "whether it is the ceremonial or the Decalogue."

[105] *opus Decalogi non justificat,* "the works of the Decalogue do not justify."

[106] *simpliciter de tota lege loquitur.* In the Latin text, Luther adds the footnote: *Paulus loquitur de tota lege,* "Paul is talking about the entire law."

[107] *opponens per antithesin justitiam fidei justitiae totius legis.*

[108] *justitiae totius legis, quae parari potest sive virtute divina sive humana ex lege.*

[109] *homo non pronuntiatur justus coram Deo.*

[110] *Iustitiam vero fidei imputat Deus gratis, per misericordiam, propter Christum.*

[111] *et tamen per ea homo non justificatur coram Deo.*

[112] *qui somniat Paulum hic loqui non de operibus decalogi, sed legis ceremonialis.*

[113] *sed de universa lege.*

it out of your own nature or through human effort or using the strength of your will power or through the gift and power of God, no matter how you keep the law, it is still unable to justify!

You see, the works of the law may be done either before or after justification. Even before the time of justification, there were many good people among the pagans. Xenophon, Aristides, Fabius, Cicero, Pomponius, Atticus, and others, before justification, performed the works of the law and achieved a good name. Cicero suffered death courageously for a good and just cause. Pomponius was a resolute man, and he loved the truth, since he never told a lie or tolerated it in others. Therefore, consistency and truthfulness are noble virtues and excellent works of the law. Even so, they don't justify anyone. After their justification, Peter, Paul, and other Christians have done and are doing the works of the law. But even so, they were not so justified by these works. "For I am not conscious of anything against myself [said Paul], but I am not justified by this" (1 Corinthians 4:4, HCSB). Thus it is evident that he is talking about the entirety of the law and the totality of the works of the law and not just about some infraction against the law.

The Theology of the Papal Scholars Commonly Known as the Scholastics[114]

Therefore, that wicked and pernicious opinion of the papal scholars[115] must be condemned because it attributes grace and remission of sins to merit for a work performed.[116] They say that a good work performed before grace grants power to obtain congruous grace [grace of agreement[117]]. However, once such grace is obtained, the following work merits eternal life as a debt owed to the person's worthiness, which they call *meritum de condigno* [merit of worthiness[118]]. For example, if a man is in mortal sin, without grace, but he does a good work out of his own natural inclination, such as saying mass or listening to mass or giving a donation or something similar, that person now merits congruous grace [grace of agreement]. Once congruous grace is received in that manner, he is now able to perform condign [worthy] works and merit eternal life. Indeed, for this first work, God does not owe him anything. But because God is just and good, it is fitting for God to approve such a good work, even though someone living in mortal sin performed it. But from here on, God is now obligated to repay with grace. In contrast with the first work, for these new works that follow, God has now become a debtor and is obligated to grant eternal life. The reason is that now it's not just a work done out of someone's

---

[114] *Theologia Sophistica.*
[115] Luther's footnote: "Meritum congrui et condigni [also *meritum de congruo*]."
[116] *operi operato.*
[117] Synonym provided by the translator of this edition.
[118] Ibid.

free will, performed according to the substance required by the work, but now these subsequent works are done by a gratifying grace—that is to say, in love.[119]

This is the theology of the reign of the Antichrist, which I expose here in order to better explain Paul's arguments. When you compare two opposing things, you can understand them better. Further, all are able to see how far from the truth these blind guides have strayed, how these leaders of the blind have veered from the path. Through this wicked and blasphemous doctrine, they have not only darkened the Gospel but vanished it and buried Christ altogether. It's like this. Let's say that I'm living in mortal sin. But I perform the smallest work that is gratifying to God. Further, I've done it not only according to the very substance of the work but also because I am capable of doing something that agrees with the will of God. For that, God gives me the grace of congruous merit.[120] Once I've received that merit then I am able to do other good works that are now according to the grace of God—that is, works done in love! As a result, I am granted the right to acquire eternal life. Why then should I now need God's grace, the forgiveness of sins, the promise, and the death and the victory of Christ? If things are truly this way, then Christ's work is worthless, and His benefit is canceled out! That is because I have the free will and the power to do good works, I earn congruous merit [merit of agreement] and then eternal life through condign merit [merit of worthiness]!

Such colossal and horrible blasphemies sound more like the arguments of Muslims or Jews. They do not belong in the church of Christ. Those arguments are clear proof that neither the Pope nor his bishops, scholars, and priests, in all their religious teachings, have the slightest knowledge or appreciation of sacred things, since they don't watch over the welfare of the flock. Instead, they abandon it but not before mauling it into pieces! For even if they had only looked through a cloud at what Paul calls sin and what he calls grace, they would have never compelled anyone to believe such abominable and damnable lies! By mortal sin, they only understood the external works done against the law such as murder, theft, and the like. But they could not see that ignoring the truth, hatred, feeling contempt for God in one's heart, ungratefulness, evil speaking about God, and aversion to God's will are also mortal sins. Neither can they see that the flesh does nothing more than think, talk, or do anything but oppose God and favor the devil. If they could have seen these horrible pests so rooted in human nature, they would not have fixed their sight on the wicked stupidities of congruous and condign merit![121]

---

[119] *sed etiam factum in gratia gratificante, hoc est, in dilectone.*

[120] The English terms "congruous merit" and "condign merit" will appear throughout this commentary to translate the Latin counterparts, *merito congrui* and *merito condigni*. The English terms still appear throughout Roman Catholic writings, and that is why they are used in this commentary.

[121] *merito congrui et condigni*. As stated previously, *merito congrui* is translated here as merit of agreement. It means a merit earned because a work has been performed in

So we have to define as simply and precisely as possible how wicked and deadly is a sinner. He is as much a hypocritical blood thirsty Holy Joe as Paul was when he traveled to Damascus persecuting Jesus of Nazareth, aiming to abolish the doctrine of the Gospel, murder the faithful, and overthrow once and for all the church of Christ. Who's going to say these weren't horrible sins? But Paul could not see them. He was blinded by a perverse zeal for God, thinking that these abominations were nothing more than perfect righteousness and excellent service rendered to God. And what shall we say, that those who defend these horrible sins are perfectly righteous in themselves and deserving grace?

Therefore, with Paul, we totally deny congruous and condign merits. We declare that these speculations are nothing more than mere deceptions of Satan. They have never been achieved, nor is there one single example as evidence. That is because God has never given to any human being grace and eternal life through congruous merit and condign merit. These claims of the papal scholars regarding congruous merit and condign merit are nothing less than toys and daydreams of empty heads. These claims serve no other purpose than to pull people away from the true worship of God. Yet this is the foundation of the entire papacy, for there is no monk that will not think like this: "Through my religious order, I am capable of meriting congruous grace and due to this work, after having received such grace, I will be able to hoard up such a treasure of merit that it not only will be enough for me to obtain eternal life but also will be enough to administer it or sell it to others." Every religious order[122] has taught and lived under that premise. And in order to defend this horrible blasphemy against Christ, the followers of the Pope come against us with everything they have. But there isn't anyone among them, no matter how sanctimonious and a merit hoarder[123] he may be, who is not the most cruel and mortal enemy of the Gospel of Christ.

The True Way of Christianity[124]

Thus the true way of Christianity is this: that man first admits before the law that he is a sinner and that it is impossible for him to do any good work. Because the law tells him, "You are a bad tree, and therefore, everything you think about, say, or do is against God." You are not able and therefore you don't deserve grace in return

---

accordance or agreement to God's will. God acts in conformity with your work and grants you merit. Thereafter any other work performed is condign merit, or merit of worthiness. Grace is infused into the soul so that you will perform more and more good works. Luther protests against this theology for it bypasses the finished work of Christ on behalf of the sinner, received by faith alone.

[122] *omnes monachi.*

[123] *iustitiarius.*

[124] *vera Christianismi ratio.*

for your works. And if you set out to do that, you will double your transgressions. Since you are a bad tree, your fruit cannot be anything else but bad, meaning your sins. "For whatever is not of faith, is sin" (Romans 14:23, WEB). Thus anyone who presumes to receive grace by performing some work previous to faith only sets out to please God with sins, for all he will do is heap pile after pile of sins, mocking God and provoking His anger. But when man permits himself to be instructed by this law, he is horrified and humbled, since he sees the greatness of his sin and can find within himself not even one spark of God's love. Therefore, he justifies God's word and confesses that he is guilty of death and eternal condemnation. The first part of Christianity then is the preaching of repentance and knowing who we really are.

The second part is this: if you want to be saved, don't attempt to be saved through your works because "God has sent His only Son to the world so that we may live through Him. He was crucified and died for you; He was given as an offering for your sins in His own body." Here, before grace, there is no equivalent work whatsoever but only wrath, sin, horror, and death, for the law does nothing else but expose our sins, intimidate us, and humble us. In this way, it prepares us for justification, pushing us along toward Christ, for God in His word has revealed to us that He will be a merciful Father toward us. Without deserving it (seeing that we deserve nothing), He will freely give us remission of sins, righteousness, and eternal life through the love of His Son. God gives gifts to His children freely for the worship and glory of His Deity. But the inquisitors and merit hoarders will refuse to receive from God freely of grace and eternal life. They will strive to merit it through their own works. For this reason, they will strip God altogether of the glory of His divinity. However, in order to retain and defend His glory, God feels compelled to send the law before His face, which like thunder and lightning from heaven will grind and break open the toughest rock.

In brief, this is our doctrine of Christian righteousness. It is contrary to the abominations and blasphemies of the papal supporters, with respect to congruous merit and condign merit, or works before and after grace. Those are the monstrous daydreams of individuals who have never fought against any temptation, have never felt the real feeling of sin, or the terror of death. Therefore, they don't know what they say or what they teach. Further, they have not been able to show any example at all of a work done before or after grace that could justify before God. Thus they are nothing more than useless toys and foolish fables with which the supporters of the Pope deceive themselves and others. Because Paul affirms here that "no one is justified by the works of the law offered before grace (that is what he is talking about here) or after grace." You can see that Christian righteousness is not an essential quality dwelling inside the human form[125] as the papal scholars imagine when they teach the following.

---

[125] *quod Christiana iustitia non est inhaerens forma.*

The Theology of the Scholastics[126]

Whenever someone does a good work, God accepts it. Then, on behalf of that work, God infuses that person with love.[127] This infused love, they say, is a quality that sticks to the heart like glue,[128] which they call formal righteousness[129] (it is necessary for you to know these terms). They can't even tolerate hearing that this quality, which embellishes the heart as whitewash on a wall,[130] is not righteousness.[131] They cannot climb any higher than these musings of human reason, that man is righteous due to his own formal righteousness,[132] which is grace that makes him acceptable—that is, a loving person![133] Thus it follows that this love that dwells and shapes you by clinging throughout your soul is a work you do according to the law. Because the law says, "You shall love the Lord your God" etc. They attribute righteousness to this form[134] and say it is worthy of eternal life.[135] Further, whoever has it is formally righteous. From there on, it becomes active. If I keep on doing good works, I am due eternal life! This is the opinion of the papal scholars,[136] yes, even their very best.

There are others who are not as savvy, such as Scotus and Occam, who said, "This infused grace given by God is not necessary to obtain God's grace. Even with his own natural strength man is able to give it all he can to achieve this grace." Scotus reasons like this: "A man is able to love another creature, the young man a damsel, the greedy loves money, things of lesser value. But he can also love God, which is the higher good. If by his own natural strength, he can love the creature, he can love the Creator so much more." The papal scholars were convinced by this argument and not one of them could refute it.

Even so, they answer back with this: "The Scripture compels us to confess," they say, "that God is not content with the natural love that He has implanted in us. He also desires self-sacrificing love, which He, Himself, gives." But with this,

---

[126] *Theologia Scholastica.*

[127] *infundit ei caritatem.*

[128] *haerentem in corde.*

[129] *formalem justitiam.*

[130] Luther refers to painting walls with lime, a practice known even today as whitewashing.

[131] *non esse iustitiam.*

[132] *homo est justus formali sua justitia.* In Roman Catholic theology, formal righteousness refers to the formation of righteousness within the individual through grace infused into the soul. Whoever has attained to this righteousness is justified.

[133] *gratia gratum facium, id est, dilectio.*

[134] *quia lex dicit, diliges dominum, etc. tribuunt iustitiam formalem, et dicunt eam esse dignam vita aeterna.*

[135] Rörer's note: *quid papistae vocent formalem iustitiam,* "which the papal scholars call formal righteousness."

[136] *sophistarum.* For lack of a more understandable modern term, I've translated this term as *papal scholars* throughout the commentary.

they only accuse God of being a tyrant and cruel despot, who is not only content with our keeping and fulfilling of His law, but on top of the law (which we are able to keep), He also requires of us that we should fulfill it adding other circumstances and adornments that will decorate our intent to fulfill the law. It's as if the lady of the house would not be satisfied that her cook prepared the most exquisite dish but then scolded her for not being decked out in the most fashionable outfit, with matching gold crown. So let's see: what kind of lady of the house is this, that when her cook has met all her obligations to perfection, she would then have to meet another requirement and dress up with a wardrobe that she doesn't even have? By the same token, what kind of God would this be if He demanded that we fulfill His law (which through our natural strength we keep and fulfill) but then adds that we dress up with a wardrobe we cannot even purchase?

But here they mark a difference so as not to be misunderstood as giving their support to contradicting arguments. They say that the law is fulfilled in two ways: first, according to the nature of the work itself,[137] and second, according to the very intent of the Lawgiver.[138] According to the nature of the work, they say, we can fulfill all the things required by the law but not according to the intent of the Lawgiver. As if saying, God is not content that you have already done all the things commanded by the law to your maximum effort, but He also requires that you fulfill the law in the spirit of divine love. Not the love that you have by nature but the love that is above nature, heavenly love, which He, Himself, gives. But what is this but turning God into a tyrant and a tormentor, who demands that we give what is beyond us to give? But then they say it's the same as saying, "If we are condemned, we are not to blame, but it's God's fault because with that condition He is demanding that we ourselves fulfill His law."[139]

I repeat these things with greater intensity so you can see how far they have strayed from the true meaning of Scriptures. Because they say that out of our own natural capabilities we can love God above all things, or at least by the work that we have performed,[140] we can merit grace and eternal life. According to them, God would not be satisfied that we fulfill the law according to the substance of the work but that it is also His will that we fulfill it according to the intent with which He gave the law. Therefore, the Holy Scriptures would demand that a supernatural quality would permeate us from heaven, which is love. That is what they say is formal righteousness by which love shapes and beautifies faith, working in order to justify.[141] So

---

[137] *secundum substanti facti.*

[138] *secundum intentionem praecipientis.*

[139] *exigit legem suam a nobis impleri.*

[140] *opere operato.*

[141] *habere habitum supernaturalem, e caelo infusum, qui est charitas, quam dixerunt esse formalem iusticiam, informantem & ornantem fidem, facientemque ut ea iustificet.*

that faith would be the body, the shell, and the color; and love would be the life, the nucleus, and the mass. These are the daydreams of the papal scholars.

However, we replace this love with faith, *even though they say that faith is like the outline of sketch*[142] *but love is the vivid color and the substance itself. However, we say the opposite:* Faith takes hold of Christ. He is the form that clothes and beautifies faith, in the same way that coloring adorns and beautifies[143] a wall. Thus Christian faith is not a lazy quality or a tiny shell in the heart that could even be in mortal sin until love comes to its rescue and infuses it with life. But true faith is a firm and assured confidence in the heart. It is a firm consent by which one takes hold of Christ so that Christ is the object of faith, but *what's more, He's not even the object, but, as it were,* Christ is Himself present in such faith.[144] Thus faith is an obscure but firm knowledge or rather a dense darkness that cannot see anything. However, when faith takes hold of Him, Christ is seated in the middle of this darkness as God on Sinai and in the temple when He revealed Himself in a "dense cloud" (Exodus 19:9; 1 Kings 8:10). That is why our formal righteousness is not the love that clothes and beautifies faith, but it is faith itself. This faith is like the reality of a cloud in our hearts. It's a constant confidence and assurance in that which we cannot see, which is Christ. Although we cannot see Him at all, even so, He is there.

Therefore, faith justifies because it takes hold and possesses this treasure, the presence of Christ in faith itself. But we cannot understand this presence because it dwells, as it were, in darkness, as I said before. Thus Christ is present even in the cloud and the darkness of faith, for there will be an assured confidence in the heart. This is the rightly shaped righteousness by which man is justified, and not by love, as the papal scholars allege.

In conclusion, the papal scholars say that love shapes and permeates faith.[145] By the same token, we say that it is Christ who shapes and permeates faith. Or rather, He is the very shape and perfection of faith. Therefore, faith,[146] taking hold of Christ and dwelling in the heart, is true Christian righteousness.[147] That is why

---

[142] Luther uses the Greek term μονόγραμμα.

[143] *informat.*

[144] *imo non obiectum, sed ut sic dicam, in ipsa fide Christus adest.*

[145] *formare et imbuere.*

[146] Luther's footnote: *reputari nos iustos propter Christum,* "regards us as righteous on account of Christ."

[147] *ergo fide apprehensus & [sic] in corde habitans Christus, est iustitia Christiana.* The meaning of the sentence is that the faith that dwells in the heart has taken hold of Christ. Luther did not teach the popular theology (rampant in evangelical Christianity today) that we are justified because Christ living in our hearts grants us grace to obey and serve Him in all things and at every moment. That theology is nothing but a carbon copy of the same Roman Catholic theology that Luther fought to defeat. Such theology is nothing more than a righteousness of works. It turns Christ into a

God counts us as righteous and grants us eternal life. In this, there is no work at all of the law; there is no love [our love] but another very different righteousness. It is a new and safe world, way beyond and above the law. Christ or faith is neither the law nor a work of the law. The papal scholars have not taught this correctly because they've never understood it properly, but we'll talk about this later. For now, let it suffice that we have shown that here Paul is talking not only about the ceremonial law but about the entire law.

LECTURE 10: Friday, August 7

As I stated before, the papal scholars promote a very pernicious error. They have taught that man obtains remission of sins and justification in the following way: if there are works that precede (which they call congruous merit), whoever performs those works merits grace, or so they say. For them, this is a quality that penetrates and sticks like glue[148] to the power of the will. It is a God-given quality that is higher and way beyond the love that we have in our natural capacities. They say that when a man receives this grace, he is formally righteous[149] and thus a true Christian. I say that this is a most wicked and foul-smelling opinion. Such a person is no Christian at all, but a Muslim, a Jew, an Anabaptist, a fanatic sectarian, and such. Why? Because is it not true that any man on his own strength (without grace) could do a good work and thus deserve grace? But that is how those wishful thinkers have turned faith into an empty quality in the soul, which by itself and without love is worthless, but when love is added, then it is effective and justifies.

The works that follow (they say) promote and earn eternal life by their very worth,[150] since God, due to the love that has been infused[151] into the will of man, accepts the work as a cause for attaining eternal life, for they say that God accepts a good work for eternal life but rejects a bad work and sends it to hell and eternal punishment. Somewhere in their daydreams, they heard something about acceptance and then they attributed it to works. All these things are false and blaspheme against Christ. But not all of them are able to express themselves even this well. As we have said, there are others who've taught that of our own strength[152] we can love God above all things. It is helpful to be aware of these things in order to see Paul's argument with greater clarity.

---

new Lawgiver demanding and commanding obedience from the heart of the believer, according to the intent of the Legislator.

[148] *inhaerens.*

[149] As in "has the form or shape of a righteous person."

[150] *de condigno.*

[151] *infundit,* or imparted.

[152] *ex puris naturalibus posse Deum supra omnia diligere.*

How to Measure the True Christian[153]

Against these empty bubbles and cherished illusions (as I have noted), we teach faith and we give the true measure of faith. First, man should learn from the law to know himself. He needs to say with the prophet, "All have sinned and are in dire need of the glory of God."[154] "They have all gone astray, they are all alike corrupt; there is none that does good, no, not one" (Psalm 14:3). Further, "Only against you have I sinned" (Psalm 51:6). On the opposite side, we warn all men to flee from congruous merit and condign merit. Thus when someone has been humbled by the law and has been taught who he really is, that's when true repentance follows. True repentance begins with the fear of God's judgment. In such a way, man realizes how great a sinner he is and that it's impossible to free himself from his sins through his own strength, works, or merits. That's when he can see what Paul described as "I am sold as a slave to sin." Also, "God has locked up all people in disobedience." He realizes that together with the whole world he is guilty before God. He can see that the entirety of the papal scholars' theology regarding congruous and condign merit is nothing but foolish and empty talk[155] and bringing the papacy to total failure.

At this, he begins to moan, saying, "Who can possibly come to my rescue?" Because he has been frightened by the law and has lost all hope, because he has no strength of his own, he looks around sighing for a mediator and savior. That is when the healing word of the Gospel comes, saying, "My child, your sins are forgiven." Believe that Jesus Christ was crucified for your sins. If you feel your sins and their heavy burden, don't let that sink you into despair. Remember that they have been transferred and placed on Christ, by whose wounds you have been healed (Isaiah 53:5; 1 Peter 2:24). Here's where salvation begins. This is how we are delivered from sin, justified, and made heirs of eternal life. It is not due to our own merits and works but through faith by which we hold on to Christ. We also recognize there is a quality and a shaped righteousness of the heart. It is not love (as the papal scholars affirm), but faith. This faith is only such faith that fixes its eyes and holds only on to Christ the Savior. Here, it's necessary for you to know the true definition of Christ. The papal scholars have made out of Christ a judge and a despot as a means to invent their foolish notions of congruous and condign merit!

However, Christ, according to His rightful definition, is no Lawgiver but the One who offers the sacrifice for your sins[156] and a Savior. Faith takes hold of this, and without doubt, it believes that He has done abundant works and obtained congruous and condign merits before and after grace. He could have wiped out the

---

[153] *Vera Christianismi ratio.*
[154] Luther's paraphrase of the text.
[155] In the Latin text, Luther used the Greek ματαιολογιαν (foolish and vain talk).
[156] *Propitiator.*

sins of the world with just one drop of His blood. But now, He has shed His blood to overflowing and provided more than enough satisfaction. "He entered the Most Holy Place once for all by his own blood" (Hebrews 9:3), and "they are justified by his grace as a gift, through the redemption which is in Christ Jesus, whom God put forward as an expiation by his blood, to be received by faith" (Romans 3:25). Thus it is a great thing to take hold of Christ, who bears the sins of the world, by faith. This faith alone is counted as righteousness[157] (Romans 3; 4).

Note that these three things,[158] faith, Christ, and acceptance,[159] or imputation, should be joined together. Faith takes hold of Christ and fastens on to Him without letting go, as the ring holds the precious stone. Everyone who is found with this trust fastened to his heart, God counts as righteous.[160] This is the means, and this is the merit by which we obtain forgiveness of sins and righteousness. "Because you have believed in me," says the Lord, "and your faith has fastened on to Christ, who I freely gave to be your mediator and high priest:[161] I declare you righteous!" Thus God does accept and count us as righteous by faith alone in Christ.[162]

This acceptance or imputation is extremely necessary,[163] first, because we are not yet perfectly righteous, but as long as we live in this life, sin remains in our flesh, and God cleanses us from this residue of sin. What's more, sometimes the Holy Spirit is withdrawn from us, and we fall into sins like Peter, David, and other saintly people. Even so, we can always count on this premise: "That our sins have been covered and that God will not count them against us" (Psalm 32; Romans 4). It's not that sin is not within us (as the papal scholars have taught us, saying that we should keep on striving until there is no fault at all within us), since sin will always be in us and the most pious will feel its power. However, sin has been snatched away,[164] and on Christ's behalf, God does not count it against us. So once we fasten on to Him, all our sins now are no longer sins. However, where there is neither Christ nor faith, sins are neither forgiven nor taken away. The only thing that remains is the accounting of sins[165] and condemnation. That is how God glorifies His Son, and through Him, He will be glorified in us.

When we have taught faith in Christ in this manner, then we also teach good works. Since you have now taken hold of Christ by faith and by Him you are

---

[157] *fides sola reputatur ad justitiam.*

[158] Luther's footnote: *Christus. Fides. Imputatio.* "Christ. Faith. Imputation."

[159] Luther's use of "acceptance" is not as it is generally understood by evangelicalism today, as "acceptance of Christ into the heart." Luther's meaning is that God accepts the sinner based on the imputation of Christ's righteousness.

[160] *reputat Deus justus.*

[161] *mediator et pontifex.*

[162] *Itaque Deus acceptat seu reputat nos justos solum propter fidem in Christum.*

[163] See the previous note on the meaning Luther gives the word *accept.*

[164] *Absconditum,* secreted away.

[165] *imputatio et damnatio peccatorum.*

now righteous, now begin to do good works.[166] You love God and neighbor, call upon Him, come before Him with thanksgiving, preach, worship Him, and confess Him. You help and serve your neighbor, and you are responsible in your duties. Indeed, these are good works that flow from this faith and from this joy born from the heart, since Christ has freely given us the remission of sins.[167]

Every cross and affliction that will come our way will be carried easily and suffered with joy "because the yoke that Christ places on us is easy and His burden is light." When sin has been forgiven, and the conscience is freed from the burden and the sting of sin, then the Christian will be able to carry all things easily. He will feel that all things in themselves are sweet and pleasant; therefore, he tolerates all things with goodwill. But when people walk in their own righteousness, everything they do is arduous and tedious because they do it unwillingly.

Thus we define a Christian in the following way. A Christian is not someone without sin but anyone to whom God does not impute sin through faith in Christ. This doctrine greatly comforts the conscience when it feels miserable and deeply stressed by profound and internal fears. Therefore, with good reason, we so often hammer home into the mind the forgiveness of sins and the imputation of righteousness on account of Christ.[168] In the same way, we insist that the Christian will not have anything to do with the law and sin, especially in the moment of temptation. Since he is already a Christian, he is above the law and sin, for he already has Christ, the Lord of the law, present and safeguarded in the heart (as I've said before), as the ring safeguards the jewel or precious stone within its circle. That is why when the law accuses him and sin hounds him, he fixes his eyes on Christ, whom he has grasped by faith. He will realize that he already has present with him the conqueror of the law, sin, death, and the devil. Christ reigns and governs over these evils so that they can no longer hurt the Christian.

Therefore, the Christian is correctly defined as someone who is free from all laws and who is no longer under submission to anything or anyone, internally or externally. That person is distinctively a Christian, even before you think of that person as a man or a woman. In other words, It is because that person's conscience has been adorned and beautified by this faith, with this great and priceless treasure, as Paul said, with this "indescribable gift" (2 Corinthians 9:15). We cannot exalt or praise this gift enough, for it makes us children and heirs of God. In this way, the Christian is greater than the entire world. He has such a gift, such a treasure in the heart, that although it may seem small, it is greater than heaven and earth because Christ, the gift, is greater than all!

---

[166] *per quem justus es, incipe nunc bene operari.*

[167] *quod gratis habemus remissionem peccatorum per Christum.*

[168] *inculcamos remissionem peccatorum et imputationem justitiae propter Christum.* We instill the forgiveness of sins and the crediting of righteousness on account of Christ.

As long as this doctrine that calms and quiets the conscience is preserved pure and without pollutants, Christians are then able to judge over all kinds of doctrines and are lords over the laws of the entire world. With all certainty, they can judge that the Muslim with his Koran is under a curse; he is not in the right path because he doesn't recognize that he is a miserable sinner, since he does not grasp Christ by faith, by whose merits he can rest assured that his sins are forgiven. In the same way, he can boldly pronounce sentence against the Pope, who together with his entire kingdom is under condemnation, for he goes around everywhere (with all his contingency of philosophers and scholars)[169] teaching that through congruous merit[170] we can come to grace, and that afterward, through condign merit,[171] we gain entrance to heaven. But the Christian says that this is not the way we are justified, nor is it the path that leads to heaven. Because I can't, he says, through my works previous to grace, merit grace[172] or, for my works after grace,[173] merit eternal life. However, he who believes in Christ receives remission of sins, and righteousness is imputed[174] to him. This truth and this righteousness make him a child of God and an heir of His kingdom. In hope, he already has eternal life; through the promise, he is sure and certain. Through faith in Christ, we are given all things, grace, peace, forgiveness of sins, salvation, and eternal life. Congruous and condign merit have no part at all.

That is why this doctrine of the scholastics,[175] regarding its congruous and condign merit, with its ceremonies, masses, and the infinity of foundational doctrines of the papal kingdom, is the most abominable blasphemy against God. Such doctrines are a sacrilege and deny Christ altogether. This was prophesied by Peter when he said, "There will be false teachers among you, who will secretly bring in destructive heresies, even denying the Lord who bought them" (2 Peter 2:1). It's as if he had said, "The Lord has redeemed and bought us with His blood so that He could justify and save us. This is the way of righteousness and salvation. But false teachers will creep in who will deny the Lord, blaspheme against the way of truth, righteousness, and salvation. They will invent new ways to falsify and destroy, and many will follow them among their damnable ways." Peter in that entire chapter, paints a most vivid picture of the papacy. Neglecting and despising the Gospel of faith in Christ, the papacy has taught the works and traditions of men, such as congruous merit and condign merit. Further, the papacy makes distinction between days, meats, vows,

---

[169] *monachis et scholis.*

[170] Congruity.

[171] *meritum condigni.*

[172] *mereri gratiam de congruo.*

[173] *consequi de condigno.*

[174] *imputatur justitia,* "imputation of righteousness."

[175] *Sententiariorum,* alumni and exponents of Peter Lombard's "Declarations," the main theological textbook of medieval times.

invokes saints, promotes pilgrimages, teaches purgatory, and similar things. The papal supporters have become so fanatic about these traditions and works that it's impossible for them to understand a single syllable of the Gospel or faith or Christ! The issue is clear all by itself. They snatch the privilege that belongs to Christ alone. He is the only one that forgives sins, the only one that grants righteousness and eternal life. But they, with all impunity and wickedness, boast that they can obtain these things by their own congruous and condign merits before and after grace. This, said Peter, is nothing but introducing damnable heresies and sects that lead to perdition. Using these means, they deny Christ, step all over His blood, blaspheme against the Holy Spirit, and despise God's grace. Therefore, no one is able to conceive the far-reaching consequences of the horrendous idolatry of the papal supporters. Just as the gift of Christ is of priceless value, to the other extreme are the abominable perversions of the supporters of the Pope. That is why these things should not be taken lightly nor forgotten but should be weighed with diligence and consideration. All this magnifies the grace of Christ and its benefit, to see that all they teach is entirely to the contrary. The more we get to know the sacrilege of the papal mass, the more its horrendous and repugnant nature appears. We can embrace the true meaning of the mass,[176] which has been taken away by the Pope, for he has put it up for sale. When Pope and priests sell it for money, they use it to their own advantage, for the Pope has said that when the priest offers mass (an apostate denying Christ and blaspheming the Holy Spirit) on the altar, he does a good work not only for himself but for others as well, the living and the dead and for the entire church, and just for the work performed and not due to any other means.

Even so, we can clearly see God's immeasurable patience. All this time and He has not destroyed the entire papacy, consuming it with fire and brimstone, as He did with Sodom and Gomorrah. But now, these charming gentlemen[177] would like nothing more than to go touring around covering up their immorality with their religious robes and decorations, but they can't fake it. Therefore, it is our duty to make known this central teaching of justification, with all diligence.[178] We need to make it shine like daylight so that it will expose all that hypocrisy and uncover their filth and shame. For this cause, we prod and urge the righteousness of faith to confound our adversaries and to establish this central teaching firmly rooted in our hearts. This is a must, for if we lose this sunlight, we will once again fall in the same darkness as before. And what's most atrocious is that the Pope himself has permitted for this to happen in the church, that Christ should be denied, trodden under foot, spat upon, and blasphemed, for the Pope has even darkened the Gospel and the Sacraments and turned them in to the most abominable abuse,

---

[176] *Missae*, the 1575 English version translates this as "Holy Communion" (per Middleton).

[177] *belli hominess.*

[178] *Summa igitur diligentia illustrare debemus articulum justificationis.*

turning them against the service of Christ, in order to establish and affirm his hideous abominations. What impenetrable darkness! How frightening the wrath of God!

VERSE 16. Even we have believed in Christ Jesus, (to what end?). So that we might be justified, etc.[179]

This is the true measure of Christianity,[180] that we are justified by faith in Jesus Christ and not by works of the law.[181] We reject the wicked whitewash of the papal scholars,[182] since they say that faith only justifies when it is woven together with love and good works. With this foul whitewash, they have blurred and corrupted this and other statements of Paul in which he clearly attributes justification to faith. But when man hears that he should believe in Christ but yet this faith will not justify unless it is woven together by love, faith will perish in no time at all. He will start to think, "If faith without love does not justify, then faith is worthless, it's not good for anything, since it is love itself that justifies. Since faith is worthless unless it's shaped and adorned with love then faith by itself is nothing."

To confirm that this is a pernicious and foul whitewash, our adversaries confront us with this passage: "If I speak in the tongues of men or of angels, but do not have love, I am nothing" (1 Corinthians 13:12, NIV). This text is their bronze fortress. These men have no understanding, and thus they can neither see nor understand anything in Paul. Not only have they falsely interpreted this text, but they have also perverted Paul's words, denied Christ, and buried all His benefits. So avoid that conclusion as a poison straight from hell. Rather, let us conclude with Paul that we are declared righteous[183] by faith alone and not by faith with the form of love.[184] *We should not grant the form the power to justify. Instead, it is faith, which in the heart grasps and possesses Christ as Savior. Thus it is faith that justifies, without love and before love ever appears.*[185]

---

[179] Luther inserts the *ad quid* (to what end?) in the Latin Vulgate text: "Et nos in Christum Iesum credimus, (ad quid?) ut justificemur, etc." This is clearly a rhetorical teaching tool that was caught and recorded by Rörer et al. We can almost see and hear Luther pause after *credimus* and ask, "Ad quid?" Another pause. Then Luther finishes the text, "ut justificemur, etc."

[180] *vera ratio Christianismi.*

[181] *fide in Christum, non operibus legis, nos justificari.*

[182] Luther adds the following footnote: *Impiam esse sophistarum glossam, fidem caritate formatam justificare*—that is, "a wicked gloss added by the sophists, that faith shaped by love is what justifies."

[183] *nos justificari.*

[184] *sola fide, non fide formata caritate.*

[185] Luther adds this footnote: *Fides iustificat sine lege,* "faith justifies without the law."

We concede the need to be taught about good works and love, however, each in its proper time and place, not when the issue is regarding the central teaching of justification.[186] Here, the issue is justification—by what means are we justified, and how may we obtain eternal life?

Here, we respond with Paul, "We are declared righteous by faith alone in Christ, not by the works of the law and love."[187] This doesn't mean we reject good works and love, as our adversaries accuse us. But we will not permit ourselves to be shoved or budged [away from justification], since that's what Satan wants more than anything. But as long as we are in the topic of justification, we reject and condemn all good works because this doctrine does not permit the intrusion of arguments that promote good works. In this matter, we simply cut away all laws and all good works of the law.

Nonetheless, the law is good, just, and holy. It is true; it is so. But when we are teaching justification, there is neither time nor place to talk about the law. Instead, the question is, who is Christ and what benefits has He obtained for us? Christ does not mean doing the law. He is not a work that I do; neither did I get Him by working according to the law. He is not mine because of my sexual abstinence, my obedience, or my poverty. He is the Lord of life and death, the Mediator, the Savior, the Redeemer of all those who are under the law. By faith, we are in Him, and He in us (John 6). The bridegroom should be alone with the bride in the secret bridal suite. Let all the servants and family members get out! But after, when they open the door and present themselves, then let all the servants and housekeepers approach to minister bread and drink. Let love then begin its work.

In order to properly define Christ, we should learn to discern among all laws, including God's law and all works. We should see that these are different from the promise of the Gospel of faith. Christ is not a new law, and therefore, He is not the Chief Debt Collector of the law and works.[188] Instead, "He is the Lamb of God that takes away the sin of the world." Faith alone grasps this.[189] It does not take hold of love, which nonetheless will follow faith with a thankful spirit. Therefore, victory over sin and death, salvation and eternal life, has not come through the law, nor by the works of the law, nor through the proper use of willpower but through Jesus Christ alone.[190] *Therefore, it is faith alone grasping onto Him, which justifies.*[191] *The following statement shows how to differentiate and understand these*

---

[186] Luther adds this footnote: *Doctrina de bonis operibus non negligenda, sed a justificatione longe removenda,* "we must not overlook the doctrine of good works, but remove it far away from justification."

[187] *sola fide in Christum nos pronuntiari justos, non operibus legis aut caritate.*

[188] *ergo nec exactor legis nec operum.*

[189] Luther's footnote: *Fides sola justificat, quia sola apprenhendit Christi beneficium,* "faith alone justifies, because it alone grasps the benefit of Christ."

[190] *sed per solum Iesum Christum.*

[191] *Ergo sola fides hoc apprehendens justificat.*

different concepts: Victory over sin and death comes only in Christ alone; thus it does not come from the works of the law, nor from our freewill, etc.[192] *Here, we will gladly tolerate it if our adversaries call us "Solarians,"*[193] *but they don't have the slightest idea of what Paul is talking about.*

VERSE 16. So that we might be justified by faith in Christ, rather than by the works of the law.

Here Paul talks not only about the ceremonial law, as we have said before, but about the entire law. The ceremonial law was just as much the law of God as the moral law. For example, circumcision, the priestly institution, the temple services and ceremonies, all had been given by God's command, as well as the Ten Commandments. Further, when Abraham received the order to offer his son Isaac as a sacrifice, it was a law. This work of Abraham pleased God as much as the other laws of the ceremonial law. However, Abraham was not justified by this work but by faith. Scripture says, "Abram believed the Lord, and He credited it to him as righteousness" (Genesis 15:6; Romans 4:3).

They say that after the appearance of Christ, it is the ceremonial law that kills and brings death. Yes, but without faith in Christ, the Ten Commandments do the same. Further, no other law should be tolerated in the conscience except the law of the Spirit and life by which we are made free in Christ from the law of the letter and death and its works and all sin. Not because the law is evil but because it has no power at all to justify us. In fact, its effect works to the contrary. It is a matter of great excellence to have peace with God, and therefore, in this matter, we need a mediator greater than Moses or the law *or our own will or even that grace they call the love of God.*[194] Here, we cannot presume we are something. We can only receive the treasure, which is Christ, and we grasp Him in our heart by faith, even though we may feel that we have never been so full of sin.

Therefore, the apostle places a great emphasis on these words: "So that we might be justified by faith in Christ and not by the works of the law."[195] The papal scholars believe these are empty words and do not profit anyone. That is why they hurry past them.

Up to now, you have heard what Paul said to Peter. With these few words, he summarized the main and central teaching of all Christian doctrine, the true

---

[192] *Victoria peccati et mortis est in solo Iesu Christo, ergo non est in operibus legis, nec in voluntate nostra etc.*

[193] *solarios.* Luther refers to those who adhere to and promote the five *solas,* or "alones," of the Reformation: grace alone, Scripture alone, faith alone, Christ alone, to God alone the glory.

[194] *charitatem Dei.*

[195] *ut ex fide Christi justificemur, non ex operibus legis.*

way of being a Christian. Now he turns to the Galatians, to whom he writes and concludes, "Since that is the way it is, that we are justified by faith in Christ, no one shall be justified by the works of the law."[196]

VERSE 16. For by the works of the law no flesh [non omnis caro] shall be justified.

"Non omnis caro" (not all flesh) is a (Latin translation of a) Hebrew expression. But it (the Latin translation) sins against proper grammar.[197] *It is a phrase that is frequently found in Scriptures, as in Genesis 4:15, "lest any finding him should kill him" (KJ21). The Greek and the Latin use a different expression. "Not all" (in Hebrew) means (absolutely) "no one"; and "not anyone" (in Hebrew) means (absolutely) "no one." But in Latin, "not all flesh" sounds like (there could be) "some flesh." However, the Holy Spirit is not bound to (the) grammatical scruples (of the Latin).*[198]

"Flesh," in Paul, does not mean the gross and obvious vices (as the papal scholars imagine). When it comes to these sins, Paul calls them by their own names: adultery, fornication, filth, and so on (see the following under 5:19–21). But by "flesh," Paul understands what Jesus explained in John chapter 3: "What is born of the flesh, is flesh" (John 3:6). Therefore, "flesh" means a person's entire nature, including reason and all the abilities that belong to humanity. "This flesh," says Paul, "cannot be justified by works, no matter if these were even the works of the law." He does not say, *"The flesh is not justified by works contrary to the law, like murder, fornication, drunkenness, and such. Instead, he says that it is not justified by works done according to the law, which are good."*[199]

Therefore, according to Paul, the flesh means all righteousness, wisdom, devotion, religion, understanding, and exercise of free will—in short, everything that exists in human nature. *If a Jew is not justified by works done according to the law of God, much less is a monk justified by his religious order, a priest by saying mass and keeping to the regulated hours, a philosopher by his wisdom, a theologian by his theology, and a Muslim by his Qur'an.* In sum, if someone could exceed all norms of wisdom and righteousness according to reason and the law of God, notwithstanding all such works, merits, masses, the most excellent righteousnesses and glorious worships, such a person cannot be justified.

---

[196] *ergo ex operibus legis non justificabitur omnis caro.*

[197] The reader must remember that Luther was lecturing in Latin and most likely using the Vulgate translation of the Bible, or one of its revisions.

[198] I have supplied the words in parentheses for additional clarity. Please also note that in *italics*, I indicate that this particular paragraph had been omitted from the first English translations.

[199] *quae bona sunt.*

The papal curia does not believe this. Instead, blind and stubborn, they defend their abominations against their own conscience and persevere in their blasphemous braggadocio still resounding their sacrilegious voices: "Whoever does this or that good work deserves the forgiveness of sins; everyone who submits to this or that order of holiness and observes the rules, we hereby promise them, with all certainty, eternal life." Words are insufficient to state what a horrible blasphemy it is to attribute eternal life to the doctrine of devils, to human decrees and regulations, to the wicked traditions of the Pope, and to the hypocritical works and merits of the monks and friars. Why? Because Paul, the apostle of Christ, rules out the law of God and its works, in order to obtain eternal life, for if by the works of the law no flesh shall be justified, even less shall anyone be justified by the orders of Benedict, Frances, and all such, in which there is not a single syllable of true faith in Christ. But this is all they urge, that whoever keeps them has eternal life.

I have often wondered long and hard at how the church has been able to persevere resisting these sects of perdition, which have reigned for so long in such great darkness and error. It was through some who God called through the Gospel and baptism (yet they remained in their assemblies). These walked with a simple and humble heart. They thought that only the monks and friars and those anointed by the bishops were holy and religious. They didn't feel worthy to be compared with them. But not finding within them a single work to offer against God's wrath and judgment, without hesitation, they fled to the death and passion of Christ and were saved in that simplicity.

God's wrath is horrendous and beyond words. For a long time now, He has been punishing the papacy for its ingratitude and for despising Christ and the Gospel. He has turned them over as an example of a lost cause because they have blasphemed and denied Christ altogether regarding their duty. Instead of the Gospel, they have created damnable rules, orders, and traditions of men. These are worshipped, honored, and preferred way above God's word. So much so that they've come to forbid marriage and have remained all tied up to this life as incestuous religious bachelors. In that condition, they have contaminated and degenerated themselves with all kinds of hideous evil, such as adultery, prostitution, impurity, sodomy, and other such abominations. This has been the fruit of their filthy lives as religious bachelors![200]

That is how God has punished sin with sin; from within, God has turned them over to their own stubborn minds. From without, He has permitted them to fall into such horrendous perversities. Justice has been done because they have blasphemed the only Son of God, in whom the Father is glorified and whom the Father gave over to death so that all who believe in Him will be saved by Him and not by their damnable rules and orders. "I will honor," He says, "those who honor me" (1 Kings 2; 1 Samuel 2:30). God is honored in His Son (John 5:23). God

---

[200] *Is fuit fructus impuri coelibatus.*

honors everyone who believes that the Son is our Mediator and Savior, for this is honoring the Father. God adorns them with His gifts, the forgiveness of sins, righteousness, the Holy Spirit, and eternal life. On the contrary, "Those who despise me," He says, "will be met with contempt."

Then this is our general conclusion: "By the works of the law no flesh shall be justified."[201] *Apply this norm far and wide including all conditions and situations of life. Ergo (therefore) no monk will be justified by his religious order, no nun by her chastity, no citizen by his integrity, no prince by his kind generosity, etc.* The law of God is greater than the entire world, since it condemns everyone, and all the works of the law exceed in excellence the works of the merit hoarders and champions of freewill. Even so, says Paul, "neither the law nor its works are able to justify, therefore only faith justifies."[202] He now goes on to confirm this assertion. His first argument turns the question around: What if the opposite were true?

LECTURE 11: Saturday, August 8

VERSE 17. But if, while we seek to be justified by Christ, we ourselves also are found sinners, is Christ therefore the minister of sin? God forbid!

These are not Latin phrases. They come from the Hebrew and have theological significance. If it is true, he says that we are justified in Christ, then it is impossible that before God we will still be counted as sinners or that God will continue to demand from us the righteousness of the law. On the contrary, if it weren't true, if we would still have to be justified by the law and the works of the law, then it's impossible that Christ could have ever justified us. One of the following two statements has to be false: either Christ is not enough for our justification or we cannot achieve our justification through the law. But the truth is that we are indeed justified by Christ. Therefore, we are not justified by the law. Paul reasons like this: "If, while we seek to be justified by Christ"—that is, "if we go to Christ to be justified, but once justified, we are still considered as sinners, then we would still be obligated to be justified by obeying the law (since we would still be considered sinners). In that case, all that Christ has ministered to us in justification is nothing but the law and sin. I say that if those who have been declared righteous in Christ are not really righteous because they still need the law to justify them, then all that Christ has ministered to them is the law and sin. If whoever is justified by Christ still needs to be justified by the law, then Christ is nothing more than a Lawgiver and a minister

---

[201] *quod ex operibus legis non justificabitur omnis caro.*
[202] *ergo sola fides justificat.*

of sin. Therefore, he who is righteous and holy in Christ is not really righteous or holy, since he still needs the righteousness and the holiness of the law."

However, we have every assurance that we are justified and righteous in Christ.[203] This is indeed the truth of the Gospel for it teaches that we are not justified by the law but that we are justified in Christ.[204] But if on the contrary, those who are justified in Christ are still considered sinners, meaning that they still belong to the law and are under the law (as taught by the false apostles), then they have not yet been justified, for the law accuses them and exposes them as sinners and requires from them the works of the law, alleging that they are necessary for their justification. Therefore, those who are justified in Christ are not really justified. From there, it follows that Christ is not the Justifier but rather the minister of sin.[205]

With these intensely passionate words, he accuses the false apostles and all merit hoarders that together they pervert everyone else. Why? Because they convert the law into grace, and grace they convert into law. They turn Christ into a Moses, and Moses they turn into Christ. They turn the figure of Moses into an image of Christ, and the figure of Christ they turn into an image of Moses. They teach that in addition to Christ, and all Christ's righteousness, the observance of the law is necessary for justification. Thus we can see in their intolerant perversity that they convert the law into a Christ. They say, "If you fulfill the requirements of the law, you will be saved. But if you do not fulfill them, you will not be justified, no matter all your faith in Christ. Thus if Christ does not justify, He is but a minister of sin (as follows from the logic of their doctrine). Christ is only a representative of the law, for He does not give us any more than what the law already gives us; He merely teaches us that we are sinners. Since Christ is the minister of sin,[206] He sends us to the law and to Moses to be justified."

Therefore, it is inevitable that the followers of the Pope[207] and all who ignore the righteousness of Christ or don't truly know it end up converting Christ into Moses and the law and the law into a Christ because this is what they teach: "It is true that faith in Christ justifies, but, even so, we must keep the commandments of God. For it is written, 'If you wish to enter into life, keep the commandments'" (Matthew 19:17). Here, right from the outset, they have denied Christ and abolished faith, since they assign to the law what only belongs to Christ. Why? Because Christ, in His true definition, is the Justifier and Redeemer of sins. But if I give that credit to the law, then the law is my Justifier and delivers me from my sins because I do its works. As it turns out, the law is now Christ, and Christ loses His name

---

[203] *Sed certe sumus justificati et justi in Christo.*

[204] *non in lege sed in Christo justificetur.*

[205] *peccati ministrum.*

[206] *doctor peccati.*

[207] First Latin edition, "Papists, Zwinglians, Anabaptists."

altogether, His function, and His glory. He becomes nothing more than a minister of the law—rebuking, intimidating, pointing the sinner to something else that will justify him because that is the function of the law.

However, once the law has declared sinners guilty, Christ's true function is to raise them up and deliver them from their sins if they have believed the Gospel, since for all who believe "Christ is the end of the law for righteousness, He is the Lamb of God that takes away the sin of the world." But the advocates of the Pope and the sectarian spirits don't hold this doctrine. They turn everything inside out. From Christ, they make a Moses, and from Moses, a Christ. And although they object, saying they really don't say that, their main argument is that Christ is indeed Moses. What's more, they make fun of us because we insist on instilling and urging faith. "Ha, ha! Wait and see if you'll get to heaven on faith alone! You must strive for far more excellent achievements! You'd be better off meeting the obligations of the law of God, since it is written, 'Do this and live' [Luke 10:28]. *You should suffer many things; shed your own blood; leave your own home, your wife, and your children; and imitate the example of Christ.* Faith, which you hold in such high esteem, turns you into nothing else but a slouch, negligent in your duties." That is why they are nothing else but ministers and workers of the law. They turn people away from baptism, faith, and the promises of Christ toward the law and its works. They turn grace into law and law into grace.

Who could possibly believe that these simple things could be so easily confused and mixed up? Surely there is no one so dense that can't see the difference between law and grace. The difference could not be more obvious and clear. The very nature and meaning of the words highlight the difference. Who can't get it through his head that these words, "law" and "grace," are different in name and meaning? The difference is so clear! The adversaries are so diabolical and perverse that they merge together law and grace. Thus they create this monstrous monstrosity[208] by transforming Christ into Moses! That is why I frequently say that this doctrine of faith is crystal clear. Anyone can see the difference between law and grace when they look at the words, but when it comes to their use and practice, it is very difficult.

The Pope and his distinguished scholars clearly confess that law and grace are unequal and distinct matters. But when it comes to their use and practice, they teach altogether the contrary.[209] According to them, faith in Christ is dead unless it is accompanied by love. Otherwise, it doesn't matter if you receive faith through the faculties or the operation and the workings of nature, whether it's infused or poured out by God within us. If this is so, whatever happened to the difference between law and grace? It's true they give them different names, but really, they have done nothing but given both the same name: "love." Everyone else that

---

[208] *monstrum monstrosissimum est.*

[209] Luther adds in a footnote: *Papa legem et gratiam confundit.*

eventually requires the keeping of the law does the same: they assign law and works to justification. Thus whoever doesn't perfectly understand the central article of justification[210] will always keep on confusing and mixing up law and grace, one with the other.

May all diligently learn above all things to recognize the difference between law and grace in deed and practice. Don't learn to mouth the words like the Pope and the fanatical sects. As far as the words, they confess they are two different things. But in actual practice (as I've said), they confuse and combine one with the other, for there's no way at all they're going to admit that faith justifies without works. But if this is true, then Christ is worthless to me, for according to them, even if my faith is beyond measure (according to their opinion), if this faith is devoid of love, I am not justified. *But if my faith is without love, love would never satisfy it because it is possible that I could always love even more.* Therefore, even if we grasp on to Christ by faith, He would not be our Justifier. Grace would amount to nothing, nor could faith be truly faith without love. *This is the same way the Anabaptists argue. They don't talk about the cross, the passion, and the shedding of blood. They claim that if I truly have love, works plus the cross,[211] then it is true faith; therefore, it justifies.*

With this doctrine, today, these lying spirits and sects of perdition darken and disfigure the benefit of Christ. They diminish the honor of the Justifier and make him a minister of sin. *They haven't learned anything from us except to mouth our words but they don't understand the subject itself. They want to make it look like they also teach the Gospel and faith in Christ as truthfully as we do, but when it comes to using and practicing it, they are teachers of the law, equal in every respect to the false apostles.*[212] Throughout all the churches, they required circumcision and the keeping of the law in addition to faith in Christ. So much so that without circumcision and the keeping of the law, they denied justification. "Unless you are circumcised," they claimed, "according to the law of Moses, you cannot be saved" (Acts 15:1). In the same way, today, these rigorous vigilantes of the law require that in addition to the righteousness of faith you must keep the commandments of God, as was said, "Do this and live" (Luke 10:28). Also, "If you wish to enter into life, keep the commandments" (Matthew 19:17). That is why there is not even one among them, no matter how wise he claims to be, that understands the difference between law and grace. *When they are brought to trial and faced with the facts, they are condemned.*

---

[210] *articulum justificationis.*

[211] *opera et crux.*

[212] Luther's footnote: *Qui legem dicunt necessariam esse ad justitiam, similes sunt pseudoapostolis,* "they allege that the law is necessary for righteousness, just like the false apostles."

However, we place the difference where it belongs. We do not question if good works should be done; if the law is good, holy, and just; or if it should be kept or not. This is another subject. We take up the matter with respect to justification, whether the law justifies or not. Our opponents will not allow this question, nor will they answer it; they do not put a marker on the difference at all. They just bellow, "You must do good works; you have to keep the law." We know that well enough. But since these are two different and distinct matters, we will not tolerate that they be merged one with the other. At a proper moment, we will deal with the subject of doing good works. But now, we are dealing with the subject of justification so that we put aside everything that has to do with good works. Our opponents get all stressed out over them, entirely assigning to good works the function of justification. However, that removes the glory from Christ and attributes the glory to one's own good works.

This is a powerful argument and one I have often used to my own comfort: "While we seek to be justified by Christ." It's as if Paul had said, "If we have been declared righteous by Christ but yet we are still not counted as justified and righteous but rather as sinners because we still need to be justified by the law, well then, let us quit looking for justification in Christ so that we may find it in the law." For if justification doesn't come from grace but rather from the law, what then did Christ accomplish through His death; preaching; victory over the law, sin, and death; and gift of the Holy Spirit? We can then conclude, "Either we are declared righteous by Christ, or He declares us sinners, guilty, and damned! However, if the law declares us righteous, then it is inevitable that Christ is the one who declares us guilty sinners, and thus Christ is nothing but a minister of sin." But if such is the case, then all you are doing is claiming this argument: "Everyone who believes in the Lord Jesus Christ is a sinner, guilty of eternal death; and unless you sprint back to the law to do its works, you will not be saved."

The Sacred Scriptures and the New Testament in particular frequently urges faith in Christ: "Everyone who believes in Him will be saved, will not perish, does not come into judgment, will not be disappointed, has eternal life." But on the contrary they say, "Everyone who believes in Him is condemned because he has faith without works, which condemns him." They pervert everything. They turn Christ into a dreary slayer but Moses into a living savior. Isn't this just a horrendous blasphemy? On top of that, they teach that good works will make you worthy of eternal life. But if you believe in Christ, you make yourself damnable and worthy of eternal death? Is this one any less horrendous: the keeping of the law will save you, but faith in Christ will condemn you?

Granted that our opponents do not use these exact words but in practice, that is their doctrine. They say that it is not infused faith (which is proper faith in Christ)[213] that frees us from sin but instead faith that comes dressed up in

---

[213] *Fide infusa*, not *gratia infusa*.

love. From this, it's obvious that faith in Christ, without the law, does not save us. This is nothing else but affirming without hesitation that Christ leaves us in our sins, under the wrath of God, and makes us guilty of eternal death. On the other hand, if you keep the law and do its works, then faith does justify you, since it has works and without works faith is worthless. Therefore, works justify and not faith. *Because the cause of something is greater than its effect; and if works are the cause by which faith justifies, therefore, works justify more than faith.* This doctrine is an overwhelming abominable blasphemy!

Paul solidifies his argument by affirming an impossibility that needs to be split up and resolved one way or another. If after we are justified in Christ we are still counted as sinners, then there is no other way to be justified except to be out of Christ, which is then, by the law. In that case, Christ cannot justify us but rather accuse and condemn us. Thus it follows that Christ died in vain and that the following and all other texts are false: "Look, the Lamb of God, who takes away the sin of the world" (John 1:29); "Whoever believes in Him should not perish, but have eternal life" (John 3:36). Given that premise, in fact, all Scripture is false, for it testifies that Christ is the Justifier and Savior of the world, for if after we have been justified we are still found to be sinners, then the conclusion is unavoidable: all who keep the law are justified apart from Christ. If this is true, then we are nothing but Muslims, Jews, or Tartars professing the name and the word of God only in appearances but in fact denying Christ and His word altogether. However, for Paul, faith is "ἀνυπόκριτον" [sincere].[214] Thus, it's a great and wicked error to affirm the following: faith justifies, but it has to be embellished by love. However, if our adversaries defend such an affirmation at all costs, why then don't they just reject faith in Christ altogether, especially since for them it is nothing more than an empty quality of the soul that is worthless without works? *Why don't they just call a spade a spade?*[215] Why don't they quit beating around the bush and come out and say that it is works that justify and not faith? And while they are at it, why don't they just come out and deny Paul and the entire Gospel as well (which in fact they do), since the Gospel attributes righteousness to faith alone and not to works? If gluing faith and works together is what justifies, then all Paul's argument is false, for Paul clearly declares, "Man is not justified by the works of the law, but through faith in Jesus Christ"[216] (Galatians 2:16, MEV).

---

[214] During his lecture, Paul used the Greek term for *sincere*.

[215] Luther uses the Latin phrase *Cur non potius appellant scapham scapham?*, or "why don't they call a skiff a skiff?"

[216] *hominem non justificari operibus legis, sed fide Iesu Christi.*

VERSE 17. Is then Christ a minister of sin? May it never be! [DLNT].

The Hebrews used this type of language. Paul uses it also in 2 Corinthians, chapter 3. There, Paul speaks magnificently and clearly of these two ministries: the ministry of the letter and the ministry of the spirit, the ministry of the law and the ministry of grace, the ministry of death and the ministry of life. "Moses," said Paul, "is the minister of the law, he has the ministry of death," which he qualifies as "wrath, death, condemnation." Paul has the tendency to call the law with rather inglorious names. Of all the apostles, he is the only one that refers to it like that. The others don't. And it is extremely necessary that all students of Sacred Scripture understand Paul's way of talking about the law.

A minister of sin is nothing more than a legislator, a teacher of the law, an instructor of good works and love. He teaches the duty to suffer the cross and afflictions and to follow the example of Christ and the saints. Whoever teaches and requires this is a minister of the law, of sin, of wrath, and of death. That is because this doctrine does nothing more than to terrify and afflict the consciences of men and slam them shut under sin. Why? Because it is impossible for man's nature to fulfill the law. Even in those who have been justified and have the Holy Spirit, the law of the members struggles against the law of the mind. What then is going to be the effect among the perverse that don't have the Holy Spirit? Whoever teaches that righteousness comes through the law understands neither what he says nor what he affirms. He keeps the law even less. Instead, he deceives himself and others. He imposes burdens on others that they cannot bear, requiring and teaching impossible things, and in the end, he drags himself and his disciples over into desperate distress.

The correct use and the purpose of the law is to accuse and condemn as guilty all those who live trusting in themselves. It is so that they can see themselves in danger of sin, wrath, and eternal death—to be filled with terror and led to the border of desperation, trembling and shuddering at the fall of a leaf! And in this condition, they are under the law. That is because the law requires perfect obedience to God and condemns all those who are not keeping it. With all certainty, no human being is capable of rendering such obedience. Nonetheless, God requires it from us. Thus the law does not justify but condemn, according to what's written: "Cursed is the one who doesn't uphold the words of this law and observe them" (Deuteronomy 27:26). Thus everyone who teaches the law is a minister of sin.

There is good reason Paul in 2 Corinthians 3 says that the law is the ministry of sin. The law exposes sin and declares what it is. Without this, the law is dead. The knowledge of sin is not the speculative knowledge of the hypocrites but a true knowledge by which we see the wrath of God against sin and feel the breath of death at our back. By this knowledge, our heart is filled with terror; we feel we're going to sink into a most horrible despair. The law kills and destroys (Romans 7:11). That is why the Scriptures call the doctors of the law and works "oppressors" and "tyrants." They are no different from old pharaoh's taskmasters who oppressed Israel with physical bondage. These new givers and vigilantes of the law oppress people into a most miserable slavery of the soul. At the end, they take them to extreme desperation and total destruction. These self-appointed scholars don't know even know themselves nor the power of the law. They can't even have a conscience at peace when they suffer great emotional pain, not even when facing death. Although they have kept the law, loved their neighbor, done many good works, and suffered great personal loss, the law always shakes them up and accuses, saying, "You never kept everything that the law ordered you because cursed is everyone who doesn't continually keep everything the law requires." Therefore, the conscience can't shake off its anguish; instead, the despair intensifies even more. And if such self-appointed scholars were not raised up by faith and the righteousness of Christ, despair and anguish would sink them deeper into unending desperation.

There is an outstanding example of this condition in "Lives of the Fathers." The story is told of a certain hermit who before his death stood still and sad for three days with his eyes fixed on heaven. When asked why he did this, he answered that he was afraid of death. His disciples tried to comfort him telling him that he had no reason to fear death, since he had lived an exceedingly holy life. But he answered, "I have certainly lived piously and have kept God's commandments, but God's judgments differ from man's." This man when confronting death, even though he had lived a spotless life and had kept God's commandments, still could not find peace for his soul. The thought occurred to him that God judges very differently from man's judgment. Thus he lost all trust in all his good works and merits and most certainly would have despaired had he not been comforted by the promise of the uplifted Christ. Therefore, the law does not achieve anything else but strips us entirely naked, and then, it locks us up as prisoners! When that happens, it is too late for counseling or help of any kind, but all is considered hopeless. In such circumstances, none of the martyred saints can help us, nor can we help ourselves!

This same scenario played out when the law was given. We can see it in Exodus 19 and 20. Moses ordered the people to come out of their tents, since they had to meet with the Lord. They had to listen to God's voice speaking from the thick cloud. But the people, astonished and trembling with fear, fled and scattered; although just before, they had promised that they would do everything God had said. Standing afar, withdrawing, they told Moses, "We can't stand the thunder and the flashes of lightning and the sound of the trumpet and the mountain smoking, you speak to us, and we will listen; but do not let God speak to us, lest we die." So the proper function of the law is to pull us out of our tents and shelters, from the quiet comfort zones of our lives, and from our own self-confidence and bring us before the presence of God. There, His wrath is displayed before our sins. Here, the conscience does not feel any confidence at all of having kept the law or that it can, nor can it bear God's wrath revealed in the law when it brings us before the presence of God, for the law brings to us fear, it accuses us and places our sins in our face. It's impossible for us to remain there. Therefore, we take off running, and like the children of Israel, we shriek, "We'll die, we'll die, don't let God speak with us, you speak to us instead."

Thus everyone who teaches that faith in Christ does not justify unless it is joined to the keeping of the law turns Christ into a minister of sin, an instructor of the law, teaching Moses' same doctrine. But when this is done, Christ is no Savior at all, no Giver of grace, but a cruel despot, requiring as did Moses what no one is able to give. Look, this is the same notion that all the merit hoarders have of Christ. They turn him into a new legislator, and the Gospel as a new volume of laws requiring new works, just like the Muslims consider their Koran. But as far as laws, Moses' are more than enough. The Gospel then is the preaching of Christ, who forgives sins, of grace, that justifies and saves sinners. Thus wherever you find commandments in the Gospel, those in themselves are not the Gospel but explanations of the law and matters that depend on the Gospel.

Further, if the law is the minister of sin, then it is also the minister of wrath and death, for the law produces terror when it reveals sin. It shows man his sin and God's wrath, it fills him throughout with a ghastly terror of death and its condemnation. Because the conscience slowly catches on: "You haven't kept the commandments; that is why God's wrath is against you. And if God is angry with you, He will destroy and condemn you forever." Then the individual comes to think that the consequence is inevitable: "I have sinned; therefore, I must die." From there, it follows that the ministry of sin is the ministry of wrath and condemnation, for once it has revealed sin, God's wrath follows, then death and condemnation. *The conscience reasons like this: "You have sinned, therefore it's just you and God's wrath, and if His wrath is against you, He will destroy and condemn you forever."* This is the reason so many cannot tolerate God's judgment and wrath, which the law exhibits so harshly; many end up killing themselves by throwing themselves off a cliff or by drowning.

VERSE 17. Certainly not.

It's as if he had said, "Christ is not the minister of sin, but the giver of righteousness and eternal life." Thus Paul places a great divide between Moses and Christ. Let Moses stay on the earth. Let him be the teacher of the letter of the law and its fulfillment. Let him be the tormentor and crucifier of sinners. But the believers, says Paul, have another Teacher in their conscience: Not Moses but Christ. He has abolished the law and sin; He has visited God's wrath and death, and taken both captive. All of us who work oppressed under all kinds of hardships are invited to come to Him. Therefore, when we flee to Christ, Moses with his law disappears. His tomb disappears from our sight; sin and death can no longer hurt us. Because Christ is our Lord over the law, sin, and death; all who believe in Him are delivered from these things. Thus Christ's proper function is to deliver from sin and death. This is what Paul teaches and emphasizes throughout his writings.

Therefore, the law kills and condemns. However, Christ justifies and gives life. The law terrorizes us and separates us from Christ. Christ reconciles us with God and opens the gate so that we may come boldly before Him, since "He is the Lamb of God that takes away the sin of the world." Well, if He takes away the sin of the world, that means He also takes away my own sins, for I have believed in Him.[217] If sin has been taken away, then God's wrath, death, and condemnation have also been removed. In place of sin, righteousness comes in. In place of wrath, reconciliation and grace. In place of death, life. Instead of condemnation, salvation. Let us learn to mark these differences not only in words but also in life and daily experience and with our own feelings. Because where Christ is to be found, without fault, you will find a joyous heart and a conscience at peace, for Christ is our reconciliation, righteousness, peace, life, and salvation. In brief, everything that an afflicted conscience could ever wish for, it finds abundantly in Christ. Paul now moves on to expand his argument and persuade in the following way.

VERSE 18. For if I rebuild something that I tore down, I demonstrate that I am a wrongdoer[218] [NIV].

It's as if he had said, "I haven't been wasting my time preaching so that now I'll backtrack and start rebuilding the things that I tore down. If I did such a thing, I would not only be working for nothing, but I'd also be guilty of doing wrong, tearing down everything, just like the false apostles—in other words, if I turn grace and Christ into law and Moses or if I convert the law and Moses into grace and Christ. Through the ministry of the Gospel, I have abolished sin, the downcast heart, wrath, and death. My teaching has been this: 'Your conscience is bound to the law, death, and sin. No man or angel could ever free you from these but now comes the Gospel and preaches remission of sins through Christ, since He has abolished the law and destroyed sin and death. Believe in Him and you will be freed from the curse of the law, the tyranny of sin and death. Thus you will be righteous and will have eternal life.'

"Through the preaching of the Gospel, I have destroyed the law so that it can no longer govern my conscience. When my new guest comes to live in the new home, He takes up residence all by Himself. Moses, the old tenant has to quit claim. He has to go somewhere else. By the same token, where the new guest

---

[217] Luther adds the following note: *Christus sublatis omnibus malis attulit omnia bona*, "Christ has removed all evil and produced everything good."

[218] Notice that Luther is using the Vulgate, which translates the Greek word παραβάτης (wrongdoer) as *praevaricator*, or "prevaricator" in English, which means one who speaks or acts falsely or evasively with intent to deceive.

comes to take up residence, there's no longer a place for sin, wrath, and death. Now only grace, righteousness, joy, life, true confidence in the Father, and assurance from Him are the new residents. The Father has now been satisfied and reconciled to us; He is kind, great in patience, and full of mercy for the sake of Christ His son. So am I then going to tear out Christ and destroy His kingdom that I have planted through the preaching of the Gospel, building once again on the law and end up setting up Moses' kingdom once again? That's what I would be doing if I now go back teaching circumcision and the keeping of the law as necessary for salvation." That's what the false apostles were doing. If I followed their example, I would be doing the same. Instead of righteousness and life, I would be establishing sin and death, for the law does nothing else but to point out sin, inciting anger and death.

Then I ask you, I plead for you to understand this, where does that leave even the best supporters of the Pope? What are they then but only destroyers of the kingdom of Christ and builders of the kingdom of the devil and sin, wrath, and eternal death? Yes, they destroy the church, what God has built, not with the law of Moses, as did the false apostles, but through the traditions of men and doctrines of devils. Even the fanatical sects of today follow on our heels. They destroy and will tear down everything that we have built. They build and will build once again what we have torn down.

However, by the grace of God, we continue to uphold the central truth of justification, knowing with all confidence that we are justified by faith alone in Christ.[219] Thus we do not mix together law and grace, faith and works. Instead, we put as much distance between them as possible.[220] Let every true Christian diligently know how to mark this difference and distance between law and grace. Let him not do it just with letters and words but in practice and in the inner experience. So that when he listens that there are good works to do and that he must follow the example of Christ, he will use good judgment and say, 'With pleasure I will do all these things.' But from that, what will follow? That therefore, you will be saved and obtain eternal life? No, not at all. I grant that I must do good works. I must suffer trials and hardships patiently, even shed my blood for the cause of Christ. But even so, I will not be justified for doing any of that, nor will I obtain salvation."

Thus we should not allow good works to stake a claim within the article of justification, as the monks have done. They do this not only with good works but also with punishments and torments meted out to criminals, telling them that they will earn eternal life by suffering them well. When they step up to the gallows or to the place of their execution, the monks tell them, "You should suffer this shameful death patiently and willingly. If you do that, you will merit forgiveness of sins and

---

[219] *Nos vero, gratia Dei, articulum justificationis tenentes certo scimus, nos sola fide in Christum justificari.*

[220] *nos confundimos legem et gratiam, fidem et opera, sed ea longissime separamus.*

eternal life." How horrible that this thief, assassin, assailant should be so miserably seduced at this point of extreme anguish and agony! At death's door, when he's about to plummet with the hangman's noose on his neck or when his head is about to be cut off, he is denied the Gospel and the sweet promises of Christ, the only words that bring comfort and salvation. Instead, they send him off trusting in forgiveness of sins as long as he takes on such a shameful death willingly and patiently, a death he suffers for his own grievous mischief! What's this? It's nothing more than piling on top of him more than what he's already suffering. It is adding extreme condemnation and damnation, since his conscience is deceived at the point of his own death. It's nothing else but sending him off on the way to hell!

Therefore, these hypocrites declare in plain daylight that they neither teach nor understand a single letter or syllable of what is grace, the Gospel, or Christ. It's only in the appearances where they retain the name of Gospel and Christ so that they can deceive people's hearts, for they deny and reject Christ and His Gospel, assigning greater value to the traditions of men. This is as true as the fact that there is so much false worship, so many religious orders, so many ceremonies, and as many who brag about the exercise of their free will. They themselves testify that all these things were set up to get a hold of grace through their merits, achieve righteousness, and eternal life. In their confessions, they make no mention at all of faith or the merits of Christ. Instead, they teach and establish how people can satisfy God doing penance and accumulating human merits. The following way of absolution is clear evidence (although here I will not mention other matters). The monks themselves practice it, since there are some who consider themselves more devout and religious than others. I think it is well to note it here so that our posterity will see how greatly horrendous is the kingdom of the Pope.

The Monks' Formula for Absolution [Forgiving Sins]: God Save You Brother!

"The merit of the passion of our Lord Jesus Christ and of the blessed Mary, virgin forever, and of all the saints; the merit of your religious order, the austerity of your religion, the humility of your confession, your contrite heart, the good works you have done and will do for the love of our Lord Jesus Christ, may they be available to you for the remission of your sins, the increase of your merit and grace, and the reward of eternal life. Amen."

We hear the merit of Christ mentioned in these words. But if you weigh them, you will see that they make Christ absolutely worthless. The glory and the name of Justifier and Savior is torn away from Him and handed over to the monks. Isn't this anything but taking the name of God in vain? Isn't this anything but confessing Christ in words only while at the same denying His power and blaspheming His name? I, myself, was once all tied up in this error. I thought that Christ was a judge (although with my mouth I confessed that He suffered and died for man's redemption). I thought that He had to be placated with the observance of my order's rules. Therefore, when I recited my prayers or said mass, I would add these concluding words: "Oh, Lord Jesus, I come to you, and I implore you that these burdens and rigors of my order and religion may be able to pay entirely for all my sins." But now, "I give thanks to the Father of all mercies, who has called me from the darkness to the light of His glorious Gospel and has given me an abundant knowledge of Jesus Christ, my Lord. Because of His love, I count all these things but loss, and I consider them as σκύβαλα[221] in order to gain Christ and that I may be found in Him, not having my own righteousness of the Augustine order but the righteousness that comes through faith in Christ, to whom together with the Father and the Holy Spirit be praise and glory, forever more without end. Amen."

Therefore, with Paul we conclude that "we are justified by faith alone in Christ, without the law."[222] Well then, once a people are justified and through faith they possess Christ, knowing that He is their righteousness and their life, they will certainly not walk around with their arms crossed. As a good tree, they will yield good fruit. Since the believers have the Holy Spirit, and the Holy Spirit does not permit laziness but provokes them to exercise devotion, love to God; to suffer patiently all afflictions; to be in prayer; to offer thanksgiving; and to show kindness toward all humankind.

We also say that faith without works is nothing and empty.[223] But the papal supporters and sectarian fanatics twist it all around: "Faith without works does not justify because you may have all possible faith, but if you have no works, it is worthless." This is false. However, faith without works according to the logic of the fanatics is mere vanity; it's a mere daydream and illusion of the heart; it is false and does not justify.

LECTURE 12: Friday, August 14

Up to now, we have dealt with Paul's first argument. He insists that it must be one of these two: the law cannot justify us; if it could, then Christ turns out to be a minister of sin, but that is impossible. That is why we conclude that justification does not proceed from the law. We have dealt extensively with this issue, as it deserves.

---

[221] "Dung." Luther cites from Philippians 3:8. Remember, Luther is lecturing seminarians and occasionally he uses Greek terms from the New Testament to emphasize his point. In Greek, the term literally means "scraps thrown to the dogs" or simply "waste."

[222] *sola fide in Christum nos justificari, sine lege et operibus.*

[223] *Quare et nos dicimus fidem, sine operibus nihili esse et inanem.* This entire paragraph is not found in Middleton's English translation but only in the Latin text.

However, we can neither overemphasize it nor drive it home sufficiently so as to make it stick to our memory.

VERSE 19. For I through the law died to the law so that I might live for God.

These are marvelous words, but in a language unknown and incomprehensible to human reason. And although they are brief, they are spoken with great zeal and a fiery spirit, as if he were highly indignant. It's as if he had said, "Why do you brag so much about the law? I don't have the slightest idea. But if you must insist in having a law, well, I also have another law." And as if the Holy Spirit had moved him to indignation, he calls grace itself "the law," giving a new name to the operation of grace, in contempt of the law of Moses and the false apostles. They contentiously insisted that the law was necessary for justification. Therefore, Paul sets law against law. These are the sweetest words, full of comfort. In the Scriptures, particularly in Paul, the law is countered with the law, sin is set against sin, death is countered with death, captivity is set against captivity, hell against hell, the altar countered with the altar, lamb against lamb, Passover countered with Passover, etc.[224]

In Romans 8 (v. 3), he says, "Through sin, he condemned sin." Then "he took captivity captive" (Psalm 68:19; Ephesians 4:8). "O death, I will be thy death: O grave, I will be thy destruction" (Hosea 13:14, GNV). In the same way, he says here that through the law, he is dead to the law. It's as if he had said, "The law of Moses accuses and condemns me. I have another law, the law of grace and liberty. This law accuses the law that accuses me. This law condemns the law that condemns." In this way, death has done away with death, but this death was in effect, life itself. Similarly, righteousness takes to itself the name of sin because it condemns sin, and this condemnation of sin is true righteousness.

Here, Paul seems to be altogether a heretic—of all the heretics, the worst, and his heresy, such as had never been heard before, for Paul says, "As long as he is dead to the law, he lives for God." The false apostles taught another doctrine: "You must be alive to the law; otherwise you are dead to God." But Paul taught the opposite: "Unless you are dead to the law, you cannot live before God." The doctrine of our adversaries today is like the doctrine of the false apostles back then. They say, "If you are to live before God, you must be alive to the law or according to the law." But we say the opposite: "If you are to live before God, you have to be totally dead to the law." Reason and human wisdom cannot understand this doctrine. They always teach it backward: "If you are to live before God, you must keep the law, for it is written, 'do this and live.'" Among all the papal scholars, this is the chosen norm: "Whoever lives according to the law, lives before God." Paul says the contrary: "We

---

[224] *Opponitur lex legi, peccatum peccato, mors morti, captivitas captivitati, diabolus diabolo, infernus inferno, altare altari, agnus agno, pasca pascati, etc.*

cannot live before God unless we have died completely to the law." Therefore, we should rise to this heavenly height so that we have the confidence that we are way above the law, so much so that we have died entirely to the law. Well then, if we have died to the law, then the law no longer has any power over us just as the law no longer has power over Christ,[225] who has freed us from the law that we may live before God. Everything moves toward that end, to prove that we are not justified by the law but by faith in Jesus Christ alone.[226]

Here, Paul is not talking about the ceremonial law. *He sacrificed in the Temple, circumcised Timothy, shaved his head in Cenchrea. He would not have done these things had he been dead to the ceremonial law. But he is talking about the entire law.* Therefore, it's just that simply the entire law, ceremonial or moral, has been abolished for the Christian because he is dead![227] But the law in itself is not dead.[228] In fact, it remains alive and reigns among the wicked. But the believer is dead to the law, as he also is dead to sin, the devil, death, and hell. These remain, as well as the world with all the wicked. Thus when the papal scholars teach that only the ceremonial law has been abolished, you should understand the flip side: that Paul and every Christian have died to the entire law, and even so, the law remains.

For example, when Christ resurrected from the dead, He remained free from the grave. But even so, the grave remains. Peter was freed from jail, the paralytic from his cot, the young man from his casket, the girl from her bed. Even so, the jail, the cot, the casket, and the bed remained. But since I am dead to the law on account of another law, that law has also died for me; but just as Christ's tomb remained, so did Peter's jail, and the girl's bed. But Christ with His resurrection has died to the tomb, Peter's rescue delivered him from jail, and the girl was freed from her bed when she received life.

Therefore, the words "I am dead to the law" are very effective. He does not say, "I am free from the law for a while, or I am Lord of the law." He simply says, "I am dead to the law." That is to say, I have nothing to do with the law. Paul could not have said anything more effective against the righteousness of the law than "I am dead to the law." He says, "I have nothing to do with the law, therefore I can't be justified by the law."

To die to the law is this: I don't live tied to the law but in freedom from the law, and I don't know it at all. Thus whoever wants to live before God let him strive to be found without the law and exit the tomb together with Christ. When Christ came out of the tomb, the soldiers were astonished. Those who saw the girl rise from the dead were astonished. In the same way, reason and human wisdom are

---

[225] *lex nihil juris habet in nos, ut neque in Christum aliquid juris habet.*

[226] *per legem nos non justificari, sed sola fide in Christum.*

[227] *Itaque simpliciter tota lex, sive sit ceremonialis sive decalogi, abrogata est christiano, quia ei mortus est.*

[228] *non quod lex pereat.*

astonished and turn senseless when they hear we are not justified unless we are dead to the law. It is impossible for them to grasp this mystery. But when from the depths of our conscience by faith we take hold of Christ, we enter within a new law, which devours the old law that held us captive. The tomb where Jesus laid remained empty after His resurrection. In the same way, when I believe in Christ and I am raised up together with Him, I die to my tomb—that is to say, to the law that held me captive there. Now the law remains as an empty tomb, for I have escaped from my prison and grave—that is, the law. Therefore, the law has no power at all to accuse me or hold me anymore within its grasp, for I have come back to life.

It is necessary to instruct people's consciences in this way so that they can understand the difference between the righteousness of the law and that of grace. The righteousness of grace and freedom of the conscience do not belong to the flesh in any way at all. The flesh cannot remain in freedom. It should stay in the grave, in jail, on its deathbed. It should be subject to the law and oppressed by the Egyptians. But the Christian's conscience should be free from the law, meaning free from the law, and should have nothing to do with it. It is good to know this. It is of great help to comfort stressed-out consciences. Therefore, when you see someone horrified and distressed by the meaning and the feeling of his sin, you can say to him, "Brother, you are not distinguishing things correctly. You have put the law in the conscience, but you should put in the flesh. Wake up, get up, and remember that you should believe in Christ the conqueror of the law and sin. With this faith, you will soar way above the law, to that heaven where there is neither law nor sin. And although the law and sin remain, they have nothing at all to do with you because you have died to the law and sin."

This is easy to say, but blessed is he who knows how to hold on to these things in times of anguish. When he feels oppressed by sin and the accusations of the law, he can say, "Are you accusing me, oh law? Of what are you accusing me, saying I have committed many sins? You are certainly right that I have committed many sins. I commit them daily so much so that I lose count. But this does not affect me at all. I am now deaf and can't hear a word you say. Therefore, you speak to me to no avail, for I am dead to you. But if you are going to accuse me because of my sins, go to my flesh with its members, my servants. Teach them, harass, and crucify them, but don't trouble my conscience, or me, which is altogether a lady and a queen. I am now dead to you, and I now live in Christ. With Him, I have another law, the law of grace, which rules over sin and the law." Through what means? Through faith in Christ, which is what Paul states in the following.

This definition seems strange and astounding: that to live to the law is to be dead to God, and to be dead to the law is to be alive to God. These two propositions are entirely opposed to reason; thus no cunning scholar or legalist can understand them. But as far as you are concerned, learn its true meaning. He who lives for the law, who strives to be justified by the works of the law, is and continues to be a sinner. Thus he is dead and condemned. Because the law cannot justify and save him. The law only accuses, terrifies, and kills him. Therefore, to live for the law is to be dead to God. On the contrary, to die to the law is to be alive toward God. That is why if you wish to live to God, you have to die to the law. If you wish to live for the law, you have to die to God. However, to live to God is to be justified by grace or faith because of Christ and without the law and its works.[229]

This then is the true and accurate definition of a Christian. He is a son of grace and the remission of sins because he is no longer under the law but above the law, sin, death, and hell. In the same way that Christ was freed from the grave and Peter from jail, the Christian is freed from the law. And there is just as great a separation between the justified conscience and the law as there is between Jesus risen from the tomb and the tomb itself as there is between Peter freed from the jail and the jail itself. Christ through His death and resurrection is dead to the tomb so that the grave has no power at all over Him, neither can it hold Him in its grasp. The stone has been removed, the seals are broken, the guards petrified. He has risen and nothing holds Him back. Peter was freed from jail and he went wherever he wanted. In the same way, by grace, the conscience is freed from the law. That is how it is with everyone born of the Spirit. The flesh doesn't even know where this comes from, or where it goes, since it cannot judge unless it is according to the law. But on the contrary, the spirit says, "Let the law accuse me, let sin and death intimidate me all they want, even so, I will not panic. I have placed the law against the law, sin against sin, and death against death."[230]

Therefore, when my conscience hurts with remorse and sin's sting, I fix my eyes on Christ, that bronze serpent hanging from the cross. There, I find the sin that opposes my sin, which accuses and devours me. This other sin is the flesh of Christ that takes away the sin of the world; it is powerful, it condemns and devours my sin. Thus my sin is condemned by another sin—that is, Christ crucified: "God made him who had no sin to be sin for us so that in him we might become the righteousness of God." In the same way, I find in my flesh a death that afflicts and kills me. But in me, I have a death that is contrary to that death. It is the death of death, since this death crucifies and devours my death!

All these are not the achievements of the law or its works but those of Christ crucified. On His shoulders were placed all humanity's evil, the law, sin, death, the devil, and hell. All these find their death in Him because by His death He has put them all to death! However, we need to receive this benefit of Christ without a vacillating faith because just as we are not offered the law nor any of its works but by Christ alone,[231] nothing else is required of us but trusting by faith. By this law, we grasp on to Christ and believe that our sins and our death have been condemned and abolished in the sin and in the death of Christ.

---

[229] *Deo justificare per gratiam seu fidem propter Christum sine lege et operibus.*

[230] *legem contra legem, peccatum contra peccatum, mortem contra mortem habeo.*

[231] *solus Christus.*

Therefore, we have stronger arguments that accurately conclude that justification comes through faith alone.[232] How could it be possible for the law and its works to contribute to justification seeing how passionately Paul counters against the law and works? He clearly says that we should be dead to the law if we are to live before God. But if we are dead to the law, and the law is dead to us, we have nothing at all to do with the law. How then could it contribute in any way to our justification? Therefore, we are compelled to say that we are declared righteous by grace alone or by faith in Christ alone without the law and its works.[233]

The papal scholars[234] are blind and cannot see this or understand it. That is why they go around hallucinating when they argue that faith does not justify unless it is accompanied by the works of love. But if such is the case, then such faith in Christ doesn't amount to anything and is worthless. That's because it tears away from faith the power to justify unless it is dressed up in love. However, let us put aside law and love until another occasion. Let us rest upon the main point of our topic: Jesus Christ, the Son of God, died on the cross; on His body, he carried my sins, the law, death, the devil, and hell. These despots are invincible enemies. They oppress, perturb, and harass. Thus I should be careful as to how I can be freed from their hands and be justified and saved. Here, I can't find any law, work, or love that could ever deliver me from such tyranny. There is none other but Christ alone who takes away the law, then kills and with His death destroys my death in His body. In this way, He plunders hell, judges and crucifies the devil, and casts him to hell. In short, Christ rose above all these, made a public spectacle of them, and triumphed over them. Now they are powerless and instead are compelled to serve me!

From this, we can clearly see that it is inconceivable for us to contribute anything at all in this matter. We need to hear that this is the way these things were done for us and without any doubt grasp them by faith. Certainly, this is faith truly formed and adorned. Now, when I have grasped on to Christ in this way by faith and through Him I am dead to the law; justified from sin; and freed from sin, the devil, and hell, only then am I able to do good works. I love God, I give Him thanks, I practice kindness toward my neighbor. But this love that has emerged neither forms nor adorns my faith. It is faith that forms and adorns love. This is our theology, which seems paradoxical[235] and wonderful, or perhaps foolish to the human way of thinking: I am not only deaf and blind to the law, but I have also been freed and given freedom from the law, as well as totally dead to it.

Paul's statement, "through the law I am dead to the law," is full of comfort. If it could only find timely entry into man's understanding and fix itself upon

---

[232] *necessario concludendum est solam fidem justificare.* Luther adds this footnote: *Lex non justificat, sed sola fides,* "the law does not justify, but faith alone."

[233] *sola gratia seu fide in Christum, sine lege et operibus justus pronuntiari.*

[234] *sophistae.*

[235] *paradoxa.*

his heart, it will yield a great effect. It will strengthen him to face all the dangers surrounding death, all the terrors of a sinful conscience, although he may be besieged, accused, and smitten to despair as never before. It is true that every man is tempted; if not throughout his lifetime, he will be at his deathbed. That is where the law accuses him and displays all his sins before him; then, his conscience will smite him: "You have sinned." But if you have grasped what Paul teaches here, you will be empowered to respond, "Yes, it's true that I have sinned."

"Then God will punish you."

"Oh no, He will not."

"And why not?"

"Because I have another law that with just one blow renders your law speechless, for I have the law of liberty."

"Who set you free?"

"Christ. Because of what Christ did, I am entirely freed from the law. Therefore, the law that is and remains as law for the wicked is instead my freedom, and this freedom ties up the law that would condemn me. In this way, the law that would want to submit me as a captive is itself tied and bound up, held captive to the law of grace and liberty. This is now my law, and it says to that law that accuses me, 'You will not hold this man bound and presume him guilty, for he is mine. I will be the one to hold you captive. Instead, I will tie up your hands so that you will not injure him, for he now lives unto Christ but is dead to you.'"[236]

To achieve this in one blow is to knock the teeth off the law, remove its venom and all its weapons, and deprive it of its strength. Even so the law continues and remains for all the wicked and unbelievers. It is also for us who might be weak; if we lack faith, the law will have power over us, and once again, it will take out its sharpened sword and show its teeth. However, if I believe in Christ, even though sin may drive me to desperation like never before, I will remain in this freedom I have in Christ. I confess that I have sinned, but it's my sin. It's a sin that has already been condemned; that sin has been placed on Christ, who is the sin that condemns sin itself. This other sin that condemns is stronger than the sin it condemns, for it is none other than grace that justifies—it is righteousness, life, and salvation. Therefore, whenever I may feel the anguish of death I say, "O death, I have nothing to do with you. I have another death that puts you to death. It is the death of my death. And this death that kills death is the stronger of the two deaths, for it has already put you to death."

---

[236] Keep in mind that what you are reading is as close as possible to a transcript of this lecture. Visualize Luther going through this monologue in front of a lecture hall full of seminarians and dialoguing with the law. Visualize yourself sitting in that lecture hall and listening to Luther's arguments. What would have been going through your head?

That is why just one single faithful believer through faith in Christ can gather himself up and conceive such a firm and strong comfort that he has no reason to fear the devil, sin, death, or any evil. And although the devil may come against him with everything he has and terrorize him with every possible fear so as to defeat him, the believer says, "Mister devil, I'm not afraid of any of your threats and terrors, for there is One whose name is Jesus Christ, in whom I have believed. He has abolished the law, condemned sin, defeated death, and destroyed hell. He is your very devil, oh Satan, for He has tied you up and holds you captive so that you will not hurt me and anyone who believes in Him." The devil cannot defeat this faith. Instead, he is defeated by it. "For this is the victory that conquers the world," says John, "even our faith." "Who is it that overcomes the world but he who believes that Jesus is the Son of God?" (1 John 5:4, 5).

Therefore, Paul, with burning zeal and indignation of spirit, gives the name of law to grace itself. Nonetheless, this law is the freedom of spirit that is ours through the exceedingly great and overabundant grace we have in Jesus Christ. What's more, he baptizes the law with a dishonorable name: he calls it dead and condemned. Let us understand that this new name is given for our comfort, for it no longer lives. Here, he presents to us a most reassuring scene to look at. He presents the law as if it were a thief and assailant who has already been condemned and sentenced to death. That's because he talks about the law as if it were a prisoner, tied up hands and feet. He has been stripped of all his power. He is no longer free to terrorize. He can no longer accuse and condemn. In this comforting view, the law becomes abhorrent and repulsive to the conscience. Thus the believer in Christ with boldness and holy pride triumphs over the law, saying, "I am a sinner. If you can do something against me, oh law, go ahead and try!" That's how powerless the law becomes; it can no longer frighten the believer.

Since Christ has already risen from the dead, why should He now be afraid of the grave? Since Peter has already been rescued from jail, why should he be afraid? When the little girl was dying, there was good reason for her to be afraid. But now that she has come back to life, why should she be afraid? Similarly, the Christian is joyful because Christ is his by faith, so why should he be afraid of the law? It is true that he will feel the tremors of the law, but they do not defeat him. Grasping on to the freedom he has in Christ, he says, "I hear your murmurs, oh law, wanting to accuse and condemn me! However, I am not bothered by any of that. You are to me what the grave was for Christ because I see you in cuffs and shackles. That's why my law was able to accomplish. Which law is that? Liberty! That is the name of that law because it doesn't tie me up. Instead, it ties up the law that had me all tied up. The law of the Ten Commandments had me all in chains. But against that law, I have another law: it is the law of grace. Although for me it is no law at all, for it doesn't tie me up, but it removes the shackles and lets me go free. And this is a law contrary to that law that accuses and condemns. This opposite law ties up the law that condemns so that it can no longer hurt me. Thus, I have another death, which is life to me; it has given me life in Christ because it opposed the death that had me in cuffs and shackles. This [greater] death frees me from my fetters and frees me from the shackles of death and with those same restraints ties up my death so that the death that had me bound and gagged has itself been firmly shackled. That which killed me was killed by death—that is to say, by life itself!"

Therefore, Christ, the sweetest name there is, is also called my law, my sin, my death in opposition to the law, sin, and death. However, in the purest reality, He is nothing but freedom, righteousness, life, and eternal salvation. For this reason, He has become the law's law, sin's sin, death's death, to redeem me from the curse of the law, justify me, and grant me life so that at the same time Christ is the law, He is also freedom. Because He became sin, He is nothing but righteous. Because He is death, He is life. By allowing the law to accuse Him, sin to condemn Him, and death to devour Him, He abolished the law, condemned sin, destroyed death, and justified and saved me. Thus Christ is poison to the law, sin, and death. And for the same reason, He is the antidote[237] that grants liberty, righteousness, and eternal life.

This way of speaking is unique to Paul and is full of comfort. In a similar way, Romans chapter 7 juxtaposes the law of the spirit over against the law of the members. This strange but marvelous way of speaking penetrates more easily into our memory and sticks to it more quickly. Further, when he says, "I through the law died to the law," it sounds more comforting than to say, "I through freedom died to the law." Before our eyes, he makes it seem as if the law were in a struggle against the law. It's as if he had said, "Oh law, accuse me if you can, tie me up, terrorize me, oppress me, but I will burden you with another law. I mean another tormentor who will accuse you, bind and gag you, frighten and oppress you! It is true that you have certainly been my tormentor. But I have another tormentor, Christ Himself who will torture you 'till you die. When you are like that, tied up, tormented, and oppressed, that is when I am set free." *In the same way, if the devil should lash me, I have a more powerful devil who in turn whips him and defeats him.*[238] Thus grace is a law, but not for me, for it won't put me in chains. Rather, it puts my law in chains. This law is bound up so well that it cannot hurt me.

Thus Paul turns away our eyes from the law, sin, death, and other evils and directs our gaze toward Christ. From that vantage point, we can admire the following happy conflict. The law battles against the law, seeking to set me free. Sin battles against sin so as to become my righteousness. Death fights against death so as to give life. Christ battles the devil and destroys hell so that I can become a child of God, for of such is the kingdom of heaven!

---

[237] *remedium.* Luther speaks of Christ as the "remedy," which is why I chose the modern medical term "antidote," although in Luther's time, there was no verifiable antidote. A more literal translation of course would be "remedy."

[238] *item, si diabolus me flagellat, habeo fortiorem diabolum, qui illum vicissim flagellet, et vincit.*

VERSE 19. That I might live to God.

With this phrase, he says how he lives before God. Thus you can see that there is no life unless it is without the law. What I want to say is to be totally dead to the law in the conscience. However, as long the flesh lives (as I have said it frequently), it needs to be exercised by laws and the harassment of the penalties required by the laws, as the Egyptians vexed the Israelites. But the inner person is not subject to the law. Rather, he is free and has been freed from the law. This human being is a dynamic person, righteous and holy, not in who he is but in Christ, because he has put his trust in Him in the following way.

VERSE 20. I have been crucified with Christ.

He adds this to declare that the law devours the law. He says, "It's not just that I am dead to the law but alive to God but also that I am crucified with Christ. However, Christ is the Lord over the law. He was crucified and died to the law. Therefore, I am also lord over the law. In what way? Because I am also crucified and dead with Christ. How so? By grace and faith. By means of this faith, I am now crucified and dead to the law. That is why the law has lost all the power it had over me, just as it had all the power it had over Christ. Christ Himself was crucified to the law, to sin, to death, to the devil so that they no longer have any power over Him. In the same way, by faith, I am now crucified with Christ in spirit. Thus I am also crucified and dead to the law, to sin, to death, to the devil so that they no longer have any more power over me. These have now been crucified and are dead to me."

Here, Paul is not talking about imitating His crucifixion as an example. To imitate the example of Christ is to be crucified with Him, but this crucifixion belongs to the flesh. That is why Peter says, "Because Christ also suffered for you, leaving you an example, that you should follow in his steps" (1 Peter 2:21). But here (Galatians 2:20), Paul is talking about a greater and higher crucifixion. In this crucifixion, sin, the devil, and death are crucified in Christ and not in me. In this crucifixion, Christ does it all by Himself. By trusting in Christ, by faith, I am also crucified with Christ so that all these things are crucified and dead to me.

VERSE 20. Nevertheless I live.

Here he speaks more clearly: "I am not talking about my death and crucifixion as if I didn't live. I live because that death and crucifixion gave me life. Because indeed I have been freed from the law, sin, and death, it is most certainly true that I live. This crucifixion and death by which I am crucified and dead to the law, to sin, and to death for me is resurrection to life because Christ crucified the devil, killed death, condemned sin, and bound the law. And when I believe this, I am set free and safe from the law, sin, death, and the devil. Thus for me the law has been tied up, killed, and crucified. For me, that means that I was tied up, put to death, and crucified to the law. That is why 'I live' by that death and crucifixion, through that grace and liberty."

Here, as I have said it before, you have to take into account Paul's particular way of speaking, for he says that we are dead and crucified to the law. In fact, it is the law itself that has been killed and crucified to us. But he purposefully expresses himself in that manner so as to provide us even sweeter comfort. Because the law, although it remains living and reigning throughout the whole world accusing every man, has been crucified and is dead only to those who trust in Christ. This glory belongs to them alone, the glory of being dead to sin, hell, and the devil.

VERSE 20. It is no longer I.

That is to say, not in my own person, not in my own substance. Here, he clearly shows how he lives and teaches what is Christian righteousness. It is that Christ lives in us and not that which is within our own person.[239] Therefore, when we discuss Christian righteousness, we should reject the person altogether.[240] *For if I fix myself on the person and talk about the person, whether it's my intention or not, I've turned that person into a doer of the law.* Here, Christ and my conscience become one body so that there is nothing before my eyes except Christ crucified and risen from the dead. But if fix my gaze upon myself, setting Christ aside, I am lost. Soon, I will slip into thinking, "Christ is in heaven, and I am on this earth. How will I approach Him? Oh, I know. I will live in holiness; I will fulfill what the law requires so that I may enter into life." But if I do this, instead of coming to Christ, I have only come around to no one but myself. I'm going to realize who I am, who I should be, and what I still have to fulfill. With all that, I lose sight of Christ, who is my righteousness and my life.[241] But if I lose Him, there is no counselor nor helping hand that can come to my rescue. What follows by necessity is desperation and devastating destruction.

---

[239] Notice that it is Christ who lives in us substitutionally before God; it is not our own person joined to any grace infused or imparted to us in order for us to live before God. See the following note.

[240] *qua Christus in nobis vivit, non quae est in persona nostra. Itaque cum disputandum est de justitia christiana, prorsus abjicientda est persona.* Notice that Luther qualifies his understanding of *Christus in nobis vivit* (Christ lives in us). The Christ within leads the sinner to fix his gaze on nothing else but "Christ crucified and risen from the dead." In other words, the *Christus in nobis* is in fact, the *Christus pro nobis.* The righteousness of Christ always remains an objective, alien righteousness, even when dwelling within the believer. See also the following discussion and footnotes. Luther will go on to say that the life of Christ in the believer is an "alien life," which is a gift received through faith alone.

[241] *qui solus est justitia et vita mea.*

This evil is very common. Such is our miserable condition that when some temptation or even death overtakes us, immediately we set Christ off to one side. We begin to look at our past and everything we've done. If we do this, unless faith picks us up once again, we will certainly perish. We should learn in such conflicts and when our conscience frightens us to forget and set aside the law, our past life, and all our works. They only move us to look at ourselves alone. The gaze must be fixed alone on the bronze serpent Jesus Christ, crucified. We must believe with all confidence that He is our righteousness and our life. Let us not fear the threats and the terrors or the law, sin, death, and the judgment of God. That's because Christ, in whom our eyes are fixed, in whom we live, and who also lives in us, is Lord and conqueror of the law, sin, death, and all evil. He reveals Himself to us as our surest and most certain comfort and gives us the victory.

VERSE 20. I live; yet not I, but Christ liveth in me [KJ21].

He says, "I live." It sounds as if Paul were speaking of his own person. But soon he corrects himself, saying, "Yet not I." That is to say, it is not my own person that lives now, but "Christ lives in me." The person lives, but not for himself, or representing himself.[242] But who is this "I" when he says, "Not I"? This is the "I" claimed by the law and who is subject to fulfill its works. It is a person separated from Christ. This person, Paul rejects. This person who lives apart from Christ belongs to death and hell. Thus he says, "Yet not I, but Christ lives in me." He is the form of my life, the ornament of my faith, as the color or the light adorns the wall. We are compelled to emphasize this. Spiritually we cannot conceive that Christ is adhered and remains[243] in us so closely and intimately as the light to the whiteness of the wall. Thus he says, "It is like this: Christ attached and joined[244] to me, abiding in

---

[242] *pro sua persona.* It seems as if Luther knew about the instrumental use of the Greek preposition εν in the Greek phrase εν εμοι (in me) when found in the dative. Recently D. A. Carson has documented that at least 30 percent of the instances of εν in the Pauline letters indicate the instrumental use rather than the locative, although the latter is most frequent. Thus here "Christ in me" could just as well be translated as "Christ lives for me," "Christ lives in my place" (which would combine the meaning of both the locative and instrumental), or "Christ represents me," as Luther implies here when he says here that the believer does not live *pro sua persona.* The translation in the instrumental case (in which Christ is the instrument on behalf of the sinner) corresponds more closely to the immediate context of justification through the substitution of the life and death of Christ on behalf of the sinner. See D. A. Carson, "The Vindication of Imputation," in *Justification: What's at Stake in the Current Debate,* ed. M. Husbands and D. J. Treier (Westmont, IL: InterVarsity Press, 2004), 46–78.

[243] *haerere et manere.*

[244] *inhaerens et conglutinatus.*

me in this very life, my doing, my living, indeed the life I live, is Christ Himself.[245] Therefore, Christ and I are one in this respect."[246]

Christ living in me abolishes the law, condemns sin, and destroys death. It cannot be any other way. At His presence, all else disappears, since Christ is eternal peace, comfort, righteousness, and life. At these, fear of the law, heaviness of heart, sin, hell, and death yield their place. Christ living and abiding in me takes away and devours every evil that harasses and afflicts me. By means of this link,[247] I am delivered from the threats of the law and sin, I am separated from myself, and I am translated to Christ and His kingdom. This is the kingdom of grace, righteousness, peace, joy, life, salvation, and eternal glory. While I live like this and dwell in Him, is there any evil that can harm me?

Meanwhile, the old man lives on the outside and is subject to the law. But insofar as justification is concerned, Christ and I need to be connected so that He can live in me and I in Him. This is a wonderful way of speaking. Now, since Christ lives in me, take a look at the type of grace, righteousness, life, peace, and salvation that there is in me. It is His, and yet it is also mine due to that inseparable union and adherence that comes by faith. By this faith, Christ and I are as if we were one in body and spirit. Inasmuch as Christ lives in me, it follows that together with Him I am a participant of grace, righteousness, life, and eternal salvation. Thus the law, sin, and death have no place in me. The law has been crucified and devoured by the law, sin by sin, and death by death. In this way, Paul drags us away from self-inspection,[248] from the law and its works, and brings us within Christ Himself where we are transplanted into the faith of Christ.[249] Therefore, we should not think there is some other reason for our justification except grace alone. That is why we should separate grace far apart from the law and works, for in this matter, these have nothing to do one with the other.

Paul has a particular way of speaking. It's not as most people speak ordinarily. It's a divine and heavenly language. No other evangelist nor any other apostle speaks as he does. Only John utilized the same type of speech. If Paul had not been the first to express himself with such clarity of words, not even the saints would have dared to speak like that, for it seems like an insolent and never-heard-before kind of speech: "I live, yet not I; I am dead, I am not dead; I am a sinner, I am not a sinner; I have the law, I don't have the law." But for those who believe in Christ, these are sweet and comforting words. Just as long as they look at themselves, they will see the law and sin. However, when they fix their gaze on Christ,

---

[245] *Christus ergo, inquit, sic inhaerens et conglutinatus mihi et manens in me hanc vitam, quam ago, vivit in me, imo vita, qua sic vivo, est Christus ipse.*

[246] *itaque Christus et ego jam unum in hac parte sumus.*

[247] *haec inhaerentia.*

[248] *abstraere ab inspeccione nostri.*

[249] *et in ipsum Christum et fidem Christi transplantare.*

they are dead to the law and have no sin. If on the subject of justification you want to stand apart from Christ, then you will be abiding in the law and not in Christ. The law will condemn you, and you will be dead before the presence of God, for you will only have this faith (according to the deluded scholars) formed by love. I speak like this by way of example, for no one has ever been saved by this faith. Therefore, all that the papal scholars have written regarding this faith is nothing more than mere toys and delusions of Satan. But for argument's sake, let's say they do have this faith. Even so, such faith would not justify them. All they have is a belief that Christ was a historical person. Even the devil and the wicked believe the same.

Therefore, a pure faith must be taught. By that faith you will certainly be connected to Christ as if truly you were one person.[250] And there won't be any way to separate you, but you will be truly attached to His very person. Thus you will always be able to say, "I exist in Christ—that is to say, in the righteousness of Christ; His victory and His life are mine." In turn, Christ declares, "I am that sinner—that is to say, his sins and his death are mine because He is adhered to me and I to him. By faith, we are one flesh, we are members of His body, His flesh, His bones" (Ephesians 5:30). This faith draws me as close to Christ as the husband to his wife. This faith is not a useless quality, but it is of such excellent value that confounds the religious scholars' illusory thinking. These only have the doctrine of a fictitious faith formed by love, their merits, or the quality of their virtue. If I could, I would only speak more clearly about these things.

LECTURE 13: Saturday, August 15

Up to this point, we have stated that this is Paul's first argument: that if one follows the logic of the false apostles, then Christ is by necessity a minister of sin. If it is not so, then the law does not justify. Having concluded this argument, he set himself as an example. He said, "He was dead to the old law due to a new law." Now he resolves to respond to two objections he would have to answer. The first is against the slander of the proud together with the scandal of the weak.

As soon as the free forgiveness of sins is preached, the evil intentioned slander against this preaching (as quoted in Romans), saying, "Why not do evil that good may come?" (3:8). As soon as people who think like this hear that we are not justified by the law, they immediately conclude with evil intentions, saying, "Let's then reject the law." And also, "if grace abounds," they say, "where sin abounds, then let's abound in sin in order to be just, and that grace may abound even more." These petulant and wicked spirits high-handedly despise and slander

---

[250] *Quare fides pure est docenda, quod scilicet per eam sic conglutineris Christo, ut ex te et ipso fiat quasi una persona.*

the Scriptures and other sayings of the Holy Spirit. They slandered Paul as well as the other apostles throughout their lifetime. But these slanderers became depraved in their own perdition, as stated in 2 Peter 3:16.

As for the rest, the weak do not have evil intentions, neither are they slanderers. They are good people but are offended when they hear that the law and good works should not be performed with an eye to justification. These folk need help. They need instruction as to why good works do not justify, how good works should be performed, and how not to do them. These should be done not as the cause but as the fruit of righteousness. Now that it is a fact that I am righteous,[251] we should do them. But not the other way around, that being wicked we should do them to become righteous. "You pick apples from a tree; you don't pick trees from an apple!"

Before, Paul had said, "I am dead," etc. Here is when the evil intentioned begin to slander. "Paul, what are you saying? That you are dead? How is it then that you are talking and writing?" The weak also have a fit. They tell him, "Paul, and then what are you? Can't we see you alive and that you are doing things in this life?" To which Paul responds, "Certainly I live, but even so, not I, but Christ lives in me." So there are two lives. "The first is mine through nature or as a living organism.[252] The other is an alien life[253]—that is, the life of Christ in me. The second life that I now live is the life of Another,[254] since my own life by nature has died. I don't live now like Paul, since Paul has died." Who is it then who lives? The Christian. Thus as far as his own life, Paul has died entirely to the law. But inasmuch as he lives in Christ, or rather Christ lives in him, Paul lives through a life that's alien to him.[255] It is Christ in Himself who speaks, works, and does everything. This no longer comes from Paul, but from the Christian's life. "But you, evil spirit, when I say that I am dead, don't slander my words any more. And you, who are weak, don't get horrified but learn to distinguish and underscore this matter correctly. There are two lives, my own and another's life that is alien to me.[256] I don't live out of my own life. If it were so, the law would have dominion over me and would hold me captive. But I have died to that law through another law; that way, the first law doesn't hold me captive and enslaved. This death has bought me someone else's life.[257] It is Christ's. This life is not mine by nature.[258] Instead, it is a gift of Christ through faith."

---

[251] *justi facti.*

[252] *naturalis vel animalis.*

[253] *et aliena.*

[254] *vivo alienam vita.*

[255] *vivens vivit alienam vita.*

[256] *mea et aliena.*

[257] *alienam vita.*

[258] *quae mihi non innata est.*

Second, the following objection could have also been made against Paul. "What are you saying, Paul? If you don't live your own life, or your life in the flesh but in Christ, why then do we see you in your own flesh, but we don't see Christ? Are you not deceiving us with your fancy talk telling us that we should not see you in your flesh, living as always and doing the things that someone does in their body just as everybody else?" Paul responds with the following.

VERSE 20. And the life that I now live in the flesh, I live by the faith in the Son of God.

It's as if he had said, "It is true that I now live in the flesh. But this life, regardless of what it means to me, I no longer regard it as life. Truly it is no real life. It is only the shell[259] of a life. In this life there lives another—that is, Christ, my true life. This life cannot be seen. It can only be heard and felt." "You hear the wind, but you don't know from where it's coming or where it's going" (John 3:8). "Even so, you can see me speaking, eating, working, sleeping, and doing other things. But notwithstanding all that, you are not seeing my life. This span of time that I now live, indeed I live it in the flesh. But I don't live it through the flesh or according to the flesh but through faith and according to faith." Paul does not deny that he lives in the flesh, since he does all the things that belong to his nature.[260] He also uses things of the flesh such as food, drink, and such things that belong to the life in the flesh. But he says this is not his life. Although he uses these things, he doesn't live through them, as the world lives through the flesh and going after the flesh. The world knows not, nor hopes for any other life.

Therefore, he says, "This life that I now life in the flesh," whatever it may be, "I live by the faith of the Son of God." This word that I now speak with the body is not the word of the flesh but of the Holy Spirit and of Christ. Whatever goes in and out of these eyes proceeds not from the flesh, it's not governed by the flesh, but by the Holy Spirit. What I hear doesn't come from the flesh, although I hear it in the flesh, but from the Holy Spirit. The Christian doesn't talk about anything else but pure, sober, and holy things that correspond to Christ, to the glory of God, and to the well-being of his neighbor. These things don't come from the flesh, neither are they done according to the flesh, but even so, they are in the flesh. I cannot teach, write, pray, or give thanks but only with these instruments of the flesh. They are necessary to carry out these works. Even so, these works don't proceed from the flesh but are given by God from heaven. Similarly, when I look at a vulnerable woman,[261] I do so with purity in my eyes, not coveting her. This manner of looking doesn't come from the flesh, although it is in the flesh, since the eyes are the carnal

---

[259] *larva.*

[260] *animalis.*

[261] *mulierculam*, a weak, little, or young woman.

instruments of the sense of sight. But to look upon a woman with purity is a vision that proceeds from heaven.

Therefore, the Christian has the use of the world and all its creatures, just as the unbeliever. In the way he dresses, eats, listens, sees, speaks, gestures, makes facial expressions, and other things, he is the same. To all appearances, it would seem that they are all one (as Paul says of Christ "being found in human form"). Nevertheless, there is a huge difference. "It's true, I live in the flesh, but I don't live from myself. What I now live, I live in the faith of the Son of God. This, what I am saying right now, flows from another fountain that you had not heard from me before." Paul's voice and tongue didn't change with his conversion. They were all the same before and after. Before, all he could do was nothing else but to blaspheme abominations against Christ and His church. After his conversion, he remained with the same flesh, the same voice and tongue as before, these didn't change. But his voice and tongue no longer proffered blasphemies but spiritual and heavenly words, praising and giving thanks to God. This proceeded from the Holy Spirit. Therefore, although I live in the flesh, I don't live according to the flesh nor after the flesh but by the faith of the Son of God.

Thus we can clearly see the source of this spiritual life. It's incomprehensible to the carnal man who cannot understand it at all, for it's unknown to him. He listens to the wind, but he doesn't know from where it comes or where it's going. He listens to the voice of the spiritual man, he knows his face, his ways, his gestures, but he cannot see where these words are coming from. Before, they were wicked and blasphemous; now, they are holy and pious. Neither does he know the source of his movements and actions. This life is in the heart by faith, where the flesh is put to death, and Christ reigns with His Holy Spirit. It's the Holy Spirit who now sees, hears, speaks, works, suffers, and does all things in him, although the flesh puts up resistance. Summing it up, this is not the life of the flesh, although it is lived in the flesh. It is the life of Christ the Son of God, who the Christian possesses by faith.

VERSE 20. Who loved me and gave himself for me.

Here, we have Paul's description of the true cause for justification and a perfect example of trusting faith. Whoever can say these words with Paul, with firm and constant faith, "I live by the faith of the Son of God, who loved me and gave himself for me," is truly happy. With these same words, Paul totally annuls and takes away the righteousness of the law and its works, as we shall discuss later. Thus we should weigh and consider these words: "The Son of God loved me and gave Himself for me." It was not that I first loved the Son of God and gave myself for Him. This is what the religious philosophers imagine when they daydream, that they love the Son of God and give themselves to Him. They teach that a person *ex puris naturalibus, that* out of his own untainted natural power, has the capacity to perform congruous merit[262] [before receiving grace] and love God and Christ above all things. They pervert the love of God and Christ, for they say that it is within them,[263] that as monks they can not only fulfill the commandments of God[264] but also observe the precepts, perform supererogatory works, and sell the surplus of their merits to the laity.[265] That's how they fantasize that they give themselves over to Christ and thus save themselves and others. That's how they twist Paul's words, "He loved me" and so on—by saying totally the contrary and adding, "We have loved Christ; we have given ourselves over to Him." However, the wicked get all puffed up with the wisdom of the flesh; they imagine that they have it in them to fulfill, to love God, to surrender to Christ. And what is it that they are doing? Nothing less than abolishing the Gospel, mocking, denying, and blaspheming Christ, even spitting and stepping all over Him. With their words, they confess that He is their Justifier and Savior. But with their deeds they tear away from Him His power to justify as well as to save. Then they attribute that power to their choice of ceremonies and religious worship. This is not to live in the faith of the Son of God but in their own righteousness and works.

Do What Is within You[266]

Thus this is not the way to justification: "Get started with what is in you." But that's an actual quote from the papal philosophers and academic scholars. They affirm that if people do what they already have within them, God will infallibly grant them grace. *They place this premise within the articles of faith. With that, they make it clear that they don't have the slightest understanding of either Paul's doctrine or the Gospel. From that assumption, they go on to declare this proverb: "Do what is within you." They really don't pressure anyone with this premise. Instead, they scatter it far and wide, intending to make it as acceptable as a truth of natural science but not quite as if it were an indivisible number of mathematics, which no one has been able to come up with.* In other words, let it suffice (they say) that it's within the power of anyone to do something that a good person would approve. *When that work is done, grace starts to flow, not just because of the nature of the congruous merit or the act itself, but also because God is infallible.* Since He is so good and just, it would be impossible for Him not to grant grace for the good that has been performed etc.[267]

---

[262] *posse facere meritum congrui.*

[263] *facere quod in se est.*

[264] *praecepta Dei.*

[265] *et laicis superflua merita vendut.*

[266] *facere quod in se est,* literally "do what is in you."

[267] *sed infallibilitate dei, qui tam bonus est et justus, ut non possit non dare gratiam pro bono etc.*

From that conjecture, the following proverb proceeds: *ultra posse viri non vult deus ulla requiri*. That is to say,

> God never requires more
> Than human strength can perform.[268]

This is a valid proposition but must be said in its proper place, such as in politics, finance, and science.[269] If I live in the kingdom of reason, it can be put into practice by the head of the household or in the construction of buildings or in a court of law. If I try to do everything that is within my possibilities, then I cannot be condemned. This kingdom has its own boundaries. Within its walls, this saying has its place: "Do what you already can until you've done everything you possibly can." But the followers of the Pope then drag these decrees to the spiritual kingdom where man can do nothing else but sin, for he is "sold under sin" (Romans 7:14). However, in external issues (such as the management of government or financial matters[270]), I am not a servant but stand as lord over them. But the papal scholars have done wickedly by dragging these political and financial premises over to the church. The kingdom of human reason should be kept far apart from the spiritual kingdom.

Nature Retains Its Integrity

What's more, they claim that nature itself is corrupt, but the qualities of nature are still whole. They even say this with respect to demons. Based on that claim, they reason like this: "If the natural qualities are intact, then the intellect is pure and the will is unsullied and whole. Consequently, all the natural qualities exist perfectly within the person."

It's important for you to know these things so that you may preserve the purity of the doctrine of faith. When they say that the natural qualities are whole and intact, I grant them that. But if based on that they infer that the human being is capable on his own to fulfill the law, love God, I deny that conclusion.

I distinguish between the natural and the spiritual qualities.[271] The spiritual are not intact but corrupt[272] to the utmost degree. Due to sin, they are totally extinct in man and devil! It's as if nothing existed there. Thus the intellect is

---

[268] *ultra posse viri, non vult deus ulla requiri*, literally "more than is possible with human strength, God in His will does not require."

[269] *de politicis, oeconomicis et naturalibus.*

[270] *politicis et oeconomicis rebus.*

[271] *distinguo naturalia contra spiritualia.*

[272] *corrupta.*

depraved[273] and the will constantly struggles against God and thinks about nothing else except how to counter Him. Yet I grant that the natural qualities retain their integrity. But what are these qualities? Someone may be steeped in sin serving the devil. Yet he has willpower, reason, free will, and the capacity needed to build a house, function as a judge, captain a ship, and perform other duties for which he is responsible, according to Genesis 1. *These following things have not been taken away from him: the power to procreate, manage civil government,[274] and administer an economy.[275] The statements we are talking about confirm the validity of these capacities. But the papal scholars have dragged them over to the spiritual realm. Undoubtedly, they came from the Fathers, but since they misunderstood them, they twisted them around as spiritual qualities. Thus they combined and confused what belongs to the civilian realm with the realm of the church. Our part is to clean and restore each to their purity and take these stumbling blocks out of the church.* We don't deny these things their proper place in the realm of the flesh. But if they are dragged into the spiritual realm before the presence of God, I reject them altogether. As I have stated, we are totally sunk and drowned in sin. Our willpower is nothing but wickedness. All our understanding is in error. Man has nothing that is spiritual, except darkness, errors, venomous cunning, a perverse will and intellect. How then is he going to do what is right, love God, and such?

Thus Paul says that we didn't begin anything, but it was Christ who took the initiative. "He! He, Himself, took delight in me and gave Himself for me." It's as if he had said, "He didn't find in me goodwill nor a proper intellect. Instead, Christ had mercy on me. He saw me wicked, erring, with an aversion to God, and always running away from Him. I had issues with God; I was captive to and governed by the devil. In His mercy he bypassed my reason, willpower, and intellect and loved me. He loved me so much that He gave Himself for me and set me free from the law, sin, the devil, and death."

Once again, these words, "He loved me and gave Himself for me," are like lightning and thunderbolts from heaven against the righteousness of the law and the doctrine of works. Such great wickedness, error, darkness, and ignorance are at the bottom of my will and intellect that it was necessary to pay an inestimable price for my freedom! Then why should I glory in the conclusions of my reasoning, of my unsullied natural qualities, of a reasoning power that dictates only what is right, and of an optimal thought process[276] that is able to keep me from evil and "do what is within me"? Why do I offer before God's wrath (according to Moses, God is "a consuming fire"[277]) this pile of straw, my horrible sins, and argue before

---

[273] *intellectus depravatus.*

[274] *politia.*

[275] *oeconomia.*

[276] *de naturalibus integris, de dictamine rationis, de ratione deprecante ad optima.*

[277] Deuteronomy 4:24.

Him that in exchange for these He should grant me grace and eternal life? When I hear this, I understand. It was because there was such great wickedness stalking around in my nature that the entire world and all its creatures were not sufficient to prevent God's indignation, but it was necessary that God's own Son should give His life for me!

Let's diligently consider this price. Carefully recognize that this captive, given over for me (as Paul says), is none other than the Son of God Himself. Observe how infinitely more valuable a price is His life than if every creature would have been offered.[278] What works are you going to offer seeing that such an inestimable price was given for you, as Paul has said? Certainly, you are not going to offer your cowl, your tonsure, your chastity, your obedience, your poverty! What do you hope to get out of all these? Or would you even offer the law of Moses and the works of the law?[279] What about the sum of good works and the suffering of all the martyrs? What of the obedience of all the holy angels compared with the Son of God's humiliation when He surrendered His life? What about the obedience of His death on the cross and His own blood shed entirely for the forgiveness of your sins? If you would only evaluate the price, you should curse, spit on,[280] consider accursed, and relegate to hell every cowl, tonsure, all vows, works, and congruous and condign merits.[281] It is an intolerable and horrifying blasphemy to pretend that any work or to presume that any of these things could appease God, seeing that there is nothing that could have appeased Him but the infinite price—indeed, the death and the blood of His Son, of which one single drop is more precious than all the creatures put together!

VERSE 20. For me.

Who is this "me"? The beloved Son of God gave Himself for me, a most miserable and condemned sinner. If I could by means of any work or merit love the Son of God and come to Him, why should He have given Himself as a sacrifice for me? The cold-heartedness with which the Pope and his followers view this is obvious, for they mistreat and mishandle the Sacred Scriptures and the doctrine of faith. If they had only studied these words, that it was necessary for the Son of God to be given for me, so many sects would not have arisen.[282] Faith itself would have given

---

[278] Luther adds the following footnote: *Quid lex Mosi etc. ad filium Deit traditum pro sobis?*, "are you going to compare the observance of the law of Moses, etc. with the Son of God who was given over for you?"

[279] *lex Mosi et opera legis?*

[280] *conspurcare, conspuere.*

[281] *merita congrui et condigni.*

[282] Luther considered the monastic orders as sects and their followers as sectarian.

the answer. Why did they choose this type of life? Why this particular order? Why these works? Don't you just do this to please God and achieve your justification? Is it impossible for you, wicked one, to hear that the Son of God gave Himself and shed His blood for you? This true faith in Christ would have resisted all these sects.

That's why I say (as I've said it before) that there is no remedy against the sects nor any means to resist them, unless it is with the article of Christian righteousness.[283] If we lose this article, it will be impossible for us to resist any error or sect. That's what we see today in these fanatical spirits such as the Anabaptists or the Sacramentarians. They have turned aside from this article, and thus they err and are always seducing others, and from them, other sects will arise without end, inventing new works. But what will all this amount to, despite the drama of so many good works, when compared with the death and the blood of the Son of God "who gave Himself for me"? Pay close attention, who is this Son of God? Fix your gaze on how glorious He is, on His power. What is heaven and earth compared to Him? Let all the Papists and founders of all sects, even if the whole world goes after them, let them all go to hell[284] with their righteousness, works, and merits so that the glory of Christ and the truth of the Gospel will remain spotless. What do they pretend when they brag about their works and merits? If I, being a miserable sinner under condemnation, could not offer a price for my rescue, why then did the Son of God consider it necessary to give Himself for me? But it was precisely because there was no price under heaven and earth for my release except that of Christ the Son of God. Thus it was supremely necessary that He gave Himself for me. What's more, He did it all from His inestimable love, for Paul says, "Who loved me."

Thus these words, "who loved me," are replete with faith. Everyone who can say this word *me* and make it his with firm faith and confidence together with Paul will be a good lawyer against the law, for He did not give sheep, bulls, gold, or silver, but God Himself in all His divinity.[285] He did it entirely and fully "for me." Yes, this "me," a miserable sinner under condemnation. According to the well-known tradition among God's children when they breathe their last, apply this "me." That is expressing the true power of faith. Those who have spent their lives in works cannot repeat, "Christ who loved me." These words express the purest preaching of grace and Christian righteousness. Paul contrasts these words to the righteousness of the law. It's as if he had said, "Let the law be a heavenly doctrine with its own glory; even so, it was not the law who loved me nor gave itself for me. The law only accuses, terrorizes, and drives you desperate. But now, I have another who

---

[283] This was Luther's name for the article or fundamental teaching of justification by faith alone.

[284] *Demergantur potius ad infernum cum suis justitiis, etc.*, literally "it would be far better for them to be buried in hell with all their righteousness, and so on."

[285] *sed quidquid erat totus Deus.*

has freed me from the terrors of the law, sin, death and has given me freedom, the righteousness of God, and eternal life. He is called the Son of God, who loves me and gave Himself for me, to whom be the glory and the praise forever and ever. Amen."

Thus as I have said, faith embraces and wraps itself up in Jesus Christ the Son of God, given to death for us, as Paul teaches here. When we grasp Him by faith, He gives us righteousness and life, *for Christ is the Son of God and out of His own pure love gave Himself for our redemption.*[286] And with these words, Paul most vividly displays the priesthood and the office of Christ. He appeases God, makes intercession for sinners, instructs and comforts them. Let us learn to define Christ correctly and not as the theologians of the great universities who seek to establish righteousness through their own works. They turn Him into a new legislator. They then teach that once He abolished the old law, He established another law more up to date. For them, Christ is nothing more than a demanding tyrant. But Christ is such as Paul defines Him here. He is the Son of God who, not because of something we deserve or some righteousness within us but out of His own mercy and will, gave Himself for us as a sacrifice for us miserable sinners, in order to sanctify us forever.

Thus Christ is no Moses or a demanding giver of new laws but the Giver of grace, a Savior, full of mercy. In brief, He is nothing more than infinite mercy and kindness, given over freely and abundantly on our behalf. When you paint a picture of Christ, you should use these colors. If you allow any other representation, you will be beaten when harassed by trial and temptation. But just as this is the greatest knowledge and secret of the Christian, it is also the most difficult. I, myself, have labored long under the brilliance of this Gospel light. For a long time, I have labored to retain this definition of Christ that Paul presents here. However, I confess that this doctrine and pestilent opinion that Christ is a legislator is still stuck to my bones. You young people, in this case, have greater reason to rejoice than us old people. You have not been infected with these pernicious errors, from which I suckled and choked since my youth. Even at the mere mention of the name of Christ, my heart shook and trembled with fear. I was convinced that He was a severe judge. Thus for me it is a double agony and trial to correct and reform this evil. First, to forget, condemn, and reject this error that is so rooted, that Christ is a legislator and judge. This evil always keeps coming back. Then to sow in my heart a new and true persuasion that Christ is the Justifier and Savior. That is why I say that you young people (if you are willing) are able to learn with less difficulty and to know Christ with greater purity and sincerity. Therefore, if you are ever feeling

---

[286] *qui ex mera caritate traditit se ipsum pro nobis redimendis.* Notice that Luther emphasizes the finished work of Christ *pro nobis.* Christ brings his *pro nobis* finished work *in nobis* to constantly reassure the believer that He is "for us" as our substitute righteousness.

oppressed by despair and anguish of heart, don't blame Christ, no matter who may come using the name of Christ. Blame the devil! He frequently shows up disguised as Christ, transforming himself into an angel of light.

Therefore, let us learn to recognize the difference between Christ and a legislator, not only in words, but also in deed and practice. When the devil shows up under the guise of Christ and in His name wants to harass us, let us be sure that it is not Christ but the devil himself, for when Christ comes, He brings to the broken and trembling heart nothing more than joy and comfort. That is what Paul testifies here. He describes it with this sweetest and comforting title when He says, "Who loved me and gave Himself for me." Christ in all reality is the lover[287] of all those who have fallen into agony and affliction, into sin, into death. This lover gave Himself for us. He is also our Most High Priest, a Mediator between God and us poor condemned sinners. What else could be said to an agonizing and afflicted conscience? Well then, if all this is true (for it certainly is, otherwise, the Gospel would be nothing but a fable), then we are not justified by the righteousness of the law or even less by our own righteousness.

Learn then with all diligence these words, "me" and "for me." Practice them within yourself so that with confident faith you will conceive and engrave this "me" in your heart. Persuade yourself that it's for you, that without doubt you are among that number to whom that "me" belongs. That Christ not only loved Peter and Paul and gave Himself for them. That same grace that is understood within that "me" embraces us and is for us as well as for them. We cannot deny that we are sinners, compelled to say that because of Adam's sin we are all lost, having become enemies of God, exposed to the wrath and judgment of God, and guilty of eternal death. At the sight of his sins, every human heart recoils with horror and confesses this truth even more than necessary. But in the same way we cannot deny that Christ died for our sins to justify us,[288] for He did not die to bring righteous people from among the righteous but to bring righteous people from among sinners,[289]

---

[287] *amator.*

[288] Here, Erasmus Middleton in his 1807 edition of this commentary incorrectly translates Luther's Latin use of the term *justification,* which he does throughout his translation into Elizabethan English. Middleton uses the English expression "to make us righteous" for Luther's Latin phrase *ut justificaremur.* However, "to justify" in Paul's writings is always "to declare righteous," not "to make righteous." But Luther himself clarifies with this footnote: *Sicut per Adam omnes rei constituimur, ita per Christum omnes justificamur* (Just as by Adam all were constituted guilty, so by Christ all have been justified). Watson (1953) followed suit by translating *iustificare* as "to make righteous" in the omitted sections.

[289] *Non enim mortuus est, ut justos faceret justos, sed ut peccatores faceret justos.* To merely translate *faceret justos* here as "to make" is a simplistic translation and does not take into account the "by faith alone in the righteousness of Christ" nature of justification that Luther is emphasizing in the context. *Faceret* also has a causative meaning, as

turning them into friends and children of God and inheritors of all the heavenly inheritance. Thus when I confess that I am a sinner on Adam's account, why then should I not also say that I am righteous on account of the righteousness of Christ, especially when I hear that He loved me and gave Himself for me? This is what Paul believed with a firm heart and thus he speaks with full certainty,[290] saying that He reached out even to us and somehow from within Himself loved us and gave Himself for us, amen.

VERSE 21. I do not nullify the grace of God.

Now Paul prepares the second argument of his epistle. Consider what he says, that to seek to be justified by the works of the law is to reject the grace of God. What sin could be more damnable and horrible than to reject the grace of God, and refuse the righteousness that is by faith in Christ! It should be enough that we are already wicked sinners and transgress all God's commandments. However, on top of that we commit the worst of all sins, which is to reject the remission of sins that Christ offers us with full assurance. This blasphemy is so horrible there are no words to describe it. The sin detested the most by Paul and the apostles is despising the grace given by Christ. It is nothing more than denying Him. But of course, no sin is more common. This is the reason Paul more than any other warns against the Antichrist. The Antichrist despises the grace of God and rejects the benefit of our great High Priest who has been offered in sacrifice for our sins. To deny Christ in this way, is it not to spit on His face, stomp all over Him, and take His place? Is it not to say, "I am the one who will justify and save you"? How? Through the celebration of the mass, the pilgrimages, the indulgences, the observation of certain rules, and such. Thus we see the high-handedness with which the Antichrist has risen up against and over God, taking the place of God, rejecting the grace of God, and denying the faith. Why? Because this is his doctrine: "Faith is worthless," he says, "unless it is coupled to works." And through this false and detestable doctrine he has disfigured, obscured, and buried altogether the benefits of Christ. In place of the grace of Christ and His kingdom, he has established the doctrine of works and the kingdom of ceremonies. He has confirmed his own kingdom with nothing but foolishness. Christ is the only one who can reign in the conscience. That is why the Antichrist has gotten everybody to march in a direction counter to Christ, compelling everyone to march straight into hell and damnation!

Therefore, we can understand what it is to reject and refuse the grace of God in order to seek the righteousness of the law. Now, who has ever heard that the

---

in "to cause, to bring about." This meaning is more compatible with Luther's concept of justification, which he describes below as "I am righteous on account of the righteousness of Christ."

[290] Here, Luther deviated from using the Latin in his lecture and used the Greek term πληροφορία, meaning full certainty, conviction, or assurance.

keeping of the law is the same as refusing grace? Are we in sin if we keep the law? God forbid! But we despise grace when we keep the law in order to justify ourselves through its observance. The law is good, holy, and helpful, but it doesn't justify.[291] Whoever keeps the law to be justified, rejects grace, denies Christ, despises His sacrifice, and will not be saved through that inestimable price. Such a person will keep on insisting that the forgiveness of his sins may be obtained through the righteousness of the law and merits grace through his own righteousness. This is blasphemy and despising the grace of God. Is it not a horrible thing to say that someone could be so diabolic as to despise God's grace and mercy? However, this is what the whole world does. But they don't judge it that way. They only think they are rendering high service and homage to God.

VERSE 21. For if justification were through the law, then Christ died to no purpose.

Here, I admonish you once again that Paul is not talking about the ceremonial law alone, as the papal scholars always imagine. Origen and Jerome were the first to promote this error, they are the professors of this perversity, and all the papal scholars follow right in step. Today, Erasmus approves and confirms such error.[292] But the faithful should totally abstain from these vain illusions, for they corrupt Paul with their perverse glosses.[293] They talk about this subject without any knowledge or expertise, as if the ceremonies were not good and holy in themselves! The ordination to the priesthood, circumcision, sacrifices, worship rituals, and similar holy works, these were all more than just mere ceremonies. Therefore, Paul is talking about the entire law.

We must diligently weigh Paul's words. Is it true that Christ suffered death or not? What's more, did he suffer in vain or not? Unless we are totally off our rockers,[294] we are obliged to say that he certainly suffered and that He did not suffer in vain but for our sake. If then he did not suffer in vain, it follows logically that righteousness does not come by the law.[295]

Take then both laws if you like: either the ceremonial and the moral or the Ten Commandments. *Imagine that you have gotten here by congruous merit, and through it, you have been given the Spirit and you have love. However, such a scenario is a monstrosity and cannot be discovered anywhere in nature! But imagine, if you please, that by doing what is in you, you have obtained grace, you are righteous, and possess the Spirit. From where? From congruous merit? If so, you don't have Christ, but He is worthless to you and indeed died in vain.*

---

[291] *sed non justificat.*

[292] Luther's footnote: *depravatores Pauli,* "perverters of Paul."

[293] *suis glossis depravant.*

[294] *nisi manifeste simus insani.*

[295] *ergo ex lege non est justitia.*

Then take even the law of the Ten Commandments itself, which commands the highest worship to God—that is, fear of God, faith in God, love to God and neighbor. But at the same time, show me someone who by obeying it has been justified. Even if you could, it would still be true that Christ died in vain, for anyone who is justified by the law of the Ten Commandments has the power within himself to obtain righteousness. They argue that if you don't put up any opposition—that is, if you do what is already within you—then you deserve grace. As a result, the Holy Spirit is poured out so that you can love God and neighbor. If that's the way things are, then Christ died in vain. Why should you need Christ who loved you and gave Himself for you? Suppose you could, without Christ, earn congruous merit to obtain grace; then work well to earn condign merits, does that make you worthy of eternal life? Will you by doing the works of the law be declared righteous? In that case, take Christ away and all His benefits, since He is totally worthless to you. Why then was Christ born? Why was He crucified? Why did He die? Why did He become a high priest? Why did He love me and give Himself as an incomparable sacrifice?[296] Why did He give His very self for me? Why did He do everything He did? Without a doubt, if righteousness comes as the papal scholars teach, then all He did was totally in vain! It's that simple. To find righteousness in the law or within myself is to find it apart from grace and Christ!

Would it not be an intolerable blasphemy to remain silent when someone says that the divine Majesty, not sparing His own Son but giving Him over to death for us all, had no serious purpose at all, but did it just for fun? Well before admitting to this blasphemy, I'd take the holiness of all the Papists and the merit hoarders and that of all the saints and holy angels and cast it all to the depths of hell for eternal damnation together with the devil! My eyes would only be fixed on this one inestimable price, my Lord and Savior Jesus Christ. As for me, He should be such a treasure, that all else should be nothing but dung compared to Him. His light shines so brightly toward me that when I grasp Him by faith I will not be aware of any law, or any sin, or any righteousness, or any unrighteousness in the world, for what is the value of all heaven and earth put together when compared to the Son of God, Jesus Christ, my Lord and Savior, "who loved me and gave Himself for me"?

Rejecting the grace of God is a most common horrible sin that reigns throughout the entire world. All those who seek righteousness through their congruous merit, or who seek to be justified by their own works and merits or through the law, reject the grace of God and Christ, as I've said before. The Pope has been the author of all these abominations. He not only has disfigured and stepped all over the Gospel of Christ but has also filled the whole world with his wicked traditions. His indulgences and bullas of forgiveness testify to the absolution of only those who are contrite, whether they have faith or not; they then confess before an accomplice, who shakes their hands only to sustain his own pomp and tradition. *All this is*

---

[296] *inaestimabilem hostiam.*

the same as testifying that Christ died in vain and that grace is null and void. Thus the abominations and blasphemies of the kingdom of the papacy are incalculable, and to this day, the papal scholars are still blind and hardened despite this great light of truth. They persevere in their wicked and vain opinions, insisting that the qualities of nature are intact and unsullied, that men can prepare to receive grace by means of their own good works and merits. And they are so far from recognizing their wickedness and errors that they continue to defend them even against their own conscience.

However, we will always affirm with Paul (because we don't nullify the grace of God) that either Christ died in vain or the law does not justify. But since Christ did not die in vain, we conclude that the law does not justify. Christ, the Son of God, of His own grace and mercy declares us righteous.[297] Consequently, the law cannot justify us. If the law could justify us, then Christ foolishly gave Himself to justify us.[298] Thus we conclude that our own works and merits do not justify us. We can do nothing presenting congruous and condign merits.[299] We are not justified through our own afflictions or by the law. Only faith in Christ justifies us.[300]

But if Christ had to pay such a high price for my salvation that He was compelled to die for my sins, then all my works with all the righteousness of the law are but mere trash and worthless compared to this inestimable price. How could I purchase with one cent what is worth an incalculable weight in gold? The law (to say nothing of other things of lesser value) with all its works and righteousness is a mere cent when you compare it to Christ. With His death He has defeated my death and thus obtained for me righteousness and eternal life. Then am I going to despise and refuse this incomparable price? Are you going to go after the law and the works of congruous and condign merit to earn the righteousness that Christ has already freely given to you through His great love? Paul has already said they are but scum and dung when compared to Christ! Am I going to reject that which cost Him such a great price that He was compelled to surrender Himself in my place? But as I have said, this is what the world does, and in particular those who count themselves among the holiest and most religious; although, the minute they open their mouths, they show their true colors. Christ dies in vain; they blaspheme Christ to the extreme, spit upon His face, step all over the Son of God, profane the blood of the covenant, and much more.

Further, when Paul mentions the fulfillment of righteousness (something he considers quite carefully), he is talking about the spiritual level. He doesn't have in mind political or administrative righteousness or acts of civil justice. However, God approves and requires their doing, providing rewards for their accomplishment.

---

[297] *Christus Dei filius ex mera gratia et misericordia nos justificavit.*

[298] *stulte egisset Christus, quod se ipsum tradidisset pro peccatis nostris, ut per hoc justificaremur.*

[299] *neque merito congrui aut condigni.*

[300] *sed sola fide in Christum nos justificari.*

Reason to some extent is capable to meet its demands. But here, Paul is imploring on behalf of the righteousness that is worthy before God, which is able to deliver us from the law, sin, death, and all evil. Paul advocates on behalf of the righteousness that makes us participants in grace, righteousness, and eternal life. Finally, this righteousness makes us as lords of heaven and earth and over all creatures. This righteousness cannot be fulfilled by the law of men or by the law of God.

The law is added above human reason, as light and help for man, to show him what he should do and what he should leave undone. However, man, even with all his strength and reason, aided by this great light of heavenly origin (I'm speaking of the law) cannot be justified. Then, if that which is of greatest excellence in the world—I'm speaking of the law, which as the brilliant sun becomes one with man's darkened reason to illumine and guide it—cannot justify him, what then can reason accomplish without the law? Look! Without a doubt, this is what the Pope has done together with all his half-asleep philosophers and all of their synagogue, monks, and much more. Just with their own traditions, they have darkened the light of just the first commandment. Not one of them can correctly understand even one syllable of the law. Instead, each one walks in the darkness of his own reason. And this error is much more pernicious than the one that proceeds from the doctrine of the works of the law.

Thus these words are spoken with great force when he says, "If righteousness comes through the law, then Christ died in vain." Here, he has nothing to say about man's natural capacity, his reason or wisdom, no matter how great they may be (the greater, the sooner they deceive man). Here, he simply states, "If by the law." That is why reason, illumined, helped, and guided by the law, even by God's law, is incapable of producing righteousness. Instead, it drags righteousness away and sells Christ off for nothing! If it were able to generate righteousness, then Christ died in vain. Thus you must simply confront every law there is with the death of Christ. Then you will be able to say with Paul, "I have no one else but Christ crucified." No other light will shine your path. Then you will be truly educated, righteous, and holy. You will receive the Holy Spirit, who will preserve in you the purity of word and faith. But turn your eyes away from the true Christ and everything else is a forgery!

LECTURE 14: Friday, August 21

Here, once again, we see the praises[301] Paul gives the righteousness of the law or self-righteousness.[302] This righteousness does nothing but condemn and reject the

---

[301] In the Latin text, Luther uses the Greek term ἐγχώμιον, "praises or commendations."
[302] Obviously, Luther is using sarcasm to emphasize his point.

grace of God; it annuls and frustrates[303] the death of Christ. Paul does not speak with great eloquence. However, if you listen quietly you will hear him develop his argument and rhetoric. Here, he becomes a great orator when he uses the expressions "[I do not] nullify grace" and "the grace of God" as well as "then Christ died in vain." But the eloquence of the entire world is not enough to describe the outrage he is talking about. To say that just anyone died in vain could be taken lightly. But to say that Christ died in vain is to erase Him from history altogether. Whoever thinks he's good at rhetoric has more than copious material here. You could expound at length on the nefarious doctrine of seeking righteousness through the law and its works, because is there any greater and more horrible blasphemy than to remove the value of Christ's death? But do those who teach the observance of the law for justification teach anything else? To say that Christ died in vain is also to say that His resurrection, His victory, His glory, His kingdom, heaven, earth, God's own majesty, and in brief, everything else are also totally worthless. Is this a small thing? *If someone were to say that the kings and kingdoms of France or the Roman Empire had been established in vain, you would say that person is insane! But that is nothing when compared to this one, to say that Christ died in vain!*

These heavenly lightning bolts with their thunder against the law and human righteousness should lead us to abhor it. *At just one lightning bolt, all the orders of monks and friars should fall flat on their face condemned, together with all monasteries, religions, and their righteousness, ceremonies, and rules of their own making.* Everyone who hears "abhor your vows, tonsures, cowls, human traditions, even the law of Moses" and doesn't spit them all out altogether has rejected God's grace and declared "Christ died in vain." When the world hears this, it can't believe it is hearing the truth. It thinks that such horrible wickedness cannot exist in the human heart, that it could reject the grace of God and consider the death of Christ as worthless. But this sin reigns as the most common. Everyone who seeks righteousness apart from faith in Christ, meaning by works, merits, satisfactions, afflictions, or the observance of the law, rejects the grace of God and despises the death of Christ. It doesn't matter how much they protest to the contrary with their mouths.

---

[303] *evacuatio et frustratio.*

Galatians 3

VERSE 1. Oh foolish Galatians!

Here, we see Paul as a diligent apostle with fervent zeal and spiritual affection for the church. Thus when he argues and refutes, he combines quiet exhortation with firm rebuke. This frame of mind agrees with his own norm given to Timothy. "Preach," he said, "the word; be urgent in season and out of season; reprove, rebuke, and exhort, with all patience and teaching" (2 Timothy 4:2). The careless reader could easily deceive himself. Thus you must read with discretion. One could think that Paul is undisciplined when he teaches. It is true that he does not comply with any of the rules of rhetoric. But as far as the spirit, he complies with a strict method and order.

Therefore, after presenting his arguments, he confirms them with two powerful arguments joined together: Christian righteousness does not come through obedience to the law but by faith in Christ.[1] In one sweep, he has refuted the doctrine of the false apostles. However, in the middle of this discourse he shifts his manner of addressing the Galatians and rebukes them. "Oh Galatians! You're either foolish or out of your minds!"[2] It's as if he had said, "I am shocked that you have fallen so disastrously low!"[3] "Oh miserable Galatians! I taught you the truth with great care and painstaking effort. How is it possible that you have abandoned it so soon? Who cast a spell on you?"

It's obvious that he firmly rebuked the Galatians because he calls them demented,[4] bewitched, and disobedient to the truth.[5] If he did it out of jealousy or compassion, I wouldn't argue either. Both would be spot on. A carnal man could interpret it as an offense, instead of a pious rebuke. Then was it that Paul gave a bad example? Or was he so resentful against the churches of Galatia that he labeled them as foolish and bewitched? Not at all! An apostle, pastor, or preacher may lawfully severely rebuke with Christian fervor the flock under his guidance. Such rebukes are pious and paternal. That is how parents with paternal and maternal affection rebuke and reproach their children. However, they would not tolerate it if someone

---

[1] *justitiam christianam non esse ex lege, sed ex fide in Christum.*

[2] *O insensati seu amentes.*

[3] *prolapsis estis.*

[4] Luther correctly translates the Greek ἀνόητοι as "demented" since ἀνόητοι means "mindless."

[5] In the original Latin, Luther, in a footnote, asks rhetorically, *num peccat apostolus, quod tam scriter objurgat galatas?*, "Does not the apostle sin by writing these rebukes to the Galatians?" *Num* anticipates a negative answer.

else would do the same. Sometimes the teacher gets upset with his student, rebukes and punishes him, who takes it for his own good although he'd not take it from anyone else. The judge gets upset in the same way. He rebukes and punishes those under his charge. This discipline is not only good but also necessary. Things would not get done properly without it. Thus unless the judge, the minister, and the father and mother become upset and as the occasion calls they scold and rebuke, they become useless and will never discharge their office properly.

Thus a strong reproof and the bitter word are as necessary in every aspect of life as any other virtue. Even so, such anger needs to be restrained so that it does not proceed from hate or ill will. Only paternal affection and zeal should flourish. It should not be childish or finicky,[6] seeking to even scores, but just enough to correct the fault. That is how the father corrects the child but not to get even, only enough to correct the child. These types of anger are good, and the Scripture calls them zeal.[7] Because when I rebuke my brother, my son, the student, or the one in my charge, I don't seek his destruction but his benefit and well-being.

It may be that here Paul rebukes the Galatians for two reasons: One, due to a fervent zeal, which sought not to destroy them but to induce them to once again take the right path. Two, out of pity and compassion. However, it's almost a lament,[8] which has caused him deep pain that they would have been so miserably seduced. It's as if he had said, "I am troubled and embarrassed upon hearing of your miserable condition and foolishness." In the same way, we rebuke the gullible. It's not to make them feel stepped on or to make them feel worse. We rebuke them out of compassion, hoping they will change. I say this in case someone slanders Paul by saying that he was haranguing the church of God and going against the precepts of the Gospel.

Christ rebukes the Pharisees in the same way, calling them snakes, generation of vipers, children of the devil. However, these are rebukes from the Holy Spirit. They are paternal and maternal, as are the reproaches of a faithful friend, as Proverbs says, "Faithful are the wounds from a friend, but the kisses of an enemy are deceitful" (Proverbs 27:6). Thus when parents rebuke with their mouths, it could be of great benefit. But if an enemy or even one of us reproves the child, it could be taken as a spiteful insult. When two people perform the same act, one might be applauded for it but the other slandered. However, when Christ and Paul rebuke, they display the same purpose and should be praised. But if a philosopher or some ordinary person were to do the same, it would be highly inappropriate and offensive. Thus in Paul's lips, a certain word is of great benefit, while the same expression coming from someone else would be a great offence.[9]

---

[6] *puerelis aut muliebris*, "neither of children nor women."

[7] Luther's footnote: *iusta ira vocatur zelus in scripturis*, "in Scripture holy wrath is called zeal."

[8] *querulantis, from querula.*

[9] *maleficium.*

There is a certain emphasis in this term, "Galatians." He does not call them brothers, as he does elsewhere. He calls them by the name of their land of origin. It seems as if foolishness[10] was the natural vice of that nation. In the same way, the foible of the Cretans was lying. It's as if he had said, "As their name, so are they." In other words, it's as if he had said, "Foolish Galatians,[11] just as you have now shown who you are with respect to the Gospel (even though you knew better), you have shown who you are by nature, you haven't changed." *Likewise, we identify nations by their quirks. Each nation has its particular fault. The Germans are always eager for something new; the Italians are conceited; etc.* Paul, to correct them, reminds the Galatians who they are by nature.

What's more, here we are admonished with respect to the flesh that certain natural faults remain in the churches and among Christians. Grace does not so change the believers so that they immediately become new creatures, perfect in every aspect. Some muck remains from their old corruption and those inherent to their nature. For example, someone who easily turns to anger is converted. Although he may be tempered by grace (the Holy Spirit filters in to his heart,[12] and he becomes more inclined to mercy[13]), even so, this fault is not fully extinguished in the flesh. Similarly, those who are stubborn by nature, even when converted to the faith, do not have that stubbornness totally extinguished in them. They retain certain relics of a hard head.[14] In the same way, the Holy Scriptures and the Gospels contain one single truth, yet they are presented in different ways by different personalities. Someone's teaching may be gentle, while another may be harsh.[15] Thus the Holy Spirit is poured out in different vessels, and it does not at once extinguish all nature's shortcomings. However, throughout a lifetime, He purifies sin, which is inherent[16] not only among the Galatians but throughout all people of all nations.

How could it be that the Galatians, having believed and given great light, then having received the Holy Spirit through the preaching of faith, still had the sludge of this fault, this kindling of foolishness, which so easily lit the flame of false doctrine? So let no one trust so much in himself, thinking that having received

---

[10] Here, Luther employs the Greek term ἀνόητοι.

[11] Ibid.

[12] *Spiritus sanctus imbuat cor ipsuius.*

[13] *ut fiat clementior.*

[14] *reliquiae istius duriciei.*

[15] *mollior in docendo, alus durior.*

[16] *sed per totam vitam purgat illud peccatum inhaerens.* Although some may take issue with Luther's use of *purgat,* or "purge sin," as referring to an additional work of Christ within the sinner to remove sin, it is well to remember that in Luther's theology the Holy Spirit applies the blood of Christ to the believer to purge or purify the sinner vicariously through the justifying passive righteousness of Christ alone. For Luther, God's declaration of "righteous" is how sin is purged from the believer, without any work of the will or of the law.

grace, he has been totally purified from his old faults. Indeed, many are still fading away within us and especially because of the serpent's head. In other words, unbelief and willful ignorance are mortally wounded. But the scaly body and the remains of sin still linger in us. Let no one think that the minute he receives faith, he is suddenly changed into a new person. No! Some of his old faults remain rooted in him, no matter how good a Christian he may be. We haven't died, yet we continue living in the flesh. It hasn't been purified and continually struggles against the spirit (Galatians 5:17; Romans 7:14). "I am carnal," said Paul, "sold under sin," "and I see another law in the members of my body which makes war against the law of my mind." Thus the faults that were in us before receiving faith remain within us after we have received faith. It is just that now they are submitted to the Spirit, which controls them with greater power so that they will not rule. However, it is not without a great struggle. But this glory is for Christ alone,[17] and this title is only His, that He is pure and without stain. "He committed no sin, and no deceit was found in his mouth" (1 Peter 2:22).

VERSE 1. Who has bewitched you not to obey the truth?

There you have it. Could there ever be anything better? You now have this remarkable message of the law and self-righteousness. It makes us despise the truth and puts a spell on us so that we will not obey the truth but instead rebel against it![18]

Regarding Physical and Spiritual Witchcraft

Paul calls the Galatians foolish and bewitched. He compares them to children who have been harmed by witchcraft. He tells them, you have been treated as children. Witches, wizards, and enchanters bewitch children with the devil's charms. Later, in chapter 5, Paul includes witchcraft among the works of the flesh, which is a type of sorcery. He clearly testifies that there is such a thing as witchcraft and sorcery and that it is practiced. Further, it cannot be denied that the devil is alive and well and that he reigns throughout the whole world. Therefore, sorcery and witchcraft are the works of the devil. With these works, he not only injures men, but whenever God permits it, sometimes, they are destroyed by them. Further, we are subject to the devil both within our bodies and in what we have. We are strangers in this world, but he is the prince and god. Thus the bread we eat, the drink we take, the clothes we wear, all the air we breathe, and what we live in the flesh is under his dominion. *Thus he is capable through his wizardry to harm children, scare them to death, bring blindness over them, steal them, or snatch them away and then place himself in the child's crib. I*

---

[17] *Solus Christus hanc gloriam.*

[18] Here, Luther uses sarcasm as a teaching method to emphasize the uselessness of the righteousness of the law.

heard the story of such a child in Saxony, where he would breast feed from five women and yet would not quit feeding.[19] *There are countless examples such as this.*

Witchcraft is nothing else than the devil's shrewdness and charms. It is said that he can take a member in the body of the young or old, injure it, and then make it look like he healed it just through his trickery. He fakes the healing of an eye or another member that appeared to have been injured, but there was never anything wrong with it. But he's only playing with the senses. He bewitches you and others who are watching fascinated to the point where no one will think it's just an illusion but will swear it's a true injury. But as time passes, he removes the injury. Then it is apparent that it was just a deception. It was not a real injury after all because a true injury could not be healed and restored just like that!

We have an outstanding example of this matter in Lives of the Fathers, *after the* Metamorphosis of the Poets. *When Saint Macarius lived in the desert, there came to him the parents of a certain virgin, who thought they had lost her. They supposed she had been turned into a cow, for all they could see was the shape of a cow. They led her to Saint Macarius and pled for him to pray so that through God's power she would be restored to human form.*

But when Macarius heard it, he said, "I see a virgin, not a cow." He had spiritual eyes. Satan could not deceive him with his tricks, as he had done with the parents and their daughter. Their eyes had been so deceived by the evil spirit that they could have sworn it was the real thing because their eyes were spinning!

But when Macarius prayed for the young woman, he didn't ask for her to be restored to the human species because she hadn't lost it! Instead, he prayed for God to remove the appearance the devil had given her. Then the eyes of the parents and the daughter were opened, and they caught on to everything. What they thought had been great harm had only been Satan making fun of them.

Such is the astuteness and power of the devil to play with our senses, just looking through a glass changes appearances and colors. Thus for him, it's so easy to deceive people with his tricks and attractions. People see things that aren't really there to see at all; they hear voices, thunderclaps, bagpipes, and trumpets that aren't there to be heard! Julius Caesar's soldiers imagined they heard the sound of a pipe or trumpet. Suetonius mentions this in his Life of Caesar. *He said that suddenly someone exceptionally tall appeared, sitting and playing a pipe. Not only most of the shepherds but also many of the soldiers left their stations, together with the buglers, to gather around to hear him play. Suddenly, he snatched a bugle from one of them and leapt over to the river's edge. There, he sounded a mighty and spirited alarm before going to the other shore. Satan has the power to negatively impact the senses so that someone could swear to have seen, heard, or touched something that was not there to see at all.*

However, he not only mesmerizes people in this crass manner. He also charms in the most subtle and dangerous way. He is a marvelous impostor. That is how Paul

---

[19] *et tamen non potuit expleri.*

relates the charming of the senses to the bewitching of the spirit. With this spiritual witchcraft, that ancient serpent bewitches not only the senses but also the mind with false and evil thinking. Those who've allowed themselves to be trapped hold to these opinions as true and pious. *Today, he shows he is able to equally deceive the fanatics, the Anabaptists, and those who blaspheme the Sacrament of the body and the blood of Christ. Their minds have become so bewitched with his delusions that they embrace lies, errors, and horrible darkness as the soundest truth and most brilliant light.*

None of them would tolerate being separated from these imaginings not even by the clearest warnings of the Scriptures. They are more than firmly persuaded that they alone have wisdom and sound judgment in sacred matters and that everyone else is blind. Thus they are no different than the parents of the girl, who once they were deceived by Satan's tricks, they could have sworn their girl was not human but bovine. They could believe nothing else than the devil's trickery and foolery. They held on tight to the testimony of all their senses: their eyes saw the shape of a cow and their ears heard the mooing of a cow etc. Even though what they saw was against their senses, they were powerless to oppose it.

But we should be at odds with our senses when the body is deceived as shown by Macarius's example. We should respond much more forcefully when it comes to spiritual witchcraft. On the outside, the devil shows up with appearances and coloring for the senses. But on the inside, he appears with an easy to believe doctrinal opinion that appears to be true. As I've said before, he deludes people's hearts so that they will swear the most untrustworthy and wicked speculation is nothing but the most reliable truth. From without, he deceives the senses with shapes and colors but from within with credible opinions with respect to doctrine. Therefore (as I have said), he charms the hearts of men to such an extent that they swear their most vain and wicked conjecture is the most certain truth. In our time, he has deceived Münzer, Zwingli, and others in this manner and through them countless others.

In brief, such is the wickedness of this sorcerer and his desire to do evil that he deceives not only those that trust in themselves with pride but also those who have a correct understanding of God's word and Christian religion. As far as I am concerned, sometimes he harasses me with such force that he oppresses me with depressing thoughts. These obscure Christ my Savior with shadows to turn my eyes away from Him altogether. In brief, there's not a one among us who at times has not been bewitched by false convictions. In other words, at times, he fears, trusts, or rejoices when he should not, or sometimes, he misses the mark when thinking about God, Christ, faith, or his own vocation.

Therefore, let us learn to recognize the subtle trickery of this magician. Otherwise, he will find us sleeping quite confidently and mesmerize us with his charms. It is true that with his charms he cannot harm our ministry, yet he is with us in spirit. Day and night, he is on the prowl, seeking how he may devour us alone. Unless he finds us sober and armed with spiritual weapons—that is, with the word of God and faith, he will devour us.

This is the reason at times he stirs up new controversy against us. But frankly, it is quite beneficial that he harasses us because he makes us exercise. Thus he causes us to be more fully confirmed in our doctrine, since he pushes us to grow in faith. We have certainly seen ourselves defeated many times, and we are still struggling in this conflict. However, we do not perish, since Christ always has triumphed and triumphs through us. That is why we hope with all confidence that we too shall obtain the victory against the devil through Jesus Christ. And this hope is our firm confidence so that in the middle of our temptations we will renew our courage and say, "Satan has tempted us and through his false illusions has provoked us to unbelief, to despise God, to despair. Even so, he has not prevailed nor will prevail henceforth. Greater is He that is in us than he who is in the world. Christ is stronger, He is the strongman who conquers the strong man who is in us and will defeat him forever." Even so, sometimes the devil defeats us in the flesh so that when we are tested with the power of the assailant, we may see the power of the stronger man and thus say with Paul, "For when I am weak then am I strong" (2 Corinthians 12:10).

Thus let no one think that it's just the Galatians alone who've been bewitched by the devil. Rather, let each one think that you yourself could have been and still could be mesmerized by him. There is no one among us so strong that could resist him, especially if you attempt it with your own strength. Job was an upright and righteous man and there was none like him on earth (Job 1:8). But did he have any power against the devil when God withdrew his hand? Didn't this righteous man have a terrible fall? That is why this sorcerer not only was powerful against the Galatians but strives to deceive if not all men as many as possible with his false persuasions and fantasies, for he is a liar and father of lies. *And with this trickery he goes at it today as I have said, bewitching the fanatical minds. He is their lord and hardens them to the point that they will not yield. They're stronger than the most solid anvil. They don't allow themselves to be taught, don't listen to any reason, nor admit the Scriptures. Their only effort is to see what they can make up with their own heads to add their own spin to the Scriptures[20] and dream up ways to defend them. This is a clear sign that they have been mesmerized by the wizardry of the devil.*

VERSE 1. Who has bewitched you?

Here, Paul excuses the Galatians and places all the blame on the false apostles. It's as if he had said, "I see that you have fallen not due to your own decision or wickedness. But the devil has sent his wizards, the false apostles, among you, my children, to mesmerize you with his doctrine of the law. That's why you now think differently about Christ than you did before when you heard the Gospel that I preached. However, through our preaching and now as I write to you, we labor to remove the spell cast on you by the false apostles and set free those who fell in those snares."

---

[20] *glossis adductos contra se scripturae.*

In the same way, we put forth every effort using God's word against the fanaticism of the Anabaptists and the Sacramentarians. We strive to release those who have fallen in their web. We want to pare them down to the pure doctrine of faith, to retain them. Our struggle has not been in vain, for we have reclaimed many of those who they charmed and delivered them from their traps. *They could have never returned through their own efforts, but we have admonished and recalled them through the word of God.*

It is impossible for someone to be delivered from the spells over his senses (just as the girl's parents could not see any other shape but a cow's before Macarius's prayer). In the same way, self-deliverance is also impossible for those who have been spiritually bewitched. Those whose minds have not been snared by that spell must deliver them. Satan's deceptions are so effective that the mesmerized boast and swear that they possess the surest truth. Meanwhile, they could not be further from confessing their error. Even though, by appealing to Scriptures, we make great efforts to convince them and especially the authors of these sects, our work is in vain. Immediately, they respond with their own interpretations with which they elude the Scriptures.

Our warnings are useless in leading them to reform. Instead, they harden and become more obstinate than before. If I didn't have the experience I do today, I would not believe how great the devil's power is. He can create a falsehood so that it looks so much like the truth. Further, and what's more horrifying, is how he prowls around overburdening the consciences that are already hurting with great anguish. They are so grieved that they cannot detect that he dresses up as Christ to afflict and tempt them even more. That is why so many simple and ignorant people are deceived and fling themselves into desperation, some even destroying themselves. They have been so bewitched by the devil that they have come to believe as irrefutable truth that they are being tempted and accused not by the devil but by Christ Himself.

That's what happened to that poor man Dr. Kraus de Halle in the year of our Lord 1527. He said, "I have denied Christ; thus He is now before the Father, accusing me." He was blinded by that illusion of the devil. It stuck so fiercely to his imagination that there was no exhortation, consolation, nor promise of God that could deliver him. Thus he lost all hope and took his life in such a miserable way. But that was just a simple lie, a spell of the devil. He believed an illusory definition of Christ, unknown to Scriptures. God's word displays Christ not as a judge, tempter, or accuser but as the Conciliator, Mediator, Comforter, Savior, and as the Throne of Grace Himself.

However, this poor man, befuddled by the devil, could not realize it. Therefore, his thinking went contrary to all Scriptures. He bought into this lie as nothing but the truth: "Christ is accusing you before the Father. He's not there for you but against you. Thus you have been condemned." This temptation is not from man, but from the devil. He's the sorcerer who powerfully attaches himself to the hearts of the tempted. But to us who are guided and taught by another Spirit, the illusion is nothing but an accursed lie and spell of the devil. But to those who are under such a spell, there's no more solid truth.

The devil is a master sorcerer of a thousand charms. He can so artfully impress upon our hearts a lie so real but shameful that we would swear a thousand times it is nothing but unfailing truth. Thus we should not get all puffed up but rather walk with fear and trembling, calling out to Christ our Savior, lest we enter into temptation. There are those people, confident and worldly, who having heard the Gospel once or twice soon imagine they have received the abundance of the Spirit and fall just the same. They did not fear God nor gave Him thanks. Instead, they presumed to uphold and defend the doctrine of true faith. At the same time, they thought they could resist every attack from the devil or any conflict, no matter how forceful. But those experiences are instruments of the devil to mesmerize them and fling them into desperation.

On the other hand, don't say, "I am perfect, I can't fall." Instead, humble yourself with fear, lest while you are standing firm today, tomorrow, you may fall. I, myself, even a doctor in theology and now a preacher of Christ and having fought for long against the devil and his false teachers, know from my own experience how difficult this is. I cannot get rid of Satan whenever I want nor grasp onto Christ as Scripture entreats. Sometimes, the devil shows before my eyes a false Christ but thanks be to God who keeps us in the word, in faith, and in prayer so that we may walk before Him in fear and humility. We cannot presume upon our own wisdom, righteousness, and power but trust in the power of Christ, who is powerful when we are weak. Thus He continually defeats and conquers through us weak and fragile creatures. To Him be the glory forever, amen.

Thus this wizardry and witchcraft are nothing but mere illusions of the devil, who impresses on the heart a false concept of Christ and even against Christ. Whoever has been bamboozled with this opinion is because he is under a spell. Thus those who have this conviction that they are justified by the works of the law or the traditions of men, are under a spell,[21] for this opinion goes against faith and Christ. Paul resorted to this word *bewitched* because he despised the false apostles who so fervently urged the doctrine of the law and its works. It's as if he had said, "What diabolic spell has done this?" Just as the senses are perverted by physical witchcraft, so the minds of men are unhinged by this spiritual wizardry.

VERSE 1. Not to obey the truth.

Initially, the Galatians heard the truth with joy and obeyed it. That is why when it asks, "Who has bewitched you?" he reveals that first they were bewitched by the false apostles, and then they had detoured from the path of truth that they had obeyed before. But when it says that they do not obey the truth, it seems as if he

---

[21] *Quod ex operibus legis aut traditionum humanarum justificentur, fascinati sunt.*

were expressing bitterness and zeal. With these words, he wants to tell them that they are under a spell and he would like to deliver them from it, but notwithstanding they neither recognize nor accept his help. It is true that he had not been able to reclaim for the truth all the Galatians, pulling them away from the errors of the false apostles. There were still some who were under their spell. Thus he uses these heated and cutting words: "Who has bewitched you?" It's as if he had said, "You are so mesmerized and bewildered that you cannot obey the truth. I fear that you will never come back to the truth."

Here, you can hear the town crier singing the praises[22] of the righteousness of the law or self-righteousness.[23] Although it holds people spellbound, they are not capable of obeying the truth. The apostles and the fathers of the early church often mentioned this subject. For instance, in 1 John 5:16, John says, "There is a sin unto death. I do not say that he shall pray about it." Also in Hebrews 6:4–6, it says, "For concerning those who were once enlightened and tasted of the heavenly gift. It is impossible to renew them again to repentance." At first, it sounds as something said by a follower of Novatian. But the apostles were forced to say things like this because of the heretics. However, unlike Novatian, they did not refuse to reinstate the backsliders to the community of the faithful through repentance. Today, we should talk the same way to the authors and teachers of errors and sects—namely, that they will never be able to return to the truth. There are some that indeed could return, but they are captive under a weaker spell. It's not like that with the leaders and champions of the spells! They should keep the title Paul gave them—that is, they will neither listen to the truth nor tolerate it. Rather, they are only eager to resist the truth and similarly to twist and elude Scripture's arguments against them. They have been taken captive and are fully convinced that they have the most precise truth and the purest understanding of the Scriptures. Whoever has this conviction neither listens nor is willing to change. Therefore, in the same way, I, myself, will not hear anything contrary to my doctrine, for I am sure and persuaded by the Spirit of Christ that my doctrine regarding Christian righteousness is certain and true.[24]

VERSE 1. Before whose eyes Jesus Christ was openly portrayed.

Before, Paul had spoken harshly. He had said they were so bewitched they could not obey the truth. Now he is even harsher, since he adds that he had portrayed

---

[22] *praeconium.* See the "Let's Hear It for Self-Righteousness and Its Fifty Select Virtues . . ." on p. xix.

[23] The reader will remember that Luther throughout this commentary is speaking to his students. Here, he resorts to the rhetorical device of sarcasm to teach the opposite: the righteousness of the law does not recommend itself.

[24] *Sum enim certus et persuasus per spiritum Christi meam doctrinam de christiana justitia veram ac certam esse.*

Christ so vividly before them. They could almost touch Him with their hands, and even so, they did not obey the truth. That's the way he attempts to convince them, resorting to the experience they had enjoyed together. It's as if he had said, "You are so bewitched and mesmerized with the perverse opinions of the false apostles that now you will no longer obey the truth. Although at the cost of great suffering and persistence, I portrayed Christ crucified so vividly before your very eyes, everything was in vain."

With these words, he goes back to his previous arguments. He had already proven that those who justify themselves with the works of the law reject God's grace and make Christ a minister of sin. Thus Christ had died in vain for them. Previously he had fervently presented these arguments to magnify Christ before them, as a painter would have painted a picture of Christ crucified before their eyes. Now, in his absence, he brings to their mind the same things, saying, "Before your eyes, Jesus Christ was openly portrayed." It is as if he had said, "There is no artist so skillful with his colors who could have portrayed Christ as vividly as I have done with my preaching. Even so, you continue under that same miserable spell!"

VERSE 1. Crucified among you.

What was the picture that I painted among you? Christ Himself. How did He look like? Crucified among you. Here, he resorts to rough and sharp words. Previously he had said that they had been seeking righteousness through the law, thereby rejecting the grace of God; as a result Christ had died for them in vain. Now he adds that they also crucify Christ, who had lived and reigned among them. It's as if he had said, "Now you not only have rejected the grace of God, not only did He die in vain for you, but now you shamefully crucify Christ among you." He makes the same declaration in the Epistle to the Hebrews: "Seeing they crucify the Son of God for themselves again, and put him to open shame" (Hebrews 6:6).

When someone just hears about a monk, his tonsure, his cowl, his regulations, it's enough to get all shaken up with fear. However, the Papists worship these abominations, and they boast that they are perfect in their religion and holiness. I, myself, and others had the same opinion before God revealed His Gospel to us. We were raised in the traditions of men. But these obscure Christ and turn Him into a worthless Christ. They should rather tremble when they listen to what Paul says, for he declares that those who seek to be justified by the law of God not only deny Christ, but they murder Him; they most wickedly crucify Him once again. Well, then, if those who crucify Christ are those who seek to be justified by the righteousness of the law of God and by the works of the law, pray tell me,[25] what

---

[25] The attentive reader will imagine Luther in suppliant gestures appealing to his students as he lectures.

will become of those who seek salvation and eternal life through the filth and dung of man's righteousness and the doctrine of devils?

However, who could ever believe or even think it could be such a horrible and abominable sin to become "religious" (that is what they call themselves) in the likes of a priest performing the mass or becoming a monk, a friar, or a nun? Without a doubt, no one. Further, they say that to become a monk is the new baptism. Could there be anything worse than the reign of the followers of the Pope who perversely spit upon the face of Christ the Son of God and crucify Him once again? Because they certainly crucify Him once again (He who was crucified and came back to life), in themselves as well as in the church and in the hearts of the faithful. They spit on Him with their wicked censures, reproaches, slanders, and offenses. With their wicked opinions, they wound and pierce Him and make Him die within them in the most shameful way. Then they replace Him with a glorious spell with which they charm and beguile so that they are unable to know that Christ is their Justifier, Reconciler, and Savior. Instead, they believe He is a minister of sin, an accuser, judge, and destroyer, who cannot be placated except through their own works and merits.

Further, from this opinion then arose the most perverse and toxic doctrine that sums up the entire papacy. It is this: if you would render service to God and merit the forgiveness of sins and eternal life while helping others achieve salvation, then you should shut yourself up in a cloister or a monastery and take vows of obedience, chastity, poverty, etc. The monks and friars, and the rest of that religious mob, puffed up with the opinion of their own holiness boast that they are the only ones who live in a state of perfection, but the others are mere ordinary Christians. They claim the latter did not perform extraordinary works, meaning more than necessary—in other words, that they did not take vows nor lived in chastity, poverty, obedience, etc. These lowly Christians had only been baptized and kept the Ten Commandments. But the doctrine of the monks is that in addition to what they have in common with other Christians, they perform works of supererogation[26] and all the counsels of Christ. Thus they hope to merit a place among the principal saints in heaven far above the rest of the Christian crowd.

Without a doubt, this is a prodigious delusion of the devil with which he has cast a spell on the entire world. And every man, no matter how pious he'd like to be, falls into the web of this charm—that is, with the pestilent persuasion of his own righteousness. It's for this very reason that we could not know that Jesus Christ was our Mediator and Savior. We thought that He was a severe judge, who could only be placated through our own works. But this was nothing else but the most horrible blasphemy against Christ. As Paul said previously, it is to reject the grace of God, cancel out the death of Christ, take away His efficacy, and not

---

[26] *supererogationis,* from the late Latin, "payment beyond what is due or asked."

only murder Him but crucify Him once again in the most shameful way. This is the correct meaning of what Christ declares in Daniel as "the abomination of desolation in the holy place." That is why every monk and member of a religious order, as well as the justifiers, who seek the remission of sins and righteousness through their own works or afflictions, is a slayer who crucifies the Christ, who today lives and reigns. This is done not to Christ's own person but in their own hearts and the hearts of others. And all who go into a monastery with a mind-set to keep the laws that will justify them do nothing else but enter a den of thieves and as such crucify Christ once again.

That is why Paul in this text employs these sharp and cutting words. He wants to infuse fear among the Galatians and draw them away from the doctrine of the false apostles. It's as if he had said, "Take into heart what you have done. You have crucified Christ once again. This is what I have painted before your very eyes so that you may see Him and touch Him with your own hands. You are crucifying Him because you seek to be justified by the law. But if righteousness comes through the law, then Christ is a minister of sin and His death has been totally worthless. If this is true, then this means that you have once again crucified Christ among yourselves."

There's a very precise reason he adds this clause "in you or among you." Christ can no longer be crucified; He does not die in His own person. But it's like he says in Romans 6, He dies in us when we reject the true doctrine of grace, faith, and the free remission of sins and seek to be justified by our own works or otherwise by the works required by the law. That is where Christ is crucified once again, in us. This persuasive doctrine is nonetheless false and perverse. It is to seek righteousness through the law and works. It's nothing else (as I have said before at length) but to follow the mirage painted by the devil. Through this illusion, he casts a spell on people so they are totally unable to recognize the benefit of Christ. It is true; they can do nothing else with their lives but deny the Lord who bought them and in whose name they were baptized, and they crucify Him among themselves once again. Let everyone who has anything left of the fear of God, or love for Christ and His true religion, flee as fast as possible from this Babylon, and let him tremble when he just barely hears the name of the papacy, for its wickedness and abomination is so horrible that no one can express it with mere words, nor can it be plainly seen except with spiritual eyes.

Paul advances these two arguments and urges and reinforces them on the Galatians. First, they are unable to obey the truth (although it is so clear before their eyes) because they have been bewitched by the devil. Second, because they crucify Christ once again in themselves. These seem to be simple and plain words spoken without great eloquence, but their power surpasses the greatest eloquence. Only in the Spirit are we able to understand how great is the wickedness that seeks to be justified by the righteousness of the law, by the righteousness and merits of man. It's nothing but being hoodwinked by the devil, it's disobedience to the truth, and crucifying Christ once again, as Paul says here. Of course, you can see how highly he recommends the righteousness of the law and self-righteousness![27]

LECTURE 15: Saturday, August 22

Thus the apostle Paul burns with fervent zeal and with bitter words reproaches and condemns faith and confidence in human righteousness. He revolts against the observance of God's law and accuses it of this wickedness that it crucifies once again the Son of God. Seeing that it is such a dangerous menace, it cannot be refuted enough nor properly condemned. This type of thinking originated no less than with Lucifer's fall. Such loss can never be recovered or estimated. Thus Paul uses such sharp and cutting words that not even God's law is spared. He raises such bitter accusations against it that it would seem he rejects and condemns it altogether. He went as far as he could in making this argument; otherwise, he would have been unable to confront the false apostles nor defend the righteousness of faith against them. Albeit the law is holy, just, and good, it puts on the costume of the greeter that bids welcome to justification by works.[28] That is why he continues with the following argument, which they already knew, and could not deny it. It says,

VERSE 2. Let me ask you only this: Did you receive the Spirit by works of the law, or by hearing with faith?

He directs these words with certain indignation and disdain toward the false apostles. If the only argument I had against you was your own experience, that would suffice. It's as if he had said, "Come on, I mentored you. Since when did you become scholars so that now you pretend to be my teachers and professors? 'Did you receive the Holy Spirit by the works of the law or by the preaching of the Gospel?'" He persuades them so convincingly with this argument that they are at a loss to respond. Their own experience accuses them. They had received the Holy Spirit not by the works of the law but by the preaching of the Gospel.

Here, once again, I put you on notice that Paul is talking not only about the ceremonial law but about the entire law. He presents his argument by correctly separating the subject matter. If he only spoke of the ceremonial law, he would not be correct in separating the issues. It's an argument that has support from two opposing sides. For the one part to be true, the other must be false—that is, you received the Holy Spirit either by the law or by hearing with faith. If it was through the law, then it was not by the preaching of faith. If it was by the preaching of faith, it could not be by the law. There is no middle ground. Everything that is not from the Holy Spirit or from the preaching of faith is from the law. Here, we enter the zone of

---

[27] Once again, note Luther's use of sarcasm as a teaching tool.

[28] *eam induere quasi personam hypocritae volentis per opera justificari.*

justification. To be justified, there is no other way but either through the voice of the Gospel or through the voice of the law. What is here generally understood by "the law" is the law set apart and separate from the Gospel. However, it's not only the ceremonial law that exists apart from the Gospel but also the moral law, or the law of the Ten Commandments. That is why Paul here is talking about the entire law.

He anchors his argument on a clear dividing line. "Tell me, did you receive the Holy Spirit by the works of the law or by the preaching of the Gospel? Answer me. Because you cannot say that it was through the law. That's because as long as you were under the law doing its works, you never did receive the Holy Spirit. Indeed, every Sabbath day you heard the law of Moses. However, it had never been seen or heard that the Holy Spirit had fallen on anyone (no matter how devout a student or disciple) through the preaching of the law. Further, you've not only taught and listened to the law, but you've also attempted with all your might to fulfill its requirements through your works. If the Spirit were given through the law almost all of you would have received it, seeing that you are not only teachers and hearers but also doers of the law. But even so, none of you can point me to the moment when that happened. However, as soon as you heard with faith the Gospel that was given to you, immediately you received the Holy Spirit. It was just by the hearing with faith, before any other work or before you demonstrated any fruit of the Spirit." In the New Testament, Luke testifies in Acts that only at the preaching of Peter and Paul, "the Spirit fell upon those who heard the word, by which they also received various gifts, so that they spoke in diverse tongues" (Acts 10:44).

Therefore, it is perfectly clear that they received the Holy Spirit only by the preaching of faith before they performed any good work or yielded any fruit of the Gospel. On the other hand, the Holy Spirit never came through the keeping of any law or even less by the hearing of the law. Thus the hearing of the law as well as that zeal and affection used in doing all the things required by the law are all in vain and useless. Let' say that someone strives with the greatest possible effort to comply with the law and all its works, even with the most fervent zeal for God, and with great strength should strive to be saved by fulfilling the law, exercising the righteousness of the law, day and night, it would all still be wearing out for nothing. Because all those who ignore the righteousness of God and "seek to establish their own righteousness," as Paul says elsewhere, do not submit to the righteousness of God. Similarly, "Israel who pursued the righteousness which is based on law did not succeed in fulfilling that law." Well then, what Paul is talking about here is the manifestation of the Holy Spirit in the early church. The Holy Spirit fell on those who believed in the same way. Through this sign, the Spirit clearly testified that He personally came through the preaching of the apostles. Further, those who heard the word of faith preached by the apostles were declared righteous before God.[29] Otherwise, the Holy Spirit would not have fallen upon them.

---

[29] *reputari iustos apud deum.*

The Argument of the Book of Acts of the Apostles

That is why we should diligently weigh and consider the impact of the argument repeated frequently in the Acts of the Apostles. This book was written with no other purpose but to confirm and establish this argument: The Holy Spirit is given only by listening to the Gospel and not by the keeping of any law. When Peter preached, the Holy Spirit came upon all who heard it. In one day, three thousand who were present when Peter preached believed and received the Holy Spirit (Acts 2). Cornelius received the Holy Spirit in the same way; not when he gave alms (although he gave them) but when Peter opened his mouth, and while he spoke, the Holy Spirit came upon those who (together with Cornelius) listened to the word (Acts 10). These are overwhelming arguments, including experiences and divine works that cannot deceive us.

Luke also writes that Paul in Acts 15, after preaching the Gospel together with Barnabas among the Gentiles and after returning to Jerusalem, set himself against the Pharisees and the disciples of the apostles. This last group urged circumcision and the keeping of the law as necessary to salvation. However, Paul stopped their mouths (Luke says) when he showed the things that he and Barnabas had done among the Gentiles; as a result, the entire church marveled when they heard him. They were especially amazed when they heard that God had worked great and marvelous miracles through their hands among the Gentiles. Those who had a zeal for the law were amazed that the uncircumcised Gentiles who did not keep the law could obtain such grace, to the extent that they were justified and received the Holy Spirit as well as the Jews who were circumcised. Here, Paul and Barnabas did not allege anything else but their own testimony regarding what had transpired. Those who heard were so astounded that they could not respond. In the same way, Sergius Paulus, the proconsul, and all those cities, regions, kingdoms, and countries wherever the apostles preached believed only through the preaching of faith, without the law and its works.

Throughout the entire book of Acts there is no other issue. The only one was that Jews and Gentiles,[30] righteous and unrighteous, must be justified by faith in Christ Jesus, without the law and its works.[31] Through their preaching, Peter, Paul, Steven, Philip, and the other apostles had made it abundantly clear, as well as by other examples given by Gentiles and Jews. Forasmuch as God had given the Holy Spirit to the Gentiles (who lived without the law) through the preaching of the Gospel alone, so it was also given to the Jews. But it was not given because they kept the law, ceremonies, and sacrifices mandated by the law. Rather, it was only through the preaching of faith. Then if the law could justify and the righteousness

---

[30] Luther's footnote: *Sola fide in Christum justificari Iudaeos et gentes.*

[31] *tam justos quam peccatores, sola fide in Christum Iesum justificari, sine lege et operibus.*

of the law would have been necessary for salvation, without doubt, the Holy Spirit would not have been given to the Gentiles because they did not keep the law. But history renders the same testimony, that the Holy Spirit was given to them without the law (as witnessed by the apostles, Peter, Paul, Barnabas, and others). Therefore, it's not the law but faith alone in Christ, as preached by the Gospel, that justifies.[32]

These matters must be diligently emphasized for the adversaries do not stop to consider the theme of the Acts of the Apostles. I, myself, in times past, when I read this book, did not understand it at all. Therefore, when you hear or read the Acts of the Apostles or whenever you find in Scriptures this term *Gentiles,* you should not interpret it literally according to the common nature of the Gentiles. This word contains a spiritual meaning, for it does not refer to those who are under the law, as were the Jews (as stated in chapter 2, "We who are Jews by nature"). Instead, it refers to those who are without the law. Thus to say that the Gentiles are justified by faith means nothing else but that those who neither observe the law nor do its works, those who have neither been circumcised nor offer sacrifices, they are those who are justified and receive the Holy Spirit. How? Not by the law and its works (for they have no law at all) but freely and without any other means other than when they hear the preaching of the Gospel.

Notice how Cornelius and the guests he invited to his house don't do anything at all; they don't stop to consider any of their previous works. However, all present receive the Holy Spirit. No one speaks but Peter. They are seated, they don't do a thing. They aren't thinking about the law or even less complying with it. They don't offer sacrifices; they don't care about being circumcised, they are just fixed on what Peter is saying. Through his preaching, he brought the Holy Spirit to their hearts, and the result was visible, "for they spoke in tongues and glorified God."

But there are those who begin to ponder at this saying, "Who knows if it really was the Holy Spirit or not?" Well, let them doubt, for it is true that it is the Holy Spirit, since the Spirit's testimony cannot lie. Rather, this testimony shows that He accepts the Gentiles as righteous and justifies them through no other means except through the voice of the Gospel or at the hearing of faith in Christ. We can also see in Acts how the Jews marveled at this that seemed so new and strange. The faithful who were from the circumcision and had come with Peter to Caesarea, were astounded when they saw the gift of the Holy Spirit poured out on the Gentiles in Cornelius's house. Also, those who were in Jerusalem complained that Peter went into the house with uncircumcised men and "ate with them." But when they heard what Peter narrated, about what had happened with Cornelius, they marveled and glorified God, saying, "Then God has also given salvation to the Gentiles."

Thus this news and report, that God had given salvation also to the Gentiles, at the beginning not only was intolerable but caused great offense even among

---

[32] *Ergo non lex, sed sola fides in Christum, quam evangelium praedicat, justificat.*

the believing Jews. They could not shake off their indignation because there was a distinction between the nations: "That they were the people of God, and that the adoption, the glory, the praise belonged only to them" (Romans 9). Further, they exercised the righteousness of the law, and they had worked at it all day long, carrying the burden and the heat of the day. What's more they had the promise with respect to the keeping of the law. Thus all they could do was murmur against the Gentiles (Matthew 20), saying, "So how is it that the Gentiles show up as latecomers, without suffering the heat or carrying the load; and even so, they get to have the same righteousness and Holy Spirit, without any works at all? Because not even with our works did we receive the Holy Spirit, not even after carrying the load and the heat of the day. It's true they have worked but merely for an hour, and with this work, they are more refreshed than tired out. Why did God then torment us with the law if it didn't help us at all to achieve righteousness? We are God's people; we have been harassed all day long. They are not even the people of God, nor do they keep any law, nor do any of its good works, yet they get the same pay!"

This is the reason the council of the apostles convened so quickly in Jerusalem, to satisfy and appease the Jews. Although they had believed in Christ, they had this deep-rooted opinion in their hearts, that they should be the guardians of the law of Moses. But once there, Peter took the opposing side presenting his own experience, saying, "So if God gave them the same gift he gave us who believed in the Lord Jesus Christ, who was I to think that I could stand in God's way?" Then he added, "God, who knows the heart, showed that he accepted them by giving the Holy Spirit to them, just as he did to us. He did not discriminate between us and them, for he purified their hearts by faith. Now, then, why do you try to test God by putting on the necks of Gentiles a yoke that neither we nor our ancestors have been able to bear?" Peter at once strikes down the entire law.[33] It's as if he had said, "We will not keep the law, for we cannot keep it. But we have believed unto salvation through the grace of our Lord Jesus Christ, just as they have." Thus Peter supports his entire argument on the testimony that God had given to the Gentiles the same grace that He had given to the Jews. It's as if he had said, "When I preached to Cornelius, I learned from my own experience, that the Holy Spirit was given to the Gentiles without the law, but only when they heard with faith. Thus they should not be burdened at all with the law. In conclusion, since it is true that neither we nor our parents were ever able to fulfill the law, it is necessary for us to repudiate this belief, that righteousness and salvation comes through the law."[34] And little by little, the Jews began to understand. But the wicked, those who felt offended by this preaching became hardened as time went on.

---

[33] *Petrus semel evertit totam legem.*

[34] *oportet et vos abjicere opinionem, quod per legem contingat justitia et salus.*

The Mission of the Book of Acts of the Apostles

Therefore, the Acts of the Apostles is a collection of the experience and preaching as well as the example of the apostles arguing against the obstinate opinion that righteousness is through the law. That is why we should love and read this book with greater diligence. It contains substantive testimony that brings us comfort and confirms us against the papacy, our own Jews. With our doctrine, we impugn their abominations and nuanced hypocrisy[35] so that we may display the benefits of Christ and His glory. They have nothing of substance to allege against us. The Jews could have alleged against the apostles, since they had received the law and all their ceremonies[36] from God. However, the Papists are no less obstinate when they defend their accursed traditions and abominations. They are no different from the Jews in defending their law (but the Jews did receive their law from God). They glory and boast that they sit as bishops, saying that they have been entrusted with the authority to govern the churches. Thus they would enslave us, bend us over, and force us to say that we are not justified by faith alone but by faith molded and adorned with love.[37] However, we oppose them with the book of Acts. Let them read this book and consider its examples. They will find that the sum of its content and its argument is one and the same: that we are justified by faith alone in Christ without works[38] and that the Holy Spirit is given to us only by hearing with faith the voice of the Gospel. It is not given by the voice of the works of the law.

Thus this is what we teach, listen: "You may fast, give donations, honor your parents, obey the judge, and so on but even with all that you will not be justified. The voice of the law, honor your parents or any other, although you may listen to it, or comply with it, does not justify. Then what? Listen to the voice of the Husband; listen to the preaching of faith.[39] Justification is in the hearing. Why? Because it brings us the Holy Spirit, who declares a person righteous."[40]

From this, we may understand and correctly tell apart the difference between the law and the Gospel. The law never brings the Holy Spirit. It only points out our duty. Thus it does not justify. But the Gospel brings the Holy Spirit because it teaches what we should receive. Thus the law and the Gospel are two doctrines opposite to each other. To establish that righteousness belongs to the law is nothing else but warfare against the Gospel. Moses with his law is an exacting bill collector. He demands that we should work and that we should give. In brief, he demands from us. But on the contrary, the Gospel does not come around demanding payment. Instead, it freely gives. It urges us to take with outstretched hands what it offers. To demand and

---

[35] *larvam.*

[36] *totum cultum.*

[37] *nos non sola fide, sed fide informata caritate justificari.*

[38] *nos sola fide in Christum sine operibus justificari.*

[39] *sermonem fidei.*

[40] *Quia affert Spiritum sanctum, qui justificat.*

to give, to exact and to offer, are two opposing actions and both cannot exist at the same time. What is given, is for me to receive. But what I give, I do not receive but I hand it over to someone else. Thus if the Gospel is a gift, it cannot require anything. On the contrary, the law does not give anything at all. Instead, it only demands and requires strict compliance even demanding the impossible.

About Cornelius in Acts 10

Our adversaries quote this passage against us, citing the example of Cornelius. He was, they say (and such is the testimony of Luke), "a devout man who feared God with all his household; he gave alms generously to the people and prayed constantly to God." Thus due to congruous merit, he was rewarded with the forgiveness of sins and could receive the Holy Spirit. I respond, "Cornelius was a Gentile, and the adversaries cannot deny it for Peter's own words confirm it in Acts 10." "And he said to them, 'You yourselves know that it is unlawful for a Jew to associate with or to visit a Gentile; but God has shown me that I should not call anyone profane or unclean.'" Thus he was a Gentile, he had not been circumcised, didn't keep the law, it hadn't even occurred to him, because the law had nothing at all to do with him. Even so, he was justified and received the Holy Spirit. This very argument, as I have said, that the law does not profit at all[41] to attain righteousness, is the argument throughout the book of Acts.

This should be enough to defend the article of justification, that Cornelius was a Gentile, had not been circumcised, and was not a keeper of the law. Thus he was not justified by the law but by hearing of faith. Therefore, God justifies without the law[42] and consequently the law does not profit at all for righteousness.[43] Otherwise, God would have given the Holy Spirit just to the Jews who had the law and kept it and not to the Gentiles who did not have the law and even less kept it. But God worked totally to the contrary, since the Holy Spirit was given to those who did not keep the law. *Thus experience clearly testifies that the Holy Spirit is given to those who do not fulfill the law.* Therefore, righteousness does not come through the law. This is the way to respond to the objection of the adversaries who do not understand correctly.

Here, once again our adversaries object and say, "It's fine that Cornelius was a Gentile and did not receive the Holy Spirit through the law. However, the text is clear, that 'he was a devout man who feared God and gave alms.' It would seem that due to these works he merited the Holy Spirit that was later given to him." I respond that Cornelius was a pious and holy man according to the Old Testament, but it was

---

[41] *quod lex nihil cooperator ad justitiam.*

[42] *Ergo Deus justificat sine lege.*

[43] In a footnote, Luther emphasizes his previous statement: *Lex non cooperatur ad justitiam,* "the Law does not contribute toward righteousness."

due to his faith in the coming Christ that he like all the patriarchs, prophets, and pious kings, was righteous. Secretly, they had received the Holy Spirit by faith in the coming Christ. But these phony philosophers can't see any difference between faith in the coming Christ and in the Christ that has now come. Therefore, if Cornelius had died before the Christ was revealed, he would not have been condemned, for he had the faith of the patriarchs who were saved by faith alone in the coming Christ[44] (Acts 15). Cornelius continued as a Gentile, uncircumcised, and without the law. However, he worshipped the same God that the patriarchs worshipped by faith in the coming Messiah. But now, once the Messiah had come, it was necessary for Him to be revealed to Cornelius by the apostle Peter, that he should no longer await Him but know for sure that He had already come.

And it is necessary that this article of faith in the coming Christ and in the Christ that has now been revealed (I only speak about this in passing) be made widely known, for seeing that the Christ has already been revealed, we cannot be saved by faith in the coming Christ, but we should believe in Him who has already come, has fulfilled all things, and has abolished the law. Thus it was necessary to guide Cornelius to place his faith not in the Christ who had not yet come, as he believed before, but in the Christ that had already been revealed. Thus faith gives way to faith: "from faith to faith" (Romans 1).

Therefore, the papal scholars are deceived when they claim (in order to support their *opere congrui,* or the work previous to grace) that Cornelius, through the natural and moral work of his reason, merited grace and exoneration by the Holy Spirit. They argue that the qualities of being pious and God fearing are qualities not of a Gentile or natural man but of a spiritual man who is already in the faith. They continue that unless he believed in God, and was a God-fearing man, he could not hope to receive anything at all through prayer. Thus the first commendation Luke mentions about Cornelius is this: "He is a devout and God-fearing man." Then he commends him for his works and donations. Our adversaries do not take this into account but only hold onto this phrase that "he gave alms to the poor." For them, that is enough to establish their congruous merit, or meritorious work they say comes before grace. But first the person, or the tree, should be commended and then the works and the fruit. Cornelius is a good tree, since he is pious and fearful of God. Then he gives good fruit and gives alms, cries out to God, and these fruits are pleasing to God, but they are due to his faith. That is why the angel commends Cornelius, due to his faith in the Christ yet to come. Then he takes him from faith to faith to the other faith in the Christ that has already been revealed, for he tells him "send for Simon, called Peter, and he will tell you what you must do." Just as Cornelius did not have the law before Christ was revealed to him so after Christ was revealed to him, he received neither the law nor circumcision. Thus just as he had not kept the law before, neither did he keep it afterward.

---

[44] *qui sola fide future Christi salvati sunt.*

This argument is affirmed by its conclusion: Cornelius was justified without the law. Thus the law does not justify.[45]

Naaman, the Syrian

Similarly, Naaman the Syrian was doubtless a good and pious man who had a reverent and religious opinion of God (2 Kings 5:1ff). And although he was a Gentile and did not belong to Moses' kingdom, which was at its height at that time, his flesh was cleansed. The God of Israel was revealed to him, and he received the Holy Spirit, for he said, "I know that there is no God in all the earth, but in Israel." Naaman does not do a thing, he does not keep the law, nor has he been circumcised. He just pleads that he may be permitted to take with him some of the soil of the land, as much as two mules could bear. Further, it seemed that his faith was not idle. He speaks with Elisha the prophet with these words: "Your servant will from now on offer neither burnt offering nor sacrifice to other gods, but to the Lord. In this matter may the Lord pardon your servant: when my master goes into the house of Rimmon to worship there, leaning on my arm, and I bow myself in the house of Rimmon, when I bow myself in the house of Rimmon, the Lord pardon your servant in this matter." At that, the prophet tells him, "Go in peace." Thus he was justified. When a Jew hears this, he murmurs furiously, saying, "What? A Gentile justified without keeping the law? Should he even be compared with us who are circumcised?"

The Gentiles Were Justified without the Law, Even When the Law and the Covenant Were Still Binding.

Therefore, God, in times past, when Moses' kingdom still reigned and flourished, revealed that He justified without the law, as was the case when He justified many kings in Egypt and Babylon. Job is included, as were people from many other Eastern nations. Nineveh, that great city, was also justified and received God's promise that it would not be destroyed. But on account of what? It was not because it heard and fulfilled the law. It was because Nineveh believed God's word preached by Jonah. That is what the prophet stated: "So the people of Nineveh believed God, and proclaimed a fast, and put on sackcloth." In other words, they repented. Our adversaries astutely fly over this word *believed*. But everything flows from that. You will not find that Jonah says, "And the people of Nineveh received the law of Moses, were circumcised, offered sacrifices, and fulfilled the vows of the law." On the contrary, it says that once they believed the word, they repented and dressed in sackcloth and ashes.

---

[45] *Cornelius sine lege justificatus est, igitur lex non justificat.*

All this happened before Christ was revealed, under the reign of the faith that trusted in the Christ yet to come. If back then the Gentiles were justified without the law and secretly received the Holy Spirit when the law still reigned, why then should the law now be a requirement as a condition of righteousness, when the Christ that has come has abolished it? That is why this is a powerful argument that has support in the experience of the Galatians: "Did you receive the Spirit by the works of the law or by hearing of faith?" That is why they were compelled to recognize that before hearing Paul's preaching they had not heard that there was even a Holy Spirit. But when he preached the Gospel, it was then when they received the Holy Spirit.

Today, we, under the conviction of our own conscience, are also compelled to confess that the Holy Spirit is not poured out due to the keeping of the law but by the hearing of faith. There are many who even to this day in the papacy have strenuously and assiduously studied, kept the law, the decrees of the fathers, and the traditions of the Pope. Some with endless exercises, prayers, and vigils have so exhausted and weakened their bodies that afterward became altogether useless. Despite all that, they achieved nothing more than to mercilessly torment and afflict themselves. They were never able to appease their consciences and obtain peace in Christ. They continually doubted God's goodwill toward them. But now, since the Gospel teaches that the law and works do not justify but faith alone in Jesus Christ, things have changed. There's now a flow of certainty in knowledge and understanding, a conscience overflowing with peaceful joy, a right judgment concerning all aspects of life, and all else. The believers can now easily judge the papacy, declaring that all its religious orders and traditions are wickedness. That's something they could not do before. Blindness was so great all over the world that we thought those works invented by men (which were not only outside of God's will but also contrary to His command) were better than those works performed by the judges, the heads of the household, the children, and those who serve according to God's commands.

Certainly, we should have learned from the word of God that the religious orders of the Papists (the ones they call holy) are wicked, for there is no commandment from God or testimony from Scripture that commands them. On the other hand, there are orders for life given by God's word and command that are holy and ordained by Him. However, at that time, we were wrapped up in such horrible darkness that we could not judge correctly with respect to anything. But now, since the clear light of the Gospel has appeared, everything in the world given to us for life is for us to judge. Boldly, we can pronounce by God's word that the status of servants, which according to the world is the lowest, before God is more pleasing than all the religious orders of the Papists put together, for according to the same word, He commends, approves, and adorns the condition of servants and not the orders of monks, friars, and the like. Therefore, this argument, rooted in experience, should prevail in our favor. Although there are many in the papacy who have performed many marvelous and great works, they were never able to be certain of God's favor toward them. Instead, they always harbored doubts. They were never able to attain to the knowledge of God nor of themselves nor of His calling. They were never able to feel the witness of the Holy Spirit in their hearts. But now that the light of the Gospel has been revealed, they are firmly instructed in all these things by the hearing of faith.

It's not without reason that I insist on these matters. Otherwise it would just seem as something insignificant, that the Holy Spirit is given by the hearing of faith, that nothing else is required of us, that we renounce all our good works and give ourselves entirely to the hearing of the Gospel. The heart of man cannot understand or believe that such a great treasure, the Holy Spirit, is given to us just as we listen with faith. It would rather understand it like this: Forgiveness of sins, freedom from death, receiving the Holy Spirit, and obtaining righteousness are matters of great import. Thus if you wish to obtain these priceless benefits, you should fulfill something equally valuable and weighty. The devil approves this opinion, and it pleases him, puffing it up in our hearts. That's why when reason hears that you can't do a thing to attain the forgiveness of sins but listen to the word of God, very soon it cries out, "I object! You hardly value the forgiveness of sins!" But this priceless gift is so great that we cannot believe it. And it's precisely because this incomparable treasure is freely offered that it's so easily despised.

However, it's necessary that we learn that forgiveness of sins, Christ, and the Holy Spirit are freely given to us with just the preaching of faith, notwithstanding our horrible sins, and lacking all merit. Further, we should not weigh the greatness of what is given to us and how much we don't deserve it at all, for the greatness of the gift and the fact that we don't merit it at all frighten us away. We should think that it pleases God to give us this unspeakable gift, which we don't deserve at all. As Christ says in Luke, "Fear not, little flock, for it is your Father's good pleasure to give you," he says, "the kingdom" (Luke 12:32). To whom? To you, undeserving, but he claims us as his little flock. If I then being so small and the gift being so great (no, the greatest ever that God has given to me), should also think that He is also great, the only great, the one who gives it. If he offers it and gives it, I should not consider my own sin and how undeserving I am, for it is the good pleasure of the Father toward me, for He is the giver. Therefore, I receive the greatness of the gift with joy and happiness. I am grateful for such a priceless gift given to me altogether freely. I emphasize that it is given to me just at the hearing of faith and that I am not worthy to receive it.

Here, once again reason is stubborn and gets offended. It scolds us, saying, "Why do you teach people that they don't have to do anything to receive such huge and priceless gift? That all they must do is listen to God's word? It seems you're doing nothing but disrespecting grace in a big way. You're teaching people to feel all assured, to become lazy and depraved, and to lean back and relax! Thus all should be cautioned to work and exercise in righteousness so that they may be able to reach and grasp the gift." Some time ago, Pelagius's followers objected in the same way against the Christians. But listen to what Paul says here in this text: "They received the Holy Spirit." They did not receive it due to their labor or tireless effort nor by the works of the law but by "the hearing of faith." In brief, listen to what Christ Himself said when He answered Martha when she was so stressed out[46] and could hardly hear what her sister Mary was listening to at the feet of Jesus as she heard His word, leaving Mary all by herself doing the chores. "Martha, Martha," He said, "Martha, Martha, you are anxious and troubled about many things, but one thing is needed. Mary has chosen the good part, which will not be taken away from her." Thus you become a Christian not because of what you do but because of what you hear. It follows then that whoever wants to exercise doing righteous works must first want to exercise by listening to the Gospel, for when you have heard and received the Gospel, then you will give thanks to God with a glad and joyful heart. Then afterward, give every effort in those good works that will follow your hearing of faith. Thus you will walk peacefully in the light, who is Christ, and resolved that you will do whatever works you wish. They will not be the works of hypocrisy but truly those works that are pleasing to God and according to what He orders. Then all your good works will condemn those hypocritical works performed under the guise of free will.[47]

Our adversaries believe that the faith by which we receive the Holy Spirit is but something insignificantly small. But from my own experience, I've come to realize that faith is immensely difficult. All those who together with me have grasped faith, share the same thought. It's easy to say that the Holy Spirit is received just at the hearing of faith. But it is not so easy when you hear the voice of faith, to grasp it, believe it, and retain it. That is why, when you hear me say that Christ is the Lamb of God sacrificed for your sins, make sure you listen effectively. Paul, right on the mark, called it the "hearing of faith" and not the "word of faith" (although there's not a great difference). It's that word that when you hear it, you'll believe it. It won't be just my voice that you hear but the voice that will penetrate your heart so that you will trust it. That indeed is the hearing of faith by which you receive the Holy Spirit. But once you have received the Holy Spirit then you will mortify your flesh!

The faithful realize from their own experience that they find happiness when they hear the word, grasp, and embrace it. They abandon this opinion of the law and their own righteousness full of faith, but in their flesh, they feel a powerful resistance against the spirit. Reason and the flesh become accomplices. They say, "You should be circumcised and keep the law." This phrase cannot be totally uprooted from our minds. Instead, it sticks firmly to the hearts of all the faithful. That is why the faithful suffer a constant conflict between the hearing of faith and the works of the law. The conscience always murmurs and thinks this is all too easy that just by hearing the word we are promised righteousness, the Holy Spirit,

---

[46] *sollicitae, genitive feminine singular of sollicitus,* "troubled, engaged, upset, disturbed, anxious, solicitous; afflicted." "Stressed out" would be the equivalent English term.

[47] *omnes larvas electiriorum operum.*

and eternal life. But once we face a difficult trial, tell me then if it's easy to hear the word of faith. Indeed, the One who gives it is great. Further, He gives many great things freely and without reproach. However, your abilities harden and your faith is weak and these war against you so that you cannot receive this gift. It only takes a murmur of objection in your conscience, and a little "you should" begins to sound without ceasing in your head. But be firm and resist, until you overcome that "you should do." That is how your faith will grow little by little, and this opinion of the righteousness of the law will also diminish. However, you cannot achieve this without great conflict.

LECTURE 16: Friday, August 28

VERSE 3. Are you so foolish? Having started with the Spirit, are you now ending[48] with the flesh?

He has concluded the argument that the Holy Spirit does not come by the works of the law but through the preaching of faith. From here on, he begins to admonish and alert them about a double danger or quandary. In the first, he says, "Are you so foolish? Having started with the Spirit, are you now ending with the flesh?" The other one follows: "Did you suffer so many things in vain?" It's as if he'd said, "You began in the Spirit," meaning "you had an excellent beginning in your religion." A while later he says, "You ran well. But where did you end up? What a pity! Now you're ending up in the flesh!"

Here, Paul sets the spirit against the flesh. As I said before, he does not refer to the flesh as lustful desires, animal passions, or sensual appetites. Here, he is not warning against lust and such fleshly desires. Here, he is pleading in favor of the forgiveness of sins, a justified conscience, obtaining righteousness before God, and freedom from the law, sin, and death. However, he says here that by abandoning the Spirit they have ended up in the flesh. Thus flesh here should be understood as that same righteousness and wisdom of the flesh, the ponderings of reason, which seeks to be justified through the law. Here, Paul calls "flesh" the highest human excellence, such as the wisdom of reason and even the efforts to be justified through the law. Whatever people call the best and most effective capabilities in one's self, Paul calls the flesh—in other words, the totality of reason's wisdom and the righteousness of the law itself!

We must pay careful attention to this text given the slander and the reasoning of the Pope's followers. They have turned this text around against us, saying that in the papacy we began well with the Spirit. But now that we are married and have a wife, we've ended up in the flesh. As if the spiritual life was contingent on

---

[48] *consummamini.*

being married or single. Even someone who is single will not be happy with just one lover, but with many. Would not that affect his spiritual life? They're out of their minds; they don't understand what's the spirit or the flesh. The spirit is all that goes on inside of us due to the Spirit. The flesh is all that is done in us according to the flesh, without the Spirit. Thus all the duties of a Christian, such as loving his wife, rearing his children, governing his home, and such things (the things they call worldly and of the flesh) are the fruit of the Spirit. But these blind vultures cannot discern between the vices and the good gifts given by God.

Take note of what Paul says here: the Galatians began in the Spirit. Now he should add the active mode: "You finished in the flesh."[49] However, he does not say it that way. Instead, he says in the passive mode, "You are being finished off in the flesh."[50] The righteousness of the law, which Paul here labels as the righteousness of the flesh, is far from justifying anyone. So much so that those who turn their backs after receiving the Spirit by the hearing of faith are all finished up and come to their wits' end—that is, they end up totally destroyed. Thus all who teach the keeping of the law for justification, even though their intention may be to appease people's consciences, in fact end up hurting them the most. They would like to think they are leading people to justification, but the truth is they've done nothing but damn them![51]

Paul is always watching out of the corner of his eyes for the false apostles. They continued urging the law, saying, "Faith in Christ alone does not remove sin, does not appease God's wrath, and does not justify. Thus if you'd like to receive those benefits, you should not only believe in Christ but also keep the law, be circumcised, observe the feasts, the sacrifices, etc. That is how you will be delivered from sin, God's wrath, and eternal death." Paul said, "On the contrary! With those actions you are establishing wickedness, provoking God's wrath, adding sin to sin, and smothering the Spirit, and in the end, you fall from grace and reject it altogether. When it's done, teachers and disciples end up in the flesh." This is the first danger of which he puts the Galatians on alert. If they continue to seek justification through the law, they will lose their spirit, and throw away their good beginning and end up in despair.

VERSE 4. Have you suffered so much in vain?

Another danger or hazard that Paul points out is this: "Have you suffered so many things in vain?" It's as if he'd said, "Notice how well you got started along the way but how miserably you wasted the first part of the race. Further, you've also lost the first fruits of the Spirit, since you've fallen once again into the ministry of sin

---

[49] *Nunc carne consummatis.*

[50] *Carne ut urne consummamini.*

[51] *dum eas justificare volunt, damnat.*

and death and in the mortifying slavery of the law. But now remember what you've already suffered for the sake of the Gospel and for the name of Christ. You have been dispossessed of your earthly goods and you have suffered endless slander and reproach, risking not only your bodies but even your lives! You were all happy and willingly were headed in the right direction. You taught a pure doctrine, you lived piously, and constantly suffered many ills for the name of Christ. But now all is lost, including the doctrine of your faith, your suffering, the Spirit, and its fruit in you."

Here, we see clearly the anguish brought by the righteousness of the law and human righteousness. Those who place their confidence in these things immediately lose countless benefits. Look around you. All the anguish and despair at having lost such priceless glory and confident conscience before God and also of having withstood such great and painful trials such as the loss of goods, wife, children, life and limb, and then having suffered all this in vain? You can gather up a lot of material in these two texts that will help you recommend[52] how great is the law and human righteousness. If only every believer would climb up on the roof of his house and from there shout about the good beginning they had in the Spirit and then retell all the trials suffered for the sake of Christ. But there is no eloquence that could express these things. Paul pleads for these priceless gifts, to wit, God's glory and victory over the world, the flesh and the devil and righteousness and eternal life. On the other hand, sin, desperation, eternal death, and hell. To think that in an instant we lose all these incomparable gifts and win all that horrible endless despair, all due to those false teachers, who lead us away from the truth of the Gospel toward that false doctrine. And they achieve it not only easily but also with great performances of pious devotion!

VERSE 4. If it really was in vain.

He adds this as if by way of correction. He wants to mitigate the previous reproof, which was quite harsh. He does it as an apostle, not wanting to frighten them beyond measure. Even though he reproves them, he always does it like this, pouring soft oil, lest he drive them to despair.

Thus he said, "If it really was in vain." It's as if he had said, "I don't leave you hopeless. But if you end up this way in the flesh, if you continue following the righteousness of the law and abandon the Spirit, as you've already changed course, then know for sure that all your glory and confidence you may have in God is in vain and all your afflictions worthless. Indeed, it is necessary for me to talk to you in this rather strong tone. I must be fervent and defensive, somewhat cutting, in

---

[52] During the lecture, Luther used the Greek εγκωμιον, "praiseworthy." Once again, Luther in front of his students uses the rhetoric of sarcasm and irony to teach the opposite.

my rebuke, due to the gravity of the subject. Otherwise, you may think it is a small matter to reject Paul's doctrine and receive another. Even so, I don't discourage you altogether so that you may repent and change course. Sickly children full of sores cannot be abandoned but must be loved and nurtured even more than those who aren't sick." Thus Paul as an astute physician lays all the blame in a certain way on the false apostles, the authors and only cause of this fatal illness. But on the contrary, he is very delicate with the Galatians, trying to cure them with his special treatment. We should follow this example in reproving the weak, to cure their illness, not forgetting to value and comfort them. However, if we are too rough with them, they can fall into despair without hope.

VERSE 5. Does he who supplies the Spirit to you and works miracles among you do so by works of the law, or by hearing with faith?

This argument, grounded on the experience of the Galatians is quite pleasing to the apostle. Once he had rebuked and shaken them, warning them of their double danger, now he repeats, expanding a bit more, saying, "He who supplies to you" etc. In other words, you've received not only the Spirit by the hearing of faith but everything they had experienced and done was given by the hearing of faith. It's as if he'd said, "It wasn't enough that God gave you the Spirit, but God Himself has also enriched you with the gifts of the Spirit and has given them growth. Thus once you received the Spirit, the Spirit would always grow, becoming more fruitful among you." Thus it is clear the Galatians had worked miracles, or at least had demonstrated the fruits of faith that disciples of the true Gospel will always display. In another place, Paul says, "Because the kingdom of God does not consist in words, but in power." This power is not only the ease of words with which to talk about God's kingdom. It is also certainly true to show that God by means of His Spirit is effective in us. Thus before, in the second chapter, he says about himself, "For God, who was at work in Peter as an apostle to the circumcised, was also at work in me as an apostle to the Gentiles" (Galatians 2).

When a preacher preaches like that, the word is never without fruit. Instead, it is effective in the hearers' hearts. In other words, when faith comes, followed by hope, love, and patience, it is because God has given His Spirit and works marvelous deeds[53] among those who hear. Similarly, Paul says here, "God has given His Spirit to the Galatians and through them has worked miracles." It's as if he had said, "Because of my preaching, God not only obtained your faith but also your pious living, many fruits of faith, and many afflictions suffered. Also, through the same power of the Holy Spirit, you who were adulterers, given to anger, impatient, covetous, and, in fact, enemies have now become generous, chaste, kind, patient, and loving toward

---

[53] *virtutes*, literally "powers." Middleton translates this as "miracles."

your neighbors." Later, he gives testimony about them that they received him as an angel from God (Galatians 4:14, 15). He speaks as if Christ Himself had sent him, and they loved him so much that they would have given their own eyes for him.

It is well and good to love your neighbor so unselfishly that you would part with your money, goods, and even your eyes and all you have for your salvation and even more to suffer patiently adversity and affliction; all these indeed are powerful virtues of the Spirit.[54] "All these powers,"[55] he says, "you received and enjoyed before these false teachers came among you. However, you received these fruits not by the law but from God who supplied them to you, and the Spirit grew daily among you. The Gospel progressed with joy among you, in the teaching and in your faith, working, and suffering. Now, seeing that you know these things (your own consciences testify it is true), why are you no longer displaying these powers as before? Why do you no longer teach with the truth? Why aren't you faithful in your belief; why won't you live piously anymore? Why will you no longer receive Paul as an angel from God or as Jesus Christ? Would you no longer give your eyes for me? What happened, I say, that this burning zeal you had has now grown cold toward me? Why do you now despise me and prefer the false apostles who seduce you mercilessly?"

The same has happened with us today. When we preached the Gospel for the first time, there were many who favored our doctrine, they held us in high esteem. After our preaching, the powers and the fruit of faith followed.[56] But then, what happened? Soon, there arose certain fanatical empty heads[57] destroying everything we had sown after investing a great deal of time and suffering much distress. They made us look repulsive before those who had loved us so much at first and at first had received our doctrine with gratitude. So much so that for them our name is the most despised. But the author of such perfidy is the devil who opposes us among his followers with contrary powers.[58] But they are struggling against the powers[59] of the Holy Spirit. Therefore, says the apostle, the experience you've had, oh Galatians, should teach you that your excellent powers did not proceed from the works of the law. You didn't have them before you heard my preaching of faith, nor do you have them now when the false apostles reign among you.

Similarly, today we ask of those who boast the name of "evangelicals" and who claim to have been delivered from the tyranny of the Pope, "Have you been delivered from the Pope's tyranny and have you obtained freedom in Christ through the Anabaptists and other fanatical empty heads or through us who preach faith in Jesus

---

[54] Rörer: *virtutes Spiritus sancti.*

[55] *virtutes.*

[56] *virtutes et fructus fide.* Middleton translates this as "the fruits and the effects."

[57] *fanatici spiritus.* Middleton translates this as "cold and sick heads"; Watson uses "light and brain-sick heads."

[58] *contrarias virtutes.* Middleton translates this as "contrary works."

[59] *virtutibus Spiritus sancti.* Middleton translates this as "works."

Christ?" If they would own up to the truth, they would confess, "No doubt through the preaching of faith." Indeed, it is true that at the beginning of our preaching, the doctrine of faith was headed in the right direction. Tumbling down went the papal pardons, purgatory, vows, masses, and such abominations, which were leading to the final ruin of the papacy. No one could rightfully condemn us, since our doctrine was pure. We lifted and comforted many ruined consciences, which for long had suffered oppression from the traditions of men under the papacy, which was nothing but the most veritable tyranny and slaughterhouse of the conscience.[60] Thus many gave thanks to God that through the Gospel (which by God's grace we were the first to preach it), they were powerfully freed from this trap and slaughterhouse of the conscience. But then these souls appeared. *They denied the bodily presence of Christ in the Supper, profaned baptism, destroyed the images, and abolished all the ceremonies, attempting to overthrow the papacy all at once. However, all they wanted was to tarnish our good name. In consequence, our doctrine got a bad reputation!* The gossip went around that there was infighting among the professors. As a result, many were greatly offended and fell from the truth. Thus they gave comfort to the papacy that we, together with our doctrine, would soon end up in nothing, and for that reason, they would recoup their previous dignity and authority once more.

Therefore, the false apostles vehemently disputed that the Galatians, now that they had been justified by faith in Christ, should go on to circumcision and observe the law of Moses. Otherwise, they could not be freed from their sins, God's wrath, and receive the Holy Spirit. However, all they did was burden them with even more sins, for sin does not disappear through the law,[61] nor is the Holy Spirit given by its observance. The law only works wrath and drives men to great terror. Thus these out of control hot heads have done nothing else but damage the church. Instead, of taking away the papacy's self-assurance, they have established the papacy.

If they would only have continued of one accord as they began, teaching and diligently urging the article of justification![62] If only they had persevered teaching that we are justified neither by the righteousness of the law nor by our own righteousness but by faith alone in Jesus Christ.[63] Without doubt, just this one article, little by little, would have overthrown the entire papacy, together with their brotherhoods, the pardons, the religious orders, relics, ceremonies, invocation of the saints, purgatory, masses, vigils, vows, and other infinite abominations. But they, in contempt of the teaching of faith and true Christian righteousness, have gone their own way, causing great damage to sound doctrine and the churches. *There's a great similarity between what's happened and the German proverb about those who*

---

[60] Luther's footnote: *Papatus carnificina conscientiarum,* "the papacy is the slaughterhouse of the conscience."

[61] *quia per legem non auferuntur peccata.*

[62] *diligenter ursissent articulum justificationis.*

[63] *quod neque legis, neque propria justitia, sed sola fide in Christum justificamur.*

fish in front of the nets. "Those who try to catch fish in front of the nets with their bare hands, go home empty handed."

Thus the papacy has lost its crest not due to the tumults of the sectarians, but due to the preaching of the article of justification.[64] *This article has not only weakened the kingdom of the Antichrist but has also sustained and defended us against its violence. If we had not taken shelter under it from the beginning, by now the sectarians would have disappeared, and we would not be far behind. But the sectarians are far from recognizing this benefit. As the psalmist says, they have returned evil for good, hate for love, and attack us with great hostility (Psalm 109:5). The article of justification, our only defense not only against the strength and wiles of men but also against the gates of hell is this: by faith alone in Christ, without any work of our own, we are declared righteous and saved!*[65] *And if we are so justified (if there was any other way we'd have to throw away the Scriptures), then without doubt it follows that we are not declared righteous because we are monks, take vows, say or hear mass, or any other work. Just with this, without abolishing anything external, without tumult, human strength, or injuring the Sacraments, but by the Spirit alone, the papacy comes toppling down.*[66] *The victory is not even ours but Christ's, whose benefit we preach and illumine.*

The issue itself confirms what I'm saying now. At that time, when the papacy began to tremble and topple, the sectarians did nothing, for they could do nothing. They didn't press the issue; they kept silent. On the other hand, we didn't teach or press anything else but this article of justification. This article is the only thing that at the beginning threatened the authority of the Pope and plundered his kingdom. But when the sectarians saw the papacy trembling and stumbling, and the fish were headed for the net, they set out to destroy and annihilate the papacy with one swift blow.[67] *They wanted to take away the glory from us and with their own hands catch the fish trapped at the net. But they took it as a sport and didn't catch a single one, all of them got away. Just as the false apostles were intent on bringing righteousness to the Galatians, so the sectarians tried to overthrow the papacy with their tumults. The images and abuses of the church would have fallen on their own weight if only they would have taught the article of justification. But they were propelled by braggadocio.*[68] *They would have been more than happy to proclaim that it was they who overthrew the papacy. Therefore, they neglected the article of justification, brewed*

---

[64] *sed per praedicationem articuli de justificatione.*

[65] *Articulus justificationis is est, sola fide in Christum, sine operibus nos pronuntiari justos et salvari.*

[66] *solo Spiritu praecipitatur papatus.*

[67] Please note that this entire section is in italics, which means it was omitted from the first English translations. As with other sections in *italics*, it is recovered here for this edition.

[68] In the Latin text, Luther uses the Greek word κενοδοξια.

up tumults that almost overwhelmed us, and confirmed the papacy's abominations. Such is the success of our achievements when we do not seek God's glory but our own.

Neither the Pope nor the devil with his demons fear these tumults but only the doctrine of faith. This is the doctrine that preaches that Christ is the only conqueror over sin, death, and the devil. That is what is feared, for it destroys his kingdom and (as I've said before) sustains and shelters us to this day against the gates of hell. And if we did not grasp onto this anchor, we would see ourselves compelled to once again worship the Pope, nor would there be any way or reason[69] to resist him. If I were to join up with the sectarians, my conscience would be confounded. Without any right, they oppose the Pope, since all they do is seek their own glory and not the glory of God. Therefore, if the only weapons we had were what they offer, I would not dare to combat the papacy or even less to plunder it.

However, they say, "The Pope is the Antichrist!" No doubt it is so. But in turn, he responds that he has a ministry of teaching that corresponds to him, that in his person resides the authority to administer the Sacraments, of binding and unbinding, and that this right is his by apostolic succession. Therefore, you won't topple him from his pedestal by creating mayhem. You overthrow the Pope like this: "Oh Pope! I would kiss your feet, acknowledge you as 'Pontifex Maximus,'[70] if only you would worship my Christ and admitted that we have remission of sins and eternal life through His death and resurrection and not by observing your traditions. If you would only concede this, I would not take away your crown and authority. But if you do not admit it, I will constantly cry out that you are the Antichrist and declare that all your worship and religiosity are not only a denial of God but supreme blasphemy against God and pure idolatry." The sectarians will not do this. By visible force they seek to remove the Pope's crown and authority, Thus their entire effort is in vain. But the wickedness and abominations of the Pope must be exposed before anything else. Why? He has deceived the entire world with his robe of holiness and religiosity. If I continue this effort, we'll see if anything remains thereafter because I will remove the kernels and leave him the cob. But on the contrary, they attempt to snatch the cob but leave him the kernels.

In summary, these powerful virtues[71] are not revealed through the works of the law, neither are they by the external works urged by the sectarians. The church gains nothing except tumults, confusion, and impediments to the Spirit. This is what experience testifies. They cannot overthrow the Pope toppling images and attempting against the Sacraments. Instead, they puffed up his pride. But through the Spirit he has been and is diminished. Meaning, by the preaching of faith, which testifies that Christ was given over for our sins. With this, the righteousness and slavery of the papal laws will fall all by themselves.

Meanwhile and nonetheless, I've often said it and will say it again that I am willing to observe the traditions of the Pope. Only if he'd just unbind the consciences of

---

[69] ratio.

[70] Latin for "High Priest."

[71] non factae sunt virtutes.

people so that they stop thinking they are justified when they keep them but condemned if they do not. But he will not do this. Because if he didn't bind the conscience to his traditions, from where would he get his power? Therefore, his only stress is to bind the consciences of men and hold them captive to his laws. That's where the following proverb comes from: "You won't be saved unless you obey the Roman Holy See, as well as the thunder and lightning of his papal bullas. Whoever is so fearless as to disobey them, let him know he will have to answer before the wrath of God Almighty!" With this, he takes away salvation from all those who will not keep his laws. On the contrary, he promises eternal life to all who keep them. That's how he pushes us toward the net of the righteousness of works, as if no one could be justified and saved without observing his laws. In brief, he does not mention faith at all, not even a word, but teaches only his issues. But if he would admit that all his laws are worthless for obtaining righteousness before God, then I, myself, would grant him much. But then his kingdom would come toppling down on its own, for if the Pope lost his power to save and condemn, that would be the final end of the Pope; he would be nothing but a mere idol. In brief, the righteousness of the heart ignores all laws, not only the Pope's but also Moses' law, for true righteousness does not proceed from the works of the law but from the hearing of faith. Then what follows are the powers and the fruits of the Spirit.

VERSE 6. So also Abraham "believed God, and it was credited to him as righteousness."

Up to now, Paul has reasoned based on the Galatians' experience, and he presses this argument vehemently. He tells them, "You have believed, and believing, you have done miracles and demonstrated notable signs.[72] Further, you have suffered many afflictions. All this is by the workings and operation not of the law but of the Holy Spirit." The Galatians saw themselves compelled to confess it, since they could not deny these things so clear before their eyes, proven by their senses. That is why this argument based on their experience is so powerful.

Now he adds the example of Abraham and reviews the testimony of Scripture. The first is that of Genesis 15:6, he "believed God" etc. Here, the apostle powerfully refutes the opposite, as he did in his Epistle to the Romans. There he said, "If Abraham was justified by the works of the law, he has a righteousness to boast about but not before God but before men" (Romans 4:2, 3). Before God, there is nothing in him except sin and wrath. But he had been justified before God not because of what he did but because he believed, for the Scripture says, "Abraham believed God, and it was counted to him as righteousness." Here, Paul highlights and expands this teaching for it is valuable. He said about Abraham, "Without weakening in his faith, he faced the fact that his body was as good as dead—since he was about a hundred years old—and that Sarah's womb was also dead. Yet he

---

[72] *virtutes.*

did not waver through unbelief regarding the promise of God but was strengthened in his faith and gave glory to God being fully persuaded that God had power to do what he had promised. Therefore, 'it was credited to him as righteousness.' The words 'it was credited to him' were written not for him alone but also for us."

With these words, "Abraham believed," Paul makes of faith the greatest worship, the greatest duty, the best obedience, and the greatest sacrifice. Whoever thinks he's a good public speaker, let him expound on this, and will see the great power of faith and that the power of faith is infinite and priceless. It glorifies God, and it is the greatest service that can be rendered to Him. To give glory to God, then, is to believe Him, declare Him to be true, wise, just, merciful, powerful. In brief, recognize Him as the author and giver of everything that is good. This is not the work of reason but of faith. Faith is the fulfillment of the divine nature (if we could say it that way); it is Divinity's creative power, not within the substance of God, but in us.[73] For without faith, God cannot find in us His glory, wisdom, righteousness, truth, mercy, etc. In summary, where there is no faith, there is no majestic worship or divine service at all that could be rendered to God. This is the most that God requires of man, that he should render to God glory and divinity. He should not take God as an idol but as God who considers, listens, demonstrates kindness, and comes to his aid. Once this is done, God has His full and perfect divinity. He has all that a faithful heart could attribute to Him. Everyone who is able to render this glory to God has the wisdom of wisdom, the righteousness of righteousness, the religion of religion, and the sacrifice of sacrifice. By this, we can perceive how exalted and excellent is the righteousness of faith. On the other hand, how horrifying and immense is the sin of unbelief.

Everyone who believes God's word, like Abraham, is righteous before God because he has faith, which glorifies God. He renders to God what God deserves (*that's how jurors define the righteous man*). Faith says, "I believe you, oh God, when you make your declarations." But what does God declare? Impossible things, lies, nonsense, absurdities, abominable, heretical, and devilish, that's what reason will tell you if you consult with it, for, what could be more absurd, foolish, and impossible than for God to tell Abraham that he'd have a son from the infertile and worn out body of Sarah, his wife?

If we were to follow the dictates of reason, God presents absurd and impossible things when the article of faith is explained to us. Reason indeed thinks it's ridiculous and foolish that in the Lord's Supper we are offered the body and the blood of Christ, that baptism is the basin of the new birth and the renewal of the Holy Spirit, that the dead will rise at the last day, that Christ the Son of God was conceived and was within the womb of the Virgin Mary, that He was born and then suffered the most egregious death on the cross, that He rose again, that He is now seated at

---

[73] *ea consummat divinitatem, et u tita dicom, creatrix est divinitatis, non in susbtantia dei, sed in nobis.*

the right hand of God the Father, that He has power over heaven and earth. For this reason, Paul called the Gospel of Christ crucified, the word of the cross and the foolishness of preaching to the Jews a stumbling stone and to the Gentiles a meaningless doctrine. Reason cannot understand that to hear the word of God and to believe it is the highest worship rendered to God.[74] Reason thinks that the things it chooses and does with good intentions (as they call them) and are of their own devotion honor God. Therefore, when God pronounces Himself, reason judges His word as heresy and as the word of the devil, for it seems foolish and ridiculous.

However, faith kills reason and beheads the beast that not even the entire world has been able to kill. But Abraham was able to kill it by God's word of faith, by which God promised him seed through Sarah, who was not only more than ninety years old but was also infertile and past her reproductive years. Faith struggled with reason within Abraham. But it was there where it won the victory, it killed and sacrificed reason, the cruelest and most pestilent enemy of God. In the same way, all the faithful together with Abraham enter into the darkness of faith, but it is then when they kill reason, saying, "Reason, you are a fool, you don't know how to taste the things that belong to God. So don't even talk to me. Keep your peace. Don't judge but listen to God's word and believe it." That's how the faithful kill such a beast, the biggest in the whole world, and offer God the greatest sacrifice and service pleasing to Him.

By comparison to this sacrifice of the faithful, all the religions of all the nations and all the works of all the monks and merit hoarders are nothing, because as I said at the outset, through this sacrifice, they demolish reason, that great and powerful enemy of God, for reason despises God, denies His wisdom, righteousness, power, truth, mercy, majesty, and divinity. Further, through that same sacrifice, the faithful render glory to God—that is, they believe that He is righteous, good, faithful, and true. They believe that He can do all things, that all His words are holy, true, living, and effective. All this is the most acceptable obedience to God. Thus there can be no greater and holier religion throughout the whole world nor any more pleasing service to God than faith itself.

On the contrary, the legalists and others like them who seek righteousness through their own works lack faith, no matter how many things they may do. They fast, pray, lose sleep, and carry crosses on their backs. But since they think they are appeasing God's wrath and through those works merit God's grace, they do not glorify God, which is to say that they don't consider Him merciful, true, and who keeps His promise. Instead, they think He is a furious judge who must be appeased with works, and through all these means, they despise God, they make Him a liar by rebuffing His promises and they deny Christ and all His benefits. In conclusion, they expel God from His throne and then sit on it. That's because when they reject and despise God's word, they choose those works that God never required. They think God is pleased with them and wait for His rewards. Thus they don't demolish reason, that powerful enemy of God. Instead, they urge reason on. They strip God

---

[74] *summum cultum esse.*

of His majesty and divinity and attribute these to their own works. But faith alone renders to God the glory, as Paul testified regarding Abraham (Romans 4:3). "He staggered not at the promise of God through unbelief but was strong in faith, giving glory to God, and was fully persuaded that what he had promised he was able also to perform. Therefore, it was imputed to him for righteousness."[75]

Christian Righteousness Consists of Faith in the Heart and Imputation[76] from God

He added this phrase from Genesis chapter 15 for good reason: "And it was imputed to him for righteousness."[77] That is because Christian righteousness consists of two parts: One, faith in the heart and two, imputation declared by God.[78] Faith indeed is the initial provision for righteousness, yet it is not enough; even after faith there remain certain residues of sin in our flesh. Abraham began with faith sacrificing reason yet the sacrifice was over only when he died.[79] Therefore, it is necessary to add the other part of righteousness—that is, the divine declaration that righteousness is imputed to us. That is how we know with all assurance that our justification is complete.[80] Faith is incomplete in its offering to God, for it is imperfect. Our faith is nothing but a tiny spark of faith,[81] which is hardly able to render to God His divine majesty. We have received the first fruits of the spirit, yet the other tenths are still missing. Further, reason does not die altogether in this life. This is true due to our lust, wrath, impatience, and other fruits of the flesh and the unbelief that remains in us. Yes, even the most pious don't experience full and continuous joy in God. They continue in their various passions, sometimes

---

[75] As in other places, Luther quotes the Scripture but does not give the Biblical citation.

[76] The biblical doctrine of imputation has been largely lost to twenty-first-century Christianity. Nonetheless, as Luther affirms in this commentary, the imputation of righteousness (or justification) is the central article or foundational truth of Christianity. *Imputation* is a term still used and understood in criminal and civil law. It means to attribute a certain action or value to an individual or a group by means of a judicial declaration. For example, in the negative sense, someone who is alleged to have violated penal law is imputed criminal charges. However, in the theological sense, imputation has a positive meaning. God declares the righteousness of His Son Jesus Christ imputed or attributed to a sinner who acknowledges God's decree by faith alone. Christ's righteousness is placed to our account as totally belonging to us, entirely by declaration. This is the meaning of imputation as Luther goes on to describe in the following discussion.

[77] *Et reputatum est illi ad justitiam.* Luther seems to be quoting Romans 4:23 from the Vulgate. "It was reputed to him for [unto] righteousness."

[78] *fide cordis et imputatione Dei.*

[79] *Sacrificium illud fidei coepit in Abraham, sed in morte tandem consummatur.*

[80] *ideoque necesse est accedere alteram partem justitiae, quae eam perficit, scilicet imputationem divinam.*

[81] *scintilla fidei.*

sad, sometimes joyful, as testified by the prophets and apostles in the Scriptures. But those faults are not taken into account due to their faith in Christ. Otherwise, no one would be saved. Thus we conclude with these words: "And it was imputed to him as righteousness."[82] The meaning is that righteousness properly begins through faith, and by faith, we have the first fruits of the Spirit. But since faith is weak,[83] righteousness is not perfected unless God imputes it to us [freely accounts it as ours].[84] Thus faith is the beginning of righteousness, but imputation [the full crediting of righteousness] maintains it complete until the day of Christ.[85]

The religious philosophers and the scholars also expound at length regarding imputation when talking about the acceptance of a good work. But in this they are totally contrary to the Scriptures for they attribute it only to works. They don't consider the filth and poison that stalks in the heart, such as unbelief, doubt, condemning others, and hate toward God. These are the most pernicious and dangerous beasts and are the source and cause of all evil deeds. That's because reason does not fear God, nor does it love God. Rather, it mistrusts God and boastfully condemns Him. Reason does not take pleasure in His words or deeds but murmurs against Him; it is angry with Him and judges and hates Him. In brief, "it is at enmity with God, nor does it give Him glory" (Romans 8:7). This pestilent beast (reason), once it cuts your throat, makes all external and gross sins seem like nothing!

That is why first and foremost we must set out through faith to knock down unbelief, hate and spite toward God, and murmuring against His judgment, wrath, and all His words and deeds. That way we debunk reason, which dies only by means of faith, because by believing God it gives Him glory, even though it may seem to reason that God says foolish, absurd, and impossible things. On His part, God Himself makes pronouncements that reason is unable to judge or conceive. That's because God announces Himself like this: "I will consider and declare you righteous, not because you have kept the law, nor for your works or merits, but for your faith in Jesus Christ, my only Son, who was born, suffered, was crucified, and died for your sins. And I will not consider whatever sin remains in you." The righteousness of faith cannot exist if reason is not demolished in this manner. Faith must condemn all human made religion and service to God invented for self-justification. Otherwise, there's no room for the righteousness of faith.

When reason hears this, it immediately feels offended. Furiously, it lets go all its evil against God, saying, "What? Then my good works are worthless? Are you telling me that I've worked under the hot sun all day long for nothing?" That's why the nations, kings, and princes roar against God and His Christ. That's because the

---

[82] *et imputatium est illi ad justitiam.*

[83] *fides imfirma est.*

[84] *eam non perfici sine imputatione Dei.*

[85] *Quare fides justitiam incipit, imputatio perficit usque ad diem Christi.*

world neither tolerates nor accepts that its wisdom, righteousness, religions, and praises are rebuked and condemned. The Pope with all his papal riffraff[86] won't even consider he's mistaken, or much even less damn himself.

Therefore, let all who devote themselves to the study of the Holy Scriptures learn from this statement: "Abraham believed God, and it was imputed to him as righteousness."[87] Thus they will be able to explain truly and correctly true Christian righteousness in the following way. It is a faith and trust in the Son of God, or rather the heart entrusts itself to God through Jesus Christ. Let them add the following phrase to set it apart from all others: that this faith and trust are imputed as righteousness for the sake of Christ.[88] For only this (as I've said before) results in Christian righteousness: faith in the heart, which is a gift of God, that confidently[89] believes in Christ. Then God accepts this imperfect faith as perfect righteousness, for the sake of Christ's imputed righteousness, in whom I am beginning to trust. Due to this faith in Christ, God does not take into account my doubts regarding His goodwill toward me, my mistrust, my heaviness of spirit, and other sins that remain in me, for as long as I live in the flesh, sin is in me. But because I am covered under the shadow of Christ's wings, as the chick under the wings of the hen, living without any fear under that measureless sky of the forgiveness of sins that has been stretched out over me, God covers and forgives the residues of sin in me. I mean that due to the faith with which I've begun to grasp onto Christ, He accepts my imperfect righteousness as if it were perfect righteousness and takes my sin as if it were no sin, although certainly it is nothing else but sin.[90]

Consequently, we take shelter under the mantle of Christ's flesh. He is our "column of cloud by day and column of fire by night," lest God see our sin. And although we ourselves see it, and because of our sin, we feel the pangs of terror in our conscience, we take refuge in Christ our Mediator and Conciliator (in whom we are complete). There we'll be safe and sound. Forasmuch as all things are in Him, so through Him we have all things. But that's not all; He supplies everything else we may lack. When we believe like this, God "turns a blind eye" at the sins stuck to my flesh and covers them as if they were no sins at all, for God says, "Since you have believed in my Son, although your sins be many, nonetheless they will be forgiven until death frees you from the body of sin."

Let Christians diligently learn to understand this article of Christian righteousness, *which the papal philosophers neither understand nor are able to comprehend but neither let them think that they can learn it all in one lesson. To that end,*

---

[86] *papa cum suis non vult videri errasse.*

[87] *Creddit Abraham Deo, et imputatum est illi ad justitiam.*

[88] *Quae fiducia imputatur ad justitiam propter Christum.*

[89] *formaliter.*

[90] *reputat justitiam imperfectam pro justitia perfecta, et peccatum pro non peccato, quod tamen vere peccatum est.*

let them learn to read Paul and read him again. Let them compare Paul fully and thoroughly with Paul himself. Then they will realize that it is true, that Christian righteousness consists of these two things: faith (which gives glory to God) and the imputation given by God, for, as I've said before, faith is weak. Thus imputation needs to join up with faith. This means that God will not count[91] the residue of our sin against us. He will not punish or condemn us (for His sake). Instead, He will cover it and freely forgive it, as if it were nothing at all. Not for our sake, for we don't even deserve it, nor by works but for the sake of Christ, in whom we have believed.

Therefore, the Christian is at the same time righteous and a sinner,[92] a friend and an enemy of God.[93] The papal philosophers will not admit these opposite realities because they ignore from where justification proceeds. For this reason, they compel all to keep on struggling without end until they no longer feel any sin within them. They are the cause why many, after struggling with all their might to be perfectly righteous without success, have gone completely insane. Yes, even countless authors of this diabolic idea, were harassed by this desperate obsession at the hour of death. The same would have happened to me, if Christ had not mercifully placed his eyes on me and delivered me from this error.

On the contrary, we teach and comfort the troubled sinner like this: "Brother, it's not possible that in this life you will reach the point where you'll be so righteous that you won't feel any sin at all neither will your body be as clear as the sun, without wrinkle or spot, since you still have so many of them. However, you are still holy." But you'll say, "How could I still be holy if I still have and feel sin within me?" I respond, "Do you feel your sin? That's a good sign, when you feel and recognize your sin. It's a healthy step when the patient recognizes and comes to terms with his illness." "But how can I be freed from sin?" "Run to Christ, the physician, who heals the brokenhearted, and saves sinners. Don't consult with reason, for it will tell you that He is angry with you. Slay reason and believe in Christ. If you believe, you are righteous, you will give glory to God, that He is all-powerful, merciful, and true. With this, you justify and praise God. In brief, confess His divinity before Him and the sin that remains in you will not be counted against you[94] but will be forgiven for the sake of Christ, in whom you have believed and who is perfectly righteous. His righteousness is your righteousness, and your sin is His sin."[95]

Here, we see that every Christian is a high priest. First, he offers and slays his own reason and the wisdom of the flesh. Then he gives glory to God, who is

---

[91] *imputare.*

[92] *christianus simul justus et peccator.* Luther emphasizes the phrase in a footnote: *christianus justus est et peccator.* This phrase became one of the earmarks of the Protestant Reformation.

[93] *amicus et hostis Dei est.*

[94] *non imputatur.*

[95] *cujus justitia est tua, peccatum tuum est suum.*

righteous, true, patient, full of compassion, and merciful. This is the daily sacrifice of the New Testament, which should be offered morning and evening. The sacrifice of the evening is to slay reason. The sacrifice of the morning is to glorify God. Therefore, the Christian should be involved in this double daily and continuous sacrifice as a spiritual exercise. There is no one who could properly explain the all-encompassing excellence and dignity of this Christian sacrifice.

LECTURE 17: Saturday, August 29

Therefore, this is a strange but marvelous definition of Christian righteousness: it is the imputation from God for righteousness, or according to righteousness, by faith in Christ, or because of Christ.[96] When the papal scholars hear this definition, they laugh, since they imagine first that righteousness is a certain infused quality that is then diffused throughout the members of the body.[97] They cannot let go of reason's vain imagination, which teaches that good judgment, a goodwill, or good intention is true righteousness. But the unspeakable gift is more excellent than all of reason put together, for God counts and recognizes man as righteous without any work at all. This righteousness is for everyone who by faith alone embraces God's Son,[98] who was sent to the world, was born, suffered, and was crucified for us.

This subject, as far as its words, is simple. Righteousness as an essence is not found within us,[99] as Aristotle contends. Instead, righteousness is found outside of us in God's grace and granted only by divine imputation[100]—that is, there is no essence of righteousness in us. All we have is a fragile faith[101] and its first fruit by which we begin to grasp unto Christ. Notwithstanding, sin certainly remains in us. Frankly, the difference is no small thing but of great weight and importance. That's because Christ, who was given for us and to whom we grasp by faith, did no small thing for us. Rather, as Paul said previously, "He loved us and gave Himself for us, and became a curse for us." That Christ gave Himself for my sins is not something made up by the imagination. He was made a curse for me so that I could be freed from eternal death. Thus God counts that faith, albeit imperfect,[102] as perfect righ-

---

[96] *Est itaque ut diximus christiana justitia imputatio divina pro justitia vel ad justitiam propter fidem in Christum, vel propter Christum.*

[97] *justitiam esse qualitatem primo infusam deinde in membra diffusam.*

[98] *Deus reputet et agnoscat sine ullis opribus illum justum, qui solum fide apprehendit filium suum.*

[99] *justitiam non esse formaliter in nobis.*

[100] *sed extra nos, in sola gratia et reputatione divina.*

[101] *imbecillem fidem.*

[102] Luther adds this footnote: *Fide in Christum reputari nos justus,* "faith in Christ counts us righteous."

teousness[103] because we have grasped the Son by faith and believed in our hearts (which itself is a gift from God).

Here, we have arrived at another world, far from the world of reason. Here, we don't discuss what we should do or which works will merit for us grace and the forgiveness of sins. Here, we are before the most exalted and celestial Deity where we hear this Gospel or good news: that Christ died for us and that we, believing this announcement, are counted as righteous, notwithstanding the sins that remain in us or however big they may be.

This is the same definition given by our Savior Jesus Christ in John regarding the righteousness of faith. "The Father Himself loves you (John 16:27). Why does He love you? It was not because the disciples were Pharisees, having a spotless righteousness according to the law, or because they were circumcised, did good works, or fasted, but because I chose you out of the world. You did nothing but love me and believed in me that I came from the Father. This Person (speaking of Himself) was sent from the Father to the world, and I was pleasing to Him. Because you have grasped and embraced the one sent by the Father, He, Himself, loves you, and in this, you are pleasing to Him." However, in another text, He calls them evil and commands them to ask for the forgiveness of sin. These things seem to be mutually exclusive: that a Christian is righteous and loved by God, and even so, he is a sinner. That's because God cannot deny His own nature. It is necessary that He should hate sin and sinners. It should be that way; otherwise, He would be unrighteous and would love sin. But then how can these mutually exclusive truths coexist with each other? I am a sinner, and no matter how much I deserve God's wrath and indignation, even so, the Father loves me? Here, no one else intervenes but Christ the Mediator. The Father, He said, does not love you because you deserve to be loved but because you have loved me and have believed that I came from the Father (John 16:27; 18:8).

Thus the Christian remains humble because he feels the effects of sin and confesses that he merits God's wrath and judgment and thus eternal death. Even so, he retains a holy pride with which he turns to Christ and overcomes the feeling of God's wrath and judgment. Further, He believes that the remnants of his sins are not imputed to him but that he is also loved by the Father, not on his own account but for the sake of Christ, the Beloved.

Thus we can see how faith justifies without works. Nonetheless, the imputation of righteousness is also necessary. Sins remain in us, which God thoroughly hates. Therefore, it's necessary that we must have the imputation of righteousness, which we obtain through Christ and because of Christ, who has been given to us and we have received by faith. Meanwhile, as long as we live here, we are carried and nourished in the bosom of God's mercy and patience until the body of sin is

---

[103] *quod Deus reputet illam fidem licet imperfectam pro justitia perfecta.*

discarded, and we are raised as new creatures on that great day. Then there will be new heavens and a new earth, which are inhabited by righteousness.

While we live under this sky, the wicked dwell here, but sin also dwells among the believers. For this reason, Paul complained that sin remained among the saints (Romans 7). However, he says in Romans 8:1, "There is now no condemnation for them who are in Christ Jesus." How can these things so contrary and incompatible be reconciled? How is it that the one who should be condemned is not condemned? That the one who deserves the wrath of God and eternal damnation should not be punished? The only one who can reconcile here is that one Mediator between God and man. This man is Jesus Christ, and as Paul said, "There is no condemnation for those who are in Christ Jesus."

VERSE 7. Therefore, be sure that it is those who are of faith who are sons of Abraham [NASB].

This is the general argument and Paul's entire dispute against the Jews. The children of Abraham are not those born of his flesh and blood but those who believe. That is what Paul vehemently disputes here and in Romans 4 and 9. This was the Jews' greatest confidence and glory: "We are the seed and children of Abraham. He was circumcised and kept the law. Therefore, if we are truly Abraham's children, we must imitate our father" and such statements. No doubt there was an excellent glory and dignity in being of the seed of Abraham. No one can deny that God spoke to Abraham and his descendants. But the unbelieving Jews did not receive any entitlements due to their lineage. It is for that reason that here Paul struggles mightily against that argument and tears away from the Jews their confidence in themselves. Paul accomplished this as no one else could have, for he was a chosen vessel of Christ. If at the beginning we ourselves had disputed against the Jews without Paul, we would have had little success against them.

Thus Paul disputes against the Jews, since they so boastfully claimed this opinion that they were children of Abraham, saying, "We are Abraham's seed. Abraham was circumcised and kept the law; we should do the same." I grant them all that. What then? Will they be justified and saved because of that? Not so. But let's go to the patriarch himself, and we shall see how he was justified and saved. Without doubt, it was not because of his excellent virtues and holy works. It was not because he left his homeland, family, and parents' house. It was not because he was circumcised and kept the law. It was not because he was about to sacrifice his son Isaac by order from God, in whom he had the promise of posterity. It was because he believed God.[104] Therefore, he was justified for no other reason than by faith alone. If you claim you should be justified by the law, well, Abraham had a much greater claim than yours to be justified by the law. However, Abraham

---

[104] *sed quia creditit Deo.*

could neither be justified nor receive the forgiveness of sins and the Holy Spirit other than by faith alone. Since this is Scripture's true testimony, why do you put so much trust on the circumcision and the law, claiming that is why you have righteousness and salvation? Was it not Abraham himself, your father, your source and fountain, in whom you so greatly boast, who was justified and saved without these but by faith alone?[105] How could this argument be refuted?

Thus Paul concludes with this phrase: "Those who are of faith are children of Abraham." Before God, neither physical nor fleshly birth makes you a child of Abraham. It's as if he had said Abraham had children according to the flesh because as a father he procreated these children before God. But God does not consider anyone as a child of Abraham (although indeed he was God's servant, chosen by God and justified by faith[106]) through carnal procreation. Instead, he was a father of faith. He justified and pleased God, not because he could procreate according to the flesh, not because he had the circumcision and the law but because he believed God. Therefore, whoever wants to be a child of Abraham the believer should himself be a believer. Otherwise, he is not a child of the elect, Abraham the beloved and justified, but only of Abraham the procreator. But in that case, that person is nothing more than a conceived human, born in the wrappings of sin, without the forgiveness of sins, without faith, without the Holy Spirit, as any other human being, and under condemnation. Therefore, such an arrogant boast, "we are of the seed of Abraham," is totally worthless.

In Romans chapter 9, Paul clearly presents this argument taking two examples from the Holy Scriptures. The first is that of Ishmael and Isaac, the two born clearly from Abraham's seed, according to the flesh. However, Ishmael was excluded. Physical conception from his father Abraham did not give him any entitlements. Rather, Scripture says, "In Isaac shall be your seed" (Genesis 21:12). The second example is Esau and Jacob. From their mother's womb, even before any of them had done right or wrong, it was said, "The oldest shall serve the younger. Jacob I have loved, but Esau I have hated" (Genesis 25:23). Clearly, only those who are of faith are children of Abraham.

Here, there are some who object (certain Jews and other wavering spirits). They say that in Hebrew this word *faith* means "truth"; thus we do not apply it properly. Further, that Genesis 15 is talking about a temporal matter, the promise of posterity, and that Paul incorrectly relates it with faith in Christ. That it should simply be understood as Abraham's faith, by which he agreed with God's promise, that he would have offspring. They conclude that nothing can be proven by appealing to Paul's arguments and evidence. They also surmise that where Paul soon after

---

[105] *sola fide justificatus ac salvatus sit.*

[106] Here, Erasmus Middleton as well as Philip Watson incorrectly translate the Latin phrase *et fide justificatus est* as "made righteous by faith" (see Watson, 230). A correct translation would be "is justified (declared righteous) by faith."

Galatians 3:1 quotes Habakkuk 2, the faith mentioned there is regarding the fulfillment of the entire vision and not just about faith in Christ, as Paul claims. Similarly, they allege that all of Hebrews chapter 11 simply talks about faith and examples of faith. That's how these arrogant and boastful spirits go hunting, seeking praise, hoping to be considered wise and scholarly, when that's what they least deserve. But due to those who are gullible and ignorant, we briefly respond to their arguments.

To the first, I respond the following. Faith is nothing more than the heart saying the truth about God. It is to have a correct and truthful opinion about God's heart. Only faith can think and understand the truth about God, reason can't. We can think correctly about God only when we believe God's word. However, when we begin to measure God without the word and strive to believe in God according to our own reasoning, we will not have the truth of God in our heart. Thus we are unable to think or judge about God as we should. For example, when a monk imagines that his cowl, tonsure,[107] and vows pleases God, and thus will receive grace and eternal life, then he does not have a truthful opinion about God but is false and full of wickedness. Truth then is faith itself, which judges correctly about God—that is to say, God does not consider our works or righteousness. That's because we are unclean! Instead, He will have mercy on us, he will look favorably on us, will accept us, and justify and save us if we believe in His Son, whom He has sent as a sacrifice for the sins of the entire world. This is a truthful judgment about God and nothing more than faith itself. My reason cannot fully confirm to me that God has given me His favor for the sake of Christ. But I hear it announced in the Gospel, and by faith, I clasp unto His grace.

To the second argument, I respond that Paul correctly quotes Genesis 15, relating it to faith in Christ. Faith must always include an unquestionable reliance[108] in God's mercy. It is vital for all to have an unwavering trust[109] in the remission of sins obtained by Christ. It would be impossible for your conscience to find rest in God's hands unless first it had the assurance that God has been merciful to you on account of Christ. Thus all the promises derive from that first promise with regards to Christ: "The seed of the woman shall wound the head of the serpent" (Genesis 3:15). All the prophets understand and teach it like this. That is why we can see that the faith of our fathers in the Old Testament and our faith now in New Testament times are all one and the same, although they differ in their external objects. Peter testifies about this in Acts when he says, "A yoke on the neck of the disciples which neither our fathers nor we were able to bear? But we believe that we are saved through the grace of the Lord Jesus, just as they are" (Acts 15:10, 11). Elsewhere, Paul said, "And all drank the same spiritual drink. For they drank of a spiritual rock that followed them, and the rock was Christ" (1 Corinthians 10:4). Christ Himself said, "Your father Abraham rejoiced to see my day. He saw it, and

---

[107] shaven crown.

[108] *fiducia.*

[109] *fidem.*

was glad" (John 8:56). Nonetheless, the faith of the fathers clung onto the Christ yet to come. Our faith clings to the Christ who has come. In his day, Abraham was justified by faith in the Christ to come. However, had he lived today, he'd be justified by faith in Christ, already revealed with His presence. As I said before regarding Cornelius, at the beginning, he believed in the Christ yet to come, but having been taught by Peter, he believed in the Christ already come. Therefore, difference in eras never changes faith, or the Holy Spirit, or His gifts, for there has always been, there is, and forever will be a mind, a judgment, and an understanding with respect to Christ, as there was in the fathers of old, the faithful of today, and those who will come tomorrow. Similarly, we have the Christ yet to come, and we believe in Him, just as the fathers did in the Old Testament. That's because we wait for His return on the final day with great glory, to judge the living and the dead, and yet we believe that He has already come for our salvation. Thus Paul's claim does not offend anyone except those blind and ignorant naysayers.

However, for us, it is unlawful to return to the Christ yet to come, except as we wait for Him at the last day, as our Redeemer will deliver us from all evil. But if you want to, go ahead and believe that Christ has not yet been revealed. Say that His revelation is still to come. But in that case, we would be denying Christ and all His benefits, denying the Holy Spirit, making God a liar, and in fact, we will be testifying that He has not yet made good on His promises, just like the Jews!

Thus as I've said, Paul is spot on when he relates this text to Genesis and applies it to faith in Christ, with respect to Abraham's faith, for all the past promises were poured on the Christ yet to come. Thus Abraham and all the fathers, together with us today, are justified by faith in Christ.[110] They are justified by faith in Him yet to come; we are justified by faith in Him who has already been revealed. That is why we insist now with respect to the essence and the manner of justification. It is all one and the same for them in the Christ yet to be revealed or in the Christ already revealed and made manifest. Thus it is enough to say with Paul that the law does not justify, but faith alone,[111] whether it's in the Christ yet to come or in the Christ already revealed.

It is the same with us today. For some, Christ has not yet been revealed. For the unbelievers, He has yet to come, and they have nothing to gain from Him at all.

---

[110] Here, once again, Middleton and Watson err in translating the Latin phrase *nos fide in Christum justificamur* as "are made righteous by faith in Christ." The correct translation should be "are declared righteous by faith in Christ." Justification declares us righteous. Justification does not make us righteous. That was Luther's contention against papal theology. Since Trent until today, Roman Catholic theology continues to allege that we are made righteous through infused or imparted grace. Instead, Paul and Luther insist that we are declared righteous through imputation, as Luther here argues on behalf of the fathers, the believers today, and those yet to come.

[111] *quod lex non justificet, sed sola fides.*

But if they hear the Gospel and believe that He has already been revealed on their behalf, He justifies and saves them.

VERSE 7. Know therefore, that those who are of faith, the same are children of Abraham [WEB].

It's as if he had said, "Know by Abraham's example and by the clear testimony of Scripture that the sons of Abraham are those of faith, be they Jews or Gentiles, without respect at all to the law or works or their carnal procreator." That's because the promise given to Abraham that he would inherit the world was not made through the law but through the righteousness of faith.[112] In his seed, all the nations[113] of the earth would be blessed, and he would be called "the father of nations."[114] So that the Jews would not wrongly interpret this word *nations*, relating it only to themselves, Scripture foresaw it, saying he'd be not only a "father of nations" but "a father of many nations." Therefore, Abraham is the father not only of the Jews but also of the Gentiles.

Here, we can clearly see that the children of Abraham are not only children of the flesh but also children of faith. That's what Paul declares: "Abraham, who is the father of us all. As it is written, 'I have made you a father of many nations'" (Romans 4:17). Paul presents two types of Abraham: Abraham the procreator and Abraham the believer. Abraham has children and is the father of many nations. Where? Before God, in whom he has believed. Not before the world, because there Abraham is the procreator.

In the world, he is a son of Adam, a sinner. Worse, he is a worker of the law, living according to reason's law—in other words, according the manner of men. That is why all this has nothing to do with Abraham the believer. This example of Abraham, given in the swaddling clothes of the Holy Scriptures, says that we are counted righteous by faith.[115] Therefore, this is a powerful and overpowering argument in two ways: one, due to the example of Abraham and two, by the authority of Scriptures.

VERSE 8. Scripture foresaw that God would justify the Gentiles by faith.

These words are concerning the previous argument. It's as if he had said, "You Jews glory too much in the law. You highly recommend Moses because God spoke to him from the burning bush etc." I, myself, have heard the Jews boast against us. They say, "You Christians have the apostles, you have a Pope, and bishops. But we Jews have patriarchs, prophets, even God Himself, for God spoke with us

---

[112] *Non enim per legem, sed per justitiam fidei.*

[113] *cognationes.*

[114] *gentium.*

[115] *quae dicit nos fide reputari justos.*

from the bush, from Sinai; He gave us the law from there and from the temple. Go ahead and make all these claims on your behalf if you can." Paul, the apostle to the Gentiles, responds, "All your boasting and arrogance profits you nothing, for Scripture foresaw, anticipating it before the law, that the Gentiles would not be justified by the law but by the blessing of Abraham's seed. This promise was made to Abraham (as Paul says thereafter) 430 years before the law was given. Since the law was given so many years after that, it was unable to do anything to prevent or abolish the promise of the blessing made to Abraham. That promise has remained in place and will remain forever." What then will the Jews say to this?

This argument, founded on the certainty of time's unceasing pace, is very powerful. The promise of the blessing was given to Abraham 430 years before the people of Israel received the law, for Abraham was told, "Since you have believed God, and given Him glory, you will be 'father of nations.'" It was then that Abraham through God's promise was named father of many nations and the inheritance of the world was given to his posterity and the seed to come before the law was given. Why then do you boast, o Galatians, that you receive the forgiveness of sins and become children and receive the inheritance through the law, which was given many years thereafter—430 years, to be precise—after the promise?

Baptism contains the promise of salvation: "He who believes . . . shall be saved." Those who deny (as the fanatics do) that righteousness and salvation is given for the first time to a newborn when he is baptized, evade the promise given in this regard, saying that baptism is only valid when children are old enough to know what they're doing and are able to do good works.[116] *They also claim that by doing good works they obtain what is offered in the promise. Further, they allege that baptism is not a sign of God's goodwill toward us, but it's only like a stamp by which believers are distinguished from unbelievers. Those who say such things strip baptism from salvation and attribute it to works. That's how the false apostles and their disciples did their work. They preached the law and its glory without measure* but paid no attention to the promise given to Abraham 430 years before the law was given and thus despised it. They would not admit under any circumstance that Abraham (of whom they nonetheless boast as the father of their entire nation), even while uncircumcised, living so many years before the law, was justified by no other means than by faith alone, for that is the testimony of the Scriptures: "Abraham believed God" (Genesis 15:6). Then when he had already been counted as righteous by his faith, Scripture mentions circumcision in Genesis 17:10, where it says, "You shall keep my covenant, you and your descendants after you throughout their generations. This is my covenant, which you shall keep." With this argument, Paul powerfully convinces the false apostles and shows directly that Abraham was justified by faith alone. He was justified without

---

[116] *cum homo ad usum rationis pervenisset, et jam bene operari posset.* I have used an idiomatic expression to convey the meaning in modern terms: literally "when a person is able to reason."

and before circumcision, as well as 430 years before the law. He utilizes this same argument in Romans 4, that righteousness was imputed to Abraham before circumcision and before being circumcised he was already righteous, way before the law.

Paul adds that Scripture foresaw and provided an argument against this glorious boasting in the righteousness of the law and works. When? Before circumcision and the law, for the law was given 430 years after the promise. Abraham not only had been justified without the law and before the law but was already dead and buried. His righteousness without the law not only prospered until the law came but also bears fruit to the end of the world. If then the father of the entire Jewish nation was justified without the law and before the law, much more the children will be justified in the same manner their father was justified. Thus righteousness comes by faith alone and not from the law.[117]

VERSE 8. Preached the gospel beforehand to Abraham, saying, "In you shall all the nations be blessed."

The Jews not only overlook but also, with their corrupt interpretations, mock these outstanding words, "Abraham believed God," "I have designated you father," and other similar words that recommend faith and contain promises about spiritual matters. They are blind and hard of heart. Thus they can't see that these texts urge faith in God and how to be righteous before God. Similarly, they evade this outstanding text regarding the spiritual blessing: "In you shall all nations be blessed." They say that to bless just means nothing else but to praise, to pray requesting prosperity, and to be seen as glorious before the world. That is how a Jew, they say, born of Abraham's seed is blessed. Therefore, they think that the blessing is nothing more than glory and praise in this world and that someone can glory and boast that he is from Abraham's seed and family. But that is to corrupt and pervert the Scriptures, not expound them. With these words, "Abraham believed," Paul defines and presents before our eyes Abraham the spiritual man—faithful, righteous, and possessing God's promise. I say that this is an Abraham who is not in error or in the flesh, for he is not born of Adam but from the Holy Spirit. Scripture speaks of this Abraham, renewed and conceived by faith, and pronounces that he would be the father of many nations and also that he would be given all the Gentiles as an inheritance, when it says, "In you shall be blessed all the nations."

This is what Paul is urging through the authority of Scriptures when it says, "Abraham believed God" (Genesis 15:6). Scriptures do not attribute any righteousness to Abraham except that he believed. All Scriptures have to say about Abraham is how he was considered righteous by God. These Scriptural phrases introduce to us a new Abraham, apart from his carnal marriage and the conjugal bed where he is a procreator, in order to present him as he really is before God. He is the believer

---

[117] *Ergo ex fide, non lege est justitia.*

justified by faith,[118] to whom God now promises because of his faith, "You shall be father of many nations" and "In you shall be blessed all the nations of the earth." This is the meaning that Paul uses to demonstrate how the Scriptures foresaw the vain supposition and bold boast of the Jews with respect to the law. Thus the inheritance of the Gentiles was given to Abraham not through the law and circumcision but many years before and only through the righteousness of faith.[119]

Therefore, to say that the Jews shall be counted and called blessed because they are the children and descendants of Abraham is nothing more than an empty boast. There is no doubt of the great distinction and glory before the world for being from Abraham's seed, such as Paul teaches in Romans 9, but not before God. That is why the Jews wickedly pervert this text regarding the blessing, relating it only to the carnal blessing, and cause great harm to the Scriptures. The Scriptures talk with great clarity about the spiritual blessing before God, and they cannot and should not be understood in any other way. This then is the true meaning of the text "In you shall be blessed." But to whom does that "you" refer? In you, Abraham the believer, or in your faith, or in the Christ (the seed) to come, in whom you have believed "all the nations of the earth shall be blessed." In other words, all the nations shall be your blessed children, just as you have been blessed, for it is written, "So shall your seed be."

Consequently, Abraham's blessing and faith is the same as ours. Abraham's Christ is our Christ, He who died for Abraham's sins died for ours. "Abraham saw my day and rejoiced" (John 8:56). Thus everything points in the same direction. We cannot tolerate the corruption of this blessing. The Jews look at the Scriptures through a veil and thus cannot understand what the promise to the fathers is all about. Nevertheless, we should heed it above all things. Thus we see that when God talks to Abraham the patriarch, God does not talk about the law or things to be accomplished. Instead, God spoke to him about the promises he was to grasp by faith. So then, what did Abraham do? He believed those promises. And what did God do with Abraham the believer? He imputed righteousness to him because of that faith. He also added many other promises, such as "I am your shield. In you shall be blessed all the nations. You shall be the father of many nations. Thus shall your seed be." These are invincible arguments, which cannot be refuted, if the texts of Scripture are considered to their depth.

VERSE 9. So then those who are of faith are blessed with Abraham, the believer [JUB].

All the weight and strength of this text is in these words: "With Abraham, the believer." It marks a clear difference between one Abraham and the other. Paul

---

[118] *credens, qui per fidem justificatur.*

[119] *per solam fidei justitiam.*

divides the same person in two. It's as if he had said, "There's an Abraham who works. There's another Abraham, the believer. We have nothing to do with the Abraham who works. If he is justified by works, he has much in which to rejoice but not before God. Let the Jews glory all they want in Abraham the procreator. That's the one who works, is circumcised, and keeps the law. However, we glory in Abraham the believer. Scripture says that he received the blessing of righteousness by means of his faith, not just for himself, but also for all those who like him are believers. That's how the world was promised to Abraham because he believed. Thus the entire world has received the blessing, which is to say, receives the imputation of righteousness,[120] if you believe like Abraham."

Consequently, the blessing is nothing more than the promise of the Gospel. "All the nations of the earth are blessed" is like saying "all the nations shall hear the blessing." That is so. God's promise shall be preached and published through the Gospel among all the nations. The prophets have understood from this text many prophecies in a spiritual sense, such as "Ask of me, and I will give the nations for your inheritance, the uttermost parts of the earth for your possession" (Psalm 2:8) and "Their voice has gone out through all the earth, their words to the end of the world" (Psalm 19:4). In brief, all the prophesies about the kingdom of Christ and preaching the Gospel throughout all the world have arisen from this text: "In you all the nations of the earth shall be blessed." Thus to say that all the nations are blessed is nothing more than to freely offer them righteousness or that they are counted righteous before God, not through the law but by the hearing of faith, for Abraham was not justified by any other means but by hearing the word of the promise, of blessing, and of grace. Thus just as Abraham obtained the imputation of righteousness by the hearing of faith,[121] it was also the same for the Gentiles, and to this very day, for the same word that was declared to Abraham was also announced to all the Gentiles.

Here, we see that to bless means nothing less than (as I said before) to preach and to teach the word of the Gospel, to confess Christ, and to make Him known among the Gentiles. And this is the priestly work, the daily sacrifice of the church in the New Testament, which distributes this blessing by the preaching, the ministering of the Sacraments, *absolving,* comforting and administering the word of grace received by Abraham. That was the same word with which he was blessed. When he believed it, he received the blessing. In the same way, we also, believing, are blessed. This blessing is of great glory, not before the world but before God, for we have heard that our sins are forgiven and are accepted before God and also that God is our Father and we are His children and that he will not be angry with us but will deliver us from sin, death, and all evil. He will give us righteousness, life, and eternal salvation. From this blessing (as I have been

---

[120] *accipit imputationem justitiae.*
[121] *imputation justitiae . . . per auditum fidei.*

saying), the prophets preach in their writings. The fathers did not receive these promises indifferently as the Jews, the papal scholars, and the sectarians of today. Instead, the prophets read and weighed them with great diligence taking from these promises what they prophesied regarding the Christ or His kingdom. That's what is stated in Hosea's prophesy: "I will ransom them from the power of Sheol; I will redeem them from death; O death, I will be thy end; O Sheol, I will be thy destruction" (Hosea 13:14, JUB). That's how other prophets in their texts repeated all these promises, which God promised our fathers the wounding of the serpent's head and the blessing to all the nations.

Further, if all the nations will be blessed, if they are counted righteous before God, it then follows they are free from sin and death, they participate in righteousness, salvation, and eternal life, not by their works but because of their faith in Christ. Thus this text of Genesis 12:3, "In you shall all the nations be blessed," does not talk about a blessing that goes no further than the mouth. Instead, it is of such a blessing that belongs to the imputation of righteousness,[122] which is of value before God, and redeems from sin and all those evils that come with sin. Thus this blessing is received by faith alone, since the text clearly says, "Abraham believed God, and it was counted to him as righteousness." However, there are some who think the blessing is simply spiritual. The world takes it as a curse, since it comes through faith alone. Nonetheless, God offers it to the world. Therefore, this is a powerful text for it says that those who are of faith participate in this promise with blessing made to Abraham the believer. In the same way, Paul preempts the arguments of the Jews who boast in Abraham the procreator and the one who works, the one who is righteous before men but not in Abraham the believer.

Well then, just as the Jews glory only in the Abraham who works, so also the Pope only presents the Christ who works, or more to the point, Christ our example.[123] Everyone who would live righteously (he says) should walk as Christ walked, according to His own declaration in John: "For I have given you an example, that you also should do as I have done to you" (John 13:15). We do not deny that the believers should follow Christ's example and do good works. But we say that following Christ's example will not justify them before God. Here, Paul is not reasoning about what we should do but about the means of our justification. He proposes only Christ[124] dying for our sins, resurrecting because He justified us, and grasp Him by faith as a gift and not as an example. Reason cannot understand this. Thus just as the Jews imitate Abraham who works and not Abraham the believer, so do the

---

[122] *quae pertinet ad reputandam justitiam.*

[123] Luther adds this note: "Papa proponit Christum ut exemplum, non ut donum" (The Pope proposes Christ as the example and not as the gift).

[124] *solus Christus proponendus.* Luther adds this note: "In causa justificationeis beneficium, non exemplum Christi considerandum est" ([Following] Christ as the example is not considered as the cause of the benefit of our justification).

followers of the Pope today. Together with him, all those who seek righteousness through works fix their eyes on and hold onto not the Christ who justifies but the Christ who works. In this way, they go astray from Christ, from righteousness, and from salvation. Just as the Jews who were saved followed Abraham the believer, it must be the same with us today. If we are to be freed from our sins and be saved, we are to grasp Christ the Justifier and Savior. Abraham himself grasped Him by faith and was blessed through Christ.

It was indeed glorious that Abraham received circumcision by order from God, was gifted with excellent virtues, and obeyed God in all things. So also, it brings great adulation and joy to imitate Christ's example.[125] That is when we work, love our neighbor, do good to those that offend us, pray for our enemies, and bear with patience the ungratefulness of those who repay good with evil. But all this is worthless as righteousness before God.[126] Abraham's excellent works and virtues were not the reason he was counted righteous before God. Neither does the imitation of Christ's example make us righteous before God.[127]

LECTURE 18: Saturday, September 5

To be justified before God requires a much more excellent price, which is neither the righteousness of man nor that of the law. For this, it is necessary for Christ to bless and save us, just as Abraham took him for blessing and salvation. How? Not by works but by faith.[128] Thus there is a great difference between Christ who blesses and redeems and Christ who works and gives the example. Well, here, Paul speaks about Christ who redeems and Abraham the believer. He is not talking about the Christ who gives the example or Abraham who works. Therefore, he purposefully adds—with great intensity—"All who are of faith are blessed with Abraham the believer."

Thus we should separate Abraham the believer from Abraham the worker as far apart as the heavens are from the earth. The first is the one who believes in Christ. He is a divine creation, for he is a son of God; inherits the world; conquers sin, death, the world, and the devil. Thus we could not praise and exalt him enough. Let's not allow Abraham the believer to remain hidden in his tomb, as he is from the Jews. Let us rather exalt and magnify him. Let us fill heaven and earth with his name so that Abraham the believer will not leave any room for us to see

---

[125] Luther adds this note: "Bonum est exempla Christi imitari, sed per hoc non contingit Justitia" (It is well to imitate Christ's example, but our righteousness is not tied to it).

[126] *sed hoc nihil ad justitiam coram Deo.*

[127] *ita nec imitatio exempli Christi nos coram Deo justus facit.*

[128] *non per opera, sed per fidem.*

Abraham the worker. When we are talking about Abraham the believer, we are in heaven. Thereafter, let's do those things done by Abraham the worker, things of the flesh and of this earth, not the heavenly and celestial (for those were gifts from God), for we will be on the earth and among men. Therefore, Abraham the believer fills heaven and earth. Similarly, every Christian through his faith fills heaven and earth so that he may not be able to see anything else but faith.

With these words, "shall be blessed," Paul puts together an opposite argument. Scripture is full of juxtapositions, opposites compared one with the other. On this issue, a certain kind of cleverness is necessary to distinguish between these contrasting matters and be able to explain them properly. This word *blessing* also points to its opposite, which is "curse." From what Scripture says about all the nations that are of faith, they are blessed with Abraham the believer, it must be deduced that all Jews and Gentiles without faith, or who appear without Abraham the believer, are under a curse. "For the promise of the blessing was given to Abraham so that all the nations will be blessed in him." Thus there is no blessing at all that we may hope for but only the promise made to Abraham, which is now proclaimed throughout the world by means of the Gospel. Therefore, everything that is not contained in that blessing is under a curse. Paul expresses this when he says,

VERSE 10. For all who rely on works of the law are under a curse.

Here, you can see that the curse is like a deluge, devouring everything there is without Abraham. That's what happens without faith and without the promise of Abraham's blessing, for if the law itself given to Moses by God's command places a curse on all those who are under it, much more so will the laws and traditions invented by man. Therefore, all those who will avoid the curse should grasp the promise of the blessing or place themselves on Abraham's faith. Otherwise, they will remain under the curse. Thus from this text, "In you shall be blessed," it follows that in his time and thereafter all are under a curse and will always remain under a curse unless they are blessed in the faith of Abraham to whom the promise was given. From his Seed, the promise has been proclaimed throughout the entire world.

It is very necessary to know these things, since they are of great help and comfort to the troubled and afflicted conscience. Further, they teach us to separate the righteousness of faith from the righteousness of the flesh, or righteousness according to the laws of the land. We should highlight here that Paul is not dealing with the subject of ethical behavior but a divine and spiritual matter.[129] He does not wish for some deranged head to say that he curses and condemns the law of the land and obedience to the magistrates. Jerome works overtime with this text and at the end says nothing. The papal scholars have also tried but are as dumb as

---

[129] *non in loco Politico, sed Theologico et spirituali.*

fish.[130] Be on notice that this text has nothing to do with the laws of the land, manners, or political issues. These have been set out by God and are good things and in other texts Scripture approves and recommends them. But this text deals with spiritual righteousness by which we are justified before God and called children of God in the kingdom of heaven. In brief, this has nothing to do with this bodily life but with eternal life. To obtain this latter we are not to wait upon any blessing or go after some certain righteousness, no matter if it is the law, or traditions, or any other thing that has a name in this life. It must only be the promise of Abraham's blessing. Let the laws and regulations of the land have their proper place and order. Let the head of the household and the magistrate devote their utmost efforts to legislate the most excellent laws. However, none of them is able to deliver any man from the curse of God's law. The kingdom of Babylon, ordered by God and through God's command was given to kings, had excellent laws, and all the nations had to obey them. However, obedience to those laws did not save them from the curse of God's law. Similarly, we obey the laws of princess and magistrates, but that does not justify us before God. Here, we are dealing with another subject.

I have good reason to diligently teach and repeat this difference for such knowledge is most necessary. Even so, there are few who emphasize it or truly understand it. Once again, to confuse and combine divine and earthly righteousness[131] is the easiest thing to do. When it comes to the laws of the land we must pay attention to the laws and their works. But with regards to the spiritual, the divine, and heavenly righteousness, we must altogether reject all laws and works. We must fix our eyes only on the promise and the blessing. These are the only ones that Christ displays before us as the giver of this great blessing and grace, as our only Savior. Thus this spiritual righteousness excludes all laws and works and gazes only on the grace and blessing given by Christ, such as was promised to Abraham and believed by him.

We can clearly see this is a powerful and irrefutable argument. If we should wait for this blessing only from Christ, then the contrary is also true, that it is not received from the law, for the blessing was given to Abraham the believer before the law and without the law. That is how Abraham believed in the Christ to come, the giver of the promise, and by the same faith we believe in the Christ who has come and who is now present. That is how today we are justified by faith, just as Abraham back then was justified by faith. Thus those who are under the law are not blessed but remain under the curse.

Neither the Pope nor his prelates believe this doctrine and want to believe it even less. That is why we should not remain silent but confess the truth and say that the papacy is under a curse. Yes, and all the laws and civil dictates of the emperor are under a curse, since according to Paul all that exists without the promise and

---

[130] Middleton and Watson's version omit the reference to Jerome and the fish.

[131] *Oeconomus et Magistratus.*

Abraham's faith is accursed. When our adversaries hear this, immediately, they pervert and slander our words. It's as if we didn't teach to honor the magistrates. They slander, saying that we urge uprisings against the emperor when we condemn all laws, that we overthrow and destroy entire nations, etc. However, all they do is cause great harm. What we do is place a difference between the material and spiritual blessings. We say that the emperor is blessed with material blessings, for having a kingdom, laws, civil regulations, a wife, children, a house, and lands, these are blessings. All these things are good things created and given by God. However, we are not delivered from eternal damnation by a material blessing, which is only in passing and must come to an end. Thus we do not condemn laws nor provoke uprisings against the emperor. Instead, we teach that he needs to be obeyed, feared, reverenced, and honored but only as far as the laws of the land are concerned. But when we talk about spiritual matters, then we boldly say with Paul, "All there is without faith and lacking Abraham's promise, is under a curse and exists under the eternal curse decreed by God." We need to fix our gaze on the life hereafter; that's the other blessing that we hope for once this life in the flesh is over.

In conclusion, we say that all earthly things are good and created by God. Therefore (as I've said) having a wife, children, goods, and political laws and rules, are blessings of God in themselves. What I mean is that they are temporal blessings that belong to this life. But the legalists and keepers of the law throughout all ages, such as the Jews, the Papists, sectarians, and such, mix and blend them altogether. They do not place any difference between the material and spiritual blessings. They say, "We have a law, and it is good, holy, and just; and it justifies us." Who could ever deny that the law is good, holy, and just? Even so, it is also the law of condemnation, sin, wrath, and death. That is why here we place a mark between the material and spiritual blessings, and we say that God grants a double blessing. One is for our bodies in this life. The other is spiritual, for eternal life. Thus to have wealth and children, we agree it is a blessing, but it is limited to this life alone. But with respect to eternal life, it is not enough to have material blessings, for even the wicked have them in abundance and more than all others. It is not enough for us to have laws of the land, or a righteousness of the law, for in these things the wicked also prosper. God distributes these things freely throughout the world and allows them to fall on both the good and the wicked, for He is generous to all. For Him, it is but a small thing to put all creatures under the feet of the wicked. "For the creation was subjected to futility, not of its own will" (Romans 8:20). Thus those who have these material blessings alone are not God's children; they are not blessed spiritually by God, as indeed Abraham was blessed. All these are under a curse, as Paul states: "All who rely on works of the law are under a curse."

Paul could have said as a general norm that all that exists without faith is under a curse. But he didn't say it like that. Instead, he names the law, which except for faith, is the best, the greatest, and most excellent among all other blessings of the world. Nonetheless, all it does is submit everyone under condemnation and keep them bound to it. Thus if God's law binds all people under a curse, much more will those inferior laws and blessings. Further, to clearly understand what Paul means by curse, he declares it through the following testimony from Scriptures, saying,

VERSE 10. For as many as are of the works of the law are under a curse. For it is written, "Cursed is everyone who doesn't continue in all things that are written in the book of the law, to do them."

Paul sets out to prove, taking this testimony from Deuteronomy 27:26, that all who are under the law, or under the works of the law, are cursed, or under damnation. That is to say, under sin, God's wrath, and eternal death, for he does not talk about a corporal curse (as I've said before) but about a spiritual curse, which is none other than the curse of death and hell. This is a marvelous way to prove what was said previously, for Paul affirms this declaration: "All who are of the works of the law are under a curse"; by means of a negation, he borrows from Moses: "Cursed is everyone who doesn't continue in all things that are written in the book of the law, to do them." Paul and Moses seem to contradict each other in these two sentences. Paul says, "Everyone who does the works of the law is under a curse." Moses said, "Whoever does not do the works of the law is cursed." How can you reconcile these two statements? Or what's more, how can you prove the one statement by the other? *Who would think to take this statement, "If you keep the commandments, you will enter into life!" and prove it with this one: "If you do not keep the commandments of God, you will enter into life"?* Can you prove one opposite with its opposite? What beautifully perfect proof indeed! Right? And yet that's precisely the proof Paul offers.[132] Indeed, there's no one who can understand this text unless you know and understand the article of justification. *Jerome sweats it out but stays all tangled up!*[133]

No doubt that when Paul was among the Galatians he had dealt fully with this matter. Otherwise, they would not have understood him, seeing that he only mentions it here in passing. But since before they had heard him say the same thing, now it comes to mind and they remember it. These two statements do not repel each other, but agree rather well. We also similarly teach: the hearers of the law are not righteous before God, but the doers of the law shall be justified (Romans 2:13). But the contrary is also true: everyone who does the works of the law is under a curse. That's because the article of justification teaches that everyone

---

[132] Neither Middleton nor Watson render the precise meaning of Luther's arguments as stated here. Both versions omit portions of the argument. Yet both translations are faithful to the intent of pointing to justification. Pelikan comes closer: "Would I not be proving one contrary on the basis of another?" Jaroslav Pelikan and Walter A. Hansen, eds., *Luther's Works, The American Edition*, 55 vols. (St. Louis: Concordia, 1963), 26:226.

[133] *Hieronymus satis quidem sudat, sed inexplicatum relinquit.*

who does not have the faith of Abraham is under a curse. Nonetheless, the righteousness of the law must be fulfilled in us (Romans 8:4). To the person who is not aware of the doctrine of faith, these two statements seem rather contradictory. *They would sound as absurd as saying: If you fulfilled the law, you did not fulfill it; but if you did not fulfill it, then you did fulfill it.*

Therefore, in the first place, we should take a look at what Paul is driving at in this verse and how he understands Moses. Here, Paul is dealing with a spiritual matter (as I said before). This is a subject apart from all laws and regulations. When he looks at Moses, he describes something much different than what the hypocrites and false apostles see. Paul expounds the law spiritually. Everything regarding this matter goes to the words "to do." Thus to do the law is not just giving the outward appearance but truly and perfectly doing the law. So then, there are two doers of the law. First are those who are of the law. These are the ones with whom Paul arduously contends throughout this epistle. The others are those of faith, of whom I will talk shortly. Thus to be of the law (or the works of the law) and to be of faith are two contrary positions. They are as opposite as the devil and God, sin and righteousness, death and life. Those who belong to the law are those who desire to be justified by the law. Those who are of faith are those who trust in God's mercy alone, on account of Christ, for their justification. Those who say that they are righteous through faith curse and condemn the righteousness of works. On the contrary, those who say that righteousness is by the law curse and condemn the righteousness of faith. Thus these two concepts are totally contrary to each other.

Here, Paul is not talking about the law and works with respect to their essence but about the use and opinion held about them by the hypocrites who seek to be justified through the law and its works.[134]

Whoever takes this into account will easily understand that to keep the law is not to give the appearance of doing what the law mandates (that's what the hypocrites think) but to keep it in spirit, which is to say, truly and perfectly. However, where shall we find such a soul that so fulfills the law? Let that person take a step forward, and we will praise him! Here, our adversaries have their answer at the ready: "The doers of the law will be justified." Very well. But first let us define who these doers of the law are. They call a doer of the law one who does works of the law; with these works breaking ground before him, he eventually becomes righteous. According to Paul, this is not a doer of the law, since to be a doer of the law and to be of faith are in opposition to each other (as I've said before). Therefore, to seek justification by

---

[134] This section in italics is not found in either Irmischer or Lufft's Latin versions. However, it is found in Watson's English version. However, Watson (1953) does not indicate his source Latin version. I am including it here for its value with respect to the history of the entire document. Pelikan (1963), however, does include it since it appears in Weimar 399:27–29. This is one of the few differences between the Weimar text *A* and the Weimar texts *C, D,* and *E*. Please see appendix "About the Latin Text."

the works of the law is to deny the righteousness of faith. That is why these legalists and workers of the law, when they keep the law, all the while deny the righteousness of faith. They sin against the first, second, and third commandments and thus against the entire law. That's because God commands that we adore Him in faith and in the fear of His name. On the contrary, they do the righteousness of works, without faith and against faith. Thus even in their so-called observance of the law, they go against the law and fatally sin to the extreme. They deny the righteousness of God, His mercy, and His promises. They deny Christ and all His benefits. In their hearts, they establish not the righteousness of the law (which they neither understand and even less observe) but a mere fantasy and idol of the law. Thus we should say that they sin not only in their doing of the law but also because they do not fulfill it. They annul all the promises of the divine Majesty. The law was not given to that end.

Therefore, by not understanding the law, they abuse it. As Paul says, "For being ignorant of God's righteousness, and seeking to establish their own righteousness, they didn't subject themselves to the righteousness of God" (Romans 10:3). They are blind and don't know what to make of faith and the promises. Therefore, without any understanding, they dash headlong into the Scriptures. There they grasp a certain portion, the law! Then they imagine they can fulfill it with their works. But that's just a strong delusion; they are only seeing a figment of their own imagination, and their hearts are under a spell. That righteousness of the law that they think they are achieving is nothing more than, by the act itself, idolatry and blasphemy against God. Therefore, there can be no other explanation. They remain under the curse.

Thus it is impossible that we should keep the law as they imagine and even less that we should be justified by the law. First, the law testifies about this, that it is totally the opposite because the law provokes more sin, produces anger, accuses, horrifies, and condemns. How then could it justify? Further, the promise teaches the same thing, for Abraham was told, "In you shall be blessed all the nations of the earth." Therefore, there is no blessing at all except in Abraham's promise, and if you find yourself without that promise, you are under a curse. And if you are under the curse, you are not fulfilling the law because you are under sin, the devil, and eternal death. All these follow the curse. To sum it up, if righteousness is to come through the law, then God gave His promise in vain. In vain, He poured out His blessing so abundantly. God saw that we could not fulfill the law and thus provided for this instance. Many years before giving the law, He gave Abraham the promise of the blessing, saying, "In you shall be blessed all the nations of the earth." By this, He testified that all the nations would be blessed not by the law but by the promise made to Abraham. That is why all those who hold on to the law and seek to be justified by keeping it, despise the promise and thus are cursed.

The first thing on our "to do" list is then "to believe," and by believing, we surpass the law.[135] First, we should receive the Holy Spirit by whom we are enlight-

---

[135] *quare facere, est primum credere, et sic per fidem praestare legem.*

ened and renewed. We begin to do works according to the law[136]—that is, we begin to love God and our neighbor. But the Holy Spirit is not received through the law[137] (because those who are under the law, as Paul says, are under a curse). Rather, it is received by the hearing of faith, which is to say, by the promise. We should be blessed only with Abraham, by the promise made to him, and in his faith. Therefore, before all else, we should listen and receive the promise, which presents Christ and offers Him to all believers. When they grasp onto Him by faith, the Holy Spirit is given to them for His sake. Then they love God and neighbor, that's when they do good works[138] and when the patiently carry their cross. This is certainly doing works according to the law.[139] Otherwise, the law would always remain without corresponding works.[140] In fact, if you would like to truly and clearly define what it means to do the law, it is nothing else but this: to believe in Jesus Christ and when by faith we receive Christ, the Holy Spirit works that which is in the law.[141] Otherwise, no one can do works according to the law,[142] for Scripture says that apart from the blessing there is no promise, not even in the law. That is why it is impossible to do works according to the law without the promise[143] and the ensuing blessing,[144] *which is the preaching of Christ. He is the one promised to Abraham, by whom the entire world would be blessed. Otherwise, we would never do works according to the law.*[145]

There is not even one person to be found in the entire world to whom this name and title belongs, "doer of the law," without the promise of the Gospel. Therefore, this phrase "doer of the law" is a fictitious term[146] that no one can understand unless he is found without the law and above it, standing on the blessing and faith of Abraham. Thus the true doer of the law is the one who having received

---

[136] *quo illuminati et renovati incipimus facere legem, hoc est, diluyere deum et proximum.* Middleton incorrectly translates this into English "wherewith we being lightened and made new creatures, begin to do the law, that is to say, to love God and our neighbor." Middleton incorrectly translates Luther's term *renovati* as "made new creatures." The phrase "new creatures" could be understood as more in keeping with the Roman Catholic concept of regeneration as part of justification, which has no place in Luther's definition of justification. Luther uses *renovati* ("renewed") to emphasize the result of the Spirit's work, and not the cause. The cause will always be the righteousness of Christ.

[137] *Spiritus sanctum autem non per legem accipitur.*

[138] *bona opera fiunt.*

[139] *Hoc vere est legem facere.*

[140] *alioqui lex perpetuo manet infecta.*

[141] *Spiritu sancto operari ea, quae sunt in lege.*

[142] *Neque aliquer lex a nobis fieri potest.*

[143] *Igitur impossibile est fieri legem absque promissione.*

[144] *oportet adesse benedictionem.*

[145] *Alioqui nunquam faciemus legem.*

[146] *terminus fictus.*

the Holy Spirit by faith in Christ begins to love God and benefit his neighbor. This phrase "to do the law" must also embrace the faith that nourishes the tree, which produces the fruit. The tree comes first, then the fruit. The apples do not make up the tree, but it is the tree that produces the apples. Therefore, to do the law without faith is to make apples of wood and clay without a tree, which is not making apples at all but mere fantasies. On the contrary, when there is a tree, or a person or doer in whom there is faith in Christ, the works will follow. The doer needs to exist before the things are made and not the things made before the doer.

A doer doesn't carry that name due to the things already done, but for the things that will be done. Christians are not made righteous when they do righteous deeds.[147] Instead, when one is already righteous by faith in Christ, righteousness works.[148] When it comes to daily life, it's the one who has done the works that is the doer or the worker. For example, someone who frequently plays the zither, as Aristotle said, becomes a zitherist.[149] But in spiritual matters,[150] workers are not made from the things they did, but it is people of faith who become workers. Paul spoke about these in Romans 2:13, when he said, "The doers of the law will be justified," which means "they have already been counted as righteous."[151]

Even the papal philosophers and scholars are compelled to confess (that's how they teach it) that a moral deed done externally, if it's not done with purity of heart, goodwill, and proper intention, is mere hypocrisy. There's a German proverb that's right to the point: "More than one kind of thief hides under a cowl." The world's most astute charlatan can impersonate the most faithful and pious in their works. Judas did the same works as the other apostles. What fault was there in his works? Didn't Judas do the same works as the rest of the apostles? But look at the response from the papal scholars and their moral philosophy. They say that although he did similar works as the other apostles, nonetheless he was already a reprobate. He was perverse in the judgment of his reasoning. That is why his works were hypocritical. They were not upright like those of the other apostles even though to all appearances they were the same. Thus they are compelled to concede that in matters of daily life and external issues, works do not justify unless they are joined to an upright heart, will, and judgment. How much more then should they not be compelled to confess the same regarding spiritual matters? For in these, before anything else, there should be a knowledge of God and faith that purifies the heart? That is why they walk among works and in the righteousness of the law, like Judas in the works of the apostles, not understanding what they said or affirmed. Although Paul clearly says everywhere that the law does not justify

---

[147] *quia Christiani non fiunt iusti operando iusta.*
[148] *sed jam fide in Christum justificati operantur justu.*
[149] Ancient musical instrument.
[150] *in Theologia.*
[151] *iusti reputantur.*

but instead brings wrath, proclaims sin, reveals God's indignation and judgment, threatens with eternal death, even while reading these things, they don't see them, and understand them even less. That's why they don't even deserve to be called hypocrites but masks and shadows of disguised hypocrites, under a miserable spell, dreaming they are justified by the works of the law. That is why as I've said before, this phrase "doer of the law" as they define it, is an invention, a true phantom, in all nature nowhere to be found!

Paul sets out to prove his statement "For as many as are of the works of the law are under a curse" by means of Moses' statement "Cursed be everyone who does not abide by all things written in the book of the law, and do them." He does not argue that one contradicts the other, as it would seem at first. Rather, he proves the text correctly and properly, for Moses wants to say and teach the same as Paul when he says, "Cursed be everyone who does not abide" etc. But there's no one that abides in the fulfilling of the law. Thus all who are of the works of the law do not keep the law. But then, if they don't observe it, they are also under a curse. But seeing that there are two doers of the law (as I said before), the true doers, and the hypocrites, the true doers must be considered separately from the hypocrites. The true doers of the law are those who through faith are the good tree that comes before the fruit, they are doers and workers before doing any works. Moses also talks about these, and unless they are of this type, they are under a curse. But the hypocrites are not in this class. They aspire to achieve righteousness through their works, and in this way become righteous and acceptable. They say, "How shall we achieve it? Through good works." They are like the foolish builder, who puts up the roof before the foundation, and who wants to pull a tree out of the fruit. When they attempt to justify themselves through their works, they propose to make a worker from the works. This is opposite to Moses, for Moses subjects such a worker to damnation. Paul does the same.

Therefore, when they get tied up in the fulfillment of the law, they aren't just not fulfilling it. They also deny (as I said) the first commandment, God's promises, the promise given to Abraham; they revoke their faith, and they promote themselves toward receiving the blessing through their own works—that is, they seek to justify themselves and thus deliver themselves from sin and death, conquer the devil, and violently take over the kingdom of heaven. But they do nothing else but renounce God, and pretend to put themselves in place of God. All these works belong to God's majesty and to no other creature, human or angelical.

That is why Paul could easily demonstrate from the first commandment, the abominations that were to come, which the Antichrist would bring to the church, for all who teach that any other worship is necessary for salvation except that which God requires from us in the first commandment, which is the fear of God, faith and love to God, are nothing more than antichrists, who put themselves in the place of God. Christ Himself predicted that these individuals would come when He said, "Many will come in my name saying, 'I am the Christ'" (Matthew 24:5).

In the same way, today we can boldly and freely declare that everyone who seeks righteousness by works without faith denies God and wants to be known as God. Such a person thinks like this: "If I do this particular work, I will be conqueror over sin, death, the devil, God's wrath, and hell and obtain eternal life." But tell me, what else is this but want to pry away that work that belongs to God, and acting like your own god? Thus it is easy for us to prophecy and judge with certainty that whoever is not of faith is not only an idolater but also an unbeliever. Such a person denies God, and puts himself in the place of God. Peter also prophesied using this same foundation when he said, "But false prophets also arose among the people, just as there will be false teachers among you, who will secretly bring in destructive heresies, even denying the Master who bought them, bringing upon themselves swift destruction."

In the Old Testament, all the prophecies against idolatry arose from the first commandment. All the wicked kings and prophets, and their unbelieving followers, did nothing more than what the Pope and all the hypocrites have always done. They cheapen the first commandment and the worship ordered by God, despise the promise of the seed of Abraham, that Seed in whom all the nations would be blessed and sanctified. They ordered a most wicked praise totally contrary to God's word. They said, "Let us serve and worship God with this praise by which God led us out of Egypt." Thus Jeroboam made two golden calves and said, "Look and behold your gods, Israel, which brought you up out of the land of Egypt!" (1 Kings 12:28 [WEB]). He said this referring to the true God who had redeemed Israel. However, he and all his people were idolaters, for they worshipped God contrary to the first commandment. They just considered the work and thought that God would consider them righteous because they had fulfilled that work.[152] And what else was this but to deny God Himself? Oh, but they confessed God with their mouths, saying, "Who brought you out of the land of Egypt"! Paul talks about these idolaters when he says, "They profess to know God, but they deny him by their actions" (2 Timothy 3:5).

Thus all the hypocrites and idolaters are busy attempting to do the works that properly belong to the Divine majesty alone, for they belong to Christ alone.[153] It's true they don't say the actual words "I am God; I am Christ." However, with their own works, they attribute to themselves Christ's divinity and office. It's the same as if they had said, "I am Christ; I am a savior; I not only save myself but others." This is not only what the monks have taught but also what they have made the whole world believe: that they are capable not only to become righteous through their own hypocritical holiness but also to make others participants of the same. Nonetheless, the rightful office of justifying the sinner belongs to Christ alone.[154]

---

[152] Through the act of worshipping, a work of their own making.

[153] *solique Christo competent.*

[154] *cum tamen justificare peccatorem sit solius Christi proprium officium.*

Similarly, when the Pope goes around sprinkling his holiness all over the world, he has denied and totally buried Christ's office and divinity.

These things must be weighed and taught well. Only then, we'll be able to judge all Christian doctrine and the person's life as well. It's also helpful to help confirm people's consciences, to understand all prophecy and the Sacred Scriptures, and to have a proper judgment over all other matters. Whoever can understand these things will understand with all certainty that the Pope is the Antichrist[155] because he teaches how to worship very differently from what is taught in the first table of the law. Such a person will know and understand perfectly well what it is to deny God, deny Christ, and what Christ meant when He said, "Many will come in my name saying, 'I am the Christ'" (Matthew 25:5). They will also be able to understand what it means for the Antichrist to sit in the temple of God as God and what is meant by the desolation of abomination that is in the holy place.

This damnable hypocrisy is not justified by the divine blessing, nor is it a creation of the Creator God. But that hypocrisy is the fountain of all mischief, for it supposes that justification is not only something passive. Instead, the believer should actively work and suffer with patience what God works within him so that God is able to receive something from him. Therefore, the hypocrite with his own works makes himself his own creator and justifier. He despises the blessing promised to Abraham and his children of faith. Thus each hypocrite is both things, matter and cause. This even goes against philosophy for one and the same thing cannot act upon itself. He is matter because he is a sinner and cause because he dons a cowl or chooses some other work to save himself and others. That is why he is at the same time creature and creator. Words are lacking to describe how abominable and horrible it is to seek the righteousness of the law through works without that blessing. It is nothing but the abomination that is in the holy place, which denies God and puts the creature in place of the Creator.

Therefore, the doers of the law are not the hypocrites, who do the works of the law for the appearances.[156] Instead, the true believers are those who satisfy it when they receive the Holy Spirit[157]—that is, they love God and neighbor. Thus the doer of the law is not the one who says he does it by his works but the person who has already done it by faith.[158] For according to theology, only the justified do righteous things. But according to philosophy, it's not that way; rather, those who are doing righteous things are becoming justified.[159] However, those of us who have

---

[155] *certo statuere potest papam esse antichristum.*

[156] *hypocritae externe facientes legem.*

[157] *qui acepto Spiritu sancto eam implent.*

[158] *ut factor legis sit, non qui ex operibus fiat factor, sed qui ex persona per fidem jam facta fiat operator.*

[159] *nam in teologia justi facti justa faciunt, non item in philosophia, ubi facientes justa justi fiunt.*

been justified by faith do good works.[160] According to 2 Peter 1:10, our calling and election are affirmed and confirmed even more each day. But since we only have the first fruit of the Spirit, for the tenths are lacking, the remnants of sin remain in us. Therefore, our doing doesn't perfectly match up to the law.[161] Nonetheless, this imperfection is not imputed to us who believe in Christ, who was promised to Abraham and has blessed us. Meanwhile, God tenderly cares for us in the bosom of divine patience, due to His love for Christ. We are that wounded man who fell among thieves, whose wounds were cured by the Samaritan, pouring oil and wine on them. Then He placed us on his beast of burden, brought us to the inn, made provision to care for us, and left us under the care of the innkeeper, saying, "Care for him." In this way, we are tenderly cared for us as if we were in the inn, until the Lord extends His hand a second time, as Isaiah says, "to deliver us."

That is why Moses' decree, "Cursed is everyone who does not abide in all the things written in this book," does not contradict Paul who pronounces a curse on all who are of the works of the law, for Moses requires such a doer who does the works of the law to perfection.[162] But where will we find such a doer? Nowhere. *Moses himself confessed he was not one of them, since he said there was no one innocent before God (Exodus 34:7).* David himself said, "Do not enter into judgment with your servant" (Psalm 143:2). Then Paul himself said, "For the good which I desire, I don't do; but the evil which I don't desire, that I practice" (Romans 7:19). That is why Moses, together with Paul, thrust us toward Christ, by whom we are accounted as doers of the law, and all record of transgression against us is annulled.[163] How can this be? First, through the forgiveness of sins and the imputation of righteousness, by means of our faith in Christ and second, by the gift of the Holy Spirit who gives birth to us into newness of life[164] and to new motivations in us so that we may be worthwhile doers of the law.[165] Whatever remains yet to be done is forgiven for Christ's sake. What's more, any sin that remains in us is not charged to our account.[166] Thus Moses agrees with Paul and says the same thing when he declares, "Anyone who does not abide in the law is cursed," for he says that they don't observe the law because they would want to be justified by keeping it. Thus he concludes with Paul that they are under a curse. Thus Moses calls for the true doers of the law, which is to say those who are of faith. In the same way, Paul condemns those who are not the true doers, which is to say, those who are not of faith. That is why there is no contradiction between them. Moses spoke in the negative, and Paul in

---

[160] *Itaque fide justificati facimus bona opera.*

[161] *legem perfecte non facimus.*

[162] *Moses enim requirit factorem, qui perfecte legem faciat.*

[163] *per quem fimus factores legis, et nullius transgressionis rei.*

[164] *parit novam vitam.*

[165] *ut etiam legem formaliter faciamus.*

[166] *non imputatur.*

the affirmative, if you can correctly define what is understood by this word *to do*. Hence both statements are true—namely, "All who do not abide by what is written in this book are under a curse" and "Those who belong to the works of the law are under a curse."

LECTURE 19: Friday, September 11

A Response to the Arguments Alleged by the Adversaries
against the Doctrine of Justification by Faith

Let me take this opportunity to say something regarding the arguments that our adversaries use against the doctrine of faith, which is that we are justified by faith alone.[167] There are many places in the Old Testament as well as the New regarding works and rewards for works. Our adversaries are emboldened by these passages and use them as arguments to overthrow altogether the doctrine of faith that we teach and sustain. Therefore, we must be well equipped and armed so that we may not only teach our brothers but also respond to the objections of our adversaries.

The papal scholars and all who do not understand the article of justification ignore all righteousness unless it is a righteousness based on the laws of the land and the righteousness of the law. Similarly, the Gentiles have certain knowledge of these laws. Therefore, they borrow certain words from the law and moral philosophy such as "to do," "to work," and others like them and then apply these to spiritual matters.[168] But this is a most perverse and wicked behavior. We should place a difference between philosophy and theology. The papal scholars themselves concede and teach that according to nature's order, being comes before doing, for naturally the tree comes before its fruits. Once again, according to philosophical thought, they concede that a moral work is not a good work unless first reason gives a proper judgment or there's goodwill or a good intention. Thus they require that reason judges correctly and that before doing a good work, there must be a good intention—that is, they require that the person must be morally righteous for the work to be good. But on the contrary, in theology and spiritual matters, where they would have an even greater obligation to pass the same judgment, they turn out to be nothing but stumbling and dim-witted mules[169] who pervert everything and turn everything upside down. They place the work before the proper judgment of reason and the good intention.

---

[167] *quod sola fide justificemur.*
[168] *in Theologiam.* Luther literally said, "Relate [or apply] them to theology."
[169] *adeo stupidi sunt asini.*

However, "doing" means something in nature, another in moral philosophy, and something else in theology. In nature, the tree needs to come first, then the fruit. In moral philosophy, the doing requires a good intention, and reason's good judgment must come before the work so as to make it a good work. But all philosophers come to this point and then get stuck. They can go no further. That is why the theologians say that moral philosophy does not place God as the final object and cause of all things. According to Aristotle, or some Sadducee, or any honest citizen, if he contributes to the public welfare, peace, and the honesty of the state, it is said he is a righteous person in his way of thinking and he does things with good intentions. A philosopher or legislator draws the limits there and goes no further. He doesn't think that through his upright way of thinking and his good-intentioned works he will achieve remission of sins and eternal life, as does the papal philosopher or the monk. Thus the pagan philosopher is much better than those hypocrites. He stays within his limits considering only the honesty and the peace of the state and does not blend together heavenly with earthly things. On the contrary, the blind religious philosopher imagines that God considers his good intention and his works. Thus he combines the earthly with the heavenly and corrupts the name of God. He learned to think like this from moral philosophy, only that he abuses it much more than the pagan.

Thus in theology, we must ascend much higher with this word *doing* than its meaning in natural things and philosophy. Now it can become something totally new, for *when you move beyond nature to morality, it is no longer the same meaning. Neither is it when you move from philosophy and the law to the theological realm.* Here, there must be a new meaning that requires proper reasoning and a goodwill, not morally but spiritually[170]—that is, "I know and believe through the word of the Gospel that God has sent to the world His Son to redeem us from sin and death." Here, "doing" is something new, something reason has never heard or known. Philosophers, workers of the law, and all others have yet to discover it, for it is wisdom hidden in mystery. Therefore, in theology, faith must come before the work.

So how shall we respond when our adversaries allege against us the declarations of Scripture regarding the law and works, where working and doing are mentioned? We should respond with words related to theology and not regarding nature or morality, for if they are related to natural things or morality, they would have to be taken out of context and its meaning. But if they are related to matters of theology, they should include such rational judgment and goodwill, which are beyond human understanding. It's that in theology, the doing should always be understood as the doing of faith. This doing of faith is like a new kingdom, apart from the natural world, or morality. Thus when we theologians talk about doing, we should talk about this doing of faith, for in theology, there is no other rational judgment, there is no other good intention, or goodwill, apart from faith.

---

[170] *theologice.*

This rule is observed in Hebrews chapter 11. There you will find a recital of the many works of holy people in the Sacred Scriptures. There is David, who killed a lion and a bear and killed Goliath. But the papal philosophers and scholars (foolish mules)[171] don't see anything else but the external work. However, if we look at David's works, we should first consider who he was before he did this work. We will then see someone whose heart trusted in the Lord God of Israel, as the text clearly testifies. "The Lord, who saved me from the paw of the lion and from the paw of the bear, will save me from the hand of this Philistine" (1 Samuel 17, NRSV). Further, "But David said to the Philistine, 'You come to me with sword and spear and javelin; but I come to you in the name of the Lord of hosts, the God of the armies of Israel, whom you have defied. This very day the Lord will deliver you into my hand, and I will strike you down and cut off your head . . . that all this assembly may know that the Lord does not save by sword and spear; for the battle is the Lord's and he will give you into our hand.'" You can see then that he was a righteous man, beloved of God, strong and constant in faith, before the doing of this work. Therefore, this work of David is not a natural or moral doing but a work of faith.

The same epistle talks about Abel, saying, "By faith Abel offered to God a more excellent sacrifice than Cain." When the scholars find this text in Genesis (where it simply explains that Cain and Abel offered their gifts but the Lord looked with favor on Abel's offerings), immediately they latch on to these words: "They offered their gifts to the Lord, and the Lord looked with favor on Abel's offerings." Then they cry out, "You see that God looked favorably upon the offerings, thus works do justify!" So these unclean pigs[172] think that righteousness is just something moral, and they look just upon the mask or the appearance of the work but not on the heart doing the work. But even so, in philosophy, they are compelled to look beyond the work by itself. They are driven to look upon the worker's goodwill. But here, they latch onto these words: "They offered their gifts, and the Lord looked with favor on Abel and his offerings." But they choose to ignore that the text in Genesis clearly says that the Lord first looked with favor upon the person of Abel, who pleased the Lord with his faith, and then came his offerings. Thus in theology, we talk about the works of faith, sacrifices, oblations, and gifts, which are offered and given in faith. This is the testimony of the Epistle to the Hebrews, which says, "By faith, Abel offered a more excellent sacrifice; by faith, Enoch was translated; by faith, Abraham obeyed God" (Hebrews 11:4). Here, in chapter 11 to the Hebrews, we then have a designated rule on a simple way to answer the arguments of the adversaries regarding faith and works. This is it: "this or that person did this or that work in faith." That way, you turn all their arguments back on them.

Thus it should be clear that in theology and spiritual matters, the work is worthless without faith, but you should have faith before beginning to work. "For

---

[171] *insulsus asinus,* literally "dumb asses."
[172] *inmundi porci.*

without faith it is impossible to please God; for whoever would approach God must believe." That is why the Epistle to the Hebrews says that Abel's sacrifice was more excellent than Cain's, because he believed. Therefore, Abel's work or sacrifice was of faith. On the contrary, Cain, who was wicked and a hypocrite, did not have faith or trust in God's grace or favor but merely boasted of his own righteousness. Thus all the effort of the work with which he sought to please God was nothing more than hypocrisy and unbelief. Therefore, the opponents must concede that all the works of the saints are preceded or presupposed by faith. That is why their works please God and are accepted by Him. Thus in theology, "the doing" has an entirely new meaning; this matter is a whole new doing, totally opposed to the moral doing.

Further, we also distinguish faith in the following way. Sometimes faith is exercised without any work at all and sometimes with the work. Just as the craftsman works with a variety of materials and as the gardener explains there are fruitless and fruit-bearing trees, so the Holy Spirit speaks of faith in the Scriptures—sometimes about an abstract or absolute faith and sometimes of a concrete, compound, or incarnate faith. An absolute faith is when Scriptures speaks in absolute terms regarding justification or how to be justified, as is evident in Romans and Galatians. But when Scripture speaks of rewards and works, then it talks about a compound, concrete, or incarnate faith. Let us review some examples of this faith. For instance, "Faith that works through love" (Galatians 5:6); "Do this and live" (Luke 10:28); "If you wish to enter into life, keep the commandments" (Matthew 19:17); "By doing them, man shall live in them" (Galatians 3:12; Leviticus 18:5); "Depart from evil, and do good" (Psalm 34:15). In these and other similar texts (and there are many of these in the Scriptures), where the doing is mentioned, Scripture is always talking about faith's doing. For instance, when it says, "Do this and live," in the first place it is saying make sure you have faith so that you have a rational judgment and goodwill—in other words, faith in Christ; and when you have it, go ahead and work!

What then? Should it surprise us if this incarnate faith, the faith that works (like Abel's, who worked faithfulness), is promised merits and rewards? And why should not Scripture talk about faith in a variety of ways, such as it also speaks of Christ in a variety of ways, as God and man? For instance, sometimes, it talks about the totality of His person and sometimes separately about His two natures or about His divine nature or of His human nature. If it speaks separately of both natures, it speaks about Christ in absolute terms. But if it talks about the divine nature united in one person to human nature, then it talks about Christ in a compound sense, or Christ incarnate. There is a common rule among the scholars regarding the properties. When the properties belong to Christ's divinity they are attributed to the human nature. We see this everywhere in Scripture. For instance, in Luke 2:11–12, the angel calls Mary's newborn, the Savior of men and the universal Lord of angels and men. In the first chapter, he calls Him the Son of God (Luke 1:32). That is why I can say with all certainty that the newborn lying in the manger and resting on Mary's bosom created heaven and earth and is the Lord of the angels. Here, it is true that I am speaking of a man, but a "man" according to this new assumption is a new word. Even the scholars themselves say it is so and is related to his divinity, which is to say that this God, who was a man, has created all things. Creation is attributed only to Christ's divinity, since humanity cannot create. Even so, it is truly said that the man created because of divinity, the only one who can create became incarnate with humanity. Thus humanity, together with divinity, share in the same properties. Therefore, it has been well said that this man, Jesus Christ, liberated Israel from Egypt, overthrew Pharaoh, and has worked all signs since the beginning of the world.

Therefore, when Scripture says, "If you would enter into life, keep the commandments of God, do this and live," we should first see what kind of keeping and doing it has in mind; for in these and other similar texts (as I've said), he talks about a concrete faith, not an abstract but compound faith and not a bare and simple faith. The meaning of this text, "do this and live," is this: You will live due to faith's doing or this doing of faith alone will give you life. Thus justification is attributed to faith alone, just as creation is attributed only to divinity. Even so, it may be said with all certainty that Jesus the son of Mary created all things. So also, justification is attributed to incarnate faith or to faith in its doing. Therefore, we should not think like the papal philosophers and the hypocrites who believe works are absolute justifiers or that the rewards are promised to the works of ethical morality. Instead, they are promised to the works of faith alone.

Thus let us allow the Holy Spirit to speak as He does in the Scriptures, about a raw, simple, and absolute faith; or of a compound or incarnate faith, for all things attributed to works belong properly to faith. Works should not be understood as the good works of moral ethical behavior but as spiritual works of faith. In theology, faith should always be the spirituality of works, and it is diffused throughout all the works of the believers just as Christ's divinity is diffused throughout His humanity. *If you feel the heat of the iron, it's because you're almost touching the iron; and whoever touches the skin of Christ is certainly touching God Himself.* Therefore, so to speak, faith is the performing agent in all the works.[173] Abraham is called faithful because faith is spread throughout the entire person of Abraham. Thus when I see him working I don't see anything of Abraham in the flesh or the agent who works but only Abraham the believer.

I repeat these things with great diligence to teach you the doctrine of faith and to instruct you on how to respond easily and correctly to the objections of the adversaries. They combine philosophy with theology and want to convert ethical moral works into spiritual theological works. A theological work is a work of faith, and a theologian is a person of faith. Similarly, a spiritual use of reason and of the will is a reason that believes and a will of faith. Faith then is divinity universally present in any work, person, and member and thus is the unique or sole cause of justification.[174]

---

[173] *Est igitur fides fac totum (ut ita loquar) in operibus.*

[174] *fides . . . ut unica causa justificationis.*

Nonetheless, it is attributed to the physical or objective shape, which is to say, the work caused by faith. Christ as a man has eternal and infinite power not due to His humanity but because of His divinity. It was divinity alone that created all things, without any cooperation from humanity.[175] *Neither did humanity overcome sin and death. Instead, it was the hook under the worm. The devil took the hook, but when he tried to devour the worm, it was the hook that conquered and devoured the devil.*[176] *Thus humanity alone could not have done it by itself. It was divinity united with humanity, which alone made all things, and humanity only due to divinity. That is how faith justifies and does all things.*[177] *The same is attributed to works, but on account of faith.*

Therefore, these words, "to do" and "to work," may be understood in three ways. Substantially (or according to nature), morally, and theologically (although the religious philosophers have come up with certain "neutral works," affirming these are neither bad or good), with respect to the substance or according to nature or in moral issues (as I've said), these words have their natural and common meaning. But in theology, they become totally new words and acquire a new meaning. Thus all the hypocrites who are out to justify themselves by the law, and give a false opinion with respect to God, belong to the moral doing. Paul argues against these. They propose works that flow from a proper rational judgment and the right use of the will. Nonetheless, they belong to the moral or rational realm. Therefore, all their works are merely moral or rational. But the believers counter with the spiritual, confined to the realm of faith.

Therefore, when you read the Scriptures, about the patriarchs, the prophets, and kings and how they did righteous works, raised the dead, and conquered kingdoms, you should remember that these and similar texts should be explained *according a to new grammar and theology,*[178] just as the epistle does: "By faith they did righteousness, by faith they raised the dead, by faith they conquered kings and kingdoms" (Hebrews 11). Faith then incorporates the work and announces, "It is done."[179] If the opponents were in good health,[180] they would not deny it but then they would have nothing to say or object. It is true that Scriptures always cry out frequently about doing and working. But we always respond that Scriptures talk about the doing of faith. First, reason should be illumined by faith before it can work. Then when reason has a true opinion and knowledge of God, it becomes

---

[175] *humanitate nihil cooperante.*

[176] Watson's footnote: "A patristic metaphor. The hook is the divinity of Christ, the worm his humanity."

[177] *sola fides justificat et facit omnia.*

[178] *dicta secundum novam et theologicam grammaticam exponenda.* Luther adds this footnote: "Locos de operibus exponendos secundum grammaticam theologicam," "the place of works is expounded according to theological grammar" (or "the grammar of faith," translator).

[179] *ut fides incorporet et informet "facere,"* Middleton incorrectly translates as "perfects it."

[180] *si sani sunt.*

incarnate and incorporated into the works. However, everything belongs to faith. Afterward, works get the credit, but they were caused by faith alone.[181]

Therefore, when we read the Scriptures, we should learn to place a difference between truth and hypocrisy, morality and believing, with respect to the doing of the law. In this way, we confidently declare the true meaning of all the texts that would seem to establish the righteousness of works. Thus the true doing of the law is the spiritual doing[182] of faith, which is lacking in those who seek the righteousness of works. That is why every doer of the law and worker of moral holiness is under a curse. They walk around boasting about their own righteousness, but it is counter to God's. At the same time, they seek justification through human reason and the use of will power, but with this doing of the law, they do nothing but transgress it—that is, the hypocrites do the law, but nonetheless, when they do the law, they don't fulfill it because they don't understand this word, "doing." That's because in the literal sense of the law, according to true Christian theology, "doing" is totally worthless. In fact, they do many things, but presuming of their own righteousness and without knowing God and faith, they are like the Pharisee (Luke 18) and Paul before his conversion. Thus they walk around blindly and miserably come short of the mark. In that condition, they remain under the curse.

Thus I once again alert you that the arguments the opponents allege from the Scriptures regarding works and rewards should be explained spiritually.[183] For instance, when they allege this statement from Daniel 4:27, "Redeem your sins with charitable donations,"[184] you should immediately consult a dictionary.[185] Make sure it's not a moral but a theological lexicon.[186] This is not a moral redemption. Instead, it is of faith—that is, a redemption that embraces faith. In the Sacred Scriptures, goodwill and proper reasoning precede works, not of a moral type, but spiritual, which is nothing else but faith. This is how you'll be able to bridle the mouths of these stubborn religious philosophers. They themselves are compelled to concede (because they have to agree with Aristotle) that each good work is preceded by the use of free will or the power of the will. If this is true in philosophy, how much more should this will power and reason guided by faith precede works in matters of theology and spirituality. Do this with all the words you see in the imperative tense and in all the words that are Scriptural mandates, in all the words taught by the law, as is clearly stated by the Epistle to the Hebrews: "By faith Abel offered."

---

[181] *sed propter solam fidem.*

[182] *Theologicum,* literally "by theology." For Luther, doing theology is always differentiating between faith and works, law and gospel.

[183] *Theologice,* literally "theologically."

[184] *Redime peccata tua eleemosynis.* Luther uses the transliteration of the Greek word *eleemosynis,* meaning "alms" or "small change donation."

[185] *grammatica.* Latin grammars included lexicons.

[186] *Statim consulenda est grammatica, non moralis, sed theologica,* literally "you should consult a grammar, not a moral but a theological."

Now, let's suppose this solution would not be enough, although it's certainly firm and to the point. In that case, the argument that conquers all arguments and the most important image on which all Christians should fix their gaze against all temptation and objection not only from the adversaries but from the devil himself is this: Christ, who is the head. Without hesitation, we must grasp on to Christ. Further, let's suppose these religious philosophers, being more astute and clever than me, could ensnare and trap me with their arguments favoring works over faith and that I could not disentangle myself (although they would find that impossible); even so, I prefer to honor and credit Christ alone than allow myself to be persuaded by all the texts they could allege to establish the righteousness of works over the doctrine of faith.

Therefore, you should simply respond, "Here is Christ, and here is the testimony of Scripture regarding the law and works. Well then, Christ is the Lord of the Scriptures and all works. He is also the Lord of heaven, earth, the Sabbath, the temple, righteousness, life, wrath, sin, death, and all things in general." Paul testifies about this, saying that "for us he was made sin and a curse." By this, I hear that there was no way at all to save me from my sin, my death, my curse, except through His death and the shedding of His blood. Therefore, I conclude that it is Christ's function alone to conquer my sin, death, and curse in His own body and not by the works of the law or through my own works. At this, reason sees itself compelled to yield and state that Christ is not the work of the law or my own work; His blood and death are not circumcision, nor observance of the law or its ceremonies, nor even less a monk's cowl or tonsure or abstinences or vows or similar things. Therefore, if He is the price of my redemption, if He was made sin and a curse to justify and bless me, then I frankly don't care if you show me a thousand texts of Scripture that support the righteousness of works versus the righteousness of faith. Go ahead and shout all the supporting Scriptures you can muster, I'm not fazed. Why? I have the author and Lord of Scriptures on my side! I prefer to be on His side than to believe in all the song and dance of the workers of the law and the merit hoarders. Nonetheless, it is impossible for Scriptures to be against this doctrine. However, it may be so among the foolish and stubborn hypocrites. But to the faithful and those who have this understanding, this doctrine testifies of Christ their Lord. Let the hypocrites see if they reconcile those Scriptures they say are contrary to my doctrine. As for me, I will stick with the author and the Lord of Scriptures.

Therefore, if anyone thinks these texts of Scripture cannot be reconciled or answered thoroughly and yet is compelled to listen to the objections and arguments of the adversaries, then respond like this with all simplicity and to the point: "You've put the servant against me—that is, the Scriptures. Yet not altogether, not even the central part, but only a few texts regarding the law and works. But I come to you in the name of the Lord Himself, who is over the Scriptures, who has been made on my behalf the merit and the price of righteousness and eternal life. I will grasp on to him, I will stick to Him, and leave you in charge of the works which nevertheless, you've never done." Neither the devil nor any religious avenger will be able to snatch or overthrow this solution. More important, you will be safe before God. Your heart has fixed its gaze on another object, who is called the Christ. He was nailed to the cross as a curse, not for Himself but for us, as the text says: "He was made sin for us" (Galatians 3:13). Grasp on to this and set it against all the statements about the law and works, saying, "Did you hear that, Satan?" Here, he will yield, for he knows that Christ is his Lord and master.

VERSE 11. Now it is evident that no man is justified before God by the law; for "He who through faith is righteous shall live" (Cf. Habakkuk 2:4; Romans 1:17).

This is another argument based on the prophet Habakkuk's testimony. It's a declaration of great weight and authority. Paul sets it against all the declarations regarding the law and works. It's as if he had said, "Is it even necessary for us to have a big argument over this? I bring to bear the prophet's most outstanding testimony, and no one can argue against it, 'The righteous through faith, shall live.'" If he lives by faith, then he does not live by the law, for the law is not of faith. Here, Paul excludes both works and the law and declares they are contrary to faith.

The religious philosophers (they're always ready to corrupt the Scriptures) twist and pervert this text like this: "The righteous will live by faith,"[187] but they add that it's about a faith that works or that has been shaped by love. But if it has not been shaped by love, then it does not justify. They, themselves, have forged this patch to the text, but they greatly injure the words of the prophet. I would not object if they called their patch "formed faith, the true and spiritual[188] faith" or, as Paul says, "faith not feigned,"[189] which God calls faith. In that case, faith would not need to be separated from love but from a false opinion of faith. We ourselves place a difference between a pretend faith and a true faith. A contrived or pretend faith hears about God, Christ and all the mysteries of the incarnation and our redemption. It also understands and takes the things it hears. Yes, it can even speak with great religiosity. Nonetheless, there is nothing in the heart except an opinion of a gospel that's empty, naked, and full of noise. In truth, it is no faith at all, for it can neither change nor renew the heart. It does not renew the human being but leaves him in the emptiness of his former opinion and way of life. This is a very pernicious faith, and it would be best not to have it at all. Better off is the philosopher with his morality than a hypocrite with this faith!

Therefore, if you wish to distinguish between formed faith and false or pretend faith, I would not object. But they talk about a faith made into the mold or

---

187 *Iustus vivit ex fide.*

188 *Theologicam*, literally "theological faith."

189 In the Latin text, Luther inserted the Greek term ἀνυποκρίτου.

shape of love and perfected by love. In this way, they create a double faith. One is a faith with a mold, and another a faith without a mold. I detest this diabolic and virulent patch altogether. Although, according to what they say, we have an infused faith, a *fides infusa*, which is a gift of the Holy Spirit. They add that we also have acquired faith obtained by our own effort, *fides acquisita, which we acquire through many acts of faith.* However, both lack their mold and perfection, which is love, and they are shaped by love. *Thus faith without love (according to their delirious thinking) is like a drawing of beautiful scenery placed in a dark place. It cannot be admired until the light, meaning love, illumines it.* But all this is giving preference to love instead of faith, and it attributes righteousness not to faith but to love. Therefore, when they don't attribute righteousness to faith unless it is combined with love, they in fact attribute absolutely nothing to faith!

What's more, these demolishers of the Gospel of Christ teach that even that faith they call infused is received neither through hearing nor by works, but is created in man by the Holy Spirit; they allege it exists together with mortal sin and that even the worst of men can have this faith. Therefore, they say, if it's alone, it is idle and worthless, even if it works miracles. That's how they strip faith away from its proper function and hand it over to love. So that faith becomes nothing unless love, which they call the mold and perfection, is linked to faith itself. *Therefore, according to this virulent invention of the religious philosophers, faith is a miserable virtue, a type of shapeless chaos; without works, it is not effective, it is lifeless, it is merely stuff waiting to be shaped.* This is a blasphemous and diabolic doctrine, which disfigures and totally overthrows the doctrine of faith, drags man far away from Christ the Mediator and from faith, which is the hand and our only means by which we can grasp unto Him, for if (according to their fantasy) love is the mold and the perfection of faith, then I am compelled to say that love is the main portion of Christian religion. However, that is precisely how I lose Christ, His blood, and all His benefits, relying totally on my moral performance, as practiced by the Pope, the pagan philosopher, and the Muslim.

However, the Holy Spirit who gives to everyone mouth and tongue knows how to speak. He could have said (as the wicked philosophers hallucinate), "The righteous shall live by faith molded and perfectly beautified by love."[190] But he omitted this on purpose, simply saying, "He who by faith is righteous, shall live." Then let those idolatrous philosophers get moving along. As for us, we will grasp and exalt this faith, which God Himself calls faith. We are talking about a sure and true faith, which does not doubt in God or in His promises or in the forgiveness of sins through Christ. That is how we will live safe and sound in Christ the object of our faith. We will keep before our eyes the passion and the blood of the mediator and all His benefits. Faith alone is that which grasps on to Christ. It is the only way we

---

[190] I have left this phrase as translated into English by the Elizabethan translators of 1575. They embellished the translation undoubtedly for clarity's sake. Instead of *love,* they used *charity.* The Latin text simply reads, *Iustus ex fide formata.*

will not lose from those benefits. That is the reason we reject that pestilent patch and accept that this text deals with faith alone.[191] Paul declares this same point and refutes the concept of a faith molded by love when he reasons in the following way.

VERSE 12. But the law is not of faith.

The religious scholars say, "The righteous shall live if their faith is molded and adorned by love." But Paul says the contrary: "The law is not of faith." However, what is the law? Is it not also the commandment to love? Yes, for the law does not command anything else but love, as we see in the text itself: "You shall love the Lord your God with all your soul" (Matthew 22:37). Again, it says, "But showing steadfast love to thousands of those who love me and keep my commandments" (Deuteronomy 5:10) and "On these two commandments hang all the law and the prophets" (Matthew 22:40). If the law issues the command to love, then it is contrary to faith. Consequently, love is not of faith. This is how Paul clearly refutes the patch crafted by the philosophers regarding their molded faith. He speaks only of faith, just as it is, isolated from the law. However, he then also sets apart the law with its love and all its requirements. What is left? Faith alone remains the thing that justifies[192] and brings back to life!

Therefore, Paul here argues, using the prophets' plain testimony that there is no human being that obtains justification and life before God. However, it is only the believer who obtains righteousness and eternal life apart from the law and its love—by faith alone. The reason is that the law is not of faith nor of anything that belongs to faith, for it cannot believe. Neither do the works of the law belong to faith, nor are they of faith. Thus faith is something very different from the law, just as the promise is something very different from the law. The promise is not obtained through performing but by believing that grasps onto Christ.

Therefore, just as in the first division of philosophy there is a distinction between substance and mixture, so in theology there is a separation between promise and law, faith and works, as far apart as the distance between heaven and earth! It is impossible then, for faith to belong to the law. Faith only leans on the promise; it only holds on to God and knows God; its confidence is only in receiving all good things from the hand of God. On the contrary, the law and works consist in minute requirements, in the doing, and in rendering service to God. When Abel offers his sacrifice, he is rendering to God; but when he believes, he receives from God. Thus Paul powerfully concludes from the text in Habakkuk that whoever is righteous by faith, and faith alone, shall live.[193] The law in no way at all belongs to faith because the law is not what is promised. Faith only rests upon the promise. So just as there is a great difference between the law and the promise, there is also between works and

---

[191] *sola fide.*

[192] *sola fides relinquitur, quae justificat et vivificat.*

[193] *justum ex fide scilicet sola vivere.*

faith. Thus that patch made up by the religious scholars is false and wicked, for it combines the law with faith. As a result, it puts out the fire of faith and replaces it with law.

You must notice that here Paul speaks about those who continually strive to keep the law in a moral sense but not in a theologically spiritual sense. Much good may be said about good works, but proper theology requires that they must simply be attributed to faith alone.[194]

VERSE 12. On the contrary, "Whoever does the works of the law will live by them."

I understand these words as containing an ironic twist. Nonetheless, I won't refute them. It's a plain moral statement—that is, that those who do the law in a moral sense, without faith, will live by them. In other words, they will not be punished but will be physically rewarded in the here and now. I also take this text in the same way; I understand what Christ said, "Do this and live" (Luke 10:28), so that there is a certain irony or egging on: "Go ahead and do it!"[195]

Here, Paul seeks to show exactly what the true righteousness of the law and of the Gospel is. The righteousness of the law[196] is to do the works of the law, according to what it says: "Whoever does these things shall live by them." However, the righteousness of faith is to believe, according to what it says: "Whoever by faith is righteous, shall live." Therefore, the law requires that we offer something to God. However, faith does not require any work from us, or that we should render anything to God. Instead, by believing God, we receive from Him. Therefore, the function of the law is to require work, just as the function of faith is to say "yes" to the promises. Faith is the faith of the promise, and the work is the work of the law. Therefore, Paul leans on this word, "does." Further, to demonstrate clearly what it is to trust in the law and to have confidence in works, he compares one with the other, the promise with the law and faith with works. He says that nothing more comes from the law except its doing. But faith is something totally to the contrary. Faith says yes to the promise and grasps onto it.

Therefore, it is necessary to distinguish perfectly between four things, for just as the law has its proper function, so does the promise. The doing belongs to the law and believing to the promise. Just as there is a wide chasm between the

---

[194] *soli fidei.*

[195] *la thue es nur.* An old German idiom that means quite the same as the modern English idiom: "Just do it," or literally "do only that now." The fact that this German idiom flows into the text is further evidence that the Latin text is a transcript. Without any warning, Luther switched from Latin into German, and the transcribers took the phrase down as he spoke it.

[196] Luther's footnote: *Iustitia legis. Iustitia fidei.*

law and the promise, there is also between the doing and the believing, *even if you understand the "doing" in a spiritual theological sense. Notice that Paul is here dealing with another topic. He urges a distinction between the doing and the believing in order to separate love from faith and to demonstrate that only faith justifies.*[197] *That is because the law, even though it is kept morally or spiritually or not observed at all, does not contribute anything to justification, for the law corresponds to doing, but faith is not of this type. Faith is a totally different species, it exists before anything else, it precedes any mandate of the law. When faith precedes everything else, that's when a beautiful incarnation is decreed.*[198]

Thus faith perpetually justifies and gives life, and still, it is not alone, it is not idle. However, in its own function and office it remains alone[199] *because it always justifies alone.*[200] *In fact, faith turns into flesh and becomes a man; in other words, it is never alone or lacking love. It is like Christ. He exists with a divine substance or nature, eternal without beginning. However, His humanity is a nature created within time. These two natures of Christ do not fuse or combine and the properties of each should be clearly distinguished one from the other. Thus it is correct to say that humanity had its beginning within time; divinity is eternal without a beginning. However, these two natures coincide.*[201] *Divinity without a beginning is incorporated into humanity with a beginning, for which I am compelled to distinguish between humanity and divinity, saying, "Humanity is not divinity, and even so, the man is God." Thus here, I also make a distinction and say, "The law is not faith, and yet faith works." Faith and works agree with each other and exist within one structure, yet each retains its own nature and function.*[202] You can see that this is what Paul is alleging in this text, that there is a great distance and separation between faith and love.

---

[197] *solam fidem sic justificare.*

[198] *tunc fiat pulchra incarnatio.* Faith precedes everything else so that the decree of "Justified!" is proclaimed without the contribution of any human effort. The beautiful incarnation refers to the justified believer apart from any behavior or sign of transformation (including love). That is why this *fiat* must be translated as a mandated decree resulting from what Jesus Christ has already accomplished in His person. The Council of Trent argued that the fiat of justification was issued as a result of the new life of love in the believer. Luther argued that the decree of justification was issued by faith alone in the finished work of Christ.

[199] *non quod non sola.* For greater clarity, I have translated the double negative as a positive statement. In Latin and its language derivatives, the double negative is easily understood. It is not easily understood in English.

[200] *fides . . . perpetuo sola justificat.*

[201] *et tamen convenient haec duo.*

[202] *conveniunt igitur fides et opera in composito et tamen utrumque habet et servat suam naturam et propium officium.*

Then let all those religious scholars perish together with their accursed fixes:[203] faith with the mold.[204] In fact, let us say these terms out loud so we will never forget them: "Faith with the mold, faith without the mold, faith acquired!"[205] These are nothing else than phantoms invented by the devil! Their only purpose is to disfigure and destroy the true Christian doctrine and faith, blaspheme and step all over Christ, and establish the righteousness of works. No doubt, works should follow faith, but faith is not to be understood as works, nor works as faith. Instead, there should be no confusion. There should be a straight dividing line between the function of the law and the boundary of the kingdom of faith.

Thus when we believe, we live simply by faith in Christ, who is without sin, who is also our covering, our mercy seat, and our remission of sins. On the contrary, when we perform the law, it is true that we work, but we don't have righteousness or life, for the function of the law is not to justify or to give life but to reveal sin and destroy. Indeed, the law says, "Whoever does these things will live by them." But where is the doer of the law? Where is that one who "loves God with all his heart, and his neighbor as himself?" Therefore, there is no one who accomplishes the law, and no matter how hard he tries, he never gets there. Thus he's still under the curse. However, faith does not work but believes in Christ the justifier.[206] Consequently, we do not live by our doing but by our believing. But whoever believes, does works according to the law, and what remains undone is forgiven through the remission of sins on account of Christ;[207] further, whatever sinfulness remains is not imputed against us.

Therefore, Paul in this text (as in Romans 10) compares together the righteousness of the law and the righteousness of faith where he says, "Whoever does these things" etc. It's as if he had said, "It would be indeed great if we could fulfill the law. However, since no one is able to do it, we must flee to Christ. He is the end of the law for righteousness to everyone who believes. He was made under the law that He might redeem us that were under the law." We begin to do the law only after we have believed in Him and received the Holy Spirit. Whatever we can't do is not imputed against us because of our faith in Christ. However, in the life to come, we will no longer need faith. We will no longer see through a glass darkly (as we do now); but we shall see face-to-face. We shall see God as He is, in the brightness of eternal glory. There will be a true and perfect knowledge of God and love for Him. We will be of sound reason and goodwill. Not in a moral

---

[203] *glossa.*

[204] Rörer's note: *fides formata, informis, etc.*

[205] *fides formata, informis, acquisita.* Taking the text as an actual transcript of the lecture, we can almost hear Luther leading the group of seminarians in the repetition of these terms!

[206] *Fides vero non facit, sed credit in Christum justificatorem.*

[207] *Remissionem peccatorum propter Christum.*

or theological sense but in a heavenly sense, divine and eternal. In the meantime, here, by our spirit in faith, we look for the hope of our righteousness. But those who seek forgiveness of sins by the law and not by faith in Christ never actually obey the law. Instead, they remain under the curse.

LECTURE 20: Saturday, September 12

Thus Paul calls righteous only those who are justified by the promise or by faith in the promise, without the law. Those who are of the works of the law, and seem to fulfill it, do not actually accomplish it. The apostle generally concludes that all who are of the works of the law are under a curse, but if they fulfilled the law they would not be in such condition. It is true that whoever does the works of the law will live by them—that is to say, will be blessed. But this fellow is nowhere to be found! Well then, there is a double use of the law, one for the law of the land (political) and another spiritual. With regards to the political, "whoever does these things shall live by them" means they may be able to keep the law—that is, if at least they appear to obey the judge or the law of the land, they will avoid punishment and death. The magistrate will have no power at all over him. But this is the political use of the law, which serves as a bridle to the rude and intransigent. But here, Paul is not talking about that use. Instead, with this text he points to the divine. Thus it's necessary to include a condition. It's as if he had said, "If men could keep the law, they would be happy." However, where are they? Thus they are not keepers of the law unless they have been previously justified apart from the law, by faith.

That is why when Paul condemns those who are of the works of the law, he is not talking about those who are justified by faith. Rather, he refers to those who seek to be justified by works, without faith in Christ. I say this because I don't want anyone to be led astray by Jerome's imagination, who was deceived by Origen, who didn't understand Paul at all but thought he was merely a civil attorney. Here, he reasoned like this: the holy patriarch, the prophets, and kings were circumcised and offered sacrifices; thus they kept the law. It would be wicked to say they were under a curse. Thus not all who are of the works of the law are under a curse. Against better judgment, he contradicts Paul and does not distinguish between the true keepers of the law who have been justified by faith and those haggardly doers who attempt to be justified by the law, apart from faith.

However, Paul here is not talking about those who are justified by faith and indeed are the true doers of the law. Instead, Paul speaks against not only those who don't keep the law but also those who sin against it, for the law demands that we should fear, love, and worship God with a faith that's true. But they don't do this. Instead, they chose other new works and a new worship. God never ordained these, thus God is not appeased. Instead, He is provoked to greater wrath according to this text: "In vain do they worship me, teaching as doctrine rules made by men" (Matthew 15:9). Therefore, they are full of wickedness; they are in rebellion against God; they are idolaters, sinning with a high hand against the first commandment over all the rest. Further, they are full of wicked lust, anger, and other great passions. In brief, there is nothing good at all in them. Rather, they just appear to be righteous and keepers of the law.

We also who are justified by faith (as were the patriarchs, the prophets, and all the saints) are not of the works of the law with regards to justification. However, because we are still in the flesh and still have the remnants of sin in us, we are under the law but are no longer under the curse. That's because the remnants of sin are not imputed against us because of Christ, in whom we have believed, for the flesh is at odds with God and the lust that remains in us not only does not fulfill the law but also sins against it, rebelling against us and taking us captive (Romans 7). Well then, if the saints don't comply with the law (but within themselves, they do many things contrary to the law), if wicked lust and the remnants of sin still remain in them (which annoys them so much that they can't fear and love God), if they can't cry out to God with full confidence that they can't praise God and reverence His words as they should, then it is much more true that whoever has not yet been justified by faith is an enemy of God and in his heart despises and hates all God's works and His words. You can then see that here Paul speaks of those who desire to comply with the law in order to be justified, even though they have not yet received faith. He does not speak of the patriarchs and the saints (as Jerome imagined) who have already been justified by faith.

VERSE 13. Christ redeemed us from the curse of the law, having become a curse for us. For it is written, "Cursed is everyone who hangs on a tree."

Once again, here, Jerome and the papal philosophers who follow him get all out of sorts and stoop to do violence against this comforting text. It seems they strive, but with a very pious zeal, to take away from Christ that scandal that declares Him abominable. They slip away from this declaration with the following. They claim that here Paul did not speak as he should. Wickedly they affirm that Paul's use of Scripture is not in agreement with itself. They try to prove it like this: "This statement from Moses quoted by Paul is not talking about Christ. Moreover, this generalized word, 'everyone,' is not found in Moses." Further, Paul skips the words "of God," which are found in Moses. They conclude that it is evident that Moses was referring to some thief or criminal who deserved to hang for his crimes, as Scripture calls for in Deuteronomy 21:22–23. Then they ask the question, "How is it possible to relate this statement to Christ that He is cursed by God by hanging from a tree, seeing that He is no criminal or thief, but righteous and pure?" There's a chance this could convince not only the simple and ignorant but also the very religious, since the religious philosophers say it not only very astutely but also with great devotion, claiming they are only defending Christ's honor and glory. They claim to be only warning all Christians to be cautious and don't think so wickedly of Christ, that He was made a curse, etc. But let's look at Paul's arguments and verdict.

Paul eloquently strengthens his words. Again, his words more than sufficiently indicate a clear distinction. He does not say that Christ was made a curse for Himself but "for us." He emphasizes the words "for us." These words mean that Christ, as far as His own person is concerned, is innocent; thus He should not hang from the cross. However, according to the law of Moses, everyone who hangs from a tree is guilty. Thus Christ Himself hung from the cross to represent the sinner and thief, not just one, but all sinners and thieves, for we are all sinners and robbers and thus guilty of eternal death and damnation. However, Christ in Himself took away all our sins and died for them on the cross.[208] Thus it was necessary for Him to be made a thief for us, as the prophet Isaiah says regarding Him, "He was counted among thieves" (Isaiah 53:12).[209]

Without any doubt, the prophets in the Spirit saw that Christ would be the greatest transgressor, assassin, adulterer, thief, rebel, and blasphemer that ever existed on earth. When He was made the sacrifice for the sins of the entire world, He is no longer innocent and without sin, He is no longer the Son of God born of the Virgin Mary but a sinner. He has and carries the sins of Paul, a blasphemer, an oppressor, and a persecutor; of Peter, who denied Christ; and of David, an adulterer and murderer (he is to blame when the Gentiles blaspheme the name of the Lord). In brief, He is the One who has and has carried the sins of all human beings on His own body, although He, Himself, did not commit them, but willingly received them. We are the authors of the sins we have committed, but they were placed on His own body so that He could satisfy[210] them with His own blood. Thus that same sentence given by Moses ["everyone"] also includes Him (although in Himself, He was innocent) because He was found among sinners and thieves. This is no different from the judge's guilty sentence pronounced against anyone found among thieves and sinners, although such an individual did not do anything worthy of death. Now, Christ was not only found among sinners, but of His own will, and by will of the Father, He was a companion of sinners. He took on Himself the flesh and blood of sinners, thieves, and those who have fallen into all kinds of sin. Therefore, when the law found Him among thieves, it condemned and put Him to death as a thief.

---

[208] *Sed Christus in sese recepit omnia peccata nostra, et pro illis in cruce mortuus est. Recepit,* literally "took away and placed on Himself."

[209] *reputari inter latrones:* Luther's own translation of the cited partial passage from Isaiah 53. *Reputari* means to be "regarded as."

[210] *pro illis sanguine proprio satisfacturus.*

This knowledge of Christ is the most tender comfort, for it assures us that Christ was made a curse for us to redeem us from the curse of the law. The papal philosophers separate Him from sins and sinners and present Him to us only as an example to follow. In this way, they not only make Christ worthless for us but turn Him into a judge and tyrant angered over our sins, condemning sinners. For our sake, we'd better make a wrapping for Christ and know that He has covered Himself with the wrapping of our sins, in our damnation, in our death, and in all our wickedness, just as He has wrapped Himself in our flesh and blood.

However, someone will say, "It's absurd and slanderous to call the Son of God a damned sinner." I answer, if you deny Him as a sinner and accursed, you should also deny that He was crucified and put to death because it is no less absurd to say that the Son of God (such as our faith confesses and believes) was crucified and suffered the pain[211] of sin and death than to say that He is a sinner and damned. If it is not absurd to confess and believe that Christ was crucified between two thieves, then it is not absurd either to say that He was accursed and, among all sinners, the worst. Paul then did not say these words in vain: "For our sake he made him to be sin who knew no sin so that in him we might become the righteousness of God" (2 Corinthians 5:21).

John the Baptist in a similar way calls Him "the Lamb of God who takes away the sin of the world" (John 1:29). He is certainly innocent, for He is the Lamb of God without spot or blemish. But since He carries the sins of the world, His innocence is burdened with the sins and the guilt of the entire world. Every single sin that I, you, and we all have committed, and will commit from here on,[212] are Jesus' own sins, just as much as if He, Himself, had committed them. In brief, our sin should become Jesus' own sin. Otherwise, we are lost forever. This true knowledge of Christ, which Paul and the prophets have handed down to us with all clarity, has been obscured and disfigured by the wicked religious philosophers.

Isaiah speaks like this of Christ: "God," said the prophet, "has laid on him the iniquity of us all" (Isaiah 53:6). We should not strip away any meaning from these words but leave them with their proper meaning. God is not entertaining us with the prophet's words. Instead, he is pleading with great love. He is saying that Christ, this Lamb of God, would carry the sins of us all. However, what does "to carry" mean? To which the religious philosophers respond, "To be punished." Very well. But why then is Christ punished? Is it not because He has sin and carries sin? Now, that Christ has sin is testified by the Holy Spirit in Psalm 40:12–13: "For troubles without number surround me; my sins have overtaken me, and I cannot see. They are more than the hairs of my head" (NIV). Then Psalm 41:5 says, "I said, 'Have mercy on me, Lord; heal me, for I have sinned against you'" (NIV). Further, "You, God, know my folly; my guilt is not hidden from you" (Psalm

---

[211] *poenas.*

[212] *et in futurum faciemus.*

69:5–6, NIV). In these psalms, the Holy Spirit speaks in the person of Christ and with clear words testifies that He had sins. This testimony is not that of an innocent voice but of a suffering Christ, who took on Himself the burden of becoming the totality of all sinners in one single person and thus was made to be guilty of all the sins of the world.

Thus Christ was not only crucified and put to death, but sin was placed on Him (for the love of God's majesty). Then when sin was placed on Him, the law came and said, "Every sinner must die. Therefore, Oh Christ, if you will answer, plead guilty and not only suffer the punishment for all sinners but the sin and the curse." Paul then correctly relates this text from the law of Moses to Christ: "Cursed by God[213] is everyone who hangs from a tree." Christ has hung from the tree; therefore, Christ is cursed by God.[214]

This is a very unique comfort for all Christians, to shroud Christ in our sins. Let us enfold Him with my sins, your sins, and the sins of all the world and see Him carrying the burden of all our sins, for when we see Him like this, all the vain dreams of the Papists regarding justification and works will easily disappear, for they do imagine (as I've said) that there is a certain faith molded and adorned by love. According to them, this faith takes away sin, and people are justified before God. But what else is this but to take away the covering from Christ, unwrapping Him from our sins, to make Him innocent? It is also to burden ourselves with our own sins and fix our eyes on them and not on Christ but us! Yes, and isn't this to dismiss Christ altogether and make Him totally worthless for us? If it is true that we take away sin through the works of the law and love, then Christ is not the one who takes them away. But if He is the Lamb of God designated from eternity to take away the sins of the world and if by His own will He is so enveloped in our sins that He became a curse for us, then it necessarily follows that we cannot be justified by works, for God has not placed our sins on us but on His Son Christ. Thus He is punished for them and becomes our peace, and through His wounds, we are healed (Isaiah 53:5). Therefore, we cannot take them away. Scripture testifies about all this. We also confess them in the articles of the Christian faith[215] when we say, "I believe in Jesus Christ, Son of God, who suffered, was crucified, and died for us."

Thus the doctrine of the Gospel (the sweetest and most comforting of all others) speaks not of our works or the works of the law but of the incomprehensible and inexpressible mercy and love of God toward us unworthy and lost human beings. That doctrine is this. Our most merciful Father, seeing that we were oppressed by the curse of the law and held under its power so that we could never have freed ourselves in our own strength, sent His only Son to the world. And He said to Him, "Become that Peter, the denier. Become that Paul, the persecutor,

---

213 *est maledictio Dei.*
214 *ergo Christus est maledictum Dei.*
215 *in Symbolo,* The Apostles' Creed.

blasphemer, and cruel executioner. Become that David, the adulterer. Become that sinner who ate the fruit in the garden. Become that thief who hung from the cross. For a moment, you must become the person that has committed the sins of every human being. Be sure you pay and satisfy the penalty for them all." Then the law appears and says to Him, "I find that you are a guilty sinner and such a great sinner that you have taken on your body the sins of all human beings. Thus I see no sins on anyone but You. Thus You must die on the cross!" Then the law lunges against Him and kills Him. But in such a way, the entire world is purified and cleansed of all sin, free from death and all evil. Now, since sin and death are abolished by this one man, God only sees throughout the whole world, especially in those who believe, not only cleansing, but righteousness! And if there remains some residue of sin, due to Christ's glory that outshines the sun,[216] God is unable to see it.

This is how we should magnify the article of Christian righteousness against the righteousness of the law and works.[217] Even so, there is no eloquence that can proclaim it as it deserves or able to magnify its infinite greatness. Thus the argument that Paul presents in this text is the most powerful against the righteousness of the law. That is because it contains this irrefutable argument: that if all the sins of the world are found in this one man, Jesus Christ, then they are no longer found in the world. What's more, if Christ is guilty of all the sins we have committed, then we are totally and entirely freed from all sin. However, not by ourselves, nor by our works or merits, but by Him. But if He is innocent and does not bear our sins, then we must bear them, and in them, we shall die and be condemned. "But thanks be to God, who gives us the victory through our Lord Jesus Christ. Amen."

Let us see how these two things so opposite can be reconciled in this one person. Not only my sins and yours but also those of the entire world—past, present, and future sins—take a hold of Him, sentence, and certainly condemn Him. Now, in Himself, He is now the worst and tops all sinners, and at the same time, there is in Him an eternal and unconquerable righteousness. There is a confrontation between the greatest and only sinner and the most exalted and only righteousness. Here, one of the two must yield to the other, since they struggle against each other with great strength and power. The sin of the whole world lunges with all its strength against righteousness itself. What will be the result of this combat? Righteousness is eternal, immortal, and invincible. Sin is also a powerful and cruel tyrant, reigning over the entire world, subjecting and submitting everyone everywhere. In fact, sin is such a powerful god that it devours all humanity—the educated, the illiterate, the saints, and the wise. This tyrant lunges against Christ to devour Him as he has done with all others. But sin realizes that Christ is a person with an invincible and eternal righteousness. In this duel, sin is compelled to concede, it is conquered and vanquished. Righteousness triumphs, lives, and

---

[216] *prae illo sole Christo*, literally "due to that sun, Christ."

[217] *magnificare articulum justitiae christianae contra justitiam legis et operum.*

reigns. Thus it is that in Christ all sin is conquered, put to death, and buried. Righteousness remains triumphant and reigns forever!

In the same way, death is an omnipotent queen and empress over the entire world, killing kings, princes, and all in general. It has a powerful confrontation with life, thinking it will overthrow it once and for all and will devour it, and whatever it sets out to do, it will certainly accomplish. But since life is immortal, even when it was conquered, life itself conquered death and obtained the victory, spoiling and killing death. *The church sings passionately about this combat: "In dread and wondrous strife, did death and life contend. Life's Captain who once died, now lives and reigns forever."* Death then is conquered and vanquished by Christ. It is only now as a matter of speaking, death in a mere painting. It has lost its sting and no longer can hurt those who believe in Christ. He is also the death of death, as the prophet Hosea said, "Oh death, I will be your death"[218] (Hosea 13:14).

It's the same with the curse, which is God's wrath over the entire world. It also goes into conflict with the blessing, which is God's eternal grace and mercy in Christ. The curse battles against the blessing; it would condemn and neutralize it, but it can't. The blessing is divine and eternal, and thus the curse must yield, for if the blessing in Christ could be defeated, then God Himself would be conquered. But this is impossible. Christ is God's power, righteousness, blessing, grace, and life. He defeats and destroys the monsters of sin, death, and the curse without weapons, only in His own body and in Himself. That's why Paul delights in saying, "He disarmed the principalities and powers and made a public example of them, triumphing over them in him" (Colossians 2:15). Then they can no longer injure those who believe.

This situation "in Himself"[219] turns this combat into a much more marvelous and glorious struggle. It demonstrates that so many things, the curse, sin, and death, were destroyed (in their place, blessing, righteousness, and life were perpetuated). They were to be placed on this one and only person, who in Himself would be the substitute for every creature.[220] Thus when I look closely at this person,[221] I see sin, death, God's wrath, hell, the devil, and every evil vanquished and destroyed.[222] As Christ reigns by His grace in the hearts of the faithful, sin, death, and the curse are made null and void. But where Christ is unknown, all these

---

[218] As quoted by Luther.

[219] *in semet ipso,* literally "in Himself." Luther is quoting from the Vulgate.

[220] *atque ita per eam mutari totam creaturam;* Middleton/Watson translate this as "the whole creature through this one person should be renewed."

[221] Rörer's note: *credentibus peccatum & mors abolitae,* "believing that all sin has been put to death and abolished."

[222] *ideo si hanc personam aspexeris, vides peccatum, mortem, iram dei, inferos, diabolum & omniva mala victa et mortificata.*

things remain. Therefore, those who do not believe lack this victory. "And this is our victory," says John, "faith" (1 John 5:4).

This is the chief article of all Christian doctrine[223] that the papal scholars have totally obscured. Today, the fanatic-minded cast darkness[224] over it as well. Given this, you can see how important it is to believe and confess the fundamental divinity of Christ. When Arius denied it, he necessarily denied the premise of our redemption.[225] To conquer the sin of the world, death, the curse, and the wrath of God in Himself is the work not of any creature but of divine power. Thus the one who in Himself has vanquished these evils can only be truly God in nature, for this breathtaking power of sin, death, and the curse (which also reigns in this world and in all creatures) could only be met with a higher and more imposing power. But unless it is the power of the sovereign and divine majesty, such power cannot be found. The power to abolish sin, destroy death, take away the curse in Himself on one side and on the other to give righteousness, bring life back again, and grant the blessing, these are solely the works of the divine majesty alone. Scripture ascribes all this to Christ. He in Himself is life, righteousness, and blessing, which is God in nature and substance.[226] That is why those who deny the divinity of Christ lose everything that is Christianity and become altogether Muslims and Gentiles. As I have often admonished you, we should diligently learn the article of justification. All other articles of our faith are found within its walls. If it is kept whole, then the others will be whole. Consequently, when we teach that human beings are justified by Christ, that Christ is the conqueror over sin, death, and eternal damnation, with all this we testify that He is God in His very nature.

Here, we can clearly see how horrible was the wickedness and blindness of the Pope's academicians. They taught that those cruel despots and tyrants, sin, death, the curse (which devour humanity whole), can be defeated, not by the righteousness of God's law (which although it is righteous, good, and holy is only able to declare people under a curse) but by the righteousness of man's works,[227] such as fasts, pilgrimages, masses, vows, and other miserly conduct. But tell me, has there ever been found anyone who by using that armor conquered sin, death, and the devil? In Ephesians 6, Paul describes another type of armor that we should use against those most cruel and furious beasts. But then, these blind leading the blind guides have stripped us naked, leaving us without armor and exposed to these extremely powerful and invincible tyrants. Not only have they handed us over into their hands to be devoured, but they also have made us ten times more

---

[223] *Hic est praecipuus locus christianae.*

[224] *fanatici spiritus denuo obscurant.*

[225] *necesse fait etiam negare eum articulum redemtionis.*

[226] *quae naturaliter et substantialiter Deus est.*

[227] *justitia operum humanorum.*

wicked sinners than thieves, prostitutes, or assassins, for the power to destroy and abolish sin, create righteousness, and give life belongs only to God. But they have attributed this divine power to our own works, saying that if you do this or that work, you will defeat sin, death, and the wrath of God. In this way, they put us in a place that belongs only to God, making us certainly even in our nature,[228] if I'm allowed to say it, as if we were God Himself! By teaching this, the Papists have revealed themselves as idolaters seven times worse than the Gentiles. They are like the hog; no sooner it's washed, it goes back to rolling in the mud. As Christ said, after they have fallen away from the faith, an unclean spirit, when he has gone out of the man, returns taking "seven other spirits more wicked than itself, and they go in and live there. And the final condition of that person is worse than the first" (Luke 11:26, NIV).

Thus let us receive this sweetest doctrine, full of comfort, with thanksgiving, with a certainty of faith,[229] which teaches that Christ has been made a curse for us (a sinner subject to the wrath of God), for He placed on Himself our own person, and placed our sins on His own shoulders, saying, "I have committed the sins that every single human being has committed." Thus He certainly was made a curse according to the law, not for Himself, but as Paul said, "for us," for if He had not taken on Himself my sins and your sins and the sins of the entire world, the law would not have had any rights over Him, for the law only condemns sinners and holds them bound to the curse. Otherwise, he could not have been made a curse, He not could have died, since the only cause of the curse and of death is sin, but He was free of these. However, since He took on Himself our sins, not because He was obligated but of His own free will,[230] it was necessary for Him to carry the burden of God's wrath and receive its punishment, not for His own person (for He was righteous and invincible and thus without guilt) but for us.

In fact, He made a very favorable exchange for us. He took on Himself our own person of sin and gave us His innocent and victorious person, with whom we are now dressed anew and freed from the curse of the law, for Christ of His own free will was made a curse for us,[231] saying, "Regarding my own person, in my humanity as well as in my divinity, I am blessed, nothing is lacking. But I will empty myself and put your person upon Myself; I will take your human nature and in like manner will walk among you and suffer death to deliver you from death." Now, since He carried the sin of the entire world on our behalf, gave Himself over, suffered, was crucified, and died, that means He made Himself a curse for us. But since He is a divine and eternal person, it was impossible for death to hold Him

---

[228] *vere et naturaliter.*

[229] *certa fiducia.*

[230] *non coacte, sed sua sponte.*

[231] Luther adds this footnote: *Christi justitia nostra, nostrum peccatum suum,* "Christ is our righteousness, we are his sin."

back. Therefore, He rose on the third day after His death and now lives forever. In all His greatness, neither our sin nor our death can be found, but only righteousness, life, and eternal blessing!

We should always keep this image before us and gaze upon it with an unwavering faith. Whoever does this will have Christ's innocence and victory, even if he is the greatest sinner! *But it cannot be acquired by the will to love but by reason illumined by faith.*[232] Therefore, we are justified by faith alone because the only way to grasp onto Christ's victory is by faith alone.[233] Then take a good look and see how much you believe this, how much you rejoice in it. If you believe that sin, death, and the curse have been abolished, then they truly have been abolished. Christ has defeated and taken them away in Himself. He wants us to believe that just as in His own person there is now no longer any resemblance of sin or vestige of death,[234] so neither are these found in us, seeing that He has fulfilled and accomplished all on our behalf.

Therefore, if sin frustrates you and death haunts you, you should think that it is only a figment of your imagination (for that's what it is) and a plain deception of the devil, for with all certainty, there is no longer any sin, curse, death, nor devil who can harm us, since Christ has conquered and abolished all these things. Consequently, Christ's victory is entirely true, and there is no defect at all in it (since above all it is true). The only defect is in our inability to believe. Reason finds it hard to believe in these riches so blessed and beyond words. Further, Satan with his fiery darts and his ministers with their false and wicked doctrine, strive to spoil us of this teaching and disfigure it altogether. They come against this article in particular, which we teach so diligently, and by which we suffer the hate and cruel persecution of Satan and the world, for Satan feels the power and the fruit of this pivotal doctrine.

When we confess daily in the Apostles' Creed, "I believe in the one holy church," we are saying that there is no longer any sin, death, or curse, since Christ already reigns. It is nothing less than if we said, "I believe that there is no sin, curse, nor death in God's church." Those who believe in Christ are not sinners, nor guilty of death, but they are holy and righteous, governing over sin and death, and living forever! But this can only be seen with faith, for we say, "I believe in the one holy church." But if you believe reason and in your own eyes, you are going to see something totally to the contrary, for you are going to see many things in the believers that will offend you. Sometimes you can see that they fall into sin; they are weak in the faith; they are subject to anger, envy, and other evil effects. Thus one could mistakenly conclude, "The church is not holy."

---

[232] *Sed ea non potest voluntate dilectionis, sed ratione illuminata fide.*

[233] *Ergo sola fide justificamur, quia sola fides apprehendit hanc victoriam Christi.* Rörer's note: *Fides sola victoriam Christi apprehendit,* "faith alone grasps Christ's victory."

[234] *nulla . . . larva peccatoris, nullum vestigium mortis.*

I reject that conclusion. If I fix my eyes on my own person, or in my brother's person, it will never be holy. But if I gaze upon Christ, who has sanctified and purified His church, then it is altogether holy, for He has taken away the sins of the entire world!

Therefore, wherever I can see and feel sins, then truly these are no longer sins. According to Paul's theology, there is no sin, nor death, nor curse anywhere in the world except on Christ, who is the Lamb of God who has taken the sins of the world. He was made a curse in order to deliver us from the curse. But on the contrary, according to philosophy and reason, sin, death, and the curse are not found anywhere else but in the world, in the flesh, or in sinners, for with respect to sin, the rhetorical theologian and the pagan philosopher say the same thing. It's just like the color, they say; it sticks to the wall. That's how sin is stuck to the world: in the flesh or in the conscience. Thus it is necessary to purify it through opposing forces—namely, love. But true theology teaches that there is no more sin in the world, since Christ, on whom the Father laid the sins of the entire world, has defeated and vanquished all of them in His own body (Isaiah 53:6). He who died for sin and was resurrected does not die again. Therefore, wherever true faith in Christ is found, sin has been abolished, put to death, and buried. But wherever there is no faith in Christ, sin still remains. And even though vestiges of sin may remain in the saints, since they still have not been perfected in the faith; these vestiges are as good as dead, since these are not imputed against them due to their faith in Christ.

This is a strong and powerful argument that Paul presents against the righteousness of works. It is Christ who rescues us from eternal damnation; it is not the law nor its works.[235] Look then dear Christian reader,[236] by God![237] Learn to distinguish between Christ and the law. Pay attention at how Paul spoke and what he said. "All," he said, "who do not continually accomplish all the works of the law are necessarily under the curse. But there is no one who always does all the works of the law." Therefore, the first proposition is true: "All human beings are under the curse." But then, he adds the other proposition: "Christ has redeemed us from the curse of the law having been made a curse for us. Therefore, the law and works do not redeem from the curse; instead, they place us under the curse." Thus love (which according to the scholastics shapes and perfects faith) was not only incapable of redeeming us from the curse; instead, it has thrust and wrapped us up more and more within the curse.

---

[235] Luther's footnote: *Christius redemit a malediction, ergo non lex,* "Christ redeemed us from the curse, therefore it wasn't the law."

[236] Obviously, this phrase directed to the "Christian reader" was added by either Rörer or Luther during the preparation of the notes for publication. The original text represents transcripts of Luther's live lectures to seminarians on the Epistle to the Galatians.

[237] *per Deum.*

Well then, since Christ is more than the law and the works of the law, so the redemption that Christ obtained on our behalf is much more than my merits or the works of the law. (Why?)[238] Because it was necessary that Christ Himself should redeem us from the curse of the law. Thus all remain under the curse if they don't grasp onto Christ by faith, neither are the papal philosophers so foolish as to say that Christ is our work or our love. Christ is much more than any other work we could ever do. It doesn't matter how crazy any follower of the Pope may be, he wouldn't dare say that the offerings they give to the poor, or the obedience rendered by the monk, is Christ, for Christ is God and man, conceived by the Holy Spirit, born from the Virgin Mary, etc. Paul said of Him that He was made for us a curse to redeem us from the curse of the law. Therefore, the law, works, love, vows, and the like do not redeem. Instead, they tie us up more around the curse and hold us down under its weight. Therefore, the more we have worked, the less we will truly know Christ and grasp onto Him.

We cannot grasp Christ through the law nor its works but through faith that illumines reason or the intellect. Grasping Christ by faith is the proper contemplative life[239] (of which the religious philosophers and the monks foolishly imagine with their heads in the clouds[240]). Rather, it is theologically driven, for it fixes its gaze upon that trustworthy and divine serpent hanging on the execution stake,[241] it is gazing upon Christ hanging on the cross for my sins, your sins, and the sins of the entire world. Therefore, it is evident that faith alone justifies.[242] But when we are justified by faith, we march on to the active life. The religious philosophers have correctly pointed to the difference between the contemplative life and the active life.[243] But if only they would have called the one Gospel and the other law! If only they would have taught that the contemplative life should be included in and guided by God's word and that our gaze should fix on nothing but the word of the Gospel. However, the active life should be sought within the law, by which man does not grasp onto Christ but is exercised in works of love toward his neighbor.

This text makes it clear that all human beings, even the apostles, the prophets, and the patriarchs, would have remained under the curse had not Christ come between sin, death, the curse of the law, the wrath and the judgment of God and defeated them in His own body, for there is no other power in flesh and blood that could have conquered these monsters. But then, Christ is not the law, nor a work of the law, but the divine human person, who took on Himself sin, the condemnation of the law and death, not for Himself but for us. Thus all the weight and force of the text are contained in these words, "for us."

---

[238] The "why" is implied in the "because" that follows. Either someone in the lecture hall asked the question or the "why" was obvious in Luther's statement.

[239] *propie est speculativa vita.*

[240] *in mirabilibus supra se.*

[241] *fidelis et divina inspectio serpentis suspensi in palo.*

[242] *Manifestum ergo est solam fidem justificare.*

[243] *vitam contemplativam et activam.*

Therefore, we should not imagine an innocent Christ as a distant and aloof person (as the scholastics, the fathers, Jerome, and all others have considered Him), holy and righteous in and for Himself alone. It is true that Christ in His person is the most pure and spotless being. However, don't stay there because you still don't have Christ, even though you may know Him as God and man. But you will most certainly have Him when you have believed that the Father has designated this Person, the most pure and innocent, to be your High Priest and Savior—what's more, even to be your Servant so that He, emptying Himself of that innocence and holiness, took your sinful person on Himself. Having done so, He took away your sin, your death, and your curse. Then on your behalf, He offered Himself as a sacrifice, having become a curse for you, and in this way, delivered you from the curse of the law.

LECTURE 21: Friday, September 18

You can then see the apostolic spirit with which Paul treated this argument of the blessing and the curse. At the same time, he not only places Christ under the curse but also says that He is made the curse. In that same way, he calls Him sin when he said, "God made him who had no sin to be sin for us so that in him we might become the righteousness of God" (2 Corinthians 5:21, NIV). It is true that these phrases could well be interpreted like this: Christ is made a curse, in other words, a sacrifice for the curse; and sin, which is to say, a sacrifice for sin. However, I think it's best to retain the proper meaning of the words because it contains great strength and passion. When a sinner comes to the knowledge of himself, he feels not only his own misery but that he is misery itself. He realizes that he is not only a sinner, under condemnation, but also sin and nothing more than damnation, for it is something terrible to carry sin, the wrath of God, the curse and death. Thus whoever truly feels these things (as certainly Christ truly felt them on behalf of all humanity) is made in fact sin, death, the curse. Therefore, Paul approaches this text with a true apostolic spirit. There is no papal philosopher, lawyer, Jew, fanatic, or anyone else that has spoken like him, for who would dare to take this text of Moses, "Cursed whoever hangs on a tree," and then relate it to Christ? Paul related this statement to Christ so we may apply it to Christ. In fact, we not only can take all of Deuteronomy 27 but put together all the curses that are found in the entire law of Moses and bind them to Christ, for as Christ is innocent with respect to this law in general, with regards to His own person, He is also in everything else. And because he was made a curse for us and hung on a tree as a criminal, blasphemer, assassin, and traitor, He is guilty with respect to this law in a general sense and guilty in everything else. All the curses of the law get piled up and placed on Him. Thus He carried and suffered for all of them in His body for us. Consequently, He was not only cursed but became the curse itself for us.

This is interpreting the Scriptures as a true apostle. No one can speak like that without the Holy Spirit. He gathers together the entire law in this one statement: "Christ was made a curse for us," and then carried its total weight on His own person. There's also the opposite. He gathers together all the promises of Scripture and says they were once and for all fulfilled in Christ. Paul takes this apostolic and invincible argument not just from certain parts of the law but from the totality of the law, on which he rests his argument.

Here, we can see how diligently Paul read the Holy Scriptures and how carefully he weighed each word of this text: "In your seed shall be blessed all the nations of the earth" (Genesis 22:18). First, from this word, "blessing," he puts together this argument: If the blessing shall be given to all the nations, then all the nations are also under the curse, even the Jews who have the law, for the Scriptures testify that all Jews who are under the law are also under the curse: "Cursed is everyone who does not abide in all the things written in this book."

Further, he weighs this clause very carefully: "All the nations." From it, he argues the following: the blessing belongs not only to the Jews but also to all the nations throughout the world. Then, since it belongs to all the nations, it is impossible that it can be obtained through the law of Moses for no other nation had the law except the Jews. And even though they had the law, they were far from obtaining the blessing through the law. That's because the more they tried to fulfill it, the more they fell under the curse of the law. Thus there should be a much more excellent righteousness than the righteousness of the law through which not only the Jews but all the nations throughout the entire world would also obtain the blessing.

Finally, these words, "in your seed," are explained in the following way. That a certain man should be born from the seed of Abraham—that is, Christ, by whom the blessing would then come over all the nations. Thus seeing that Christ would be the one who would bless all the nations, it would also be He who would take away their curse. But He could not take away the curse through the law because the law magnifies the curse even more. Then what did He do? He joined Himself to the company of the accursed, taking their flesh and blood on Himself, intervening as Mediator between God and humanity, saying, "Even though I am flesh and blood and now dwell among the damned, even so, I am that blessed One by whom all people are to be blessed." It's in that manner how in one person God and humanity are united, and having joined Himself to us who are under the curse, He becomes a curse for us. He hid His blessing in our sin, in our death, and in our curse, which then condemned and put Him to death. But since He was the Son of God, these could not hold Him back. Instead, He defeated them, and took captivity captive triumphing over them. That which clung to His flesh[244] was what He had taken from

---

[244] *et quidquid adhaesit carni.*

us and then carried it within Himself. Therefore, all who cling[245] unto His flesh are blessed and freed from the curse—that is, from sin and eternal death.

There are those who do not understand this benefit of Christ (which is the Gospel's uniquely urgent call[246]), and they don't know any other righteousness unless it is the righteousness of the law. When they hear that the works of the law do not exist as necessary for salvation but that instead all receive it only by hearing and believing that Christ the Son of God became flesh and has joined Himself to the accursed to bless all the nations, they (I say) are deeply offended.[247] That's because they don't understand a thing about all this or otherwise understand it in the flesh. Their minds are occupied in pondering other fantasies of their imaginations. Thus they think these things are unexplainable.[248] Even we, who have received the first fruits of the Spirit, find it impossible to perfectly understand these things, for they engage our reason in a powerful struggle.

In conclusion, we would have been swept away by the flood of evil, as the wicked will be flooded away forever. But Christ made Himself the transgressor of all laws on our behalf. He made Himself to be guilty of all our condemnation for all our sins and wickedness. He intervenes as mediator and embraces us all wicked and damnable sinners. He took on Himself and carried all our wickedness, which would have oppressed and tormented us forever. These momentarily overwhelmed Him as passing waters over His head, as the prophet personified Christ groaning, "Your wrath lies heavy upon me, and you overwhelm me with all your waves" (Psalm 88:7, NRSV). Also, "Your wrath has swept over me; your dread assaults destroy me" (Psalm 88:16, NRSV). In this way, through Christ, we are delivered from these eternal dreads and sufferings and will enjoy an eternal and unspeakable peace and happiness if we believe.

These are the deep mysteries of Scriptures, which lead us to worship. Moses also revealed them beforehand in some texts but darkly. The prophets and the apostles also showed the same knowledge and handed it down to their posterity. The saints of the Old Testament rejoiced in this knowledge and benefit of Christ much more than we do now, although He reveals Himself to us with great comfort. Certainly, we ourselves recognize that this knowledge of Christ and that the righteousness of faith is a priceless treasure, but we cannot conceive the fullness of joy experienced by the prophets and the apostles. That is why there arose from them and from Paul such an abundant and diligent exposition of this article of

---

[245] *itaque omnes illi carni adhaerentes.*

[246] *de quo evangelium propie concionatur.*

[247] Rörer adds this footnote: *Hypocritae offenduntur doctrina evangelii,* "the hypocrites are offended by the doctrine of the Gospel."

[248] *aenigmata.*

justification,[249] for the proper function of an apostle is to display the glory and the benefit of Christ and thus raise up and comfort guilty consciences everywhere.

VERSE 14. That in Christ Jesus the blessing of Abraham might come upon the Gentiles, that we might receive the promise of the Spirit through faith [RSV].

Paul's eyes are always focused on this phrase: "In your seed." That's because the blessing promised to Abraham could not reach the Gentiles except through Christ alone, who is the Seed of Abraham. For this to be accomplished, it was necessary that Christ should become a curse so that this promise made to Abraham, "In your seed will all the nations of the earth be blessed," could be fulfilled. Thus there was no way at all the promise could be fulfilled unless Jesus necessarily became a curse and joined Himself to the accursed Gentiles,[250] to take away their curse and by His blessing bring them righteousness and life. Here, I emphasize (as I forewarned you) that this word *blessing* is not in vain, as the Jews have imagined. They explain it away, saying that it's just a greeting passed on by word of mouth or in writing. But here, Paul is referring to sin and righteousness, life and death before God. Consequently, he is talking about priceless and incomprehensible things when he says, "So that Abraham's blessing would come on the Gentiles, through Jesus Christ."

Further, look at the type of merit that we offer and how we obtain this blessing. These are indeed congruous and condign merits all in one; it is the preparatory work by which we obtain this righteousness: "That Jesus Christ was made a curse for us." It is due to our own indifference that we don't know God, that we are enemies of God, that we are dead in our sins and under the curse. What then, is it that we merit? What else can the damned deserve, who don't take God into account, who are dead in their sins, and who are subject to God's wrath and judgment? When the Pope excommunicates someone, everything that person does is considered accursed. How much more could we say is someone damned before God (as we all are before knowing Christ), who does nothing else but that which is under a curse? There is no other way to avoid the curse except to believe, and with assured confidence say, "You, Christ, are my sin and my curse," or rather, "I am your sin, your curse, your death, your wrath of God, your hell." The opposite is true as well: "You are my righteousness, my blessing, my life, my grace of God, and my heaven." The text says it clearly: "Christ was made for us a curse." Therefore, we are the cause by which He was made a curse. No! Rather, we are His curse!

This is an excellent text and it is full of spiritual comfort. And although it does not satisfy the blind and hard-hearted Jews, it does satisfy us who have been baptized and received this doctrine that powerfully concludes that we are blessed

---

[249] *articulus justificationis.*
[250] *gentibus maledictis.*

by Christ's curse, sin, and death. By these, we are justified and brought back to life.[251] Because as long as sin, death, and the curse remain in us, sin torments us, death kills, and the curse condemns us. But when these are transferred and placed on Jesus' back, then these evils are entirely His, and all His benefits are ours. Thus let us learn in all temptation to transfer sin, death, the curse, and all other evil that oppresses us from us to Christ and in the same step to transfer from Him to us righteousness, mercy, life, and blessing, for He carries all our evil and misery. "God the Father has placed all our iniquities," as the prophet Isaiah says, "on Him" (Isaiah 53:6). He has taken them of His goodwill, even though He was not guilty. But He did it fulfilling the will of the Father, by which we are sanctified forever.

This is the infinite and immeasurable mercy of God, which Paul magnified with great joy, eloquence, and abundance of words. However, the diminished capacity of the human heart cannot understand and even less mutter anything coherent about God's boundless and burning love for us.[252] Certainly, the incalculable greatness of God's mercy engenders not only resistance in us to believe but unbelief itself. Because I hear not only that the Almighty God, the Creator and Maker of all things, is good and merciful but also that this supremely great and sovereign majesty cared so much for me, a condemned sinner, a son of wrath and eternal death, that God did not withhold His own Son. Rather, He gave Him over to the cruelest death so that He, hanging between two thieves, would become a curse and sin for me, an accursed sinner, so that I could be blessed as a son and heir of God. Who could sufficiently exalt and praise this great kindness of God? Not even the angels in heaven. Thus the doctrine of the Gospel speaks about other issues much higher than any book of morality or philosophy, even more than the book of Moses. The Gospel speaks of God's most divine and inexpressible gifts that surpass the capacity and understanding of angels and any human even though it were to be added up altogether to its greatest sum.

VERSE 14. So that by faith we might receive the promise of the Spirit [NIV].

This is a phrase from the Hebrew language: "The promise of the Spirit," or the promised Spirit. The Spirit is freedom from the law, from sin, from death, from the curse, from hell, and from God's wrath and judgment. Here, there's no congruous or condign merit or anything of value on our part. Instead, a promise given freely as a gift through Abraham's seed so that we may be freed from all evil and obtain everything that is good. This freedom and gift of the Spirit we don't receive due to any merit but by faith alone, for it is only faith that can grasp the promises

---

[251] *justificati et vivificati simus.*

[252] *abyssum profundissimam et zelum ardentissimum divinae caritatis erga nos non potest angustia cordis humani comprehendere, multo minus eloqui.*

of God, as Paul says in this text: "So that by faith we might receive the promise of the Spirit, not by works, but by faith."

This is indeed a true and sweet apostolic doctrine, for it shows all that has been accomplished on our behalf. It has all now been given to us. Many prophets and kings desired to see and hear it. Texts like these summarize many declarations from the prophets who from times past, in the Spirit, saw that all things would be changed, restored, and governed by this man, Christ. None of the prophets or rulers of God's people gave any new law. Elijah, Samuel, David, and all other prophets remained under the law of Moses. They did not legislate new tables of the law, or a new kingdom, or priesthood, for that new kingdom, priesthood, law, and worship was related to and reserved only to Him. Long before, Moses had prophesied about Him: "The Lord your God will raise up for you a prophet like me from among you, from your fellow Israelites. You must listen[253] to him" (Deuteronomy 18:15, NIV). It's as if he had said, "Listen only to Him and no one else."

The fathers understood this well. No one could teach greater and loftier themes than Moses himself, who made laws about great and lofty matters, as are the Ten Commandments. Look at the first commandment: "I am the Lord your God . . . You shall have no other gods before me. You shall love the Lord your God with all your heart, and with all your soul, and with all your might." This law regarding love to God also encompasses the angels. Thus it is the fountain of all divine wisdom. Nonetheless, it was necessary for another Master to come—that is, Christ. He would bring and teach something that would surpass those excellent laws—in brief, grace and the remission of sins. Thus this text is replete with power. In this brief statement, "that we may receive the promise of the Spirit by faith," Paul pours out all at once everything he could have said. When he cannot go any further (for he could not have said anything greater or sublime), he cuts off and stands on what he said.

VERSE 15. To give a human example, brethren: no one annuls even a man's will, or adds to it, once it has been ratified.

After this main and invincible argument, Paul adds another one based on the similarity to someone's last will and testament. This argument is seemingly weak and of such nature that the apostle should not have used it to confirm such an important subject. In such great and weighty matters, we should confirm human issues with divine matters and not the divine with such earthly and mundane concerns. *It so happens that once Cicero said, "Homer transferred things human to the gods: I would rather transfer things divine to us."* And indeed, it's true these are the weakest of all arguments, when we argue from the human to the

---

[253] Luther adds this footnote: *Christi doctrina longe melior Mosi,* "the doctrine of Christ is far better than Moses."

divine,[254] as does Scotus. "Man," he said, "is capable of loving God above all things, for he loves himself above all things. Therefore, how much more then, he certainly is able to love God above all things; since something good, the greater it is, can be loved so much more." From here, it is inferred that man is capable, *ex puris naturalibus—that is,* from his own natural strength, to easily fulfill that lofty commandment: "You shall love God from all your heart," etc. "Thus," he said, "man can love the lesser things above all things, even to the point of denying his own life (which exacts from him the highest cost) for the love of filthy lucre. But since that is true, he can do so much more for God's sake."

You have frequently heard me say that civil law and the rules of the home are from God, since God has ordained and permitted them, just as He has done with the sun, the moon, and other creations. Thus an argument taken from the ordinances given by God to the creatures is good, if we use it properly. In this vein, we find the prophets frequently using examples and comparisons to the creatures. They call Christ the sun, the church the moon, the preachers and teachers of the word stars. There are also many comparisons in the prophets involving trees, thorns, flowers, and the fruits of the earth. Similarly, the New Testament abounds with such examples. Thus wherever we may find an ordinance of God for His creatures, we could find an argument that could lend itself to compare with divine and heavenly matters.

Thus it was that our Savior Christ in Matthew 7:11, arguing from earthly to heavenly things, said, "If you then, who are evil, know how to give good gifts to your children, how much more will your Father who is in heaven give good things to those who ask him!" Paul also said, "We must obey God rather than men." Jeremiah also says in chapter 35, "The Rechabites obeyed their parents, how much more will you not receive my instruction to obey my words?"[255] Well, all these things are given by God and are his teachings that the parents should pass on to their children and that the children should obey their parents. Thus these are good arguments when they are based on God's commands. However, if their starting point is the corrupt affection of men, they are null and void, for that is Scotus's argument: "If I can love that which is of lesser value, then so much more I can love that which is of greater value." I reject such a conclusion. My love is not according to what God commands but rather a diabolical corruption.[256] It is true that I should have that kind of love, that I, loving myself or some other creature, should love God the Creator even more, but it is not so. The love with which I love is corrupt and contrary to God.[257]

---

[254] *cum ab humanis ad divina argumentamur.*

[255] Luther summarizes Jeremiah 35 in this quote.

[256] *quia meum diligere non est ordinatio divina, sed depravatio diabolica.*

[257] *quo diligo me ipsum, est vitiosus et contra Deum.* Luther adds in his own footnote, *amor nostri vitiosus,* "our love is polluted."

I say this so that no one starts to think that an argument taken from corruptible things and related to divine and spiritual matters would not have any of value, *neither am I disputing if the argument may be rhetorical or dialectic. I only say this, that the argument that begins with human matters and relates them to God has sufficient strength if it is founded on a command of God, as we see is the case here.* Civil law, which has been ordained by God, says that it is not lawful to annul or change a person's last will and testament.

It is true that if the testator still lives, the will is not ratified, but when he dies, any change is illegal. But this is said not de facto *but* de jure—*that is, with respect to what should be done and is done properly because the law upholds that a testament should not be changed. The laws themselves decree that anyone's last will and testament should be religiously observed and is one of the most sacred traditions among humankind.*[258]

Thus using this tradition of the human last will and testament as a foundation, Paul argues in the following way. Why is man obeyed but not God? With respect to the civil laws of the land regarding testaments and other things, people carefully observe these matters. Nothing is changed; nothing is added or taken away. But then they do take the liberty to change and add to God's testament—that is, His promise regarding the spiritual blessing, heavenly and eternal matters, which the entire world should not just receive with great gratitude but also reverent worship. This has great persuasive power, to argue using human law as an example. Thus he says, "To give a human example"—that is, I bring to you an example taken from human ways and traditions. "The human will and testament and other corruptible matters are rigorously enforced and that which the law commands is diligently kept and enforced. But when a man declares his last will and testament, giving away his lands and goods to his heirs, and subsequently dies, that testament is confirmed and ratified by the death of the testator. From then on, nothing may be added or taken away, according to all the laws of the land. No more legal consultations will take place, and it is for everyone's benefit to submit to the testament. Thus I ask, 'If such respect and loyalty is shown a human testament, so that nothing is added or withdrawn, certainly God's last will and testament promised and granted to Abraham and his seed should be much more strictly obeyed!'"

With Christ's death, the testament was validated. But after His death, God's last written will and testament was unsealed, which is to say, "The blessing promised to Abraham was then preached among all the nations scattered throughout the entire world." This was God's last will and testament, the great testator, validated by the death of Christ.

Thus no one should change it or add anything to it. But they who teach the law and the traditions of men do just that. They say that unless they are circumcised, keep the law, do many works, and suffer many things, they cannot be saved.

---

[258] *inter sacra humana.*

This is not God's last will and testament. He did not say to Abraham, "If you do this or that, you will receive the blessing, or those who are circumcised and keep the law will receive it." Instead, He said, "In your seed shall all the nations of the earth be blessed." It's as if he had said, "I, out of pure mercy, promise you that Christ will come from your seed. He will pour out the blessing over all the nations oppressed by sin and death." That is, He will free the nations from eternal damnation, sin, and death, receiving this promise by faith: "In your seed shall all the nations be blessed."

Just as the false apostles of the past, the Papists and legalists of today are perverse annihilators, not of the testament of men (for it is forbidden them by law) but of God's testament. They don't fear Him at all, even knowing that God is a consuming fire, for such is the nature of all hypocrites that they observe the law of the land to the letter but despise God's laws and sin with the greatest impunity. But the day will come when they will have to bear with a terrible judgment. They will feel what it is to scorn and destroy the testament of God. Therefore, there is more than sufficient strength in this argument, since it is based on God's ordinances.

VERSE 16. Now the promises were spoken to Abraham and to his seed. He does not say, "And to seeds," as referring to many, but rather to one, "And to your seed," that is, Christ [NASB].

Here, he uses a new name, "a testament," for God's promises made to Abraham regarding Christ, who would bring the blessing to all the nations. Certainly, the promise is nothing more than a testament, it was not yet revealed, the seal was still intact. Well then, a testament is not a law but a grant, given freely. That is because the heirs do not expect to receive laws, requirements, or any burden imposed on them by the testament; rather, they come to find the inheritance that has already been ratified.

Therefore, from the outset, he explains the words. Thereafter, he relates the example and leans on this word, "seed." He says that Abraham was not given laws but a testament. The promises were declared to him with respect to a spiritual blessing. Thus something was promised and granted to him. If then, a person's testament is respected, why is God's testament disrespected? The human testament is but a mere allegory.[259] But if we observe the sign,[260] why don't we safeguard the things to which they point?

Now, then, the promises were made to Him, not to all the Jews but to one Seed only, who is Christ. The Jews don't accept this interpretation of Paul. They say that the singular was used here in substitution for the plural, one for many. But we receive Paul's meaning and interpretation joyfully, who frequently repeats

---

[259] *allegoria.*
[260] *signa.*

this word, "seed," and explains that this Seed is Christ, as moved by his apostolic spirit. Let the Jews deny it all they want. As for us, we have arguments of sufficient strength, as presented by Paul who confirms this matter, and they cannot deny it. So far, we have dealt with the issue of the likeness of the allegory described,[261] the human testament. Now he continues explaining and expanding on the same subject.

VERSE 17. My point is this: the law, which came four hundred thirty years later, does not annul a covenant previously ratified by God, so as to nullify the promise [NRSV].

Here, the Jews might object, saying, "God was not only satisfied with giving the promises to Abraham but after 430 years, He also gave the law." It's as if they said, "Therefore, God, not quite trusting in His own promises, as if they were insufficient to justify, added something better: the law! The law came as a better successor to the promises because then not the idle but the doers of the law would be justified." With this argument, they come to a different conclusion: "The law, given after the promise, did indeed nullify the promise." The Jews are always looking to turn and twist around these texts.

The apostle Paul responds well and to the point to this objection, which He refutes rather firmly. The law, he says, came 430 years after the promise "in your seed" was given. That is why the law could neither nullify nor invalidate the promise. The reason is that the promise given so many years before the law is God's testament, confirmed by God Himself in Christ. Thus what God had promised and validated in the past could not be revoked and rescinded but would forever retain its validity.

Then why was the law added? It was certainly given after so many years to Abraham's descendants but not with the purpose of helping them obtain the blessing. That's because the function of the law is not to bless but to put people under a curse. Rather, the law was given to bring to the world a group of people who would have the word and the testimony of Christ and from whom Christ Himself would be born according to the flesh. Further, so that people, locked up under the law, would groan and sigh to be redeemed by Abraham's Seed, who is Christ. He is the only one who should and could bless—that is, to deliver all nations from sin and eternal death. What's more, the ceremonies ordained by the law pointed to Christ. Thus the promises were abolished neither by the law nor by the ceremonies of the law. Instead, these things themselves, as if they were certain seals, for a time would testify of Him

---

[261] *similitudo vel pictura allegorica.*

until He, Himself (the promise), as a letter sent, could be opened and through the preaching of the Gospel scattered throughout all the nations.[262]

However, let us allow the law and the promise to encounter each other in a face off and then we'll see which of the two is the strongest—that is, if the promise is able to abolish the law or the law abolishes the promise. If the law can abolish the promise, then it follows that we make God a liar through our works; the promise is indeed nullified, for if the law justifies us and can deliver us from sin and death and our works and strength fulfill the law, then the promise made to Abraham is totally null and void. In that case, God turns out to be a liar and a scammer. But it is impossible for the law to declare God a liar or that our works nullify the promise. No, instead it is necessary for the promise to be unmoved and established forever (for God doesn't promise in vain), even if we were able to serve and satisfy the law. And if we were to concede that all men were as holy as the angels so that they would not need the promise (which is totally impossible), even so, we should think that the same promise remains true and sure. Otherwise, God would be a liar, since He would have promised in vain or could not fulfill His promises. Therefore, just as the promise existed before the law so it is of greater excellence than the law.

God was so purposeful in giving the promise such a long time before the law. He did it on purpose and to this end so that afterward it could not be said that righteousness was given by the law and not by the promise, for if He would have wanted us to be justified by the law, then He would have given the law 430 years before the promise or otherwise together with the promise. But now, at the outset, He does not say a single word with respect to the law. Instead, after a long passage of time—after 430 years—He gives the law. Throughout all that time, God spoke only about His promises. Therefore, the blessing and the free gift of righteousness were given before the law and through the promise. That is why the promise is of greater excellence than the law. Thus the law does not abolish the promise. It is faith in the promise (by which even the believers before Christ were saved), which is now proclaimed by the Gospel throughout the globe of the earth. Thus when the promise is grasped by faith, the law is destroyed[263] so that it can no longer make sin abound, terrify sinners, or drive them into desperation.

You will also note here a slight overemphasis—or an irony, perhaps—since there's a reference to the exact number of 430 years. It's as if he had said, "If you know anything about math, then count with your fingers all the time that went by between the giving of the promise and the giving of the law. It's clear that Abraham received the promise way before the law, for the law was given to the people of

---

[262] First edition (1535): "for the promises contained in Scripture were letters, and afterwards, seals were placed on them."

[263] *destruit legem.* Luther's footnote: *Lex non abrogat promissionem, sed fides apprehendens promissionem destruit legem.*

Israel 430 years thereafter." This is an invincible argument, since it's founded and centered on a specific period of time.

Here, he does not talk about the law in a general way but only about the written law. It's as if he had said, "God cannot gaze in marvel on our rituals and works of the law, and then grant righteousness on the doers. The law was not given requiring certain religious observances and works here and there in return for its promise of granting life, for the law says, 'Everyone who does them shall live by them'" (Leviticus 18:5). But even with that promise, it does not consequently follow that we can obtain those promises, for it clearly says, "Everyone who does them." Well then, it is obvious that there is no one who can do them. Further, Paul said that the law cannot nullify the promise. Therefore, the promise made to Abraham 430 years before the law remained firm and constant. For a better understanding, I'll give you an example. Let's say that someone very wealthy (without any obligation) adopted a son whom he doesn't know and to whom he owes nothing. Further, he names him heir over all his lands and goods. After several years of having granted him such a benefit, he imposes on the adopted son the burden to comply with this or that law. The son cannot say then that he merits the benefit received and credit it to his own works, since many years before, without asking, he had freely received the benefit. Neither can God look with favor on our works and merits before righteousness, since the promise and the gift of the Holy Spirit were given 430 years before the law. Thus Paul, through irony, promotes this argument.

Thus it is perfectly clear that Abraham did not obtain righteousness before God through the law because no law had been given yet. If the law did not exist, then neither was there any work or merit. Then what was in place? Nothing but the simple promise. Abraham believed this promise, and it was counted to him for righteousness. In the same way as father Abraham obtained this promise, the children receive and keep it. Thus today, we say, "Our sins were purged by the death of Christ more than fifteen hundred years back, when there were no religious orders or canons or penitential rules or congruous and condign merits. Thus there is no way we are now going to purify our sins with our own works and merits." That is how Paul brings together firm and solid examples with timelines and persons. There's no one who could deny them. Thus let us arm and fortify our consciences with these arguments, firm and solid on every side; it is so helpful to have them handy when temptation comes to visit. They lead us from the law and works to the promise and faith, from punishment to grace, from sin to righteousness, and from death to life.

Therefore, these two things (as I always emphasize), law and promise, should be carefully separated. With regards to time, place, and person and in any other circumstance, they exist as far and separate one from the other as heaven and the earth, as the beginning of the world to its final day. Certainly, they are close neighbors, since they live within the same human being. However, with regard to our affections for them, and their actual function, they should be kept separate from the other. Thus let the law have its dominion over the flesh, but let the promise placidly reign over the conscience. When you have assigned each one their own place, then you will be able to walk between them with all confidence, on the planet of the law and throughout the heavens of the promise.

In the Spirit, you will walk in the paradise of grace and peace. In the flesh, you will walk on the land of works and suffering affliction. But the trials that the flesh must necessarily bear will not seem difficult because the promise is so delightful that it will comfort and greatly rejoice your heart. But now, if you confuse and combine these two, placing the law in the conscience and the promise of freedom in the flesh, then you will have created confusion (as the papacy has done). The result is that you will not know which is which. You won't be able to tell apart the law from the promise or sin from righteousness!

Thus if you are to be rightly explaining the word of truth, you should discern the great difference between the promise and the law and see how each affects your emotions in their entirety. It is not in vain that Paul pursues this argument so diligently. He foresaw in the Spirit that this mischief would wiggle its way through the back door into the church, to confuse God's word—that is, the promise would get mixed up with the law, resulting in the total loss of the promise, for when the promise is combined with the law, it turns out to be nothing but pure law. Thus it should become your practice to put a clear boundary between the promise and the law, even with regards to its operation in time. When the law shows up and accuses your conscience, you should confidently say, "Madame Law, you've arrived before your time; you got here way too early. Why don't you wait another 430 years? Then after they've gone by, then yes, come back and condemn. But if you wait that long, it will be too late for you. Because the promise got here 430 years before you did." With that testimony, I rest confidently and sweetly. "So Law, I have nothing to do with you. I don't hear you. I now live with Abraham the believer or, better yet, with Christ, who is my righteousness and who has removed you." This is how you should always fix your gaze on Christ. Likewise, keep in your heart a summary of all the arguments with which to defend the righteousness of faith against the righteousness of the flesh, the law, and all works and merits!

LECTURE 22: Saturday, September 19

Up to this point, I have reviewed almost all the arguments that the apostle Paul presents in this epistle, but especially those that confirm this doctrine of justification. Of all these, the weightiest argument is with respect to the promise made to Abraham and the other patriarchs; it is also the most efficacious. This is the argument that Paul advocates with greater diligence here as well as in the Epistle to the Romans. The words to which he attributes greater weight and emphasis are with respect to time periods and the persons involved. He also leans on this word, "seed," relating it to Christ. Finally, he declares that the law has an adverse function—that is, it places all human beings under the curse. In this way, he strengthens the article of Christian righteousness[264] with strong and powerful arguments. In addition, he defeats the arguments of the false apostles, which they used to defend the righteousness of the law. Paul takes these arguments and turns them upside down on their own heads. In other words, since they argued stubbornly that righteousness and life come through the law, Paul demonstrates that what the law gives us is nothing but damnation and death. You argue, "But the law is necessary for salvation. By chance, have you not read that it says, 'Whoever does them shall live by them'?" (Leviticus 18:5). But who does it? Nobody![265] Thus "all who rely on works of the law are under a curse." Further, "The sting of death is sin, and the power of sin is the law" (1 Corinthians 15:56). Now he moves on to the conclusion of all these arguments.

VERSE 18. For if the inheritance comes from the law, it no longer comes from the promise.

That's what he also affirms in Romans 4: 14: "If it is the adherents of the law who are to be the heirs, faith is null and the promise is void." It cannot be otherwise, for this difference is clear: The law is something very different from the promise. Yes, even reason in its natural state (although it is always blind) is compelled to confess that it is one thing to promise and another to demand. It is one thing to give and another to receive. The law requires and demands works from each of us. The promise of the Seed offers us spiritual and eternal benefits given by God and is entirely free because of Christ. Therefore, we obtain the inheritance of the blessing through the promise and not by means of the law, for the promise says, "In your seed shall be blessed all the nations of the earth." Therefore, those who have the law still do not have enough because they do not yet have the blessing; without it, they necessarily remain under the curse. Thus the law cannot justify, since the blessing is not added unto it. Further, if the inheritance came through the law, then God would be a liar, and the promise was given in vain. Once again, if the law was enough to attain the blessing, then why did God give this promise, "In your seed," and so on? Why didn't He say instead, "By keeping the law, you will merit eternal life"? Therefore, this argument has

---

[264] *articulum de justitia christiana.* Luther of course is referring to the article of justification.

[265] *Quis autem facit? Nemo.* Use your imagination. Luther is lecturing. His finger sweeps over the lecture hall filled with students. Suddenly he stops in front of a student and asks, "But Who does it?" There is a long pause, and slowly a chorus of timid voices begins to answer "Nobody." Luther affirms in a booming voice, "Nobody!"

two opposing parts. The inheritance ensues from the promise. Therefore, it is not from the law.

VERSE 18. But God gave it to Abraham by a promise.

It cannot be denied before the law was given, God gave Abraham the inheritance or the blessing through the promise—that is, the forgiveness of sins, righteousness, salvation, and eternal life—so that we could be children and heirs of God and coheirs with Christ. Genesis could not say it any clearer: "In your seed shall be blessed all the nations of the earth" (Genesis 22:18). Thus the blessing is freely given, without even a glance at law or works. That's because God gave the inheritance before Moses was born or before any thought about the law had occurred to anyone for the first time! Why then, do they boast about righteousness coming from the law seeing that righteousness, life, and salvation were given to their father Abraham without the law? Yes, even before there was any law at all? Whoever is not broken to the heart with these things is blind and stubborn. However, I've already dealt at length with this argument of the promise. Thus here I'll just briefly run through it.

Up until now, we have heard the main part of this epistle. Now the apostle demonstrates the use and function of the law, adding certain examples of the tutor, the small heir, as well as the allegory of Abraham's two sons, Isaac and Ishmael. At the end, he sets out certain rules of behavior. The epistle concludes with Paul appealing instead of teaching.

VERSE 19. Why then the law?[266]

When we teach that man is justified without the law and works, the following question necessarily follows: If the law does not justify, then why was it given? Further, why did God require and impose the burden of the law if it does not give us life? For what reason does the law exercise and harass us so arduously if those who work for just one hour are given the same consideration as those of us who've carried the heat and the burden of the law all day long? Because no sooner is grace displayed by the Gospel, and its announcement proclaimed to us, that this great murmur is heard, and without it, the Gospel cannot be preached. The Jews had this opinion, that if they kept the law, they would be justified. Thus when they heard the Gospel regarding Christ, who came to the world to save not the righteous but sinners, and that sinners would enter the kingdom of heaven before them, they were greatly offended. They complained that they had carried the heavy weight of the law for so many years with such great efforts and sweat and that they had been harassed and oppressed under the tyranny of the law without any profit, even to their own

---

[266] *Quid igitur lex?*

loss and further that the Gentiles who were idolaters obtained grace without works or misfortunes. Likewise, the Papists today murmur, saying, "What good have we gotten out of living in cloisters for the past twenty, thirty, or forty years? We who have taken vows of chastity, poverty, obedience and who have recited countless psalms, done penance with ceaseless canonical hours,[267] and said so many masses! Why have we punished our bodies with fasts, prayers, and humiliations if any husband, woman, prince, governor, tutor, teacher, student, day laborer, pitiful sack carrier, or sweeper woman is not only our equal, but God considers them better and worthier than us?"

Thus this is a hard question, and reason has no answer for it, except that it feels greatly offended. Reason understands to some extent the righteousness of the law. It also teaches and promotes it, imagining that the doers of the law are righteous. But it does not understand the function and purpose of the law. That is why when it hears this statement from Paul (for it is strange and unknown in the world), "that the law was given because of transgressions," it utters the following judgment: "Paul abolishes the law, for he said that we are not justified by it. Then he is a blasphemer against God who gave the law, for Paul says, 'The law was given because of transgressions.'" So then, let us live like the Gentiles who have no law. Yes, "let us sin and live in sin that grace may abound!" That's followed by "Let us do evil so that good may come from it." This happened to the apostle Paul. The same happens to us today. When common people hear from the Gospel that righteousness comes from the pure grace of God, by faith alone, without the law, and without works, immediately, they suppose as the Jews in times past, "If the law does not justify, then let's not do anything," which indeed they do quite well.

Then what shall we do? This wicked stubbornness drives us out of our minds, but there's no remedy for it. Even when Christ preached, He had to hear that He was blaspheming and was seditious—that is, that through His doctrine He was deceiving people and made them rebel against Cesar. The same happened to Paul and the other apostles. Should it surprise us then if the world similarly accuses us today? So let it accuse us, slander us, persecute us mercilessly. But that's no reason for us to keep quiet. Rather, let us speak freely so that afflicted consciences will be freed from the devil's traps. Let's not pay attention to foolish and wicked people who will abuse our doctrine, for there's no remedy for them whether they have the law or whether they don't. But let's look and see how to comfort those with afflicted consciences, lest they perish with the crowd. If we look the other way and say nothing, there won't be any comfort for those discouraged and stressed out consciences, who are so snared and tangled up in the traditions and laws of men that there's no way they will get untangled by themselves.

When Paul saw that some resisted his doctrine and others sought to give the flesh free rein and when both got worse, he comforted himself like this: that

---

[267] Marking the divisions of the day in periods of fixed prayer at regular intervals.

he was an apostle of Jesus Christ sent to preach the faith to the chosen of God and that he should suffer all things for the sake of the elect so that they would obtain salvation as well. In the same way, today, we do everything for the sake of the elect, for we know they will be built up and comforted by our doctrine. But as far as the dogs and the pigs (the first are those who persecute our doctrine and the others are those who trample the freedom we have in Christ), I am so incensed by them that for their own good and for the rest of my life I will not cross words with any of them, for I would rather wish that these pigs together with our adversaries the dogs would still be subject to the tyranny of the Pope than having them walk around blaspheming God's holy name.

Thus it's not only foolish and ignorant people but also those who consider themselves supremely wise that argue like this: "If the law does not justify, then it is something useless and worthless." However, that's not true. Along that same kind of thinking, would the following also be worthless? Money doesn't justify or make anyone righteous, and therefore, it is worthless; the eyes do not justify, and therefore, they should be pulled out; the hands do not make anyone righteous, and therefore, we might as well cut them off. Neither is it true that the law does not justify, and therefore, it is useless. However, we must concede it has its own function and use. Thus we do not destroy or condemn the law, we only deny that it justifies. Instead, we answer the question "Why then the law?" differently than our opponents, since they wickedly and perversely falsify the function and use of the law with something that it doesn't have.

We dispute against this abuse and falsified function of the law, and together with Paul, we respond, "The law does not justify." But as we say it, we do not affirm that the law is worthless as they immediately understand it. They say, "If the law does not justify, then it was given in vain." But no, that's not so because it has its own function and use. But it's not what our opponents imagine, that it is given to make people righteous. Instead, it accuses, terrifies, and condemns. With Paul, we say that the law is good if it's used properly—in other words, if the law is used as law. If I give the law its proper function and retain it within the perimeter of its correct function and use, then it's something excellent. But if I assign it another use and attribute to it what I should not, then I pervert not only the law but also all theology.[268]

Therefore, Paul here struggles against those pestilent hypocrites who would not tolerate this statement: "The law was given because of the transgressions," since they believe the law's function is to justify. Further, among the papal philosophers and throughout the entire world, this is the generalized opinion of human reason throughout the whole world, that righteousness is attained through the works of the law. There is no way reason will tolerate that anything will take from its grasp this pernicious opinion because it does not understand the righteousness of faith. That is why the Papists foolishly and wickedly say, "The church has God's law,

---

[268] *totam theologiam.*

the traditions of the fathers, the Conciliar Decrees, and whoever lives by them thus is holy." No one will be able to persuade these people that by keeping these things God will not be pleased. In fact, they provoke Him to anger. In short, all who trust in their own righteousness[269] imagine they are appeasing God's wrath through their worship of their own choices and of their own free will.[270] Therefore, this opinion regarding the righteousness of the law is the pit of all evil, and the sin of all sins the world over. Gross vices and sins may be exposed, but the judge remedies and contains them with punishments. But this sin, the sin of the opinion of one's own righteousness, they do not discard as sin but instead value it as the greatest religion and righteousness. Thus this pestilent sin is the strength of the power of the devil over the whole terrestrial globe,[271] the serpent's head itself, and the snare with which it entangles and lassos all human beings into captivity, for naturally, all people have this opinion, that they are justified by keeping the law.[272] Paul then, in order to show the true function and use of the law and uproot from the hearts of men this false opinion of the law, responds to this objection, "Why then the law?" in the following way: "The law was not given to justify men," he said, but

VERSE 19. It was added because of transgressions.

So just as there is variety and distinction in all things so their use is also varied and different. These functions should not be mixed together. Otherwise, the result is confusion. The woman may not use man's clothing and man may not use women's garb. Let men do the things corresponding to men and women those that correspond to women. Let everyone do what is required by their profession and labor. Let the pastors and preachers teach God's word with purity. Let the magistrates govern their subjects and the subjects obey their magistrates. Let each thing serve in its own and proper place. Let the sun shine during daytime and the moon and the stars by night. Let the fish surge from the sea, the grain from the earth, wild beasts from the forests and trees, etc. In the same way, let not the law usurp the function and use of justification; let it leave that alone for grace, the promise, and faith. What then is the function of the law? Transgressions. That's what he also said in another text: "The law," he said, "the law entered, so that sin might increase." Shall we say, what a delightful function, right?[273] "The law," he said, "was added because of transgressions." That is, it was added apart from and after the promise until Christ the Seed should come to whom it was promised.

---

[269] *omnis iustititarius.*

[270] *suis electitiis cultibus et voluntaria.*

[271] *toto orbe terrarum.*

[272] *omnes . . . legem justificare.*

[273] Once again, Luther is using irony.

Regarding the Double Use of the Law

Here, you should understand the double use of the law. One is the civil use. God has ordained all civil law, all laws, to punish crimes. Every law is given to prevent sin. But if it can prevent sin, doesn't it then justify?[274] No, not in the least. When I don't kill, I don't commit adultery, I don't steal, or desist from committing other sins, it's not because I do it willingly or because I'm in love with virtue. Rather, it's because I fear getting locked up in jail, the sword, or hanging on the executioner's noose. These regulations act like a bridle on me and hold me back from sinning, just as the chains hold back the lion or the bear so that it won't destroy and devour everything in its path. Thus to abstain from sinning is not righteousness; rather, it is a sign of unrighteousness. Because just as a bear or rabid beast must be chained, so also the law acts as a bridle on those who give free reign to their lusts, to keep them from sinning. But this bridle clearly shows that those who need the law (everyone without Christ) are not righteous. Instead, they are the wicked and brazen; they must be held back with shackles and prison so they won't sin. Thus the law does not justify.

Therefore, we must understand that the first use of the law is to bridle the wicked, for the devil reigns over the world and compels all to commit all kinds of horrifying wickedness. Therefore, God has ordained magistrates, parents, ministers, laws, shackles, and all kinds of civil regulations to at least bind the devil's hands, if nothing more. That's so the devil won't wander about in his captives satisfying the madness of his lusts. The demon possessed, in whom the devil reigns powerfully, must be bound with straightjackets and chains, lest they hurt others. It's the same with the world, it's possessed by the devil; it goes headlong into all kinds of wickedness. That is why the magistrate comes with his shackles and handcuffs; his laws bind hand and foot—otherwise, many people would lunge into all kinds of barbaric acts! Whoever can't tolerate this bridle then goes out of his mind. This bridle of civil law is a must and is ordained by God to preserve the peace of the land. But its special purpose is to protect the spread of the Gospel so that the tumult and treachery of the wicked, the savage, and the proud won't hinder its course. But here, Paul is not advocating in favor of this use and function of the civil law. It is true that it is indeed necessary, but it does not justify. The demon possessed or those deranged are not free from the shackles of the devil; neither do they enjoy mental health just because they are bound hand and foot and cannot damage anything. In the same way, even though the law will bridle and bind the world from wickedness and atrocities, even so, the world will not be righteous, for it will continue to be wicked. The bridle itself clearly demonstrates that the entire world is perverse and savage, incited and driven to all kinds of wickedness by its prince, the devil. Otherwise, it would not need the bridle of the law to keep it from sinning.

---

[274] *ergo iustificat?*

Another use of the law is divine and spiritual. As Paul put it, it is "that sin might abound"—in other words, to show man his sin, blindness, misery, wickedness, ignorance, hate, disregard for God, death, hell, judgment, and well-deserved wrath of God. The apostle urges this use of the law especially in Romans 7. This is a totally unknown use to the hypocrites, the papal philosophers and scholarly theologians, and all those who walk in the opinion of the righteousness of the law, or their own righteousness. God had to bridle and knockdown this monster, this wild beast, which is nothing more than the presumptuous opinion of human righteousness with its religion. This belief naturally fills men up with pride and puffs them up so that they think they themselves can greatly please God. Thus it was necessary for God to send some Hercules that could defeat this monster, using great strength and courage to defeat it and destroy it altogether. In other words, God was compelled to give the law on Mount Sinai, with great majesty and terrifying demonstration of power so that the great multitude was struck with terror (Exodus 19:20).

This is the main and proper use of the law. It is very beneficial and supremely necessary. That is because anyone who is not a murderer, adulterer, thief, and to all appearances abstains from sin, as the Pharisee mentioned in the Gospel, would swear up and down that he is righteous (since he is devil possessed). Thus he is cherishing the opinion of his own righteousness and boasting of his own good works and merits. God has no other way to bring these individuals down to size except only through the law, for it is the hammer of death, the thunder from hell, and the lightning from God's wrath that grinds into powder all stubborn and foolish hypocrites. Thus this is the proper and true use of the law, through lightning, storms, and the sound of Sinai's trumpet that terrifies and, through its thunder, knocks down and tears into pieces that beast called the opinion of self-righteousness. Thus God said through the prophet Jeremiah, "My word is like a hammer that breaks the rock in pieces" (Jeremiah 23:29), for as long as the opinion of self-righteousness remains in man, there will remain in him an incomprehensible pride, presumptuousness, arrogance, hate toward God, disregard for His grace and mercy, and ignorance of the promises and of Christ. The preaching of the free remission of sins through Christ cannot enter the heart of such an individual; he will always resist it. Neither can he taste it as longs as he cherishes that huge rock and immovable boulder of self-righteousness that has him cornered and won't let him out.

The opinion of self-righteousness is a great and horrible monster, a rebellious beast, headstrong, and hardheaded. To overthrow it, God needs a powerful hammer: the law. When used correctly and with its proper function, it accuses and reveals sin like this. "Look, you have broken all God's commandments!" It penetrates the conscience with terror so that it feels that God is truly offended and angered; it feels guilty and fears eternal death. At this point, the pitiful afflicted sinner feels the intolerable weight of the law and is crushed almost beyond hope. Now, feeling oppressed with great anguish and fear, the sinner desires death or otherwise seeks his own destruction. That demonstrates that the law is that hammer, that fire, that horrible wind, and that terrible earthquake that tears mountains apart and breaks up mighty boulders (1 Kings 19:11–13)—in other words, the proud and stubborn hypocrites. Elijah covered his face with his robe, for even he was incapable of bearing the terrors of the law and its meaning. Nonetheless, when the storm he had witnessed was over, there came a gentle whisper,[275] and the Lord was in it. However, it was necessary for him to go through that tempest of the fire, the wind, and the earthquake before the Lord revealed Himself in that quiet murmur that followed the breeze.[276]

The terrifying and majestic demonstration through which God gave His law on Mount Sinai did represent the true use of the law. There was a certain air of holiness in the people of Israel that left Egypt. They gloried and said, "We are God's people. All that the Lord has spoken, we will do." Further, Moses ordered the people to sanctify themselves. He commanded them to wash their clothes, not to touch their wives, and be ready for the third day. There was not even one in the whole bunch who was not jam-packed with holiness. On the third day, Moses brings the people from their tents to the mountain before God's sight for them to listen to His voice. What happened then? When the children of Israel saw that terrifying sight of the mountain going up in flames and smoke, the dark clouds and the lightning shining through all that darkness from top to bottom, when they heard the clarion call, each time longer and more resonant, with an ever-increasing drum roll, as they heard the thunder and lightning, they were panic-stricken. Moving farther away, they said to Moses, "We will willingly do all things, but let the Lord not speak with us, lest we die and this great fire consume us. You speak with us, and we will listen." I plead with you to tell me, what did all the purifying, the white robes, and not touching their women amount to? Absolutely nothing. Not one of them could remain standing before God's majesty and glory. Instead, all of them panicked and shook with fear; they fled as if the devil himself had driven them away. "For the Lord your God is a devouring fire" and no one can stand before His presence.

Therefore, God's law has that uniqueness shown on Mount Sinai when it was given for the first time. Those who heard it had washed and were cleansed; they were upright, purified, and chaste. Nonetheless, it led that holy people to a knowledge of their profound misery; terrified, they fled headlong to desperation and death. There was no purity or holiness that could save them. What was in them was such a feeling of their own filth, unworthiness and sin, and judgment and God's wrath that they fled from the presence of the Lord, not even able to tolerate His voice. "For who is there of all flesh, that has heard the voice of the living God speaking out of the midst of fire, as we have, and has still lived?" This day, we have seen that God speaks with man and still lives. Now, their talk was quite different from just a while before when they said, "We are God's holy people,

---

[275] *sibilos.*

[276] *susurro lenis aurae sequebatur.*

for the Lord has chosen for Himself a peculiar people, from among all the nations of the earth. All the things the Lord has spoken, we will do." At the end, it's the same with all legalists, who while drunk with the opinion of their own righteousness think they are out of temptation's reach, that they are loved by God and that God considers their vows, fasts, prayers, and the works of their will power[277] and thus God is under obligation to grant them a crown in heaven. But when that thunder, lightning, fire, and the hammer breaks them into pieces, meaning God's law, then suddenly God's wrath and judgment overwhelms them showing them their sin. They experience the same as the Jews at the foot of Mount Sinai.

Here, I warn all who fear God, and particularly those who will teach others, to diligently learn from Paul the true and proper use of the law. I fear that after our time that knowledge will be stepped all over and totally abolished by the enemies of truth. Even today, while we still have life and diligently dedicate all our efforts to expound on the function and use of the law as well as the Gospel, there are but few, even among those who count themselves as evangelicals[278] and claim to profess the Gospel together with us, who understand these things correctly as they should. What do you think will happen when death takes us away from here? I say nothing about the Anabaptists, the new Arians, and other spirits who blaspheme against the body and blood of Christ.[279] They are no less ignorant about these things than the Papists, although they would say completely the opposite. But they have revolted against the pure doctrine of the Gospel, ending up in laws and traditions and thus they no longer teach Christ alone. They boast and swear they don't want anything else but Christ's glory and the salvation of their brothers, claiming they teach God's word in its purity. But in their deeds, they truly corrupt and stretch it until it snaps. Then they give it another meaning that is more in tune with their own imaginations. Thus taking shelter under the name of Christ, they teach nothing more than their own fantasies and under the name of the Gospel, nothing but laws and ceremonies. They all look alike and continue in the same thing. In other words, they are nothing but monks, workers of the law, wise in teaching nothing but ceremonies, only that they invent for themselves new names and new works.

It's no small thing, then, to correctly understand the law and its true use and function. Since we diligently and faithfully teach these things, we testify that we do not reject the law and works as our opponents falsely accuse us. Instead, we entirely establish the law, we require its works and say that the law is useful and beneficial but within its proper use—that is, first, to bridle the civil transgressions and second, to reveal and make the spiritual transgressions abound. Thus the law is also a light that illumines and reveals not the grace of God, not righteousness and life but sin, death, and God's anger and judgment. On Mount Sinai,

---

[277] *electia opera sua.*

[278] *pii;* first edition (1535), *evangelici.*

[279] *spiritibus blasphemis in Sacramentum corporis et sanguis Christi.*

the thunder, lightning, the dark and dense cloud, the mountain top in flames and covered with smoke, and that terrible sight neither brought joy nor gave life to the children of Israel. Instead, it frightened and terrified them. It showed them how incapable they were despite all they purity and holiness to remain standing before God's majesty who spoke to them from the cloud. In the same way, the law, when properly used, does nothing more than uncover sin, generate wrath, accuse and terrify people bringing them to the edge of desperation. This is the proper use of the law, and it ends here and it should go no further.

On the contrary, the Gospel is a light that illumines, enlivens, comforts and uplifts frightful minds. It reveals that God, for the sake of Christ, is merciful toward sinners, even the most unworthy, if they believe that through His death they are freed from the curse, which is to say, from sin and eternal death. Through His victory, the blessing is freely granted, which is to say, grace, forgiveness of sin, righteousness, and eternal life. In this way, by placing the difference between the law and the Gospel, we give each its proper use and function. But this difference between the law and the Gospel is nowhere to be found in the books of the monks, in the Canons, in the writings of the theological scholars, or in the books of the ancient fathers. In short, throughout many years, there was a deafening silence regarding this difference in all the universities and churches, placing the human conscience at great risk. But on the contrary, when people are aware of the difference, then they also understand how indeed they are justified. It is not a difficult matter to discern between faith and works, between Christ and Moses, and between all the civil laws of the land. All things without Christ are nothing more but the ministry of death given to punish the wicked. Thus Paul responds to the question in the following way:

VERSE 19. It was added because of transgressions.

In other words, so that the transgressions would abound, be made known, and would be easy to see. Indeed, it is so. Because when sin, death, God's wrath and judgment, and hell are revealed to man through the law, it is impossible for man not to become impatient. He murmurs against God and despises his own will. He cannot tolerate God's judgment, his own death, and condemnation. However, he cannot avoid them. Consequently, at this point, he has a great downfall and begins hating God and blaspheming against Him. Before, when he was not facing temptation, he was a top saint.[280] He worshipped and praised God; he prayed on bended knee, thanking God like the Pharisee (Luke 18). But now when his sin and death are revealed, he wishes God did not exist at all! The law itself brings along with it a special hatred of God. That's how sin is revealed and made known through the law, and it causes it to increase and inflate; it ignites

---

[280] *magnus Sanctus.*

and is magnified[281] through the law. That is why Paul said, "But sin, that it might be shown to be sin, by working death to me through that which is good; that through the commandment sin might become exceedingly sinful" (Romans 7:13). There he appeals in a big way in favor of these consequences of the law.

Thus Paul responds to this question: "If the law does not justify, what is it good for?" He said that although it does not justify it is very beneficial and necessary. In the first place, it is a civil bridle to the flesh driven, rebellious, and obstinate. Further, it is a mirror that shows man who he is: a sinner, guilty of death, and worthy of God's wrath and eternal indignation. What's the good of this humiliation, these blows and afflictions[282] given by the hammer of the law? It has this purpose: that we may have an entrance into grace, for God is the God of the humble, the miserable, the afflicted, the oppressed, the hopeless, and those who are drowning in their poverty. It is His nature to exalt the humble; feed the hungry; give sight to the blind; comfort the miserable and afflicted, the bruised and brokenhearted; justify sinners; give life to the dead; and save the most desperate and condemned. He is the powerful almighty Creator who makes all things out of nothing. But that pernicious and pestilent opinion of self-righteousness doesn't recognize he is a sinner, unclean, miserable, damnable. Instead, he thinks of himself as righteous and holy and does not tolerate that God will do what is natural and proper. Therefore, God needs to take that mallet in hand (I'm talking about the law) to knock down and demolish, turning this beast into nothing with its empty confidence, wisdom, righteousness, and power. That's how it will finally learn through its own misery and foolishness that it has been left totally to its own doings, lost and condemned. This is when the conscience suffers the horror brought on by the law, sent from the Gospel and grace, which comfort and lift it up, saying, "Christ came to the world not to break the bruised reed, nor to quench the smoldering flame, but to preach the Gospel of great joy to the poor, heal the broken and contrite heart, preach forgiveness of sins to the captives."

However, the difficulty of this whole issue is resolved here. When a man is horrified and feels totally defeated, he can then rise again and say, "Now I've been bruised and afflicted more than enough by the time of the law. But now is the time for grace. Now is the time to listen to Christ and the words of grace and life than proceed from Him. Now is the time to fix our gaze not on the flames and smoke of Mount Sinai, but on Mount Moriah. There your will find the throne, the temple, God's mercy seat—in other words, Christ Himself, who is the King of righteousness and peace. There, I will hear what He has to say, for He speaks nothing but peace to His people."

But no, the foolishness of the human heart is so huge that in this conflict of the conscience, when the law has fulfilled its function and exercised its true

---

[281] *per stensionem augeri, inflari, incendi & magnificari peccatum.*

[282] *contusion et contrito.*

function,[283] this individual then not only throws aside the doctrine of grace, which assured him the forgiveness of sins on account of Christ, but also digs up more laws with which to comfort himself.[284] "If I'm able to live," he says, "I'm going to put my life together. I will do this and that. I will enter a monastery; I will live most frugally and content just with bread and water; I will go barefoot; etc." Here, you must do the complete opposite. You must send away Moses and his law. Send him to the confident, the proud, and the stubborn. In the middle of your anguish and fears, grasp onto Christ, who was crucified and died for your sins then you will find the fact of your complete salvation.[285]

Thus the incidental function of the law is toward justification. It does not justify but propels us toward the promise of grace and becomes his sweetest and most desirable comfort. Thus we do not abolish the law. Instead, we demonstrate the true function of the law. That is, it is an extremely useful minister[286] that propels you to Christ. Thus once the law has humbled, terrified, and defeated, you completely,[287] so that now you feel as if you were at the edge of desperation, you must pay attention and learn the proper use of the law, for its function and use is not only to reveal sin and the wrath of God but also to drive you to Christ. The Holy Spirit in the Gospel reveals this use of the law, where He testifies that God reveals Himself to the afflicted and brokenhearted. Thus if you have been crushed[288] by this mallet,[289] don't react perversely to your humbling,[290] by burdening yourself with more laws. Instead, listen to Christ, who tells you, "Come to me, all who labor and are heavy laden, and I will give you rest" (Matthew 11:28). When the law has gotten you down and so depressed that you are about to despair, remember this: it is driving you to Christ to cry out for help. Thus the proper function of the law is to serve the Gospel, aiding toward justification.[291] This is the best and perfect use of the law.

LECTURE 23: Friday, September 25

That is why Paul here begins to urge the law and defines what it is, taking care not to contradict what he had said before, that the law does not justify. Because reason, as soon as it hears this, immediately infers, "Then God gave the law in vain." Thus

---

[283] *usum.*

[284] *sibi consolere velit.*

[285] *plane actum est de salute tua.*

[286] *utilisima ministra.*

[287] *contrivit.*

[288] *contritus.*

[289] *malleo.*

[290] *contritio.*

[291] *et servit per evangelium ad justificationem.*

it was necessary to define the law properly and to show what the nature of the law really is and how it should be understood so that it would not be considered as something more imposing and severe than what it really is. There is no law, he said, that of itself is necessary for justification. Therefore, when we reason regarding righteousness, life, and eternal salvation, the law should be totally removed from our sight, not as if it had never been or never should be but as if it were nothing at all, for regarding justification, no one can sufficiently remove the law from his sight or fix his sight enough only on the promise of God, as he should. Thus I've said before that the law and the promise should be sharply separated within one's most profound feelings, although indeed they are almost together.

VERSE 19. Until the Seed to whom the promise referred had come.

Paul does not argue that the law is perpetual. Instead, he said that it was given and added to the promises because of the transgressions. In other words, to bridle them with respect to the laws of the land but particularly to reveal the transgressions and make them abound spiritually, although not forever but only for a time. Here, it is important to know for how long the power and the tyranny of the law should extend, which reveals sin and shows us what we are and reveals the wrath of God. There are some hearts that are so sensitive with regards to these matters that they would perish suddenly if they would not receive this comfort. Therefore, if the days of the law would not be shortened, no one would be saved. It is proper to place time periods and fix limits on the law, after which it could no longer reign. How long then should the dominion of the law be extended? Until the Seed should come—that is, the Seed about whom it was written, "In you shall be blessed all the nations of the earth" (Genesis 22:18). The tyranny of the law should then be extended until the fullness of time and until that Seed should come bringing the blessing, not that the law would be able to bring this Seed or that it could give righteousness but instead that it should bridle the rebellious of the land, the stubborn, and lock them up, as if it were, in prison and then spiritually to reprove them of sin, humiliate, and terrify them. Then when they were so humbled and defeated, it would compel them to fix their sight above on that blessed Seed.

We can then understand the continuity of the law with respect to the letter, as well as its spiritual function. According to the letter, it's like this: the law would continue until the time of grace. "The law and the prophets," Christ said, "prophesied until John, until that day, the kingdom of God suffers violence, and the violent take it by force" (Matthew 11:12, 13). This was the time when Christ was baptized and began to preach. It was also at that time when, according to the letter of the law, all the ceremonies of Moses came to an end.

Spiritually, the law is to be understood like this: it should not reign in the conscience beyond the time allotted to it but only until the assigned time for the appearance of this blessed Seed. When the law teaches me my sin, terrifies me, and reveals the judgment of God thus I begin to tremble and lose hope. The limits and time of this law last only up to a point and then it comes to an end. From this moment on, it forever ceases to exert its tyranny because when it has fully accomplished its function then it has sufficiently revealed God's wrath and then that's it, its reign of terror is over. When we come to this point, we should say, "Law! Enough, it's over. You've already crushed me and caused me enough grief." "All your waves have inundated me" (Psalm 88:8).[292] "Do not hide your face from your servant. Do not reprove me in your fury nor punish me with your wrath" (Psalm 6:2). When these terrors and trials have come, then the time and the hour have arrived for the appearance of the blessed Seed, then let the law have its place, which certainly was added to reveal and make sin abound and yet not forever but only until that blessed Seed should come. But once the Seed has come then let the law depart, and let it no longer uncover sin nor continue with its terrors, and let it turn its kingdom over to another—that is, to the blessed Seed who is Christ, for His are the lips of grace, which do not accuse or frighten, but speaks of better things than the law. These are grace, peace, forgiveness of sins, victory over sin, death, condemnation, all of which is obtained by His death and passion for all who believe.

Thus Paul shows with these words, "until the Seed to whom the promise referred had come," the time frame allowed to the law's literal and spiritual functions. According to the letter, it ceased once the blessed Seed came to the world, taking our flesh on Himself, giving the Holy Spirit, and writing a new law in our hearts. But in its spiritual time frame, the law does not end immediately but continues firmly rooted to the conscience. Thus it is a difficult matter for someone who has been exercised in the spiritual use of the law to see the law come to an end. When the mind is overwhelmed with the terror and feelings of sin, it cannot conceive there is hope. But the hope is that God is merciful and will forgive sins on account of Christ. The mind only judges that God is angered toward sinners and that He accuses and condemns them. At this point, faith must lift up once again this afflicted and anguished conscience, as Christ said, "Where two or three are gathered together in my name" (Matthew 18:20). But if there is no faithful brotherly hand through God's word to comfort such a depressed and defeated soul with God's word, then hopelessness and death will follow. It is a dangerous thing for someone to be alone. "Woe to him who is alone when he falls," said the Preacher, "and has not another to lift him up" (Ecclesiastes 4:10). Therefore, those who put together the regulations for those monks who live in solitude have been the occasion for many to fall into hopelessness, for if man separates from the companionship of others for a day or two to exercise in prayer (as we read about Christ, who sometimes would go alone into the mountain and was in prayer all night), there is no danger in that. But when a person is compelled continually to live a solitary life,

---

[292] The versification corresponds to the Vulgate, which Luther was using.

that's the devil's own device, for when someone is tempted and is found alone, that person is not able to get up on his own, no, not even at the slightest temptation.

VERSE 19. It was ordained through angels by the hand of a mediator.

This is but a minor digression from his main purpose. He doesn't explain or conclude the statement but only mentions it in passing and then moves on. He takes up his main purpose when he says, "Is the law then opposed to the promises of God?" This was the text that caused his digression. When Paul placed a difference between the law and the Gospel, there was also a difference not only with respect to time but also with respect to its author and effective cause, for the law was delivered by angels (Hebrews 2:2), but the Gospel by the Lord Himself. Thus the Gospel is much more excellent than the law because the law is the voice of the servants, but the Gospel is the voice of the Lord Himself. Thus to reduce and diminish the authority of the law and to exalt and magnify the Gospel, he says that the law was a doctrine given to cover a brief period. It only lasted until the fulfillment of the promise, until the blessed Seed came and fulfilled the promise. However, the Gospel endures forever. All the faithful have always had just the one Gospel, since the beginning of the world by which they have been saved. However, the law is much inferior to the Gospel, since it was ordained by angels who are only servants and its time span was brief. On the other hand, the Gospel was ordained by the Lord Himself, and it is to continue forever (Hebrews 1:2), since it was promised before the beginning of the ages (Titus 1:2).

Further, the word of the law was ordained not only by angels as servants but also by another servant way below the angels—in other words, by a man, as it says here, by the hand of a mediator who was Moses. Now, Christ is no servant at all, but the Lord Himself. He is no mediator between God and man according to the law, as was Moses. Instead, He is the Mediator of a new covenant. Therefore, angels as servants ordained the law since Moses and the people heard God, who spoke from Mount Sinai. They heard angels speaking on behalf of the person of God. That is why Stephen said, "You who received the law as delivered by angels and did not keep it" (Acts 7:53). Further, the text of Exodus 3:2 clearly says that the angel appeared to Moses in a flame of fire and spoke with him from within the burning bush. *(Here, the Latin text is misleading, since it doesn't have the word* angel *but* Lord. *Due to the ignorance of the Hebrew language, a dispute has arisen from this text with respect to whether it was the Lord Himself who spoke with Moses or if it was an angel).*

Thus Paul makes it understood that Christ is the Mediator of a much better covenant than Moses'. Here, he brings to memory the story of the Exodus and the giving of the law, which tells how Moses led the people from their tents and brought them to the foot of Mount Sinai. That was a charged and terrifying spectacle. The whole mountain burned in flames. When all the people saw that great display, they began to tremble, since they thought that they would surely be suddenly destroyed by that frightening storm. Since they could no longer resist the horrendous blare from the law that came from Mount Sinai (since the law's terrifying voice would have destroyed the people), they said to Moses, their mediator, "You go there and listen to what the Lord has to say, and you speak with us." And he answered, "I, myself," he said, "was a mediator who stood between God and you." In these texts, it is clear that Moses had been designated a mediator between the people and the voice of the law.

Paul takes this story and proposes (rather covertly) that it is impossible for righteousness to come through the law. It's as if he had said, "How can the law justify seeing that all the people of Israel, having been purified and sanctified, yes, even Moses himself, the mediator between God and the people, were afraid and shook at the voice of the law?" That's how the Epistle to the Hebrews relates it (chapter 12). Was there anything else besides fright and trembling?[293] But what kind of righteousness and holiness is this that it neither can tolerate nor is capable or willing to listen to the law but takes off running, hating it, as if there were no more hateful and abominable thing in the world? The story testifies all too clearly that the people when they heard the law hated nothing else but the law, and instead of listening to the law, they rather wished to die!

That is what happens when sin is uncovered and exposed. It's as if the spotlight from the lighthouse shone its powerful beams on the heart. There is nothing more hateful and intolerable to the human being than the law. Here, people prefer death rather than facing the law even for an instant. This is the most precise proof that the law does not justify, for if the law could truly justify, then without any doubt, people would love it. They would delight in it and take great pleasure in it; they would embrace it with overflowing goodwill. But where is this goodwill? It's nowhere to be seen. It's not in Moses or in anyone among the entire people. They all freaked out and fled. So how could it be that man runs away from what he loves the most? He does not delight in it, but instead he turns away in revulsion and hates it to the max![294]

Therefore, their flight shows there is infinite hate in the heart of man toward the law and thus against God Himself, the author of the law. Further, if there were no other argument to prove that righteousness does not come through the law, this single story would be enough, which Paul remembers with these few words: "By the hand of a mediator." It's as if he had said, "Don't you remember that your fathers were so incapable of listening to the law that they fled to Moses as their mediator?" (Hebrews 12). But when he was assigned such an office, they were so far from loving the law that, together with their mediator, they would have dug through an iron mountain to get back to Egypt! That's how much they detested the law. But they were all closed in;

---

[293] Luther's note: *Lex perterrefacit, ergo non justificat,* "the law terrifies to the extreme; therefore, it does not justify."

[294] *Maxime exosum habet.*

there was no way to escape. That is why they cried out to Moses, "You speak to us for if we hear the voice of the Lord our God any longer, we shall die." Thus if they could not tolerate the voice of the law, how were they ever going to keep it?

Thus if the people of the law[295] saw themselves compelled to seek a mediator, then it follows as an infallible consequence that the law had not justified them. Then what was the law good for? It's as if Paul had said, "The law came in to increase the trespass" (Romans 5:20). Thus the law was a light and a sun that shone its beams on the hearts of the children of Israel. That's why they were frightened and were so smitten with the fear of God that they hated the law as well as its author with terrible wickedness. Now, are you going to say those people were righteous? Absolutely not! They are righteous if they listen to the law and with goodwill embrace it and delight in it. But the story of the giving of the law testifies that all people of the world, no matter how holy they are (especially seeing that they had purified and sanctified themselves and still were incapable of listening to the law), are horrified of the law and flee from it. They would rather there were no law at all. Thus it is impossible for people to be justified by the law. Instead, it has the completely opposite effect.

As I've said, even though Paul here touches on this subject only in passing and does not plumb its depths, or conclude it, every attentive and diligent reader will easily understand that he speaks well of both mediators—that is, of Moses and Christ, comparing one with the other, as we shall see later. If he had followed up on this topic, this text would have given him a great argument and more than sufficient reason to write another epistle. This story of Exodus 19 and 20 regarding the giving of the law would also yield sufficient material to write a new volume, although few would read it and with little devotion. Those who are ignorant of the true use of the law and its function would find it rather sterile when compared to other parts of sacred history.

Seeing all this, if all the inhabitants of planet earth had been standing around the mountain together with Israel, they also would have hated the law and taken off running, as they did. Thus the entire world is an enemy of the law, hating it to death. But the law is holy, just, and good, and it is the straight forward will of God.[296] How could then someone be righteous who not only despises and detests the law but also flees from it? On top of that, he is also an enemy of God who is the author of the law! The truth is that the flesh can do no other, as Paul testifies, "because the mind of the flesh is hostile towards God; for it is not subject to God's law, neither indeed can it be" (Romans 8:7, WEB). Thus it is extreme insanity[297] to hate God and His law so that you can't even tolerate hearing it and at the same time insist that we are justified by the law.[298]

---

[295] *legis populus.*

[296] *rectitudo divinae voluntatis.*

[297] *extrema dementia.*

[298] Luther's footnote: *caro odit legem Dei, ergo non justificat,* "the flesh hates God's law; therefore, the law does not justify."

Therefore, the papal scholars are totally blind and understand nothing about this doctrine. They only stare at the great external appearance of the law,[299] thinking that it is fulfilled through satisfying moral norms[300] and that those who give the appearance of such moral behavior are righteous before God! But they cannot see the true spiritual effect of the law. It is not to justify, quiet and pacify tormented consciences. Instead, it is to make sin abound,[301] frighten the conscience, and bring out the wrath. By ignoring this, the boast that man has a goodwill and a reason capable to judge correctly how to fulfill God's law. But whether this is true or not, you must ask the people of the law, with their mediator, who heard the voice of the law from Mount Sinai. Ask David himself, who often laments in the Psalms that his heart failed before the very face of God, who felt he was in hell itself, and who felt horrified and depressed at the greatness of his sin, feeling God's wrath and indignation. He did not trust in the sacrifices, not even in the law itself, to defend him from these great tyrants. Instead, he was lifted and comforted only by God's mercy freely given to him. Thus the law does not justify.[302]

If the law would serve my affections—that is, if it would only give credence to my hypocrisy; if it would only prove the opinion of my self-righteousness; if it would only concede that without God's mercy and faith in Christ I could be justified before God, strengthened only by its power (for that's how the entire world thinks about the law); if it would only say that God is appeased and moved by its works and has the obligation to compensate its workers; if the law would also help me shed my need for God, I could then be my own god and merit grace as a reward for my works; despising Christ, I could be saved through my own merits; if I were to say that the law should pamper my own feelings then I would find it sweet, a delight, and a great pleasure altogether, and reason would have great motivation to congratulate itself! However, this kind of thinking must be short lived. The law came with its proper function and use. Thus it is evident that reason cannot tolerate those rays of light from the law. Someone like Moses had to approach and intervene as mediator, although without any fruit at all, as I will explain momentarily.[303]

To this end, that text in 2 Corinthians 3:13, regarding Moses covering his face, is applicable. Here, Paul takes up the story of Exodus 34 to point out that the

---

[299] *Intuentur tantum externam legis larvam.* This is a good example of the task involved in choosing a synonym for a transcript/translation. *Intuentor* may be translated with any of these words: look at, consider, regard, admire, or stare. However, given the context of Luther lecturing for maximum visual effect, it is more likely that if Luther would have been speaking modern English, and given his dynamic and graphic style of delivery, he would have said "stare," while mimicking a stare before the audience of seminarians.

[300] *civilibus moribus satisfieri.*

[301] *sed augere peccatum. Augere* may also be translated as "promote."

[302] *Ergo lex non justificat.*

[303] The reader must remember that Luther was delivering a lecture to the seminarians at Wittenberg.

children of Israel not only ignored but could not even tolerate the proper spiritual use of the law. First, Paul says, they could not understand the purpose of the law due to the veil worn by Moses to cover his face. They could not even look directly at Moses' face, due to the glory of his appearance, for when Moses spoke with them, he covered his face with a veil. Without it, they could not tolerate his words. To put it another way, they could not listen to Moses, their mediator, unless he, himself, placed another mediator between them, a veil. How then could they listen to the voice of God, or of some angel, when they could not even listen to Moses' voice, who was not only a mere man but also their mediator, unless he covered his face? Therefore, unless that blessed Seed should arise to comfort those who heard the law, they would perish out of desperation, hating the law, hating and blaspheming God, and daily offending Him more and more. Because when this fear and confusion in the conscience brought by the law penetrates more and more, the longer it lasts, the more hate and blasphemies increase against God.

Therefore, this story demonstrates that so called power of free will.[304] The people panic, tremble, turn around, and flee. What happened to their free will? Where did that goodwill disappear? What happened to that good intention, that upright choice of reason, of which the Papists brag so much about? What good did it do all those purified and sanctified beings to have free will?[305] Free choice had nothing to choose![306] However, how it makes reason go blind and perverts the will itself! It cannot receive or greet or joyfully embrace the coming of the Lord to Mount Sinai with thunder, lightning, and fire. It cannot tolerate the voice of the Lord. On the contrary, it says, "Let not the Lord speak to us lest we die!" We can then see how powerful and strong was free will in the children of Israel who despite all their washing and sanctifying could not tolerate one syllable or letter of the law. Thus these extremely high recommendations of the Papists about their free will are nothing but rubbish!

VERSE 20. Now a mediator involves more than one party [NRSV].

Here, he compares these two mediators with startling brevity. Nonetheless, it should suffice the attentive reader[307] who will understand that this word *mediator* is a general term. Paul is speaking about the meaning of mediator in general and is not specifically referring to Moses. "A mediator," he said, "involves more than one party." But the word necessarily refers to both the offended and the offender, where just one of them needs the intercession and not the other. Thus a mediator is not just for one but for two in disagreement. Thus Moses (using this generalized

---

[304] *liberi arbitrii.*

[305] *Quid hic in purificatis et sanctis liberum arbitrium valet?*

[306] *Nihil habet consilii.*

[307] "Attentive reader" was used for the printed version. Originally Luther directed his remarks to the "attentive student."

term) is a mediator, for he fulfills the role of interceding between the law and the people who cannot tolerate the spiritual use of the law.[308] Thus the law must put on a new face and change its voice—that is, the spiritual voice of the law,[309] or the law that brings panic to the inner affections, needs to put on a mask. With this mask, the law becomes tolerable and audible through the human voice of Moses.

So then, outfitted in this disguise,[310] the law no longer speaks with its own majesty but through the voice of Moses. But in this outfit, the law no longer fulfills its function; it no longer afflicts the conscience. This is also the reason it is neither understood nor valued. That is why they've become self-assured, negligent, and arrogant hypocrites. Even so, one of two things is necessary: that the law does not fulfill its function and that it covers itself with a veil (but then, as I've said, it becomes a creator of hypocrites). Otherwise, the law should fulfill its function without the veil, but then it kills. That's because the human heart cannot bear the power of the law. Then you'd better grasp onto that blessed Seed by faith. In other words, you should look beyond the end of the law toward Christ, who is the fulfill-ment of the law. Here, He will say to you, "Enough of living fearful of the law, be of good cheer my child, your sins are forgiven you (I'll say more about this shortly). Otherwise, you will have Moses as mediator and with his veil."

For this reason, Paul says, "A mediator involves more than one party." It can-not be that Moses is only a mediator on God's behalf, for God does not need a mediator. Further, he is not only the people's mediator, but he functions as a medi-ator between God and the people, who felt distressed by God. It is the mediator's function to appease between the offended and reconcile him to the offending party. Although Moses is such a mediator (as I've pointed out already), he does nothing more than change the voice of the law. He makes it more tolerable so that the peo-ple can bear hearing it. But he does not give them any power at all to fulfill it. In short, he is the mediator of the veil and thus cannot grant any power to fulfill the law. All he does is wear a veil. His disciples will always be hypocrites, since he is the mediator of the veil.

However, what do you think would have happened if the law had been given without Moses, either before or after Moses, without any mediator at all? Further, if the people had been neither allowed to flee nor permitted a mediator? In that case, the people stricken with an irresistible fear would have perished immediately. Or if the people had fled, some other mediator would have intervened between the law and the people. In this way, the people could survive and the law remained in force. Reconciliation would also be made between the law and the people.[311] Moses indeed came at the right moment and was made a mediator. He places a veil

---

[308] *Theologicum usum legis.*
[309] *Theologicum vocem legis.*
[310] *larvata.*
[311] *et populo cum lege convenisset.*

to cover his face, but he still cannot deliver the conscience from the anguish and fright brought by the law.[312] Thus what hope is there for the poor sinner at the hour of death or when his conflicted conscience feels God's wrath and judgment against sin, which the law has exposed and multiplied? The law should then have another mediator who will push Moses aside to protect the sinner from his desperation and say to him, "Although you are a sinner, you will stand." In other words, "you will not die." Nonetheless, the law and its wrath remain.

This mediator is Jesus Christ. He does not change the voice of the law, nor covers it with a veil as Moses did, nor pushes me away from the law so that it won't notice me. Instead, He, Himself, faces the wrath of the law and takes it away. He satisfies the law in His own body, within Himself. Through the Gospel, He then says to me, "Certainly the law threatened you with God's wrath and eternal death; but do not fear, do not flee. I supply and fulfill all things on your behalf. I satisfy the law on your behalf." This is a much more excellent mediator than Moses, for he comes between God, the offended party, and the offending ones. Here, Moses' intercession is worthless. He has already accomplished his function, and now he, together with his veil, has disappeared. At this point, the suffering sinner in all his desperation (or someone breathing his last) and the offended God encounter each other. A mediator far different than Moses is needed who can satisfy the law and take away its wrath; the offended God must be reconciled with that miserable and damnable sinner, guilty of eternal death.

Paul speaks briefly about this mediator when he says, "A mediator involves more than one party." This word *mediator*[313] refers to someone who mediates between the offended and offending parties. We are the offending party. God and His law are the offended ones. The offense is of such magnitude that neither can God forgive it nor can we make it right. Therefore, between God (who in Himself is one) and us there is an irreparable breach. Further, God cannot revoke His law but insists that it be observed and fulfilled. On the other hand, we who have transgressed the law cannot flee from the presence of God. Christ then has come as a mediator between these two opposing parties, hopelessly driven apart by an infinite and eternal separation; yet He has brought them together and reconciled them once again. And how did He accomplish it? As Paul said in another text, "Wiping out the handwriting in ordinances which was against us; and he has taken it out of the way, nailing it to the cross; having stripped the principalities and the

---

[312] The entire Old Testament testifies to keeping the law for the sake of the veil. Thus the Old Testament also testifies that the law is completely incapable as a method of justification, because the veil always stood between the law and the conscience. The conscience could convince itself that it was fulfilling the law, but it was only for the sake of the veil. Christ's life removes the veil, and what is seen is the life of Christ, who is true righteousness, imputed to the sinner by faith alone in Jesus Christ.

[313] *mediatorem agit.*

powers, he made a show of them openly, triumphing over them in it" (Colossians 2:14, 15, WEB). Therefore, He is a mediator not just of one party but between the two who were in total disagreement.

This is also a text replete with power and efficacy to disarm the righteousness of the law and teach us that with respect to justification, it should be removed totally from our sight. This word *mediator* also yields enough evidence to prove that the law does not justify. If it did, why do we need a mediator? We then see that human nature cannot tolerate the hearing of the law and even less is it capable of fulfilling the law or coming to an agreement with the law. Therefore, the law does not justify.[314]

This doctrine (which I repeat so often, and even though I'll bore you, I'll keep hammering it over your heads) is the true doctrine of the law. Every Christian should learn it diligently so that he may truly define what is the law, what is its proper use and function, what are its limits, what is its power, its timeframe, and its end, for its purpose is totally different from what everyone thinks it is. Nearly all have this pernicious and pestilent opinion rooted in them by nature that the law justifies. That's why I fear that when we have passed on, this doctrine will once again become disfigured and obscured, for the whole world will once again be covered with darkness and errors before the coming of the final day.

Thus let all who are able to comprehend it let them understand this: that the law, in true Christian theology and in its true and proper definition, does not justify. Instead, it has the completely opposite effect. It uncovers and reveals who we truly are. It manifests the wrath of God; it troubles us and not only exposes sin but also makes it grow out of control. Where sin was once only a small thing, through the law that brings it to light, now, sin becomes exceedingly sinful. The person begins to hate the law and flee from it. With perfect hate, it despises God, the giver of the law. This is not to be justified by the law (logic concedes the same). Instead, it is to sin twice against the law: first, not only for having a will at such great disagreement with the law that it cannot even hear it but also because it does what is against its commands and, second, because the will hates the law so much that it desires the law's abolishment together with God, its author, although He is infinitely good.

Now, what great blasphemy, what more horrendous sin could be imagined than to hate God, despise His law, so that you don't even want to hear it, even though it is entirely good and holy? History clearly testifies that the people of Israel refused to listen to that excellent law, those extremely pleasant words:[315] "I am the Lord God your God who brought you out of the house of Egypt, a house of slaves. You will not have other gods before me. I am merciful toward thousands. Honor your father and your mother so that your days may be long upon the land that the Lord your God gives you."[316] Further, they needed a mediator. They could not toler-

---

[314] *Ergo lex non justificat.*

[315] *in sua natura iucundissimas voces.*

[316] Luther's paraphrase of both texts.

ate that great divine wisdom of maximum excellence and perfection, this doctrine full of grace, sweet, and gracious. "Let not the Lord speak with us," they said, "lest we die. You speak to us" etc. Doubtless, it is quite astounding that man doesn't even want to hear those things that are for his maximum and sweetest good[317]—that is, that he has a merciful God who will show mercy upon thousands of generations etc. Further, he cannot even tolerate that which is the best for his own defense and security: "You will not kill, you will not commit adultery, you will not steal." Through these words, the Lord has defended and built a walled city around the life of man, his wife, his children, and his goods against the strength and violence of the wicked.

The law then cannot do anything else but to shine a light upon the conscience so that it may know sin, death, judgment, and God's wrath. Before the law came, I felt confident, I was not aware of sin at all. But when the law came, sin, death, and hell were revealed to me. This is not being righteous but guilty; this is to be declared an enemy of God, condemned to death and eternal fire. Thus the main point of the law in true Christian theology is not to make people better but worse! That is, the law exposes their sin. When they get to know it, they are humbled, troubled, mauled, and broken. Then they are driven to seek comfort and make their way to the blessed Seed. This is the sum of Paul's argument regarding the term *mediator*, on which he had digressed.

VERSE 20. But God is one.

God offends no one and thus does not need a mediator. Instead, it is we who offend God and thus need a mediator, not Moses but Christ, who speaks to us of better things. Here, Paul concludes his digression and continues with his main topic.

VERSE 21. Is the law, therefore, opposed to the promises of God?

Before, Paul had said that the law does not justify. Then are we going to get rid of the law? No, not at all. It brings with it a certain value. What is it? It leads people to know who they really are. It uncovers and increases sin. However, an objection comes up at this point: "If the law does nothing more than make people worse, since it shows people their sins, then it is opposed or contrary to the promises of God, for through the law, God is offended and provoked to anger. Thus He neither considers His promises nor fulfills them. However, as Jews, we think the opposite. We are bridled and subjected through that external discipline, and that is why God is moved and hastens to fulfill His promise, because through that discipline we are made worthy of the promise."

---

[317] *summum ac suavissimum bonum.*

Paul responds, "Nothing like it. If you pay attention to the law, you are instead blocking the promise." It is natural reason that offends God, who has faithfully promised. It's the same logic that refuses to hear that His law is holy and good, for it says, "Let not the Lord speak with us." Then how can God fulfill His promise with them who not only reject His law and discipline but also, with moral hate, despise it and flee from it? Therefore, as I said, at this point, this objection comes up: "Is the law opposed to the promises of God"? Although only in passing, Paul responds to this objection, saying,

VERSE 21. Absolutely not! [NIV].

Why this answer? First, because God does not promise us due to what we deserve or because of our merits or our good works but due to His own unquenchable kindness and eternal mercy. He does not say to Abraham, "In you shall be blessed all the nations of the earth because you have kept the law." However, when he was still uncircumcised, without any law, and was still and idolater (Joshua 24:2), He said to him, "Go from this land; I will be your shield." Further, "In you shall be blessed all the nations of the earth." These are absolute and pure promises that God freely gave Abraham, without any condition, nor expecting works, either before or after.

This goes against the Jews who think that God's promises are thwarted due to sins. Paul said, "God does not delay His promises due to our sins, nor does He hasten them due to our righteousness or merits. He does not take either of them into account." Therefore, even though we become worse sinners and because of the law we despise and hate God even more, God is not deterred from His promise. God's promise does not rest on our worthiness and righteousness but only on His kindness and mercy. Thus when the Jews say, "The Messiah has not come yet because our sins delay Him," they are showing an abhorrent imagination. As if God would become unrighteous due to our sins or turn out to be a liar because we are liars. He is always righteous and true. Therefore, His truth is the only reason he keeps and brings His promise to fruition.

Further, although the law reveals and increases sin, even so, it is not contrary to God's promises. Instead, it confirms the promises, for when it is used correctly regarding its proper work and function, it humbles and prepares man to groan and seek for mercy. Because when sin is revealed to man and the law multiplies it within him, then man begins to perceive the wickedness and hate in his heart toward the law and God Himself, the author of the law. Then he certainly feels that besides not loving God, he also hates God and blasphemes against Him, who is the fullness of kindness and mercy, and against His law that is holy above all. That is when the law compels man to recognize there is nothing good in him. It is then when he is totally defeated and humbled by the law, that he recognizes that in himself he is the most miserable and damnable being. Thus when the law has compelled the sinner to declare his own wickedness and to confess his sin from the depths of his heart, then the law has properly achieved its purpose and its time has been fulfilled. Then it is time for the season of grace, when the blessed Seed arrives just in time to encourage and comfort through the Gospel all who have been defeated and humiliated by the law. In this way then, the law is not contrary to God's promises, for in the first place, the promise does not hang from the law but from God's own truth and mercy alone.

Second, when the law performs it main purpose and function, it humbles man, and when he is humbled, it makes him sigh and groan to seek the hand and the help of his Mediator. Thus in His grace and mercy he experiences it as supremely sweet and comforting (as it has been said, "Your mercy is sweet" [Psalm 109]) and His gifts as precious and inexpressible. Counter to its usual purpose, it enables the sinner to receive Christ.[318] As the poet says, *Dulcia non meruit, qui non gustavit amara:*

No one deserves the sweet until they've tasted bitter.

There is also that common proverb: "Hunger makes the best chef."[319] As the parched earth covets the rain so the law causes the afflicted and distressed to thirst after Christ. These souls find in Christ a sweet flavor; for them, He is nothing more than joy, comfort, and life—that is when you truly begin to know Christ and His benefit.

Then this is the supreme use of the law. When man comes to use it in this way, it humbles him and makes him thirst for Christ. Christ indeed calls for thirsty souls. He attracts and calls them in the most loving way and full of grace. He says, "Come to me, all who labor and are heavy laden, and I will give you rest" (Matthew 11:28). He delights in watering these parched lands. He doesn't pour out his torrents on flooded and fetid lands; they must be dry and desire water above all. His benefit is without price. Thus He only gives to those who need and fervently desire His gifts. He preaches good news of great joy to the poor; He makes the thirsty to drink. "If anyone is thirsty, let him come to me and drink!" "He heals the broken in heart" (John 7:37; Psalm 146:8). He comforts the bruised and battered by the law. Therefore, the law is not opposed to the promises of God.

VERSE 21. If a law had been given which could make alive, then righteousness would indeed be by the law.

Paul makes it understood with these words that there is no law that of itself can bring or grant life. Instead, it only kills. Therefore, neither those works performed

---

[318] *Atque sic nos Christi capaces reddit.*

[319] *Dulcia non meruit, qui non gustavit amara. Fames optimus cocus est.* Luther cites two common proverbs of his day.

according to the laws and traditions of the Pope nor those according to the law of God justify anyone before God. Instead, these works only make them into greater sinners. They do not pacify the wrath of God. Instead, they provoke it. They do not obtain righteousness. Instead, they hinder it. They do not give life. Instead, they kill and destroy. That is why when he says, "If a law had been given that could make alive," he is clearly teaching that the law does not justify but has the completely opposite effect.

Although Paul's words are more than clear, they are obscure and totally unknown to the Papists. Indeed, if they had understood them, they would not magnify their free will, their own natural strength,[320] the observance of decrees, the supererogatory works, etc. However, in order not to give the impression that they are brazenly wicked unbelievers, denying the words of the apostle of Christ with such impudence, they have the following misleading interpretation[321] always at the ready. With it, they pervert the texts of Paul where he says that the law—in other words, the Ten Commandments—reveals sin and generates sin. They bring out their touch-up paint and say that Paul is only talking about the ceremonial law and not about the moral law. But Paul speaks clearly when he says, "If a law had been given," without making an exception for any law at all. Thus this touch-up used by the Papists is not even worth batting an eye. That is because God had also ordained the ceremonial laws and they were to be kept as strictly as the moral laws. The Jews observed circumcision as rigorously as the Sabbath day. Thus it is obvious that the apostle is talking about the whole law.

In the papacy, they sing and repeat Paul's words throughout their churches. Nonetheless, they teach and live the complete opposite. Paul simply says that no law was ever given to enliven or engender life. But the Papists teach the complete opposite and affirm that many, indeed an infinite number of laws, are given to enliven and give life! Although they don't say it in so many words, their deeds expose their opinion. Such is the testimony of their monastic life and many other laws and traditions of men, their works and merits offered before and after grace,[322] and their countless wicked ceremonies and false worship made up in their own heads. This is all they have preached, stepping on the Gospel, and nonetheless they guarantee grace, forgiveness of sins, and eternal life to those who observe and fulfill them. This, I can say, cannot be denied, since their books still circulate and testify all that is true.

On the contrary, we affirm with Paul that there is no law at all, whether it's man's or God's, that could ever give life. Thus we place a great difference between the law and righteousness, as great as there is between life and death, between heaven and hell. The reason we cannot budge from here is this text from Paul, where he

---

[320] *vires humanas.*

[321] *glossa.*

[322] *opera et merita congrui et condigni.*

clearly says that the law has not been given to justify, to give life, or to save; it's only been given to kill and destroy. Every man's opinion may be to the contrary, since naturally they could not have any other judgment regarding the law except that it has been given to work out righteousness and to give life and salvation.

LECTURE 24: Saturday, September 26

This difference between the function of the law and the Gospel safeguards the totality of Christian theology[323] within its true and proper use.[324] It also enables the believer to have criteria over all ways of life, over all laws and teachings judged as dogma,[325] and to discern all types of spirit. On the other hand, the Papists, since they confuse and combine the law and the Gospel cannot teach with any certainty regarding faith, works, how to live, or how to discern spirits. Today, the fanatical minds do exactly the same.

Thus once Paul has sufficiently refuted their arguments, and in good order, he teaches that the law (if examined in its true and perfect use) is nothing more than a tutor to lead us to righteousness.[326] It humbles, prepares, and readies sinners to receive the righteousness of Christ. When it fulfills its proper work and function, it makes them feel guilty, terrifies them, and leads them to the knowledge of sin, wrath, death, and hell. When it has accomplished all this, the opinion of man's righteousness and holiness disappears and Christ and all His benefits begin to taste sweeter. Thus the law is not contrary to God's promises. Instead, it confirms them. It's true that it does not fulfill the promise, nor does it bring righteousness. Notwithstanding, it humbles us with its function and office, we feel greater thirst, and it makes us more apt to receive the benefit of Christ. Thus he says, if a law had been given that could have brought righteousness and through righteousness life (for no one is able to attain to life unless he is righteous), then righteousness would come through the law. Further, if there were some way of life, some work, some religion by which man could achieve remission of sins, righteousness, and life, then these things would indeed justify and grant life. But that is impossible, since

---

[323] *conservat in vero usu universam sinceram theologiam.*

[324] In a footnote, Luther asks: *Ad quid prosit tenere legis et evangelii discrimen, et econtra etc.,* "which is better, to place a difference between the law and the gospel, or the opposite, etc."

[325] *super omnes omnium hominum leges et dogmata judices.*

[326] *paedagogiam quandam ad justitiam.*

VERSE 22. But the scripture imprisoned all[327] under sin [LEB].

Where? First, in the promises themselves regarding Christ, as in Genesis 3, "The seed of the woman will crush the serpent's head" (Genesis 3:15). Also, in Genesis 22:18, "In your seed." Then wherever in Scripture you find a promise made to the fathers regarding Christ, therein a blessing is promised, which is to say, righteousness, salvation, and eternal life. Thus the opposite is evident: those who are to receive the promise are subject to the curse, which is to say, sin and eternal death. If it were not so, why then was it necessary to promise the blessing?

Second, Scripture locks up everything under sin and under the curse, especially by the law. The law has its own special function. It is to reveal sin and stir up wrath. That is what we've seen throughout this epistle but particularly in this statement of Paul: "For as many as are of the works of the law are under a curse." There is also this text where the apostle argues based on Deuteronomy 27:26: "Cursed be everyone who does not abide by all things." These declarations in such simple words lock up everything under sin and under the curse, not only those who sin openly against the law or that to all appearances don't observe the law. Instead, they also lock up everyone who is under the law, including those who make extreme efforts to fulfill the law, such as the Jews I mentioned before. What's more, in the same text, Paul locks up under sin and under the curse all the monks, friars, hermits, Carthusians, and so on with all their professions, regulations, and religious orders. To all these, they attribute holiness, they fantasize that once they professed their vows when they die they will fly straight to heaven! But listen, here, Scripture locks up everything under sin. Therefore, neither the vow nor the most perfect religion of the Carthusian is righteousness before God, since everyone is under a curse and condemnation. Who dictates that sentence? The Scriptures. But where? First, in the promise—"the seed of the woman shall wound the serpent's head," "in you will be blessed," and similar texts. Further, within the entire law, for its main function is to accuse everyone of sin. Therefore, there is absolutely no monk, nor Carthusian, nor Celestine who is able to crush the serpent's head, but they themselves are crushed and broken by the head of the serpent—that is, under the power of the devil. Who is able to believe this?

In brief, everything that is outside of Christ and His promises, be it God's law or man's law, the ceremonial or the moral, everything without any exception, is locked up under sin because Scripture binds up everything under sin. So it was well said by the one who wrote "all," for it allows no exceptions. Therefore, we conclude with Paul that the norms and laws of all nations, although they are good and necessary, with all ceremonies and religions, without faith in Christ, are and remain under sin, death, eternal condemnation unless they are accompanied by

---

[327] *omnia,* "all things."

faith in the promise of Christ, as follows in the next text. But we've already spoken at length about this issue.

Therefore, the following is a true proposition: Faith alone justifies[328] (which our adversaries cannot tolerate). That is because Paul here powerfully concludes that the law neither engenders life nor grants life, because it was not given to that end. If the law neither justifies nor gives life, then works justify even less. Because when Paul says that the law does not give life, he means that works do not grant life either, for it means more to say that the law engenders and grants life than to say that works engender and give life, for if the fulfillment of the law itself (although it is impossible for the law to be fulfilled in that manner) does not justify, then works justify even less.[329] Therefore, faith alone justifies, without works.[330] Paul cannot tolerate this misleading interpretation: that faith together with works justifies. Instead, he simply proceeds from the negative (Romans 3:20), as well as from the second chapter: "Therefore, by the works of the law, no one will be justified" as well as "The law was not given to grant life" (Galatians 2:16).

VERSE 22. "So that what was promised, being given through faith in Jesus Christ, might be given to those who believe" [NIV].

Previously, he had said that Scriptures had locked up everything under sin. What? Forever? No! Only until the fulfillment of the promise. Now, the promise is the inheritance itself or the blessing promised to Abraham. It is this: to be rescued from the law, sin, death, and the devil and brought to the free gifts of grace, righteousness, salvation, and eternal life. This promise, he said, is not achieved by means of acquiring any merit or by the keeping of any law or by performing any work. Instead, it is given. To whom? To those who believe. In whom? In Jesus Christ, who is the blessed Seed, who has redeemed all the believers from the curse so that they may receive the blessing. These are not obscure words, they are clear enough. Nonetheless, we should diligently emphasize them and weigh their strength and weight, for since all has been locked up under sin, it follows that all the nations are under the curse and dispossessed from God's grace. It also means that they are under the wrath of God, the power of Satan, and that no one person may be rescued from these through any other means but by faith in Jesus Christ. Therefore, with these words, Paul powerfully lambasts against the illusions of the Papists and all the legalists with respect to the law and works when he says, "So that the promise by faith in Jesus Christ, might be given to those who believe."

---

[328] *Sola fides justificat.*

[329] Luther's footnote: *Si lex non justificat, multo minus opera, etc.,* "if the law does not justify, then works justify even less."

[330] *Ergo sola fides sine operibus justificat.*

Now, how should we respond to the statements regarding works and rewards? I've already said enough about that. But the subject now does not compel us to say anything about works, for here we have not taken up the matter of advocating works but justification. The fact is that it is not obtained through the law and works, since all things are locked up under sin and under the curse. Instead, it is obtained through faith in Christ. When we leave the subject of justification, we will not be able to praise and magnify sufficiently those works ordained by God, for who can recommend and sufficiently expound on the benefit and fruit of just one work done by a Christian through faith and in faith? Certainly, it is more precious than heaven or earth. Thus the entire world would not be able to reward the worthiness of such a good work. Yes, the world does not have the grace to magnify the holy works of the believers such as they deserve and even less to reward them, for they don't even pay attention to them, and if they do, they don't consider them as good works but as the most wicked and repugnant transgressions. They eliminate from the world those that do them, as if they were the deadliest plagues to ever trouble humanity.

That's how it was with Christ, the Savior of the world. As a reward for His incomprehensible and priceless benefit, He suffered the most shameful death on the cross. It was the same with the apostles, who brought the word of grace and eternal life to the world; they were called the world's greatest καθάρματα and περίψωμα.[331] This is the reward given by the world for such great and unspeakable benefits. But the works done without faith, albeit done with great display of holiness, are under a curse. Although those performers think that by them they deserve grace, righteousness, and eternal life, they are in fact piling sin on top of sin. That is how the Pope works, that man of sin and son of perdition and all his followers. It is the same with all those merit hoarders and all the heretics who have fallen away from the truth.

VERSE 23. But before faith came.

Here, he goes on to state the benefit and need of the law. He had said before that the law was added because of the transgressions, not that God had in mind giving a law just to bring death and condemnation. As Paul says in Romans 7:13, "Did that which is good, then, bring death to me? By no means!" The law then is a word that leads us to life and drives men to live. Thus it is given not just as a minister

---

[331] *katharmata* and *peripsoma*. What are these two Greek words doing here? Luther was lecturing along. Suddenly he realizes he's about to use two very offensive words. Instead of using the Latin words, he chooses their Greek equivalents, perhaps to tone down the shock effect. Only those students who knew their Greek caught the harshness of the words. Otherwise they were caught off guard by the Greek terms and realized what Luther meant. καθάρματα = bastards; περίψωμα = filthy scum.

of death. Instead, its main function and use is to reveal death so that sin might be known and seen in all its horror. Nonetheless, it does not reveal death as if it had no other purpose but to kill and destroy. Instead, it reveals death with this purpose: when people see themselves horrified, defeated, and humbled, then they should fear God. This is declared in Exodus 20:20, where Moses said, "Do not fear; for God has come to prove you, and that the fear of him may be before your eyes, that you may not sin." Thus the function of the law is to kill but only so that God may revive and once again give life. Notice, then, that the law is not given simply to kill. Instead, since man is proud and imagines he is wise, righteous, and holy, it is necessary to be humbled by the law so that this beast, the opinion of self-righteousness, is put to death. Otherwise, no human being could ever obtain life.

Then although the law kills, God uses that consequence of the law and puts it to good use, which is to give life! God knew that the most fatal plague that afflicts the entire planet is people's opinion of their own righteousness, their hypocrisy and confidence in their own holiness. Thus God gave the law to defeat this plague. However, people are not to remain defeated forever. Once they are down, they can get up again when they hear this voice: "Do not fear. I didn't give the law or kill you by the law for you to remain in this death but instead so that you may fear me and live." However, boasting in good works and self-righteousness cannot have a place next to the fear of God. Where there is no fear of God there cannot be any thirsting after grace for eternal life. That is why God needs that powerful hammer, or a powerful mallet, to break up the rocks, a burning fire in the middle of heaven to knock down mountains to destroy this furious and obstinate beast (I'm talking about self-pride). Thus when people are bruised and broken by the law until they are nothing, then they lose hope in their own strength, righteousness, and holiness. When they feel so desperate and thirsty, that's when they will cry out for mercy and the remission of sins.

VERSE 23. Now before faith came, we were imprisoned and guarded under the law until faith would be revealed [NRSV].

Before the time of the Gospel and grace had come, the function of the law was to lock us up and guard us within it, as if it were a prison. This is a beautiful analogy that shows how the law makes people righteous![332] Thus it is necessary to weigh it carefully. There is no thief, assassin, adulterer, or any other criminal who loves the chains and shackles, the dark and repugnant prison where he's bound tightly. Rather, if he could, he would destroy his prison blow by blow with his irons and shackles until there was nothing left but rubble! True, while he's confined in prison, he refrains from doing evil. But it's not due to his goodwill, not for the sake of righteousness. Instead, it's because prison binds him so that he can't do

---

[332] Luther is using a bit of sarcasm here.

anything. But while he's bound hand and foot, he does not hate his thievery and murderous ways. Instead, he feels all bitter that he can't be out robbing, assaulting, cutting and slicing throats. This man hates prison, and if he could escape, he would go back to stealing and killing as before.

The Law Imprisons People in Two Ways: In the Secular and the Spiritual[333]

Such is the strength of the law and the righteousness that comes through the law, that people are driven to give the appearance of being good. Why? It threatens the transgressors with death or any other punishment. Indeed, we then obey the law but fearing the punishment—in other words, not out of our goodwill but rather greatly offended. But what kind of righteousness is this, when we abstain from evil because we fear the punishment? Therefore, this righteousness of works is nothing more than loving sin and hating righteousness, detesting God and His law, and worshipping evil in all its entirety.[334] Look at all the goodwill the thief shows! Look at how he loves his prison and hates his thievery. It is the same with us when we so "gladly" obey the law, fulfilling what it ordains, and avoiding what it prohibits.[335]

Nonetheless, the law yields a profit,[336] even though the hearts of men continue hardened in sin. First, in the external and the secular, for in a certain way, it helps to keep in check thieves, assassins, and other criminals, for if they did not believe and understand that sin is punished in this life by prison, the gallows, the sword, and such and in the hereafter with eternal damnation and hellfire, no magistrate, parent,[337] or teacher could bridle the fury and rage of those who are not bothered by laws, shackles, or chains. But the threats of the law castigate with terror the hearts of the wicked so that they will be bridled to a certain extent and will not go from here to there all out of their minds doing all kinds of evil, as indeed they certainly would if they could. However, they would prefer the absence of any law, punishment, hell, and, why not, God. If God had no hell or did not punish the wicked, He would be loved and praised by all men. But since He punishes the wicked, and all are wicked, since all are locked up under the law, they have nothing else left but to blaspheme God and hate Him to death.

---

[333] *Theologice,* literally "the Theological."

[334] *et summam malitiam adorare.*

[335] The *gladly* in quotation marks is to point out Luther's use of irony or even sarcasm as he says this. This further corroborates the transcript nature of the Latin text, for only as we listen to the sarcasm in "libenter" are we able to understand its use. Otherwise, Luther would be teaching us that we should be glad when obeying the Law. Instead, he is describing our inner resistance to the law.

[336] *hoc commodi habet lex.*

[337] *paterfamilias.*

Further, the law locks up everyone under sin, not only in the secular, but also in the spiritual.[338] The law is also a spiritual[339] prison and, as it were, a hell itself. Because when it reveals sin and it threatens death with God's wrath, man cannot avoid it or find any comfort in it, for no one has the power to shake off these horrible fears that arise in the conscience or any other anguish or bitterness of spirit. Thus we find these, the complaints of the saints found throughout the Psalms: "Who will praise you from the grave?" (Psalm 6:5). That's how it is when someone is found tied up in the prison from which there is no escape, neither can he see how he shall be freed from those shackles, meaning those horrible terrors.

Thus the law is a prison in the secular as well as in the spiritual. First, it restricts the wicked so they won't be going around out of their heads following the impulses of their own lusts, getting into all kinds of evil. In the spiritual, it also points out our sin, it harasses and humbles us so that we many know our own misery and damnation. This is the true function and use of the law; thus it is not perpetual. Since this locking up and subjecting under the law should not last any longer once faith arrives. When faith has come, then this spiritual prison should come to an end.

Here, we can see once again that although the law and the Gospel should be placed far apart and utterly opposed to each other, regarding the affections of the soul, they are right next to each other. Paul demonstrates this when he says, "We were imprisoned and guarded under the law until faith would be revealed." Therefore, it is not enough for us to be kept locked up under the law, for unless something greater came along, we would lunge toward desperation and die in our sins. Nonetheless, Paul adds that we are locked up and kept under the tutor (the law) but not forever. The purpose is to take us to Christ, who is the end of the law. Thus these terrors, this humiliation, and this prison should not continue forever but only until faith is revealed. Let it continue only as long as it is for our benefit and salvation; up until we are beaten and humbled by the law, sin, and death. But then let grace, the remission of sins, and deliverance from the law, from sin and death, bring us the sweetest comfort. However, this is not found through works but through faith alone.[340]

When the moment of temptation comes, put together these two things so contrary to each other. In other words, when you have been so harassed and defeated by the law, then you should know that the law has come to an end. The time for grace has come, or the revelation of faith. This is the true use of the law. All the wicked are ignorant, since they altogether disavow this knowledge and keen perception. Cain did not acknowledge that he was locked up in the prison of the law feeling the gravity of his sin. At first, he was outside the prison. Although

---

[338] *Theologice.*

[339] *spiritualis.*

[340] *quae operibus non accipiuntur, sed sola fide apprehenduntur.*

he had already killed his brother, he was not afraid. Instead, he subtly covered up the matter, thinking God would not notice it. "Am I my brother's keeper?" he asked. But when he heard these words, "What have you done? Listen! Your brother's blood cries out to me from the ground," he definitely began to feel the walls of the prison closing in. What did he do? He stayed locked up in prison. He did not tie the Gospel to the law, but instead, he said, "My wickedness is so great, that it cannot be forgiven."[341] He only showed respect to the prison. He did not recognize that his sin had been revealed to him with this one and only purpose: to flee to God and receive mercy and forgiveness. Therefore, he panicked and denied there was a God.[342] He could not believe that he had been locked up with this one purpose, to receive the revelation of grace and faith. He only believed that he had to stay locked up under the law.

These terms, "kept under" and "locked up," are not empty and useless words but are deeply insightful and carefully chosen. They refer to true and spiritual fears, when the conscience is imprisoned, although it may go looking throughout the world for a way out where it will feel safe and sound. As long as these terrors last, the conscience feels such anguish and sadness that even if heaven and earth were ten times longer and wider, they still would feel as tight and narrow as a mouse hole. Here, man feels totally deprived of all wisdom, strength, righteousness, counsel, and aid. The conscience is very delicate and when it feels so locked up under the prison of the law, it cannot see any way out. This narrowness gets more constricted with each passing day; it seems as if there is no end in sight. That's when man feels God's wrath, infinite and incalculable. No one can escape it, as Psalm 139:7 testifies: "Where will I flee from your presence?"

Just as in this world the secular prison afflicts the body so that the recluse cannot have the free use of his body, in the same way, the spiritual prison[343] afflicts the mind with anguish so that the recluse cannot enjoy quietness of heart and a peaceful conscience. But even so, it is not to last forever (as reason is inclined to think when it finds itself in this prison) but only until faith is revealed. Therefore, this stunted conscience needs to be revived and comforted in the following way: "Brother, you are indeed locked up, for it is written, 'We are locked up until that faith is revealed.' You have been tormented in this prison, but it has not been to destroy you but for you to be comforted by the blessed Seed. The law has killed you so that through Christ you can live again and be restored to life. Therefore, do not despair like Cain, Saul, and Judas. When they realized they were all locked up and could not see beyond their dark prison, they stayed there. Thus they fell prey to desperation. However, you must think differently when you feel these torments within your conscience. You must know that it has been for good, and it

---

[341] *Maior est iniquitas mea, quam ut veniam merear.* Luther quotes the Vulgate.
[342] *negavit se deum habere.*
[343] *Theologice carcer est.*

has been for your benefit to have been so locked up that you have been confused and defeated. Therefore, use this prison time properly, as it benefits you, so that once the law has fulfilled its function, faith will then be revealed, for God does not afflict you with the sole purpose of tormenting you. He will not kill you for you to remain in death. 'I do not wish the death of the wicked,' he says through the prophet Ezekiel (Ezekiel 33:11). But He will afflict you to humble you and that you will come to understand your need for mercy and the benefit of Christ."

This prison time under the law should not last forever but only until the arrival or the revelation of faith. This delightful psalm teaches that "the Lord takes pleasure in those who fear Him," which is to say in those who are in the prison of the law. However, he immediately adds, "In those who hope in His mercy" (Psalm 147:11, NKJV). Therefore, we need to bring these two things together, even though they are opposed to each other. Because what else could be so contrary than to hate and abhor God's wrath but then to trust in His kindness and mercy? One is pure hell, the other is precious heaven, but the two must closely come together in the heart. In theory, one could easily tie them together. But in the experience and in practice, it is the hardest thing to do. I, myself, have proven this in my own experience. But the Papists and the fanatics don't know anything about this matter. Thus these words of Paul to them are dark, and they don't know their meaning at all. Then when the law reveals to them their sins, it accuses and torments them; they cannot find any comfort, rest, help, or aid. Instead, they fall into despair, like Cain and Saul.

Thus seeing that the law (as I said) is our prison and executioner, it is true that we have no love for it. Instead, we hate it. Because everyone who says he loves the law is a liar and doesn't know what he's saying. Thieves and assailants would be considered crazy if they loved their prison, shackles, and chains. Seeing then that the law locks us up and keeps us in prison, it cannot mean anything else but that we are bitter enemies of the law. In conclusion, we love the law and its righteousness just like a murderer loves his musty cell, the shackles, and the irons. How then is it possible that we could ever be justified by the law?

VERSE 23. We were imprisoned and guarded under the law until faith would be revealed [NRSV].

Here, Paul speaks with respect to the fullness of time completed when Christ came. But we should relate it not just to this time but also to the interior man. The fulfillment of the coming of Christ is the story of the abolishment of the law, the coming of light, freedom, and eternal life. This happens every day in every Christian's life. Some are always found in the time of the law and others in the time of grace. Each Christian has a body in whose members (as Paul said elsewhere) sin dwells embattled. I understand that sin is not only the act or the work but also the root and the tree, together with the fruit, as Scripture says referring to sin. It is not only rooted in the baptized flesh of every Christian but also at mortal war within him, and holds him captive. Although he may not consent to sin, or to do the works of sin, even so, it prevails, exerting great power over him. The Christian may not fall in external and gross sins such as murder, adultery, theft, and such. However, he is not free from impatience, complaining, hate, and blasphemy against God. These sins are totally ignored by the carnal mind's ability to reason. These things compel him to sin even against his own will and to detest God's law. They drive him to flee from God's presence, they harass him until he hates and blasphemes against God. Just as carnal desire is strong in a young person, in their years of maturity, people feel the desire and love for glory, and when they reach old age, people deal with greed. In the same way, in the faithful and holy believer, impatience, complaining, hate, and blaspheming against God prevail powerfully. We find examples of this in the Psalms, in Job, in Jeremiah, and throughout the Scriptures. Therefore, when Paul describes and expounds on this spiritual battle, he uses burning words and much to the point, such as struggle, rebellion, locked up, and taken captive.

These two periods (I'm referring to the law and the Gospel) are found in the Christian, in his interior emotional life. The time for the law is when the law vexes and torments me with a despairing heart, it oppresses me and takes me to the knowledge of sin, and makes it abound. Here is where the law is exerting is true and perfect use, and the Christian will feel it frequently throughout his life. That is why the apostle Paul was given a thorn in the flesh, "a messenger from Satan to buffet me." He would have happily preferred to feel constant joy in his conscience, his heart's laughter, and the sweet savor of eternal life. He would have felt more than happy to feel free of all trial and anguish of spirit; that is why he desired the removal of this temptation. Nonetheless, it was not so. Instead, the Lord told him, "My grace is sufficient for you, for my power is made perfect in weakness" (2 Corinthians 12:9). Every Christian is aware of this struggle. In my own experience, I spend many hours arguing with and berating God, and I resist him impatiently. God's wrath and judgment are not pleasing to me. On the other hand, my impatience, complaints, and such sins are also displeasing to Him. This is the time of the law, under which every Christian continually lives, according to the flesh. "For the desires of the flesh are against the Spirit, and the desires of the Spirit are against the flesh" but in some more than others.

The time of grace is when the heart comes to life again through the promise of God's freely given mercy, and says, "Why are you cast down, O my soul, and why are you disquieted within me?" (Psalm 42:6). Can you see nothing more than the law, sin, terror, despair, hopelessness, death, hell, and the devil? Have you not heard there's grace, forgiveness of sin, righteousness, comfort, joy, peace, life, heaven, Christ, and God? Don't oppress me anymore, oh my soul. What is the law, what is sin, and what is all the evil of the world put together when compared with these? Trust in God, who has not held back His only beloved Son but who has given Him over to death on the cross for your sins. Consequently, we are locked up under the law according to the flesh, not forever, but only until Christ is manifested. Thus when you feel beaten, tormented, and afflicted by the law, then cry out like this: "Madam Law, you are all alone and neither are you all things. There are many other better and more important things than you; for instance, grace, faith, and the blessing. Grace, faith, and this blessing do not accuse me or afflict me; they don't condemn me. Instead, they comfort me and urge me to trust in the Lord. They promise me victory and salvation in Christ. There is no reason at all for me to live in anguish or despair."

This is an art and everyone who knows how to use it with ability and shrewdness may well call himself a theologian. Today, the fanatical minds and their disciples constantly boast of the Spirit and persuade themselves to know it inside and out. However, there are others who together with me have just begun to learn its basic principles. It is true that one can learn but as long as the flesh and sin shall last, it can never be learned to perfection, and so it should be. Thus the Christian finds himself divided between the two times. With respect to the flesh, he is under the law. With regards to the spirit, he is under grace. Lust, greed, ambition, and pride always cling to the flesh. Ignoring and despising God, impatience, complaining, and resenting God are all the same. God obstructs and destroys our plans because He does not immediately punish the wicked, rebellious, and proud. This type of sin is rooted in the flesh of the faithful. Therefore, if you just look at nothing more than the flesh, you will always find yourself in the time of the law. But these days should be cut short; otherwise, no one would be saved. The law should have its designated timeframe with its end. Thus the time for the law is not perpetual but has its end, who is Jesus Christ. But the time for grace is eternal, "for we know that Christ being raised from the dead will never die again; death no longer has dominion over him." He is eternal. Therefore, the time of grace is also eternal.

We cannot overlook such exceptional statements by Paul. The Papists and the sectarians overlook them to their loss. These declarations contain words of life that comfort and confirm the troubled conscience. Those who know and understand them well can judge with respect to faith, they can discern between false and true fears, they can judge regarding the internal affections of the heart and discern every spirit. The fear of God is something holy and precious, but it should not last forever. The Christian must certainly feel it, since sin will always be within him; but he should not remain alone. Otherwise, it will become like the fear of Cain, Saul, and Judas—in other words, a submissive and desperate fear. Therefore, the Christian should overcome fear through faith in the word of grace; he should withdraw his eyes from the time of the law and fix his gaze upon Christ and the faith yet to be revealed. *Then his fear turns into a sweet experience and mixed with nectar so that he no longer fears God but begins to love God.* At this point, fear begins to feel like something sweet within us and leads us to delight in God. But if man only fixes his gaze on the law and sin, putting faith aside, he will never be able to separate himself from fear but fall prey to desperation.

Thus Paul clearly distinguishes between the time of the law and the time of grace. Let us also learn to distinguish these times not only in words but also in the deepest emotions, which is something difficult to do, for even though these two exist totally separate from each other, they are found almost united within a single heart. Nothing is as closely bound together as fear and trust, the law and the Gospel, sin and grace. They are so close together that one absorbs the other. Therefore, there is no mathematical conjunction[344] quite like this.

In the passage "Why then the law?" Paul began to argue regarding the law, as well as it use and abuse. He builds on what he had affirmed before, that the faithful grasp righteousness by grace and the promise but not by the law.[345] This argument gave rise to the question "Why then the law?" That's because reason, hearing that righteousness or the blessing is obtained by grace and the promise, immediately infers, "Then the law is worthless." Thus the doctrine of the law should be considered with great attention so that we may judge why and how we should esteem it, lest we reject it altogether. That's what the fanatical heads did in the year 1525, inciting the people to revolt,[346] saying that the law of liberty given by the Gospel freed everyone from all kinds of laws.[347] Otherwise, the power to justify is attributed to the law. Both ways offend the law. On the one hand, the one that says the law justifies and on the other, the one that says that we should be freed altogether from the law. Therefore, we should walk along the royal highway,[348] where we neither reject the law nor attribute to it more than necessary.

What I have repeated often regarding the uses of the law, the secular and the spiritual, should be enough to state that the law is not given to the righteous but as Paul said elsewhere (1 Timothy 1:9), to the wicked and rebellious. Of the latter, there are two types, those who are to be justified and those who are not to be justified. Those who are not to be justified should be bridled by the secular use of the law because they need to be restrained with the shackles of the law, as beasts are restrained with ropes and chains. This use of the law has no end, and Paul says nothing about this use of the law. But those who are to be justified are exercised in the spiritual use of the law for some time (but not forever, as it is with the secular use); they fix their eyes on the faith that is to be revealed, and when Christ comes, the law comes to its end. That is why we can clearly see that all Paul's declarations where he urges the spiritual use of the law should be understood as relating to those who are to be justified and not to those who are not. Those who have been justified, since they remain in Christ, are above the law. Thus the law should be imposed on those who are not yet justified, to keep them under prison until the righteousness

---

[344] *matematica coniunctio.*

[345] *quia asseruit justitiam credentibus contingere ex gratia et promissione, non lege.*

[346] A reference to the Peasants' Revolt (1524).

[347] *libertate Evangelicam absolvere homines ab omibus legibus.*

[348] *regia via.*

of faith reaches them. However, the law is not imposed to attain righteousness (that would not be a proper use of the law but would be to abuse it). Instead, once they have been defeated and humbled by the law, they should flee to Christ, who is "the end of the law for righteousness to everyone who believes."

Well then, in the first place, those who abuse the law are the legalists and hypocrites, since they have the illusion that people are justified by the law. That's because this use of the law does not exercise and drive a person to the faith that is to be manifested. Instead, it makes them arrogant and careless hypocrites, puffed up and presuming of the righteousness of the law, putting an obstacle to the righteousness of faith. In the second place, those who abuse the law are those who release the Christian from the law, as the fanatical spirits who stirred up the peasants to revolt. There are many of this type who claim to profess the Gospel together with us today. They think that because they have been delivered from the tyranny of the Pope by the doctrine of the Gospel that Christian liberty is dissolute and carnal freedom to do whatever they wish. These (as Peter said in 1 Peter 2:16) claim freedom of the spirit to cover up their evil intentions. They are the reason the name of God and of Christ's Gospel are slandered everywhere. Thus they will suffer punishment but only once for their wickedness. In the third place, there are those who also abuse the law, for when they feel the stress of the law, they don't understand that these terrors should not continue but instead should flee to Christ. This abuse makes them fall into desperation, for the arrogance and pride of the hypocrites will lead them there.

On the contrary, the true use of the law can never be sufficiently esteemed and magnified, as it deserves. When the conscience feels the narrow walls of its prison closing in, it should not despair. Instead, in the middle of its fright, the Holy Spirit comes to instruct it. Then the conscience declares, "It is true that I am locked up under the law, but it's not forever. Instead, this period of captivity will turn into a great benefit for me. How could this be? Because through this confinement I am compelled to groan and seek the hand of a Savior." As such, the law is a soldier that drives the hungry toward Christ, so Christ may satisfy them with His good gifts. Therefore, the true use of the law is to show us our sins, to have us plead guilty, to humiliate us, to kill us, to take us to hell, and finally, to strip us of all help, all aid, all comfort but only with this one purpose: for us to be justified, exalted, brought back to life, transported to heaven and made recipient of every good gift. Thus it not only kills but kills so that we may have life.

VERSE 24. Therefore, the law was our schoolmaster to bring us unto Christ.

Here, once again with respect to the affections of the inner heart, he places the law and the Gospel side-by-side, which up until now had been completely separate, for he says, "The law was our schoolmaster to bring us to Christ." The example of the schoolmaster also deserves our attention. Although a disciplinarian is very helpful and necessary for the instruction and upbringing of children, show me just one child or student who loves his disciplinarian. What kind of love and obedience did the Jews show Moses when at that same hour (according to the testimony of history) they would have stoned him to death without remorse? Therefore, it's not possible for the student to love his disciplinarian. How can he love the one who keeps him locked up in prison and doesn't allow him to do whatever he wants? And should he wish to violate his commands, he is immediately scolded and punished and then to top things off he is forced to kiss the punishing rod? So go ahead and tell me, what kind of wonderful obedience is this? The student obeys the schoolmaster due to such severe and dire threats that he even kisses the rod? But does he do it out of goodwill? As soon as the schoolmaster turns his back, he breaks the rod or throws it in the fire. If he had any power over his schoolmaster, he would not only fend off the punishment, but he'd turn around and land his own blows on the disciplinarian! However, the student has a great need for the schoolmaster, to instruct and discipline him. Otherwise, the child would be totally lost without discipline, instruction, and a good education.

LECTURE 25: Friday, October 9

Thus the tutor is designed to instruct, care for, and keep the child locked up in prison so to speak. But to what purpose and for how long? Is the idea for the tutor's rough treatment to last forever, or is the child to remain locked up forever? Not at all; it's only for a time so that this obedience, this prison and correction, turns into something worthwhile for the child so that when the time comes, he is able to become his father's heir, for it is not the father's will that his child will always be subject to the tutor receiving blows from the rod. Instead, due to his stern teachings and discipline, he may be empowered and formed to be his father's successor.

It's as if Paul said, "The law is nothing but a schoolmaster, but it's not to last forever, its job is over once it has taken us to Christ." This is what he had previously said, "The law was added because of transgressions until the coming of the Seed"; "we were held in custody under the law, locked up until the faith that was to come would be revealed." That is why the law is not only a schoolmaster but a schoolmaster to take us to Christ because what kind of a schoolmaster is that who is always tormenting and beating the student if he can't teach him anything? Even so, in the past, there were such schoolmasters who were cruel tyrants, nothing more than butchers. The children would always be beaten, they learned with great pain and constant anguish, but they all turned out to be good for nothings! The law is not such a tutor. It not only annoys and perturbs but also, with its rod, drives us toward Christ (unlike the foolish schoolmaster who beats his students but doesn't teach them anything). The law is like a good schoolmaster, who instructs and exercises his students in reading and handwriting. That way they will have a good command of letters and other beneficial matters. When they are adults, they delight in what before they were forced to do and was contrary to their will.

By this excellent example, Paul demonstrates the true use of the law. It is as follows: The law does not justify hypocrites because in their conceit and self-confidence they continue without Christ. On the other hand, the law does not abandon the contrite of heart in death and the curse if they properly use the law, for, as Paul teaches, the law drives them toward Christ. But those who continue in their wickedness (notwithstanding their fears and terrors), and do not grasp on to Christ by faith, will eventually fall prey to panic. Thus Paul in this allegory of the schoolmaster vividly describes the true use of the law. The schoolmaster reproves his students. He afflicts them and places heavy burdens on them, but not to keep them in such captivity forever. Rather, when the children are well educated and properly instructed, its function comes to an end. Further, once they see themselves without the annoyance of the tutor, they enjoy their freedom and the goods of their father. Similarly, those who are harassed and oppressed by the law, let them know that these terrors and harassments will not continue forever but that this is how they are prepared to come to Christ, who will be revealed to them and will grant them freedom of spirit etc.

VERSE 24. That we might be justified by faith.

The law is not a tutor to lead us to another lawgiver who demands good works but to Christ our Justifier and Savior[349] so that by faith in Him we might be justified and not by works. But when someone feels the strength and the power of the law, he does not understand or believe the law's real message. That's why he says, "I've lived in wickedness, since I've broken all God's commandments, and thus I am guilty of eternal death. If God would only grant me a few more years of life, or at least a few months, then I'll mend my ways and from then on I will live in holiness." But with this, he abuses the proper function of the law by turning the law right back on himself. Reason, when it sees itself penned in by these fears and dire straits, has the audacity to promise God it's going to fulfill all the works of the law. That is the reason so many sects and swarms of religious hypocritical monks, countless ceremonies, and works without end were invented to merit grace and the forgiveness of sins! But those who came up with these inventions didn't think the law was a schoolmaster to lead them to Christ. No, they've made up a new law and a new Christ as a Lawgiver and not as He who has abolished the law.

However, the true use of the law is to teach me that I am a sinner until I, myself, will admit it and be humbled by it so that I may come to Christ and be justified by faith. But faith is not any kind of law or work at all but a firm confidence

---

[349] *Christum justificatorem et salvatorem, ut per fidem in ipsu, non per opera justificemur.*

that takes hold of Christ, who "is the end of the law" (Romans 10:4). In what way? It's not that He has abolished the old law in order to give us a new law or that He is a judge that must now be appeased by works, as the Papists have taught. Instead, He is the end of the law unto righteousness for all those who believe[350]—that is, everyone who believes in Him is righteous;[351] the law will never have any reason to make any accusation against him. The law then is good, holy, beneficial, and necessary if we use it properly. But those who abuse the law, in the first place are the hypocrites who grant it the power to justify. Second, those who despair and will not understand that the law is a schoolmaster to lead them to Christ, the law humbles them, not to destroy them but to lead them to their salvation, for the fact is that God wounds in order to heal and kills in order to give life.

Then as I've said before, Paul talks about those who are going to be justified and not about those have already been justified. Thus when you set out to reason with respect to the law, you must take the issue of the law and direct it to those over whom the law still reigns—the sinner and the wicked, who are not justified by the law. The law puts their sin right before their eyes; it knocks them down and brings them to a knowledge of themselves. It opens their eyes to hell, wrath, and God's judgment. This is certainly the proper function of the law. From this, we may know that this is the function of the law. Next, the sinner sees that the law does not reveal his sin and humbles him in order for him to despair but rather that through its accusations and pushing and shoving it leads him to Christ the Savior and Comforter. When this takes place, then he is no longer under the school-master. But this use is very necessary. Seeing that the entire world is overflowing with sin, it needs this ministry of the law to reveal sin. Otherwise, no one would ever attain to righteousness, as we have previously and thoroughly stated. But is there any function for the law in those who have already been justified by Christ? Paul answers the following as a supplement to what he has already stated.

VERSE 25. But now that faith has come, we are no longer under a tutor [WEB].

In other words, we are free from the law, from its prison, and from our schoolmaster because when faith is revealed, the law ceases to terrorize and torment. Here, Paul is talking about the faith that was preached and announced by Christ when the time designated beforehand had come, for Christ, taking on Himself human nature,[352] came at His appointed time to the world. He abolished the law with all its consequences and freed from eternal death all those who receive His benefit by faith. Thus if they fix their gaze on Christ and on what He has done, they will

---

[350] *sed finis est legis ad justitiam omni credenti.*

[351] *Omnis, qui credit in eum, est justus.*

[352] *humana natura.*

now see that the law is no longer.[353] At the appointed time, He took away the law.[354] Now, since the law has disappeared, we are no longer under its tyranny. Rather, we live in joy and assurance under Christ, who now sweetly reigns among us by His Sprit. Now, where the Lord reigns, there is liberty. Thus if we could only perfectly grasp on to Christ, who through His death has abolished the law[355] and reconciled us with the Father, the schoolmaster will no longer have any power over us. But the law of the members rebels against the law of the mind and gets in our way so that we cannot perfectly grasp on to Him. However, the fault does not reside in Christ but in us who have not yet put aside this flesh to which sin is adhered, as long as we are in this life. Thus as far as we are concerned, we are somewhat free from the law and somewhat under the law. According to the Spirit, together with Paul, we serve the "law of God, but according to the law of the flesh, the law of sin" (Romans 7).

From here, it necessarily follows that with respect to the conscience we are fully freed from the law and thus that schoolmaster should no longer rule. In other words, the law should no longer afflict the conscience with its terrors, threats, and captivity. And although the law will always attempt it, the conscience should not be perturbed, for it has Christ crucified before its eyes, who has removed all the chambers of the law from the conscience,[356] "having wiped out the handwriting of requirements that was against us" (Colossians 2:14, NKJV). Thus just as the virgin who has not known any man at all, so the conscience should not only be unaware of the law but also be totally dead to the law and similarly the law to the conscience.[357] This cannot be attained by any work or through the righteousness of the law but by faith, which fixes its gaze on Christ and grasps on to Him. Nonetheless, sin is still stuck to the flesh, as far as its emotions are concerned, which at times accuse and afflict the conscience. As long as the flesh has life, this schoolmaster also remains, which sometimes afflicts the conscience and burdens it with its weight when it reveals sin and threatens with death. However, it revives daily when Christ comes. Just as He came once to the world, at the precise moment that had been determined from before, to redeem us from the rough and harsh slavery to the schoolmaster, so He comes every day to us spiritually so that we may grow in faith and in His knowledge, so that the conscience may grasp onto Christ more perfectly day after day and so that the law of the flesh and sin, with the terrors of death and all the ills brought along by the law, will be diminishing within us with every passing day. Then just as long we are living in this flesh, which is not free from sin, the law will often return and perform its task, in some more than others, according to their faith, strong or

---

[353] *nulla amplius lex est.*

[354] *verissime totam legem sustulit.*

[355] *Quare si possemus Christum, qui legem abrogavit.*

[356] *Christum crucifixum, qui abstulit omnia officia legis e conscientia.*

[357] *conscientia non solum legis ignara, sed etiam ei prorsus mortua ese debet, et vicissim lex conscientiae.*

weak, but not to destroy but for their salvation, for this is the operation of the law in the saints, the continuous mortification of the flesh, reason, and our own strength, and for the daily renewal of our minds (2 Corinthians 4).

Then we also receive the first fruit of the Spirit. The yeast is hidden in the dough but not all the dough has been leavened; the leavening has barely begun. If I fix my eyesight on the yeast, I will see nothing but pure yeast. But if I look at the entire mass of dough, I can see that the yeast has not yet taken hold—that is, if I fix my eyes on Christ, I am entirely pure and holy, totally unaware of the law, for Christ is my yeast. But if I fix on my own flesh, I feel within me envy, lust, wrath, pride, and arrogance; as well as fear of death, despair, hate, murmuring and impatience with God. The more these sins are present within me, Christ will be absent even more. Or, if He is indeed present, we are aware of Him, but very little. Thus there arises the need for a schoolmaster, to exercise and frustrate this stubborn mule, the flesh. Through this exercise, the sins will diminish, and the way is prepared for Christ. Christ came once in the flesh, and at the appointed time, He abolished the entire law, conquered sin, and destroyed death and hell. In the same way, He comes spiritually without ceasing, and daily, He douses these sins and puts them to death in us.

I say this so you may answer if someone objects as follows: "Christ came to the world and once and for all took away all our sins and cleansed us with His blood. Why then must we hear the Gospel, the need for absolution and the Sacraments?" It is true that if you fix your eyes on Christ, the law and sin have been abolished. But Christ has not yet come to you, or if He has, there are residues of sin that remain in you. You have not yet been entirely leavened, for wherever you find lust, despair of spirit, and fear of death, there you will also find the law and sin. Christ has not yet come altogether. However, when He comes indeed, He takes away fear and despair and brings peace and quiet to the conscience. Then in the same measure that I grasp Christ by faith, the law is abolished for me. But my flesh, the world and the devil, harass faith within me so that it cannot be perfect. I would be more than happy for that tiny light of faith that is found in my heart to be scattered throughout my body and all its members. It barely begins to disperse, but it is not dispersed immediately everywhere. Meanwhile, we have this comfort, the first fruit of the Spirit has just now begun to leaven us; however, we shall be fully leavened when this body of sin is dissolved, and together with Christ, we will be raised again.

Then although Christ is the same yesterday, today, and forever (Hebrews 13) and although Adam and all the faithful before Christ had the faith and Gospel, Christ appeared only once at the appointed time. Faith also came when the apostles preached and announced the Gospel throughout the entire world. Further, Christ also comes spiritually every day. Faith as well also comes daily through the word of the Gospel. Now, when faith comes, the schoolmaster is also forced to give up his place with his heavy and painful function. Christ also comes spiritually when we come to know Him more and more, as we grow in grace and in knowing Him (2 Peter 3:18).

VERSE 26. For in Christ Jesus you are all sons of God, through faith.

Paul as a true and excellent teacher of faith always has these words in his lips: "through faith, in the faith, from faith" that is in Christ Jesus. He doesn't say, "You are God's children because you have been circumcised, because you have listened to the law, and because you have done its works (as the Jews imagine and as taught by the false apostles)." No, it is by faith in Jesus Christ.[358] The law then does not make us God's children; even less, the traditions of men. It does not engender in us a new nature or a new birth. Instead, it fixes our eyes on the old birth, by which we were born to the kingdom of the devil. However, it prepares us for a new birth that is by faith in Jesus Christ and not through the law. The apostle Paul clearly testifies about this: "For in Christ Jesus you are all sons of God, through faith" etc. It's as if he had said, "Although you have been tormented, humiliated, and put to death by the law, the law has not made any one of us righteous nor made us into God's children. This is the work of faith alone." What faith? Faith in Christ. Therefore, it is faith in Christ then that makes us children of God and not the law.[359] John testifies about this as well: "To all who did receive him, to those who believed in his name, he gave the right to become children of God" (John 1:12, NIV).

Bring to this location the preachers who will speak about the unspeakable grace and glory that we have in Jesus Christ; let them expound and magnify it. Let them show how we miserable sinners, by nature children of wrath, have attained this honor: that by believing in Christ, we should be children and heirs of God and coheirs with Christ, lords over heaven and earth. The time is yours; preach on! However, there is no language, neither human nor angelical, that could ever possibly preach about this magnificent glory!

VERSE 27. For as many of you as were baptized into Christ have put on Christ.

Putting on Christ can be understood in two ways: according to the law or according to the Gospel. According to the law, as Romans 13:14 says, "clothe yourselves with the Lord Jesus Christ"—that is, imitate the virtues of Christ and suffer as He suffered. Also in 1 Peter 2:21, "Christ also suffered for you, leaving you an example, so that you should follow in his steps" (NRSV). Look well at Christ's infinite patience, gentleness, love, and admirable moderation in all things. Clothe yourselves with these ornaments of Christ—that is, we should imitate His virtues, as well as the lives of the saints.

However, to be clothed with Christ according to the Gospel does not consist in imitation but in a new birth and a new creation—that is, I clothe myself with

---

[358] *Per fidem in Christum Iesum.*

[359] *Fides ergo in Christum efficit filies Dei, non lex.*

Christ Himself. I am clothed in Christ's innocence, His righteousness, His wisdom, His power, His saving wholeness, His life, and His Spirit. We are all clothed with Adam's garb of skins. This is a perishable garb and attire of sin, for we are all subject of sin, sold under sin. There is within us horrible blindness, ignorance, rejection, and hatred toward God, including evil lust, impurity, covetousness, etc. This attire, this corrupt and sinful nature we receive from Adam and Paul often calls it "the old man." This old man should be shaken away with all his works (Ephesians 4:22; Colossians 3:9) so that the children of Adam can become children of God. This cannot be changed as easily as putting on a different piece of clothing nor by keeping any law or doing a certain work. Rather, it is by a new birth and a renewal of the interior being, which is what happens at baptism. As Paul said, "For as many of you as were baptized into Christ have put on Christ" and "He saved us, not because of deeds done by us in righteousness, but in virtue of his own mercy, by the washing of regeneration and renewal in the Holy Spirit" (Titus 3:5). In those who are baptized, besides being reborn and renewed by the Holy Spirit to a celestial and eternal life, there emerges a new light and a new fire, new and holy affections arise, such as the fear of God, a true faith, and a sure hope, etc. There's also the beginning of a new will. This is to be truly clothed with Christ and according to the Gospel.

Thus in baptism we are not given the righteousness of the law or that of our own works but Christ Himself is our robe.[360] Now, Christ is no law at all, nor a lawgiver, nor any work, but a divine and priceless gift that God has given to us. He is given to us as our Justifier, our Lifegiver,[361] and our Redeemer. Thus to be clothed with Christ according to the Gospel is not to be clothed with the law, or with works, but with an incomparable gift—that is, the remission of sins, righteousness, peace, comfort, joy of spirit, salvation, life, and Christ Himself.

Keep this well in mind, since the fanatics have nothing better to do but go around diminishing the majesty of baptism, slandering its meaning. Paul, on the contrary, urges it and describes it with honorary titles, calling it "the washing of rebirth and renewal by the Holy Spirit" (Titus 3:5). And here he has said that all who are baptized have put on Christ. It's as if he had said, *"Through baptism you have not received just a password*[362] *by which you are enrolled in the list of Christians, as in our days so many fanatic hot heads suppose. They have made of baptism a mere sign, meaningless and empty. But Paul says, all you who have been baptized in Christ have put on Christ"*—that is, you have been removed from the law and taken to a new birth, which is testified through baptism. Therefore, you are no longer under the law, but you have been dressed anew with a brand-new robe, the righteousness of Christ. *Thus Paul teaches that baptism is not a sign*

---

[360] *Christus fit indumentum nostrum.*

[361] *Vivificator.*

[362] *tesseram.* This word has several synonyms: die, square tablet marked with watchword, countersign, token, or ticket. In our digital world, Luther may well have said, "Password."

but the robe of Christ itself. No! There's more! Christ Himself is our robe.[363] That is why baptism is something of great power and efficacy. Now, once we are clothed with Christ, with that robe of righteousness and salvation, that is when we should be clothed with Christ as the garment of example and imitation. But I've already dealt elsewhere more fully with this issue, which is why I'm only summarizing here.

VERSE 28. There is neither Jew nor Greek, there is neither slave nor free, there is neither male nor female; for you are all one in Christ Jesus.

Here, one could add many other names of people and functions ordained by God, such as these: there is neither magistrate nor subject, teacher nor listener, tutor nor pupil, lord nor servant, nor lady nor lady in waiting, for in Christ Jesus, all states of life, even those ordained by God, are nothing. In fact, man, woman, subject, free, Jew, Gentile, prince, or servant all are good creatures of God. But in Christ, with respect to salvation, all things are nothing, with all their wisdom, righteousness, religion, and power.

Thus with these words, "neither Jew," Paul powerfully considers the law as abolished, for here, things have that nature, that when someone has been declared a new person by baptism[364] and has been clothed with Christ, there is neither Jew nor Greek. Here, the apostle is not talking about the Jew regarding his nature and substance. He calls "Jew" anyone who is a disciple of Moses and subjects himself to the law, is circumcised, and, with all his strength, strives to worship[365] as ordained by the law. But he says that when one is clothed with Christ, there is no longer such a type of person as a Jew, nor circumcision, nor any ceremony ordained in the law, since Christ has abolished all the laws of Moses that ever existed. Thus the conscience that has believed in Christ should be so fully persuaded that the law has been abolished, with all its terrors and threats, that it should be totally unaware that there ever was a Moses or any law or any Jew at all because there is no way at all that Christ and Moses could ever agree. Moses came with the law, with many works and ceremonies. But Christ came without any law at all, nor did He require any work; instead, He came giving grace and righteousness and so on, "for the law was given through Moses, but grace and truth came through Jesus Christ" (John 1:17, NKJV).

Further, when he says, "nor Greek," he also rejects and condemns the wisdom and righteousness of the Gentiles. Among the Gentiles, there were many of great renown: Xenophon, Themistocles, Marcus Fabius, Atilius Regulus, Cicero, Pomponius Atticus, and many others who were gifted with outstanding virtues.

---

[363] *imo ipsum Christum indumentum nostrum ese.* More likely, Luther speaking twenty-first-century English might have used the colloquial phrase "But wait, there's more!"

[364] *ubi novus homo in baptismo fit.*

[365] *cultum.*

They governed their territories with great excellence and did many other works worthy of preserving for posterity. Even so, all these were as nothing before God with all their wisdom, power, their outstanding works, their excellent virtues, laws, religions, and ceremonies, for we should not think that the Gentiles condemned all honesty and religion. Yes, all nations scattered throughout the entire world throughout all the ages have had their laws, religions, and ceremonies without which it would not have been possible to govern humanity. Therefore, all righteousness regarding the governance of families, territories, or divine matters (as in the righteousness of the law), with all obedience, fulfillment, and holiness, no matter how perfect it might be, is worthless before God. What then is of value? The robe of Christ with which we are clothed at baptism.[366]

Then if the servant carries out his duties, obeys his master, serves in his vocation with all diligence and faithfulness; if those who enjoy freedom exercise authority and govern over territories or guide their families praising them; if a man fulfills his responsibility when he marries a woman, when he governs his family, obeys the magistrates, behaves decently toward all; if a woman lives virtuously, obeys her husband, watches over her home, educates her children in the fear of the Lord (these are certainly excellent gifts and holy works), even so, all these things are nothing when compared to that righteousness that stands before God. In summary, all laws, ceremonies, religions, righteousness, and works of the entire world (even beginning with the Jews, who were the first to claim the kingdom and priesthood designated by God with their holy laws, religions, ceremonies, and praises)—all these do not remove sin, free from death, or save you.

Therefore, oh Galatians, your false apostles subtly deceive you when they teach you that the law is necessary for salvation. With that argument, they rob you of the sublime glory of your new birth and adoption. They do nothing but call you once again to your old birth, which is that miserable slavery to the law, converting you from God's children living in freedom to slaves of the law, making exception of persons according to the law. There certainly are differences in the law and in the world and that is proper and good but not before God. "For all have sinned and fallen short of the glory of God." Therefore, Jews and all Gentiles of the world, you must keep quiet in the presence of God. God certainly has many commands, laws, levels, and grades in which to live, but these are worthless to merit grace and obtain eternal life—that is, because all who are justified are justified not because they have kept man's or God's law but by Christ alone, who has abolished all law. The Gospel has been prepared for Him to be the one who appeases the wrath of God by the pouring out of his own blood, as our Savior. Without faith in Him, the Jew will not be saved by the observance of the law, nor the monk due to his order, nor the Greek by his wisdom, nor the magistrate or the lord because they govern properly, nor the servants due to their obedience.

---

[366] *Quid tum? Indumentum Christi, quem in baptismo induimus.*

VERSE 28. For you are all one in Christ Jesus.

These are excellent words. In the world and according to the flesh, there are great differences and inequalities among people, which need to be carefully guarded. If the woman wanted to be a man, if the son the father, if the servant the owner, if the subject the magistrate, confusion would reign everywhere in all kinds of things. But on the contrary, in Christ there is no law, there are no differences between people. There is no Jew or Greek, but all are one, for there is one body, one spirit, one hope in the calling. There is only one Gospel, one faith, one baptism, one God and Father of us all, one Christ and Lord of all.[367] We all have the same Christ, you and me, and all the faithful such as Peter, Paul, and all the saints. *We also have one baptism for all infants.* Consequently, here the conscience owes nothing to the law but only has Christ before its eyes. Thus Paul always wishes to employ this phrase, "in Christ Jesus," for if they take Him away from our sight, we cannot see our salvation.

The fanatic hotheads of today have the same talk as the papal theologians, for they dream up the teaching that faith is a quality affixed to the heart, without Christ. This is a diabolic error, for Christ should be presented in such a way that you won't be able to see anything else but Him and only Him; you should only think that there is nothing else that could come close to you or nearer to your heart than what He is, for He is not idly sitting in heaven but is present with us, working and living in us; as Paul said before in Galatians 2:20, "I live, but it is no longer I who lives, but Christ who lives for me."[368] It is the same here: "You are clothed in Christ." Thus faith is an unwavering gaze that cannot fix its sight on anything else but Christ, the conqueror over sin and death, the giver of righteousness, salvation, and eternal life. This is the reason Paul names and presents Jesus Christ so frequently in his epistles, yes, in every verse. But he does it through the word, for Christ cannot be understood, except by trusting in the word.

This was vividly represented by the bronze serpent, which is a figure of Christ. Moses commanded the Jews who were bitten by the serpents in the desert to do nothing else but fix their sight on the bronze serpent and not allow it to waver. Those who did so were healed by that constant and unwavering gaze at the serpent. On the contrary, those who did not obey Moses' command died; they had fixed their sight on their own wounds and not on the serpent. So that if I wished to find some comfort when my conscience is troubled, or if I should come to death's doorstep, I should do nothing else but grasp onto Christ by faith, and say, "I believe in Jesus Christ the Son of God who died, was crucified, and died for me; in whose wounds, I see my sin—in His resurrection, victory over sin, death and the devil, as well as righteousness and eternal life. Apart from Him, I see nothing, I hear nothing." This is the genuine faith of Christ and in Christ[369] by which we are made members

---

[367] Luther paraphrases Ephesians 4:4–6 as he lectures.

[368] See previous note.

[369] *fides Christi et in Christum.*

of His body, flesh of His flesh, and bone of His bones. In Him, we live, we move, and have our being. *Thus the fanatics in vain wickedly speculate regarding faith. They imagine that Christ is in us spiritually or imagine He is in us, but He is really in heaven.* Christ and faith should be totally united. We should be in heaven and Christ should live and work in us. Now, He lives and works in us, not due to our imagination and speculative knowledge, but through a present and efficacious reality.[370]

VERSE 29. If you belong to Christ, then you are Abraham's seed, and heirs according to the promise [NIV].

In other words, if you believe and are baptized in Christ. If they believe, I say, that He is that Seed promised to Abraham who brought the blessing to the Gentiles, then they are children of Abraham, not by nature but through adoption. Scripture attributes to him children not only according to the flesh but also through adoption and by the promise, but those who are not will be sent out of the house. Paul, in just a few words, transfers all the glory of Lebanon (meaning the Jewish people) to the desert (meaning the Gentiles). A special comfort emerges from this text. The Gentiles are children of Abraham and consequently the people of God. However, they are children of Abraham, not because they have been conceived according to the flesh but according to the promise. The kingdom of heaven then, life and the eternal inheritance, belong to the Gentiles. Long before, Scripture had underscored it when it said, "For I have made you the father of a multitude of nations" (Genesis 17:5, WEB). And again, "In your seed will be blessed all the nations" (Genesis 22:18). Now, since the Gentiles have believed and by faith received the blessing promised to Abraham and realized in Christ, the Scriptures call us children and heirs of Abraham, not according to the flesh but according to the promise. Thus this promise "in your Seed" belongs as well to all the Gentiles; accordingly, Christ now belongs to us.

It is true that the promise was given only to the Jews and not us, the Gentiles: "He declares his word to Jacob . . . He has not dealt thus with any other nation" (Psalm 147:19, 20). Nonetheless, what was promised to us reaches us by faith alone and only by faith can we grasp onto God's promise. Although the promise was not made to us, even so, the promise was given regarding us and for us, for we are named in that promise: "In your seed all the nations shall be blessed." The promise clearly shows that Abraham would be the father not only of the Jewish nation but of many nations. He would inherit not just the Jewish nation but many nations. He would inherit not just one nation but the entire world (Romans 4:13). In this way, the glory of Christ's entire kingdom is directed toward us. Thus all laws are abolished in the Christian's heart and conscience, although they remain in the flesh. We've already spoken about this at length.

---

[370] *non speculative, sed realiter, praesentissime et efficacissime.*

Galatians 4

LECTURE 26: Saturday, October 10

VERSES 1-2. I mean that the heir, as long as he is a child, is no better than a slave, though he is the owner of all the estate; but he is under guardians and trustees until the date set by the father.

Look at how Paul feverishly sweats as he calls on the Galatians to turn back.[1] Consider the strong arguments he takes up in debating the subject. By way of example he takes hold of Abraham's experience, the testimony of Scriptures, and similar matters. It seems he is starting the whole argument all over again. Previously, it seemed that he had completed his argument regarding justification, concluding that people are justified before God by faith alone.[2] But now, since he offers this example from civil law regarding the small heir, it's because he wishes to confirm the subject. He is rather astute, for he seems to catch the Galatians by surprise with a certain holy cleverness, since the ignorant are persuaded more easily with examples and similar things than with profound and well thought out arguments. They prefer to gaze at the image of a well-painted picture than to read a well-written book. Thus Paul, after presenting the argument of a man's will, as well as the tutor, now takes up this example of the heir (which is known and familiar to every man). He only wishes to move and persuade them. There's a great deal of truth and value in being well equipped with such examples and metaphors, which not only Paul but also the prophets and Christ Himself frequently employed. [The Latin text here indicates some sort of pause, for it has this phrase: "From here to the end of the epistle, he is constantly appealing." It's as if Luther was responding to a student's question].[3]

You can see, he said, that civil law ordains that an heir, even though he is lord and master of all his father's goods, is no different from a servant. True, his hope in the inheritance is guaranteed, but before he becomes an adult, his tutors keep him subject to their authority, as a pupil to his tutor. They don't turn over to him the handling of his own goods. Instead, they force him into service watching to see how he handles his things as if he were a servant. Therefore, as long as this subjection continues, if he is under tutors and disciplinarians, he is no different from a servant.

---

[1] *ardeat et aestuet ad revocandos.*
[2] *concludebat homines sola fide justificari coram Deo.*
[3] Loose sentences such as these throughout the text, although rare, are further evidence of the transcript nature of the Latin text.

But this subjection and work of a servant is of great benefit to him. Otherwise, due to his own foolishness, he would soon squander all his goods. This slavery does not last forever but is for a certain limited time as designated by the father.

VERSE 3. So with us; when we were children, we were slaves to the elemental spirits of the universe.

In the same way, when we were little children, we were heirs. We had the promised inheritance that would be fulfilled for us through Abraham's seed. The promise is Christ, in whom all the nations of the earth would be blessed. But since the fullness of time had not yet come, Moses was sent as our tutor, governor, and teacher. He had us subject to slavery, bound hand and foot, so that we could not manage or possess our inheritance. However, just as the hope of freedom is nurtured and kept alive in the heir, so Moses nurtured us with the hope of the promise that would be revealed at the designated time—that is, when Christ would come and through His coming would put an end to the time of the law and install the time of grace.

Thus the time of the law came to its conclusion in two ways. First, as I've said, Christ came in the flesh at the appointed time by the Father. "But when the fullness of the time came, God sent out his Son, born to a woman, born under the law, that He might redeem those who were under the law, that we might receive the adoption of children." "He entered with His blood, thus securing an eternal redemption." Also, the same Christ who once came at the appointed time also comes in spirit to us every day and every hour. Indeed, only once and with His own blood, He redeemed and sanctified all. However, because we are not yet altogether perfectly pure (since the remnants of sin cling to our flesh and struggle against the spirit), He comes spiritually to us every day, fulfilling more and more the times appointed by the Father and abolishing and taking away the law.[4]

That's how He also came to the Old Testament patriarchs, before He appeared in the flesh. They had Christ in spirit. They believed in Christ who was to be revealed, just as we believed in Christ who has already been revealed. They were saved by Him, just as we are, according to what has been written: "Jesus Christ is one, yesterday, today, and will forever be the same"[5] (Hebrews 13:8). Yesterday refers to the seasons before the appointed time for Him to come in the flesh. Today, when He has already been revealed at the appointed time; now and forever, He is one and the same Christ, for it is only through Him alone by whom all the faithful have been, are, and will be freed from the law, justified, and saved.

"In the same way," he said, "we as well were slaves to the elemental spirits of the universe." That is, the law had dominion over us and kept us in strict slavery, as slaves and captives. First, it bridled all who were driven by the flesh. Also, those

---

[4] *abrogate et tollit legem.*

[5] Luther's paraphrase of Hebrews 13:8 as he taught extemporaneously.

of a rebellious nature were kept from going headlong into all kinds of evil. The law threatens delinquents with punishment, and if they have nothing to fear, there's no end to the mischief they would do. The law reigns and governs over everyone it can restrain in that manner. Further, it accused, frightened, killed, and condemned us spiritually before God. This was the central power the law held over us. Thus just as an heir is subject to his tutors, as he is beaten and forced to diligently follow their mandates, so also the conscience of men before the coming of Christ was oppressed with demanding servitude to the law—that is, the law accuses, harasses, and condemns. But this dominion, or better said, this tyranny of the law does not last forever but should continue only until the time of grace. Thus the function of the law is to reprove and make sin abound; it is not to bring righteousness. It is to kill and not to give life, for "the law is a schoolmaster to bring us to Christ."

Tutors deal with the heir during his childhood, governing him harshly and strictly, ordering him around as if he were a servant. Consequently, he will have no other choice but to be under their rule. In like manner, the law accuses, humbles, and takes us captive so that we will be servants of sin, death, and God's wrath, all of which is the most miserable captivity. The power of the tutors subjecting and enslaving the small heir is not forever but comes to an end at the time appointed by the father. When that time comes, the heir no longer needs the government of the tutors. Neither does he remain subject to them, but he enjoys his inheritance in freedom. In the same way, the law has dominion over us; we see ourselves servants and slaves of its dominion. However, it's not forever, for this phrase follows: "But when the fullness of time had come, God sent his Son." Christ, the one promised, came and redeemed us from our oppression under the tyranny of the law.

On the other hand, the coming of Christ profits neither the careless hypocrites, nor the wicked who condemn God, nor the desperate who think they have no other option but to suffer the terrors of the law. His coming only benefits those who for a time have been tormented and afraid—that is, for those who do not lose hope notwithstanding those great internal torments stirred up by the law, but who with unwavering confidence come to Christ, to the throne of grace, who has redeemed them from the curse of the law, having made Himself a curse for them. There they will find mercy and grace.

Thus there is a certain passion in this phrase: "We were slaves." It's as if he had said, "Our conscience was subject to the law, which held us bound as slaves and captives, as a tyrant dominates his prisoners. We felt its lashes and with great power the law exerted its tyranny over us—that is, it made us feel great terror and oppression of spirit. It made us tremble feeling we were at the border of desperation, threatening us with eternal death and condemnation." This spiritual slavery[6] is very painful and bitter, but (as I've said) it doesn't last forever but is only for the season of our childhood—that is, while Christ is absent. While He is absent, we

---

6 *theologica servitus.*

are servants, locked up under the law, stripped of grace, faith, and all the gifts of the Holy Spirit. But when Christ arrives, jail and slavery suddenly cease.

VERSE 3. Under the elemental principles of the world.

Some have thought that Paul is talking here about those elemental forces: earth, wind, water, and fire. But Paul has a unique way of speaking. Here, he is talking about nothing less than God's law, which he calls the elements or rudiments of the world so that it seems his words are quite heretical. In the same way, in other texts, he tends to diminish and lower the authority of the law in a big way when he says that the letter kills, that it is the ministry of death and condemnation, and that the power of sin is the law. These odious names clearly show the power and use of the law, but he chooses them to warn us. When we find ourselves in the terror of sin, wrath, and God's judgment, let us not trust in our own righteousness or in the righteousness of the law, seeing that the law in its main use cannot do anything else but accuse our conscience. It makes sin abound and threatens with death and eternal damnation. That is the reason this uncomplimentary treatment of the law refers to the negative conflict it causes within the conscience. It applies neither to the civil law nor to those whose heart is already at peace.

Therefore, he calls the law "the elemental principles of the world"—that is, the external laws and traditions written in a certain book, for although the law of the land bridles evil people and forces them to do what's good, even so, this kind of observance neither delivers them from sin, nor justifies, nor prepares the way to heaven but leaves them in the world. I don't obtain righteousness and eternal life because I don't kill, I don't commit adultery, I don't steal, and other virtues. These external qualities and honest ways of living are not the kingdom of Christ nor heavenly righteousness; instead, they are the righteousness of the flesh and of the world. The Gentiles also had this righteousness and not just the merit hoarders, as were the Pharisees of Christ's time and the friars and monks in ours. Some do observe this righteousness to avoid the punishment of the law. Others observe it to be praised by men and be considered righteous, consistent, and patient. Thus they should call this righteousness "hypocrisy painted in water colors" instead of righteousness.

Further, when the law fulfills its main function and puts it to use, it can do no other but to accuse, terrorize, condemn, and kill. But where such terror exists and those sentiments of sin, death, wrath and God's judgment prevail, there is no righteousness or anything heavenly or godly because all these things are mere things of this world. This world (since it's the kingdom of the devil) is nothing but a puddle of sin, death, hell, and all the evil felt by the fearful, stressed out, and heavy hearted, but the self-confident and self-appointed judges who condemn don't feel them. Therefore, the law at its best and more perfect use does nothing more than point out sin and make it abound. The law beats us up with the fear of death but all these things belong to the world. Thus Paul very much to the point calls the law "the elements or rudimentary principles of the world."

Although Paul calls the entire law "the rudiments of the world" (for so it seems according to what I've already said), he reserves a disdain for the ceremonial laws. These don't profit much; even so (he says), they only consist in external matters such as meats, drinks, dress, places, times, the temple, the feasts, ritual washings, sacrifices, etc. These belong only to this world; they are matters ordained by God only for use in this present life but not to justify or save before God. Thus through this phrase, "the rudimentary principles of the world," he rejects and condemns the righteousness of the law, which consists in these external ceremonies, which were ordained through God's command to be observed for a while, and gives it an insignificant name calling it "the rudimentary principles of the world." In the same way, the laws of the emperor are rudiments of this world, for it deals with matters of this world; that is, things dealing with this life such as goods, possessions, inheritances, murders, adulteries, robberies, and so on, things that the second table of the Ten Commandments also mentions. With respect to the canons and papal decrees, which prohibit marriage and meats, Paul in another place calls these "doctrines of devils." These are also rudiments of the world for they are the ones that most wickedly submit people's consciences to the observance of external matters, contrary to the word of God and faith.

Therefore, the law of Moses deals with nothing else than worldly matters—that is, it only shows there is evil in the world, whether it's dealing with civilian society or spiritual matters. However, if used in its true sense, it compels the conscience through terrifying fears to seek and thirst after God's promise and look to Christ. But for that to happen, you need the Holy Spirit's help who can say to your heart, "It is not God's will that after the law has performed its work in you, you should continue paralyzed and dead. Instead, when through the law you come to know your misery and condemnation, you should not lose hope but put your faith in Christ, who is 'the end of the law, that everyone who has faith may be justified.'" At this moment, there is no longer any earthly thing, but everything of this world and every law comes to its end. However, everything heavenly begins to appear, for as long as we are under the rudiments of the world, that is under the law, which is not only incapable of granting righteousness and peace to the conscience (but instead reveals and increases sin, stirs up wrath), we are entirely subject to the law as its servants even if we have the promise of the blessing to come. Indeed, the law said, "You shall love the Lord your God," but the law cannot give me such love, nor can it take my hand to grasp on to Christ.

I say this not for the law to be despised, for neither is that Paul's intent, but that it should be held in great esteem. However, since Paul is dealing here with the subject of justification, it was necessary to talk about the law as something despicable and hateful, for justification is another subject that greatly differs from the law. When we are dealing with this subject, one must keep on talking about the law as insignificant and detestable. Thus when the conscience finds itself in conflict, then it should fix its gaze on nothing else but Christ and Christ alone. Then the law must be removed entirely from sight, and we must embrace nothing else but the promise regarding Christ. But this is easier said than done. However, in the moment of temptation, when the conscience struggles in God's presence,[7] it is the most difficult thing to achieve—that is, when the conscience accuses you, harasses you, perturbs you, reveals your sin, threatens with God's wrath and eternal death, with all the strength of mind and body, respond as if there had never been any law or any sin but Christ alone, sheer grace, and redemption.[8] You could also say, "Oh law, I am not going to pay any attention to you, for you stammer and are slow of speech. Further, the fullness of time has come and thus I am free; I will no longer, not even for one more second, put up with your tyranny!" Here, you can see how difficult it is to separate the law from grace.[9] Once again, how divine and heavenly it is to hope against all hope and how true is Paul's declaration that "we are justified by faith alone."[10]

So that when it comes to the topic of justification, learn to talk about the law with the greatest disdain possible, following the example of the apostle who calls the law "the rudiments of the world," pernicious traditions, the power of sin, the ministry of death, etc. If you allow the law to dominate and reign over your conscience when you find yourself in God's presence fighting against sin and death, then the law is nothing more than a bottomless pit of every evil, heresy, and blasphemy, for it cannot do anything more than stir up sin, accuse and trample the conscience, threaten with death, and leave you exposed to a wrathful God who rejects and condemns sinners. Therefore, here, if you are to be wise, banish far from you that stammering and stuttering Moses together with his law and don't let yourself be moved at all by his terrors and threats. Here, you must hold him as a suspect, as a heretic, as excommunicated and condemned, worse than the Pope and the devil himself, and thus you must absolutely not give him an audience.

However, outside of the topic of justification, together with Paul we should think reverently about the law, highly recommend it, call it holy, just, good, spiritual, and divine. When it's outside the realm of the conscience, we should deify it but when it impinges upon conscience, it's the very devil himself. In the tiniest temptation, it is incapable of lifting and comforting the conscience. On the contrary, it smothers, oppresses with despair, and snatches from the conscience the assurance of righteousness, life, and the greatness of God's favor. That is why Paul soon after calls it "the weak and miserable elemental principles." Thus under no circumstance should we allow the law to govern in our conscience, especially seeing that Christ paid such a great price to free our conscience from the tyranny of the law, "for He was made for us a curse in order to deliver us from the curse of the law." Thus let the godly learn that

---

[7] *cum Deo agit.*
[8] *solus Christus, mera gratia et redemtio.*
[9] *legem a gratia discernere.*
[10] *sola fide justificari.*

the law and Christ are incompatible, for one cannot tolerate the presence of the other. When Christ is present, there is no circumstance at all in which the law can reign, but it should abandon the conscience, get out of bed (for it is so narrow that there is no room for the two, as Isaiah 28:20 says), and leave its place to Christ alone.[11] Let Him alone reign in righteousness, peace, joy, and life; let the conscience sleep and rest joyfully in Christ without any feeling regarding the law, sin, and death.

Paul here uses the figurative phrase "elements of the world." By using this phrase, he vigorously minimizes the glory and authority of the law to catch our attention. Every careful reader of Paul will realize that he calls the law "the ministry of death," "the letter that kills," etc. Yet immediately, the question arises: "Why does he refer to the law with such odious names, that to one's reason it would seem to border on blasphemy, although it is a doctrine that has been revealed from heaven?" But Paul answers that the law is both just and good, and that it is also the ministry of sin and death, but from different aspects. Before Christ's coming, it is holy. After Christ has come, it is death. Therefore, once Christ has come there's no reason for us to come to an understanding with the law, unless it is in this one aspect: that it has power and dominion over the flesh, to bridle it, to keep it under subjection. Here, there is a conflict between the law and the flesh (the yoke of the law is hard and grievous) for as long as we live.

Of all the apostles, only Paul calls the law "the rudiments of the world," "the weak and poor elements," "the power of sin," "the letter that kills," and such. The other apostles never talked about the law using those words. Then let everyone who wishes to be a scholar in Christian theology,[12] observe diligently this manner of speech used by the apostle. Christ calls him a "chosen vessel" and thus gave him an exquisite vocabulary—unique among the apostles—so that he, as a chosen vessel, could faithfully establish the foundations of the article of justification and be able to clearly expound it.

VERSE 4. But when the fullness of time had come, God sent his Son, born of a woman, born under the law, in order to redeem those who were under the law.[13]

In other words, once the time of the law came to its end and Christ was manifested; it is the time when He delivered us from the law and the promise was proclaimed among all the nations.

Observe carefully how Paul defines Christ. He said that Christ is the Son of God and of a woman, born under the law for us sinners to redeem us who were under the law. With these words, he encompasses the person of Christ as well as His function. His person consists of His divine and human nature. He clearly demonstrates it

---

[11] *soli Christo.*

[12] *studiosus Christianae Theologiae.*

[13] Here, Luther includes the first part of v. 5 within the text of v. 4.

when he said, "God sent His Son, born of a woman." Therefore, Christ is God of very God, and man of very man. His office is highlighted with these words: "Born under the law to redeem those who were under the law" etc. Here, it would seem that Paul, as if in reproach, calls the Virgin Mary only "a woman." Thus Christ is very God and very man. His true mission is described by these words: "born under the law, in order to redeem those who were under the law."

It appears that Paul took some heat from those who were offended that he had not called her a virgin, or the mother of God. Instead, he just called her "a woman." Some of the ancient fathers would have also wanted him to call her a virgin. They would have preferred him to call her a virgin instead of a woman. But in this epistle, Paul's focus is a matter of greater importance: The Gospel, faith, and Christian righteousness. The emphasis includes the person of Christ Himself, His function, that which He took upon Himself on our behalf, and the benefits that He has granted to us miserable sinners. Thus due to the excellence of such an exalted and wonderful matter he did not consider Mary's virginity. For him, it was sufficient to expound on and preach on the inestimable mercy of God than to say that God's Son was born from the dignity of that gender. Thus he makes no mention of the dignity of the gender but only of the gender. And as far as his mention of the gender, what he wants to say is that Christ became man of very man, born of a woman. As if he said, He was not born of a man and a woman but only of a woman. Thus he names only "a woman," saying, "Born of a woman," as if he had said, "Made from a virgin." John the Evangelist, when expounding about the Word, says that "in the beginning, He became flesh," without saying a word about His mother.

Further, this text also testifies of Christ, for when the fullness of time for the law has come, Christ causes it to be abolished. He frees those who were oppressed by the law but makes no mention at all of a new law that would come thereafter, or of some other law on the same footing as Moses' ancient law. That is why the monks and the papal scholars don't err any less and blaspheme Christ, for they imagine that He has given a new law in agreement with the law of Moses. The Muslims do the same when they boast about their Mohammed, as a new legislator after Christ and better than Christ. So according to them, Christ did not come to abolish the law but to create a new one. But Christ (as Paul says here) was sent from the Father to the world to redeem all who were enslaved under the law. These words paint a true and precise word picture of Christ for they don't attribute to Him the function of creating a new law but that of redeeming those who were under the law. Christ Himself said, "I judge no one." And in another text, He said, "I have not come to judge the world, but to save the world" (John 8:15; 12:47). It's as if He said, "I didn't come to bring any new law, nor to judge people with respect to the law, as Moses and other lawgivers. I have a greater and better function. The law killed them, but I in turn judge, condemn, and kill the law, as to deliver them from its tyranny."

We who are older have suckled on this pernicious doctrine of the Papists. We conceived an opinion quite contrary to what Paul teaches here, for although with our mouth we confessed that Christ redeemed us from the tyranny of the law, even so, it is true that in our hearts, we thought of Him as a legislator, a tyrant, and a judge, more fearful than Moses himself. And even today, notwithstanding the great light of the truth, we cannot altogether reject it due to the things we were forced to learn in our youth; it has remained rooted to our hearts. However, you are still young and have not been infected with this pernicious opinion. You can learn who Christ is with greater purity. With less difficulty than us older folk, you can uproot from your minds these blasphemous imaginations that we have conceived about Him, even though you have not escaped the deceptions of the devil altogether, for although you have not yet been infected with this accursed opinion that Christ is a lawgiver, you still have the root that nourishes it—that is, you still have the flesh, reason, and a corrupt nature that cannot pass any other judgment except that Christ is a lawgiver. Thus you should make every effort, utilize everything within your power to learn who Christ is and to know Him, grasping Him as Paul presents Him in this text. But if in addition to this natural corruption, you would add corrupt and evil teachers (who overwhelm the world), this natural corruption will grow, and the evil will be redoubled—that is, the wicked teaching will increase and confirm the pernicious error of blinded reason, which naturally judges that Christ is a lawgiver. Reason will then powerfully impress that error upon our minds and cannot be banished except with great struggle and difficulty.

Thus it is to our great benefit that we always keep in mind this sweet and comforting declaration and others like it that present a living and true Christ. May we, throughout our entire life, when facing every danger, when confessing our faith before tyrants, and at the hour of our death boldly and confidently declare, "Oh law, you have absolutely no power over me, thus in vain, you accuse and condemn me, for I believe in Jesus Christ the Son of God who the Father sent to the world to redeem unworthy sinners oppressed by the tyranny of the law. He gave His life and spilled His blood for me. Thus when I feel your terrors and threats, oh law, I plunge my conscience in the wounds, the blood, the death, the resurrection and victory of my Savior, Christ. Apart from Him, I will see nothing, I will hear nothing."

This faith is our victory by which we overcome throughout great conflicts, the terrors of the law, sin, death, and every evil. Here is where true godly believers daily exercise themselves in the face of great temptations, in true sweat and blood. Frequently, they are harassed with the thought that Christ accuses and argues against them, that He will require them to give an account for their past life, and that He will condemn them; they cannot be assured that He has been sent by His Father to redeem us from the tyranny and the oppression of the law. And where does this come from? The saints have not yet cast aside the flesh that rebels against the spirit. Consequently, we experience the terrors of the law and the fear of death. These and other sad and depressing sights visit us frequently and become an obstacle to our faith. As a result, our faith cannot grasp onto Christ's benefit (who has redeemed us from slavery to the law) with all possible confidence.

But for what reason and in what way has Christ redeemed us? This is how He achieved our redemption: He was "born under the law." When Christ came, He found us all captive, living under disciplinarians and tutors—that is, locked up and trapped in prison under the law. Then what did He do? Even though He was the Lord of the law and thus the law had neither authority nor power over Him (for He is the Son of God), of His own free will, He submits to the law. Then comes the law and exerts over Him all the tyranny that it exerted over us. It is the same with which it accuses and condemns us. And in doing it, it is altogether within its right, for we are all sinners, and by nature we are children of wrath. But on the contrary, "Christ committed no sin; neither was there found deceit in His mouth." Therefore, He was not subject to the law. But the law was no less cruel against this righteous, blessed, and innocent lamb than it was against us accursed and condemned sinners. Instead, it was even more demanding! It accused Him of sedition and blasphemy! It made Him guilty before God for all the sins of the world. The law terrorized and oppressed Him with so much despair and anxiety of spirit that His sweat turned into blood, and for a brief span, the law condemned Him to death and death on the cross.

This was truly an astounding combat. The law being but a creature lunges against its Creator with all its power. It exerted all the tyranny it had imposed over us children of wrath and imposed it on the Son of God against every right and principle of equity. Thus since the law had so horribly and with such great damnation sinned against its God, it has consequently been brought before the judgment seat to answer for itself. There, Christ said, "Oh law, powerful queen and cruel sovereign over all humanity, what have I done for you to so accuse, intimidate, and condemn me seeing that I am innocent?" At this point, the law that before had condemned and annihilated every human being is left defenseless and exposed, for it has been condemned and defeated, for it has lost all its rights, not only over Christ (whom it cruelly affronted and killed), but also over all those who have believed in Him, for Christ has said to them, "Come to me all those who have been worked over by the yoke of the law."[14] I could have defeated the law with just my absolute power, without my own wisdom for I am the Lord of the law, and thus it has no power over me. But I have made myself subject to the law on behalf of those who were under the law, taking their flesh on me—that is, out of my own overabundant love, I humbled myself and surrendered to the same prison, tyranny, and slavery of the law under which you served as captives and slaves. I permitted the law to have dominion over me. Although I was its master, I allowed it to frighten me, submit me, and make me captive to sin, death, and the wrath of God, as it should have never happened. Therefore, I have twice defeated the law, by right and authority. First, as Son of God and Lord of the law and second, in your own person, for it is as if you yourselves would have defeated the law, for my victory is your victory.

---

[14] Luther's paraphrase of the text.

Everywhere Paul speaks like this of this amazing combat between Christ and the law. To make the topic more delightful and real, he tends to represent the law by means of a rhetorical device called *prosopopoeia*,[15] as if it were a certain powerful character that had condemned and killed Christ. However, once Christ conquered death, He also defeated and condemned this character "thereby bringing the hostility to an end" (Ephesians 2:16). Further, "You have ascended on high, You have led captivity captive" (Psalm 68:18, NKJV). He also employs the same figure in his epistles to the Romans, Corinthians, and Colossians: "He condemned sin in the flesh." Thus through this victory Christ banished the law from our conscience so that now it can no longer disturb us in God's sight, harass us with hopelessness, or condemn us. Indeed, it never ceases to bring our sin out in the open, to accuse and harass us. But the conscience taking hold of the apostle's words, "Christ has redeemed us from the law," is reassured by the hand of faith and receives great comfort. Further, it triumphs over the law with certain holy pride, saying, "I don't care about your terrors and threats, for you have crucified the Son of God, and in the most unjust manner. Therefore, the sin you have committed against Him cannot be forgiven.[16] You have lost your right and sovereignty and more than ever you have not only been defeated, condemned, and put to death not only by Christ but also by me for I have believed in Him, who has also given me His victory." For us then, the law has died forever, only that we abide in Christ.[17] Thus thanks be to God who has given us the victory through our Lord Jesus Christ.

These things also confirm the doctrine that we are justified by faith alone.[18] When this combat was fought between Christ and the law, not one of our works or merits intervened. It was Christ alone[19] who clothed Himself in our own person. He then made Himself subject to the law and in perfect innocence suffered all its tyranny. Thus the law, as a criminal commits sacrilege against God's Son and thus loses all its rights. It deserves such condemnation that wherever Christ is found, or His name is uttered even once, it has no recourse but to hide and flee, just as the devil flees from the cross (as the Papists imagine). Thus if we believe, we are freed from the law by means of Christ, who triumphed alone over it. Therefore this glorious victory, purchased for us by Christ, is not obtained by means of any of our works but by faith alone grasping unto Him.[20] Thus only faith justifies.[21]

---

[15] Personification.
[16] *est irremissibile.*
[17] *modo in Christo permaneamus.*
[18] *quod sola fide justificemur.*
[19] *sed solus Christus.*
[20] *sed sola fide apprehenditur.*
[21] *Ergo sola fides justificat.*

These words then, Christ was "born under the law," not only are brief and moving but also express a certain fervor, thus they merit to be considered diligently and attentively. This phrase declares that the Son of God, having been born under the law, not only complied with a couple of works of the law, not only was circumcised and presented at the temple or went up to Jerusalem at the appointed times, or not only lived under the law of the land but, what's more, suffered the entire tyranny of the law, for the law, summoning all its strength and power, lunged against Christ and besieged Him so ferociously that He felt such anguish and terror as will never be experienced by another human being on the face of the earth. This is more than evidenced by the blood in His sweat, the comfort given to Him by the angel, that powerful prayer He uttered in the garden, and, briefly, that pitiful cry from the cross: "My God, why have you abandoned me?" (Matthew 27:46). He suffered all this to redeem those who were under the law—that is, in profound distress, anguish, and terror, at the point of desperation, He suffered for all who are oppressed by their heavy burden of sins, as most certainly all are oppressed because regarding the flesh we sin daily against all God's commandments. But Paul grants us great comfort when he says, "God sent His Son."

Thus it was that Christ, a divine and human being, destined by the eternal God and within time born of a virgin,[22] did not come to create a new law. Instead, He came to feel and defeat the greatest fears caused by the law and in Himself remove it altogether.[23] He was not made a doctor of the law but an obedient disciple of the law[24] so that through His obedience He could redeem those who were under the law.[25] This goes contrary to the doctrine of the Papists for they have made a Legislator out of Christ, much more strict and severe than Moses himself. Here, Paul teaches entirely the contrary—that is, that God humbled His Son under the law; God compelled Him to bear the judgment and curse meted out by the law, sin, death, and the like, for Moses—the minister of the law, sin, wrath, and death—arrested, bound, condemned, and killed Christ, and Christ suffered it all.[26] Therefore, as he stands before the law, Christ is passively on the receiving end. He is not on the active side enforcing it as a legislator, neither is he a judge according to the law. Rather, He is subject to the law, under its condemnation, and thus delivers us from its curse.

Christ in the Gospel delivers teachings and instructs on the law or rather interprets it. However, these do not belong to the doctrine of justification but to the doctrine of good works. Further, it is not Christ's function to teach the law (it is not the main reason He came to the world), but rather, it is an incidental or resulting function, such as healing the sick or raising the dead. These indeed are excellent and divine

---

[22] *natus ex Deo ab aeterno, ex Virgine in tempore.*

[23] Luther's footnote: *Christu non venit, ut legem conderet, sed ut eam abrogaret,* "Christ did not come to establish a new law, but to abolish it."

[24] *Non factus est doctor legis, sed discipulus obediens legi.*

[25] *sua obedientia redimeret eos, qui sub lege erant.*

[26] *Moses . . . cepit, ligavit, condemnavit et occidit Christum, hoc ipse pertulit.*

works, but they are neither unique to Christ nor His major works, for the prophets also taught the law and worked miracles. But Christ is God and man. As He struggled against the law, He suffered the law's greatest cruelty and tyranny. But He conquered it within Himself by remaining firm before the law, and that is why He was raised from the dead. The law was our bitterest enemy, but He condemned it and took it away. Now it is impossible for the law to condemn or kill. Thus Christ's true and proper function is to wrestle against the law and against sin and death for the whole world. Through this struggle, which He sustained and dealt within Himself, He conquered and abolished the law. Thus the believers are delivered from the law and every evil. Therefore, to teach the law and work miracles are special benefits from Christ, but they are not the main motive for which He came to the world. Indeed, the prophets and particularly the apostles did greater miracles than Christ Himself (John 14:12).

Seeing then that Christ has conquered the law in His own person, it is necessary for Him to have a divine nature.[27] There is no one else, man or angel, who is over the law but God alone. But Christ is over the law, since He has defeated it. Consequently, He is the Son of God and has a divine nature. If you grasp on to Christ in the way Paul has painted Him here, you will neither err nor fall into confusion. Further, you will easily be able to judge with regards to all manners of living, of all religions and ceremonies throughout the entire world. However, if this true representation of Christ is disfigured or obscured in some manner, then what follows is confusion in all things, for the natural man cannot judge with regards to God's law. This is the point where the shrewdness of the philosophers, the canonical scholars, and all men fail altogether, for the law has power and dominion over every man. Thus the law judges man and not the other way around, as if man could judge the law. Only the Christian has a proper and true judgment regarding the law. And what is that? That the law does not justify. Then why was the law created if it does not justify? Righteousness before God, which is received by faith alone, is not the means to an end as to why Christians obey the law. They obey to keep peace in the world, in thanksgiving to God, and as a good example so that others may be invited to believe in the Gospel. The Pope has so confused and combined the ceremonial law, the moral law, and faith and mixed them all together so that at the end he has preferred the ceremonial law instead of the moral law and the moral law instead of faith.

LECTURE 27: Friday, October 16

VERSE 5. So that we might receive adoption as sons.

That is, we are children of God. Paul expounds and greatly expands this text of Genesis 22:18: "In your seed all the nations of the earth shall be blessed." A short

---

[27] *necessario sequitur eum esse natura Deum.*

while before he had called this blessing from Abraham's seed "righteousness, life, the promise of the Spirit, freedom from the law, the will," and the like. Here, he calls it "adoption and eternal life." The word blessing embraces all these things, for when the curse (sin, death, etc.) is abolished then its place is taken over by the blessing—that is, righteousness, life, and every good gift.

However, through what merit have we received this blessing, this adoption and inheritance of eternal life? Absolutely through none of our own, for what merit could be earned by those who are tied up under sin, subject to the curse of the law, and worthy only of eternal death? We have received this blessing freely, totally unworthy of it, yet not without any merit at all. Whose merit could this be? Not ours but the merit of Jesus Christ the Son of God, who was born under the law, not for Himself but for us (as Paul had said before that "He was made a curse for us") and redeemed us who were under the law. Therefore, we have received this adoption only through the redemption obtained for us by Jesus Christ the Son of God. He is our overabundant and eternal merit, without any consideration of our congruous or condign merits or whether they come before or after grace. And together with this free adoption, we have also received the Holy Spirit, who God has sent to our hearts, crying out, "Abba, Father," as follows.

VERSE 6. And because you are children, God sent out the Spirit of his Son into your hearts.

The Holy Spirit has been sent in two ways. In the early church, He was sent with a visible and expressible appearance. That is how he came over Christ in the Jordan, with the appearance of a dove, and with the appearance of fire over the apostles and other believers. This was the first sending of the Holy Spirit, and it was necessary to send it in this manner for it was necessary that it would be established through many miracles due to the unbelievers, as Paul testifies. "Tongues, then, are a sign," he said, "not for believers but for unbelievers" (1 Corinthians 14:22). But once the church was called together and confirmed by these miracles, it was no longer necessary for this visible outpouring of the Holy Spirit to continue.

Second, the Holy Spirit is sent out through the word to the hearts of the believers, as stated here: "God sent the Spirit of His Son." This sending is no longer any visible manifestation. Instead, when we hear the external word we receive a certain fervor and internal light by which we are moved and we come to exist as new creatures. In the same way, we also receive a new way to judge, a new feeling, and new emotions. This change and this new judgment is due not to the work of reason or the power of man, but it is the gift and the workings of the Holy Spirit that comes with the preaching of the word that purifies our hearts through faith and awakens in us a new spiritual motive. Thus there is a great difference between us and those who violently and astutely persecute the doctrine of the Gospel. But we, by God's grace, can judge through the word, the will of God toward us, every law and doctrine, our own life, and the lives of others.

On the contrary, the Papists and sectarians cannot give a solid judgment about anything, for they corrupt, persecute, and blaspheme the word. Well then, without the word, man cannot judge confidently about any matter whatsoever.

Although it may not appear before the world that we have the renewal of our minds and that we have the Holy Spirit, nonetheless, our judgment, our kind of speech, and our confession give more than ample evidence that we have the Holy Spirit with its gifts in us. Before, we could not judge properly with respect to anything. We didn't speak like we now do. We did not confess like we now do in the true knowledge of the light of the Gospel, that all our works were sin and were worthy of damnation and that Christ was our only merit, both before and after grace. Therefore, let's not allow any of this to cause us any grief, that the world (and we testify that its works are evil) judges us as the most pernicious and seditious heretics, destroyers of religion, and disturbers of the common peace, possessed by the devil, allegedly speaking in us and governing everything we do. Against this world's perverse and malicious judgment, let the testimony of our conscience suffice, by which we know with all assurance what is the gift of God, that we not only believe in Jesus Christ but also preach and confess Him before the world. Just as we believe with our heart, so we also confess Him with our mouth according to what the psalmist said, "I believed, therefore I spoke" (Psalm 116:10, NKJV).

Further, we exercise ourselves in the fear of God and avoid sin in every way possible. If we sin, we don't sin purposely but due to ignorance, and we are sorry that we did. Perhaps we slip up, for the devil harasses us day and night. We also have the remnants of sin that without reprieve stick to our flesh. Therefore, with respect to the flesh, we are sinners, yes, even after we have received the Holy Spirit. Further, there is no great difference between the Christian and an honest man who keeps the law of the land. The Christian's external works to all appearances are basic and simple. He fulfills his obligations as called by his vocation, he guides his family, tills the land, gives good advice, and comes to the aid of his neighbor. The carnal man does not sufficiently appreciate these works, but rather thinks that they are common to all men, for even the pagans do them, for the world does not understand the things pertaining to the Spirit of God and thus judges wickedly regarding the works of the faithful. But they hold in great esteem the monstrous superstitions of the hypocrites and their works displaying great will power. They count them as works of holiness and don't think twice about giving them their support. On the contrary, the works of the faithful to all appearances may even seem contemptible and worthless. Nonetheless, they are certainly good works, acceptable to God because they are done in faith, from a joyful heart, and with thankful obedience before God. These works, I say, are not only despised as good works but also rejected as the most wicked and abominable works. Consequently, the world does not in the least believe that we have the Holy Spirit. However, when a great trial arises, or the cross, or the moment of confessing our faith (which is the proper and main work of the faithful), when it is necessary to abandon wife, children, goods, and even life itself, or otherwise we would deny Christ, that is when the confession of our faith is made plain, confessing Christ and His word by the power of the Holy Spirit.

Thus we should not doubt if the Holy Spirit dwells in us but be fully confident that "we are temple of the Holy Spirit" as Paul said (1 Corinthians 3:16)—that is, anyone who within himself feels love toward God's word and willingly listens, speaks, writes, and thinks about Christ should know that this is not the work of his will or reason, but the gift of the Holy Spirit, for it is impossible to do these things without the Holy Spirit. On the other hand, where there is hate and God's word is despised, the devil reigns therein, for "the god of this world has blinded the minds of the unbelievers, to keep them from seeing the light of the gospel of the glory of Christ." This is what we generally see in people today. They don't have any love for the word but condemn it, as if it had nothing to do with them. But all who feel love or desire for the word should recognize with thanksgiving that this affection is poured out on them by the Holy Spirit, for we don't create this affection and desire within us, neither are there rules that teach how we should receive it. Instead, it is simply and entirely the work of the Almighty's right hand. Therefore, when with goodwill and joy we hear the preaching of the word regarding Christ the Son of God, who for us became a man and made Himself subject to the law to deliver us from the curse of the law, hell, death, and damnation, then let us be confident that through this preaching, God most assuredly sends the Holy Spirit to our hearts. Thus it is the duty of the faithful to know that they have the Holy Spirit.

I say this to refute that pernicious doctrine of the Papists and the monks who teach that no one may know with full assurance (notwithstanding how pious and without blemish someone might be in this life), whether he has God's favor or not. This common verdict was a special norm and article of faith in all the papacy. Through its use, they totally disfigured the doctrine of faith, tormented the consciences of people, plundered the churches of Christ, obscured and denied all the benefits of the Holy Spirit, abolished the worship of God, imposed idolatry, scorned God, and blasphemed against God in the hearts of men, *for they who doubt in God's will toward them, and have no assurance at all that they are under grace, cannot believe they have the remission of sins, that God looks out for them, and that they can be saved.*

Augustine said it well, and piously, that "everyone may certainly see his own faith, if indeed he has it." They deny this. They say, "God forbid that I would give myself the assurance that I am under grace, that I am holy, and that I have the Holy Spirit; even if I lived piously and did any number of good works." You are still young[28] and have not yet been infected with this pernicious opinion (on which the papacy's kingdom is based). Take a good look at it, and flee from it as if it were the most horrible plague. We who are old and were nurtured in this error, since our youth, and have suckled there, have it deeply rooted in our hearts. Thus it takes us just as much labor

---

[28]   The reader is reminded that these are live lectures and Luther is addressing young seminarians.

to uproot it and forget it as it does to learn and grasp onto the truth. But we should be fully assured and have no doubt at all that we are under grace on account of Christ, that God is pleased with us, and that we have the Holy Spirit. "Anyone who does not have the Spirit of Christ does not belong to him." *Further, anything that proceeds from doubt, whether it's thoughts, words, or deeds, is sin, for anything that is not of faith is sin.*

Thus if you are a minister of God's word, or a municipal judge, you should be entirely assured in your mind that God is pleased with your work. But you'll never be able to think like this unless you have the Holy Spirit. However, you may say, "I have no doubt that God is pleased with my work, since it is ordained by God, but I have doubts regarding my own person if God is pleased with me or not." Here, your recourse is God's word that teaches and assures us that not just the person's vocation but also the person himself is pleasing to God, for such person has been baptized, has believed in Christ, has been cleansed by His blood of his sin, and lives in the communion and fellowship of his church.[29] Further, he not only loves the pure doctrine of the word but is also overjoyed when he sees it advancing and believers growing in numbers. At the same time, this person will detest the Pope and all the sectarians with their wicked doctrine, according to this saying of the psalmist: "I hate vain thoughts, but Thy law do I love" (Psalm 119:113, KJ21).

Therefore, we should be fully assured that not just our labor but also our very own person[30] is pleasing to God. Yes, everything I say, do, or think in private[31] is pleasing to God not because of us but because of Christ, who was born under the law on our behalf. On that basis, we are fully confident that Christ is pleasing to God and that He is holy. Thus since Christ is pleasing to God, and we are in Him, we are then also pleasing to God and are holy. And even though sin remains in our flesh and we fall and offend daily, grace abounds even more and is stronger than sin. God's mercy and truth does forever reign over us. That is why sin cannot terrify us and lead us to doubt that God's grace is in us, for Christ, that powerful giant, has not only abolished the law but also condemned sin and conquered death and every evil. As long as He is at God's right hand, interceding for us, we cannot doubt of God's grace and favor toward us.

Further, God has also sent the spirit of His Son to our hearts, as Paul says here. In the same way that Christ in His own spirit is confident that He pleases God, so it is also with us. Having the same spirit of Christ, we should be assured of His favor; more than enough has already been given that we may have full confidence. I have said this with respect to the internal witness by which the Christian's heart should feel plenty persuaded that he is under grace and has the Holy Spirit. But the external signs (as I've said before) are: joy when hearing of Christ, preaching and teaching Christ, giving thanksgiving to Him, praising, confessing Him, yes, even at the loss of

---

[29]   *in societate Ecclesiae.*

[30]   *sed etiam personam nostrum.*

[31]   *privatim.*

goods and life. Another sign is to fulfill our duty according to our vocations, in keeping with our capacity, fulfilling it with faith, joy, and the like. Neither is it to meddle in someone else's business, but in our own, to help our brother in need and comfort the brokenhearted. Through these signs, as well as through certain effects and consequences, we have full confidence and confirmation that we are under grace. The wicked also imagine they have the same signs, but they have nothing at all.

Here, we can clearly perceive that the Pope with his doctrine doesn't do anything else but to disturb and torment people's consciences and at the end plunge them into desperation. Thus as the psalmist says, "There is no truth in their mouth" (Psalm 5:9), and in another text the psalmist says, "Under his tongue are mischief and iniquity" (Psalm 10:7).

Here, we may see that the believers are still very weak in the faith, for if we were fully convinced that we are under grace, that our sins have been forgiven, that we have the spirit of Christ, that we are God's children, then without any doubt, we would be joyful and thankful to God for this infinitely valuable gift. But because we feel opposing emotions, fear, doubt, anguish, and depression and others like them, we cannot give ourselves full assurance. Yes, even our conscience dictates that it is great presumption and pride to grant ourselves such great honor. Thus if we are to understand this matter correctly, as we should, we should put it into practice, for without experience and practice we will never learn it.

That is why everyone should practice it so that in his own conscience, he will be fully assured that he is under grace[32] and that his own person, as well as his works, is pleasing to God. And if he should have any lingering questions or doubts, then persevere in the struggle to gain greater strength and confidence in the faith. Then you will be able to say, "I know that I am accepted and that I have the Holy Spirit, not because I am worthy of it or because of my works or my merits but because of Christ, who for us[33] subjected Himself to the law and took away the sin of the entire world. I believe in Him. If I am a sinner and make mistakes, He is righteous and cannot err. Further, I am happy to hear, read, sing, and write about Him and wish for nothing else than for His Gospel to be known throughout the entire world and that many be converted to Him."

These things give clear witness that the Holy Spirit is for us. The human heart is able to do these things through neither human strength nor ritualistic exercises or painful labor. Instead, Christ alone obtains them. First, He justifies us through the knowledge of Himself in His holy Gospel. Then he creates a new heart in us, brings us new motivations, and grants us the confidence that we are assured that we please the Father because of Him. Further, He gives us a proper way to judge things; on this basis, we prove or attempt to do what we didn't know before or else we despised altogether. That is why now it is our duty to fight against this uncertainty,

---

[32] *quod certo statuat se esse in gratia.*

[33] *sed propter Christum, qui propter nos.*

to overcome it daily more and more, and reach a full persuasion and assurance of God's favor toward us. We must uproot from our hearts this accursed opinion that man should doubt of God's grace and favor, for this doubt has infected the entire world, *for if we are not sure that we are in grace and that because of Christ we please the Father, then we are in fact denying that Christ has redeemed us and denying His benefits altogether. You who are young may easily grasp the doctrine of the Gospel and keep clear from this pestilent opinion that has not yet infected you.*

VERSE 6. Crying, "Abba! Father!"

Paul could have said, "God sent the Spirit of His Son to our hearts invoking,[34] 'Abba, Father.'" But he didn't say it that way. Instead, he said, "Crying,[35] 'Abba, Father,'" so that he could show and describe to the tempted Christian, that he is still weak, and that he believes but with weakness. In Romans chapter 8, he calls these cries "unutterable groans." "Likewise the Spirit also helps in our weaknesses. For we do not know what we should pray for as we ought, but the Spirit Himself makes intercession for us with groanings which cannot be uttered" (Romans 8:26, NKJV).

It is extremely comforting when he says, "The Spirit of Christ has been sent to our hearts, crying 'Abba, Father'" and also that he "helps us in our weakness" and that the "Spirit himself intercedes for us through wordless groans" (NIV). Every believer who has this trust will not be defeated by any trial, no matter how powerful the affliction. But there are many things that hinder this faith in us. First, our heart is born in sin. Further, this evil is grafted in us by nature, that we doubt of God's goodwill toward us[36] that we cannot believe with full assurance that we please God. Above all this, the devil our adversary goes all around us roaring horribly, saying, "You are a sinner; thus God is angry with you and will destroy you forever." Against all these horrible and intolerant roars, we have nothing but to grasp and lean on but the word alone; it presents before us Christ the conqueror over sin and death and over all evil. However, the difficulty is in grasping firmly to the word in these temptations and terrors of the conscience. At those times, there is no feeling at all that can perceive Christ. We cannot see Him. Our heart does not feel His presence nor help in temptation. Instead, it seems as if He is furious with us and that He has abandoned us. Further, when we are under temptation and feel afflicted, we feel the power of sin, the weakness of the flesh, and doubt; we feel the fiery darts of the devil, the terror of death, and God's wrath and judgment. All these things cry out horribly against us so that we cannot see anything else but hopelessness and eternal death.

But even so, in the middle of these terrors of the law, the thundering of sin, the threats of death, and the roars of the devil, the Holy Spirit (says Paul) cries out in

---

[34]   *invocatem.*

[35]   *clamantem.*

[36]   *de divino favore.*

our hearts, "Abba, Father!" This cry overpowers the cries of the law, sin, death, the devil, and such. It penetrates heaven's thickest clouds and ascends to the ear of God.

With these words, Paul wants to say that there are still weaknesses in the believers. This is how he also talks in Romans 8, when he says, "The Spirit helps us in our weakness." Just as negative feelings and emotions harass us without end, when we feel God's displeasure more than His favor and goodwill toward us, so is the Holy Spirit sent to our hearts, which not only groans and intercedes for us but also cries out powerfully, "Abba, Father." The Spirit Himself pleads for us according to God's will, with tears and groans that are too deep to be heard. And how can this be?

When our conscience is in the middle of terrors and conflicts, we grasp onto Christ and believe that He is our Savior. But that is when the law and sin harass and torment us more than ever. Further, the devil besieges us with all his warfare and fiery darts, and is committed with all his power to take Christ, our comfort, away from us. Here, we must not succumb to despair. We are nothing but a bruised reed and dimly burning wick (Matthew 12:20). Nonetheless and meanwhile, the Holy Spirit comes to our aid in our weakness and intercedes for us with inexpressible groans and affirms to our spirit that we are children of God. That is how our mind overcomes those terrors: looking to its Savior and exalted Pontiff,[37] Jesus Christ. That is how the weakness of the flesh is defeated, how its comfort is conceived and says, "Abba, Father." Paul calls this a cry and a groan that fills heaven and earth. Yet that is still the cry and the groan of the Spirit's call. The Spirit stirs the same cry in our hearts when we are feeling overwhelmed with weakness and temptation.

The law, sin, and the devil cry out against us like never before. With great and fearful roars, they seem to overwhelm heaven and earth and muffle almost completely the moaning of our own hearts. Yet they will never be able to inflict on us any damage at all, for the more furiously they accost, accuse, and torment us with their clamors, the more we will sigh. As we sigh, we grasp onto Christ and cry out to Him with our mouth and heart. We will cling to Him believing that He was born under the law to deliver us from the curse of the law and destroy sin as well as death. When by faith we have taken hold of Christ, we cry out to Him "Abba, Father." This, our cry, by far overwhelms the roaring of the devil and all else.

However, our sighs are so drowned out by our fears and our weakness that we hardly perceive them as sighs, for our faith, which in temptation sighs for Christ, is very weak if we consider our own feelings, so we cannot hear its great cry. But we have the word, by which we grasp Him in the middle of our conflict, and the groan we breathe is so slight we can barely hear it. Indeed, it is a mighty cry, but we cannot hear it. This is true, for as Paul says, "He who searches the hearts of men knows what is the mind of the Spirit" (Romans 8:27). To this searcher of the hearts, this weak and pitiful cry (as it seems to us) is a great shout, an inexpressible groan. By comparison, the great and fearful roars of the law, sin, death, the devil, and hell are as nothing and

---

[37] Luther uses the Latin word commonly reserved for the Pope.

can no longer be heard. Paul has good reason to call this sighing of the heart arising from the faithful, a cry and groan of the spirit that cannot be expressed, but it fills all heaven so that the angels think it's impossible to hear anything else!

However, in us, there is a totally different feeling, for it seems to us that our pitiful cry does not even break through the clouds and there's no way God in heaven or His angels could ever hear it. We think the worst and especially during the time of temptation, when the devil roars fearfully against us, when heaven and earth tremble, and when we fear they will fall on us, that every creature threatens to destroy us, and that hell has opened and it's ready to devour us. This feeling is in our heart, these horrible voices come from the spectacle we see and hear. This is what Paul says in 2 Corinthians 12:9, that "the power of Christ is made perfect in our weakness." Now it's when Christ appears in all His power. That is when He truly reigns and triumphs in us, when we are so weak that a pitiful moan barely escapes from us. But Paul says that this sigh in God's ear is the most powerful cry that fills heaven and earth!

Christ also in Luke 18, in the parable of the unrighteous judge, calls this faint sigh of the heart, a cry, yes, such a clamor that cries out unceasingly day and night before God. He said, "And will not God bring about justice for his chosen ones, who cry out to him day and night? Will he keep putting them off? I tell you, he will see that they get justice and quickly." Today, we find ourselves in great persecution and opposition from the Pope, tyrants, and sectarians who fight against us from the right as well as the left. We have no recourse but to cry out with such groans. These have been our firearms and artillery, which for many years we have used to diffuse the strategies and projects of our adversaries, by which we have also begun to overthrow the kingdom of the Antichrist. These will also hasten the day of Christ's glorious coming, when He will put His enemies under foot. Amen.

In Exodus chapter 14, the Lord speaks to Moses at the Red Sea, saying, "Why do you cry out to me?" But Moses had not cried out. Instead, he trembled and had almost lost all hope for he was in a great predicament. It seems that unbelief reigned within him rather than faith, for when he saw the people of Israel surrounded and besieged by the Egyptian armies and the sea, there was no way out. At this point, Moses did not dare open his mouth. When was it then that he cried out? Thus we should not judge according to the feelings of our heart but according to God's word. It teaches us that the Holy Spirit is given to the afflicted and the fearful and those ready to despair so as to lift and comfort them so they will not be overcome by temptations and afflictions but may escape victorious but not without great fear and affliction.

The Papists in their illusions have thought that "the saints" had the Holy Spirit, so they never felt or had any temptation. Today the fanatics say practically the same: "They were only surmising about the Holy Spirit." But Paul says, "The power of Christ is made perfect in our weakness, and the Spirit helps us in our weakness. It intercedes for us with inexpressible groans." Not only that, but when we have the greatest need for help and comfort from the Holy Spirit, that is when He is most ready to help us, when we are in our greatest weakness and at the point of despair. If anyone suffers affliction with a persevering and joyful heart, then it is when the Holy Spirit has done His work in him. Certainly, the Spirit has fulfilled its proper function in those who have suffered great terror and affliction and have come near, as the psalmist says, to death's door. Moses says the same when he saw death in the waters, when he saw himself cornered. At this moment, he felt extreme anguish and desperation. No doubt he had felt in his heart that powerful outcry from the devil, saying, "This entire people will perish because they have no way out; and you are the only author of this great calamity. Aren't you the one who brought them out of Egypt?" However, above all, the people cried out against him, saying, "Was it because there were no graves in Egypt that you brought us to the desert to die? What have you done to us by bringing us out of Egypt? Didn't we say to you in Egypt, 'Leave us alone; let us serve the Egyptians'? It would have been better for us to serve the Egyptians than to die in the desert!" The Holy Spirit was with Moses not just in his imagination but in factual reality. The Spirit interceded for him with inexpressible groans so that he groaned to the Lord, saying, "Oh Lord, by your command, I have led this people so help us!" This moan or lament before God is called a great cry in Scriptures.

I have dealt extensively with this subject to clearly show the role of the Holy Spirit, and how the Spirit carries out its function. In temptation, we should not judge in any way according to our own feelings or emotions nor due to the cries of the law, sin, devil, and the like, for if we allow ourselves to be guided by our own feelings, and we listen to those outcries, we will think that we are out of reach from all help and aid from the Holy Spirit and totally cast out from God's presence. No, instead, let us remember what Paul said: "The Spirit helps us in our weakness" and other comforting texts. The Spirit also cries out, "Abba, Father"—that is, He expresses a faint and pitiful sigh from the heart (for so it seems to us) that nonetheless is a loud cry and an unutterable groan before God. Thus when you find yourselves in the middle of temptation and weakness, grasp onto Christ alone and groan before Him for He gives the Holy Spirit that cries out "Abba, Father." This pitiful sigh is a great cry in God's ear that fills heaven and earth in such a way that God hears nothing else and drowns out the outcries from all other voices.

Pay close attention to what Paul said. The Spirit intercedes for us when we are tempted, not with an abundance of words or long prayers but with just a sigh that cannot even be expressed in words. He does not cry out with a great shout, "Have mercy on me, oh God" (Psalm 51:1). Rather, it's only a weak and faint sigh that escapes, as in "Ah, Father!" This is just a tiny word, but nonetheless, it reaches out beyond all space. It is not the mouth that speaks. It is the feeling from the heart that sighs: "Although I may be oppressed by anguish and horrible fears from one extreme to the other and it seems to me that I've been abandoned and cast out from your presence, even so, I am your child, and you are my Father on account of Christ.[38] I am loved in the Beloved." That is why this little word, "Father," effectively

---

[38] *tu pater propter Christum.*

conceived in the heart surpasses all the eloquence of Demosthenes, Cicero, and the most eloquent orators that have ever existed on the face of the earth. This matter is not expressed with words but with sighs and such sighs that cannot be expressed with words or oratory, for there is no tongue at all that is able to express them.

LECTURE 28: Saturday, October 17

I have used many words to say that Christians should give themselves the firm assurance that they enjoy God's favor and that the Holy Spirit cries out from their hearts. I have said it this way so that we may learn to repudiate that fatally toxic opinion[39] that reigns throughout the kingdom of the Pope, for he has taught all believers to have insecurity and harbor doubts regarding God's favor and grace toward them. When this opinion works its way in, then Christ amounts to nothing, for whoever doubts of God's favor will also doubt of God's promises. Consequently, they will also doubt of God's will and of the benefits of Christ. These are that He was born, suffered, died, and was resurrected for us, and on it goes. But there can be no greater blasphemy against God than to deny His promise, which is to deny God Himself and deny Christ etc. Therefore, it is not just extreme insanity but a horrible wickedness when the monks so arduously seduce the young. They take young men and women over to their monasteries and their holy orders (as they call them) with the pretext that if they join them they gain a more assured entrance to salvation. However, once they accomplish their purpose, they order them to doubt of God's grace.

Further, the Pope has called people throughout the entire world to obey the Holy Roman Church, as if it were a state of holiness by which they with all certainty attain salvation. However, once it has them submissively obeying its laws, the church commands them to doubt in their salvation. There you have it. That's how the kingdom of the Antichrist works. First, the church boasts and inflates the holy law, promising eternal life to all those who observe it and in addition the ordinances and regulations of its order. But then, when these poor wretched people begin to afflict their bodies with long vigils, fasts, and such practices according to the traditions and commands of men, all they get in return is uncertainty. They ask themselves whether God was pleased with their obedience or not. That is how Satan, in the most horrible way, through the Pope, is responsible for the death and destruction of these souls. Thus the papacy is nothing more than a slaughterhouse of consciences and the very kingdom of the devil!

Well, to establish and confirm this pernicious and damnable error, they allege Solomon's proverb as its foundation: "The upright and the wise and their works are in the hand of God; and men may not be certain if it will be love or hate;

---

[39] *repudiare pestilentissimam opinionem.*

all is to no purpose before them" (Ecclesiastes 9:1, BBE). Some understand this to say that it's talking about the hate that is yet to come, others about hate in the here and now. But not one of them understands Solomon, for in this text, what they imagine is the last thing he wants to say. Further, all Scripture teaches us above all things that we should not doubt. Instead, it calls us to trust and believe without any doubt that God is merciful, kind, and patient, that He is no double-dealer or deceiver, and rather that He is faithful and true and keeps His promise. Indeed, He has already kept what He promised in giving to us His only Son to die for our sins so that whoever believes in Him should not perish but have eternal life! Here, we cannot doubt but believe that indeed God is pleased with us. We may believe with all certainty that He has reconciled us, that God's hate and wrath have been taken away, seeing that He allowed His Son to die for us unworthy sinners. Even though this topic is expounded and repeated throughout the entire Gospel, it means nothing to them. This proverb of Solomon, perversely understood, has prevailed more (especially among those who take vows and become the strictest hypocrites of all their orders) than all the promises and comforts of Scripture; yes, even more than the sayings of Christ Himself. They abused the Scriptures to their own destruction and were justly punished for despising the Scriptures and disregarding the Gospel.

It is worth our while to know these things: First, because the Papists boast of their holiness as if they had never committed any wrong. Thus they must be convinced of their own abominations with which they fill up the entire world such as their own books, which do nothing but accuse them, and these books are infinite. Second, we may be fully assured that we have the pure doctrine of the Gospel. The Pope cannot glory of this assurance in his kingdom, even if all his other doctrines were correct. This monstrous doctrine of doubt in God's grace and His favor surpasses all other monstrosities. It is obvious that the enemies of the Gospel of Christ teach falsehoods, since they command that people should live with doubt in their minds, yet they condemn and kill us as heretics because we dissent from them. Instead, we teach matters that leave no room for doubt. But they persecute us with diabolical fury and cruelty as if they were truly certain of their doctrine.

Thus we should thank God that today we have been freed from this monstrous doctrine of doubt. Now we can be sure that the Holy Spirit clamors and stirs within our hearts with unspeakable sighs. This is our anchor, our foundation: the Gospel does not command us to be looking at our service, our perfection, but to God who promises and in Christ the Mediator. Quite the contrary, the Pope orders us to look neither on the God who promises nor to Christ our exalted Bishop but to our works and merits. In consequence, all this produces nothing but doubt and despair. However, in the Gospel, we hear God say: "Look, I gave my Son over to sin and death. By His blood He redeemed you from your sins and eternal death." That being the case, I cannot doubt unless I were to deny God altogether. This is the reason for the certainty of our doctrine because it takes us out and away from ourselves. We are not to trust in our own strength, our own conscience, our own feelings, our own person, or our own works. Instead, we will trust in that which is outside of us[40]—that is, in God's promise and truth. These cannot deceive us. The Pope ignores this, thus he wickedly imagines that no one can know, no matter how righteous and good they may be, whether they are worthy of love or hate. However, if they were indeed righteous and good, they would know with all certainty that God loves them; otherwise, they would neither be just nor wise.

Further, Solomon's declaration says nothing regarding God's hatred or favor toward men. Instead, it's an ethical declaration condemning people's ingratitude, for such is the world's perversity and ingratitude that the more a person is worthy, the less that person is honored, and sometimes the one who should be one's best friend becomes one's worst enemy. But those who are less worthy seem to be valued the most. This happened to David, a holy man, and a good king, but he was banished from his own kingdom. The same occurred with the prophets, Christ, and the apostles, whose lives were cut short. In conclusion, the history of all the nations gives testimony that many people in their own land, even though they deserved the best, were banished by their own citizens. They ended up living in great indignity and some went through great shame and humiliation, finally perishing in the dungeon. In this text Solomon is not talking about the conscience and its relationship to God. He is not talking about God's favor or judgment. Neither is he talking about God's love or hatred. Instead, he is talking about how people judge each other and the emotional relationships among them. It's as if he had said, "There are many righteous and wise people that God uses to do a lot of good and bring about peace and quiet among them. But others, far from recognizing them for their efforts, repay them in the grossest and most discourteous way for their works, which merit nothing but praise." Thus although certain people may do things right and go beyond and above, they don't know if they will be the object of hatred or praise among their fellow citizens for their diligence or faithfulness.

That is how it has been with us today. We thought we would find favor among our German compatriots, for we preached to them the Gospel of peace, life, and eternal salvation. However, instead of finding favor, we have encountered bitter and cruel hate. It is true that at the beginning many were greatly delighted with our doctrine. They received it joyfully. We thought they had become our friends and brothers and that together with us they would have sown and preached this doctrine to others. But now we realize they are false brothers and have become our mortal enemies, who sow and scatter false doctrine everywhere. What we teach correctly and faithfully, they pervert and overthrow wickedly, sparking controversies that offend the churches. Therefore, all who fulfill their duty faithfully and piously, regardless of their vocation, and no matter how much good they do, get nothing in return; instead, they can look forward to people's rejection and hatred. Let them not be perturbed or distressed but say with Christ, "They hated

---

[40] *Quod est extra nos.*

me without cause" and "They have also surrounded me with words of hatred and fought against me without a cause. In return for my love, they are my adversaries, but I am in prayer" (Psalm 109:3, 4).

Therefore, the Pope with his diabolical doctrine with which he commands people to doubt of God's favor toward them has taken away from the church of God all His promises, buried all Christ's benefits, and abolished the eternal Gospel. Inevitably and consequently, there followed all kinds of errors for then people do not lean on God's promises but on their own works and merits. Thus when they cannot trust in God's goodwill toward them, the result is that they will doubt and at last will lose all hope. No one may understand what God's will is or what is pleasing to Him except by the word of God. This word assures us that God has banished all hatred and displeasure toward us when He gave His only Son for our sins. *The Sacraments, the power of the keys, also confirms it, for if God did not love us, He would not have placed these in our hands. We are overwhelmed by the infinite amount of testimony regarding His favor toward us.* Therefore, we should totally abandon these diabolical doubts with which the papacy is poisoned. Let us have full assurance that God is merciful toward us and that we have the Spirit of God who intercedes for us with those inexpressible groans and sighs.

The true cry and sigh is when someone in temptation cries out to God. The cry is not as if He were a tyrant, judge, or executioner but a father. The sigh may be ever so soft and secret that it can hardly be perceived, for when temptation is supremely strong and the trial comes, when the conscience struggles against the judgment of God, it tends to call God not as Father but as an unjust judge and irate and cruel tyrant. But this is the moan that Satan stirs up in the heart and it surpasses the cry of the Spirit, and it is felt with great force. It's then when it seems that God has forsaken us and will cast us into hell. The faithful sometimes bemoan, as in the Psalms: "I am cut off from your sight." Also, "I am like a broken vessel" and others. This is not the moan that cries out "Abba, Father," but the roar of God's wrath that cries out in panic, "Oh cruel judge, oh tormentor." This is the moment when you should look away from the law and works, from the feelings of your own conscience; this is the time to grasp the promise through faith—that is, take hold of the word of grace and life, which lifts the conscience upright so that it now begins to moan and say, "Although the law accuses me and sin and death harass me as never before, even so, oh my God, you promised me grace, righteousness, and eternal life through Jesus Christ." That is how the promise brings a sigh and a moan that cries out, "Abba, Father."

Here, I do not reject those who affirm that Paul uses these two words intentionally; one is in Hebrew and the other one in Greek, since both Jews and Greeks constituted the church. These two groups used different languages for God's name, "Father." However, the sigh of both peoples is one and the same, since both cry out, "Abba Father."

VERSE 7. Therefore you are no longer a slave, but a son.

This is the conclusion and finishing touch of what he had said. It's as if he had said, "Since this is true, that we have the Spirit because the Gospel by which we cry out 'Abba, Father,' and since this decree has been issued from heaven itself, there is no longer any slavery but only freedom, adoption, and sonship." But how did we come to life? Certainly, it was due to that sigh. And how did it happen? The Father offered it to me because of His promise, His grace, and His fatherly favor. What's still lacking? For me to receive this grace. But this happens when once again and with a child's heart I nod, saying "yes" to this name, "Father." Here, then, is when the father meets the son, and the wedding feast goes on without pomp and circumstance—that is, nothing intervenes between them, neither law nor work is required. But what's to be done with the terrors and the horrible darkness of temptation? Here, there is nothing more than to respond with the sigh "Father" and thus receive His promise who through Christ (born under the law) calls me His son. Here, I simply respond with the sigh, "Father." There are no demands made here, just the slight moan of a child. This little child grasps Him by faith in affliction and says, "You promised and told me that I am your child on account of Christ; that is why I call you Father." This is certainly what it means to be His children, simply, without any works. But these things cannot be understood without experience and putting them into practice.

In this text, Paul makes use of this word *servant* as he had done before in chapter 3 (v. 28), when he said, "There is neither slave nor free." Here, he uses the phrase "a servant of the law, subject to the law, as he had just said, 'We were enslaved under the rudiments of the world.'" Consequently, to be a servant according to Paul in this text is to be guilty and captive under the law, under God's wrath and death, and to look upon God not as a merciful Father but as an executioner, an enemy, and a tyrant. This is certainly to be bound hand and foot and in Babylonian captivity and, in that confinement, receive cruel torments, for the law does not deliver from sin and death. Instead, it reveals sin and puts a strangle hold on you, and rage goes to work. This slavery has come to an end; it no longer oppresses us nor causes us grief. Paul firmly says, "You are no longer a slave." But the statement takes on further meaning if we generalize it: "In Christ, there will no longer be any slavery but only freedom and adoption, for when faith arrives, slavery ends," as I had previously said in 3:25.

Well, since by Christ's spirit our hearts cry out, "Abba, Father," we are no longer slaves but children then it follows that we are freed not only from the Pope and all the abominable traditions of men but also from the dominion and the power of God's law. Consequently, we should not in any way tolerate the rule of the law in our conscience, and even less should we tolerate the Pope with all his empty threats and terrors. Indeed, he roars powerfully like a lion

(Revelation 10:10)[41] and threatens all who do not obey his laws with the wrath and indignation of God Almighty and of his blessed apostles. But here, Paul lends us weapons and comforts us against these roars when he said, "You are no longer a slave but a son." Grasp this comfort by faith, saying, "Oh law, your tyranny cannot occupy any space at the throne where Christ is seated as my Lord. I cannot hear you there (even less the Antichrist's monstrous voice), for I am free and I am a son and as such I am not subject to any yoke or in servitude to any law." Don't let Moses go up with all his laws (and with greater reason the Pope with his) into the bedroom suite—that is, don't let him reign over the conscience—for Christ has freed it from the law so that it will no longer be subject to any yoke. Let the servants remain down in the valley below with the mules. Let no one else but Isaac go up into the mountain with his father Abraham—that is, let the law have dominion over the body and over the old man, let him remain under the law and suffer whatever burden is placed on him, let him get to work and stress out over the law, let the law put limits on him and recite to him what he must do, and let him learn what he must suffer and how he should live and behave among men. But let it not stain the bed where only Christ is to find rest and sleep. Let not the law perturb the conscience, for it should live alone with its husband, Christ, in the kingdom of freedom and adoption.

Since then, he said, by Christ's spirit, we cry out, "Abba, Father," then we most certainly are no longer slaves but children in full use of our freedom. We are without the law, without sin, without death; in other words, we are already safe and sound and have been delivered from all evil. Thus adoption brings with it the eternal kingdom and every possible heavenly inheritance. The result is that the human heart cannot conceive how priceless is the glory of this gift, much less express it. In the meantime, we can perceive it but in the shadows, as if it were far away. We have this small sigh of faith that only finds its rest when it hears the voice of Christ proclaiming His promise. *With respect to what we feel and what emotions are central to us, these should concern us the least. On the other hand, Christ's promise belongs on the highest and infinite level. Thus what the Christian has in Christ is the greatest, in fact, infinite! However, what he can perceive and feel is minimal and finite.* However, we cannot measure it using human reason and emotion. Rather, we should think about it in terms of a circle—namely, the God who promises. He is infinite, thus His promise is infinite. His promise is surrounded by moments of anguish, like narrow straights (so to speak), *but His word is like the compass at the center.* Once we only saw the narrow passes but now we only see the center. Thus nothing now remains to accuse, frighten, or oppress my conscience, for servitude has given way

---

[41] The Latin text has Revelation 10:10 as the reference. Did Luther mean Revelation 10:3? A typo, perhaps? A slip of the tongue as he spoke that was not corrected in Rörer's notes?

to adoption, which brings us not only freedom from the law, sin, and death but also the inheritance of eternal life, which is expressed as follows.

VERSE 7. But a son; and if a son, then an heir of God through Christ.

Since he is a son then he must also be an heir. Due to his birth, he merits to be the heir. There is neither work nor merit by which he could obtain the inheritance. It is his only by the mere fact of his birth. He is only a passive agent and not an active agent,[42] not because he conceived, worked, or looked after things but only just because he was born; this is what enables him to be an heir. *He spent no effort in being conceived but was only a passive agent.* That is how we obtain the eternal gifts: forgiveness of sins, righteousness, the glory of the resurrection, and eternal life. We do not acquire these as active agents but as passive agents, not by doing but by receiving. Here, there is nothing that intervenes; it is faith alone that grasps onto the offered promise. Just as according to the civil laws a son is an heir only by virtue of his birth, so here, it is faith alone that proclaims us God's children, born from the word, which is God's womb, in which we were conceived, carried, born, nurtured, and so forth. Thus it is by this birth, through this passion,[43] that we are declared new creatures, formed by faith in the word. Now, since we are heirs, we are delivered from death, sin, and the devil. Because we are heirs, we have righteousness and eternal life.

Further, this surpasses all human understanding, that He should call us heirs, not from some wealthy or powerful prince, nor from the emperor or from the world, but from the Almighty God, Creator of All Things. Thus this is the worth or our inheritance! There are no words to describe it, as Paul says somewhere else (2 Corinthians 9:15), for when a person begins to understand the great excellence of this doctrine, that is when he becomes a son and heir of God. All who believe this with constant faith would consider all the power and wealth of the world as filthy dung when compared with this eternal inheritance. They would abhor whatever the world considers worthy of the highest praise and of the greatest glory. Yes, the greater the pomp and glory of the world, the more he would despise it. In conclusion, all that the world esteems as the highest and magnificent is to their eyes the most abhorrent and abominable filth, for what is the entire world with all its power, its riches and glory, if we compare them with being a

---

[42] *mere passive, non active contingit ei haereditas.*

[43] *hac ergo nativitate, hac passione . . . fili et heredes Dei per Christum.* Note that Luther ties or connects our "new birth" to Christ's passion. We are born again because of and in Christ's birth, life, passion, and resurrection. Luther's teaching on the new birth points in this direction. Our new birth is like our baptism, we are baptized into Him, and we are also born in Him.

son and heir of God? Further, with Paul we would wish with all our heart to be free and be with Christ; nothing else would be so welcome than to die without delay. We would embrace our death as our most joyful peace, knowing it would then end of all our misery and thereby we would take hold of our inheritance. Yes, whoever should perfectly believe this would not survive for long but would be swallowed up by unrestrained and extreme joy.

However, the law of the members, in combat against the law of the mind, blocks faith in us and does not allow it to attain perfection. Therefore, we need the aid and comfort of the Holy Spirit, which in our trials and afflictions will intercede for us with inexpressible groans, as I've said before. Sin remains in the flesh. Sometimes it oppresses the conscience and gets in the way of faith so that we cannot look upon, wish for, and enjoy with perfect joy those eternal riches that God has given us through Jesus Christ. Paul, himself, aware of his own struggle between the flesh and the Spirit, exclaims, "Wretched man that I am! Who will deliver me from this body of death?" He accuses his own body, which nonetheless is required to love and gives it a dreadful name, his death. It's as if he said, "My body afflicts me to no end; it ambushes me more than death itself." It blocked that joy in the Spirit in him. He did not always feel that sweet joy at the thought of the coming heavenly inheritance. Instead, he often felt great depression of spirit, anguish, and terror on all sides.

Here, we can clearly see how difficult faith is for us. We do not easily and quickly perceive this. There are certain lazy and puffed up minds, which imagine other things, and would like to swallow all Scriptures in one gulp. But the great weakness of the saints testifies to the weakness of their faith, for a perfect faith quickly creates a sense of disdain and world weariness with this life. If we could grant ourselves full confidence and believe that God is our Father and we His children and heirs, then we would condemn this world without hesitation, with all its glory, righteousness, wisdom, power, with all its royal scepters and crowns, and with all the riches and pleasures it affords. We should not live stressed out with this life; we should not be so addicted to the world and the things of the world,[44] confiding in them when we have them and complaining and despairing when we lose them. Instead, we should do all things with great love, humility, and patience. However, we do quite the contrary, since the flesh still has great strength, faith is feeble and the spirit is weak. Thus Paul said it well that in this life we only have the first fruit of the spirit; the other tenths would come later![45]

---

[44] *non sic adhaereremus corde corporalibus rebus,* literally "nor should our heart be glued to material things."

[45] Luther throws in a bit of humor during his lecture.

VERSE 7. Through Christ.

Paul always has Christ on his lips and cannot forget Him, for he anticipated that Christ and His Gospel would be most ignored in the world (even among professed Christians). Thus he mentions Him directly and continually places Him before our eyes. And every time he talks about grace, righteousness, the promise, adoption, and the inheritance, he tends to add "in Christ" or "through Christ" and, in a veiled way, devalues the law. It's as if he had said, "These things are ours not through the law nor by the works of the law, and even less through our own strength, nor by the traditions of men but through Christ alone given for us."

VERSES 8 and 9. However at that time, not knowing God, you were in bondage to those who by nature are not gods. But now that you have come to know God, or rather to be known by God, why do you turn back again to the weak and miserable elemental principles, to which you desire to be in bondage all over again? [WEB].

Here, Paul concludes his disputation. From here to the end of the epistle, he doesn't have much more to dispute but only gives certain ethical precepts for one's behavior. Nonetheless, he reproves the Galatians a great deal. He is very hurt that they dispelled this divine and heavenly doctrine so quickly from their hearts. It's as if he had said, "You have teachers that will once again lead you to the captivity of the law. That is not what I did. Instead, through my doctrine, I called you from darkness, from ignorance regarding God, to His marvelous light and knowledge. I removed your yoke and set you free as God's children. I accomplished this by preaching to you not the works of the law nor the merits of men. Instead, I taught you God's grace and righteousness and the outpouring of heavenly and eternal blessings through Christ. Now, seeing that this is true, why then did you abandon the light so quickly and return to darkness? Why did you allow them to so easily lead you from grace to the law, from freedom to slavery?"

Once again, we can see here (as I've said before) that to fall from faith is rather easy,[46] as attested by the Galatians' example. The Sacramentarians, the Anabaptists, and others attest the same. For our part, we promote this doctrine of faith by constantly traveling, preaching, reading, and writing. We clearly and transparently distinguish between the Gospel and the law, and even so, we don't gain much ground. This comes from the devil, who goes prowling around with all possible deceits seducing all and locking them up in error. He cannot tolerate the existence of the true knowledge of grace and faith in Christ. Therefore, to

---

[46] *facillimum ese lapsum in fide.* Rörer adds, *Lapsus in fide facilis,* "to fall from faith is easy."

remove Christ completely from sight and from the heart, he places before people certain grandiose performances with which he deceives them. Then little-by-little, he leads them away from faith and the knowledge of grace to topics regarding the law. When Christ is taken away, the devil has achieved his goal. It is with good reason then that Paul speaks so often and so much about Christ. That is why he is committed to expound with all purity the doctrine of faith, for this is the only way by which righteousness is attributed to anyone. He takes righteousness away from the law, declaring that the law has a totally opposite effect—that is, it stirs up lust, makes sin abound, etc. Paul joyfully persuades us not to let anyone to remove Christ from our heart, as the wife would not allow anyone to pull her husband away from her arms. Instead, she seeks to be always in his embrace grasping onto him, for once He is present there is no danger. All that may be heard are faithful sighs regarding our heavenly Father's will, our adoption, and our inheritance.

However, why does Paul say that they had relapsed to the weak and poor rudiments or ceremonies—that is, the law? But they had never received the law, for they were Gentiles (although he also wrote these things to the Jews, as we will see later). Or why didn't he write to them like this: "In the past, when you did not know God, you served those things which by nature are not gods. But now that you know God, why do you return to them, abandoning the true God to worship idols?" Is it that Paul understands that all is but the same thing, that to fall from the promise to return to the law, from faith to works, is no different than serving gods that by nature are not gods? I answer, "Everyone who falls from the article of justification does not know God and is an idolater. Therefore, it is all the same thing: to return to the law or to worship idols. It is all the same thing regardless of the name they give it: monk, Muslim, Jew, or Anabaptist. Because when this article is removed from the center, all that remains is nothing else but error, hypocrisy, wickedness, and idolatry. It doesn't matter what appearance they take. They all pretend to sustain the same truth, whether it is service to God, true holiness, or whatever."

The reason is that God does not allow Himself to be known, nor can God be known by any other means except through Christ;[47] according to what John said, "the only Son, who is in the bosom of the Father, he has made him known" (John 1:18). He is the seed promised to Abraham in whom God has rooted all His promises. Christ is the only means, and as you might say, the mirror in which we can see God and by whom we can also know His will, for in Christ, we see that God is no cruel and demanding judge but a Father of extremely goodwill, loving and merciful. In order to bless us—that is, to deliver us from the law, sin, death, all evil, and to grant us grace, righteousness, and eternal life—He "did not spare his own Son, but gave him up for us all." This is the true knowledge of God, the divine

---

[47] *Quia Deus non vault neque aliter potest cognesci, nisi per Christum.* Luther adds this footnote: *Deus congnoscitur per Christum,* "God is known through Christ."

persuasion that does not deceive us but paints us a trustworthy picture of God, other than this there is no God.[48]

Those who have fallen from this knowledge have fallen because they necessarily have conceived this fantasy in their heart: "I will serve God doing this and doing the other; I will become a monk of a certain order; I am going to perform this or that work; and that is how I will serve God. I don't have any doubt that God will accept these works and through them He will reward me with eternal life, for He is merciful and generous, giving all things even to those who don't deserve them and are grateful for them. Therefore, God will much more grant me grace and eternal life due to my many and great good works and merits earned." This is the highest wisdom, righteousness, and religion that reason could ever invent, which is common to all nations, whether they are Papists, Muslims, heretics, and all else! They cannot go any higher than where the Pharisee was standing mentioned in the Gospel. They are ignorant of Christian righteousness, or the righteousness of faith, because the natural man neither perceives nor needs the things of God. Thus there's no inner difference at all between Papists, Jews, Muslims, heretics, and everyone else. True, there is some diversity between peoples, places, rites, religions, works, and types of worship.[49] However, the same reasons, the same heart, the same opinion, and the same thought processes belong to them all, for the Muslim thinks the same as the Carthusian[50]—that is, if I do this or that work, God will be merciful to me. If I don't accomplish it, I have His wrath. There's no middle ground between human works and the knowledge of Christ. If this knowledge is obscured or disfigured, everything becomes the same thing, no matter if you're a monk or a pagan.[51]

That is why it is such insanity that the Papists and the Muslims battle among themselves about which of the two is the true religion and what is acceptable service to God.[52] They argue among themselves that they both have the true beliefs and the correct way to worship God. Neither do the monks come to an agreement among themselves! Some of them consider themselves holier than the others because they fulfill certain foolish acts they call ceremonies, and even so, in their hearts, they are all have the same conviction, for if you've seen one egg, you've seen them all, for all of them have this delusion: "If I fulfill this work, God will have mercy on me; if I don't, His wrath will find me out." That is how everyone who becomes rebellious against the knowledge of Christ will by default fall into idolatry. They will conceive mistaken notions about God, which are not in agreement with God's nature.[53] That

---

[48] *extra quam non est Deus.*

[49] Luther's footnote: *Nulla differentia est inter Turcas, Iudaeos, papistas, etc.,* "there's no difference between Muslims, Jews, Papists, etc."

[50] *Turca, quod Carthusianus.*

[51] *sive sis monachus, sive ethnicus, etc.*

[52] *papistae & Turcae inter se digladiantur de religione & cultu Dei.*

[53] *quia necesse est eum de Deo fingere formam, quae nusquam est.*

is how it is with the monk in his monastery of great renown, who he enters to fulfill the requirements of his order, and with the Muslim in obeying his Qur'an.[54] All of them grant themselves the same confidence, that they are pleasing God, and consequently, they will receive some reward for all their efforts.

Such a God that forgives sin and justifies sinners cannot be found anywhere. All they have is a vain imagination, a dream, and an idol in their heart, for God has not promised that He will save and justify people due to their religion, practices, ceremonies, and regulations designed by men. Yes! There's nothing God abhors more (as Scriptures testify) than these works of will power, such as observances, rites, and ceremonies. In fact, for this, God has overthrown entire kingdoms and empires. Therefore, all who trust in their own strength and righteousness serve a certain god but a god of their own imagination and that for sure is not God in God's own nature,[55] for the true God in His own nature[56] speaks like this: "There is no righteousness, nor wisdom, nor religion that pleases me, except that one by which the Father is glorified through the Son. Everyone who takes hold of the Son takes hold of me, and my promise is that I will be their God. I, the Father, accept, justify, and save such persons. Everyone else remains under wrath, because they worship that which by nature is not God."

All who abandon this doctrine necessarily fall from the knowledge of God. They cannot understand what the true meaning of Christian righteousness, wisdom, and worship of God is. They are idolaters, living under the law, sin, death, the power of the devil, and all they do is under a curse and condemnation. That is why the Anabaptists imagine they please God if they rebaptize; if they abandon their homes, wives, and children; if they mortify their flesh and suffer great adversity, even death itself. However, they don't have one drop of the knowledge of God. Nonetheless, they expel Christ, dream only about their own works and how to get rid of their goods, and increasing their affliction and physical suffering. When they get to this point, they are no different than the Muslim, the Jew, or the Papist in the spirit of their hearts. The only difference appears in the external works and the ceremonies, which are of their own choosing. All the monks and holy orders have this same confidence, although there is some difference in their garb and other appearances.

Today, there are many like them who nonetheless would pass themselves off as true teachers and professors of the Gospel. Further, with regards to their words, they may teach that sinners are freed from their sins by the death of Christ. But since they teach this faith in such a way that they give more credit to love than to faith itself, they greatly dishonor Christ and wickedly pervert His word, for they contrive the delusion that God values and accepts us due to our love for God and neighbor. But if this were true, then we would not need Christ at all. Such people

---

[54] *Turca propter observationem Alcorani.*

[55] *qui natura Deus est.*

[56] *verus et naturalis.*

do not serve the true God but a mere idol in their own hearts, designed all by themselves. In fact, the true God neither values nor accepts us for our love, virtues, or newness of life but only on account of Christ.[57]

However, they protest with this argument: "But Scripture commands that we should love God with all our heart etc." That's true. But who fully obeys that commandment? Thus although God commands it, it doesn't follow that we fully obey it. If we loved God with all our heart and such, then no doubt we would be justified, and we would live by that obedience, as it is written: "Whoever does these things will live by them" (Leviticus 18:5). But the Gospel says, "You don't do these things; therefore, you will not live by them." That's because this statement, "You shall love the Lord your God," requires a perfect obedience, a perfect fear, perfect trust, and love to God. People neither do nor can fulfill these things as long as they live in this corrupt nature. Therefore, this law, "You shall love the Lord your God," does not justify but accuses and condemns everyone, according to what is written: "The law stirs up wrath" (Romans 4:15). But on the other hand, "Christ is the end and the fulfillment of the law for righteousness to everyone who believes."[58] We have already spoken a great deal about this.

The Jews keep the law with this same notion in mind, that they please God with their obedience.[59] But that is not serving the true God but idolatry. They are worshipping an illusion and an idol in their own heart, an idol that is nowhere to be found. The God of their fathers, who they say they worship, promised Abraham "a seed" by which all nations would be blessed. Thus God is known and His blessing is given, not through the law, but through the Gospel of Christ.

Paul directed his words, "not knowing God, you served," mainly and precisely to the Galatians because they were Gentiles. However, the same words also pertain to the Jews. Although to all appearances the Jews had rejected their idols, in their hearts they worshipped them more than the Gentiles themselves, as it says in Romans, "Detesting idols, do you commit idolatrous acts?" (Romans 2:22, CJB). The Gentiles were not the people of God, they did not have His word, and thus their idolatry was more crass. But the Jews covered up their idolatry with the name and the word of God. This is precisely what the legalists do today because they seek righteousness through the efforts of their works. With this external theater of holiness, they deceive many. Thus idolatry, the holier and more spiritual, is the more damaging.

However, how can these two apparently contradictory statements by the apostle be reconciled? "You did not know God" and "worshipped God"? I answer that all people have by nature this general knowledge of God, according to

---

[57] *sed propter Christus.*

[58] *Christus est consummatio legis ad iusticiam omni credenti.*

[59] Luther's note: *Non per legem sed Evangelium cognoscitur Deus, & donatur bene-dictio,* "God is not known through the law, but God is known and His blessing received through the Gospel."

Romans 1, that there is a God, "since what may be known about God is plain to them, because God has made it plain to them" (Romans 1:19, 20, NIV). God was revealed to them in the invisible things of God that appeared through the creation of the world. Further, the ceremonies and religions that have always existed sufficiently testify that people everywhere have had a certain general knowledge of God. Whether they had this knowledge through nature or through the traditions handed down from their ancestors, I will not argue here.

But at this point, some will once again object: "If they all knew God, why then does Paul say that the Galatians didn't know God before the preaching of the Gospel?" I answer that there are two ways of knowing God. One is general, the other particular.[60] Everyone has a general knowledge—that is, that there is a God that created heaven and earth, that He is righteous, and that He punishes the wicked. However, regarding what God thinks about us (His will toward us), what He will give or do to deliver us from sin and death, and how to be saved (for certain, this is the true knowledge of God), they don't know any of this. In the same way, I may know someone by sight but not thoroughly because I don't fully understand that person's feelings toward me; that is how people by nature know there is a God. But what is His will and what is not His will,[61] they have no idea! For it is written, "There is no one who knows God." And in another text, "No one has ever seen God" (John 1:18)—that is, no one has known the will of God. Now, what good is there in knowing there is a God but not knowing what is God's will toward you? Here, some think one thing, others something else. The Jews imagine that God's will is to be worshipped according to Moses' requirements; the Muslim[62] if he observes his Qur'an; the monk if he is faithful to his order and fulfills his vows. However, they are all deceived. They become vain in their own thoughts, as Paul says, not knowing what pleases or displeases God (Romans 1). Thus instead of the true and natural God, they worship the dreams and illusions of their own heart, which are nothing.

This is what Paul meant to say when he said, "When they knew not God"; when they didn't know the will of God, they served those who by nature are not gods—that is, they served the illusions and imaginations of their own heart. These led them to think, without the word, that God should be worshipped with this or that work, with this or that ceremony. It's from this starting point that all understand through nature that there is a God. However, without this natural knowledge of God, idolatry would have never arisen. Since people had this natural knowledge of God, they conceived vain and wicked imaginations regarding God, without and against the word. But they valued their own thoughts, holding them as nothing but truth itself. Thus they imagined God was just like they fancied Him to be, even though in Himself God

---

[60] *generaalis et propia.*
[61] *quid velit, quid non velit.*
[62] *Turcae.*

is not who they think God is. However, this is exactly how the monk imagines God, that in exchange for fulfilling his vows, God will forgive his sins and grant him grace and eternal life! But this God is nowhere to be found because this God simply does not exist! Thus the monks do not render service to the true God but to that which by nature is not God—that is, the imagination and the idol of their own hearts. It is their own and false opinion about God, which they imagine is such a great truth as to be free from all doubt. Well, since when does an opinion look like God to you? Reason itself will deny such foolishness![63] Thus anyone who proposes to worship God without His word does not render service to the true God (as Paul says) but to something that by nature is not God.

Therefore, although you may say that here "rudiments" refer either to the law of Moses or to the traditions of the Gentiles (although here he specifically talks about Moses' rudiments), there is no great difference, for whoever has fallen from grace and gone back to the law doesn't fall with any less danger than the one who falls from grace to idolatry, for without Christ, there is nothing else but pure idolatry and vain and false illusions regarding God no matter what name you give it: law of Moses, papal bulls, the Muslim's Qur'an, etc. Therefore, he says with certain astonishment,

VERSE 9. But now that you have come to know God.

It's as if he had said, "Now, this is quite astounding; you who once knew God through the preaching of faith now rise up so suddenly against the knowledge of His will. I was so convinced that you were firmly grounded in that knowledge that it never even occurred to me that you would be so easily defeated. Now, instigated by the false apostles, you once again have returned to the feeble and beggarly ceremonies to which you now render tribute. Through my preaching, you have heard that God's will is to bless all nations, not through circumcision or through the observance of the law but through Christ, the One promised to Abraham. Those who believe in Him will be blessed together with Abraham the believer. You are children and heirs of God. That is how I say that you have come to know God."

VERSE 9. Or rather to be known by God.

Here, Paul takes his own rhetoric to task. First, he corrects the previous statement: "Now that you have come to know God" with "Or rather to be known by God," for he fears that they had lost God altogether. It's as if he had said, "What? Have you fallen so low that after you have known God that you now turned back from grace to the law? However, God still knows you." Indeed, our knowledge is more passive than active—that is, it consists in this: instead of knowing God, we are known by God.

---

[63] Alternate translation: "reason itself will compel us to confess that someone's opinion is no God at all!"

Our only doing is allowing God to work in us. He sends the divine word, and when by faith we grasp it by faith, we are born children of God. Thus the meaning is this: "You are known by God"—that is, they have been guests of the word; they have been gifted with faith and the Holy Spirit by which they have been revived. Even with these words, "known by God," he takes away all the righteousness of the law and refutes the claim that we can attain the knowledge of God through the virtue of our own works. "No one knows who the Son is except the Father, or who the Father is except the Son and any one to whom the Son chooses to reveal him" (Matthew 11:27). Also, "By his knowledge my righteous servant will justify many, and he will bear their iniquities" (Isaiah 53:11, NIV). Thus our knowledge of God is merely passive.[64]

LECTURE 29: Friday, October 23

Therefore, he marvels greatly seeing that they had come to know the true God through the Gospel. Yet through the persuasion of the false apostles, they very quickly had returned to the feeble and beggarly rudiments. I would also be astonished if our church (which by God's grace has been spotlessly instituted[65] in the purity of its doctrine and in the faith) would be seduced and perverted by some fanatical and pretentious head. With just a pair of sermons, they could get my congregation to no longer accept me as their pastor. However, this will happen someday, if not while we live, it will happen after death separates us, for then, many will rise up as teachers and scholars who under the colors of the true faith will teach a false and perverse doctrine and quickly overthrow everything that it has taken us so much time and effort to build. We are no better than the apostles who during their own lifetime saw how the churches revolted, the very same churches they had planted through their ministry. Thus we should not feel aghast if today we were compelled to see the same evil occur. Those churches where the sectarians reign, once we die, will take possession of the churches we have planted and raised through our ministry. They will infect and incite them with their poison. Nonetheless, Christ prevails and will reign to the end of the world, amazingly, as the church prevailed throughout the papacy.

It seems as if Paul is talking about the law with a great deal of disdain, for he calls it "the rudiments (principles)" (as he had done before at the beginning of this chapter). But now he not only calls it "rudiments." He calls it "weak and miserable elemental rudiments (principles) and ceremonies." But is it not blasphemous to call God's law such loathsome names? In its proper use, the law should serve the promises and support the promises and grace. However, when the law enters into combat with these, it is no longer the holy law of God but a false and

---

[64] *notitia nostra de Deo est mere passiva.*
[65] *pulcherrime instituta.*

diabolic doctrine. It does nothing but hurl people into madness and thus should be repudiated.

Thus when he calls the law the "weak and miserable elemental rudiments (or basic principles)," he talks about the law as understood by the proud and self-important hypocrites who seek to be justified by the law. He does not talk about understanding the law spiritually, in the sense that it generates wrath. The law (as I've often said) when used properly accuses and condemns. In this respect, it isn't only a strong and prosperous rudiment. Instead, it's an opulent magnate, yes, an invincible and luxurious potentate. If you here compare the conscience with the law, then the conscience is extremely fragile, for the smallest sin distresses and perturbs it so that it becomes totally desperate, unless it can be once again be reassured, for the law in its proper use is so powerful and opulent that neither heaven nor earth can contain it, for only one dot or jot is able to annihilate all humanity, as testified by the giving of the law by Moses (Exodus 19, 20). This is the true and divine use of the law, but that's not what Paul is talking about here.

Paul here calls out the hypocrites who have fallen from grace and those who have not yet taken hold of grace. Both abuse the law and attempt to be justified by the law. They exhaust themselves day and night performing their own works. This is what Paul testified about the Jews: "For I can testify about them," he said, "that they are zealous for God, but their zeal is not based on knowledge, since they did not know the righteousness of God" (Romans 10:2, 3, NIV). These hope to be strengthened and made wealthy by the law. Then they believe they can offset God's wrath and judgment with their power and wealth, which they think they have obtained through the righteousness of the law. They believe they can appease God and be saved by the law. But to this, we affirm that the law is a feeble and beggarly rudiment, meaning that it cannot even bring aid or rescue.

Those who wish to expand on this theme, whether it's active, passive, or neutral. As active, the law is a feeble and beggarly rudiment because it weakens and impoverishes people even more. Because of its nature, the law has neither power nor riches through which to grant or bring righteousness. This is because it not only is feeble and beggarly but makes people weak and indigent. As passive, it has neither power nor wealth to grant or convey righteousness. As neutral, it is weak and beggarly itself. How then could it prosper and strengthen those who before were both weak and indigent? Therefore, to endeavor to be justified by the law is as if someone already weak and beggarly attempts to overcome his own weakness and poverty by attempting some greater harm, which would anyhow result in self-destruction. It's as if someone who has fallen prey to some malignant plague seeks remedy by catching a deadlier scourge! Or it's as if a leper would come to heal another leper or a beggar to make another beggar wealthy. *Here, as the saying goes, "one milks the goat and another holds the colander"!*

This is a perfect example of tapinosis.[66] Paul wants to say that those who endeavor to be justified by the law have this helpful little tool: every day they get feebler, fainter, and more impoverished. They are already in themselves weak and beggarly—that is, they are by nature children of wrath, subject to death and eternal condemnation. Notwithstanding, they hang on to weakness and poverty, expecting these to strengthen them and fill them up with riches. Thus all those who have fallen from the promise to the law, from faith to works, don't do anything else but take on a greater weight when they are already weak and unsteady. They cannot carry the weight (Acts 15:10), but get ten times weaker while they're at it so that at the end they plunge into desperation unless Christ comes and grants them freedom.

The Gospel also testifies about this when it talks about the woman tormented by the flow of blood for twelve years, suffering a great deal at the hands of many doctors, spending on them all she had without finding a cure. The longer she was under their care, the worse she got (Mark 5:25ff). Everyone who strives to be justified by doing the works of the law accomplishes nothing more than becoming twice as wicked as before—that is (as I've said before), more feeble and impoverished and more inept to do any good work. I've confirmed this truth in my own person as well as in many others. I've known many monks in the papacy who with great zeal have done many grandiose works to achieve righteousness and salvation. However, they became more impatient, weaker, more miserable, more unbelieving, more fearful, and closer to desperation than anyone else. The judges in charge of the law of the land were always busy carrying weighty and important matters, but they were not so impatient, fearful, depressed, superstitious, and unbelieving as these legalists and merit hoarders.

Thus everyone who goes after righteousness through the law by repeating the same works *only gets into the habit*[67] *of starting them all over again from the beginning!* They imagine that an angry and vengeful God will be placated with those works. Once they have conceived this illusion, they get to work. But they will never be able to find enough good works to quiet their conscience. They will only wish for more! They find sin in all those works they had done before. Thus they will never have assurance in their conscience. Instead, they will always live in doubt, thinking within themselves, "You've not sacrificed enough as you should; you've not prayed well enough, you have left this or that undone, you have committed this or that sin." Here, their heart trembles and feels oppressed by countless sins, to which they keep adding without end, so that they stray further away from righteousness. At last, all they get is the nasty habit of falling into despair.[68] "I am

---

[66] Suppose you were a student in Luther's lecture hall. Would you know what this is? They didn't have the luxury of an immediate online search!

[67] Luther used the Greek term ἕξιν during his lecture. It is found in Hebrews 5:14 and typically means a habit or way of doing things through repetition.

[68] *acquirat habitum desperationis.*

nothing but misery itself! I have not fulfilled my vows. Where shall I flee from the wrath of Christ, that furious judge? Oh, if God would only send me into a herd of pigs!" Or "I am the most wicked and damned of all the world!"

That is how the monk at the end of his days is weaker, more destitute, more unbelieving and fearful than at the beginning when he entered his order for the first time. The reason is that he sought out weakness as a source of strength and poverty as a source of wealth. The law or the traditions of men or the rules of his order should have cured all his ills and made him wealthy notwithstanding his poverty. But he has become weaker and more destitute than publicans and prostitutes. These have not piled up mounds of miserable tedious works[69] in which to trust, as the monks have done! Yet since they feel the weight of their sins (as all the monks, nuns, and friars have never felt), they can cry out like the publican, "Lord, have mercy on me, a sinner!" (Luke 18:13). However, the monk has spent his lifetime among the weak and beggarly rudiments. Yet he comes to this conclusion: if I keep the rules of my order, I will be saved. With this false conviction, he gets so razzle-dazzled[70] that he cannot understand grace. No! He cannot even think there's such a thing as grace. So despite all the works he does or has done, however great and plentiful, he will always think they're not enough and will always be eyeing some new work to do. In this way, he goes on piling on works striving to appease God's wrath and justify himself until he arrives at the edge of panic. Thus everyone who lets go of faith to hang onto the law is like Aesop's dog who let go of the prey to bite its shadow!

It's impossible that those who strive for righteousness and salvation through the law (as humans are naturally inclined) will ever find peace and quiet for their conscience. Instead, all they accomplish is to pile up laws stacked up on top of more laws with which to torment themselves and others. They afflict the consciences of other people with so much gloom and doom that many die before their time due to extreme anguish in their hearts. That's because where there's one law, it soon gives birth to ten more and so on, increasing exponentially forever more! *This is testified in the countless Summae (that special creation of that little devil they call "Angelicus"), where laws of this type are gathered and expounded ad infinitum!*[71]

In brief, whoever strives to be justified by the law struggles for what he will never attain. Here, we can relate what the Fathers said regarding the proverbs of wise and illustrious men working in vain, such as "Rolling the stone," "Drawing water with a colander," and such. I believe with these phrases and parables the Fathers wanted to emphasize the difference between the law and the Gospel. They wanted to show that

---

[69] *infelicem illam operum.*

[70] Luther used the Latin colloquialism *dementatus et captus est,* which figuratively means "fooled by foolery," thus the closest English equivalent expression is "razzle-dazzled."

[71] Luther refers to Thomas of Aquinas's *Summae*. Aquinas was *called* the "Doctor Angelicus."

when people fall from grace, no matter how much effort they exert with their ceaseless and tiring struggles, all their work is in vain. You can truly say about them that they spend their time rolling a stone—that is, their efforts are in vain, as the poets wrote about Sisyphus, who while in hell, rolled a stone up to the summit of a mountain only to have it roll back down, and also drawing water with a sieve—that is, to get all fatigued with useless and endless efforts, as the poets described the daughters of Danaus, who once they got to hell had to carry water in broken clay pitchers to fill a bottomless jug.

I wish for you who study the sacred subjects to store up parables such as these so that you may retain a better way of seeing the difference between the law and the Gospel. That way you may use these to illustrate that attempting to be justified by the law is like counting coins from an empty purse, serving yourself from an empty platter, drinking from an empty cup, and seeking strength and wealth where there is only weakness and want, placing a load on someone who's already crushed by the weight he carries, paying a bill for one hundred gold coins without a single penny, taking the shirt off a naked man, oppressing the sick and needy with greater sickness and hardship.

Well, who would have thought that the Galatians, having learned a doctrine so sound and pure from such an excellent apostle and teacher, would have so suddenly departed from it permitting themselves to be entirely perverted by the false apostles? There's a good reason I repeat it so often that to fall from the Gospel is the easiest thing to do. The reason is that people do not value, no, not even the faithful value, how excellent and precious a treasure is the true knowledge of Christ. Therefore, they make no great and diligent effort to store it and retain it. Further, a great number of those who hear the word are not persecuted due to the cross, nor do they suffer affliction. They don't struggle against sin, death, and the devil but live within their safe house without any conflict at all. These, since they have been neither tried nor refined by fire when tempted, are not armed with God's word against the wiles of the devil. They can never feel the power nor know the use of the word. It is true; whenever they are surrounded by faithful ministers and preachers, they follow their words, they repeat the same things they say, persuaded that they understand the doctrine of justification perfectly. But when they are all alone, and the wolves arrive dressed in sheep's clothing, they experience what happened to the Galatians—that is, they are seduced so quickly that they easily return to the feeble and beggarly rudiments.

Here, Paul has a unique way of speaking altogether different from the other apostles. Not one of them except Paul gave the law such names—that is, that it is a feeble and beggarly rudiment and in other words totally useless to achieve righteousness.[72] Frankly, I would not describe the law with such names. I would have thought it great blasphemy against God if Paul had not done it before. But I have already dealt at length with this topic, pointing out when the law is weak and beggarly and when the law is powerful and opulent.

---

[72] *legi . . . plus quam inutile ad justitiam.*

Well, if God's law is weak and ineffective for justification,[73] how much weaker and useless are the papal decrees for justification.[74] *It's not that I reject and condemn all his laws, for I say that many are useful as an external discipline so that all things in the church may be done properly and in order. They are useful in avoiding dissension and arguments in the same way the laws of the emperor are good for the nation's welfare. But the Pope is not content with this proper recognition of his laws but requires our consent that by keeping them we are justified and saved. Therefore, we deny all that* and condemn such rules, regulations, and papal decrees with great boldness and conviction as Paul did against God's law. We say that such regulations are not only feeble and impoverished, totally useless for righteousness, but they are repulsive, accursed, diabolical, and damnable, for they blaspheme grace, overthrow the Gospel, abolish faith, and remove Christ altogether.

Then when the Pope demands that we keep his laws as requirements for salvation, he is the Antichrist himself and the vicar of Satan.[75] All those who take hold of him, confirm his abominations and blasphemies; and those who keep them with the end goal of meriting forgiveness of sins are servants of the Antichrist and the devil. Well then, this has been the doctrine of the papal church for a long time, saying that these laws must be kept as necessary for salvation. That is how the Pope sits in the temple of God, claiming that he, himself, is God, opposing God, exalting himself against everything that is called God, and allows himself to be worshipped as God (2 Thessalonians 2:4, NIV). Thus people's consciences show more reverence and fear for the Pope's rules and laws than for the word of God and its commands. That is how he made himself lord of heaven and earth, hell, and wears a triple crown on his head. The cardinals and bishops, his creatures, were also made kings and princes of this world. Therefore, if he had not oppressed people's consciences with his laws, he would not have been able to sustain his horrible power, dignity, and riches for such a long time, but his entire kingdom would have come tumbling down in no time at all.

The text that Paul explains here is of great weight and importance; therefore, it must be carefully noted—that is, those who fall from grace and return to the law lose altogether the knowledge of truth. They do not see their own sins. They don't know God or the devil or themselves. Further, they don't understand the strength and the use of the law, although they brag without end that they keep and observe it, for without the knowledge of grace—that is, without the Gospel of Christ—it is impossible to define the law in such terms, that it is a feeble and beggarly rudiment, worthless for righteousness. Instead, they have an understanding totally contrary regarding the law. They believe that it not only is necessary for salvation but also strengthens the weak and prospers the poor and beggarly—that is, all who obey and keep it will be able to merit righteousness and eternal salvation. But if this opinion

---

[73] *lex Dei infirma et inutilis est ad justificationem.*

[74] *multo magis leges papae sunt infirmae et inutiles ad justificationem.*

[75] *papa . . . est antichristus et Satanae vicarious.*

prevails, God's promise is denied, Christ is evicted, and every lie, wickedness, and idolatry is established. Well then, the Pope with all his bishops, their schools, and their entire synagogue has taught that his laws are necessary for salvation. Thus he was a teacher of the feeble and beggarly elements with which he has made the church of Christ far and wide the most feeble and beggarly—that is, with the wickedness of his laws he has miserably burdened and tormented the church, disfiguring Christ and burying His Gospel. *Thus if you are going to observe the laws of the Pope without consulting your conscience, then do it with the thought that it's not going to avail you for righteousness, for righteousness is given through Christ alone.*[76]

VERSE 9. Do you want to be slaves to them all over again?

He adds this to declare that he is talking about the hypocritical and proud who strive to be justified by the law, as I have shown before. Otherwise, he calls the law holy and good, as well as "the law is good if one uses it properly" (1 Timothy 1:8, NIV)—that is, in its secular use to bridle the criminals and spiritually to increase the transgressions[77] (Galatians 3:19). Everyone who observes the law to obtain righteousness before God changes the law from something good into something that condemns and harms. He reproves the Galatians because they have wanted to return to slavery under the law, but it does not remove sin. Instead, it multiplies it, for as long as sinners who are already weak attempt to justify themselves by the law, they cannot find anything in it but weakness and poverty. This is like two sick and feeble beggars getting together, but neither can help the other. All they do for each other is to get in the other's way!

We, strengthened in Christ, would willingly serve the law, not the law that is feeble and impoverished but the law that is powerful and productive—that is, the law that exercises control over the body. Let us serve the law only in our body and exterior members but not in our conscience. However, the Pope demands that we obey his laws with this in mind: that if we do this or that, we are righteous. Otherwise, we are condemned. Here, the law is nothing more than a feeble and beggarly principle, for as long as the conscience remains in slavery under the law there cannot be any other condition but weakness and poverty. Therefore, the whole weight of the matters falls on this word *slavery*. What Paul wants to say is this. He will not allow the conscience to serve the law as a slave. The conscience will be free and will have dominion over the law, for through Christ, the conscience has died to the law and the law to the conscience. In chapter 2, we explained this at great length.

---

[76] *justitiae ea namque per solum Christum donatur.*

[77] *quod lex bona sit, si quis ea legitime utatur, scilicet politice ad coercendos malos, theologice ad augendas transgressiones.*

VERSE 10. You observe days, and months, and seasons, and years!

With these words, he clearly shows the teaching of the false apostles: It's all about the observance of days, months, seasons, and years. *Almost all the scholars have interpreted this text relating it to the days of Chaldean astrology. They say that the Gentiles when closing business deals or to celebrate matters of daily life, observed certain fixed days, months, etc. They claim that the Galatians did the same at the urging of the false apostles. Even Saint Augustine, and others who followed him, explained these words of Paul in relation to the traditions of the Gentiles, although later he interpreted them as the days, months, and so on of the Jews.*

But here Paul is instructing the conscience. Thus he cannot be talking about the traditions of the Gentiles regarding the keeping of days or matters related to the body. Instead, Paul is talking here about God's law and the keeping of days, months, and so on according to the law of Moses—that is, with respect to religious days, months, and seasons that the false apostles observed as necessary for justification. The Jews had the command to sanctify the Sabbath day; new moons; the first day of the month; the seventh; the three appointed feasts, which are the Passover, the Feast of the Weeks, the Feast of the Tabernacles; and the Year of Jubilee. The false apostles taught that they had the obligation to keep these ceremonies as necessary for righteousness. Thus he says that they, having lost grace and the freedom they enjoyed in Christ, had returned to the slavery of the weak and beggarly rudiments. The false apostles had persuaded them that they were required to keep these laws and that in keeping them would obtain righteousness, but if they did not observe them, they would be condemned. But on the contrary, Paul cannot tolerate in any way the tying of people's consciences to Moses' law; rather, he urges that they will always be freed from the law. "Now I, Paul [he says soon after in 5:2], say to you that if you receive circumcision, Christ will be of no advantage to you." He also says, "Therefore, do not let anyone judge you by what you eat or drink, or with regard to a religious festival, a New Moon celebration or a Sabbath day" (Colossians 2:16, NIV). Christ, our Savior, also said, "The coming of the kingdom of God is not something that can be observed" (Luke 17:20, NIV). Much less then should the consciences be burdened with the traditions of men.

Here, someone could say, "If the Galatians sinned by observing days and times, why isn't it a sin when you do the same?" I respond, "We observe the Lord's day, the day of His Nativity, the Passover, but in plain use of our freedom. We do not burden the conscience with these ceremonies, nor do we teach them as the false apostles and now the Papists have done, for they teach that they are necessary for justification or that by observing them we cleanse our sins. We keep them so that everything will be done orderly and without tumults in the church. Further, so that our external fellowship will not be broken (for we agree in spirit). We don't do as Victor, that Roman pontiff, who excommunicated all the churches in Asia for no other reason except that they had celebrated Easter on a different date than the church of Rome. Irenaeus reproved Victor for that, for it was reproachable. It was extreme insanity to deliver all the Eastern churches over to the devil for such an insignificant matter. The true knowledge of the meaning of these days and times was unknown even among the most important men. Jerome didn't have it and Augustine would not have acquired it had the followers of Pelagius not harassed and perturbed him.

"However, we observe such feasts so that the ministry of the word will be preserved so that people will meet together on certain days and times and listen to the word. Further, so that people will come to the knowledge of God, to participate in holy communion, to pray for every need, and to give thanks to God for all His material and spiritual benefits. I believe it was especially for this last one that the Fathers instituted the observance of the Lord's Day, Easter, Pentecost, and others."

VERSE 11. I fear for you, that somehow I have wasted my efforts on you [NIV].

Here, Paul shows himself to be greatly troubled because of the Galatians' fall. He would reprimand with more severity except that he feared that greater severity would have worsened the situation; it might have offended them to the point of completely alienating him against them. Therefore, as he writes, he changes his tone and softens his words. Since he bears the main responsibility, he says, "I am afraid for you, lest I have labored for you in vain," meaning that he had preached the Gospel among them with such diligence and faithfulness yet has seen no fruit come from it. Nevertheless, while showing them a very fatherly and loving affection, he still rebuked them rather sharply yet very subtly. When he says that he had "labored in vain" or had preached the Gospel without obtaining fruit, he is subtly showing one of two things: one, that they were obstinate unbelievers or on the other hand, that they had fallen from the doctrine of faith. Both unbelievers as well as backsliders from the doctrine of faith, are sinners, wicked, unrighteous, and damned. Such people obey the law in vain: they uselessly observe days, months, and years. Contained within these words, "I am afraid for you, lest I have labored for you in vain," there is a secret excommunication, for by this, the apostle means that the Galatians were excluded and separated from Christ, unless they quickly returned to the sound and whole doctrine. Yet he doesn't pronounce an open condemnation against them because he perceives that no good would be accomplished with severe language. Therefore, he changes his tone and speaks to them evenhandedly, saying,

VERSE 12. Brethren, I urge you to become like me, for I became like you.

This text is not about back-and-forth arguments;[78] *it is full of affection and should be understood as an effort to persuade.*[79] Up to this point, Paul has had his hands full dealing with doctrine. He was moved by the enormous and wicked rebellion of the Galatians. He felt vehemently furious with them and bitterly reproved them. He has called them foolish, bewitched, unbelievers of the truth, crucifiers of Christ, and other things. Well, as he draws his epistle to a close, he realizes he has been too harsh with them. Therefore, he is careful not to cause further harm with stern language and demonstrates that his strong reproaches proceed from a fatherly affection and a true apostolic heart. Thus he tones down his rhetoric with softer and more affectionate words as if perhaps he had offended someone (as indeed some had been offended). He attempts to mitigate the effect with these soft and loving words.

Here, with his own example, he admonishes all pastors and ministers. They should have both a maternal and a paternal affection, not as if they were dealing with ravenous wolves but with a delicate herd of sheep, pitifully seduced and wayward, carrying patiently their faults and weaknesses, instructing and restoring them with a gentle spirit. There's no other way to bring them back to the good path. If he rebukes them too much, he'll provoke them to anger or otherwise plunge them into despair but not into repentance. By the way, take note that such is the nature and fruit of true and sound doctrine that when it has been taught and understood well it unites the hearts of people with the same sentiment. But when people reject the faithful and sincere doctrine, they embrace errors and that unity and sentiment of mutual accord is soon broken. Therefore, as soon as you see your brothers seduced by haughty and fanatical spirits, and you see them fall from the article of justification, you will soon see them persecute the faithful with bitter hate, the very same ones who used to love you with devoted affection.

Today, we've proven this with our experience. Our false brothers and other sectarians[80] at the beginning of the Gospel reformation[81] heard us gladly. They read our books and fervently and affectionately recognized the grace of the Holy Spirit in us. They respected us as true ministers of God. Some also, for a time, lived among us as one family. Their behavior was sober and modest. However, when they separated from us and were perverted by the wicked doctrine of the fanatics,[82] they quickly let it be known that they were our most bitter enemies, against our doctrine and name, equal to none. The Papists hate us but not as bitterly as they do. Frequently, I, myself, wonder where they conceived such mortal

---

[78] Literally *Hic locus non est dialecticus.*

[79] *qui tractandi sun rhetorice.*

[80] *sacramentariis et Anabaptists.*

[81] *initie caussae Evangelicae.*

[82] *per phanaticus spiritus.*

hatred against us, since before they had loved us with a great deal of affection and loving care. After they so lovingly embraced us, they dropped us although we neither offended them at all nor gave them occasion to despise us. They were even compelled to confess that what we want more than anything is to let God's glory be known, that Christ's true benefit be proclaimed, and that the truth of the Gospel is taught in all purity. This is the truth that in our days God has revealed through us, which should provoke them to love us instead of hating us. I am astounded, then, and not without reason, about the source of such a change of heart. Indeed, there's no other reason than they've acquired new teachers and have paid attention to new instructors who have infected them with their poison; for their hatred against our work and passion is implacable.

This was situation of the apostles and all those who have been faithful ministers ever since. When their disciples and hearers are infected with the errors from the false apostles and heretics, they turn against them and become their enemies. Among the Galatians, there were but very few who followed in the sound doctrine of the apostles. All others, having been seduced by the false apostles, no longer recognized Paul as their pastor and teacher. No, for them, there was nothing more objectionable than Paul's name and doctrine. My belief is that there were very few who renounced their error as a result of this epistle.

If the same thing should happen to us—that is, if we were to depart for some time and our church were seduced by the fanatical hotheads and we were to write not one or two, but many epistles—we would have little to no success. Our men (except for the strongest) would behave no different toward us than those who've allowed themselves to be seduced by the sectarians. They would sooner worship the Pope than obey our warnings or support our doctrine. No one could convince them that when they reject Christ they returned once again to the feeble and beggarly elements and to those rudiments that by nature are not divine. They would not tolerate that their teachers, who have seduced them, are committed to overthrowing the Gospel of Christ and perturbing not only people's consciences but also the entire church. They say, "The Lutherans don't hold the corner on wisdom; they're not the only ones who preach Christ; they're not the only ones who have the Holy Spirit or the gift of prophecy or the true knowledge of Scriptures. Our teachers are no less than theirs. No, they're even superior because they follow the leading of the Spirit and teach about spiritual topics." However, they've never tasted true theology but are stuck on the letter, and thus they have nothing else to teach but the catechism, faith, love, and these matters.

LECTURE 30: Friday, October 30

Thus (as I've frequently said), to fall from faith is rather easy but ominously dangerous. It is to fall from the highest heaven to the depths of hell's abyss. The fall is not as it may commonly appear, as it would in murders, adultery, and the like. However, it is nothing but Satanic, and it comes from the devil himself.[83] Those who have that kind of fall cannot be quickly restored but commonly will continue perversely and obstinately in their error. They end up right where they started, just as Christ, our Savior, testified when He said, "When the unclean spirit has gone out of a man, he passes through waterless places seeking rest; and finding none he says, 'I will return to my house from which I came.' And when he comes he finds it swept and put in order. Then he goes and brings seven other spirits more evil than himself, and they enter and dwell there; and the last state of that man becomes worse than the first" (Luke 11:24ff).

Paul then, perceived by revelation of the Holy Spirit the possible negative consequences that could arise in the minds of the Galatians. Although previously he had rebuked them as foolish and bewitched and so on, now, he sees that such stern rebukes would cause them to turn against him even more instead of turning back to him. Further, now Paul knew for sure that the false apostles were among them. The false teachers would take Paul's stern rebukes, which proceeded from his fatherly affection, and twist them around in a different light making this allegation: "Now you can clearly see who Paul is, the one you praise so much, as he really is and the spirit that leads him, for when he was with you, he treated you with such fatherly love but now in his absence, his letters arrive, but they show he's really a tyrant." Thus Paul feels very troubled and doesn't know what to say or write to them, for it is quite dangerous to defend your cause against absent accusers now that they have begun to despise him and allowed themselves to be convinced by others that his cause is worthless. Therefore, he is quite disconcerted, for he says shortly thereafter, "I am perplexed about you"—that is, I don't know what to do or how to deal with you.

VERSE 12. I plead with you, brothers and sisters, become like me, for I became like you [NIV].

These words need to be understood not with regards to doctrine but to the affections. Thus the meaning is not "be like me" so that you share my doctrinal thinking but that you love me as I love you. It's as if he said, "Perhaps I have rebuked you too harshly, excuse my harshness; don't judge my heart by my words, but judge my words according to the affection of my heart. My words seem stern, and my punishment severe, but my heart is loving and fatherly. Thus, oh Galatians, take my rebukes in the same way that I feel about you, for the topic compelled me to show you my harsh and severe side."

We could say the same thing about us. We correct harshly and our style of writing is vehement and stern, but what proceeds from our heart is not bitterness or envy or desire for reprisals against our adversaries. Instead, we care for you with

---

[83] *Neque humanus, ut lapsum in homicidium . . . sed Satanicus est.*

caring devotion and a concerned spirit. We neither hate the Papists nor wish evil on others who promote error or wish their destruction. Rather, we wish for them to return once again to the straight path and be saved together with us.

The teacher punishes the student, not to hurt him, but seeking to correct him. The rod is harsh but correction is necessary for the child, and the heart of the parent is loving and friendly. That is how the parent punishes the child, not to destroy him but to bring about his change and reform. Discipline is very painful for the child, but the father does not punish to destroy the child, he is not uncaring about his welfare, abandoning the child to perish. So to correct one's children is a sign of fatherly affection and is profitable for them. That is how, my Galatians, I've treated you. Then don't judge my rebukes as harsh and bitter but as profitable for you. "For the moment, all discipline seems painful rather than pleasant; later, it yields the peaceful fruit of righteousness to those who have been trained by it" (Hebrews 12:11). Thus I plead that the same affection I have for you, you will also have toward me. I carry you lovingly in my heart and wish you would do the same with me.

Therefore, he speaks to them softly and continues in the same way, to quiet their minds for they were quite agitated against him due to his harsh words. However, he does not take back his words. He certainly confesses that his words have been harsh. But it was necessary for him (he says) because he saw himself obligated to speak to them somewhat harshly and severely, but "I did it from a sincere and loving heart toward you." The doctor gives his patient the bitter medicine, not to hurt but to cure him. The doctor doesn't blame himself for the bitterness of his patient's medicine, but he blames the medicine itself, as well as the illness. Likewise, judge my harsh and severe rebukes.

VERSE 12. I plead with you, brothers and sisters . . . You did me no wrong [NIV].

He has called them disobedient to the truth. He has told them they have crucified Christ. Now, he pleads with them? It looks more like a very strong rebuke. However, and to the contrary, Paul says it's no rebuke at all but a burning plea. He's certainly right. It's the same as if he had said to them, "I confess that I have rebuked you with certain bitterness, but it's for your good and you will realize that these, my rebukes, are not rebukes at all but instead pleas and prayerful appeals." If a father likewise corrects his son, it's as if he said, "My son, I plead with you to be a good son etc." It certainly looks like discipline, but if you could see the father's heart, it is only a soft and passionate plea.

VERSE 12. You have done me no wrong.

It's as if he had said, "Why should I get upset with you or talk trash about you with bad intentions, since you have not offended me at all?" To which they reply, "But then, why do you say that we've become perverted, that we have abandoned your doctrine, that we are foolish and bewitched? These things testify that you do feel offended by us." He responds, "You have not harmed me, but only yourselves. Thus I am troubled, not because of something I've done but because of the love I have for you. Thus don't think that I've rebuked you with bad intentions, nor because I have bad feelings toward you. I have God as my witness that you have not caused me any harm. Instead, you have overwhelmed me with abundant benefits."

Having spoken to them gently, he prepares their minds to tolerate his fatherly discipline with the affection shown little children. This is like softening the wormwood[84] or putting honey and sugar to a bitter brew in order to sweeten it. That is how parents speak gently with their children after punishing them. They give them apples, pears, and other similar things. That is how children understand that their parents really love them and that they seek their well-being, in spite of the harsh discipline.

VERSES 13 and 14. You know that it was because of a physical infirmity that I first announced the gospel to you; though my condition put you to the test, you did not scorn or despise me, but welcomed me as an angel of God, as Christ Jesus [NRSV].

Now he declares the joys he had received from the Galatians. "The first benefit that I value, he said, is the best of them all, and it is this. When I first began to preach the Gospel among you, it was because of a weakness of the flesh and great temptations. However, you were not offended by the cross I carried. Instead, you were loving, kind, and offered me your friendship. Thus you were not offended by the weakness of my flesh, with my temptations and sufferings, even though I felt almost over-whelmed by them! But you loved me tenderly and received me as an angel of God, no, as Jesus Christ Himself." This is indeed a great compliment to the Galatians who received the Gospel from a man such as Paul, who was despised and afflicted everywhere he went, for wherever the Gospel was preached, Jews as well as Gentiles murmured and became furious with him, for all the powerful, wise, religious, and scholars, hated, persecuted, and blasphemed against Paul. Notwithstanding all that, the Galatians were not bothered in the least. They did not pay attention to this weakness, those temptations and dangers. No. Not only did they pay attention to this poor, despised, suffering, and afflicted Paul, but they also declared themselves to be his disciples and received him as an angel from God, yes, even as Jesus Christ Himself. This is a well-deserved compliment that points to a particular virtue of the Galatians. Indeed, it is a compliment that was not given to any of the other recipients of his other letters; it was given only to these Galatians.

---

[84] Of all herbs, it is probably the bitterest, although it is thought to have therapeutic and medicinal value.

Jerome and others among the ancient Fathers explain Paul's weakness of the flesh as some physical ailment or some lustful temptation.[85] These men lived during a time when the church was going through an apparent prosperous and peaceful era, without a cross or persecution. It was when the bishops began to hoard up wealth, esteem, and glory in the world. This was a time when many also governed as tyrants over their subjects, as testified by church history. Very few fulfilled their duties, and those who gave the appearances abandoned the doctrine of the Gospel and proclaimed their own decrees to the people. Well, when the daily task of the pastors and the bishops is not God's word but they put aside the sincere and pure preaching of the word, it is inevitable for them to fall into a false sense of security. In this condition, they are not fighting against temptations, they are not suffering for the cross and persecution because these always and inevitably follow when the word is preached in all its purity. Therefore, it was impossible for them to understand Paul. But by God's grace, we uphold a sound and sincere doctrine, which we also freely preach and teach. Thus we are forced to suffer the bitterness of hate, the afflictions, and persecutions from the devil and the world. On the outside, tyrants and sectarians with power and treachery harass us. On the inside, the terrors and fiery darts of the devil accost us. Were it not for these, we would also be in the dark; we would not understand Paul. That's how it has been in the past throughout the world, and these things are still unknown by the Papists, the fanatical spirits,[86] and other of our adversaries. Thus the gift of knowledge, interpretation of Scripture, and our own study, together with internal and external temptations open for us Paul's meaning and the meaning of Scriptures.

Thus Paul does not call this weakness of the flesh a physical ailment or identify it as the temptation of lust. Instead, it's the suffering of his affliction that he carried in his body, which he confronts by means of the virtue and power of the Spirit. But let it not seem as if we are twisting and perverting Paul's words. Listen to his own voice: "Therefore, I will boast all the more gladly about my weaknesses, so that Christ's power may rest on me. That is why, for Christ's sake, I delight in weaknesses, in insults, in hardships, in persecutions, in difficulties. For when I am weak, then I am strong" (2 Corinthians 12:9, 10, NIV). Further, he says, "I have worked much harder, been in prison more frequently, been flogged more severely, and been exposed to death again and again. Five times I received from the Jews the forty lashes minus one. Three times I was beaten with rods, once I was pelted with stones, three times I was shipwrecked, I spent a night and a day in the open sea" (2 Corinthians 11:23–25, NIV). He calls these afflictions that he suffered in his body "weakness of the flesh" and does not give them the name of a particular illness. It's as if he said, "When I preached the Gospel among you, I

---

[85] *tentatio libidinis.*

[86] *Papistis & fanaticis spiritibus.* Middleton's translation has "Papists and Anabaptists."

was oppressed with various temptations and afflictions. I was always at risk among Jews and Gentiles, as well as from the false brothers and sisters. I suffered hunger and want in everything. I was perceived as the worst scum[87] and filth of the world." He also talks about his weakness in many other texts, such as 1 Corinthians 4:2 and 2 Corinthians 4:9, 11, 12.

Then we see that when Paul talks about afflictions, he refers to the weaknesses of the flesh that he suffered in the flesh, as also suffered by all the other apostles, the prophets, and all the faithful. The power of Christ resided in him, which always reigned and triumphed for him, as he testifies in 2 Corinthians 12:10 with these words: "For when I am weak, then I am strong." Further, he says, "Therefore, I will boast all the more gladly about my weaknesses, so that Christ's power may rest on me" (2 Corinthians 12:9). Then also, in the second chapter, he says, "But thanks be to God, who always leads us in triumph in Christ" (2 Corinthians 2:14, NASB). It's as if he had said, "Indeed, the devil, the Jews, and the Gentiles roar with cruelty against us. Nonetheless, we persevere invincible against all their attacks and whether they like it or not, our doctrine will prevail and triumph." This was the power and the strength of Paul's spirit, but from within, he suffered the weakness and the captivity of the flesh.

Now this weakness of the flesh among the faithful is what offends reason most astonishingly. That is the reason Paul so highly compliments the Galatians, because they had not been perturbed either by this scandalous weakness or by that despised and repulsive cross they saw in him. Instead, they received him as an angel, even as Christ Himself. Christ Himself armed the faithful against this despised and repulsive cross in which He revealed Himself when He said, "Blessed is anyone who does not stumble on account of me" (Matthew 11:6). Indeed, it is a wonderful thing for those who have believed in Him to confess Him as Lord of all and Savior of the world, notwithstanding that they have heard that He was the most pitiful of all men—of all, the most despised, disgraced, and demeaned. Although for a short time he was despised and hated by all, condemned to death on a cross—even by His own people and particularly by those who considered themselves the very best, the wisest, and holier than the rest—it is worthy of great consideration that they didn't consider these repulsive traits. They overlooked them without condemning him at all but instead held this poverty-stricken Christ in great esteem, so highly mocked, spat upon, lashed, and crucified. They valued Him more than the riches of the wealthiest magnates, more powerful than all the strong, with all the crowns and scepters of all the kings and princes of the entire world. Thus Christ has every reason to call them "blessed" for they did not make a scandal out of Him.

Thus it was quite astonishing that the Galatians were not ashamed of such strong offense and those despicable ways of the cross they saw in Paul. Instead, they received

---

[87] κάθαρμα, περίψημα (scum, excrement you scrub off your sandals).

him as an angel and as Jesus Christ Himself. Further, just as Christ told His disciples to watch in temptation, so Paul said that the Galatians did not despise the temptations he carried in the flesh. Thus Paul has good reason to grant them so many compliments.

Well, Paul had not only temptations from the outside (which I already mentioned) but also internal and spiritual temptations, for example, Christ's temptations in the garden. Paul in 2 Corinthians 12:7 complains that he felt "the thorn [σκόλοψ (escolops)] in my flesh, a messenger of Satan, to torment me." By the way, I say this because the Papists translated it to the Latin as *stimulus carnis;* then they have explained this stimulus as harassment of fleshly lust. But in the Greek, σκολοψ (escolops) means a stinger or a pointy stake. Thus it was a spiritual temptation. Here, there's no contradiction, for this word qualifies the other word, flesh, saying, "I was given a thorn in my flesh." The Galatians and others who knew Paul well had often seen him in great depression, anguish, and distress.

Thus they[88] experienced not only physical temptations but also spiritual temptations. This is what Paul also confesses in 2 Corinthians 7:5: "Conflicts on the outside, fears within." Luke also says in the last chapter of Acts that Paul, having suffered several storms at sea as well as the affliction of his spirit, was comforted once again and recovered his strength when he saw the brothers who came from Rome and met with him in the market of Appius and the Three Taverns (Acts 28:15). In Philippians 2:27, he confesses that God had been merciful to him, for He had restored Epaphroditus, whose exhaustion had him at death's door; however, he was restored to health, avoiding grief upon grief. Thus in addition to conflicts without, the apostles also suffered great anguish, depression, and horrible distress.

However, why does Paul say that the Galatians did not despise him? It would seem they despised him when they abandoned his Gospel. Paul himself explains it: "When I preached the Gospel among you for the first time (he said), you did not behave like others who had been greatly offended by my weakness and temptations of the flesh, who did despise and reject me." Truth is, this repulsive and unattractive form of the cross soon offends man's reason. Reason judges as insane all those who, having these afflictions, try to comfort, aid, and care for others in need. Further, despite their distress, they boast of their great wealth—that is, of righteousness, power, and victory over sin, death, and every evil, as well as claiming to have joy, salvation, and eternal life. However, they suffer great physical needs, weakness, sadness, rejection, abuse, and even death itself (not by the crowd but at the hands of the highest civil and religious authorities,[89] who consider them as pure venom.) Those who kill them think they have rendered God the highest service. Thus when they offer others eternal treasures, while they themselves perish so mercilessly before the world, they are held as the laughingstock of the world. They are mocked and forced to hear, "Doctor, heal thyself." Therefore, the lament

---

[88] Luther is referring to the apostles in general. See the bottom of the paragraph.

[89] *in administracione politica et ecclesiastica.*

heard throughout the Psalms goes up: "But I am a worm, and no man . . . Be not far from me, for trouble is near, and there is none to help" (Psalm 22:11).

Therefore, it is a great tribute to the Galatians that they were not offended with Paul's weakness and temptations but received him as an angel of God, yes, as Christ Himself. Indeed, this is a great virtue that deserves a great tribute, particularly when pertaining to the apostles. But it is even greater and a true Christian virtue to welcome Paul in the condition he came before the Galatians. He was poor, weak, and abhorrent (as he, himself, says). Yet they received him as an angel from heaven and honored him as if he had been Christ himself and did not allow themselves to be offended by his great sufferings, since they were many and abundant. Thus with these words, he greatly praises the virtue of the Galatians and tells them he will never forget them and values them so highly that he desires for the entire world to know about them. However, even as he exalts so greatly their benefits and virtues, he tacitly shows how fully they loved him before the coming of the false apostles. That is why he urges them to continue as before and embrace him with no less love and respect as before. Here, it seems that the false apostles had taken on greater authority among the Galatians than Paul himself, for the Galatians, compelled by their authority, had given them greater preference than Paul, who before they had loved so much and received as an angel of God.

VERSE 15. What happened to this sense of being blessed you had?[90] [HCSB].

It's as if he had said, "Do you remember how happy you were? All the compliments and tributes you received?" This is the same expression we find in the song of the Virgin Mary: "Henceforth all generations will call me blessed" (Luke 1:48). The words "What happened to this sense of being blessed you had?" contain a certain passion. It's as if he said, "Not only were you blessed but you were blessed in everything and highly praised." He speaks like this to moderate and soften the acrimony of his bitter herbs—that is, of his harsh rebukes. He feared the Galatians had been greatly offended, since he knew in detail that the false apostles would slander him and scornfully would interpret his words, for such is the caliber and nature of these snakes. They will slander and pervert with evil intentions all the words that proceed from a simple and sincere heart, tearing away their proper sense and meaning. In this, they are astute craftsmen, way ahead of the astuteness and eloquence of the greatest speakers of all times. An evil spirit that bewitches them leads them. They are inflamed with a diabolical fury against the faithful and will do no less than give a false interpretation and wickedly twist their words and writings. Thus they are like the spider that sucks the venom of the flowers' sweet delights. But the poison proceeds not from the flowers but from their own venomous nature that turns into venom everything

---

[90] *quid erat beatitudo vestra?*

that is in itself good and right. Thus with these sweet and soft words, Paul attempts to prevent the false apostles from afterward taking some occasion to slander and pervert his words, much like this: "Paul mistreated you. He called you foolish, bewitched, disobedient to the truth, which is evidence that he does not desire your salvation but considers you worthy of Christ's condemnation and rejection."

VERSE 15. I can testify that, if you could have done so, you would have torn out your eyes and given them to me [NIV].

His praise to the Galatians may sound like an overstatement. With all courtesy, he says, "You not only cared for me and with all respect received me as an angel of God, but if necessary, you would have also gouged out your own eyes and given them to me." It is true that the Galatians put their lives on the line for him, since when they received Paul and gave him sustenance (to whom the world held as the most despised and accursed), they put their hands on the fire for him, receiving on their own heads the hate and indignation of both Gentiles and Jews.

So it is today. The name of Luther is most hated before the world. Anyone who dares praise me is a worse sinner than an idolater, blasphemer, perjurer, fornicator, adulterer, assassin, or thief. Thus the Galatians were well established in the doctrine and faith of Christ seeing that at such a great personal risk they received and provided for Paul, who was hated by the entire world. Otherwise, they would have never been able to bear that cruel hatred from the entire world.[91]

VERSE 16. Have I now become your enemy by telling you the truth? [NIV].

Here, he uncovers the reason he addresses the Galatians with great kindness. He suspects they already hold him as an enemy, since he had rebuked them so harshly. "I plead with you," he said. "Don't pay attention to these rebukes as an excuse to renounce the doctrine. That way you will realize that my intention was not to rebuke you but to teach you the truth. It is true and I confess that my epistle is harsh and severe. Yet it is with the same somber reason that I propose to call you back to the truth of the Gospel, from which you have fallen, and that you will abide in it. Therefore, don't relate this harshness and bitterness to your own persons but to the disease that you suffer. Do not judge me as an enemy when I rebuke you so severely, but think about me as your father, for if I did not love you so dearly as my children, knowing that you love me as well in the same way, I would not have rebuked you so severely.

---

[91] To illustrate the point that Paul came to the Galatians hated and rejected by Jews and Gentiles, Luther briefly refers to his own rejection and hatred by those close to him. It's as if he had wanted to say more about his own personal situation but relinquishes that line of thought to continue focusing on Paul and the Galatians.

"It is one's duty to freely admonish a friend if he takes a step in the wrong direction. When that happens, if the one who receives the rebuke has any wisdom at all, they will not be bothered for having been admonished with such kindness, speaking the truth; rather, he will thank the other. In general, one can see that in the world the truth stirs up hate and whoever speaks the truth becomes the enemy. But it should not be so between friends, even less among Christians. Thus seeing that it was out of love that I rebuked you, don't be offended with me, nor lose the truth, nor think that I am your enemy due to my fatherly rebukes; otherwise, treat them as coming from a friend." Paul says all these things to confirm what he had said before: "I plead with you, brothers and sisters, become like me, for I became like you. You did me no wrong."

VERSE 17. Those people are zealous to win you over, but for no good [NIV].

Here, he rebukes the flattery of the false apostles, for Satan attempts through his ministers, using well-camouflaged and armed subtleties, to deceive the simple minded. As Paul said, "By smooth talk and flattery they deceive the minds of naive people" (Romans 16:18). Well, first they make a grandiose protest that they want nothing more than to advance God's glory. Then they allege that the Spirit moves them, saying that the people feel abandoned or they are not being taught the truth in all its purity. From there, they dictate that they are the ones who teach the infallible truth so that through them the elect will be saved from error and come to the light and the knowledge of all the truth. Further, without any doubt, they promise salvation to those who receive their doctrine. Unless the faithful and alert pastors reject these voracious wolves, they will cause great harm to the church under the pretense of piety, for they come dressed as furry lambs, for the Galatians could have said, "Why do you come against our teachers with such invectiveness, seeing that all they have is our best interest? Everything they do is with pure zeal and love, this should not bother you." "True (he said), they have zeal for you, but it is a zeal that is worthless to you." *In this same way, today we are compelled to listen to the Sacramentarians who claim that due to our stubbornness we offend love and break up the peace among the churches, for we reject their doctrine of the Lord's Supper. It would be better, they say, that we would overlook it, that there is no danger at all in it. They claim that due to this one and only article of the doctrine (but it's not the primary) so many great discords and arguments should surge within the church. They argue that they do not dissent from us in any other article of the doctrine except in this one regarding the Lord's Supper. To which I respond, "Cursed be that love and agreement that is sealed and preserved at the cost of God's word!"*[92]

---

[92] *Maledicta sit caritas et Concordia, propter quam conservandam periclitatur verbum Dei.*

That is how the false apostles pretended to ardently love the Galatians and that they were moved toward them with a special divine zeal. Here, it must be observed that to have zeal for or to be jealous of refers to an offended love, or perhaps it could be said, to a pious covetousness. Elijah said, "I have been very jealous for the Lord, the God of hosts" (1 Kings 19:14, RSV). That is the kind of jealousy the husband has for his wife, the father for his son, brother toward his brother, because their love for the other is measureless. However, they hate their vices, and they take great pains to correct them. The false apostles pretended to have this kind of love for the Galatians. It's true that Paul admits that they had great zeal for the Galatians, but this zeal (he said) was not good. That is how these shadows and subtleties seduce the simple minded, for these tempters lead them to believe they have great zeal for them, since they appear to work so much for them. Thus Paul here admonishes us to distinguish between a zeal that's for the good and another that seeks evil. I have zeal for you (said Paul), just as they do. Now you judge which of our zeal is more helpful, mine or theirs, which one is pious and good, which one is vile and of the flesh. Thus don't let yourselves be so easily seduced by their zeal.

VERSE 17. Those people are zealous to win you over, but for no good. What they want is to alienate you from us, so that you may have zeal for them [NIV].

It's as if he had said, "Frankly, they have much zeal for you but that's because they want you to be zealous for them and thus reject me. If their zeal were indeed pious and sincere, then they would be more than happy for you to love me, and they would also love me. But they hate our doctrine and wish for its rejection altogether; they are eager to replace it with their doctrine. Well, to make this happen, they attempt through that zeal to tear them from my heart, make them hateful toward me so that when they finally hate me and my doctrine, you will shower them with your affection and zeal just for them, loving them and no one else so that you will not receive any other doctrine but theirs." Thus he raises suspicion regarding the false apostles among the Galatians, showing them that with those pious pretenses they are trying to deceive them. That's also how Christ our Savior warned us, saying, "Watch out for false prophets. They come to you in sheep's clothing, but inwardly they are ferocious wolves" (Matthew 7:15, NIV).

Paul suffered the same temptations as we do today. He felt tremendously upset at the way things had gone. Soon after the preaching of his divine and holy doctrine, he looked on as so many sects, commotions, overthrown kingdoms, changes in others, and many other similar events occurred that brought about infinite evils and hostilities. He was accused by all the Jews of being pernicious, stirring up sedition throughout his entire nation, and that he was the leader of the Nazarene sect. It's as if they had said, "This is a seditious and blasphemous individual. He preaches such things that not only would overthrow the Jewish nation (an excellent organization founded on God's laws) but he also pretends to abolish the Ten Commandments, God's religion and its ceremonies, and our priesthood and spread throughout the entire world this doctrine he calls the Gospel. However, from his teachings all kinds of evils have arisen: seditions, hostilities, and sects." In Philippi, he was also compelled to listen to the Gentiles who cried out against him, alleging that he stirred up trouble in the city and preached unlawful teachings impossible for them to accept (Acts 16:20, 21).

Jews as well as Gentiles attributed wars, strife, and sectarian struggles to Paul and the other apostles' doctrine. They were also held responsible for problems confronting civilian governments, such as tragedies and famines, for these reasons, they were persecuted; they were treated as a common plague and enemies of civilian peace and religion. However, the apostles did not surrender their commitment but with greater persistency preached and confessed Christ. They knew that it was better to obey God instead of men and that Christ should be preached even if the entire world were to be stirred up with commotions; neither would they allow one soul to be passed over or perish for lack of its preaching.

Undoubtedly that was a heavy burden for the apostles to bear, for they were not made of iron. They felt immense pain if the people with all their gifts were to perish, those for whom Paul had been willing to sacrifice even if torn from Christ in order to attain their salvation. They saw that great uprisings and changes in governments would result because of their doctrine. Further, they felt even more grief than death itself (especially Paul) when they realized that many sects would arise even from among them. Paul felt an enormous burden when he heard the news that the Corinthians were denying the resurrection of the dead; that the churches he had sown with his ministry were now in great upheaval; and now, that the Gospel had been overthrown by the false apostles and all Asia together with many great figures had revolted against his doctrine.

However, he knew that his doctrine was not the cause of these discords and sects, thus he was not discouraged. He did not abandon his calling but kept moving forward knowing that the Gospel he preached was the power of God unto salvation to all who believe. It didn't matter to him that Jews and Gentiles thought it was a foolish and offensive doctrine. He knew that those who are not ashamed by this word of the cross are blessed, whether they are teachers or hearers. Christ Himself said, "Blessed is anyone who does not stumble on account of me" (Matthew 11:6, NIV). However, he knew that those who judge this doctrine as foolish and heretical are under condemnation. Thus fully convinced[93] of his own doctrine, he said together with Christ regarding both the Jews and the Gentiles who were offended

---

[93] In his lecture (and in the Latin text), Luther used the Greek term πληροφορία, which means fully convinced or assured.

by his doctrine, "Leave them; they are blind guides. If the blind lead the blind, both will fall into a pit" (Matthew 15:14, NIV).

Today, we cannot help but hear the same that was said of Paul and the other apostles—that is, that the doctrine of the Gospel, which we profess, is the cause of many and great calamities, seditions, wars, sects, and countless crimes. Yes, today's problems are attributed to us.

What is obviously clear is that we don't teach heresy or wicked doctrine, but we preach the Gospel of Christ, that He is our Pontiff and Redeemer.[94] Further, our adversaries are constrained to admit this (if they confess the truth), that through our doctrine we have not given any cause for seditious uprisings, wars, or commotions. Instead, we have always taught honor and respect for the magistrates because God has so ordered it, neither are we the authors of crimes, but if the wicked commit crimes when they are offended by us, the fault is theirs and not ours. God has assigned to us the preaching of the doctrine of the Gospel, without paying attention to any offense against us. But since this, our doctrine, condemns the wicked and idolatrous doctrine of our adversaries, they feel provoked and stir up infighting among themselves. Even the scholars have said that these offenses would occur and should not be avoided, since they are inevitable.

Christ taught the Gospel without fearing the Jew's offenses. "Leave them alone," He said, "they are blind, leading the blind" (Matthew 15:14). The more the priests prohibited the apostles to preach in the name of Christ (whom they had crucified), the greater witness the apostles gave of that same Jesus; they testified that He is Lord and Christ and that everyone who invokes His name will be saved, that there is no other name given among men under heaven by whom we should be saved. In the same way, we proclaim Christ today, without a care for the wicked papal outcries and those of all our adversaries who cry out alleging that our doctrine is seditious and full of blasphemy and that it disturbs civilian governments, overthrows religions, teaches heresies, and, in brief, is the cause of all evil. The same was said of Christ and His apostles' preaching by the boastful and wicked Jews. Soon thereafter, the Romans came and destroyed their place as well as their nation, according to Christ's own prophecies. Therefore, let the enemies of the Gospel today take heed, lest they be overthrown by the same evils they themselves have prophesied.

They have gathered a heap of scandalous practices. For instance, that priests and monks should not marry, that no one should eat meat on Fridays, and many similar ones. But they don't think they offend at all with their wicked doctrine when they seduce and destroy countless souls; when by their evil example, they cause the weak to stumble; when they blaspheme and condemn the glorious Gospel of the Almighty God and persecute and kill those who study the sound doctrine. But they don't think they're stirring up any trouble. Instead, they think

---

[94] *Pontifex & redemptor noster.* Luther referred to Christ by the Latin term *Pontifex,* which at the time was reserved exclusively for the Roman pontiff, the Pope.

they are offering acceptable service and sacrifice to God. However, we have no recourse but to let them go on because "they are blind, leading the blind." "He that is unjust, let him be unjust still." But we, because we believe, will continue to speak and present the wonderful works of the Lord as long as we have breath and endure the persecutions of our adversaries until that time when Christ, our Pontiff and King, returns from heaven. Further, our hope is that He will soon return as a Judge bringing retribution on all those who do not obey the Gospel. Amen.

Then let not the faithful worry about absolutely anything, notwithstanding all these offenses alleged by the wicked, for they well know that what the devil hates the most is the pure doctrine of the Gospel. Thus he sets out to disfigure it with countless aggravations and thus tear it away from people's hearts forever. Before, when the church taught nothing else but the traditions of men, the devil would not attack with such fury, for as long as the strong man watched over his house, all his possessions were safe. But now, when the stronger man has come, who has defeated and tied the strong man and has ransacked his house, then he begins to attack unceasingly. These attacks are infallible signs that the doctrine we profess is from God. Keep in mind, as Job says in chapter 40, "the Behemoth[95] sleeps and hides secretly under the shadows of the reeds."[96] But now it is out and about, roaring like a lion, and ignites such whirlwind and dust devils that it is nothing but an obvious sign that he feels the power of our doctrine.

When Paul says, "Those people are zealous to win you over, but for no good," he shows in passing, the identity of the authors of the sects—that is, those jealous spirits who always overthrow the true doctrine and perturb the peace of the people. These are the ones that suddenly appear with a perverse zeal, they imagine they have a certain particular holiness, modesty, patience, and doctrine superior to all others and thus they think they are able to provide salvation for all people. They believe they teach profound and profitable matters, that they prepare better services and ceremonies than anyone else; they despise all others as if they were nothing next to them and they diminish all other authority and corrupt teachings that have been taught with all purity. The false apostles had this type of wicked and perverse zeal, founding sects, not only in Galatia but everywhere Paul and the other apostles had preached. In their wake, countless crime and astonishing scandals suddenly appeared. "For the devil [as Christ said] is a liar and a murderer." Thus his only intention is to distress the consciences of people with false doctrine and spark commotions, seditions, wars, and all kinds of mischief.

Today in Germany there are many who are possessed with this kind of zeal. They pretend great religiosity, modesty, doctrine, and patience. However, in their deeds, they are all rapacious wolves; with their hypocrisy, they seek nothing else but to discredit us; they warn that no other doctrine should be accepted save theirs

---

[95] In the Latin text, Luther used the Hebrew for "Behemoth": בְּהֵמוֹת.

[96] Luther's translation from Hebrew into Latin.

alone. Now, since these men have such a great opinion of themselves and despise the rest, the only thing that can come out of that is horrible dissensions, sects, divisions, and seditions. But what should we do? No amount of prohibitions could stop it. Not even Paul, in his own time, was able to contain it. However, he succeeded in winning back some who heeded his warnings. In the same way, I hope we have been able to rescue some from the errors of the fanatics.

VERSE 18. It is fine to be zealous, provided the purpose is good, and to be so always, not just when I am with you [NIV].

It's as if he said, "I praise you for this, for you were zealous for me without bounds when I preached the Gospel in the weakness of my flesh. Now that I am absent, you should have the same loving affection toward me, as if I had never left, for if I am absent in body, you nonetheless have my doctrine. You should always retain it and safeguard it, seeing that through it you received the Holy Spirit. Keep this thought present among you, that when you have my doctrine Paul will always be present with you. Thus I don't rebuke you for zeal that you have. Instead, I praise you for it, for it is fervor from God or from the Spirit and not from the flesh." Well, the zeal of the Spirit is always good, for it is an intense zeal to do something good, and thus it is not the zeal of the flesh. That is why he praises the devotion of the Galatians, for he seeks to soothe their emotions, hoping that they will patiently accept his discipline. It's as if he had said, "Accept my discipline's good side, for it does not come from my annoyance but from a sad heart that is eager for your salvation." This is a living example as to how to teach all ministers to care for their flock and to watch over their every word so that whether it's given with rebuke, affection, or by pleading, they may retain their sheep in the sound doctrine and abandon their crafty seducers and false teachers.

LECTURE 31: Saturday, October 31

VERSE 19. My children, for whom I am again in labor until Christ be formed in you! [NABRE].

He has this rhetorical principle in mind, that soft and tender words will soothe the mood of the Galatians. These are sweet terms when he seems to exaggerate calling them "my little children." Every word is calculated to move their affection and endear himself to them with kindness.

When he says, "For whom I am again in labor," it is to be understood as an allegory, for the apostles take the place of parents as well as teachers, regarding their position and calling, for in the same way as the parents give shape and form the body, they also shape the mind. Well, the form of the Christian mind is faith, or that confidence of the heart that grasps on to Christ and takes hold of Him and nothing else! That heart that has conformed to this excellent confidence or assurance, that on account of Christ we are declared righteous, has Christ's true form.[97] This form is granted through the ministry of the word, as it says in 1 Corinthians 4:15, "For in Christ Jesus I became your father through the gospel"—that is, in spirit so that you may know Christ and believe in Him. Also in 2 Corinthians 3, it says, "You are a letter from Christ, the result of our ministry, written not with ink but with the Spirit of the living God, not on tablets of stone but on tablets of human hearts" (2 Corinthians 3:3, NIV), for the word emerges from the mouth of the apostle or the minister and enters the heart of the hearer. The Holy Spirit becomes present there and engraves the word in the heart, and the heart consents to it. Therefore, every faithful teacher is a father that inseminates and goes on to form the true figure in the mind of the Christian, through the ministry of the word.

Further, he relates these words, "For whom I am again in labor," to the false apostles. It's as if he had said, "I fathered you as it should be, through the Gospel. But these corrupt men have given you new eyesight in your hearts, but it is no longer Christ's but Moses'.[98] Your confidence no longer rests upon Christ but upon the works of the law." This is not Christ's true form but that of a stranger and totally diabolical. Paul does not say, "For whom I am in labor pains until my semblance is formed in you, but until Christ be formed in you"—that is, I suffer in labor pains until you once again may receive the form and the semblance of Christ and not Paul's. With these words, he once again rebukes the false apostles, for they had abolished Christ's form in the hearts of the believers and had designed for them another form, their own, as he says in chapter 6, "They want you to be circumcised that they may boast about your circumcision in the flesh" (Galatians 6:13, NIV).

He also speaks of this image of Christ in Colossians 3:10: "[You] have put on the new self, which is being renewed in knowledge in the image of its Creator" (NIV). Thus Paul attempts to repair the form of Christ[99] among the Galatians that had been disfigured and perverted by the false apostles. That divine image of Christ is this: to have one's sentiments, understanding, and will conform to God's will, whose thought and will are the forgiveness of our sins and the granting of eternal life through Jesus Christ. He has sent His Son into the world to be the sacrifice for our sins, indeed, those of the entire world and that through Him we are reconciled to God and acknowledge that we are His sons and He is our merciful Father. Those who believe this have the divine likeness—that is, they think as God thinks in all things. Thus at the very heart of our affections, we have the same image in our minds as that of God or Christ. According to Paul, this is what

---

[97] *propter Christum simus justi, habet veram formam Christi.*

[98] *finxerunt novam faciem in corde vestro, non Christi, sed Mosi.*

[99] *reparare formam Christi;* first edition, *imaginem dei seu Christi.*

it means to be renewed in the spirit of our minds and to put on the new man who is created according to God (Ephesians 4:23, 24).

Thus he says he suffers with labor pains once again for the Galatians. However, his struggle is not to stamp the figure of the apostle on the children or for them to look like Paul, Cephas, and others but to resemble another Father—that is, Christ. He says, I will form Him in you so that you will have the same mind that was in Christ. In brief, "I suffer for you"—that is, I work tirelessly to call you back to the faith you had before that which you have lost, having been deceived by the trickery and subtleties of the false apostles and having gone back to the law and works. Therefore, now, once again, I need to take great pains to have you return from the law to faith in Christ. This is what he calls to suffer with birth pangs.

VERSE 20. How I wish I could be with you now and change my tone [NIV].

These are the true concerns of an apostle. A common proverb says that "a letter is like a dead messenger,"[100] for it can't deliver more than it carries. There's no epistle or letter ever written so thoroughly that could still say something more. Circumstances vary. Times, places, people, customs, and affections vary; thus a letter cannot express all these completely. Therefore, the reader reacts in different ways. One will feel sad and the other joy according to each one's disposition. If something is said too harshly, or untimely, the live speaker is able to explain, soften, or correct what's been said. Thus the apostle wishes to be with them to soften and change his tone according to what he would see is necessary depending on the reactions of his hearers, for if he could see that some are too distressed, he could soften his words to not discourage them with more negativity. On the contrary, if he could see that some are too arrogant, he could rebuke them harshly, for they could become too confident and careless.

That is why he could not be sure how to deal with them through letters, since he was absent. It's as if he said, "If my epistle is too harsh, I'm afraid I'll offend even more instead of correcting some of you." Further, "If I am too soft on you, it will have no effect on the perverse and stubborn, for dead letters with their words cannot give more than what they already contain. On the contrary, the voice of a live person, compared to an epistle, is altogether regal. It can add or reduce, it can adapt to all kinds of feelings, times, places, and peoples. In brief, it would be well if my letters would convert you to return from the law to faith in Christ, but I'm afraid I won't be able to achieve that with my dead letters. However, if I were with you, I could change my tone, I would be able to harshly rebuke the obstinate and comfort the weak with sweet and loving words according to the occasion."

---

[100] *epistolam mortuum nuncio.*

VERSE 20. I am perplexed about you.

In other words, "I am troubled in my spirit and I don't know how to present myself to you in my letters." Here is a vivid description of a true apostle's affection. He leaves no stone unturned. He rebukes the Galatians, he pleads with them, he speaks softly to them, praises their faith, making all efforts to try to have them return to the truth of the Gospel and free them from the traps of the false apostles. These are passionate words that proceed from a heart moved and inflamed with a burning zeal and thus should be noted carefully.

VERSE 21. Tell me, you who want to be under the law, are you not aware of what the law says?

Paul didn't want to write anymore and would have concluded his epistle here. He preferred to be present among the Galatians and talk to them in person. But he felt greatly perplexed and giving this matter the attention it deserved takes hold of this allegory that has come to mind. People delighted in allegories and parables. Christ Himself used them at times. They are, as it were, word paintings that present matters as if drawn before simple people's eyes. Thus they greatly move and persuade, especially among the simple and innocent. Thus first he moves the Galatians with words and arguments. Second, he paints the issue before their eyes with this good allegory.

Paul was a marvelous craftsman of allegories. He tends to relate them to the doctrine of faith, grace, and Christ but not regarding law and works, as did Origen and Jerome. They deserve rebuke because they altered the simple words of Scripture into allegories that didn't go anywhere, didn't correspond or make any sense at all. Thus the use of allegories tends to be quite risky. Unless one has a perfect knowledge of the Christian doctrine, allegories cannot be properly used.

However, why does Paul quote the book of Genesis from which he extracts the allegory of Ishmael and Isaac and refers to it as "the law"? However, this book does not contain anything regarding the law and especially the passage that he cites does not talk about any law but instead contains a story obviously about Abraham's two sons? Paul tends to call the first book of Moses "the law," according to the Jewish custom. This book does not contain any law at all except the law of circumcision. However, its main teaching is about faith and testifies that the patriarchs pleased God with their faith. Notwithstanding, the Jews, due to the law of the circumcision it contains, called the book of Genesis together with the other books of Moses "the law." Paul did the same, since he was a Jew. Further, Christ Himself includes the Psalms under the name of the law and not just the books of Moses, as in this text: "They hated me without a cause" (John 15:25; cf. Psalm 35:19).

VERSES 22–23. For it is written that Abraham had two sons, one by the slave woman and the other by the free woman. His son by the slave woman was born according to the flesh, but his son by the free woman was born as the result of a divine promise. [NIV].

It's as if he had said, "You abandoned grace, faith, and Christ and defected back to the law. Thus since you have decided to go back to the law, and through it you will make yourselves wise, then I will talk to you about the law." I plead with you to take the law into account. You will see that Abraham had two sons, Ishmael from Hagar and Isaac from Sara. Both children truly came from Abraham. Ishmael was just as truly a son of Abraham as was Isaac, for both came from one father, from one flesh, and from the same seed. So what was the difference? Paul says, the difference is not in that one's mother was free and the other a slave (although it fits the allegory). Instead, Ishmael who was born from the slave was born according to the flesh—that is, without the promise and God's word. However, Isaac was born not only from the free but also according to the promise. Isaac was also physically from Abraham's seed just as Ishmael. I concede that both were sons of the same father. However, there is a difference, for although Isaac was also born from Abraham's flesh, when God promised Isaac, God also gave him a name. Paul was the only one who had noticed this difference, which he had seen in the following passage from Genesis.

The way that Hagar got pregnant and conceived Ishmael was not through God's word, which predicted the future, but because Sara permitted Abraham to come into her servant Hagar. Sarah, since she was infertile had given her over to Abraham as wife, as it says in the book of Genesis. Sara had heard that Abraham through God's promise would have seed in his body, and she hoped to be the mother of that seed. But having waited for the promise for so many years with great anguish of spirit and seeing that the promise had been delayed, her hopes were dashed![101] Therefore, this holy woman, renounces her place of honor beside her husband, and yields it to her slave. She does not allow her husband to marry another woman from her own family but hands him over in marriage to her slave so that through her she may build her future. That's what is stated in the story: "Now Sarai, Abram's wife, had borne him no children. But she had an Egyptian slave named Hagar; so she said to Abram, 'The Lord has kept me from having children. Go, sleep with my slave; perhaps I can build a family through her'" (Genesis 16:1–2). This was a very humiliating for Sara, to feel pressured to lower herself like that. In a certain way, she assumed responsibility for that temptation and trial of her faith, for she thought like this: "God cannot lie, what He promised my husband, He will indeed fulfill. But perhaps God does not wish for me to be the mother of

---

[101] *se spe sua frustratam esse.*

that seed. I will not be offended if Hagar bears that honor; that is why I will allow my husband to go in to her, for perhaps through her, I will build my family."

Therefore, Ishmael is born without the word, just at Sara's request. There's no word from God that grants the command to accomplish the act, nor is a son promised. Instead, everything takes place due to Sara's "perhaps." "Perhaps," she says, "I will have children through her." Abraham had not received any word from God regarding the time when Sara would bear the promised child. The only word had been Sara's "perhaps." Thus it is evident that Ishmael was a son of Abraham only according to the flesh,[102] without the word. Thus he was born out of a "perhaps," a child that ordinarily is expected and born, as any other child. Paul looked at this carefully and does well to take it into account.

In Romans 9, he promotes the same argument he repeats here and presents an allegory with the powerful conclusion that not all Abraham's children are God's children. He says that Abraham had two types of sons. Some are born according to his flesh and blood. However, the word and God's promise came before, as in Isaac. Others are born without the promise, as in Ishmael. Therefore, the children according to the flesh, he says, are not the children of God but only the children of the promise. With this argument, he powerfully shuts the mouths of the boastful Jews, who gloried that they were of the seed of Abraham and thus his children. Christ said the same in Matthew 3 and John 8. It's as if he had said, "Your affirmations or deductions are not correct when you say, 'I am of the seed of Abraham, therefore, I am a child of God,' 'Esau is the firstborn, and thus he is the heir.'" It is not so; instead, it's the other way around. Those who wish to be children of Abraham will not be considered as such just because of their natural birth, but they who have believe the promise are the true sons of Abraham and, in consequence, of God.

Therefore, since God did not promise Ishmael to Abraham, he is a child only according to the flesh and not according to the promise. That's because he was born from a "perhaps," as any other child, for there is no mother who may know if she will ever have a child or when she is pregnant if the child will be a boy or girl. However, Isaac was explicitly assigned a name: "Sara, your wife," the angel said to Abraham, "will give birth to a son, and you shall call his name Isaac." Here, both the son and the mother are explicitly named (Genesis 17:9). However, Sarah dispossessed herself of her maternity rights and suffered being despised by Hagar (Genesis 16). However, God restored her honor and she became the mother of the promised son.

---

[102] Today Luther might have written, "Ishmael was just Abraham's biological son."

VERSE 24. Now this is an allegory.[103]

In theology, allegories do not carry a great deal of persuasive power. However, they are used as paintings; they beautify and help in the presentation of the topic. If Paul had not previously confirmed the righteousness of faith against the righteousness of works utilizing strong and conclusive arguments, this allegory would have hardly served any purpose at all. But since he had already strengthened his cause previously with invincible arguments, taken from experience, from Abraham's example, from the testimony of Scripture, and from similar matters, now at the end of his debate, he adds an allegory but only when a good foundation has been laid and the matter proven to great depths, for as a painting is an ornament to decorate and beautify a home already built so an allegory is a light that shines on the topic that already has been proven and confirmed.

VERSES 24–25. Now this is an allegory: these women are two covenants. One is from Mount Sinai, bearing children for slavery; she is Hagar. Now Hagar is Mount Sinai in Arabia; she corresponds to the present Jerusalem, for she is in slavery with her children.

Abraham is a figure of God, who has two sons—that is, two types of people represented by Ishmael and Isaac. These two are born through Hagar and Sara, who represent the two covenants, the Old and the New. The Old is from Mount Sinai, which engenders slavery, which is Hagar. The Arabs in their language give the name of Hagar to the same mount the Jews call Sinai (which seems to have that name due to its many thorns and thistles). Ptolemy and the Greek scholars witness to this in their comments. In the same way, there is a diversity of names given to the many mountains, according to the diversity of nations. Thus the mountain that Moses called Hermon, the Sidonians called it Sirion, and the Amorites called it Senir.

All this is beautifully appropriate! Mount Sinai in the Arabic language means female servant, and I believe that the similarity of this name gave Paul light and occasion to present this allegory. Just as Hagar the slave gave Abraham a child, not an heir but a slave, so also Mount Sinai is an allegory of Hagar, that gave God a son—that is, a people in the flesh. Further, just as Abraham was the true father of Ishmael, so also the people of Israel had the true God for Father who gave them His law, His decrees, His religion, true service, and the temple, as it says in Psalm 147:19, "He has revealed his word to Jacob, his laws and decrees to Israel" [NIV]. However, this was the only difference: Ishmael was born from the slave according to the flesh—that is, without the promise—and thus could not be the heir. Thus the mystical Hagar—that is, Mount Sinai where the law was given and where the Old Covenant was ordered—gave birth to a people for God (in the allegory Abraham

---

[103] *per Allegoriam.*

represents God) but without the promise, for the promises regarding Christ, the giver of all blessing, and regarding freedom from the curse of the law, sin, and death, as well as regarding the freely given remission of sins and righteousness and eternal life are not added to the law because the law says, "Keep my decrees and laws, for the person who obeys them will live by them" (Leviticus 18:5, NIV).

Therefore, the promises of the law are conditional, they promise life, but are not freely given; they are only for those who fulfill the law. Thus they leave uncertainty in the minds of the people, for there is no human being who fulfills the law. But the promises of the New Covenant neither attach any conditions, nor require anything from us, nor depend on our virtue as a condition but bring to us freely given forgiveness of sins, grace, righteousness, and eternal life on account of Christ, as I've said elsewhere more fully.

Thus the law, or the Old Covenant, contains only conditional promises, for it always has conditional attachments such as these: "If you obey my voice, if you keep my ordinances, if you walk in my ways, you shall be my people, etc." The Jews, without taking note of it, grasped onto these conditional promises as if they had been absolute and without any conditions attached. They thought that God would never revoke them but would be forced to fulfill them. Therefore, when they heard the prophets predicting the destruction of the city of Jerusalem, of the appointed time, of the kingdom and the priesthood (who could have well discerned between the material promises of the law and the spiritual promises regarding Christ and his kingdom), they persecuted and killed them as heretics and blasphemers of God. They could not see that this condition was attached: "If you keep my commandments, it will go well for you."

Thus Hagar, the servant, gives birth to a slave. That is why Ishmael is not the heir. Although by nature he is a son of Abraham, he continues as a slave. What does he lack? The promise and the blessing of the word. Thus the law is given on Mount Sinai, yes, the Arabs call it Hagar, but it only gives birth to slaves. But the promise given regarding Christ did not have the law attached as a condition. Thus, Oh Galatians, if you abandon the promise and faith, you will fall once again into the law and works, you will always continue as slaves—that is, you will never be free from sin and death but will always live under the curse of the law, for Hagar does not conceive the seed of the promise with her heirs—that is, the law does not justify, it does not bring the adoption and the inheritance. Instead, it gets in the way of the inheritance and stirs up wrath![104]

---

[104] *lex non justificat, non affert filiationem et hereditatem, sed potius eam impedit et iram efficit.*

VERSE 25. Now Hagar is Mount Sinai in Arabia; she corresponds to the present Jerusalem, for she is in slavery with her children.

This is a marvelous allegory. Just as Paul moments before had connected Hagar with Sinai, now, he would have greatly desired to connect Sara with Jerusalem. However, he doesn't dare; besides, he could not. Instead, he sees himself constrained to connect Jerusalem with Mount Sinai, for he writes, "Now Hagar is Mount Sinai in Arabia, which hill is joined to it that is now Jerusalem, for she is in slavery with her children" (RSV, WYC). It is true that there is a mountain range that extends from Arabia Petrea to Cadesh-barnea of the Jews. Then he says that the city that is now Jerusalem—that is, this earthly and temporary Jerusalem is not Sara. Rather, it belongs to Hagar, for there she reigns as queen. Within the city is the law conceiving children into slavery; there, you will find the worship and ceremonies, the temple, the kingdom, the priesthood, and all else that was ordered in Sinai by the mother, who is the law. Nothing else takes place in Jerusalem. That is why he related her to Sinai and summarized it in just one word: "Sinai," or Hagar.

To handle this allegory in such a manner seems to me way too presumptuous. I would have preferred for him to call Sara "Jerusalem" or the "New Covenant," since that's where the preaching of the Gospel first began, that's where the outpouring of the Holy Spirit took place and the people of the New Covenant were born. Had he given the allegory such an interpretation, I would have thought him to be right on the mark. But it is not in man's hands to use allegories as he pleases, for even a very pious appearance soon deceives the heart and causes it to err. Who would not have thought it was more than adequate to call Sinai "Hagar" and Jerusalem "Sara"? It is true that Paul relates Jerusalem to Sara but not this earthly Jerusalem, which he simply connects to Hagar. Instead, he connects Sara to that spiritual and heavenly Jerusalem where no law reigns at all, nor will you find the people of the flesh dwelling there, for they dwell in that other Jerusalem that continues in slavery with her children. But in the spiritual Jerusalem, the promise reigns and that's where you will find a free and spiritual people.

For the law to be fully abolished, together with its entire kingdom as established in Hagar, God permitted the horrible destruction of the earthly Jerusalem together with all its ornaments, the temple, the ceremonies, and everything else. Well, although the New Covenant began there and from there it has dispersed throughout the world, the city belongs to Hagar. That is the city of the law, the ceremonies, and the priesthood instituted by Moses. In summary, Hagar the slave conceived it and thus she is in captivity with her children—that is, she walks in the works of the law and will never attain to freedom of the spirit. It will continually remain under the law, sin, a sinful conscience, God's wrath and judgment, and the sentence of death and hell. True, it enjoys freedom according to the flesh for it has an earthly kingdom; it has its magistrates, wealth, goods, and similar things. But we are talking about freedom of the spirit where we are dead to the law, sin, and death and live and reign in grace, the forgiveness of sins, righteousness, and eternal life. The earthly Jerusalem cannot obtain any of this, thus it remains with Hagar.

VERSE 26. But the Jerusalem that is above is free, and she is our mother [NIV].

He says that this earthly Jerusalem, the one below, which has the rules and ordinances of the law, is Hagar and dwells in slavery with her children—that is, it has not been delivered from the law, sin, and death. But the Jerusalem above—that is, the spiritual Jerusalem—is Sara (although Paul does not add Sara's proper name but gives her another name, "the free [woman]"). She conceives us in freedom and not in slavery like Hagar. Well then, this heavenly Jerusalem that is above, is the church—that is, the faithful scattered throughout the world, who have the one and the same Gospel, one same faith in Christ, the same Holy Spirit, and the same Sacraments.

Therefore, I do not relate this word *above,* αναγωγικός (anagogicós), to the church triumphant (as the scholastics call her) in heaven but to the church militant here on earth, for it is said of the faithful that their life is in heaven, "Our πολίτευμα [citizenship] is in heaven" (Philippians 3:20), but not as a location but in the believing Christian who grasps on to those priceless, heavenly, and eternal gifts that are in heaven: "Who has blessed us in the heavenly realms with every spiritual blessing in Christ" (Ephesians 1:3). Thus we should differentiate between the heavenly or spiritual blessings and the earthly. The earthly blessing is to have a good civilian and economic government[105] and to have children, peace, wealth, fruits of the land, and other bodily comforts. But the heavenly blessing is to have been freed from the law, sin, and death; to be justified and reborn to life; to have peace with God; to have a faithful heart, a joyous conscience, and spiritual comfort; to know Jesus Christ; to have the prophecy and revelation of Scriptures; to have the gift of the Holy Spirit and rejoice in God; and more. These are the heavenly blessings that Christ has given to the church.

Thus the Jerusalem αναγωγικός (above)—that is, the heavenly—is the church now in the world; it is not our country in the future life. Neither is it the church triumphant as the illiterate and bogus scholars imagine, who teach that the Scriptures have four meanings: the literal, the moral, the allegorical, and the symbolic.[106] They have foolishly interpreted almost all the words of Scripture according to these meanings. According to them, the word *Jerusalem* literally would indicate the city with that name; morally, a pure conscience; allegorically, the church militant; symbolically, the heavenly city or the church triumphant. With these foolish and frivolous fables, they have torn Scriptures to pieces in so many diverse meanings that impoverished minds could not receive any doctrine at all with any certainty.

---

[105] *bonam politiam et oeconomiam.*

[106] *Literalem, Tropologium, Allegoricum et Anagogicum.*

But here, Paul says that the ancient and earthly Jerusalem belongs to Hagar and is in slavery with her children and has been totally abolished. However, the new and heavenly Jerusalem is a queen that joyously delights in her freedom. God has designated her so that on earth and not in heaven she will be a mother to us all by whom we have been conceived and, even so conceived from day to day. Thus it is necessary that she, our mother, belong on earth among men, just like her offspring. Nonetheless, she conceives by the Holy Spirit through the ministry of the word and the Sacraments and not according to the flesh.

I say this so that regarding this topic we will not get off track with musings about the hereafter but so that we may know that Paul places the Jerusalem above in contrast with the earthly Jerusalem—not physically, but spiritually, for there is a distinction between spiritual matters and those that are bodily or earthly. Spiritual things belong above, but the earthly belong below. The Jerusalem above is distinguished from the fleshly and passing Jerusalem, which is below, not in location (as I've said) but spiritually, for this spiritual Jerusalem that had its beginning in the earthly Jerusalem has no place it calls its own as the other has, which is in Judea. Instead, it is scattered all over the world and could well be found in Babylon, Turkey, Tartary, Scythia, Judea, Italy, Germany or in the islands of the sea, in the mountains and valleys, and throughout the world wherever men and women have the Gospel and believed in Jesus Christ.

Sara (or Jerusalem) is our mother in freedom. She is the church itself, the wife of Christ, from whom we have all been born. This mother unceasingly conceives children to the end of the world, if she preaches and proclaims the Gospel, for that is what it means to conceive. In the following way, we are all delivered from the curse of the law, sin, death, and all evil through Jesus Christ but not through the law nor works. Therefore, the Jerusalem above—that is, the church—is not subject to the law or works. Instead, she is a mother who lives in freedom without the law, without sin, and without death. Well then, as the mother, so are the children she conceives.

Thus this beautiful allegory teaches that the church should do nothing else but preach and teach the Gospel in truth and sincerity and through these means it should conceive offspring. That is how all of us are parents and children from each other, for we are generated from among ourselves. I am conceived by another through the Gospel and then I conceive another, who will conceive another, and this conceiving will go on to the end of the world. But when I talk about conceiving, I am not talking about Hagar the slave, who conceives her slaves through the law, but of Sarah the free, who conceives heirs without the law and without works or human efforts. Since Isaac is the heir and not Ishmael (although Abraham fathered both), Isaac had the inheritance through the word of the promise: "Your wife Sarah will bear you a son, and you will call him Isaac" (Genesis 17:19). Sara understood this quite well for she said, "Get rid of that slave woman and her son" (Genesis 21:10, ERV); Paul also quotes these words. Thus just as Isaac has his father's inheritance only through the word and his birth, without the law and without works, in the same way, we are born the true heirs of the promise from that free woman Sara—that is, the church—through the Gospel. She instructs us, nourishes us, and carries us in her womb, on her lap, in her arms. She comforts us and molds us to the image of Christ so that we may present everyone perfect in Him. Thus all things are fulfilled through the ministry of the word. Therefore, the function of the woman living in freedom is to conceive children to God through her husband, without ceasing and without end—that is, those children who are sure they are justified by faith and not through the law.[107]

VERSE 27. It is written, "Be glad, woman, you who have never had children. Shout for joy and cry out loud, you who have never had labor pains. The woman who is all alone has more children than the woman who has a husband." (Isaiah 54:1) [NIRV].

Paul here refers to Isaiah the prophet, completing the allegory. He says, "It is written that the mother who has many children and has a husband will get sick and die. But the infertile woman who has no children will have children in abundance." Ana in her song takes up the same theme, from which Isaiah took his prophecy: "The bows of strong soldiers break, and weak people become strong. People who had plenty of food in the past must now work to get food. But those who were hungry in the past now grow fat on food. The woman who was not able to have children now has seven children. But the woman who had many children is sad because her children are gone" (1 Kings 2; 1 Samuel 2:4–5, ERV). This is something wonderful, he says, "The fertile will become infertile, and the infertile, fertile. Further, those who before were strong, full, wealthy, glorious, righteous, and blessed will become weak, hungry, poor, despised sinners, subject to death and condemnation. But on the contrary, the weak and hungry, will become strong and satisfied."

By means of this allegory from the prophet Isaiah, the apostle shows the difference between Hagar and Sara—that is, between the synagogue and the church or between the law and the Gospel. The law is the husband of the fertile woman, or the synagogue, that conceives many children. Because throughout human history, not only the foolish but also the wisest and the greatest (i.e., all humanity except for the free woman's children) cannot see or know any other righteousness except the righteousness of the law, much less will they care to consider a more excellent righteousness. Therefore, they regard themselves righteous if they keep the law and to all appearances perform its works. *Further, when I use this word* law, *I include all law, human and divine.*

Well then, although these may yield fruit, have many disciples, and shine with the righteousness and glorious works of the law, nonetheless they are not

---

[107] *tales filios, qui fide, non lege norunt se justificari.*

free, but slaves, for they are Hagar's children who are conceived into slavery. Well, if they are slaves, they cannot participate in the inheritance but will be cast out of the house, for the servants do not stay in the house forever. Yes, they have been cast out of the kingdom of grace and liberty: "He who does not believe is condemned already." Thus they remain under the curse of the law, under sin and death, under the power of the devil, and under God's wrath and judgment.

Well, if the moral law itself, or God's Ten Commandments, cannot do anything else but conceive slaves—that is, it cannot justify but only intimidate, accuse, condemn, and plunge people's consciences into despair, how then, pray tell me, will all men's laws, or the Pope's laws, justify, which are nothing but doctrines of devils? Therefore, all who teach and put forward the traditions of men, or God's law, as necessary to obtain righteousness before God, do nothing else but give birth to slaves! Notwithstanding all this, such teachers are counted among the very best; they earn the favor of the world and are the most fertile mothers, for they acquire countless disciples. Why? It is because human reason cannot understand what is faith or true devotion and thus it rejects and despises these. It is naturally addicted[108] to superstition and hypocrisy—that is, to the righteousness of works. Well, since this righteousness shines and flourishes everywhere, it is a most powerful empress over the entire world. Thus those who teach the righteousness of the works of the law give birth to many children. To all appearances, they are free and display a glorious show of excellent virtues, but in their conscience, they are all tied up as slaves of sin. Thus they must be thrown out of the house into condemnation.

On the contrary, Sara the free—that is, the true church—appears infertile, for the Gospel which is the word of the cross and affliction preached by the church, does not shine with as much brilliance as the doctrine of law and works; thus it does not have as many following disciples. Further, she has been labeled with the tag that she forbids good works; that she makes believers complacent, lazy, and careless; that she stirs up heresies and uprisings; and that she is the cause of all mischief! Therefore, she cannot brag about bringing success or prosperity. Instead, to all appearances, she is infertile, desolate, and a lost cause. Thus the wicked are quite convinced that the church and its doctrine will not last much longer. The Jews were confident that the church planted by the apostles would be overthrown and gave it the odious name of "sect." Thus they spoke with Paul like this in Acts 28:22: "For with regard to this sect we know that everywhere it is spoken against." In the same way, how often (pray tell me) have not our adversaries been left disappointed when some pointed to the occasion and others to the time when we would certainly be destroyed? Christ and His disciples were oppressed, but after His death, the doctrine of the Gospel scattered further than during His days. In the same way,

---

[108] Luther used the Latin *afficitur*, which means "influenced, affected, afflicted, or weakened." The closest modern English term to encompass these meanings could well be *addicted*.

our adversaries today may oppress us, but the word of God remains forever. Then, however much the church might seem infertile and abandoned, seem weak and despised, suffer persecution, and further is compelled to hear the slander that its doctrine is heretical and seditious, that much more only she is fertile before God. She conceives through the ministry of the word an infinite number of children, heirs of righteousness and eternal life, and although externally she suffers persecution, in spirit, they enjoy the greatest freedom. Her children not only judge over all doctrine and works but are also the most glorious conquerors over the gates of hell!

Thus the prophet concedes that the church is in mourning; otherwise, he would not have exhorted her to rejoice. He grants that before the world she is infertile; otherwise, he would not have called her infertile and abandoned, without children. However, before God, he said, she is fertile and thus urges her to rejoice. It's as if he had said, "It is true that indeed you are despised and infertile, and because you don't have the law as your husband, you don't have any children. But rejoice because even if you don't have the law as your husband, you will be the mother of countless children. This is a faithful promise even though while you were still a virgin you were abandoned on the eve of your marriage (for he does not call her widowed). You would have a husband had he not abandoned you or had he not been killed. But your husband, the law, did not fulfill his obligation and left you alone and forgotten; that is why you are no longer under the obligation to enter into marriage with the law." Thus even though the people or the church of the New Covenant is totally free from the law regarding the conscience, it would seem to have been totally abandoned according to the world's opinion. However, although she has never been as infertile as she appears today without the law and without works, before God she is the most fertile conceiving an infinite number of children, not into slavery but into freedom. But through what means? Not through the law but through the word and the Spirit of Christ that is given through the Gospel, through which she conceives, gives birth, and educates her children.

Thus through this allegory, Paul clearly distinguishes between the law and the Gospel: first when he calls Hagar "the Old Covenant" and Sara "the New"; further when he calls one "the slave" and the other "the free"; and also when he says that the one who is married and fertile has become infertile and cast out of the house with her children. In contrast, he says, the infertile and despised has become fertile and gives birth to an infinite number of children who are also heirs. These differences represent two types of people: those of faith and those of the law;[109] that is what I want to make clear. The people of faith do not have the law as their husband; they don't serve in slavery, for they have not been born from that mother who is the present Jerusalem. However, they have the promise and they are free, for they have been born from Sara the free.

---

[109] *Hae differentiae essentiales sunt populi fidei et legis.*

Thus he separates the spiritual people of the New Covenant from the other people of the law when he says that the spiritual people are not the children of Hagar the married slave but of Sara the free, who is not aware of the law. In this way, he places the people of faith way above the law and without it.[110] Well then, if they are beyond and apart from the law, then they are justified merely due to their spiritual birth, which is only through faith alone and not through the law or its works. Well, since the people of grace do not have the law, nor could they, so the people of the law do not have, nor can they have, grace.[111] That is because it is impossible for the law and grace to exist paired up as one![112] Thus we must be justified by faith and lose the righteousness of the law; or we must be justified by the law and lose the righteousness of faith.[113] But this is a great and dreadful loss, to lose grace in order to go back to the law. However, it is a pleasant and blessed loss to let go of the law in order to grasp on to grace.

Thus we (following Paul's example and exacting care) attempt by every possible means to clearly identify the difference between law and Gospel, which is rather easy to put into words. Who can't get it that Hagar is not Sara, and Sara is not Hagar? Also, that Ishmael is not Isaac and that he doesn't have what Isaac does? It may be easy for anyone to tell these apart. But in the middle of great terrors and in the anguish of death, when the conscience struggles against God's judgment, the most difficult thing to say with all confidence, assurance, and unbreakable hope is this: "I am not a child of Hagar but of Sara—that is, I cannot claim that the law is mine because Sara is my mother, and she gives birth not to slaves but to heirs who live in freedom." But this is all difficult to accept.

LECTURE 32: Friday, November 13

Paul then, through Isaiah's testimony, has proven that Sara—that is, the church—is the true mother and she gives birth to children who are heirs in liberty. On the contrary, Hagar who is the synagogue indeed conceives many children but they are slaves and should be cast out. Further, since this text also talks about Christian liberty and abolishing the law, it should be noted with a great deal of attention, since the main and special tenet of the Christian doctrine is to know that we are justified

---

[110] *populum fidei longe supra et extra legem.*

[111] *populus gratiae non habet nec potest habere legem, ita populus legis non habet nec potest habere gratiam.* Luther adds this footnote: *Populus gratiae sine lege, populus legis sine gratia,* "the people of grace without the law; the people of the law without grace."

[112] *impossibile est legem et gratiam simul posse exsistere.*

[113] *Aut igitur fide justificari nos oportet, et justitiam legis amittere, aut lege, et gratiam et justitiam fidei amittere.*

and saved through Christ and, antithetically, to insist and uphold the abolishment of the law.[114] This doctrine helps to confirm our doctrine of faith. It also grants the conscience full consolation and assurance of its security by knowing that the law has been abolished. This is especially true when the conscience feels great fear and is going through serious conflicts.

As I've frequently said, I'll say it again (for it cannot be repeated often enough), when Christians grasp on to Christ's benefits by faith, they have no law at all. For them, all law has been abolished with its torments and anxieties. This text from Isaiah teaches the same and thus it is extraordinary and full of comfort. It urges the infertile and abandoned to rejoice, the one who according to the law deserved only scorn or pity. According to the law, the infertile woman was under a curse. But the Holy Spirit inverts this condemnation and declares the infertile worthy of praise and blessing. On the other hand, the fertile and those who procreate children are accursed, for it says, "Sing, barren woman who has never had a child! Burst into song, shout for joy, you who have never been in labor! For the deserted wife will have more children than the woman who is living with her husband."[115] However, before the world, Sara the church seems to be abandoned and infertile without the righteousness and works of the law. Notwithstanding, she is the most prolific mother conceiving countless children before God as the prophet testifies. On the contrary, although it appears that Hagar has never been so prolific, conceiving so many children, her child bearing years are over; that's because the children of the slave have been cast out of the house together with their mother. Thus they do not receive an inheritance with the children of the free, as Paul goes on to say.

Therefore, since we are children of the free, the law who is our former husband has been abolished (Romans 7). As long as he had dominion over us, it was impossible for us to conceive children who are free in the Spirit or that would know grace, but we remained in slavery together with the former one. Indeed, as long as the law reigns, people are not indolent, but work tirelessly, carrying the burden and the heat of the day. They conceive and procreate many children but both parents and children are illegitimate and don't belong to the mother that enjoys her freedom. Therefore, at the end, together with Ishmael, they are thrown out of the house without an inheritance. They die while under condemnation. Therefore, it is impossible for people to obtain the inheritance—that is, to be justified and saved through the law—regardless of how much they work or how great their offspring. Thus cursed be that doctrine, life, and religion that attempts to achieve righteousness

---

[114] *Nam ut summus et praecipuus christianae doctrinae articulus est, nosse, quod per Christum justificemur et salvemur, it per antithesin multum refert, probe tenere locum de abrogationae legis.*

[115] The English quote is from Isaiah 54:1, CJB.

before God by means of the law or its works.[116] However, let us continue with our task at hand, regarding the abolishment of the law.

Thomas[117] and other scholastics, when talking about the abolishment of the law say that the judicial and ceremonial laws bring death, since the coming of Christ and thus these are the ones abolished but not the moral law. These ignorant doctors didn't know what they were talking about. If you are going to be talking about the abolishment of the law, talk about the law itself, of its proper use and function in its spiritual sense. But at the same time, tie together the totality of the law[118] without making fine distinctions between judicial, ceremonial, and moral, for when Paul says that we are delivered from the curse of the law through Christ, he means the entire law, and mainly the moral law, for this is the only one that accuses, damns, and condemns the conscience; the other two do not have these roles. Thus we say that the moral law or the law of the Ten Commandments does not have the power to accuse and distress the conscience because Christ reigns there with His grace, for He has wiped it away.

It is not that the conscience won't feel all the anguish caused by the law (indeed it feels it), but the law can no longer condemn it nor hurl it into desperation. "There is therefore now no more condemnation for those who are in Christ Jesus" (Romans 8:1). Further, "So if the Son makes you free, you will be free indeed" (John 8:36). Then it doesn't matter how much distress Christians will feel when the law shows them their sin, they will not despair, for they have believed in Jesus Christ and have been baptized in Him and have been washed by His blood and have remission of all their sins. Well, when our sin is forgiven through Christ, who is the Lord of the law (sin is forgiven because He gave His life to attain that forgiveness), the law, seeing that it is but a mere slave, no longer has the power to accuse and condemn of sin because we have been forgiven. We are now free because the Son has freed us from our bondage. Therefore, the law has been entirely abolished for those who have placed their faith in Christ.

However, you will say, "So I don't do anything at all." True, you cannot do anything at all to free yourself from the tyranny of the law. But listen to this joyous news brought to you by the Holy Spirit through the words of the prophet, "Rejoice, oh barren one." It's as if he had said, "Why are you so depressed, why do you grieve so much, since you have no reason at all to moan?" "But I am infertile and rejected." "Well, no matter how infertile and terminally ill you may feel without the righteousness of the law, Christ is your righteousness. He was made to be a curse for you, to free you from the curse of the law. If you believe in Him, the law has died for you. And since Christ is so much more superior to the law, your righteousness

---

[116] *Maledicta sit igitur omnis doctrina, vita, religio, quae conatur lege aut operibus parare justitiam coram Deo.*

[117] Thomas of Aquinas.

[118] Luther's footnote: *Lex tota abrogate est,* "the entire law is abolished."

is much more excellent than the righteousness of the law.[119] Further, you are fertile and not barren, for you have many more children than the one that has a husband."

There is still another abolishment of the law, which is external. Moses' civil laws do not apply to us. Thus we should not reestablish them nor tie ourselves superstitiously to them, as some have done in the past unaware of this freedom. Well then, although the Gospel does not subject us to Moses' judicial laws, it does not exempt us from obeying the laws of the land. Instead, it subjects us to this bodily life, to the laws of the governments wherein we live—that is, it commands us all to obey the governor and his laws, "not only to avoid God's wrath but also for the sake of conscience" (1 Peter 2; Romans 13). The emperor or any other prince should not cause us any harm if they should implement any of Moses' civil laws. Yes, let them use them freely, and without offense to us. Thus the papal scholars are deceived, for they imagine that Moses' civil laws are harmful and ill-fated since Christ came.

Just as we are not under any obligation to observe Moses' ceremonial laws, much less are we bound to the Pope's ceremonies. But in this bodily life, we cannot do without all ceremonies. Certain instruction is necessary, thus the Gospel allows the church to have certain regulations regarding days, times, and places. The people need to know the day, hour, and place of meeting to listen to God's word. It also allows the structuring of lessons and readings, as in the schools, especially for the instructions of children and the illiterate. These things are allowed so that everything may be done decently and in order within the church (1 Corinthians 14:40). However, the keeping of these regulations does not merit the remission of sins. Further, they may be changed or omitted without sin at all so that the weaker believer will not be hindered. *Neither is it true that after Christ's revelation the Mosaic ceremonies bring on death; otherwise, Christians would have sinned observing the feasts of Passover and Pentecost, instituted by the ancient church following the example of the law of Moses (although celebrated differently and for another purpose).*

Well, Paul here talks about the abolishment of the moral law, which should be carefully noted. He talks against the righteousness of the law, to establish the righteousness of faith. This is his conclusion: if only grace or faith in Christ justifies, then the entire law is simply abolished.[120] Isaiah's testimony confirms this for he calls on the infertile and despised to rejoice, for she has no any children, nor hopes to ever have any—that is, she has no disciples, nor the favor, nor the nods of approval from the world because she preaches the word of the cross of Christ crucified against all the wisdom of the flesh. But you, infertile (says the prophet), don't stress over that at all. Instead, lift up your voice and rejoice for the despised has more children than the one who is living with her husband—that is, the married

---

[119] *et quo major est ipse Christus lege, hoc meliorem habes justitiam legis justitia.*

[120] *Si sola gratia seu fides in Christum justificat, ergo total ex simpliciter abrogate est.*

woman has a great number of children but she will be weakened, and the despised will have a countless multitude of children!

He calls the church infertile because her children are not conceived through the law, nor by works, nor by the diligence of human effort, but by the word of faith through God's Spirit. All one has to do is to be born, without any work at all. But on the contrary, those who yield fruit do nothing but work and put out great efforts to conceive and give birth. All you will find here is nothing but exertion and no one is born. However, they do nothing but work in order to obtain the rights of children and the inheritance through the righteousness of the law, or by their own righteousness, but they are slaves and never receive the inheritance. No! It doesn't matter if their exhaustion leads them to death by exertion. Their attempts to obtain through their own works are against God's will because God out of His free grace will grant the inheritance to all the believers on account of Christ.[121] The faithful also work but that is not the reason they are declared children and heirs, for that was theirs at birth. However, what they do now that they are children and heirs is to glorify God with their good works and lend a helping hand to their neighbor.

VERSE 28. Now you, brothers and sisters, like Isaac, are children of promise [NIV].

In other words, we are not children of the flesh like Ishmael or like all Israel that boasted they were of the seed of Abraham and the people of God. However, Christ answered, "If you were Abraham's children, you would do what Abraham did, but now you seek to kill me, a man who has told you the truth" (John 8:39ff, NIV). Further, "If God were your Father, you would indeed love me and receive my word." It's as if he had said, "Brothers and sisters who are born and reared in the same home know each other by their voice, but 'you are of your father the devil.' We are not such children," he says, "who continue in slavery and at the end will be thrown out of the house. But we are children of the promise, as was Isaac"—that is, of grace and faith, born only from the promise. But I've already talked at length on this matter, in chapter 3, when dealing with this text, "In your seed shall be blessed all the nations of the earth." Thus we are declared righteous, not by the law, nor by works, nor by our own righteousness, but by God's pure mercy and grace.[122] Paul frequently repeats this and takes great pains to present the promise that is only received by faith, for he saw the great need to make it known.

Up to this point, we have dealt with the allegory in Genesis to which Paul adds the text from Isaiah as its interpretation. Now he relates the story of Ishmael and Isaac for our example and comfort.

---

[121] *quod Deus ex mera gratia propter Christus.*

[122] *Ergo non ex lege, operibus, justitia propia pronuntiamur justi, sed ex mera gratia.*

VERSE 29. At that time the son born according to the flesh persecuted the son born by the power of the Spirit. It is the same now [NIV].

This text contains a deeply felt comfort. Everyone who is born and lives in Christ rejoices in his birth and inheritance received from God and has Ishmael as his enemy and persecutor. We have learned this today by experience, for we see that the entire world is embroiled in tumults, persecutions, sects, and hostilities. Therefore, if we would not equip ourselves with this and other similar reassurances from Paul, without a good understanding of the article of justification, we would never be able to resist Satan's violence and subtle trickeries. Who would not be distressed by all these cruel persecutions from our adversaries and with these sects and infinite hostilities stirred up today by these agitated and fanatical spirits? True, it causes us no small grief when we are forced to hear that everything was peaceful and calm before the preaching of the Gospel but that since the Gospel is preached everything has turned into a whirlwind and the entire world seems to be caught up in uprisings so that everyone takes up arms against everyone else. When those who have not received God's Spirit hear these things, they are quickly offended and judge that the disobedience of the citizens against their leaders, the seditions, wars, plagues, famines, overthrown governments, kingdoms, countries, sects, aggressions, and countless other evils arise from the preaching of the Gospel.

We should take solace against such immense accusations and equip ourselves with these sweet, reassuring words, that the faithful must carry this name and label before the world: "They are seditious and divisive, and authors of endless evil. That is why our adversaries believe they can mount a proper case against us, yes, they even think that they will render God great service when they hate, persecute, and even kill us." There is no other alternative then but that Ishmael will persecute Isaac and not that Isaac persecutes Ishmael, for those who are not persecuted by Ishmael cannot confess they are Christians.

However, let out adversaries (who so greatly magnify these evils today) declare the many good things[123] that followed Christ and the apostles' preaching of the Gospel. Is it not true that what followed was the destruction of the Jewish kingdom? Is it not true that the Roman Empire was destroyed? Is it not true that the entire world was caught up in great strife? However, the Gospel was not to blame, for Christ and His apostles preached for the benefit and salvation of men and women and not for their destruction. These things happened because of peoples' wickedness. Nations, kings, and princes, possessed by the devil, would not listen to the word of grace, life, and eternal salvation. Instead, they detested and condemned it as the most malevolent and harmful doctrine to religion and governments. It is proper for these things to happen, for the Holy Spirit said beforehand

---

[123] Once again, Luther is using irony and a bit of sarcasm.

in David's words: "Why do the nations rage; and the peoples plot a vain thing?" (Psalm 2:1ff, WEB).

We hear and see such commotions and disturbances today. The adversaries blame our doctrine. But the doctrine of grace and peace is not what stirs up these evils. Instead, it is peoples, nations, kings, and the princes of the earth (as the psalmist said). They roar and murmur, conspire and consult, not against us (as they think) nor against our doctrine, which they blaspheme as false and seditious, but against the Lord and His anointed. Thus their conspiracies and maneuvers are and will be frustrated and neutralized. "The One enthroned in heaven laughs; the Lord scoffs at them" (Psalm 2). Thus let them lash out all they want, saying that we are the cause of such commotions and disturbances. However, this psalm reassures us because it says that they themselves are the authors of these evils. They won't believe and even less accept that they are the ones who murmur, rebel, and conspire against the Lord and his anointed. No! Instead, they think they are the ones who support God's cause, who defend His glory, and who believe that when they persecute us they render a pleasant offering before Him. But the psalm does not lie and will continue to be confirmed in like manner until the end of time. At this, we do nothing at all but suffer, as the Holy Spirit testifies in our conscience. Further, the doctrine by which such commotions and uprisings occur is not ours but Christ's. We cannot deny this doctrine, nor can we abandon its defense, seeing that Christ said, "For whoever is ashamed of me and of my words in this adulterous and sinful generation, of him will the Son of man also be ashamed" (Mark 8:38).

Thus all who preach Christ in truth, confessing that He is our righteousness, should be content when they hear they are called perverse, causing trouble everywhere. "These men who have turned the world upside down have come here also . . . acting against the decrees of Caesar" (Acts 17:6, 7), said the Jews of Paul and Silas. Further, in Acts 24:5, it says, "We have found this man to be a troublemaker, stirring up riots among the Jews all over the world. He is a ringleader of the Nazarene sect" (NIV). The Gentiles had the same complaint in Acts 16:20: "These men are throwing our city into an uproar" (NIV). It is no different today when they accuse Luther of upsetting the papacy and the Roman Empire. But if I keep silent, then nothing the strong man has would be disturbed. The Pope would stop persecuting me. But to desist would be to tarnish the Gospel of Jesus Christ and disfigure it. If I speak, the Pope is annoyed and roars cruelly. Thus we should lose either the Pope (an earthly and mortal being) or God immortal, Jesus Christ, life, and eternal salvation. Or do you think you are just choosing between the lesser of two evils? Then let the Pope perish in the dust of the earth and Christ reign in heavenly places forever and ever![124]

Christ Himself in the Spirit saw the great evils that would follow His preaching, but this reassured Him: "I have come to bring fire on the earth, and how I

---

[124] *ruat igitur potius papa terrenus et mortalis, quam Christus coelestis et aeternus.*

wish it were already kindled!" (Luke 12:49, NIV). In the same way, today we see the great evils that follow the preaching of the Gospel through the persecution and blasphemy of our adversaries and the ingratitude of the world. This matter hurts us; sometimes, according to the flesh and reason's judgment, we think it would have been better had the Gospel never been preached because due to its preaching the peace of the land has been so greatly upset. But according to the Spirit, we can boldly say with Christ, "I have come to bring fire on the earth, and now, it is already kindled!" Well then, once the fire is kindled, great disturbances follow. But it is not a king or emperor who is provoked but the god of this world, a great and powerful spirit and lord over the earth. This phrase, which seems so fragile, "preaching Christ crucified," falls on top of this powerful and terrible adversary. This Leviathan, when he feels the divine power of this word, incites all his members, shakes his tail, and makes the depths of the seas boil over as if it were a pot (Job 41:22). This is the source of these disturbances, all those cruel and vicious hostilities throughout the entire world.

Therefore, don't let it trouble you that our adversaries are offended and cry out that no good comes out of the preaching of the Gospel. They are unbelievers, blind, and obstinate; therefore, it is impossible that they will reap any fruit from the Gospel. Rather, we who believe are the ones that see the inestimable profits and fruits of the Gospel. Although for a time, we may be accused of countless evils, despised, spoiled, slandered, and condemned as rejects and the περίψημα among all people.[125] It may even be that we will be put to death or inwardly afflicted with the consciousness of our own sin[126] and harassed by devils, for we live in Christ in whom and by whom we have become kings and lords over sin, death, the flesh, the world, hell, and all evils. In whom, and through whom, we also tread beneath our feet that dragon and viper who is the king of sin and death. How is this accomplished? By faith, because the blessedness for which we now hope has not yet been revealed. But meanwhile, we patiently wait for that revelation. However, we are most confidently it is now ours by faith.

Thus let us diligently learn the foundational truth of justification,[127] for it is the only truth that can sustain us against such endless slander and insults. It also reassures us in all our temptations and persecutions. Also, it's impossible for the world not to be offended by this doctrine of the Gospel. The world will continually cry out that it serves no useful purpose. "The person without the Spirit does not accept the things that come from the Spirit of God but considers them foolishness and cannot understand them because they are discerned only through the

---

[125] περίψημα. Luther used this Greek term during his lecture, and it was included in the Latin text. It means the foul scraping on one's sandals after stepping on some kind of dung.

[126] *conscientia peccati.*

[127] *Discendus est igitur diligenter articulus justificationis*, the article of justification.

Spirit" (1 Corinthians 2:14, NIV). These persons only pay attention to external evils, calamities, rebellions, assassinations, sectarianism, and other similar things; they are offended and blinded when these arise, and they finally fall despising and blaspheming God and His word.

On the contrary, we should comfort and reassure ourselves with this: our adversaries will not accuse and condemn us for some patently wicked deed we have committed such as adultery, murder, theft, and similar things. No! Let them accuse and condemn us for our doctrine. And what is this that we teach? Christ, the Son of God, by His death on the cross has redeemed us from our sins and eternal death. Thus they cannot bring us into disrepute for anything in our lives, but our doctrine is not about us but about Christ.[128] Thus Christ, not us, has committed the misdeed for which they accuse us. Fine then, if they are going to condemn Christ and cast Him out of heaven as heretical and seditious, let them look well at what they are doing. As far as we are concerned, we will entrust this, His cause, into His own hands. We will remain quiet looking to see if Christ or they will triumph. Indeed, according to the flesh, it hurts us that these Ishmaelites hate and persecute us so furiously. However, according to the Spirit, we glory in these sufferings, on the one hand, because we know that we suffer not because of our sins, but for Christ's cause, whose benefit and glory we preach, and on the other, because Paul's previous warning is also confirmed, that Ishmael would ridicule and persecute Isaac.

The Jews explain the text in Genesis 21 cited by Paul, where Ishmael derides and persecutes Isaac in the following way. They allege that Ishmael forced Isaac to commit idolatry. If that happened, I don't believe it was such crass idolatry as the Jews imagine—that is, that Ishmael made images out of clay like the Gentiles and then forced Isaac to worship them. Abraham would not have tolerated such a thing. However, I believe that to all appearances Ishmael was a pious man. He was just like Cain who also persecuted his brother and at the end killed him. They did not quarrel over some possession but because Cain saw that God held his brother in greater esteem. In the same way, Ishmael loved to be religious; he sacrificed and worked at doing the right things. But he ridiculed his brother Isaac and wanted to pass himself off as the better one for two reasons: first, due to his own religion and service to God and second, because according to the law of the land, he held command[129] and thus the claim to the inheritance. He thought that the kingdom and the priesthood belonged to him by right, according to God's law, as the firstborn. Thus he persecuted Isaac in the spiritual sense due to his religion and in the material sense due to the inheritance.

This persecution will always be present in the church, especially when the doctrine of the Gospel is in bloom—that is, the children of the flesh deride the children of the promise and persecute them. The Papists today persecute us for no

---

[128] *sed doctrinam nostram, imo non nostram, sed Christi.*
[129] *civilem dominationem.*

other reason than we teach that righteousness comes through the promise. The Papists become resentful seeing that we don't worship their idols—that is, we don't value their righteousness, their works, and their worship, designed and ordained by men as a means to obtain grace and forgiveness of sins. For this cause, they plan to cast us out of the house—that is, they boast that they are the church, the children and the people of God, and that the inheritance belongs to them. But on the other hand, they excommunicate and banish us as heretics and seditious; and when they can, they kill us all the while thinking they are rendering an acceptable service to God. Thus they make every possible effort to cast us out of this life and from the life to come. The fanatical spirits[130] hate us to death because we detect and despise their errors and heresies, which they scatter everywhere, daily renewing them in the church. For this reason, they judge that we are worse than the Papists and thus have infused themselves[131] with a more cruel hatred against us than against the Papists.

Therefore, as soon as God's word comes to light, the devil is enraged and uses all his strength and trickery to persecute it and erase it altogether. Thus he has no other option but to raise up countless sects, horrible crimes, cruel persecutions, and abominable murders. He is the father of lies and a murderer. He spreads his lies throughout the entire world utilizing false teachers and stirs up tyrants to kill people everywhere. Through these means he is the landlord who dwells in the spiritual as well as the material kingdoms: in the spiritual kingdom, by means of false lying teachers (constantly stirring up people through his fiery darts to invent heresies and wicked opinions) and in the material kingdom, through the tyrants' sword. That is how this father of lies and murderer stirs up persecution on every side, spiritually as well as materially, against the children of the free. We see ourselves forced to suffer intolerable spiritual persecution at the hands of the heretics who cause us great grief. This is due to the infinite insults and slander of the devil devoted to disfiguring our doctrine. We are compelled to hear that all the heresies and errors of the Anabaptists, Sacramentarians, and other heretics and every other enormous falsehood proceed from our doctrine. The physical persecution in which the tyrants lie in wait to take our lives and goods is more tolerable. They persecute us not for our sins but for our witness to God's word. Thus let us learn even from the title Christ gave the devil, that he is the father of lies and murder (John 8:44). It is when the Gospel flourishes and Christ reigns that these sects of perdition will rise up, as well as murderers persecuting the Gospel, bellowing everywhere, for Paul says, "There must also be sects among you, that the approved may become manifest among you" (1 Corinthians 11:19, DARBY). Whoever who is not aware of all this will soon become offended and, turning away from the true God and the true faith, will return to their gods of old placing their faith in falsehoods.

---

[130] *fanatical spiritus.*

[131] *praesertim Anabaptistae* (1st edition, 1535).

Thus in this text, Paul predelivers weapons to the faithful so that they will not be offended by these persecutions, sects, and insults, for he says, "The son born according to the flesh." It's as if he said, "If we are children of the promise, born according to the Spirit, then indeed we must expect that our brother will persecute us because he was born according to the flesh—that is, not only those who are openly wicked will persecute us, but even those who at the beginning were our dear friends, with whom we shared as family together living in the same house, who together with us received the true doctrine of the Gospel, will turn against us as our mortal enemies and persecute us without end, for the brothers according to the flesh will persecute their brothers born according to the Spirit." Christ in Psalm 41:9 bemoaned regarding Judas: "Even my close friend, someone I trusted, one who shared my bread, has turned against me" (NIV). However, this is our comfort, that we have not given the Ishmaelites occasion to persecute us. The Papists persecute us because we teach the pure and proper doctrine of faith,[132] which, if we ceased to preach, they would also cease to persecute us. Further, if we gave the sectarians our nod of approval, they would praise us. But since we detest and abhor the wickedness of the ones as well as the others, it's impossible that they will not hate and persecute us.

However, Paul is not the only one (as I mentioned before) to prepare us with weapons against such persecutions and aggressions. Christ Himself reassures us with great tenderness. He says in John 15:19, "If you belonged to the world, it would love you as its own. As it is, you do not belong to the world, but I have chosen you out of the world. That is why the world hates you" (NIV). It's as if He had said, "I am the cause of all the persecutions you suffer; and if they kill you, I am the reason they kill you, for if you didn't preach my words and confessed me, the world would not persecute you." But this is a sign they are walking in the right path, for "a servant is not greater than his master."

With these words, the Lord takes all the blame upon Himself and delivers us from all fear. It's as if He had said, "You are not the reason why the world hates and persecutes you. Rather, it is my name that you preach and confess, that is the reason." "But take heart! I have overcome the world." This comfort upholds us; thus we have no doubt that Christ's power is sufficient not only to bear the burden but also to subdue all the cruelty of the tyrants and the subtle trickeries of the heretics. That is what He stated when He displayed His power against the Jews and the Romans, whose tyranny and persecutions He tolerated for some time. He also bore the subtleties and the deceitful practices of the heretics, but in His own time and place, He overthrew them, enduring as king and conqueror. Then let all the Papists rage all they want; let the sectarians slander and corrupt the Gospel of Christ all they may. Nonetheless, Christ will reign eternally and His word will remain forever, but all His enemies will be destroyed. Further, the fact that Ishmael's persecution against

---

[132] *propter doctrinam pietatis.*

Isaac will not last forever is a very special comfort; it will be but brief, and when it ends the following sentence will be pronounced:

VERSE 30. But what does the scripture say? "Cast out the slave and her son; for the son of the slave shall not inherit with the son of the free woman" (Genesis 21:10).

Abraham was deeply hurt by these words of Sara. No doubt when he heard this statement, his fatherly affection was moved with compassion toward his son Ishmael, for he had been conceived from his flesh. Scripture clearly testifies about this when it says, "The matter distressed Abraham greatly because it concerned his son" (Genesis 21, NIV). However, God confirmed the sentence pronounced by Sara, saying to Abraham, "Do not be so distressed about the boy and your slave woman. Listen to whatever Sarah tells you, because it is through Isaac that your offspring will be reckoned."

In this text, the Ishmaelites hear the sentence pronounced against them. It's a decree that defeats all the Jews, Greeks, Romans, and everyone else that persecutes the church of Christ. This same sentence will overthrow the Papists and all those who justify themselves through their own works,[133] those that today boast they are God's people and the church. It includes those who have total confidence that they will receive the inheritance and judge us. While we confidently rest in God's promise, they allege not only that we are infertile and abandoned but also that we are heretics and outcasts from the church and that it is impossible for us to be sons and heirs. However, God dismisses those judgments and pronounces this sentence against them: "Because they are children of the slave, and persecute the children of the free, they will be cast out of the house and will have no inheritance whatsoever with the children of the promise, for that inheritance belongs solely to them, since they are children of the free." That sentence has now been ratified and can never be revoked. Thus with all assurance, that's how it will be: our Ishmaelites will lose not only the ecclesiastical and political government they now have but also eternal life, for Scripture has predicted that the children of the slave will be cast out of the house—that is, from the kingdom of grace—for they cannot be heirs together with the children of the free.

Well, in this text, we can see that the Holy Spirit refers to the people of the law and works, with an apparently derisive name, the "son of the slave." It's as if he had said, "Why do you boast of the righteousness of the law and works, and why do you glory that you are the people and children of God resorting to the same pretexts? If you don't know whose children you are, I will tell you: 'You are slaves born from a slave.' And what kind of slaves? Slaves to the law and consequently slaves to sin, death, and eternal condemnation. And since the slave is no heir, he is cast out of the house." Therefore, the Pope with all his kingdom and all other legalists (who to all appearances would lead you to believe they are the essence of

---

[133] *omnes, quincunque tandem sunt, iustitiarios.*

holiness), who believe they have the hope of obtaining grace and salvation keeping human or divine laws, are children of that slave and have no inheritance at all with the free. However, I am not talking now about the Popes, cardinals, bishops, and monks, for they are openly wicked, they have made a god out of their bellies and committed such atrocious sins that in good faith I will not mention. Instead, I am talking about the very best among them, such as I and others were among them, living piously and with great effort and suffering we struggled to keep the monastic orders, placate God's wrath, and merit the forgiveness of sins and eternal life. Here, let all who have heard their name hear their sentence: "They are children of the slave and should be cast out of the house together with their slave mother."

Since we take these statements seriously, we remain confident in our doctrine and confirm ourselves in the righteousness of faith over and against the doctrine and righteousness of works,[134] which the world embraces and magnifies, condemning and despising the other. However, this perturbs and offends the weak minded. Although they can clearly see the wickedness and abominable evil of the Papists, they are not easily convinced that the masses of people who have taken the church's name are mistaken. There are very few among them who have a sound and correct opinion of the doctrine of faith. If the papacy would live today with the same holiness and austerity exercised by the ancient fathers Jerome, Ambrose, Agustin, and others, when the clergy had not yet gotten a bad reputation for its simony, lavishness, lust, power, fornication, sodomy, and countless other sins but instead to all appearances lived in accordance to the regulations and decrees of the fathers, and in celibacy, is there anything we could say today against the papacy?

Celibacy, to which the clergy submitted so rigorously in the time of the fathers, before everyone's gaze turned mere men into the semblance of angels! That is why the apostle Paul in Colossians 2:18 calls it the religion of angels. The Papists sing about their virgins like this: "They lived an angelical life in the flesh because they lived contrary to the flesh." Further, the life they call "contemplative" (the clergy devoted themselves fully to it, neglecting all civil and family responsibilities) was quite a theatre of showmanship holiness. If that theatrical performance of holiness from the papacy's former times, with all its outward show, remained to this day, perhaps our doctrine of faith would not have made a dent on it. Yet even though that theater of holiness and severe discipline has disappeared, we hardly prevail today when all you can see in the papacy is but a mere pit and cesspool of vice and abominations.

However, let us suppose that the papacy's old religion and discipline still existed. It still would be our duty (given Paul's example who relentlessly persecuted the false apostles who presumed to be great and holy men) to fight against the merit hoarders of the papacy's kingdom and say, "Although you live in celibacy, consuming and wearing out your bodies with endless self-inflicted tribulations, walking humbly in the religion of angels, nonetheless, you are still slaves of the law,

---

[134] *doctrina et iusticia fidei, contra doctrinam et iusticiam operum.*

sin, and the devil and should be cast out of the house; for you seek righteousness and salvation through your own works and not through Christ."[135]

Thus we should not be distressed over the sinful life of the Papists but keep an eye on their abominable and hypocritical doctrine, and our struggle against it is very specific. But then, what if the papacy's old religion and discipline still flourished today, what if it were still observed with such severity and rigor as before (*by the hermits, Jerome, Augustine, Gregory, Bernard, Francis, Dominic, and many others*)? We would still have this to say: "If all you have to offer before God's wrath and judgment is that life of holiness and chastity, it is proof indeed that you are nothing but children of the slave who should be cast out of the kingdom of heaven and suffer condemnation!"

Today, they themselves do not defend their life of sin. No! Instead, their best and most wholesome detest it. Their struggle is to retain and defend their doctrine of devils, the hypocrisy, and the righteousness of works. Today, they claim the authority of the Councils and the examples of the holy fathers, alleging they were the authors of the holy orders and their regulations. Thus we should not fight against the obvious wickedness and abomination of the papacy. Instead, we should fight against the highest holiness and piety of their saints, for they think they are living the angelical life and fantasize they keep not only God's commandments but also the teachings of Christ; they think they do supererogatory works and others they are not called to do at all. We say all this is to work in vain, unless they take hold of "this one thing," which Christ said "is necessary," and together with Mary choose the better part that will not be taken away from them.

Bernard actually did it. He was a man so pious, holy, and chaste deserving commendation and preference above all others. On a certain occasion, he was so sick and had lost all hope to survive. But he did not put his trust in his life of celibacy in which he had lived with all chastity nor in his good works and works of charity, of which there were many. Instead, he cast them all away from his sight and taking hold of the benefit of Christ through faith said, "I have lived a life of perdition, but you Lord Jesus Christ have twice the right to the kingdom of heaven. The first is yours because you are the Son of God and the second, because you have bought it with you blood and passion. The first is yours by birthright. The second you grant to me, not for any right I have due to my works but by your right and your grace." He did not offer his life as a monk and angelical life before God's wrath and judgment but took hold of "this one thing" that was "necessary" for him and thus was saved. I also believe that Jerome, Gregory, and many others of the fathers and hermits were saved in the same way. Further, there's no doubt that also in the Old Testament many of the kings of Israel and other idolaters were saved likewise. At the hour of death, they stripped themselves off their vain trust they had placed in their idols and took hold of God's promise regarding Abraham's seed that was to come—that is, in Christ

---

[135] *non per Christum quaeritis justitiam et salutem.*

in whom all the nations would be blessed. Today, if there's a Papist that would be saved, he would simply have to lean not on his own works and merits but only in God's mercy offered to us in Christ. With Paul, he should say, "And be found in him, not having a righteousness of my own, based on law, but that which is through faith in Christ, the righteousness from God that depends on faith" (Philippians 3:9).

VERSE 31. Therefore, brothers and sisters, we are not children of the slave woman, but of the free woman.

Here, Paul concludes his allegory about the infertile church and the fertile people of the law. He said, "We are not children of the slave." In other words, we are not under the law that conceives children into slavery, for it terrifies, accuses, and leads to desperation. Instead, Christ has delivered us from it. Therefore, it cannot frighten or condemn us. We've already dealt with this topic before. Further, although the children of the slave incessantly persecute us for a time, nonetheless, we are comforted with the following assurance. At the end, they will be cast out into the dense darkness and will be compelled to leave the inheritance to us, for it is ours, since we are children of the free.

Thus Paul employed these words, "the slave" and "the free" (as we've heard), to reject the righteousness of the law and confirm the doctrine of justification. He uses the term *the free* purposefully and passionately proclaims and magnifies it, especially at the beginning of next chapter. He uses the occasion to explain Christian liberty, whose knowledge is extremely important. The Pope has overthrown its meaning altogether and subjected the church to the traditions and ceremonies of men, taking it captive to a most miserable and filthy slavery. However, that liberty with which Christ has bought us is for us a mighty fortress,[136] in which we defend ourselves from the tyranny of the Pope. Therefore, we should diligently consider this doctrine of Christian liberty, in order to confirm the doctrine of justification and to lift up and comfort weakened consciences against many trials and misfortunes that our adversaries impute to the Gospel. Well then, Christian liberty is something very spiritual that the carnal mind is unable to understand. Even those who have the first fruits of the Spirit and are able to explain it well can hardly retain it in their hearts. To reason, it seems it's a topic of little importance. Therefore, if the Holy Spirit did not magnify it to the value it deserves, it would be condemned.

---

[136] *firmissimum praesidium.* Two years before these lectures, in 1529, Luther had written a hymn by that name. The hymn is still sung throughout Christian churches today.

Galatians 5

LECTURE 33: Saturday, November 14

Nearing the end of his epistle, Paul now passionately and heatedly argues in defense of the doctrines of faith and Christian liberty against the false apostles. They are the enemies and slayers of these doctrines. But he directs and hurls these words as lightning bolts seeking to defeat them altogether. With all this, he exhorts the Galatians to flee from their malicious doctrine and avoid it as the deadliest plague. As he exhorts them, he combines warnings, threats, and promises, for at all costs, he will attempt to keep them in the liberty with which Christ purchased them, saying,

VERSE 1. For freedom Christ has set us free. Stand firm, therefore, and do not submit again to a yoke of slavery [NRSV].

He wants to tell them, "Stand firm." Peter urged the same: "Be alert and of sober mind. Your enemy the devil prowls around like a roaring lion looking for someone to devour. Resist him, standing firm in the faith" (1 Peter 5:8). He said, "Don't be careless. Don't budge. Be consistent." Don't lie down to sleep but stand up. It's as if he had said, "It's better to be alert and unwavering so that you may keep and retain that freedom with which Christ has liberated you. Those who think they are safe, get careless and cannot keep their freedom. That's because Satan hates to death the light of the Gospel—that is, the doctrine of grace, freedom, confidence, and life. Thus as soon as he sees, it is surging, he springs into battle against it utilizing all his strength and power, stirring up storms and hurricanes to obstruct it and at the end overthrow it altogether." That is why Paul now admonishes the faithful not to sleep or get careless. Instead, consistently and courageously resist Satan so that he will not strip them of that liberty with which Christ has purchased them.

Here, every word manifests a striking passion. "Stand firm," he said. It's as if he had stated, "In this respect, you stand in great need to be alert and vigilant." "In the liberty." What liberty? Not in any of the freedoms granted by the emperor but in that freedom by which Christ set us free. The emperor has given, or rather was pressured to give, the Roman bishop[1] a city, free of charge, and other lands. He also granted immunities, privileges, and prerogatives, among others. This is also

---

[1] *Romano Pontifici.*

liberty, but it is respecting civil liberties, by which the Roman Pontiff[2] together with all his clergy are exempt from all public taxes. There is also a freedom of the flesh, or rather a diabolical liberty through which the devil reigns practically throughout the world. Those who enjoy this freedom do not obey either God or God's laws but instead do whatever they please. This is the freedom that people seek and embrace today. It is the same with the sectarians, they see themselves at liberty to give their opinions and display all their works so that with impunity they may teach and do whatever they imagine is right. All these stand firm in the liberty with which the devil has made them free. But here, we're not talking about this freedom, although the entire world doesn't care one bit about any other freedom, neither are we talking about the liberty granted by civil law. We are talking about another freedom that surpasses it, which the devil hates and resists.

This is the liberty that Christ has given to us. It is not from an earthly yoke nor from the Babylonian captivity or the tyranny of the Muslims but from God's eternal wrath. And where is it given? In the conscience. There is where our freedom rests, there's no need to go any further. Christ has made us free not politically, nor in the flesh, but theologically or spiritually[3]—that is, we are free because our conscience has found peace and freedom, without fear of the wrath to come. This is that great and priceless liberty. If we compare its magnitude and majesty with all the rest (political freedom and freedom of the flesh), they are but a drop of water in the endless sea, for, having such confidence within the heart, who can adequately describe how wonderful it is that they are not nor ever will be objects of God's wrath? Instead, because of Christ,[4] God will be a merciful and loving Father toward them. This is indeed a marvelous and incomprehensible freedom that the most exalted and sovereign Majesty would show us such favor! In this life, God not only defends, sustains, and comes to our rescue but also, with respect to our body sown in corruption, dishonor, and illness, will set it free, resurrecting it incorruptible, in power and glory! Therefore, this is a priceless freedom that we are forever freed from God's wrath. It is a freedom that surpasses heaven, earth, and all creatures.

From this freedom follows another in which Christ has freed us from the law, sin, death, the power of the devil, hell, and more. Just as God's wrath can no longer distress us for Christ has delivered us from it, so also the law, sin, and the like cannot accuse and condemn us. Although the law may accuse us and sin perturbs us, they cannot plunge us into desperation, for faith, which overcomes the world, appears immediately and says, "These things no longer belong to me, for Christ has freed and delivered me from them all. Death, the most powerful and fearful foe in all the world,[5] has been defeated and cast out from the conscience

---

[2] Ibid.
[3] *Theologice seu espiritualiter.*
[4] *propter Christum.*
[5] *qua nihil potentius et horribilius in mundo est.*

by the Spirit's freedom." Thus the majesty of this Christian liberty needs to be held in high esteem and carefully considered, for it is quite easy to say, "Freedom from God's wrath, sin, and death" and so on, but in the battleground of temptation,[6] when the conscience agonizes, it is much more difficult to put into practice.

Therefore, we must be charged with courage. When we feel the law accusing us, the terrifying power of sin, the horror of death, and God's wrath, we will be able to cast out these despairing thoughts and dreadful fantasies from our sight. In their place, we will place the freedom with which Christ[7] has bought us, the forgiveness of sins, righteousness, life, and God's eternal mercy. And although we may feel something radically different, we are assured that it will not be for long, according to what the prophet said, "In overflowing wrath for a moment I hid my face from you, but with everlasting love I will have compassion on you" (Isaiah 54:8). But in fact, this is so difficult to do! That freedom that Christ purchased for us is not something you believe as soon as you hear it. If it could be assimilated with a firm and constant faith, that would be the end of worldwide anger and fear caused by the law, sin, death, or the devil, be it ever so enormous, for immediately, it would be absorbed as a tiny drop of water in the vastness of the ocean. Indeed, this Christian liberty absorbs immediately and dissolves the greatest pile of troubles, whether they be from the law, sin, death, God's wrath, and very shortly the serpent itself with its head where its power resides. Christian freedom replaces all those with righteousness, peace, and eternal life. But blessed are those who understand and believe!

Therefore, let us learn to magnify this, our freedom, for it was no emperor, neither patriarch nor prophet nor any angel from heaven, that attained it for us but Jesus Christ the Son of God, for whom all things were created in heaven and in earth. He has bought this freedom with no other price but that of His own blood, to set us free, nor from any bodily yoke nor temporary situation but from a spiritual and eternal slavery under the cruelest and invincible tyrants, which are the law, sin, death, and the devil; Christ freed us to reconcile us with the Father. Now, since these enemies have been defeated and we have been reconciled with God through the death of His Son, with all certainty, we are righteous before God, and all that we do[8] pleases Him. And although certain remnants of sin remain in us, they are not held against our account but are forgiven[9] because of Christ.[10]

Because Paul utilizes such passionate and powerful words, they must be carefully examined. "Stand firm (he said) in the liberty by which Christ has made us free." This freedom then is not given to us through the law or due our own righteousness but freely because of Christ, who set us free. This is the same as testified and declared

---

[6] *in certamine.*

[7] *libertatem Christi.*

[8] *omnes actiones nostras.*

[9] *non imputari, sed condonari.*

[10] *propter Christum.*

by Paul throughout his entire epistle. Christ also, in John 8, said, "So if the Son makes you free, you will be free indeed" (John 8:36). He is the only one who stands between us and the evils that distress and assail us on every side. He has defeated and removed them so that they can no longer oppress nor condemn us. Instead of sin and death, He grants us righteousness and eternal life. In this way, He exchanges in our conscience the yoke and terrors of the law with the freedom and the reassurance of the Gospel that says, "Take heart, my son; your sins are forgiven" (Matthew 9:2). Therefore, everyone who believes in Christ has obtained this freedom.

Reason is unable to perceive the excellence of this fact. But when the spirit takes it into account, you will see how priceless it is! Who can conceive in his mind such a great and unspeakable gift!? It brings the forgiveness of sins, righteousness, and eternal life! This gift replaces the law, sin, death, and God's wrath, bringing the assurance that God is merciful, and forever shows His favor. The Papists and the hypocrites who strive after the righteousness of the law, or their own righteousness, they indeed boast that they also have this freedom, which they promise to others as well. But by their deeds, they serve corruption, and at the hour of temptation, all their confidence evaporates in an instant. Why? Because they place their confidence in works and their compliance but not in God's word nor in Christ. Therefore, it is impossible for the self-justifiers who strive to earn heaven, life, and salvation through their meritorious works to know what it is to be free from sin.

On the contrary, our freedom has Christ Himself for its foundation, who is our eternal High Priest, seated at God's right hand and who intercedes for us. That is why the forgiveness of sins, righteousness, life, and liberty that we have received from Him are certain and perpetual so that our confidence will not waver. Therefore, if we grasp on to Christ with a firm faith and remain in that liberty by which He made us free, we will obtain those priceless gifts. But if we are careless and neglectful, we will lose them. There's a very good reason why Paul urges us to be vigilant and resist. He knew that the devil does not want anything else but to rob us from that freedom for which Christ paid such a great price and, through his ministers of slavery, snare us once again with his yoke according to the following explanation.

VERSE 2. And don't let yourselves be tied up again to a yoke of slavery.

Paul most effectively and with great depth declared himself in favor of grace and Christian liberty. With exalted and powerful words, he exhorted the Galatians to abide in them, for they are easily lost. Therefore, he urges them to resist and remain firm lest due to negligence or a false sense of security they fall from grace and faith into the law and works. Now, since reason (whose preference is the righteousness of the law instead of the righteousness of faith) doesn't see any danger in it at all, Paul, with certain indignation, indicts God's law and, with great disdain, calls it a yoke, yes, a yoke of slavery! Peter refers to it with the same terms: "Now then, why do you try to test God by putting on the necks of Gentiles a yoke that neither we nor our ancestors have been able to bear?" (Acts 15:10). In this way, he turns everything upside down. The false apostles discredited the promise and magnified the law and its works in the following way: "If indeed you want to be free from sin and death (they said), in order to attain righteousness and life, then you must fulfill the law; be circumcised; observe days, months, times, and years; offer sacrifices; and do similar things. Then that kind of obedience to the law will justify and save you." However, Paul goes against them. "They," he said, "those who teach the law in this way, are not able to free the consciences of sinners; instead, they entrap and entangle them with a yoke, yes, and with nothing less than a yoke of slavery!"

Thus he talks about the law with a great deal of disdain and contempt, calling it an insufferable slavery and a humiliating yoke. He wouldn't talk like this about the law unless he had a mighty good reason, for this pernicious opinion about the law, that the law justifies making people righteous before God, clings so tenaciously to human reason, and all humanity is so entangled in it, that it is very difficult to get away from its grip sane and sound. In order to strip the law from the glory of justifying, Paul seems to compare those who seek righteousness through the law with the oxen who are tied to the yoke. The oxen pull from the yoke with great effort, yet they receive no reward except grass and hay, and when they can no longer pull from the yoke, they are slated for the slaughterhouse. That is just exactly what happens to those who strive after righteousness through the law; they are captives and oppressed by the yoke of slavery—that is, with the law. But when they are all worn out by years of the works of the law with great pain and effort, their final reward is none other than remaining forever under the yoke of slavery, for as we've said before, the law does nothing more than bring out, increase, and aggravate sin; it accuses, terrorizes, condemns, and stirs up wrath. In the end, it plunges the conscience into desperation, and this is the most miserable and insufferable yoke there could ever be (Romans 3, 4, 7).

Thus he uses very vehement words because what he would want the most is to persuade them not to suffer this intolerable burden that the false apostles wish to impose on them or for them to be tangled up once again with the yoke of slavery. It's as if had said, "We are here for no small matter but for one of two things. It's either for eternal freedom or for an endless slavery," for just as freedom from God's wrath and all evil is not according to a temporal political decree from the flesh but is given forever, so also the yoke of sin, death, the devil, and such is not temporary or from the flesh but unending (a yoke that oppresses all those who strive for justification and salvation through the law), for all those workers (of the law) who commit themselves to meticulously and precisely fulfill and perform in all things (Paul is talking about them) will never have peace and quiet in their conscience.[11] As long as they live, they will have doubts about God's goodwill toward them, they

---

[11] *numquam quieti et pacati sunt.*

will always be fearful of death and God's wrath and judgment; and when this life is over, they will be punished with eternal condemnation for their unbelief.

Therefore, the doers of the law[12] are properly called (as the proverb goes) "the martyrs of the devil."[13] These impose on themselves greater toil and trouble to purchase hell than the Christian martyrs do for heaven, for they torment themselves in two ways: First, they afflict themselves miserably while they are here, doing many arduous tasks and grand works. But everything is in vain. Second, after they die, they pile on themselves a reward of eternal damnation. They are the most miserable martyrs, in this life as well as the next, and their slavery is eternal. On the contrary, the faithful suffer trials in the world, but they have peace in Christ because they have believed that He has overcome the world. Therefore, we must resist, firmly persevering in that freedom that Christ bought for us with His death. We should be alert so that we won't get tangled up again with that yoke of slavery. This is what has happened with the fanatical spirits. Having fallen from faith and this freedom, they have purchased for themselves here a transitory slavery, and in the coming world, they will be oppressed with an eternal yoke. As far as the Papists, most have slowly degenerated in nothing else but Epicureans.[14] That is why they sing that little ditty that they have chosen as their freedom in the flesh: *Ede, bibe, lude, post mortem nulla voluptas*—that is, "Let us eat, drink, and play, for there are no pleasures beyond the grave" for that is how they are in themselves the slaves of the devil who holds them subject to his slavery doing nothing else but his will. Therefore, they will feel this eternal bondage in hell. Up to this point, Paul's exhortations have been vehement and passionate, but that's nothing compared to what lies ahead.

VERSE 2. Mark my words! I, Paul, tell you that if you let yourselves be circumcised, Christ will be of no value to you at all [NIV].

Here, Paul is greatly moved with zeal and fervor in spirit and thunders against the law and circumcision. These fiery words proceed from great indignation stirred up by the Holy Spirit when he says, "Mark my words! I, Paul." "Since I have received knowledge of the Gospel that has been given to no one else, but by revelation of Jesus Christ, and I have been duly authorized from on high to publish and preach it, I declare this new but unequivocal truth:[15] 'If you circumcise yourselves, you will have achieved the same as if you had declared that Christ was altogether worthless to you.'" Here, we have a very powerful statement, when Paul says that to circumcise

---

[12] *operadores legis.*

[13] *vocantur diaboli (ut mere vulgi loquar) martyres.* In a footnote, Luther summarizes *martyres diaboli*, "the devil's martyrs."

[14] *papistas . . . major et potior pars degenerat hodie paulatim in Epicuraeos.*

[15] *sententiam novam quidem, sed certam et veram.*

is the same as saying that Christ was just a loafer,[16] not in Himself, but with respect to the Galatians. Having been deceived by the subtle arguments of the false apostles, they had come to believe that in addition to faith in Christ it was necessary for the faithful to circumcise; otherwise, they could not attain to salvation.

This text is like a foundation stone. It allows us with all certainty and freedom to judge every doctrine, works, religions, and ceremonies performed by all. Everyone who teaches that anything is necessary for salvation (whether Papists, Muslims, Jews, or sectarians) in addition to faith in Christ or should invent any other work or religion[17] or observe any regulation, tradition, or ceremony at all, thinking that due to such things will attain to the forgiveness of sins, righteousness and eternal life, should listen in this text to the sentence pronounced by the Holy Spirit against them all by means of the apostle Paul: "Christ is worthless to you."[18] Seeing that Paul dares to issue this sentence against the law and circumcision, which were ordained by God Himself, what would he say today against the hay and soot of human traditions?

Therefore, this text thunders mightily against the Pope's entire kingdom. All of them, priests, monks, and hermits, have deposited their confidence and all their faith in their own works, righteousness, vows, and merits (their very best) and not in Christ. However, with all wickedness and blasphemy, they imagine Him to be an irate judge, who accuses and condemns. Therefore, let them hear their verdict here: "To them Christ was a worthless person,"[19] for if they are able to remove their sins and merit the forgiveness of sins and eternal life through their own righteousness and right living, then, why was Christ born? What benefit do they receive from His passion and shedding of blood, from His resurrection, victory against sin, death, and the devil, believing that they have been able to defeat these monsters with their own stubborn tenacity? And what tongue could ever express (or heart conceive) how dreadful it is to take away Christ's benefits? Thus the apostle pronounces these words greatly annoyed and highly indignant: "If you let yourselves be circumcised, Christ will be of no value to you at all."[20]—that is, you will gain nothing from all His benefits for in vain did He pour them out over you all.

It is sufficiently clear here that there is nothing under the sun more harmful than the doctrines of men and their works. That's because in one blow they overthrow the truth of the Gospel, faith, true worship to God, and Christ Himself to whom the Father has delivered all things: "In whom are hidden all the treasures of wisdom and knowledge," "for in Christ all the fullness of the Deity lives in bodily form" (Colossians 2:3, 9, NIV). Therefore, all the authors or supporters of

---

[16] *Christum otiosum fieri.*

[17] *cultus.*

[18] *quod Christus illis simpliciter non prosit.*

[19] *quod Christus sit illis otiosus.*

[20] *Christus vobis nihil proderit.*

the doctrines of works are oppressors of the Gospel, they remove from Christ the benefit of His own death, stain and disfigure His Sacraments, they strip them of their proper use. In summary, they are blasphemous, enemies and deniers of God and of all His promises and benefits. Whoever is not moved by these words of Paul (which call the law a yoke of slavery) and refutes the observance of circumcision as necessary for salvation robs Christ of His benefit. Such people remain stuck in the law and circumcision (and what about the traditions of men?). Therefore, the only thing they are left with is the trust they have deposited in their own righteousness and works; that is why they cannot be moved at heart to seek this freedom there is in Christ. Their heart is harder than stone.

This verdict could not be any clearer, that Christ is worthless, that He was born, crucified, and resurrected without any value for those who are circumcised— that is, for those who have placed their confidence in circumcision, for, as I've said before, here, Paul is not talking about the work of circumcision itself (which brings no grief at all to those who don't trust it will bring them righteousness). However, he is talking about the use of the work—that is, regarding the confidence and righteousness attributed to the work, for we should understand Paul regarding his subject matter, or according to the argument he presents, that people are not justified by the law or works or circumcision or anything like it. He does not say that the works in themselves are nothing but that the confidence and righteousness of works are nothing. This is what it means that Christ is of no value at all. Thus to everyone who is circumcised, believing that it is necessary for justification, Christ has been of no value at all.

Let us keep this well in mind when temptation visits us in private, when the devil accuses and harasses our conscience to lead us to despair. He is the father of lies and the enemy of Christian liberty. He torments us at every instant with false fears so that when our conscience has lost this Christian liberty, it will be forced to feel guilt for sin and feel condemned and thus continue in anguish and great panic.[21] When that great dragon (I say), that ancient serpent the devil (who deceives the entire world accusing the brothers and sisters day and night before the presence of God),[22] comes and accuses you, saying that you have done nothing good and have also transgressed God's law, respond like this: "You distress me with the memory of my past sins; you also remind me that I have done nothing good. However, for me, all that means nothing. Because if on the one hand I trust in my good works and on the other I lack assurance because I haven't done them, either way Christ would be of no value to me. Therefore, if you rub my sins on my face or my good works, I accept neither one of them. I put them all far away from my sight and rest alone on this freedom with which Christ has set me free. I know that He is of value to me, thus I will not be the cause for Christ to be worthless to me.

---

[21] *ut semper sit in metu, ac sentiat reatum et pavores.*

[22] Revelation 12:10. Luther included the reference in the Latin text.

However, that would happen if on the one hand, I would presume that I could buy God's grace and eternal life[23] through my good works and on the other, I would distress about my salvation due to my sins."

Therefore, let us learn diligently to distance Christ from all works, be they bad or good; from all law, be it God's or man's and from all feelings of anguish in the conscience, for Christ has nothing to do with these. I do admit that He does have something to do with anguished consciences but not to torment them but to lift them up and comfort them when they are deeply troubled. Therefore, if Christ comes to you in the likeness of an angry judge or a legislator that demands a strict accounting of our past life, then we must assure ourselves that that is not Christ but a demon out of control. Scripture draws a picture of Christ as the place where we have been forgiven,[24] as our Advocate and our Comforter.[25] That is how He is and forever will be. Jesus cannot change in the very essence of who He is.

The devil (transformed into a likeness of Christ) will argue with us in the following way: "You should do this, for thus says my word, you should have done it, but you have not, and you should not have done the other, but you did it; that is why I will vent my vengeance on you." However, don't even blink. Immediately, we should think, "Christ does not speak like that, He does not pile distress upon distress"; "He will not snap off a broken reed or snuff out a smoldering wick" (Matthew 12:20). He certainly speaks harshly to those with a hard heart, but He attracts the anguished and afflicted with the greatest love and kindness, saying, "Come to me, all who labor and are heavy laden, and I will give you rest" (Matthew 11:28). "I came not to call the righteous, but sinners" (Matthew 9:13). "Take heart, my son; your sins are forgiven" (Matthew 9:2). "Be of good cheer, I have overcome the world" (John 16:33). "For the Son of man came to seek and to save the lost" (Luke 19:10). Therefore, let's be alert, lest we are deceived by the trickeries and subtleties of Satan and we receive an accuser and condemning judge instead of a Comforter and Savior. That is how a false masked Christ could appear—that is, the devil—to lead us to push Christ aside so that He will be of no value to us. We have said all this with respect to the private and particular temptations and how we should behave when they come upon us without warning.

VERSE 3. I testify again to every man who receives circumcision that he is bound to keep the whole law.

The first drawback is certainly quite significant, since Paul says here that for the circumcised Christ is of no value at all. But this text that follows is no less important, for it says that those who are circumcised are obligated to keep the entire law.

---

[23] *consecuturum gratiam et vita aeternam.*

[24] *propitiatorem.*

[25] *propiciatorem, interpellatorem et consolatorem.*

He says these words with such spirited passion and vehemence that he confirms them by uttering an oath: "I testify"—that is, "I so swear by the living God." But these words may be understood in the negative as well as the positive in the following way: In the negative, "I testify to every man who receives circumcision that he goes into debt that cannot be repaid unless he keeps the entire law"[26]—that is, that by the mere fact of circumcision, he is not really circumcised, and even in the observance of the law, he does not fulfill it but transgresses against it. It seems to me this is Paul's simplest and truthful meaning in this text. Thereafter, in chapter 6, he explains, saying, "Not even those who are circumcised keep the law" (6:13). He says the same thing previously in 3:10 "Those who are of the works of the law are under a curse." It's as if he had said, "Even though you have been circumcised, nonetheless, you are not righteous and free from the law (this is what we saw before in 3:10).[27] Instead, by that mere fact you become debtors and slaves to the law. The more you attempt to satisfy the law and be free from the law, the more you get entangled and trapped in its yoke, giving the law greater power to accuse and condemn you. This is nothing but racing backward against the crab and trying to clean up dung with dung."

I say this in relation to the words of Paul. I, myself, have learned this by my own experience and in that of others. I have seen many who have painfully labored and conscientiously have done everything possible. They fasted, prayed, and covered themselves with hair, punishing and tormenting their bodies with various oppressive exercises (by which they are totally exhausted, although at the beginning they seemed to be made of iron) and all this to put their conscience at ease. However, the more they struggled, the more they were assailed with panic, especially at the hour of death; they were so fearful that notwithstanding all the holiness in their lives, I have seen many murderers and other criminals condemned to death die with greater courage.

That is why it is an established truth, that those who keep the law do not fulfill it, for the greater their efforts to fulfill the law the more they transgress against it. Our judgment with regards to the traditions of men is similar. The more people attempt to pacify their conscience in such a way the more they afflict and torment it. When I was a monk, I lived in accordance to the strict regulations of my order in every way possible. I confessed with great devotion and took into account all my sins (even before getting started I was already contrite!). I would frequently return to the confessional and fulfilled to the letter every penance imposed on me. However, notwithstanding all that, my conscience never assured me, but I always doubted: "You didn't do this or that quite well enough; you didn't have enough contrition and remorse; you omitted this one and the other sin in your confession;

---

[26] *debitor est totius legis servandae.*

[27] Here, Luther is cross-referencing his students to a previous lecture, dealing with Galatians 3:10.

etc." Thus the more I attempted to help my feeble, fickle, and afflicted conscience with the traditions of men, the more feeble, doubtful, and distressed I felt. Thus the more I observed the traditions of men, the more I transgressed against them; and attempting to attain righteousness through my order, I never reached it, for it is impossible (as Paul said) to appease the conscience through the works of the law, and even less through the traditions of men, without the promise and the good news found in Jesus Christ.

Therefore those who attempt to be justified and revived by the law are so much more distanced from righteousness and life than the publicans, sinners, and prostitutes, for these do not put their trust in their own works seeing that their deeds bring no hope at all of ever receiving grace and forgiveness of sins, for if the righteousness and works done according to the law do not justify, how could there ever be justification in the sins committed against it? But in this regard, they are in a better spot than the justifiers, for they do not trust in their own works, which greatly hinder true faith in Christ. On the contrary, the justifiers to all appearances abstain from sin and live in holiness without stain as the world looks on. Thus they have quite the opinion of their own righteousness, but without true faith in Christ, it will all collapse! For this reason, they feel even more distraught than the publicans and prostitutes who do not present their good works before God to remove His displeasure so that through them He will reward them with eternal life (as the justifiers expect) because they have nothing to offer; instead, all they want is for their sins to be forgiven on account of Christ.[28]

Therefore, those who strive to do the works of the law with this opinion, that they wish to be justified by the law, become debtors to the entire law. However, they don't even fulfill one letter of the law. That is because the law has not been given to that end, to justify, but to uncover sin, to terrorize, to accuse, and to condemn. Thus however much people try to appease their conscience with the law and works, to that same extent, they leave their conscience in doubt and confusion. Ask the monks (who at great pains and with much devotion attempt to quiet their conscience through the practice of their traditions) if they can with all assurance affirm that their way of life pleases God and if from all their efforts they have found grace before God. If they confess truthfully, they will respond, "Although I may live a blameless life and most diligently observe the rules of my order, it's impossible for me to say with all assurance if God is pleased with my obedience or not."

I've already mentioned Arsenius. We read about him in Life of the Fathers. *He had spent a long time living in the greatest holiness and abstinence. However, when he felt that death was approaching, he began to feverishly fear, lament, and panic.[29] When he was asked why he was so fearful of death, he gave this answer: "Although I*

---

[28] *propter Christum.*

[29] *affici.* In twenty-first-century English, Luther might have said, "He began to lose it."

have fulfilled my contract,[30] *with no letup serving God throughout my life, I answer that according to people's judgment I have lived a blameless life. But God's judgments are totally different than the way people judge. Through my holy and austere life, I have not gained anything but fear and horror of death. If I am going to be saved, I must part with all my righteousness and lean only on God's mercy. 'I believe in Jesus Christ the Son of God, our Lord, that He suffered, was crucified, and died for my sins.'*[31]

The other explanation is to the affirmative. Whoever is circumcised is committed to keeping the entire law. Those who receive Moses in one point have the obligation to receive him in all points. It is worthless to say that only circumcision is necessary and not the remaining laws of Moses because for the same reason you were circumcised, you must also keep the entire law. Well, whoever makes a commitment to keep the entire law does nothing but demonstrate that in fact Christ has not yet come. But then if this is true, we are also obligated to keep all the Jewish ceremonies and the laws that regulate meats, places, and times. We must also keep on waiting for Christ's coming to abolish the Jewish kingdom and priesthood and establish a new kingdom throughout the world. But all Scripture testifies, and its outcome clearly states, that Christ has already come, that He has already abolished the law, and that He has entirely fulfilled all things as the prophets said about Him. Thus having abolished and removed the law from the middle, He has replaced it with grace and truth. Consequently, we are not justified by the law or its works but by faith in Christ, who has already come.[32]

There are some today who fancy some laws of Moses more than others and would like to bind us to them! That is just what the false apostles did in Paul's time. But there's no way at all this should be tolerated, for if we permit Moses to rule us in any one matter, we place ourselves under the obligation to obey him in all things. Thus we will not allow anyone to impose on us any of Moses' laws. We permit Moses to be read among us and that he be heard as a prophet and witness who testifies about Christ. Further, we can take good examples from his excellent laws and morals.[33] But there is no way we are going to allow him to take over our conscience. In that case, let him stay dead and buried, and let no one know the place of his grave.

The negative explanation, the first, shows itself to be the most apt and spiritual. However, both are fine and both condemn the righteousness of the law. The first is this: we are so incapable of achieving justification through the law,[34] that the more we

---

[30] *transegisset.*

[31] *Credo in Iesum Christum filium Dei, dominum nostram passum, crucifixum, mortuum pro peccatis meis etc.* Luther begins reciting the Creed to his astonished students, the Creed he repeated many times throughout his monastic life, and now as Gospel theologian.

[32] *Non igitur lex neque opera ejus, sed fides in Christum, qui jam venit, justificat.*

[33] *exempla optimarum legum et morum.*

[34] *tantum abesse, ut lege iustificemur.*

try to fulfill the law the more we violate it. The second is this: those who commit to fulfill any portion of the law are obligated to fulfill the entire law. To sum it all up, for those who strive to be justified by the law, Christ avails them nothing.[35]

Paul's most outstanding argument here is that to put confidence in the law is to deny Christ altogether.[36] However, it is quite daring to affirm that Moses' law, given by God to the people of Israel is to deny Christ.[37] Then why did God give it? It was necessary before Christ came and before He was manifested in the flesh because the law is our schoolteacher to lead us to Christ. But now that He has been manifested, by which we have believed in Him, we are no longer under the schoolteacher. We've already spoken at length about this in chapter 3. Therefore, all those who teach that the law is necessary for righteousness teach a complete denial of Christ and all His benefits.[38] They have made God a liar and even made a liar out of the law, for the law testifies of Christ and of the promises made to us regarding Christ and predicts that He would be a King of grace and not of law.

VERSE 4. You who want to be justified by the law have cut yourselves off from Christ.[39]

Paul explains here and further demonstrates that he is not just talking about the law or simply about circumcision. He is talking about the confidence and opinion that people have, that they will be justified through the law. It's as if he had said, "I do not entirely condemn the law nor circumcision (for it is lawful for me to drink, eat, and keep company with the Jews according to the law; it is lawful for me to circumcise Timothy). However, what I condemn is your attempt to justify yourselves through the law, as if Christ had not yet come. And even now that He has come, you still claim that unaided He alone is unable to justify. That is what I condemn, for it is nothing but to cut yourselves off from Christ." Thus he says, "You have separated yourselves"—that is, you are like the pharaoh of old, for you have said, "Let Christ go free, let Him go!" Thus Christ is not in you; He is no longer working in you. You are no longer participants of the knowledge, the Spirit, the fellowship, the favor, the liberty, the life, or the works of Christ. Instead, you have completely cut yourselves off from Christ so that He no longer has anything to do with you nor you with Him.

These words of Paul should be heeded with a great deal of attention. He says that to strive after righteousness through the law is nothing else but to cut yourself

---

[35] *summa, Christum nihil prodesse iis, qui lege justificri volunt.*

[36] Luther's footnote: *Qui lege conantur justificari, negant Christum,* "whoever strives to justify himself through the law, has denied Christ."

[37] *negationem Christi.*

[38] *Itaque qui legem necessariam ad justitiam docet, negationem Christi et omnium beneficiorum ejus docet.*

[39] *evacuati estis.*

off from Christ and accomplish nothing, except making Christ totally worthless for you. What else could be said more forcefully against the law? What could ever withstand this lightning and thunder? That is why it is impossible for Christ and the law to coexist in the same heart,[40] for one must give way to the other: It's the law, or it's Christ.[41] But if you believe that faith in Christ and confidence in the law can live together, then it's clear Christ is not living in your heart. Instead, it's the devil living in your heart,[42] taking the appearance of Christ, accusing and perturbing you. The devil will always demand from you the law and its works as righteousness. But the true Christ (as I've said before) neither calls you to give an account for your sins nor urges you to trust in your good works. The true knowledge of Christ, or of faith, does not argue if you have done good works with an eye to righteousness or if you have done bad works by which you will be condemned. Rather, it simply concludes the following: if you have done good works, you will not be justified by them or if you have done bad works, you will not be condemned because of them. I don't remove from good works their praiseworthiness, nor do I recommend bad works. But with respect to justification, I say, we must be sure that we have grasped on to Christ. Otherwise, if we strive to be justified through the law, we will achieve nothing except making Christ worthless to us, for it is Christ alone who justifies me, over against my bad works and without my good works. If I have this conviction regarding Christ, I am grasping on to the true Christ. But if I think that He requires from me the law and good works to attain righteousness, then He is worthless to me, and I cut myself off entirely from Him.

These are fearsome statements and threats against the righteousness of the law and self-righteousness. Further, they are also the strongest principles that sustain the article of justification. Therefore, at the end, we come to this conclusion: Either we lose Christ or we lose the righteousness of the law.[43] If you are left with Christ, you are righteous before God. But if you hold on to the law, Christ avails you nothing.[44] Further, you are left with the obligation to keep the entire law and the verdict against you has already been pronounced: "Cursed is anyone who does not uphold the words of this law by carrying them out" (Deuteronomy 27:26, NIV). And everything we've said about the law, we extend to the traditions of men. The Pope and all his religious followers must renounce all that they have ever trusted; otherwise, Christ will also avail them nothing. That is why we can say without hesitation how pernicious and pestilent is the doctrine of the Pope; he

---

[40] Luther's footnote: *Christus et lex non cohabitant.*

[41] *Ergo impossibile est Christum et legem simul habitare in corde. Aut enim legem aut Christum cedere oportet.*

[42] *Si vero in ea persuasione es, Christum et fiduciam legis cohabitare posse in corde, tum certo scias non Christum, sed diabolum in corde tuo habitare.*

[43] *Aut Christum amitte, aut justitiam legis.*

[44] *Si Christum retines, justus es coram Deo. Si legem, Christus nihil tibi prodest.*

has in fact achieved Christ availing nothing. In Jeremiah 23, God complains about the prophets because they prophesy lies and dream dreams arising from their own hearts leading people to forget His name. The false prophets departed from the correct interpretation of the law and from the true doctrine regarding Abraham's seed in whom all the nations of the earth would be blessed. Instead, they preached their own dreams so that people would forget their God. In the same way, the Papists drive away the entire world from Christ; they have obscured and disfigured the doctrine of Christ to the extent they have canceled out His power, teaching and expounding only the doctrine of works. Those who wholeheartedly take this entire issue into account will have no other response but to fear and tremble.

VERSE 4. You have fallen away from grace.

In other words, they are no longer in the kingdom of grace. When someone falls overboard from a ship and drowns, it doesn't matter from which side they fell off. In the same way, those who fall from grace will perish. Thus those who strive to justify themselves through the law have already fallen into the sea and placed themselves at risk of eternal death. *And what could ever be more insane and wicked than to decide to keep the law of Moses and thus lose grace and God's favor? If you should do this, you would heap on yourself wrath and all kinds of evil!* Well then, if those who strive to justify themselves through the keeping of the moral law have fallen from grace, where, then, I ask, will those who strive to justify themselves through their own vows and traditions end up? They will end up at the depths of hell. Oh no! Who said that? Instead, they go straight to heaven, for that is how they taught us: "Everyone who lives (that's what they say) according to the orders of Saint Francis, or any other, may God's peace and mercy be on him." Further, "Those who keep and persevere in chastity, obedience, and so on will have eternal life." Put this empty and wicked nonsense behind you! Listen here to what Paul teaches and Christ's instruction: "Whoever believes in the Son has eternal life, but whoever rejects the Son will not see life, for God's wrath remains on them." Also, "Whoever does not believe stands condemned" (John 3:18).

By the way, just as the doctrine of the Papists regarding the traditions of men, works, vows, and merits has become the most popular throughout the world, so also it is considered the best and closest to the truth; that is why the devil has built and established his kingdom with such great power. Thus when we impugn and defeat this doctrine with the power of God's word, it flees as chaff blown away by the wind. But then, we should not be astounded that Satan turns against us with such cruelty, stirring up slander and trouble everywhere, turning the whole world against us. That's when some will say that it would have been better for us to have kept quiet for then all those devils would not have been stirred up. But we are more concerned about holding God's favor in the highest esteem (whose glory we declare) than about the fury of the world that persecutes us, for who is the Pope and the entire world compared to God, *who we should indeed magnify and prefer above all creatures? Further, the wicked enlarge the tumults and troubles that Satan has provoked to destroy, or at least to disfigure, our doctrine. But on the contrary, we magnify the priceless benefit and the fruit of this doctrine, which we prefer above all upheaval, sectarian divisions, and scandals.* It is true that we are like children, weak, yet we are pregnant[45] with the divine treasure in fragile vessels of clay, but regardless of how fragile we are, the treasure is infinite and beyond our understanding.

These words, "you have fallen from grace," are not to be taken with indifference as if they mattered little. They have great weight and importance. Whoever has fallen from grace has totally relinquished the value of Christ's sacrifice,[46] the forgiveness of sins, righteousness, freedom, life, and everything else that Christ achieved as merits in our favor through His death and resurrection. On the other hand, to fall from grace is to acquire God's wrath and judgment, sin, death, the devil's bondage, and eternal damnation. This text here powerfully confirms and fortifies the defense of our faith, or the article of justification, and marvelously comforts us against the cruel fury of the Papists who persecute and condemn us as heretics because we teach this article. Indeed, this text should bring fear to the enemies of faith and grace—that is, to all who strive after the righteousness of works so they won't persecute and blaspheme the word of grace, life, and eternal salvation. They have been so obstinate and hard-hearted that seeing they cannot see and hearing they don't listen. When they hear this terrible sentence pronounced by the apostle against them, they don't understand it. Then let them stay that way, for they are blind and blind guides of the blind.

LECTURE 34: Friday, November 20

VERSE 5. But we by the spirit, because of faith,[47] await the hope of righteousness.[48]

Here, Paul puts the final stitch on the fabric with an astounding declaration: "You strive to justify yourselves through the law, circumcision, and through works, but we do not seek to be justified through those means, lest Christ avail us nothing. In that case, we will owe a huge debt to the entire law and most certainly be fallen

---

[45] *gestantes thesaurum coelestem in testaceis vasis.*

[46] *expiationem.*

[47] *spiritu ex fide.*

[48] Translator's note: The Greek reads, ἡμεῖς γὰρ Πνεύματι ἐκ πίστεως ἐλπίδα δικαιοσύνης ἀπεκδεχόμεθα. The literal English translation is "we by the spirit, because of faith [or from faith], await the hope of righteousness." This translation agrees with Luther's translation used throughout his Latin lectures (Jerome's Vulgate): *nos enim spiritu ex fide spem iustitiae expectamus.*

from grace. Rather, in the spirit, and through faith, we await the hope of righteousness." Here, we should pay attention to every word, for they are stated with great eloquence. Here, he doesn't just say as he normally does that we are justified by faith or in the Spirit by faith, but he adds, "We await the hope of righteousness." He includes hope in order to embrace the entire subject of faith. *When he says, "We in the spirit because of faith," there is an opposing part in the word spirit. It's as if he had said, "We do not strive to be justified in the flesh, but thankfully, by the Spirit. This spirit is not according to the fanatics who claim that each one is his own teacher, that's how the heretics boast about the Spirit. But our Spirit is from faith." He had already spoken fully about the Spirit. Here, he not only says, "The Spirit justifies us by faith," but also adds, "We await the hope of righteousness," which is something new.*

According to the Scriptures, hope must be understood in two ways. First, hope centers on its object, the very thing you are waiting for. The other expresses the emotion of waiting. Colossians chapter 1 tells us about what we are waiting for: "Because of the hope laid up for you in heaven" (Colossians 1:5)—that is, what you wait for. Regarding the feeling while you wait, it is understood from Romans 8:24, 25: "Hope that is seen is not hope; for who hopes for what he already sees? But if we hope for what we do not see, with perseverance we wait eagerly for it."[49] This last text may also be understood in two ways, and thus has a double meaning. The first is as follows: "Our spirit, from faith, hopes for our awaited righteousness"— that is, we await our righteousness, which most certainly will be revealed in its own time. The second is this: Our spirit, from faith, awaits with longing for the righteousness we have hoped for—that is, we are righteous. However, our righteousness has not yet been revealed; it is still pending from hope, but "in hope we have been saved" (Romans 8:24).

However, as long as we live here, sin remains in our flesh. There is also a law in our flesh and our members that rebels against the law of our mind and leads us captive to serve sin. Well, when these feelings of the flesh become furious and govern, we on the other hand through the Spirit, strive against them creating a space for hope. It is certain that we have begun declared righteous by faith. That is how we received the first fruit of the Spirit. The mortification of the flesh has also begun within us but righteousness has not been fully perfected in us. Then what is still lacking is for us to be made perfectly righteous, and this is what we await with longing. Thus although we have not yet been made righteous, we already are, through hope.[50]

This is most sweet and solid assurance. All distressed consciences that feel their sin and are horrified by every fiery dart of the devil may receive this wonderful assurance. The sense of sin, God's wrath, death, hell, and any other terror is oppressively powerful when the conscience is conflicted, as I, myself, know all

---

[49] NASB.

[50] *nondum est in re, sed adhun in spe.*

too well, having learned from experience. Then all those who are terribly afflicted should be given the following counsel in the middle of their distress: "You desire to experience your justification with your feelings[51]—that is, you desire to feel God's favor in the same way as you feel your sin, but this cannot be. Instead, your righteousness must exceed every feeling of sin.[52] Your righteousness or justification to which you grasp is not built on what can be seen or felt.[53] Instead, your hope is based on this: before the presence of God you are righteous.[54] Thus your righteousness cannot be seen or felt. In God's own time, your righteousness will be made visible and revealed in its fullness. Thus you should not judge according to the feelings of sin that distress and frighten you but according to the promise and the doctrine of faith by which you are promised Christ, who is your perfection and eternal righteousness."[55] As I hope, I long for the feelings of hope, in the middle of my fearful anguish due to my sense of sin. Yet hope provokes and lifts up my faith by which I trust in Him, my righteousness. Then hope in that for which we hope is this: although we are unable to see our righteousness, at the appointed end time it will be revealed.

Any of the two meanings fit. But the first, which penetrates to one's inner desires and feeling of hope, brings a greater assurance, for the righteousness that there is in me is not yet perfect, nor am I able to feel it yet. Even so, I won't panic, for faith allows me to see Christ in whom I trust, and when by faith I have grasped on to Him, I am fighting against the fiery darts of the devil. Thus hope revives me against the feelings of sin and assures me that in heaven there's a perfect righteousness ready and waiting for me. Thus both meanings are true, that I am already righteous through that righteousness by which I am already on my way. Also, I gather strength against sin through that same hope and wait for the final consummation of that perfect righteousness in the heavens. However, these things are properly understood only when they are carried over into life.

What Is the Difference Between Faith and Hope?

At this point, the question arises, what is the difference between faith and hope? The papal academicians and scholars have struggled at length with this topic but have never said anything with any certainty. Yes, it's even difficult for us who diligently study the Scriptures, as well as with greater fullness and power of the Spirit (I say this without any boasting), to find any difference. There's great affinity between faith and hope. One cannot separate one from the other. However, there's

---

[51] *sensitivam iusticiam.*
[52] *Sed tua justitia debet transcendere sensum peccati.*
[53] *tua Justitia non est visibilis, non est sensibilis.*
[54] *coram Deo justum esse.*
[55] *Christus, qui est perfecta et aeterna justitia tua.*

a difference between them, which is due to their differing functions, different ways through which they operate, and their purposes.

First, they differ with respect to the subject—that is, the foundation on which one each rests. Faith rests on the understanding and hope on the will. But they can never be separated one from the other, since the two cherubim on the mercy seat could not be separated.

Second, they differ with regards to their function—that is, in how they operate. Faith communicates the tasks ahead: it teaches, prescribes, and directs; it is something made known.[56] Hope is an exhortation that provokes the mind to find strength, to be inspired with boldness and courage. It strengthens it to suffer and persevere in adversity and in that state of mind to wait for better things to come.

Third, they differ regarding their object—that is, that special object on which they fix their gaze. Faith has truth as its object, teaching us to cling to it, having its gaze fixed on the pledged word and the promise. Hope has as its object God's kindness and looks on all things that have been promised in the word—that is, on those things that faith teaches we are to wait for.

Fourth, they differ in their order. Faith is the beginning of life at the outset of all tribulation (Hebrews 11). However, hope follows and proceeds from the tribulation (Romans 5:3, 4).

Fifth, they contrast each other. Faith is our teacher and judge; it fights against errors and heresies and judges spirits and doctrines. But hope is, as it were, the commanding general in the battle field, struggling against tribulations, the cross, impatience, despair, weaknesses, hopelessness, and blasphemy and yet anticipating better things, even when surrounded by all evil.

Therefore, when faith instructs me through God's word, I grasp on to Christ, believing in Him from the bottom of my heart (but this doesn't happen without the will), then I am righteous through this knowledge. When I am justified by this faith or by this knowledge, the devil immediately appears. He is the father of deceit and attempts to extinguish my faith through trickery and subtleties—that is, through lies, errors, and heresies. Further, since he is a murderer, he goes around to violently oppress our faith. Here, hope comes out fighting; it grasps onto that which faith has prescribed and defeats the devil, who wars against the faith. After this victory, peace and joy in the Holy Spirit follows. Thus in reality faith and hope are barely discernible one from the other, yet there is a certain difference between them. To have a better understanding of this matter, I will try to explain it with an example.

In the civil government,[57] restraint and a firm hand differ. Yet these two virtues are so close they cannot be pulled apart. Firmness is an unyielding will, which is not set back in adversity; instead, it perseveres courageously and hopes for better things. But if firmness rejects the good advice of restraint, it is nothing more than

---

[56] *notitia.*

[57] *in politia.*

recklessness and foolhardiness. On the one hand, if firmness were not to join with restraint, such restraint would be in vain and totally worthless. In the same way as in government, restraint is empty without a firm hand, so in theology faith without hope would be nothing. However, if hope perseveres and is constant in adversity, at the end it will conquer all evil. On the other hand, just as firmness without restraint is nothing but recklessness, so also hope without faith is nothing but presumption of spirit; it is tempting God. That is because it does not know Christ and the truth taught by faith; thus it is only blind recklessness and arrogance. That is how every faithful person should see to it that his understanding is taught by faith.[58] In this way, his mind will be guided in trials so that he can hope for those better things that faith has revealed and taught.

Faith is the dialectic that conceives the idea regarding the object of its belief. Hope is the rhetoric that magnifies, urges, persuades, and beckons to persevere so that faith will not fail in the hour of temptation but should keep a firm grip on the word and not let it go. Dialectic and rhetoric[59] are different skills that nonetheless are so closely related as to be inseparable. Without dialectical arguments, the orator has nothing to teach with any conviction. Without the skills of a public speaker, the debater does not move his audience. However, those who put them together teach and persuade. In the same way, faith and hope are different states of mind, for faith is not hope, nor is hope faith, but due to their great affinity, they are inseparable. Thus just as dialect and rhetoric go hand in hand joined in purpose, so faith and hope are similarly understood. Therefore, there is the same difference between faith and hope in theology as between understanding and volition in philosophy, restraint and firmness in government, and dialectic and rhetoric in oratory.[60]

In summary, faith is conceived through teaching, for instruction brings the truth into the mind. Hope is conceived through exhortation, for exhortation revives hopefulness in the middle of affliction. Hope confirms those who have been justified by faith; this confirmation strengthens them to resist adversity in the face of defeat. Nonetheless, if the spark of faith were not to illumine the will, it would not be persuaded to cling onto hope. We who have faith then, by which we understand its teaching, are given understanding into heavenly wisdom, grasp on to Christ, and persevere in grace, for as soon as we grasp Christ through faith, we confess Him. Immediately, our enemies, the world, the flesh, and the devil

---

[58] *intellectum fide informatum.*

[59] Argumentation and public speaking.

[60] This entire paragraph reminds us that Luther was lecturing a group of well-schooled seminarians trained in the skills he mentions. Here, I have left intact the academic register of the language. This way, the reader gets a glimpse of the academic level of both students and lecturer. However, the academic register of this paragraph is not descriptive of Luther's style throughout the lectures. Luther's style, although in Latin, was not classical or even academic Latin. Only rarely (as in this example) did he surprise his students with academic rhetoric.

conspire against us, hating and persecuting us most cruelly, in the body as well as in the spirit. Thus we, believing and justified by faith, in spirit await the hope of our righteousness.[61] We wait patiently, for all we see and feel is totally to the contrary, for the world, together with its prince the devil, is a powerful prowler, hunting us down from within and from without. Further, sin remains within us and it pushes us into hopelessness. However, even facing these threats, we will not surrender. Instead, through faith, we will gather strength and lift our minds, for faith teaches, guides, and lights our way. That is how we persevere, firm and without wavering, defeating all adversities through Him who loved us until our righteousness is revealed, in which we have believed and awaited.

Just as we first believed, we continue to hope and through revelation will receive all things. As long as we live here, we will stand firm in our belief, we will teach the word, and we will proclaim the knowledge of Christ to others. In this our daily task, we patiently suffer persecution (according to this text, "I kept on believing, even when I said, 'I am completely crushed'" [Psalm 116:10, GNB]) but are strengthened and encouraged through hope. That is because Scriptures exhort us to hope with the sweetest and most comforting promises, for they are revealed and taught by faith. That is how hope surges and increases in us "so that through the endurance taught in the Scriptures and the encouragement they provide we might have hope" (Romans 15:4, NIV).

Thus there is good reason Paul joins patience in tribulations together with hope in Romans 5 and 8 as well as in other places, for they awaken hope. However, faith (as I've already shown) comes before hope, for it is the beginning of life and comes before any tribulation, and it learns from Christ and grasps on to Him, without the cross of affliction. However, the knowledge of Christ cannot last long without the cross, without trials and conflicts. In this case, the mind should be provoked to have an unwavering spirit (for hope is nothing more than spiritual strength, as faith is nothing more than spiritual discernment), for it consists in suffering, according to the saying "that through patience." These three things then live together among the faithful: faith, which teaches the truth and defends from heretical error; hope, which suffers and conquers every adversity of body and spirit; and love, which works what is good in everything, as follows from the text. And that is how a person is whole and perfect in this life, within and without, until the awaited righteousness is revealed, which will be a perfectly fulfilled righteousness,[62] lasting forever and ever.

Further, this text contains a unique doctrine as a source of comfort. With respect to doctrine, it demonstrates that we are justified not by works, sacrifices, or the ceremonies of Moses' law, much less by the works and traditions of men,

---

[61] *Ideo sic credentes, justificati spiritu ex fide expectamus spem justitiae nostrae.*
[62] *consummata.*

but by Christ alone.[63] Therefore, all that the world values as good and holy without Christ is nothing more than sin, error, and flesh. Thus circumcision and the keeping of the law, as well as works, religions, the vows of the monks, and all who trust in their own righteousness, are nothing but flesh. But we (says Paul) are above all these things in the spirit and the inner man, for Christ is our possession through faith and in the middle of suffering, through hope, we wait for that righteousness that by faith is already ours.

The comfort is this: in the great and terrifying conflicts, when the sense of sin, hopelessness of spirit, desperation, and such are so great (for they pierce the heart to its depth and attack it with great power), you should not follow the inclination of your own feelings. Otherwise, you will say, "I feel the terrifying horrors of the law and the tyranny of sin; these not only conspire against me but also tie me up and take me captive so that I feel neither comfort or righteousness at all. Thus I am a sinner, not righteous. If I am a sinner, then I am guilty of eternal death." But you should fight against this feeling, saying, "No matter how much I may feel entirely drowned and absorbed by sin and my heart should say that God is offended and angered with me, that is nothing but a pure lie, these are just my own feelings and emotions judging me." God's word (which I should follow in the face of these terrors and not my feelings) teaches something much better—that is, "The Lord is near to the brokenhearted, and saves the crushed in spirit" and "A broken and contrite heart you, God, will not despise." Further, Paul demonstrates here that those who are justified in spirit by faith alone, hope for righteousness not because they feel it but because they anticipate it.

Therefore, when the law accuses you, and sin distresses, you and all you feel is God's wrath and judgment, notwithstanding all this, do not lose hope. Instead, take on God's armor, the shield of faith, the helmet of hope,[64] and the sword of the spirit and show your worth as a good and courageous fighter. By faith, grasp on to Christ, who is the Lord over the law and sin and all things that come with these. Believing in Him you are justified but reason and the feelings of your own heart will not tell you this, only God's word says it. Further, in the middle of these conflicts and terrors that so frequently turn against you and fluster you, through hope, patiently wait for righteousness, which is now by faith alone; it has just begun and is imperfect, until in its own time it is fully revealed as perfect and eternal. "It's that within myself I don't feel any righteousness at all or at least feel it but little." However, it is not about feeling but believing that you are righteous.[65] And unless you believe that you are righteous, you greatly offend Christ, who has cleansed you "by the washing with water through the word." He is the one who also died on the cross, condemned sin, and killed death itself so that through Him you may obtain righteousness and

---

[63] *sed per solum Christum.*

[64] *galeam spei.* Luther paraphrases the text and changes "salvation" to "hope."

[65] *Non sentire, sed credere debes te justitiam habere.*

eternal life. You cannot deny these facts (unless you openly declare yourself to be totally wicked, blaspheming against God, despising God altogether, rejecting all His promises and Christ with all His benefits). Consequently, you cannot deny that you are righteous.[66]

Therefore, let us learn that in the middle of great and terrible distress, when our conscience can no longer be aware of anything else but sin, and to our judgment, God is angry with us, and we feel that Christ has withdrawn His face from us, we are not to pay attention to the feelings or emotions of our heart. Let us rather grip onto God's word that says God is not angered but instead looks upon the afflicted, the poor and humble of spirit who tremble at His word (Isaiah 66:2) and that Christ does not turn His back of the weary and heavy burdened but renews and comforts them. These texts clearly teach that neither the law nor works grant us righteousness or any comfort.[67] Instead, this is the work of the Holy Spirit through the faith of Christ, who lifts up our hope, which defeats all distress and tribulation, and perseveres in conquering all adversity. There are very few who know how weak and fragile are faith and hope when they suffer the cross and when undergoing conflict, for it seems that the flickering flame is about to go out when the winds flare up. The faithful are those who believe amid these terrors and injuries, hoping against hope. Utilizing faith in the promise with respect to Christ they fight against the feelings of sin and God's wrath. But it is not until the aftermath when by experience they understand that this spark of faith, no matter how small (for thus it will seem to reason, for reason is barely aware of it), is a powerful fire and absorbs all our sins and fears.

There is nothing in the whole world that is dearer or more treasured to the truly pious[68] than this doctrine, for all those who understand this doctrine know what the entire world ignores. To wit, sin, death, and all misery, affliction, and calamity of body and spirit are reversed and turn for the benefit and gain of the elect. Further, they know that God is nearer to them when He seems the most distant. When it seems to us that He is angered, when it seems He would afflict and destroy, that is precisely when He is a merciful High Priest and loving Savior, for they also know they have an eternal righteousness, which they await through hope as a certain, sure possession set apart for them in heaven, even when they feel the horrible terrors of sin and death. What's more, that is when they are lords over all things, when they feel they are destitute of everything, according to what is written: "Having nothing, and yet having all things" (2 Corinthians 6:10). Scripture says that this is what it means to receive comfort through hope. But this insight is not learned without great and repeated temptations.

---

[66]   *ideo neque te justum ese negare potes.*
[67]   *legem et opera non afferre justitiam et consolationem.*
[68]   *vere pii.*

427

VERSE 6. For in Christ Jesus, neither circumcision nor uncircumcision counts for anything, but only faith working through love[69] [NABRE].

The papal scholars[70] twist this text around to their opinion, for they teach that we are justified by love or works. They say that faith,[71] although it is infused from above (I am not talking here about faith acquired[72] through our effort), does not justify unless it is shaped by love,[73] for they call love "that which makes grace gracious"[74] or justifiable (to use our own word, or rather Paul's). Then they say that love is acquired[75] through our congruous merit[76] etc. Further, they affirm that even faith is on the same level as mortal sin.[77] That is how they totally strip away justification from faith and through this means attribute it only to love (that's how they reason). They attempt to validate their argument through this text from Paul: "Faith working through love,"[78] as if Paul had said, "Look, faith does not justify, no, it's really nothing in itself, unless you add to it the worker called Love,[79] which then gives shape to faith."

However, all these things are monstrosities, invented by cowards, for who is going to tolerate that faith, which is God's gift through the Holy Spirit infused into our hearts, could be on the same level as mortal sin? If they spoke of faith acquired through our own effort or a historic faith or an opinion conceived from history, they could even be tolerated, yes, even with respect to a historic faith they could be speaking the truth. But when they think like that about faith given from above, they confess that they totally lack all correct understanding of faith. Further, they read this Pauline text through a colored glass (as the proverb says) and pervert the text according to the dreams of their own fantasies.[80] The reason is that Paul does not say, "Faith which justifies through love" or "Faith which makes one acceptable through love." They invent such a text and force it here into this place. Paul even less says, "Love that makes one acceptable." He does not say that, but rather, he says, "Faith which works through love."[81] He says that the works are done by faith through love and not that the person is justified by love. But who could be so lacking in grammar as to

---

[69] *per charitatem eficax.*

[70] *sophistae.*

[71] Luther's footnote: *Sophistarum dogma de justificatione.*

[72] *fides acquisita.*

[73] *informatam per charitatem.*

[74] *gratia gratum faciens.*

[75] *acquiriri.*

[76] *nostro merito congrui.*

[77] *peccato mortali.*

[78] *per caritatem operatum.*

[79] *operatix caritas.*

[80] Luther inserts the following footnote: *Sophistae depravatores Pauli,* "the papal scholars corrupt Paul."

[81] *ex fide per caritatem.*

not understand the meaning of the words themselves, that it is one thing to be justified and another one to work? Paul's words are clear: "Faith that works through love."[82] *Thus it is clear fraud when they invalidate Paul's clear meaning and interpret "work" as "justified" and "works" as "righteousness," for even in moral philosophy, they are compelled to confess that works are not righteousness but that the works arise from righteousness.*

Further, Paul here is not dealing with faith as if it were a shapeless chaotic mass, purposeless and useless. Rather, he attributes the working to faith itself and not to love. He does not fantasize that faith is some crude and formless quality. Instead, he affirms that it is effective and diligent, not as a vacant substance but (as it is called) a formed substance, for he does not say, "Love is effective" but "Faith is effective." He does not say, "Love works" but "Faith works." Here, he describes love as an instrument of faith, through which faith works.[83] *And who is not aware that an instrument's strength, movement, and action does not come from itself but from the worker, operator, or agent? Who is going to say that the carpenter's hand is moved by the power and motion of the saw? Or that the helmsman gets his bearings from the sails and turns the helm aided by their power? Or deducing from Isaiah's example, who will say, "Can an ax or a saw overpower the one who uses it? Can a wooden pole lift whoever holds it?" (Isaiah 10:15, CEV). There's very little difference when they say that love is the form of faith or that it imparts strength and motion to faith or that it justifies. But seeing that not even Paul attributes works to love, how is it possible that he would attribute justification to love? Thus a great offense is indeed committed not just against Paul but also against faith and love when this text is twisted against faith to favor love.*

But this is what happens when careless readers and others of their kind bring their own assumptions to the reading of the Holy Scriptures. They should rather come with empty hands to receive the thoughts of the Scriptures. Further, they should diligently consider the words, comparing the ones that come before with the ones that follow them, attempting to reach a complete understanding of each text and not rummaging around for words and phrases that are more agreeable with their own dreamy fantasies, for here, Paul has set out to declare neither the nature of faith nor what is profitable before God. Here, he is not disputing (I say) regarding justification (for he had already done that quite extensively). Instead, as he summarizes his argument, he briefly demonstrates what the Christian's life itself is, saying, "In Christ Jesus, neither circumcision nor uncircumcision counts for anything, but only faith working through love"—that is, that faith is not feigned or hypocritical but instead it is real and alive. This is the faith that puts love into action doing good works and urges others to do them as well. It is the same thing as saying, those who desire to be true Christians, who belong to God's kingdom, should be true believers. If the works of

---

[82]   *per caritatem operatur.*

[83]   *Caritatem vero facit fidei velut instrumentum, per quod operatur.*

love do not follow their faith, they will not be true believers. So on either side, the right as well as the left, Paul shuts the door of Christ's kingdom to the hypocrites. On the left, he leaves out the Jews and all those who strive to work for their salvation, saying, "In Christ, neither circumcision"—that is, neither works nor liturgies nor any type of lifestyle in the world but faith alone, without any kind of confidence in works or merits, is worth anything before God. On the right, he leaves out the loafers and the lazy who say, "If faith justifies without works, then let's do nothing at all, just believe and do whatever we please." "It's not like that, enemies of grace," said Paul to the contrary. And although it is true that faith alone justifies, here, he is talking about another aspect of faith—that is, once faith has justified you, faith is not idle; instead, it gets busy working through love.[84]

Thus in this text, Paul presents the entire sum of Christian living—namely, that inwardly, it consists in faith toward God and externally, in love and good works toward our neighbor. In this way, the Christian is inwardly perfect through faith in God that has no need for our works and then, externally, before men to whom our faith brings no benefit at all. But on the other hand, they are benefitted by our love and works. Thus when we hear or understand this way of living the Christian life through faith and love (as I've explained it), we have not yet made any statement with respect to the nature of faith or the nature of love, for that's another topic. Regarding faith, or its internal nature, the strength and use of faith, Paul has already stated it before when he demonstrated that faith is our righteousness, or rather our justification before God. Here, he ties together love and works—that is, he talks about the external function of faith that provokes us to good works, to yield the fruits of love, for the benefit of our neighbor. *Therefore, since this text speaks about the Christian's way of life, no one with good judgment should understand it as justification before God. That would be a most poorly constructed dialectic. It would be the fallacy of composing in order to divide so what is said about one of the parts is then used to describe the whole. Dialectical thinking cannot tolerate (in contrast to rhetorical exposition) the figures of synecdoche and hyperbole. Dialectical thought is the master teacher that defines, separates, and concludes (as can be done with precision in these matters). But is this any kind of dialectic? "The human being is soul and body, neither can man exist without soul and body; therefore, the body understands but the soul all by itself does not understand." It is the same as the following dialectic: "Christian life is faith and love or faith working through love; therefore, love justifies, not just faith all by itself." But the human mind keeps on making things up!*

This text also teaches how horrible the darkness of the Egyptians who despise not only faith but also love is. These so-called Christians replace them with agonizing works of will power, tonsures, annoying coverings, meats, and countless other

---

[84] *Verum est sine operibus solam fidem justificare, sed de fide vera loquor, quae, postquam justificaverit, non stertet otiosa, sed est per caritatem operosa.*

masked performances. But all they do is pretend they are Christians! But here, Paul stands with great freedom and openly and clearly declares that what makes a person a Christian is faith working through love. He does not say, "A Christian consists of a cowl, a tonsure, fasts, special clothes, ceremonies but a true faith in God which loves one's neighbor and does what is good." It doesn't matter if one is a servant or lord, king, priest, man, or woman dressed in royal blue or rags or if one eats meat or fish; none of these things without exception makes the person a Christian but only faith and love. Everything else is falsehood and nothing but idolatry. Nonetheless, nothing is more despised than these among those who would like to be super Christians and belong to a holier church than God's own church! Once more, they admire and brag about their theatric performances and power of the will mockeries that they utilize to cover up their horrible idolatry, wickedness, greed, filth, hatred, homicides, and hell's entire kingdom of the devil! Such is the vehement power of hypocrisy and superstition throughout the ages from the beginning to the end of the world!

VERSE 7. You were running well; who hindered you from obeying the truth?

These words are clear. Paul affirms he has taught them the truth; it was the same as he had taught them before. They had run well as long as they had obeyed the truth, that which they had rightly believed and lived. But now, that was no longer the case, since the false apostles had led them astray. Further, he uses here a new figure to talk about the Christian life as a way, a path. Among the Hebrews, to run or walk is the same as to live, or to have understanding. The teachers run when they teach with purity and those who hear, or the students, run well when they receive the word with joy and when the fruits of the Spirit follow. All this was well and good as long as Paul was present, as testified before in chapters 3 and 4. Here, he says, "You ran well"—that is, things went well and there was joy among you. You lived well; you were headed to eternal life, as promised by God's word.

These words, "You ran well," are particularly comforting. Sometimes, there is a certain temptation that assails the faithful, but it seems to them that instead of running they barely drag themselves along. However, don't let that annoy you if you remain in the proper doctrine and walk in the Spirit. It may seem things move awfully slow, or rather that you are crawling along. But God judges otherwise, for what to us seems as barely creeping, or hardly moving, in God's sight we are running a speedy race. Once again, that which to us is only grief, hurt, and death before God is joy, rejoicing, and true happiness. That is why Christ said, "Blessed are those who mourn and grieve, for they shall be comforted; you will laugh"[85] (Matthew 5:4). All things will improve for those who believe in the Son of God, be

---

[85] Luther's own paraphrase of the text. Actually, Luther joins the last part of Luke 6:21 to Matthew 5:4.

it pain or death itself. Thus the true racers are those who, regardless of what happens, run well and keep on going forward, aided by the Holy Spirit of God, who knows no such thing as creeping along.

VERSE 7. Who hindered you from obeying the truth?

In this race, those who are hindered are those who let go of faith and grace to fall into the law and works, as occurred to the Galatians. They were hindered and seduced by the false apostles, to whom he gives a thinly disguised reprimand: "Who hindered you from obeying the truth?" In this text, Paul also demonstrates in passing that people can be powerfully mesmerized with false doctrine, that they embrace lies and heresies instead of the truth and spiritual doctrine. They say and swear that the sound doctrine that they loved before is error. However, they claim the error they defend with all their might is nothing but sound doctrine. That is how the false apostles led the Galatians (who had run well at the beginning) to this opinion, to believe they had been mistaken when they were marching slowly forward when Paul was their teacher. But then, having been seduced by the false apostles, they fell so brazenly from the truth. They were powerfully seduced by the deception of the false apostles that they came to believe they were now happy and were now running well. The same happens today to those who have been seduced by the sectarians and fanatical spirits. That is why I am compelled to say that to fall from the doctrine does not come from man but from the devil. It is extremely dangerous, for it is to fall from the highest heaven to the depths of hell. Those who continue in error are so far from admitting their sin that they affirm that sin itself is the grandest righteousness. That is why it is impossible for them to be forgiven.

VERSE 8. This persuasion is not from him who calls you.

This is a great comforting thought and a doctrine without parallel. In it, Paul shows how false persuasions in those deceived by wicked teachers can be uprooted from their hearts. The false apostles were very charming fellows. They seemed to outshine Paul's education and piety. The Galatians, having been deceived by this theatrical performance of piety, thought that when they heard them speak they were hearing Christ Himself. They came to believe that the false apostles' persuasiveness came from Him. But on the contrary, Paul shows that this persuasion and doctrine did not come from Christ, who had called them in grace. Instead, it came from the devil. Through this argument, he was successful in leading many out of that false persuasion. In the same way, today, we lead many out of the error that deceived them when we show their opinions are nothing but fanaticism and wickedness.

Once again, this comfort belongs to all the afflicted who due to temptation conceive a false opinion regarding Christ. The devil is an expert in persuasion and knows how to exaggerate the smallest sin, yes, even the most diminutive, so that those being tempted will think they have committed the most horrible and heinous crime that merits eternal damnation. Here, the distressed conscience must be comforted and lifted up just as Paul did with the Galatians—that is, such exaggerations or persuasive arguments do not come from Christ, since they combat the word of the Gospel. That is because the Gospel presents Christ not as an accuser, cruelly calling all to render an account, but as a Savior and Counselor, meek, merciful, and humble of heart.

However, Satan (a very astute conniver who stalks on every side) can crush your comfort into dust, countering with the word and the example of Christ in the following way. "It is true that Christ is meek, humble, and merciful, but only with the devoted and religious. Nevertheless, He threatens sinners with wrath and destruction (Luke 13). He also declared that the unbelievers are already under condemnation (John 3:18). Further, Christ did many good deeds, suffered many evils, and now commands us to follow His example. But if your life is not in agreement with the word of Christ and you neither follow His example, then these statements that Christ pronounced as an angry judge are for you. These comforting statements that show He is a loving and merciful Savior are not for you. That's because you are a sinner; you don't even have faith. In fact, you have done absolutely nothing right." Everyone who may be tempted in this way, seek the following comfort.

Scripture presents Christ to us in two ways: First, as a grant, a gift. If I grasp onto Him in this way, "I shall not want," "for in Christ are hidden all the treasures of wisdom and knowledge" (Colossians 2:3). With everything that is found in Him, "He is the source of your life in Christ Jesus, whom God made our wisdom, our righteousness and sanctification and redemption." Therefore, although I may have sinned, many times and grievously, even so, if I believe in Him, all will be absorbed by His righteousness. Second, Scripture presents Him as an example to follow. However, I am not going to allow this Christ (the Christ as an example) to appear until afterward, when the time of happiness and rejoicing arrives, when I am out of temptation (that's when I'll scarcely be able to follow one thousandth of his example). Then may I have Him as my mirror to see what I still lack, lest I get overconfident and careless. But in the time of trial, I will neither listen nor admit Christ except as a gift. When He died for my sins, I was granted His righteousness.[86] He has fulfilled and achieved everything that was lacking in my life. "For Christ is the end of the law for righteousness to everyone who believes."

It is good for us to know these things. It's good so that each of us may have a sure and certain remedy at the time of temptation with which to throw away that venom of desperation given to us by Satan to poison us. Further, it also helps us resist the fury of the sectarians and separatists of our time, for the Anabaptists find nothing more glorious in their entire doctrine than to severely urge the following of Christ's example and to carry the cross; they obsess on Christ's statements when He entrusted the disciples to carry the cross. Thus we must learn how to resist this

---

[86] *impertiit mihi suam justitiam.*

Satan who transforms himself into an angel of light. We will resist him if we know how to put a difference between the Christ who appears to us as a gift and sometimes as an example. But if we cannot mark this difference, the preaching of the Gospel turns into poison instead of the announcement of salvation.

Therefore, all those who are worked over and injured by their heavy burden of sins should be presented with Christ as a Savior and a gift, not as an example and lawgiver. But to the self-confident and stubborn, He should be presented as an example. In the same way, should the severe admonishments of Scriptures be presented, as well as the horrible examples God's wrath, as when the entire world was flooded,[87] Sodom and Gomorrah were destroyed, and other similar incidents, that they may repent. Therefore, let all Christians when they are left frustrated and afflicted learn to shake off the false opinion that they have imagined about Christ. Let them say, "Oh you cursed Satan, why do you start arguing with me about works and efforts seeing that my sins are already distressing and afflicting me? No! I am not going to listen to you because you are an accuser and a destroyer, seeing that now I am worked over and heavy burdened. Instead, I will listen to Christ, the Savior of humanity, who said He came to the world to save sinners; to comfort those who live in terror, agony, desperation; and to announce liberty to the captives. This is the true Christ, and apart from Him, there is none other. I can admire the examples of the pious lives of Abraham, Isaiah, John the Baptist, Paul, and other holy people. But they cannot forgive my sins, they cannot deliver me from the power of the devil and death, they cannot save and grant me eternal life. These things belong only to Christ, of whom the Father says, 'This is my beloved Son, in whom I am pleased, listen to him'" (Matthew 3:17; Mark 9:7). Let us learn to find comfort in this way through faith when temptation and false doctrine seems to overwhelm us. Otherwise, the devil will attempt to seduce us through his ministers, or kill us with his fiery darts.

VERSE 9. A little yeast works through the whole batch of dough [NIV].

Jerome and all who came after him indict Paul. They allege that sometimes he changed the sayings of the Holy Scriptures, distorting them with another meaning. Thus they say that certain issues that Paul advocates, given their own context, are nothing to argue about. However, they accuse the apostle without merit. Paul very correctly and wisely takes generalizations and relates them to particulars or the other way around. For instance, previously in 3:10, he takes this general declaration, "Cursed is everyone who hangs from a tree," and very fittingly relates it to Christ. He also takes this statement, "a little leaven," and generalizes it relating it to doctrine (as

---

[87] *ut diluvii.*

in this text where he advocates on behalf of justification) and issues of life and bad moral practices (1 Corinthians 5:6).

This entire epistle abundantly testifies how Paul suffered due to the falling away of the Galatians and how often he had hammered into their heads (sometimes reproving, sometimes imploring) the great and horrible enormities that would follow their fall unless they repented. But Paul's paternal and apostolic devotion did not move them at all, for many of them no longer accepted Paul as their teacher but highly preferred the false apostles. They thought they had received the true doctrine from them and not from Paul. Further, the false apostles (no doubt) slandered Paul among the Galatians, saying that he was a contentious and hardheaded, who for just a trifle was creating disunity among the churches, for no other reason than to exalt his own wisdom and to be honored above everyone else. By means of these false accusations, they got what they wanted; among them, Paul was considered a very despicable man.

Some who had not abandoned his doctrine altogether thought there was no danger in dissenting from him just slightly regarding the doctrine of justification by faith. Therefore, when they heard that Paul made such a big fuss over something they thought was small and insignificant, they were shocked and thought like this: Although we may have slightly digressed from Paul's doctrine, and perhaps are mistaken somewhere, the difference is so unimportant that he should have looked the other way or at least not blow it up so much that the unity of the churches would be at stake for something so insignificant.

LECTURE 35: Saturday, November 21

That is why he responds with this statement: "A little yeast leavens the whole mass." Paul leans on this watchword or admonition. Today, we value it just as much, for *the Sacramentarians, who deny the presence of Christ in the Supper,* likewise protest against us, saying that we are contentious, obstinate, and immovable when defending our doctrine, alleging that *for just this one article regarding the Sacraments we tear apart Christian love and shred the accord between the churches. They say we should not make such a fuss over this small point of doctrine, which is obscure and remained somewhat unclear in the apostles' statements. Further, they say that in particular, we do not respect the totality of the Christian doctrine or the joint agreements prudently worked out between the churches, since we have a reasonable understanding among ourselves.*[88] *Using this very plausible argument, they not only stir up jealousies, but what's more, they sabotage us, since in their judgment we dissent out of pure stubbornness or some personal preference.* But these are subtle

---

[88] *neque totius christianae doctrinae neque generalis omnium ecclesiarum concordiae rationem habeamus.*

trickeries of the devil with which he attempts to overthrow *not only this article but also the entire Christian doctrine.*

To all this, we respond with Paul, "A little yeast leavens the entire batch of dough." In philosophy, a small fault at the outset, results in a huge and serious fault at the end. It is the same in theology. A small error overthrows the entire doctrine. That is why we need to interject a great separation between our lives and the doctrine so that one is as far as possible from the other. The doctrine is not ours, but God's; and we are called to be its ministers. Therefore, it's impossible for us to yield or change by even one dot. The life is ours. Thus in this regard we will hold together all that the Sacramentarians[89] require of us. We should accept, forgive, and bear with them, as long as the doctrine and faith remain unharmed. That is why we will always reply with Paul, "A little leaven." *In this matter, we cannot yield by even a hair. The doctrine is like a mathematical point, which is indivisible—that is, it cannot be subjected to either subtraction or addition. On the other hand, life is like a point in natural philosophy, which will always be divisible; it will always yield to some degree.*

The tiniest speck will injure the eye. That is why the Germans have a saying about eye remedies: "Nothing in the eye is good."[90] Our Savior said, "Your eye is the lamp of your body. When your eyes are healthy, your whole body also is full of light. But when they are unhealthy, your body also is full of darkness" (Luke 11:34, NIV). "Therefore, if your whole body is full of light, and no part of it dark, it will be just as full of light as when a lamp shines its light on you" (Luke 11:36, NIV). Through this allegory, Christ wants to say that the doctrine should be the most simple, clear, and without any darkness at all, without fog, etc. James the Apostle said (not from his own thinking but without a doubt from what he heard the apostles say), "Whoever is guilty in one point is guilty of all" *(James 2:10). Therefore, the doctrine should be as a golden circle, round and whole in which there is not a single fissure, for wherever they may be the slightest gap, the circle's wholeness is lost. What does it profit the Jews to believe in only one God, even in the Creator of all things, or that they believe in all the articles and accept all the Scriptures when they deny the Christ? "Thus whoever is guilty in one point is guilty of all."*

This text must be carefully observed for it goes against their false accusations. They allege that we break apart the harmony of love, causing great damage and hurt to the churches. However, we are certainly ready to keep the peace with love for all, if they keep our doctrine of faith safe and sound. *If we cannot obtain this, then in vain do they require love from us. Cursed be that love that is preserved at the loss of the doctrine of faith.*[91] However, all must yield to that faith, be it love, apostle, or even an angel from heaven. *Therefore, their slander more than testifies*

---

[89] *sacramentarii.* Here, Middleton translates "adversaries" instead of "Sacramentarians."

[90] *nichts ist inn die Augen gut,* an old German proverb.

[91] *Maledicta sit caritas, quae servatur cum jactura doctrinae fidei.* Other viable translations: "at the expense of the doctrine of faith"; "by throwing away the doctrine of faith."

how they dilute the majesty and magnificence of God's word. If they would truly believe it is God's word, they would not play games with it. Instead, they would hold it in high regard, and without arguments and doubts, they would put their trust in it, knowing that one word of God is the whole, and the whole is one. Similarly, one article of doctrine encompasses all, and all are found in the one so that if one is missing, all are eventually lost. They are bound together and held by the same link.[92]

Then let them exalt Christian love and harmony all they want. But as for us, let us magnify the majesty of the word and faith. Love may be left unattended for a certain time and place. But not so with word and faith. Love suffers all things; it yields its place to everyone. On the contrary, faith suffers nothing; it does not yield its place to anyone. When love yields, it believes, gives, and forgives, but sometimes it is also betrayed. Moreover, when it is deceived, it loses nothing of what could be called a real loss—that is, it does not lose Christ, thus it is not offended. Instead, it is constant in doing what is good, yes, even toward the ungrateful and unworthy. On the contrary, with respect to faith and salvation, when people teach lies and errors under the banner of truth and seduce many, there is no place here for love at all. Here, we don't lose any benefit granted to the unworthy. Rather, we lose the word, faith, Christ, and eternal life. *Thus if you deny God in just one article, you have denied Him in all, for God is not divided into many articles but is all in one and one in all the articles of faith. Thus we always must respond to the Sacramentarians, who accuse us of negligence in love, with this saying from Paul, "A little leaven" and so on, as well as with the common proverb, "Don't play around with my reputation, my faith, or stick your finger in my eye."*[93]

I have spoken at length about these issues to support our people and teach others who may be offended by our persistence. They don't think that we have firm and strong reasons for our perseverance. Thus let us not be moved by their great urging to safeguard love and harmony, for whoever does not love God and His word, no matter who they love or how much they love, they love in vain.

Therefore, through this declaration Paul warns both teachers and their hearers. They should be careful not to consider faith as something insignificant, as something with which they can meddle as they please, for this doctrine is as a ray of light that is heaven sent, it illumines, directs, and guides us. Well then, just as the world with all its wisdom and power cannot stop or deflect the rays of light that come from the sun to the earth so also nothing may be added or taken away from the doctrine of faith. That would be to disfigure and overthrow it altogether.

VERSE 10. I have confidence in you in the Lord [NASB].

It's as if he had said to them, "I have taught, admonished, and reproved you more than necessary so that by now you should have listened to me. Nonetheless, I wish

---

[92] *cohaerent enim et quodam communi vinculo continentur.*

[93] *nor patitur ludum fama, fides, oculus,* a proverb from that era.

you well in the Lord." However, a question arises from this text. Was Paul right in saying that he had hope or confidence in the Galatians in view that the Scriptures prohibit reliance on men? Faith as well as love have their confidence and their belief but in different ways due to the varying nature of their objects. Faith trusts in God, thus it cannot be deceived. Love believes in another human being and thus it is quite often betrayed. Yet this faith that proceeds from love is necessary in this present life. Without this faith, life in this world could not exist, for if one person could not believe and trust another, what kind of life would we live on this earth? True Christians are more prone to believe and value through love even more than the children of this world. Faith toward another is a fruit of the Spirit or of Christian faith among the faithful. Yes, Paul here had confidence in the Galatians, even though they had veered away from his doctrine; still they were in the Lord. It's as if he had said, "I have confidence in you as long as the Lord is in you and you in Him—that is, as long as you remain in the truth. But if you come tumbling down from there, seduced by Satan's ministers, I will stop believing in you. Thus it is lawful for the faithful to trust or believe in men."

VERSE 10. That you will take no other view [NIV].

In other words, with respect to the doctrine of faith as I have taught it to you and have learned from me. Further, I have hopes that you will not receive any other doctrine contrary to mine.

VERSE 10. However, the one who is troubling you will suffer God's judgment, whoever he is [ISV].

With this declaration, Paul sits as a judge on the bench. He condemns the false apostles and calls them with a disgraceful name, "the troublers" of the Galatians. Notwithstanding, the Galatians considered these men as very pious and better teachers than Paul. From there, he shakes up the Galatians with this ominous declaration with which he boldly condemns the false apostles. He wants the Galatians to flee their false doctrine as the most terrible plague. It's as if he had said, "What are you doing paying attention to these pestilent subjects who instead of teaching you do nothing but trouble you? The doctrine they have delivered to you is nothing more than distress for the conscience. Thus no matter how assumingly important they appear, they will be condemned."

Well, one could understand with these words, "whoever he is," that the false apostles in their outward appearance were very pious and sanctified fellows. By coincidence, any one of them could be a distinguished disciple of one of the apostles, of great name and authority. There must be a reason for his vehement and cutting words. Further, in chapter 1, he uses the same words, saying, "But even if we or an angel from heaven should preach a gospel other than the one we preached to you, let them be under God's curse!" (Galatians 1:8, NIV). Without doubt, many were offended by this intensity, thinking, "Why is the apostle tearing up the bond of love like that? Why is he so stubborn about something so small? Why does he so pronounce so abruptly eternal condemnation against those who like him are also ministers of Christ?" Paul is not moved at all by this. Rather, he boldly curses and condemns all who pervert the doctrine of faith, no matter how highly they may be regarded, no matter how much they appear to be sanctified and highly schooled.

In the same way, we consider as excommunicated and damned all those who say that the article regarding the Sacrament of Christ's body and blood is uncertain or that this article does violence to Christ's words regarding the Supper. Without hesitation at all, we insist that all the articles of the Christian doctrine, both small and great (although for us none are small), should be sustained as pure and firm. And this is so much more necessary for the doctrine is our only light that lights and guides the path to heaven and it is of such a nature that if it is partly undermined, all it will come tumbling down. When this happens, neither love nor agreement with the Sacramentarians will possibly save us but only the pure doctrine of faith.

Otherwise, with pleasure we would retain love and agreement with them, all who together with us have the same understanding regarding all the articles of the Christian faith. And what's more, as far as we are concerned, we will keep the peace with our enemies and pray for them, for they ignorantly blaspheme our doctrine and persecute us. However, we cannot do so with those who knowingly and against their conscience injure one or more articles of the Christian faith. Because of that, Paul teaches us by his own example to be as obstinate in our teaching as the false apostles and their disciples appeared, for Paul believed, "I am right and true in what I teach." They thought, "We are right and true in what we believe"; this is not just a trifle but something that has been taken completely out of proportion. Regardless, they will be brought into judgment.

Thus (as I frequently admonish), we should diligently discern between doctrine and life. The doctrine is heavenly. Life belongs to this earth. In life, there is sin, error, impurity, and depravity mixed up with vinegar, as the saying goes. Thus it befits love to do its work and look the other way, to tolerate, to be betrayed, to believe, to hope, and to suffer all things. From love, let the forgiveness of sins prevail as much as it can so that sin and error will not be defended or sustained. However, in the doctrine where there is no error, there is no need for the forgiveness of sins. Therefore, there is no comparison at all between the doctrine and the life. A little point of doctrine is of greater value than heaven and earth and thus we should not tolerate that the smallest dot should be corrupted. But we can well look the other way to life's offenses and mistakes, for every day we err in life and behavior, as we so passionately confess in the *Our Father* and in the articles of our faith. But our doctrine, God be praised, is pure. We have all the articles of our faith rooted upon the Holy Scriptures, which is why the devil eagerly wishes to corrupt and overthrow them. That is why he so astutely prowls around us with the pious argument that we should not break up the bond of love and the unity among the churches.

VERSE 11. Brothers and sisters, if I am still preaching circumcision, why am I still being persecuted? In that case the offense of the cross has been abolished [NIV].

Paul resorts to every possible resource striving for the Galatians' return. He now reasons using his own example. "Because I remove righteousness away from circumcision, my reward has been (he says) the hate and persecution of the priests and elders and of all my nation. If I were to attribute righteousness to it, the Jews would not only stop persecuting me, but they would also love and highly congratulate me. But since I preach the Gospel of Christ and the righteousness of faith, abolishing the law and circumcision, I suffer persecution. But on the contrary, to avoid this cross and the cruel hate of the entire Jewish nation, the false apostles preach circumcision and thereby obtain and retain the goodwill of the Jews"; as he says in chapter 6, "Those . . . compel you to be circumcised" (Galatians 6:12). Further, they would want nothing more than the lack of dissension, only peace and agreement between Jews and Gentiles. But it is impossible to achieve that without losing the doctrine of faith, which is the doctrine of the cross, which is full of scandalous offenses.[94] Thus when he says, "If I am still preaching circumcision, why am I still being persecuted? In that case, the offense of the cross has been abolished," he wants to say that it would be great foolishness and cause for great indignation if the cross would no longer cause a scandal. He states the same when he says, "For Christ did not send me to baptize but to preach the gospel, and not with eloquent wisdom, lest the cross of Christ be emptied of its power" (1 Corinthians 1:17). It's as if he had said, "I will not allow the abolishment of the scandal of the cross of Christ."

Here, some will say, "Then Christians are really crazy, for of their own free will, they plunge directly into danger, for what else are they doing when they preach and confess the truth? Don't they realize they are doing nothing else but engaging the hate and enmity of the entire world and stirring up scandals?" This, said Paul, does not offend nor perturb me in the least. Rather, I grow bolder and I'm granted hope by the joyous success and increase of the church, which blooms and grows under the cross, for it is necessary that Christ, the head and husband of the church, reign among His enemies (Psalm 100:2). But on the contrary, when the cross is abolished and the tyrants and heretics' fury ceases on the one hand and the scandals on the other and everything is at peace, that's when the devil is watching over the entrance to the house; that's a sure sign that he has removed the pure doctrine of God's word.

When Bernard considered this topic, he said that when Satan besieges the church on every side, be it by subtleties or violence, that's when the church is at its best condition. But on the contrary, it's at its worst when surrounded by great calm, and to that end, he alludes to Hezekiah's declaration in his song: "Lo! My bitterness

---

[94] *plena scandalis.*

is most bitter in peace" (Isaiah 38, WYC). He then applies this text to the church in times of peace and calm. Thus Paul is clear that whatever is preached in times of peace is clearly not the Gospel. On the other hand, the world takes it as the surest sign that the Gospel is the most heretical and seditious doctrine because great tumults appear, protests, hostilities, divisions, and similar things. Therefore, God sometimes takes the disguise of the devil, and the devil disguises as God; however, God will make Himself known when He appears in the likeness of the devil, but the devil will be unmasked and condemned when he appears disguised as God.

"The stumbling block of the cross" is understood both actively and passively. The cross immediately follows the doctrine of the word according to this text: "I believed when I said, 'I am greatly afflicted'" (Psalm 116:10, NASB). Well then, the cross of the Christians is persecution, with slander and dishonor, without any mercy; therefore, it causes a great deal of pain because people will take offense at its message. First, Christians suffer as the most pernicious criminals of the world and that is how Isaiah himself spoke regarding the Christ: "He was counted among the transgressors" (Isaiah 53:12). Further, the assassins and thieves are sentenced to certain time limits and then receive mercy. But on the contrary, the way the world judges Christians is to condemn them as the most pestilent and pernicious people; they think no punishment is sufficiently severe to punish them for their horrendous crimes, neither is the devil moved with compassion toward them, for they are punished with the most shameful and dishonorable death there could ever be. Thus the world thinks they deserve a double reward. First, they imagine that by putting Christians to death they render a great service before God. Second, they believe that the common peace and calm are restored and established when such plagues are eliminated. Consequently, the death and the cross of the believers are replete of such humiliations. But Paul says we should remain firm no matter how long we suffer persecution for the cross of Christ and its shame; instead, it should confirm us, for as long as the cross endures, it will go well for Christianity.

In the same way, Christ comforts his disciples in Matthew 5:11–12: "Blessed are you when people insult you, persecute you and falsely say all kinds of evil against you because of me. Rejoice and be glad, because great is your reward in heaven, for in the same way they persecuted the prophets who were before you" (NIV). The church cannot permit for this joy to be snatched away from its hands. Thus I would not wish to enter into a joint agreement with the Pope,[95] the bishops,

---

[95] *Quare non libenter velim, quod papa, episcopi, principes et fanatici spiritus nobis-cum concords essent.* Indeed, this is Luther's anticipated and preemptive response (nearly five hundred years before) to the Joint Declaration on the Doctrine of Justification by the Lutheran World Federation and the Catholic Church and other protestant and evangelical organizations. See https://www.lutheranworld.org/sites/default/files/Joint%20Declaration %20on%20the%20Doctrine%20of%20Justification.pdf. See also http://www.vatican.va/ roman_curia/pontifical_councils/chrstuni/documents/rc_pc_chrstuni_doc_31101999

the princes, and the sectarians,[96] for if we had such a joint agreement it would be an unmistakable sign that we have lost the true doctrine.[97] In brief, as long as the church teaches the Gospel, it will suffer persecution. That's because the Gospel presents God's mercy and glory, it brings to light the evil shrewdness and trickeries of the devil and it paints him just as he is and tears away from him the mask of God's majesty with which he appears and deceives the entire world—that is, the Gospel exposes as evil and demonic all worship, religious orders invented by men, and traditions regarding celibacy, meats, and other such things, which men think make them worthy of the forgiveness of sins and eternal life. Then there is nothing that irritates the devil more than the preaching of the Gospel, for it tears away the mask he uses to appear as God; he is exposed just as he is, the devil and not God. Therefore, it cannot be any other way but as long as the Gospel flourishes, the cross and its offense will follow; otherwise, no one has put a hand on the devil, he's barely been tickled! But if he's hit with well-placed blows, he does not rest; he begins to roar out of control and stirs up scandals everywhere.

Then if Christians are to uphold the word of life, don't be afraid or offended when you see the devil is out and about, roaring everywhere; when you see the world agitated, dictators practicing their cruelty, and sects on the rise. On the contrary, be assured that these are not frightful signs but signs of joy, as Christ Himself said, "Rejoice and be exceedingly glad." Would to God then that we don't lose the scandal of the cross; that's what would happen if we preached what the prince of this world and his cronies would want to hear with delight, the righteousness of works! In that case, we would have a kinder devil, a favorable world, a Pope full of grace, merciful princes. But since we present Christ's benefits and glory, they persecute and strip us of our goods and lives!

VERSE 12. I wish that those who disturb you would cut themselves off [WEB].

Does this also belong to the tasks of an apostle? Not only to denounce the false apostles as troublers of the church, condemn them, and turn them over to Satan but also to wish for them to be totally uprooted and perished? And what else could this be but to swear and curse? Paul (I suppose) alludes here to those of the

---

_cath-luth-joint-declaration_en.html. Also please note https://www.firstthings.com/blogs/firstthoughts/2010/03/a-betrayal-of-the-gospel-the-joint-declaration-on-the-doctrine-of-justification.

[96] *Quare non libenter velim, quod papa, episcopi, principes et fanatici spiritus nobiscum concordes essent.* Middleton adds between brackets "unless they would consent to our doctrine," although this phrase is not in the Latin text. Most likely, it was the first English translators who added the phrase, and it remained unchanged in ensuing versions.

[97] *Ea enim Concordia certa significatio esset nos amisisse vera doctrinam.*

circumcision. It's as if he had said, "They force the cutting off the foreskin of the flesh, but I would rather that they themselves would be totally cut off by the root."

Here, a question comes up, is it lawful for Christians to swear? Why not? Although not always, nor for just any reason. However, when the matter reaches this point, that someone speaks offensively of God's word, His doctrine is blasphemed and consequently God Himself. Then we should arrive at this sentence and say, "Blessed be God and His word, and whoever is found without God and His word, let them be cursed! Yes, it doesn't matter whether it's an apostle or an angel from heaven." That is what he had already said before in chapter 1: "But even if we or an angel from heaven should preach a gospel other than the one we preached to you, let them be under God's curse! As we have already said so now I say again: If anybody is preaching to you a gospel other than what you accepted, let them be under God's curse!" (Galatians 1:8, 9).

Thus you can see how Paul here shows the grave consequences of a little leaven and for the same reason dared to curse the false apostles, for they appeared to be men of great authority and holiness. Let us not consider the doctrine of a little leaven as a small matter. Although it appears as a small matter, if we neglect it, it will lead us little by little to lose the truth and salvation, and we found denying God Himself, for when the word is corrupted and God is denied and blasphemed (which is what follows when the word is corrupted), there will remain no hope of salvation. But as for us, if we are cursed, harangued, or beheaded, there remains One who can lift us up again and deliver us from the curse, death, and hell.

Thus let us learn to promote and exalt the majesty and authority of God's word, for it is no small thing (as the fanatics claim today), but each jot is greater than heaven and earth. Therefore in this regard, we have no consideration for Christian love, or agreements. Instead, we sit as judges (to put it this way) on the throne—that is, we curse and condemn everyone who in the least promotes any doctrine that disfigures and corrupts the majesty of God's word, for "a little yeast leavens the entire batch of dough." But if they would leave us with God's word whole and sound, we are not only ready to keep love and peace with them, but we also offer ourselves as their servants and do whatever we can on their behalf. If it cannot be so, then let them perish and be thrown into hell, and not only them, but the whole world as long as God and His word endure forever, for as long as He endures, life, salvation, and the faithful will also endure.

Thus Paul does well when he curses those who trouble the Galatians and pronounces sentence against them—that is, that they are cursed with all they teach and do. Further, he does well when he wishes for them to be cut off, especially that they will be uprooted from God's church and that God will not provide support or prosper their doctrine or their works. This curse proceeds from the Holy Spirit. That is also the source for Peter's curse on Simon the sorcerer in Acts 8: "Your money perish with you." The Holy Scriptures sometimes pronounces curses against those who trouble people's consciences. Notice this particularly in the Psalms, such as

"Let death take them by surprise; let them go down alive into hell" (Psalm 55:15[98]) and "Let the wicked turn into hell, and all nations that forget God."[99]

Up to this point, Paul has strengthened the place of justification with strong and powerful arguments. Further, so that he will not omit anything, here and there, he interjects reproaches, praises, exhortations, threats, and the like. At the end, he adds his own example, that due to this doctrine he suffers persecution. That is why he admonishes the faithful not to dismay or be troubled when they see great uprisings, sects, and insults arise from the preaching of the Gospel. Instead, they should rejoice and be happy, for however much the world roars against the Gospel, so much more the Gospel prospers and joyfully marches on ahead.

Today, this comfort should encourage us, for it is true that the world hates and persecutes us for no other reason than we profess the truth of the Gospel. It does not accuse us of theft, murder, prostitution, and the like. However, it detests and despises us, since we faithfully and with purity teach Christ and will not budge an inch in defense of the truth. Thus we can put away all doubt, since this our doctrine is holy and from God, and that is the reason the world hates it so bitterly. On the other hand, there is no doctrine so wicked, so foolish, and pernicious that the world will not gladly admit, embrace, and defend and, what's more, will not reverently serve, esteem, praise its scholars, and do whatever it can on their behalf. The world only despises the true doctrine of the Gospel, life, and salvation together with its ministers and works all kinds of spite it can invent against them. Thus it is an obvious sign that the world so cruelly comes against us for no other reason than its hate against the word. Consequently, when our adversaries accuse us that nothing proceeds from this doctrine except wars, seditions, trouble, sects, and an infinity of outrageous things, we respond, "Blessed be the day when we see these things, for the entire world is in tumult. And so be it, for it the world would not be troubled if the devil would not be roaring and stirring up such quagmires against the pure doctrine of the Gospel. The Gospel cannot be preached without these entanglements and tumults as a result. Therefore, whatever you may count as great evils, we receive them with great joy."

The Doctrine of Good Works

Now he proceeds to the exhortations, the precepts concerning life and good works. It is the custom of the apostles, once they have taught the faith and instructed the conscience, to add precepts regarding good works through which they enjoin the faithful to practice the duties of Christian living toward each other. Reason itself, in a certain way, teaches and understands this part of the doctrine; but it knows nothing regarding the doctrine of faith. Thus to make it clear that the

---

[98] Luther's own paraphrase of Psalm 55:15.
[99] Luther's rendering of the text.

Christian doctrine does not destroy good morals or oppose civil law, the apostle also exhorts us to practice moral living, to live honestly and unpretentiously, to safeguard love and live in accord with each other. Thus the world cannot be fair when it accuses Christians alleging they destroy good works, that they disturb the peace, or that they are dishonest in their daily life, and so on, for Christians teach good works and all other virtues better than all the philosophers and magistrates of the world, since they urge to add faith to all they do.

VERSE 13. You, my brothers and sisters, were called to be free. But do not use your freedom to indulge the flesh; rather, serve one another humbly in love [NIV].

It's as if he had said, "Now that you have obtained freedom through Christ—that is, you are already above all law regarding the conscience and before God are blessed and saved—Christ is your life. Therefore, although the law, sin, and death perturb and horrify you, they cannot harm you, nor plunge you into desperation. This is the excellent and priceless freedom you have received. Now it's in your hands to be attentive and be careful so that you will not use that freedom as an occasion for the flesh."

This is a common evil and the most pernicious that Satan has conjured up through the doctrine of faith. In many, he turns this freedom inside out, the freedom with which Christ set us free, and turns it into freedom for the flesh. The apostle Jude also laments in his epistle, "For certain individuals whose condemnation was written about long ago have secretly slipped in among you. They are ungodly people, who pervert the grace of our God into a license for immorality and deny Jesus Christ our only Sovereign and Lord" (Jude 4, NIV). The flesh is totally unaware of the doctrine of grace—that is, it is unaware that we are righteous, not by works, but by faith alone and that the law has no authority over us. Thus when it hears the doctrine of faith, it abuses it and turns it into immoral living. Immediately, it calculates this way: "If we have no law, then let us live however we please; let us not do what is right or help the needy, let us not suffer at all, for there is no law to require it of us nor tie us to anything."

Therefore, there is danger on both sides, although one is tolerated more than the other. If grace and faith are not proclaimed, no one would be saved, for it is faith alone that justifies and saves.[100] On the other hand, if faith is preached (as we must), most people understand the doctrine of faith according to the flesh and relate the freedom of the spirit to the freedom of the flesh. We can see this in all lifestyles, whether it's those of high society or among the most ordinary people. All boast that they are evangelicals,[101] belonging to Christian freedom. However, they serve their own lust and they give themselves over to their own greediness,

---

[100] *fides enim sola justificat et salvat.*
[101] *Evangelicos.*

pleasures, pride, envy, and other similar vices. There is no one who dutifully fulfills his task or their duty to serve their brothers. I get so impatient with this state of affairs that sometimes I wish that such pigs that tread precious pearls would still be under the tyranny of the Pope, for it is impossible for the Gospel of peace to govern this people of Gomorrah.

Further, those of us who teach the word don't know how to discharge our duty with as much passion and diligence in light of the Gospel as we did before when we were ignorant and in darkness, for the more we are assured that Christ purchased our freedom, so much more cold and negligent we become in studying the word, in prayer, in doing what is good, and in suffer adversity. If Satan did not frustrate us inwardly with spiritual temptations and outwardly with the rejection and ingratitude of our own colleagues, we would become totally negligent and averse to any good work. In this way, with the passing of time, we would lose the knowledge and the faith in Christ. We would lose the ministry of the word and would dedicate ourselves to a life more suited to the flesh. Many of our men have already begun to live like this. They struggle in the ministry of the word, for they cannot live from their work. They must also live with the humiliating treatment at the hands of those they were able to rescue from their slavery to the Pope through the preaching of the Gospel. These men then abandon Christ, who lived in poverty and rejection, and become entangled in the things of this life, serving their own bellies instead of Christ. But they will receive no other reward than what is stored for them in the time to come.

We know that the devil besieges us even more because we hate the world; the rest he keeps as slaves according to his will. Further, he works with all his might to take away our freedom of spirit or at least turn it into lust. We exhort, according to Paul's example, not to use this freedom of the spirit, bought by the blood of Christ but freely given to us, as occasion to give free reign to the flesh or, as Peter says, as a cover up for their evil intentions (1 Peter 2:16). Instead, through love let us serve one another.

Thus to prevent Christians from abusing this liberty (as I've said before), the apostle places a yoke of service over his own flesh through mutual love. Then let the faithful remember that in their conscience and before God they are free from the curse of the law, sin, and death on account of Christ. But regarding the flesh, they who are servants should serve each other through love, according to this command from Paul. Then let everyone strive to diligently fulfill his duty according to each one's calling and come to the aid of his neighbor with all his might. That is what Paul here requires from each one of us, "Through love, serving one another." These works do not free the saints. Instead, they bind them as servants, with respect to the flesh.

Further, this doctrine of mutual love, which we should retain and practice toward each other, cannot get through the heads of carnal people; there's no way to persuade them! But those who are Christian do joyfully receive and obey this doctrine. However, as soon as freedom is preached, others immediately deduce, "If I am free, I will do whatever I please. What I have here is mine, why should I not sell it and get out of it as much as I can? Further, seeing that we do not obtain salvation through our works, why should we give anything to the poor?" In this way, they shake off the yoke and servitude given to the flesh and turn the freedom of spirit into dissolute living and freedom of the flesh. These are careless judges because they don't believe us but laugh and scoff at us. They use their bodies and goods according to their own lusts. That's the way they truly are, since they don't help the needy. Instead, they deceive their fellow believers by bartering, taking what belongs to others, hoarding, and, cost what may, grasping the object of their greed. However, we say to them (says I), that they are not free no matter how much they boast of their freedom. Rather, they have lost Christ and Christian freedom, they have made themselves slaves to the devil and are seven times worse than when the devil left them, for the devil has taken another seven demons worse than before and has returned once again to live among them. Thus the end of such people is worse than their beginning.

Regarding us, we have God's mandate to preach the Gospel. It offers all people freedom from the law, sin, death, and God's wrath freely because of Christ if they have faith. It is not within our power to hide or revoke this freedom that the Gospel now proclaims, for God has freely given it to us and has bought it with His death, for we can neither hold back those pigs that plunge headlong into every lust puddle and immoral work nor force them to help others with their bodies or goods. Therefore, we do what we can—that is, we diligently admonish them regarding their duty. If we get nowhere with these admonitions, we leave the matter in God's hands, and He will reward these scoffers with a just punishment in due time. Meanwhile, this is our comfort, that with respect to the faithful, our work is not in vain, for doubtless, there are many who through our ministry have been freed from the devil's slavery to live in the freedom of spirit. These (who notwithstanding are few) recognize the glory of this freedom of spirit. On their part, they are ready to serve men and women with love and know they are indebted to their brothers and sisters according to the flesh. That is why they give us greater joy than the countless multitude of those who abuse this freedom and would discourage us.

Here, Paul opted for timely yet eloquent words when he says, "Brothers and sisters, to freedom you were called." However, so that no one will dream he is talking about freedom for the flesh, he explains what kind of freedom he's talking about, saying, just "do not use your freedom to indulge the flesh, rather, serve one another humbly in love." Therefore, let all Christians know that with respect to the conscience Christ has made them lords over the law, sin, and death, thus these have no power over them. However, let them know that there is an external servitude imposed on their bodies, with the purpose of serving their neighbor out of love. Those who understand something else by Christian liberty may enjoy the benefits of the Gospel but to their own destruction, and they are worse pagans (using the name of Christ) than they were before under the Pope. Now Paul proceeds to declare, beginning with the Ten Commandments, what it means to serve one another through love.

LECTURE 36: Friday, November 27

VERSE 14. For the entire law is fulfilled in keeping this one command: "Love your neighbor as yourself" [NIV].

Once Paul lays down the foundation of the Christian doctrine, he proceeds to build it with gold, silver, and precious stones. Well then, there is no other foundation (as he, himself, had said to the Corinthians) except Jesus Christ, or the righteousness of Christ (1 Corinthians 3:11). Now, on top of this foundation, he builds the good works that indeed are good works, for these are all that are embraced by this unique precept: "You shall love your neighbor as yourself" (Leviticus 19:18). This is indeed correct interpretation of Scriptures and the commandments of God. *The opinion of the papal scholars regarding this word* love *is cold and totally empty, for they say that love is nothing more than to wish someone well*[102] *or that love is an inherent quality of the soul,*[103] *with which a person may evoke a feeling from the heart, or a certain gesture that is called goodwill.*[104] *That kind of love is naked, fruitless, and mathematical; it cannot become flesh (so to say it), nor does it get to work. Rather, Paul says that love should be a servant, and unless it has the function of a servant, it is not love.*

Well then, when he provides these instructions regarding love, he covertly refers to the false teachers. Paul has been engaged in a powerful confrontation with them to defend and establish his doctrine of good works against them. It's as if he had said, "Oh Galatians! Up to now, I have taught you the true and spiritual life. Now I will also teach you what are truly good works. I will do this so that you may see how vain and foolish are the works of ceremonies urged by the false apostles, they are much inferior to the works of love, for such is the foolishness and the craziness of all false teachers and fanatical minds. They not only put aside the true foundation and the pure doctrine but also, following their own superstitions, never really accomplish good works." Thus (as Paul says in 1 Corinthians 3:12) they build with just wood, hay, and stubble on the foundation. Thus the false apostles, who were the greatest defenders of works, did not teach or require the works of love. The works of love urge you to quickly aid your neighbor in every need, not only with goods, but also with your body—that is, with your tongue, hand, heart, and all your strength. But the false apostles only required circumcision and the observance of days, months, and the like. Concerning good works, they had nothing to teach. Once they destroyed the foundation, which is Jesus Christ, and obscured the doctrine of faith, it was impossible that there would remain a truly good use, practice, or opinion of good works. If the tree is cut down, the fruit perishes as well.

---

[102] *bonum alicui velle.*

[103] *animo.*

[104] *bene velle.*

Today, the sects are similarly bewitched by the doctrine of good works. They are driven to teach all kinds of phenomenal and superstitious works. They have stolen away Christ; they have cut down the tree. They have overthrown the foundation. As Paul says, they have built on the sand and cannot build with anything else but wood, hay, and dead leaves. They offer a great performance of love, humility, and so on, but in reality, they love, as John says, "not in deed and in truth" (1 John 3:18). When it comes to love, all they offer is an abundance of words!

They also make a great display of holiness. They parade their fake holiness before everyone so that people will judge their works as the most grandiose and pleasing to God. But if you look carefully at these works under the light of the word, you will realize that they are mere toys. These ridiculous and empty trifles are only regarding times, places, dressing up, paying people homage, and such. That is why it is necessary for the teachers of truth to expound on the doctrine of good works as well as the doctrine of faith. Satan hates both and bitterly attacks both. However, one must first plant faith, for without faith, it is impossible to understand what is a good work or what it is that pleases God.

Thus we can see how Satan loathes the true doctrine of good works or how to practice them. All human beings have indeed a certain knowledge implanted in their minds by which they naturally perceive they should treat others as they would want to be treated. We call this and other similar opinions natural law. They are the foundation of human rights and every good work. However, human reason is so corrupt and blinded due to the devil's vices that it does not understand it was born with this knowledge. Or having been admonished by God's word and understood its duty, such is Satan's power that reason knowingly neglects and condemns it. Further, there is this other evil. The devil so afflicts all the legalists and heretics with such insanity, that neglecting the true doctrine of good works, they urge only infantile ceremonies or grotesque works of their own invention. Reason, not taking faith into account, magnifies these wonders and delights in them.

That is how the Papists unnecessarily invent foolish and useless works that God neither orders nor requires. Today, we see this same zeal for uselessness among the sectarians and their disciples, and particularly in the Anabaptists. But in our churches where the doctrine of good works is taught with greater diligence, it never ceases to amaze how indolence and lethargy are kings! The more we exhort people to do what is good, to serve each other with love, and to put aside the obsession to fill their bellies the more the practice of piety becomes a huge task and misses the mark. Therefore, Satan bitterly hates not only the doctrine of faith but also good works and gets in the way of both! On the one hand, he stands in the way preventing our people from learning it, or if they know it, he prevents its practice. On the other hand, the hypocrites and heretics ignore them altogether and supplant them with foolish ceremonies or certain ridiculous and fanatical works with which they bewitch and entertain others,[105] for the world will not be governed by the Gospel and faith but by the law and superstitions!

---

[105] *capiuntur et delectantur homines.*

Therefore, the apostle diligently exhorts Christians to engage in good works once they have heard and received the pure doctrine of faith. The remnants of sin remain even in the justified; and since they are contrary to faith, they obstruct and prevent us from doing good works. Further, human reason and the flesh, which in the saints resists the spirit and in the wicked reigns supreme, naturally delights in pharisaic superstition—that is, it takes more delight measuring God by its own imagination than by His word. Reason will do the works of its own choosing, with much more passion than those ordered by God. Accordingly, it is necessary for pious preachers to sweat teaching and urging the doctrine of love not feigned and endorsing good works. The teaching of true faith points to these as well.

Thus let no one pretend to think he knows the depth of this command: "You shall love your neighbor as yourself." It is certainly brief and easy regarding its words. However, show me the teachers and trained instructors who while they teach it also learn from it, live it, practice it, and fulfill it correctly. So the words "Serve one another in love" as well as "You shall love your neighbor as yourself" are eternal and none of the faithful truly take them into account. Neither do they sufficiently urge, practice, and fulfill them properly. But the faithful have this temptation (and this is astonishing), if they omit a tiny duty they should have done, immediately they are conscience stricken! However, they are not at all moved in the same way if they are negligent toward the duties of love (as happens daily), nor is their love toward their neighbor sincere as to a brother or a sister. That's because they don't consider the commandment to love more than their own superstitions, nor are they able to free themselves from these throughout their life.

Paul then reproves the Galatians with these words: "For the entire law is fulfilled in keeping this one command." It's as if he had said, "You have drowned in your superstitions and ceremonies respecting places and times, which have no benefit for either you or others; meanwhile, you neglect love, the only thing you should observe." What insanity is this? Jerome put it this way: "We degrade and consume our bodies with vigils, fasts, and tasks, but we neglect love which is the only wife and lady of works." This may be seen quite clearly in the monks. They strictly observe the traditions regarding their ceremonies, fasting, vigils, wearing certain clothes, and such. In this regard, if they omit some trifle, it is mortal sin. But when they not only neglect love but also hate each other to death, they don't sin or offend God at all?[106]

Thus through this commandment, Paul not only teaches good works but also condemns fanatical and superstitious works. He not only builds with gold, silver, and precious stones on the foundation but also knocks down anything built with wood and burns up the hay and dead leaves. *It is true that God did well in giving the Jews so many ceremonies. Through them, He makes it understood that the human mind is naturally superstitious, that it doesn't care about love at all, but*

---

[106] Luther is using a bit of sarcasm as well as pointing out the obvious irony.

it gets wrapped up in ceremonies[107] *and delights in the righteousness of the flesh.* Meanwhile, God testified through examples in the Old Testament that which God has always valued: love. His wish is that the law itself and its ceremonies would yield their place to love. When David and those with him were hungry and had nothing to eat, they ate the consecrated bread, which by law the people could not eat, except for the priests. Christ and His disciples broke the Sabbath (as the Jews themselves stated) when He healed the sick on the Sabbath. All these things demonstrate that love must be preferred above all law and ceremonies and that what God only requires is love to neighbor. Christ similarly testified, "And a second is like it" (Matthew 22:39).

VERSE 14. For the whole law is fulfilled in one word. "You shall love your neighbor as yourself."

It's as if he had asked, "Why do you put on the yoke of the law?" Why make such a great effort and get all perturbed by the ceremonies of the law, with respect to meats, days, places, and other things? Why also worry about what to eat, what to drink, and observing feasts and sacrifices? Leave these foolish things alone and listen to what I'm telling you: The entire law is summed up in this saying: "You shall love your neighbor as yourself." God does not delight in the observance of ceremonies of the law,[108] nor does God need them. The only thing He requires from your hands is this: "That you believe in Christ, whom He has sent, in whom you are fully perfect,[109] and all things are yours." But if to faith you are going to add laws, then be assured that all laws are wrapped up in this brief precept: "You shall love your neighbor as yourself." Strive to keep this commandment, for when you keep it, you have kept all laws.

Paul is the finest exponent of God's commandments for he resumes all of Moses in just one sum, showing that all his laws (which in a certain way were infinite) don't contain anything else except this brief statement: "You shall love your neighbor as yourself." Human reason is offended with the simplicity and economy of these words, for it doesn't take long to say, "Have faith in Christ" and then "you shall love your neighbor as yourself." Accordingly, reason despises the doctrine of faith as well as that of good works. Nevertheless, that simple and despicable word of faith (that's what reason believes), "Have faith in Christ," is the power of God for the faithful; by it, they conquer sin, death, the devil, and all else, and through it, they attain eternal life. Therefore, to serve one another in love is to point the lost in the right direction, comfort the afflicted, lift up the weak, come to the aid of your neighbor with every means possible, tolerate his blunders and

---

[107] *sed alligatum ese ceremoniis.*
[108] *rituum legalium.*
[109] *consummati estis.*

lack of consideration, bear the trials, the tasks, the ingratitude and rejection in the church and, in daily life, obey the rulers, give due honor to your parents, be patient at home with a petulant wife and a family out of control, and the like. These (I say) are works to which reason attaches no value. But they are certainly such works that the entire world is unable to understand their excellence and value, for reason measures neither works nor anything else by God's word but by the judgment of a reason that is wicked, blind, and foolish. Yes, it is unaware of the value of the most insignificant works that could be done and that are truly good works.

Thus when people imagine they understand well the commandment of love, they are wandering all over the sky! It is true they have it written in their heart, since by nature they are aware of one's duty toward the other, as they wish would be done to them. But then it doesn't follow that they understand it. If they did, they would certainly fulfill it and would give love priority in their works. They would not value their superstitious toys as much, such as walking around with a long face, hunched over, living in celibacy, subsisting on bread and water alone, living in the desert, dressing in rags, etc. They consider these horrible and superstitious works (of their own design and making) as holy and excellent. Further, they think they surpass and even obscure love, but love is, as it were, the sun of every good work. How great and incomprehensible is the blindness of human reason! It not only is incapable of judging correctly regarding the doctrine of faith but also errs with respect to daily living and its works. Thus we should combat mightily against the opinions of our own heart, for we are more inclined to hear them regarding the doctrine of salvation than God's own word. We should also combat the pious theatre where we perform disguised with a false mask our own works of will power. Let us learn to magnify the works that all perform in their own vocation, no matter how simple and insignificant they may seem, for they have the approval of God's word. On the contrary, we should despise the works chosen by reason without God's command, no matter how excellent, painful, great, and holy they may appear.

Elsewhere, I have fully urged this instruction so that now I will only touch it in passing. It is true that one can quickly say, "You will love your neighbor as yourself." However, it is much to the point and purpose. No one can provide a better example, more on the mark and apt than one's self, *neither could there be a more noble or profound disposition than love nor an object of love more excellent than one's neighbor. Therefore, the example, the disposition, and the object are supremely noble.* Therefore, if you wish to know how you should love your neighbor and see a clear example, take note of how you love yourself. If you were in need or in danger, you would feel joyous to have the counsel, goods, and strength of every possible person and creature. Thus you don't need any book to teach and admonish you how you should love your neighbor, for you have with you an excellent law book; it is the one you have in your own heart. You don't need a tutor in this subject, just consult your own heart and it will teach you more than enough about how to love your neighbor as yourself. Further, love is an excellent virtue, which predisposes anyone to the service of one's neighbor with one's tongue, hand, money, and material resources, as well as one's own body, even with one's own life. When you do all this, you are not motivated by any reward or consideration at all, and neither are you prevented by negative consequences or ingratitude. That is how a mother feeds and cares for her baby, only because she loves her child.

Finally, there is no other creature[110] to whom you should show your most noble love than to your neighbor. He is no devil, lion, bear, wolf, stick, or stone but the creature that is most like you. No one on earth is more pleasant, kind, useful, gracious, more comforting, and necessary than your neighbor. This love is the tastiest spice for our civilization and society. In all creation, there is no one more deserving of our love than our neighbor!

But the devil is a most prodigious magician, for he is able to obscure these most noble subjects and cast them far from each other's hearts. Not only that, but he is also able to persuade your heart to an opposite opinion. That way you will judge your neighbor as the one who above all deserves bitter hate instead of love. The devil achieves this very easily, with just one whisper: "Look, this person has had issues in his job, this one is always sick, this one has criticized you, the other one has gotten in your way, etc." Then this person you once thought so noble becomes so extremely disgusting that he is no longer your neighbor worthy of your love but an enemy deserving of your hate. In this way, Satan performs his astounding magic by which he changes our heart's willingness to love. Instead of loving our neighbor, we become defamers, agents of hate, and persecutors, up to the point where nothing else remains of this precept, "You shall love your neighbor as yourself," but bare and empty letters and syllables!

Well then, my neighbor is every person, particularly those who need my help, as Christ explains it in Luke chapter 10. Even though he may have harmed me or somehow injured me, nonetheless, he has not stripped away his human nature; he has not ceased to exist in flesh and blood. Among all God's creatures he is the one most like me. In brief, he has not ceased to be my neighbor. Then, as long as human nature remains in him, just as long remains the command to love him. That which is required from my hand is for me to neither despise my own flesh nor repay evil with evil. Rather, one must conquer evil with good; otherwise, love will never become what Paul describes in 1 Corinthians 13.

A body's sick limb is not amputated, but it is treated and cured. On the least honorable members, we grant the greatest and most abundant honor (1 Corinthians 12:23). The devil's venom has corrupted human nature so that it is blinded and perverted. Consequently, the children of this age may know someone due to his many gifts and virtues. However, as soon as they spot the smallest fault in him, they will discredit him just for that one reason and all his gifts and virtues are soon forgotten.

---

[110] *animal.*

You can also see buffoons and crass performers who don't show any consideration toward those who they don't agree with but mock them with some insulting nickname such as the man in Terence who used to call others "slant-eyes, hook nose, cabbage ears," and other insults like these. In summary, the world is the devil's kingdom and with great fury despises faith, love, and condemns God's assuring words and works.

Therefore, Paul entrusts the Galatians with love, together with all the faithful for they are the only ones who can truly love. He urges them that through love they will serve one another. It's as if he had said, "You don't need to haul on your backs the burden of circumcision, together with Moses' ceremonies. Instead, above all things persevere in the doctrine of faith you have received from me. Thereafter, if you are going to do good deeds, I tell you in one single word the greatest and most important of all works and how you can fulfill the law: 'Serve one another in love.' You will never run out of people to serve with love, for the world is full of those who need help from others." This is a perfect and sound doctrine of faith and love; it is also the shortest but broadest in all theology. It is the shortest with respect to the words and sentences. But with respect to its use and practice, it is the broadest, the widest, the deepest, and the highest in the entire world.[111]

VERSE 15. But if you bite and devour one another, be careful that you don't consume one another [WEB].

With these words, Paul testifies that if the foundation of faith in Christ were to be overthrown by the false teachers, there would be no peace or accord within the church in either doctrine or how to live. But it is inevitable that various opinions and discrepancies will arise every now and then in doctrine, works, and life. *But once harmony is broken within the church, there is no end to that split, for the authors of schisms enter into disagreements among themselves. One teaches that this one work must be done and others that the other work is necessary to obtain righteousness. Everyone affirms his own opinion and superstition and reproves the other.* What happens is that one bites and devours the other—that is, the one judges and condemns the other until at the end all consume one another. Many examples can be found in Scripture as well as throughout the course of history. Once the Manicheans perverted Africa, the Donatists arose immediately but these could not agree among themselves so at the end they were divided into three different sects. *In our day, the Sacramentarians were the first to abandon us then the Anabaptists and neither agrees with the other. One sect gives birth to another, and then each one condemns the other. According to the mathematicians, once the unity of the number is broken, the breakdown goes on forever. Therefore, when the unity of*

---

[111] Luther's footnote: *Doctrina de fide et caritate brevissima et longissima,* "the doctrine of faith and love is the shortest and the longest."

the spirit is broken, it is impossible to come to any agreement in doctrine or in ethics.[112] Rather, every day new errors will arise, without measure or end.

We also see this in the papacy. Once they abandoned the doctrine of faith, it was impossible to retain harmony in spirit. In its place, through the doctrine of works, there arose countless sects of monks. When they could no longer agree between them, they measured their holiness according to the severity of their orders. Not agreeing among themselves, they measured their holiness by the austerity of their orders and the difficulty of the superstitious works they themselves had devised. Others believe they are due more respect than the others.

Further, the monks of various persuasions dissented not only among themselves but also within the same orders! So as one potter envies another so the Minorite[113] envied the Minorite etc. In conclusion, within one monastery, there were as many opinions as there were monks! Between them, they nourish their rivalries, arguments, squabbles, toxic slanders, biting, and chewing up on one another to the point that as Paul says, they devour one another.

However, those who uphold the doctrine of faith, love one another according to Paul's instruction. They don't shame the others' lifestyle and works.[114] Instead, each one approves of the other's lifestyle[115] and duties carried out in their respective professions. None of the faithful thinks that the office of magistrate is better before God's sight than the ordinary citizen, for they know that both are ordained by God and carry out God's command. The believers do not discriminate between the office or task of a father and a son, a tutor and his pupil, a master and his servant, etc. Instead, they confidently confess that God is pleased with these if they are properly done in the faith and obedience to God. No doubt that before the sight of the world these lifestyles and their vocations are not similar. However, this external inequality does not stand in the way of unity in the Spirit, through which they all think and believe the same regarding Christ—that is, we are certain that only through Him that we obtain the remission of sins and righteousness.[116] Further, with respect to lifestyle and duties, one neither judges the other nor denounces his works; neither does anyone praise his own works as if they were much better. Instead, united in voice and spirit, they confess that they have the same and only Savior, Christ, before whom there is no exception of persons or works.

Those who neglect the doctrine of faith and love and teach superstitious works find it impossible to make such a statement! The monk does not concede that the works of the layperson, which are done in fulfillment of his profession, are as good

---

[112] *moribus.*

[113] A Franciscan friar.

[114] *non vituperant alii aliorum genus vitae et opera.*

[115] Ibid.

[116] *qua omnes idem de Christo sentiunt et credunt, scilicet per eum solum nobis contingere remissionem peccatorum et justitiam.*

and pleasing to God as his own. The nun would rather have her own life and works instead of the works of the lady of the house who lives with her husband; she judges that her works merit grace and eternal life but not that of the wife. In this way, these persons, as accursed as is greed for gold, have vehemently condemned and persuaded the entire world that their level of life and works are greater and more pious that those of the layperson, for if up to this day they did not defend and grasp the opinion that their works are holy, they could not retain their honor and riches. Thus there is no monk or legalist who could ever be convinced that the works of an ordinary Christian, a husband, a wife, a maid, or a servant, could be carried out in faith and obedience toward God. They could never admit that these simple roles are better than and more pleasing to God than those monstrous and superstitious works or their own choosing. Because once they remove Christ, the corner stone, those who strive after salvation through works cannot give any other judgment than they alone are those who fulfill such great and spectacular works that indeed are pleasing to God. That is how today the Anabaptists hallucinate that they, the poor, suffering hunger and cold and dressed in rags, are holy but those who have goods are not. Thus it is impossible that the legalists and the authors of sects keep the peace with those who do not approve of their opinions. Instead, they will keep on biting and devouring themselves.

On the other hand, Paul admonishes that such occasions for discord should be avoided and shows how to avoid them. He says, here's the way to unity and accord: Let everyone fulfill their duty in life according to the calling received from God. Don't climb over others or rummage through the faults of others and then applaud your own virtues, but let each serve one another in love. This is a very simple and true doctrine with respect to good works. Those who have shipwrecked their faith don't teach this and have conceived nothing but fantasies respecting faith and good works. Thus they have disagreed among themselves regarding the doctrine of faith and good works, they bite and devour one another—that is, they accuse and condemn among themselves, as Paul says here of the Galatians: "If you bite and devour one another, be careful that you don't consume one another." It's as if he had said, "Don't accuse and condemn each other regarding circumcision, the observance of sacred days, or other ceremonies. Instead, give yourselves over to service and mutual help for love's sake." Otherwise, if you continue biting and devouring each other, be careful you don't consume yourselves—that is, you will perish altogether, yes, even bodily, as frequently happens, especially among the founders of the sects and as happened to Arius and others and several in our time. Those who have laid their foundation on sand and built with hay, dry leaves, and such things no doubt will fall and be consumed, for all these things have been ordered to the lake of fire. I am not saying that after biting and devouring in this manner ruin and destruction will befall just one city but entire nations and kingdoms will come to ruin, that's what will happen. But now the apostle proceeds to show what it means to serve one another in love.

It is something dangerous and difficult to teach; we are righteous by faith alone, without works, and notwithstanding, also require works. Here, unless Christ's ministers are faithful and wise agents dispensing the mysteries of God, rightly handling the word of truth, they will immediately confuse faith with works. Both these doctrines, faith and works, should be taught and urged diligently. However, each one should remain within its limits. Otherwise, if they teach only works (as is done in the kingdom of the papacy), faith is lost. If they teach only faith, then carnal minded people will start to think that works are not necessary.

Not long ago, the apostle had exhorted them to good works; he had taught that the entire law was fulfilled in only one word, "You will love your neighbor as yourself." Here, someone will say, "Throughout this entire epistles Paul strips away the righteousness of the law, for he said, 'a person is not justified by the works of the law' as well as 'For all who rely on the works of the law are under a curse.' But now when he says that the entire law is fulfilled in just one word, it seems he forgot the entire subject he urges throughout his epistle. It now seems he gives an opinion to the contrary: 'Those who do the works of love fulfill the law and therefore are righteous.'" To this objection, Paul responds with the following.

LECTURE 37: Saturday, November 28

VERSE 16. So I say, walk by the Spirit, and you will not gratify the desires of the flesh [NIV].

It's as if Paul had said, "I have not forgotten my previous discourse regarding faith, nor do I revoke it when I exhort you to mutual love, saying that 'all the law is fulfilled by love.'" I still think the same, I am still of the same opinion. Then, so that you can clearly understand me, I will add, "Walk by the Spirit, and you will not gratify the desires of the flesh."

A Refutation of the Scholastics' Argument: "Love Is the Fulfillment of the Law, Thus the Law Justifies"

Although Paul speaks here with great simplicity and clarity, to many today it seems he has not achieved a great deal. That's because the papal scholars misunderstand Paul's words, "Love is the fulfillment of the law," and construe the following: "If love is the fulfillment of the law, then it follows that love is righteousness. Thus if we love, we are righteous. These charming fellows[117] argue with tremendous depth from the word to the work, from the doctrine (or precepts) to life. This is their line of thinking: 'The law decrees the command to love. Thus works

---

[117] *belli homines.*

will immediately follow. But this is an absurd conclusion, for it argues that works issue directly from the commandments."[118]

Indeed, we should fulfill the law and be justified through its fulfillment. But sin gets in the way. It is true that the law prescribes and commands us to love God with all our heart and so on and that we should love our neighbor as ourselves. But from there, it doesn't follow that "it is written, so we did it!" or "the law commands us to love, thus we love!" There is no human being on the entire face of the earth that loves God and his neighbor as required by the law. However, in the life to come where we will have already been purified from every vice and sin and where we will be made as pure and clear as the sun, we will love perfectly and we will be righteous through perfect love. But in this life, the flesh is an impediment to attain such purity, for as long as we have life, sin remains stuck to our flesh. Our corrupt self-love is so powerful that it surpasses our love for God and neighbor. Meanwhile, in this life, we are righteous because Christ is our mercy seat and throne of grace. Because we have believed in Him, sin is not counted against us.[119] Thus faith is our righteousness in this life.[120] But in the coming life, when we have been fully purified and freed from all our sins and lusts, we will no longer need anything from faith and hope. It is then when we will love perfectly.

However, it is an error of great magnitude to assign justification or righteousness to love, which is nothing, for if it were really something, it would still lack sufficient greatness to appease God, since love even in the faithful (as I've said) is imperfect and impure. Remember that nothing impure shall enter the kingdom of heaven. However, in the meantime, we are sustained by this confidence and assurance: that Christ, the only one who did not commit sin and in whose mouth was found no deceit, covers us with the shadow of His righteousness. Once we are sheltered under this cloud, we are covered by this shade. It is our heaven, where our sins have been forgiven and we live at the throne of grace. It is only then when we begin to love and do works according to the law. But not even by these works are we justified or accepted before God, as long as this life shall last. But once Christ has delivered the kingdom to God His Father and abolished all principalities and God is all in all and above all then faith will cease and love will be perfect and perpetual (1 Corinthians 13). The papal scholars don't understand this matter. Thus when they hear that love is the sum total of the law, immediately they conclude: *ergo*, the law justifies.[121] Also, when they read in Paul that faith justifies the person, they say, "Yes, because faith has been formed and adorned by love." But this is not Paul's meaning, as I've explained before.

---

[118] *a praeceptis argumentari et conludere ad opera.*

[119] *ut et in hac vita justi simus, habemus propitiatorium et thronum gratiae, Christum, in quem credentes, peccatum nobis non imputatur.*

[120] *fides justitia nostra in hac vita.*

[121] *ergo dilectio justificat.*

If we were already purged of all sin and ablaze with a perfect love to God and neighbor, then we would certainly be righteous and holy through love, and God would ask nothing else of us. However, this is not fulfilled in this life but is postponed until the life to come. Here, we certainly receive the gift and the first fruits of the Spirit so that we begin to love, but scarcely so. But if we truly and perfectly love God as required by His law that says, "You will love the Lord your God with all your heart, and with all your soul, and with all your strength," then we would be satisfied for richer or for poorer, in pain or in pleasure, in death or in life. Yes, whoever indeed is able to love God in truth and perfection, would not last much longer in this life but would immediately be absorbed by that love.

However, since human nature is so corrupt and drowned in sin, none of its senses can have a proper regard for God. It doesn't love God but hates God to death. Thus it is just as John says: "This is love: not that we loved God, but that he loved us and sent his Son as an atoning sacrifice for our sins" (1 John 4:10). Further, in Galatians 4:4–5, "God sent his Son, born under the law, to redeem." Once we have been redeemed and justified by the Son then it is when we begin to love, according to what Paul said in Romans 8: "For what the law was powerless to do, God did by sending his own Son, in order that the righteous requirement of the law might be fully met in us" (Romans 8:3, 4, NIV)—that is, could begin to be fulfilled. Thus what the Sophists and papal scholars teach regarding the fulfillment of the law is but a mere illusion.

Therefore, with these words, "walk in the Spirit," Paul lets us understand how he would like for us to grasp the text where it says, "In love serving one another." Also, "Love is the fulfillment of the law" etc. It's as if he had said, "When I instruct you to love one another, this is what I'm asking of you, to walk in the Spirit, for I know that you will not fulfill the law, since sin will live within you as long as you live, thus it is impossible for you to fulfill the law. However, in the meanwhile, diligently strive to walk in the Spirit—that is, fight in the Spirit against the flesh and pursue the spiritual life."

It is apparent then that he has not forgotten the subject of justification, for when he urges them to walk in the Spirit, he denies that works justify. It's as if he had said, "When I talk about fulfilling the law, I don't mean that you are justified by the law. What I'm saying is that there are two contrary captains within yourselves, the Spirit and the flesh. God has sprung a battle in your bodies; it's a struggle and a fight. The Spirit combats the flesh, and the flesh struggles against the Spirit. Here, I don't ask from you for anything else but to follow the Spirit as the captain and guide; to resist the captain of the flesh, for that is all you'll be able to do. Obey the Spirit and fight against the flesh. Thus when I teach you to keep the law, I am exhorting you toward mutual love. Don't think I am turning my back on what I've already taught you regarding the doctrine of faith or that I am now attributing justification to the law or to love. What I want to say is that you should walk in the Spirit and not practice the desires of the flesh."

Paul utilizes very apt and precise words. It's as if he had said, "We have not yet arrived at the fulfillment of the law. That is why we should walk in the Spirit and exert ourselves in Him so that we may think, say, and do those things that are of the Spirit and resist those things that are of the flesh." Thus he adds:

VERSE 16. So I say, walk by the Spirit, and you will not gratify the desires of the flesh [NIV].

It's as if he was saying, "The desires or the lust of the flesh are not quite dead in us. Instead, they spring up over again and fight against the Spirit." The flesh of the faithful is not so pious[122] that as soon as it is offended, it does not begin to bite and devour or at least to turn a blind eye to some detail of God's law. At the first annoyance, he cannot control himself but gets angry with his neighbor, seeks out vengeance, and hates him as his enemy or at least does not love him as he should, although the commandment requires it. This happens in the faithful.

Thus the apostle has given this mandate to the faithful: "Serve one another in love, bear each other's burdens, forgive one another. If you cannot bear with each other and tolerate one another, it is impossible for peace and harmony to remain among Christians. Otherwise, it will always be like this: You will offend and be offended. You will see many things in me that will offend you. As for me, I see many things in you that I don't like. In this case, if we cannot bear each other in love, there will be no end to the disagreements, discordance, envies, hatred, and ill will."

Consequently, Paul want us to walk in the Spirit; otherwise, we risk satisfying the desires of the flesh. It's as if he were saying, "Although you feel stirring up within you anger and disgust toward your brother that offends you or if he were to do something against you, even so, through the Spirit, resist and suppress these violent emotions. Bear with his weakness and love him according to the commandment, 'You will love your neighbor as yourself.' Your brother does not cease to be your brother when he slips or because he offends you. Instead, that's when he most needs you to show him your love. Further, this commandment, 'You will love your neighbor as yourself,' requires the same from you—that is, do not obey the flesh because when it feels offended that's when it hates, bites, and devours. Rather, fight against it in the Spirit, and in the same way, persist in loving your neighbor, even though you may not discover within him anything worthy of your love."

The papal scholars surmise that the desire of the flesh is the body's lust. It is very true that even the faithful, especially the young, are tempted with the lusts of the flesh. Yes, even those who are married (the flesh is so corrupt and perverse) have no lack of such carnal lusts. This applies to all, but now, I'm speaking particularly to the faithfully married, men and women, to examine yourselves in depth,

---

[122] *nullius sancti.*

and no doubt, you will find the same within yourselves. The beauty and conditions of another man's wife please him more than those of his own woman. He feels annoyed and upset with his own legitimate wife and loves what is not lawful. Men despise what they have and fall in love with what they do not. As the poet said, *Nitimur in vetitum semper, cupimusque negata*—that is,

> *Always scrapping for the unlawful,*
> *and languishing for the forbidden.*

I don't deny that the desire of the flesh includes the lust of the flesh, but it's not just about that. The desires of the flesh encompass all other corrupt passions. The faithful are infected with all that—some more, some less. These are pride, hate, greed, impatience, and other like these. Yes, even Paul places in the list of the works of the flesh not only these gross vices but also idolatry, heresy, and others like them. Thus it is clear that he talks about all lusting of the flesh and the entire dominion of sin, which still surges within the faithful who have received the first fruits of the Spirit, opposing the dominion of the Spirit. Accordingly, he includes not only carnal lusts, pride, greed, and so on but also unbelief, lack of assurance, loss of hope, hatred, contempt toward God, idolatry, heresies, and the like when he says, "And don't satisfy the desires of the flesh." It's as if he had said, "I write to you so that you will love one another. But you do not, nor can you, since the flesh infected and corrupted with lust not only stirs up sin in yourselves but it is sin itself, for if you had perfect love, there would be neither despair nor adversity no matter how great that could damage or perturb that love, but instead, it would be diffused throughout the whole body. There would be no wife no matter how plain that her husband would not be madly in love with her, despising all other women no matter how beautiful and gracious they might be. However, they cannot love like that because it is impossible to be made righteous through love."

"Therefore, don't think that I am revoking and taking back my words on my teaching regarding faith, for faith and hope must remain so that by the one, we may be justified and by the other, we will rise up when distressed and persevere until the end. What is more, we serve each other through love, since faith is not idle, but love is weak and very small. Thus when I urge you to walk in the Spirit, I make it more than clear that we are not justified through love.

"Thus when I exhort you to walk in the Spirit and not to fulfill the desires of the flesh, I don't require you to be entirely rid of the flesh or destroy it but to bridle it and submit it, for it is God's wish for the human race to last until the final day, but that would not be possible unless there are parents who conceive and raise children. Thus it is necessary for men and women to procreate so that the flesh will endure. Consequently, the flesh will sin, for the flesh cannot exist without sin. Thus with respect to the flesh, we are sinners; but regarding the Spirit, we are righteous. However, our righteousness abounds much more than our sin because Christ's holiness and righteousness abound so much more. He is the place where we find mercy,[123] and it abounds much more than the sins of the entire world. The forgiveness of sins has been given to us through Him. He is so great, so immense, and infinite that He easily devours all sin so that we can walk according to the Spirit."

Here, it may be noted that Paul does not write these things only to the hermits and monks who live in celibacy but to all Christians. I say this so that we will not err together with the Papists, who fantasized with the idea that this commandment belongs only to the clergy, believing that the apostle exhorts them to live in celibacy, subduing the flesh with sleepless vigils, fasts, tasks, and the like to avoid satisfying the desires of the flesh—that is, carnal lust. However, they were never able to suppress and control it regardless of all the shackles they tried to impose on the flesh.

Jerome, who led others in a life of silence, greatly loved and defended celibacy. However, he openly confessed: "Oh [he said], how often have I imagined that I am right in the middle of the pleasures and delights of Rome, even though I found myself in the most desert wastelands, under the sun's burning rays, a most deplorable place to live, suitable only for monks." He went further: "Yet I, who for the fear of hell had condemned myself to such a prison frequently imagined that I was dancing among delightful virgins, when I had for company nothing but scorpions and wild beasts! My face was pale from fasting, but my mind was inflamed with the desires of my cold body; and even though my flesh was half dead, the flames of this carnal lust boiled up within me." If Jerome himself, living only on bread and water in the desert wasteland, felt these flames of carnal lust, what do our Holy Joes feel, who worship their bellies, the clergy, stuffed to the hilt with all kinds of delightful delicacies? It's a wonder their bellies don't explode! Thus all these things were written not for the hermits, nor for the monks (as the Papists imagine), nor just for worldly sinners, but for the universal church of Christ and for all the faithful. They are the ones that Paul exhorts to walk in the Spirit and not satisfy the desires of the flesh, as in lust, anger, impatience, and the like. However, he refers not just to these but also to the spiritual feelings such as doubt, blasphemy, idolatry, hatred and rejection of God.

Paul (as I've said) does not require the faithful to rid themselves entirely of the flesh but to bridle it so that it is subjected to the Spirit. In Romans 13:14, he urges us to value the flesh.[124] Just as we cannot be cruel with other's bodies, so we should not be cruel with our own bodies (Ephesians 5:29). Thus according to Paul's teaching, we should care for our own flesh so that it can withstand the struggles of the mind and body but only what is necessary and not to satisfy the desires of the flesh. Thus if the flesh begins to get out of control, through the Spirit, repress and bridle it. If you cannot, marry a woman for it is better to be married than burned. As you do this, you

---

[123] *Propiciatoris nostri.*

[124] *favore carnem*, Romans 13:14. Here, Luther translates this to the German: "Care for the body, but don't let it get out of control."

will walk in the Spirit—that is, you will be following God's word and doing His will. *But (as I've said) this command to walk in the Spirit and so on does not belong just to the hermits and monks but to all Christians, even though some may think lust does not apply to them!*[125] *Thus the prince does not satisfy the desires of the flesh when he diligently fulfills his duty and governs his subjects fairly, punishing the guilty and defending the innocent. Here, the flesh and the devil resist him and tempt him, provoking him to declare unjust wars and to obey his greed. If he follows the direction of the Spirit and the good and sound admonitions of God's word regarding his duty, he will not be satisfying the desires of the flesh etc. In this way, let each one within his calling walk according to the Spirit and not satisfy his lustful flesh or any other work of the flesh.*

VERSE 17. For the desires of the flesh are against the Spirit, and the desires of the Spirit are against the flesh.

When Paul tells us that the desires of the flesh are against the Spirit and the Spirit against the flesh, he warns us that we will feel the lust of the flesh—that is, not just carnal lust but also pride, anger, despair, impatience, unbelief, and others like these. But just as he wishes for us to be aware that we will be impacted by these temptations, at the same time, he wishes that we will not give them our consent nor fulfill those desires. In other words, that we should not even think, talk, or do any of those things that provoke our flesh. Accordingly, if we are provoked to anger, we should become angry as Psalm 4:5 teaches us: "Angry but without sin." It's as if Paul were saying, "I know that the flesh will provoke you to anger, envy, doubt, unbelief, and other temptations. But resist through the Spirit so that you will not sin, for if you abandon the Spirit's guidance and follow after the flesh, you will fulfill the desire of the flesh, and you will die," as Paul says in Romans 8:13. The apostle's statement then is to be understood not only regarding lust but also regarding the entire kingdom of sin.

VERSE 17. For these are opposed to each other, to prevent you from doing what you want [NRSV].

These two captains or leaders (he says), the flesh and the Spirit, are antagonists within the body so that you cannot do what you would like. This text clearly testifies that Paul writes these things to the faithful—that is, the church of believers in Christ, baptized, justified, and renewed, and who have received full forgiveness of sins. However, he says, they have the flesh in rebellion against the Spirit. In the same way, he declares in Romans 7:14, "I am carnal," he says, "sold under sin." Further, he says, "But I see another law at work in me, waging war against the law of my mind and making me a prisoner of the law of sin at work within me."

---

[125] Can you hear some seminarians snickering at Luther's sarcasm?

Further, he adds, "What a wretched man I am! Who will rescue me from this body that is subject to death?" (Romans 7:23, 24, NIV).

Here, not only the papal scholars but also some of the ancient fathers get all upset looking for a way to excuse Paul. It seems to them that it is absurd and improper to say that a chosen vessel of Christ would have sin. But we give credence to Paul's own words where he clearly confesses that he is sold under sin, that he is taken captive by sin, and that the flesh in him serves the law of sin. Here, they respond that the apostle is the spokesperson for the wicked. But the wicked don't complain that their flesh is in rebellion or about any battle or conflict or regarding spiritual captivity because sin reigns powerfully within them. Thus that is Paul's plain lament, as well as of all the faithful. So those who have tried to excuse Paul and all the faithful, saying that they have no sin, have done something wicked. With this argument (that proceeds from ignoring the doctrine of faith), they have robbed the church of a special comfort: they have abolished the forgiveness of sins and annulled the efficacy of Christ.

Thus when Paul says, "I see another law in my members," he does not deny that he has flesh and the vices of the flesh in him. Accordingly, it is very true that he sometimes felt the stirrings of carnal desire. What's more (no doubt), in him these feelings were well suppressed, due to the great and painful trials and temptations of mind as well as in the body by which in a certain way he was continually tried and perturbed, as stated in his epistles. Or if in another moment he felt happy and strong, he felt the lust of the flesh, anger, impatience, and other similar feelings, even so, he would have resisted by the Spirit and not allowed for these passions to rule over him. Thus let us not allow these texts (where Paul describes the battle of the flesh against the Spirit and within his body) to be corrupted by these comments in the margins. The scholars, the monks, and others like them have never felt any spiritual temptation. They have only attempted to repress and overcome carnal lust and morbid thoughts. They have felt proud of a victory they have never won and think of themselves as better and holier than married men. No! I would say that with that performance of holiness they only fed and nurtured all kinds of terrible sins, such as discord, pride, hate, disdain and contempt for their neighbors, confidence in their self-righteousness, pretentiousness, contempt for all piety and God's word, unfaithfulness, blasphemy, and similar sins. They never struggled against these sins. No, instead they got around the idea that those were not sins at all. They fixed their righteousness on the observance of their foolish and wicked vows. However, their wickedness was to ignore and not condemn such foolishness.

However, this should be our foundation and anchor: Christ is our supreme, finished, and perfect righteousness.[126] If we have nothing left in which to trust, these three things remain (as Paul says): faith, hope, and love (1 Corinthians 13:13). Therefore, we should always believe and never lose hope. We should always grasp

---

[126] *capitalem, rotundam et perfectam.*

on to Christ as the head and the foundation of our righteousness. Everyone who believes in Him will not be ashamed. Further, we should always strive to be externally righteous—that is, not to consent to the flesh, which always seduces us toward some evil. Rather, we should resist it through the spirit. We must not allow ourselves to be overcome by impatience, by people's ingratitude and disdain, and then by those who scorn us because they are abusing their Christian liberty. Instead, through the Spirit, we should overcome this and every other temptation. Look well, then, that we are actually fighting against the flesh through the Spirit so that we may be externally righteous, although this righteousness does not commend us before God.

Then don't let anyone despair when they feel that the flesh lets loose another attack against the Spirit or if immediately you cannot subdue the flesh taking it into the obedience of the Spirit. I also would like to have a more courageous and persistent heart to more boldly oppose the threats of the tyrants, the heresies, the damage, and the tumults stirred up by Satan and his soldiers, enemies of the Gospel. How I wish that I could immediately shake off the frustration and anguish of spirit, at least for a short while not to feel the sting of death but welcome it and embrace it as if it were a most welcome guest. But I find that there is another law in my members that rebels against the law of my mind etc. There are others who struggle with lesser temptations such as poverty, humiliation, impatience, and others like them.

Therefore, let no one be surprised or greatly frightened when you feel within your body this battle of the flesh against the Spirit. Instead, let him take courage within his heart and comfort himself with these words of Paul: "The flesh lusts against the Spirit," and also, "These are opposed to each other, to prevent you from doing what you want." With these statements, he comforts the tempted. It's as if he had said, "It's impossible for you to follow the Spirit's guidance in everything without feeling the opposition of the flesh.[127] Here, it is enough if you resist the flesh and don't satisfy its desires—that is, if you follow the Spirit and not the flesh, for the flesh easily defeats the spirit with impatience, the desire for vengeance, biting, resentment, hatred toward God, anger against Him, hopelessness, and other things." Thus when you feel this ongoing battle between the Spirit and the flesh, don't sell yourself out.[128] Instead, resist in the Spirit, saying, "I am a sinner and I feel sin. I have not yet been stripped of my flesh, which is glued to sin as long as I live. But in the Spirit, I will not humor the flesh—that is, I will take hold of Christ's faith and hope, stand firm on His word, and will not bring to fruition the lusts of the flesh."

It is very helpful for the faithful to be aware of this and keep it well in mind for it is a timely comfort when they are tempted. When I was a monk, if at any time I felt the desire of the flesh, I would immediately think that I would be stripped away of my salvation—that is, if I felt a bad feeling, carnal lust, anger, hate, or envy against any brother. I would try some new way to fight, I admit, every single day! I

---

[127] *impedimento carnis.*

[128] *abjiciat.*

accomplished nothing! Carnal lust and the desire of the flesh would always find their way back. I could not find any rest but always felt overwhelmed by these thoughts: "You have committed this or that sin; you are infected with envy, impatience, and other similar sins. Thus you have entered this order in vain and all your good works have been in vain." If back then I would have understood these statements from Paul, "The flesh desires what is contrary to the Spirit, and the Spirit what is contrary to the flesh," I would not have tormented myself so miserably. Instead, I would have thought to myself, as I now do, "Martin, since you have flesh, you will always find sin within you, thus you will feel the battle of the flesh according to what Paul said, 'The flesh desires what is contrary to the Spirit.' Thus do not despair but resist and don't satisfy its desires. In this way, you will not be under the law."

I remember that Staupitz used to say, "I have sworn a thousand times before God that I would become a better man but was never able to fulfill my oath. From here on, I will not take such an oath, for now I have learned by experience that I cannot fulfill it. Thus unless God for Christ's sake extends His favor and mercy to me and grants me that happy and blessed hour when I will bid farewell to this miserable life, I could not go before Him bringing along all my vows and good works." This is not only true, but it was a pious and holy despair, and one that all the saved should confess with their mouths and from their hearts, for all the faithful do not trust in their own righteousness but with David say, "Please don't bring your servant to judgment, because no living thing is righteous before you" (Psalm 143:2, CEB) and "If you kept track of sins, Lord—my Lord, who would stand a chance?" (Psalm 130:3, CEB). They fix their gaze on Christ, their place of mercy,[129] who gave His life for their sins. Further, they know that although there are remnants of sin in their flesh, these are not accounted against them[130] but are freely forgiven. However, in the meantime, the Spirit struggles against the flesh within them, lest the flesh satisfy its desires. Although they feel that the flesh roars and rebels against the Spirit and they themselves sometimes fall into sin due to weakness, they are not discouraged, nor do they think their condition or way of life and the works they have done in their calling displease God. Rather, they rise up and stand through faith.

Therefore, the faithful are greatly comforted through this doctrine from Paul, by which they understand that in themselves they are on the one hand flesh and on the other spirit. Notwithstanding, the Spirit rules and the flesh stays subdued so that righteousness reigns and sin is submitted as a slave. Whoever ignores this doctrine and thinks the faithful should not have any defects at all, all the while feeling the opposite, at the end, will be absorbed by sadness and despair. But whoever knows this doctrine well and uses it correctly, even bad things inevitably work together for good, for when the flesh provokes them to sin, for that same reason, they will

---

[129] *Propiciatorem*. In English translations of the Bible, this is commonly translated as "mercy seat."

[130] *non imputari*.

be moved and compelled to seek the forgiveness of sins for the sake of Christ and embrace the righteousness of faith. Otherwise, they would not value it so greatly nor seek it out with such a burning desire. Thus it is greatly beneficial for us to sometimes feel the sinfulness of our nature and the corruption of our flesh so that through this means we will awaken and take courage in faith and cry out for Christ. In this way, a Christian becomes a powerful artisan and wonderful creator. From despair, he creates joy and from fear, comfort; from sin, righteousness; and from death, life when in such a way he represses and bridles the flesh, subjecting it to the Spirit.

Therefore, those who feel the desire of the flesh don't despair of your salvation. Let them feel it with all its power so that they will not consent to it. Let them be shaken by the passions of lust, anger, and other vices so that they will not be defeated. Let them be besieged by sin so that it will not conquer them. Yes, and however more pious is the believer that much more he will feel the intensity of the battle. That is why we find all the pitiful complaints of the faithful in the Psalms and throughout all Scripture. But the hermits, the monks, the scholars, and all those who strive for righteousness and salvation through works have no idea of what this battle is about. However, here someone could say that it is a dangerous thing to teach that people are not under condemnation if they are not immediately victorious over the passions of the flesh. It is alleged that if this doctrine spreads throughout the common people, they will become careless, stagnant, and listless. However, keep in mind what I've said before. If we teach faith, carnal people will neglect works. But if we urge works, then people will lose faith and a conscience at peace. Here, we cannot dictate over anyone nor prescribe a specific rule. But let us examine ourselves carefully to see which passion of the flesh hurts us the most. Once we detect it, let's not be complacent; let's not excuse it. Instead, let us watch and in the Spirit struggle against it. If we cannot completely control it, at least we will not bring it into fruition.

All God's children have wrestled in this struggle of the flesh against the Spirit, and we also have experienced it. Those who go and dig within their conscience, if they're not hypocrites, will see the same thing that Paul says here: the flesh opposes the Spirit. Then let each of the faithful feel and confess that their flesh resists and fights against the Spirit, and that these two are contrary to each other. Within the faithful, these two are so set against each other that do what they may, they will never do all they would like to do. Therefore, the flesh stands in the way so that we cannot fulfill God's commandments, love our neighbor as ourselves, and much less love God with all our heart. Thus it is impossible for us to be ever justified[131] by the works of the law. There's certainly within us goodwill and so it should be (for the Spirit itself resists the flesh), for its greatest wish is to do what is right, fulfill the law, love God and neighbor, and similar things, but the flesh does not obey this goodwill but resists it. However,

---

[131] *Ideo impossibile est nos legis operibus justificari.*

God does not count this sin against us, for He is merciful to all those who believe on account of Christ.[132]

However, it does not follow from here that you should minimize sin or normalize it,[133] thinking that God will not impute it. It is true that God does not impute it, but to whom and on account of whom? Not to the hard-hearted and self-assured but to all those who sorrowfully by faith grasp onto Christ, the mercy seat. Because of Him, all their sins are forgiven; even the remains of sin that are left in them are not imputed against them. That does not take away the importance of their sin. Instead, it is amplified and exposed for what it is, for they know that they cannot take it away with satisfactions, works, righteousness, but only by the death of Christ. Even so, the greatness and enormity of their sin does not lead them to despair but to trust that they are forgiven on account of Christ.[134]

I say this lest someone assume that after receiving faith, they will think that sin is not great and powerful. Sin is certainly sin, whether it's committed before the knowledge of Christ or thereafter. God will always hate sin. Yes, all sin is under condemnation, insofar as the deed itself. However, whoever believes has not been condemned to death, for this comes from Christ, the mercy seat, who by His death has taken away sin. But whoever does not believe in Christ, not only are all his sins condemned, but also his good works are under condemnation according to what is written: "All that is not of faith, is sin" (Romans 14:23). Therefore, the scholastics' error is most perverse for it makes a difference between the sins done according to the deeds and not according to the person. The sins of the believers are just as huge[135] as the sins of the unbelievers. But for those who believe, they are forgiven and not imputed. For the believer, they are venial sins. For the unbeliever, they are mortal and condemn him, not because there is a difference between sins or because the believer's sin is of minor consequence and the unbeliever's is more severe but because they are different persons. The believer has the assurance within himself that through faith his sin has been forgiven, that was the reason Christ gave Himself. Therefore, although he still has sin in him and sins daily, he continues to be faithful. But the unbeliever, on the contrary, continues to sin. This is the believers' true wisdom and comfort, that although they have committed and commit sins, they know that for Christ's sake they are not imputed to them.[136]

I say this to comfort the faithful, for they certainly only feel that they have committed and commit sins—that is, they feel that they don't love God with as much fervor as should be the case; they think they don't trust in Him with as much devotion as they should but instead doubt if God watches out for them; they are

---

[132] *propter Christum.*

[133] *extenuare aut contemnere.*

[134] *propter Christum.*

[135] *magnum.*

[136] *propter fidem in Christum non imputari.*

impatient, and in trials, they get angry with God. As I've said, that's the source for all the mournful laments of the faithful in the Scriptures and especially in the Psalms. Paul himself complains that he is "carnal, sold under sin." Further, here, he says that the flesh resists the Spirit and rebels against it. But since they are putting to death the works of the flesh through the Spirit (Romans 8:13), "they crucify the flesh with its passions and desires" (Galatians 5:24), these sins do not penalize them or condemn them. However, if they obey the flesh, satisfy its desires, then they do lose faith and the Holy Spirit; and if they do not abhor their sin and turn back to Christ (who has given power to His church to receive and lift up the fallen that they may recover faith and the Holy Spirit), they die in their sins. Thus we are not talking about those who fantasize they have faith and remain in their sins. These people have already received their sentence: for those who live according to the flesh will die (Romans 8:13). Also, "The acts of the flesh are obvious: sexual immorality, impurity and debauchery; idolatry and witchcraft; hatred, discord, jealousy, fits of rage, selfish ambition, dissensions, factions and envy; drunkenness, orgies, and the like. I warn you, as I did before, that those who live like this will not inherit the kingdom of God" (Galatians 5:19–21).

That is how we can understand who the true saints are. These are not made of wood and stone (as the monks imagine) so that nothing could ever move them or that they will never feel any lust at all or the desires of the flesh. Instead, as Paul says, the desire of their flesh is against the desire of their spirit, and thus they have sin and can sin. Further, Psalm 32:5–6 testifies that the faithful do confess their wickedness and pray for the forgiveness of the evil of their sin. That is why it is written, "I will confess my transgressions to the Lord. And you forgave the guilt of my sin. Therefore, let all the faithful pray to you while you may be found." Further, the entire church, which is holy, prays for the forgiveness of sins and believes in the forgiveness of sins. In Psalm 143:2, David pleads, "Enter not into judgment with thy servant: for in thy sight shall no man living be justified" (Psalm 143:2, KJV). Further, it says in Psalm 130, "If you kept track of sins, Lord—my Lord, who would stand a chance? But forgiveness is with you—that's why you are honored" (Psalm 130:3, CEB). That is how the first among the saints and God's children talk and pray like David, Paul, and others. Thus all the faithful talk and pray for the same and with the same spirit. The papal scholars don't read the Scriptures, or if they read them, they have a veil over their eyes. Therefore, they cannot judge correctly with respect to any matter at all, thus they are unable to properly judge with respect to what is sin or holiness.

VERSE 18. But if you are led by the Spirit you are not under the law.

Paul cannot forget the doctrine of faith but continues to repeat it; he hammers it over their heads, yes, even when dealing with the subject of good works. Someone here could object, "Why are we not under the law? Because, Paul, you nonetheless teach that the desire of our flesh is against the Spirit and struggles against us; it torments us and turns us into slaves! Further, we certainly feel sin and cannot be freed from it no matter how much we faint striving for our freedom. Isn't this really to be under the law?" However, he says, "Don't let this annoy you. Only strive to be led by the Spirit—that is, be disposed to follow and obey that goodwill that resists the flesh and does not satisfy its desires (for this is what it is to be guided and attracted by the Spirit). Then you will not be under the law." That is how Paul talks about himself: "I of myself serve the law of God with my mind" (Romans 7:25)—that is, in the Spirit, I am not subject to any sin but even so, in my flesh, I serve the law of sin. The faithful then are not under the law, they are in the Spirit, for the law cannot accuse them nor mandate the death sentence against them even though they feel sin and confess they are sinners, for the condemnation of the law has been removed by Christ, who was "born under the law, to redeem those who were under the law." Thus the law cannot accuse the faithful that there is sin within them, although indeed there is sin and is committed in transgression of the law.

Then the power and dominion of the Spirit are so great that the law cannot accuse the believers although they commit what is certainly sin, for Christ is our righteousness, and we take all of Him by faith. He is entirely without fault, and thus the law cannot accuse Him. If we adhere to Him, we are guided by the Spirit and are free from the law. In this way, the apostle, even though he may be teaching good works, does not forget regarding justification but always demonstrates that it is impossible for us to be justified through our good works.[137] The remnants of sin may be nailed tight to our flesh and thus as long as flesh shall live, it will never cease to wish everything that is contrary to the Spirit. But there's nothing to fear from any danger because having been freed from the law, we are now walking in the Spirit.

With these words, "If you are led by the Spirit you are not under the law," you can be greatly comforted and comfort others who are going through difficult temptations, for it happens that at times someone is so doggedly harassed by anger, hate, impatience, carnal desire, an anguished and horrified spirit, or some other desire of the flesh that they cannot be shaken off, no matter how hard they try. What should be done in this case? Should you despair? No! God forbid! Instead, he should say to himself, "Your flesh is fighting against the Spirit. Let it roar all it wants, only come what may, let its desires pass you by. Instead, walk with wisdom and follow the Spirit's guidance. When you do this, you are free from the law. It accuses and annoys you, but its efforts are in vain. Thus in this conflict of the flesh against the spirit, there is nothing better than to uphold God's word before your eyes and from there reach for the Spirit's comfort."

Those who suffer this temptation, don't dismay. The devil is able to aggravate you, exaggerating your sin during the conflict so that you will go down shaking,[138]

---

[137] *sed semper indicat impossibile esse nos operibus posse justificari.*

[138] *succumbere in paroxismo.*

be unable to feel anything else but God's anger, and then despair. In this instance, under no circumstance should you pay attention to your own feelings. Rather, take hold of Paul's words, "If you are led by the Spirit"—that is, if you are lifted up and comforted by faith in Christ—you will not be under the law. You will have a strong shield with which to deflect all the fiery darts from the evil one who holds you under siege. Then it doesn't matter how much the flesh roars and boils, such feelings and powerful emotions can neither hurt nor condemn, for the believers following the leading of the Spirit neither consent to the flesh nor satisfy its desires. Therefore, when the feelings of the flesh roar with fury, the only remedy is to take the sword of the Spirit. This is the word of salvation, which says that God does not desire the death of sinners. Then they should go on and fight against those desires. As we do this, let us not doubt that we shall be victorious, although as long as we are in the middle of the battle, we will feel totally the opposite. But let them push aside the word out of sight, and they've lost every possible comfort.

Consequently, I speak out of my own experience. I have suffered many great passions, and these have been intense and enormous. However, as soon as I have taken hold of any text of Scripture, staying there as if it were my anchor, my temptations immediately vanished. However, without the word, it would have been impossible to persevere, not even for a short while, and much less overcome them.

LECTURE 38: Friday, December 4

Then the sum or effect of all that Paul has taught in this dispute or discourse regarding the conflict or battle between the flesh and the spirit is this: that God's holy or elect cannot fulfill the desires of the Spirit, for the Spirit wishes to be altogether pure, but since the flesh is joined to the Spirit, it does not allow it. Nonetheless, they will be saved by the remission of sins there is in Christ Jesus. Further, since they walk in the Spirit and are led by the Spirit, they are not under the law—that is, the law cannot accuse or terrify them no matter how hard it tries, it will never cast them into despair.

VERSE 19. The acts of the flesh are obvious . . . [NIV].

This text is no different from Christ's statement, "By their fruit you will recognize them. Do people pick grapes from thorn bushes, or figs from thistles? Likewise, every good tree bears good fruit, but a bad tree bears bad fruit." Paul teaches no differently from Christ. Whether the trees are good or bad is testified by their works and fruits—that is, if people are following the leadings of the flesh or of the Spirit. It's as if he had said, "I'm going to make sure people won't say to themselves they don't understand me. So since now I am dealing with the topic of the battle between the flesh and the Spirit, I will show before their eyes the works of the flesh, which are known even among the wicked and then the works of the Spirit."

Paul does this, since there were many hypocrites among the Galatians (as there are among us today). On the outside, they appear to be pious and boast a great deal about the Spirit. Yet they don't walk according to the Spirit but according to the flesh, doing its works. That is how Paul clearly convinces them that they are not as devoted as they boasted. Thus he issues this fearful warning. If they despise it, they would not inherit the kingdom of God; but once admonished, they would mend their ways.

Every stage of life, even for the faithful, has its own particular temptations. Carnal lust[139] besieges man during his entire youth. Once he matures, it is ambition and recognition. In old age, don't be surprised: it is greed in action.[140] There has never been a believer so holy who, sometime during his life, has not felt provoked by the flesh toward impatience, anger, conceit, and the like. Thus Paul is talking about the faithful in this text, saying that the flesh desires against the Spirit and such things. That is why they will never find themselves without the desires and the struggles against the flesh. Nonetheless, they will not be harmed. But we should judge like this: It is one thing to be provoked by the lust of the flesh and refuse to yield to it but instead walk and resist in the Spirit. It is another thing to consent to the flesh without fear or remorse and do its works and remain in them, all the while acting holy and boasting in the Spirit. The first, Paul comforts when he says they are led by the Spirit and are not under the law. The others, he threatens with eternal destruction.

However, sometimes it happens that even the saints will fall as well and satisfy the desires of the flesh. That's how it was when David fell horribly into adultery. He also caused the death of many men when Uriah was killed at the battlefront. With that, David also gave occasion for the enemies to glory and triumph over God's people, worship their idols, and blaspheme the God of Israel. Peter also fell grievously and horribly when he denied Christ. But although these were great and horrifying sins, they were not committed in contempt of God or due to a willful mind determined to commit wicked deeds but due to feebleness and weakness. However, when they were admonished, they did not remain obstinate in their sins but instead they repented. He urges such believers in chapter 6 to be welcomed, instructed, and reestablished, saying, "Brothers and sisters, if someone is caught in a sin, you who live by the Spirit should restore that person gently. But watch yourselves, or you also may be tempted" (Galatians 6:1). Thus those who sin and fall due to weakness are not to be denied forgiveness so that they may rise again and not continue in their sin, for of all things, to persist in sin is the worst. But if they do not repent but remain obstinately in their wickedness, satisfying the desires of the flesh, that is a sure sign that there is deceit in their spirit.

Thus there is no one alive who lives free from lust. As long as people live in the flesh—and for that very reason—no one will ever be free from temptation.

---

[139] *libido.*

[140] *avaritia praecipue exercet.*

However, some are tempted in one way or another, according to the differences between people. Someone may be impacted by the most egregious and grievous desires, with greater bitterness and anguish of spirit, or blasphemy, mistrust, and despair. Others are beset with more crass temptations, such as fleshly lust, anger, envy, greed, and other such things. But in this case, Paul requires from all that we walk in the Spirit and resist the flesh. However, to all who obey the flesh and persist without a remorseful conscience satisfying the lust and its desires, let them know that they don't belong to Christ. No matter how much they may brag in the name of Christ, they are self-deceived, "for all who are of Christ crucify their flesh with its desires" (Galatians 5:24).

Who Are the Properly Called Saints and Who Are Saints Indeed?

This text (as I've already mentioned) contains a special comfort, for it gives notice that the saints and the most faithful of this world cannot live without lust, nor without temptations of the flesh, nor even yet without sin. Therefore, he admonishes us that we should pay attention. This will prevent us from becoming like others that Gerson writes about; they struggled to achieve such perfection, attempting to empty themselves of all feelings of temptation or sin, as if they were tree trunks and stumps. The monks and the academics had the same image of their saints, as if they had been mere sticks without feelings and lacking all emotion. The Virgin Mary would feel great pain and grief of spirit when she would no longer have her son (Luke 2:35). In the Psalms, David complains that he was almost drowning in grief due to the enormity of his temptations and sins. Paul also complains, saying, "We were harassed at every turn—conflicts on the outside, fears within," and that in his flesh he serves the law of sin. He says he carries the burden of all the churches and that God has shown him great mercy; He has delivered Epaphroditus, who was so close to death and was once again raised to life so that he would not suffer grief upon grief. Therefore, the holier-than-thou papal scholars[141] are like the stoics who imagined their wisdom was a rarity in the natural world. But this foolish and evil persuasion arises from ignoring Paul's doctrine; accordingly, the papal scholars cast on themselves as well as numberless others, nothing but infinite despair!

When I was a monk, sometimes, with all my heart, I wished to have the joy of seeing a real saint or pious man up in real life and see how he lived. While I waited for that moment, I imagined that such a saint lived in the brush, abstaining from food and drink, and living only on the roots of herbs and cold water. That is what I had learned to think regarding these monster saints, not only from the books of the papal scholars and academicians, but also from the books of the fathers. It was Jerome who wrote this in a certain place: "Regarding food and drink, I have nothing to say, for their use is already excessive; thus even the feeble and listless should

---

[141] *sophistarum.*

only drink cold water or anything that has been diluted." However, now in the light of the Gospel, we can clearly see who are those that Christ and the apostles called saints. They are not the ones who live alone and in celibacy or who abstain strictly regarding days, foods, dress, and other similar things or who externally appear to do great and monstrous works (as we read about many in *Lives of the Fathers*). Instead, it is those who, having been called by the Gospel and baptized, believe they have been sanctified and cleansed by Christ's death and blood. That is why Paul in his writings calls them saints, children and heirs of God, and the like. Thus everyone who believes in Christ, whether it is man or woman, free or slave, all are saints. They are not saints through their own works but through God's works such as His word, His Sacraments, Christ's passion, His death, His resurrection, His victory, and the outpouring of the Holy Spirit. In summary, they are holy through a holiness they freely receive. However, it's not through a holiness that they themselves have achieved through their own productivity, good works, and merits. In brief, you are holy through a passive righteousness and not through an active righteousness.

The ministers of the word, the local judges, parents, children, teachers, and others are those who are truly saints—that is, if first and foremost, they possess full assurance that Christ is their wisdom, righteousness, sanctification, and redemption, and second, they fulfill the duty of their vocation according to what is ordered in God's word and do not humor the flesh, restraining their lustful longings through the Spirit. Although not all have the same strength to resist temptation but in most people their weakness and frailties are obvious, these do not hinder their holiness. Thus their sins do not proceed from a will determined to do what is evil but only from weakness and frailty, for (as I've said before) the faithful indeed do feel the desires and lusts of the flesh, but they resist so that they don't satisfy its desires. Further, if at any time, they unbecomingly fall into sin, even so, they obtain forgiveness if by faith they rise up again unless we push them away. Instead, let us seek them out and bring them home as stray and lost sheep. Thus God forbid that I immediately judge the weak in their faith or morals,[142] supposing they are profane or wicked, when it is obvious they love and revere God's word; they come to the Lord's Supper, for God has received them and counts them as righteous through the remission of sins.[143] That is how they stand or fall. This is how Paul speaks everywhere about the saints.

Thus I joyfully thank God that He has abundantly and overwhelmingly granted what I had so earnestly requested when I was a monk. He has now given me the grace to see not just one but many saints, yes, even an infinite number of true saints, not those who are the invention of the papal scholars but such as Christ Himself and the apostles describe, and I, myself, have the assurance that

---

[142] *moribus.* May also be translated as "behaviors" or "habits."

[143] *reputat eos iustos per remissionem peccatorum.*

I belong to such a number, for I am baptized, and I do believe that Christ is my Lord; through His death, He has redeemed and delivered me from all my sins and has given me eternal righteousness and holiness. And let those be accounted as accursed who do not give this honor to Christ and believe that through His death, His word, and Sacraments that they are already justified and sanctified.

Therefore, let us reject this stupid[144] and wicked notion regarding the title of saints. In the papacy and our ignorance, we thought that it pertained only to the saints in heaven and on earth, to the hermits and monks who achieved certain wonderful and strange works. Instead, let us learn now through the Holy Scriptures that all who faithfully believe in Christ are saints. The world has had great admiration for the holiness of Benedict, Gregory, Bernard, Francis, and others. The world has heard what they have done, in the outward appearance, and in the world's opinion they have achieved great and excellent works. No doubt Hilary, Cyril, Athanasius, Ambrose, Augustine, and others were also saints but did not live as strictly and rigorously as the first. Nonetheless, they lived among others, ate common foods, drank wine, used clean and simple clothing. There was no difference between them and other honest people regarding their daily habits and the use of necessary things for this life. So then, were they preferred above the others? The latter taught Christ's doctrine sincerely and with purity, without any superstitions; they resisted heretics and purged the church from countless errors. Many were benefitted by their companionship and friendship, especially the afflicted and despondent who they lifted up and comforted through the word of God. They did not separate from the companionship of others but carried out their duties even in places where there were all kinds of people. On the contrary, the others not only taught things contrary to the faith, but they themselves were the authors and inventors of many superstitions, errors, abominable ceremonies, and wicked acts of worship. Thus unless at the hour of death they would have grasped on to Christ and rested their entire trust on His death and victory, their strict and painful life counted for nothing.

All this demonstrates sufficiently clear who are the true saints and who have received the calling to live a pious life. It is not those who withdraw to caves and dens, who emaciate their bodies with fasting, dress in hairs, and do other things with the persuasion and assurance that they will obtain some special reward in heaven over and beyond all other Christians. However, the pious life describes those who have been baptized and believed in Christ, depriving the old man and his works, although not altogether, for lust and desire remain in them while they live. However, those feelings do not harm them at all if they are not permitted to govern them but rather submit them through the Spirit.

This doctrine brings great comfort to pious minds. Consequently, when they feel the darts of the flesh with which Satan attacks their spirit, they should

---

[144] *stulta.* This was a strong word. It could be softened to "foolish," but "stupid" catches the full force of Luther's opinion on the matter.

not despair, as happened to many in the papacy for they thought they should not feel the lust of the flesh. However, although they had Jerome, Gregory, Benedict, Bernard, and others (who the monks set out as perfect examples of chastity and all Christian virtue) who were never able to reach the point where they could no longer feel lust or the lusts of the flesh, indeed, it is true that they felt them and very powerfully, which they confess and clearly admit in various places in their books. *Thus God did not impute these small faults to them, not even those pernicious errors that some of them brought to the church. Gregory was the author of the private mass, such a great abomination that there has never been anything like it in the New Testament church. Others invented the monastic life with their wicked acts of worship, which they invented all by themselves! Cyprian demanded that those who had been baptized by heretics should be rebaptized.*

Therefore, let us properly confess the articles of our faith whereby we confess there is one holy church. Since it is invisible and dwells in a place out of everyone's reach, its holiness cannot be seen. God hides and covers its weaknesses, sins, errors, and various ways of understanding the scandal of the cross. Before God, these just aren't there! All who ignore this, when they see the frailties and sins of the baptized who have the word and believe it, immediately get offended and judge that they don't belong to the church. At the same time, they dream with the illusion that the hermits, monks and those who shave their heads are the church. Although they honor God with their lips, in vain do they honor Him, for they do not follow God's word but the doctrines and commandments of men and teach others to do the same. Since they teach certain superstitions and grotesque works, carnal flesh amplifies them and values them beyond measure. Thus they judge that they alone are holy and that they are the church. When they do this, they change and totally turn upside down this article of faith: "I believe there is one holy church." In place of this statement, "I believe," they replace it with "I see." These types of righteousness and holiness are men's own inventions. They are nothing else but spiritual witchcraft with which they blind people's eyes and minds and lead them far from the knowledge of true holiness.

However, we teach that the church has no spot or wrinkle. Instead, it is holy but only by faith in Christ Jesus,[145] once again, that it is holy in its life and way of living as it abstains from the desires of the flesh and by exercising in yielding spiritual fruit.[146] But not in such a way that it will be free from all evil desire or purged from all wicked error and opinion, for the church always confesses its sins, prays for the forgiveness of its trespasses, and believes in the forgiveness of sins.[147] Thus the saints sin, they fall, make mistakes, but due to their ignorance, for they do

---

[145] *ecclesiam non habere maculam aut rugam, sed esse sanctam, per fidem tamen in Jesum Christum.*

[146] *exercitium spiritualium fructum.*

[147] A reference to the third article of the Apostles' Creed.

not willingly deny Christ or abandon the Gospel; thus they have the remission of sins. Further, if due to ignorance they err in the doctrine, this is forgiven as well, for at the end, they recognize their error, and lean only on God's truth and grace offered in Christ. Such was the case with Jerome, Gregory, Bernard, and others. Thus let Christians avoid the works of the flesh, but they will not be able to avoid the desires and the lusts of the flesh.

Thus it is very beneficial for the godly to feel the impure desires of the flesh lest they get all puffed up with some empty and wicked opinion about the righteousness of their own works, as if they were accepted before God on their account. The monks, all swollen with this opinion, regarding their own righteousness, thought they were so holy that they sold their righteousness and holiness to others although the witness of their own hearts convinced them of their impurity. That is how pernicious and foul smelling is the poison of thinking that man can trust in his own righteousness, as well as thinking that you can clean up after yourself. However, the pious, those who feel the impurity in their own hearts, cannot place their confidence on their own righteousness. This feeling leads them to bow down, to humble themselves, realizing they cannot find assurance in their own good works but instead see themselves compelled to flee to Christ, their mercy seat.[148] He does not have a corrupt and sinful flesh but the purest and most perfect flesh, which He has given for the life of the world. In Him, they find a lasting and perfect righteousness;[149] that is how they persist in humility. It is not the pretend righteousness of the monks but true and without disguise, since impurity remains in them. Consequently, if God were to judge them strictly, He would find them guilty, worthy of eternal death. But since they don't puff up proudly against God but with broken and contrite heart humble themselves owning up to their sins, they rest entirely on the benefit granted them by Christ the Mediator. That is how they come before God's presence and pray for the forgiveness of sins on account of Christ. Thus God covers them with an infinite sky of grace and does not account their sins against them for the sake of Christ.[150]

I say this so that we will keep our eyes open to see the pernicious errors of the Papists regarding holiness in our life. They can really tie up our minds in knots to such a point that it becomes extremely difficult to untie those knots. Thus strive diligently to discern and you will be able to judge properly between true righteousness and holiness and the hypocritical. Then you will see the kingdom of Christ with different eyes than those of carnal reasoning—that is, with spiritual eyes—and judge properly as to who are the real saints: they are those who have been baptized and believed in Christ. Thereafter, in the same faith with which

---

[148] *Christum propitiatorem.*

[149] *In illo inveniunt justitiam solidam et perfectam.*

[150] *expandit super eos Deus immensum coelum gratiae, ac peccata propter Christum non imputat eis.*

they have been justified and their past and present sins have been forgiven, they abstain from the desires of the flesh. But they don't remain entirely clean from these desires, for the flesh opposes the Spirit. Nonetheless, these impure and rebellious desires remain within them to this end, to humble them. Once humbled, they will feel the sweetness of grace and the benefit of Christ. Then the remaining impure desires and sins will not harm them at all but instead are great benefits to the faithful, for the more they feel their weaknesses and sins that much more they will flee to Christ, to the throne of grace, and with greater desire, they will long for His help and aid—that is, for Him to adorn them with His righteousness, that He will increase their faith, that He will gift them with His Holy Spirit. Then through the Spirit's guidance and direction they may overcome the desires of the flesh so that they may not be ruled and governed by them but that they themselves will bring them into subjection. Thus true Christians will constantly strive against sin. Yet as they fight against them, they are not overcome but obtain the victory.

I have said this so that you may understand, not through illusory dreams but through God's word, who are the true saints. Then we will see the extent to which Christian doctrine helps to lift up and comfort those who struggle with a weak conscience. It is not about robes, hoods, tonsures, shaved heads, fraternities, and similar toys. It is about weighty and lofty matters, how we can overcome the flesh, sin, death, and the devil. This doctrine is unknown by the legalists and all who trust in their own works. But through the doctrine of works, it is impossible to instruct and set back on track a vagabond or stray conscience or placate and comfort that conscience when it is found in the middle of despair, panic, or desperation.

VERSE 19. Now the works of the flesh are plain: fornication, impurity, licentiousness, idolatry, sorcery . . .

Paul does not call out a list of all the works of the flesh. He names some in particular, but they represent an indefinite list. First, he recounts all kinds of lust,[151] such as adultery, fornication, impurity, dissipation, etc. Well then, the desire of the flesh is not the only work of the flesh as the Papists imagine. They have also called marriage a work of the flesh (so chaste and holy are these men), although God Himself is the author of marriage and they themselves count it among their Sacraments. Instead, the apostle also includes within the works of the flesh (as I've said before) idolatry, witchcraft, hate, and others as follows. But this text is sufficient to demonstrate extensively what Paul wants to say by "the works of the flesh." These words are so well known they don't need any interpretation at all. *However, those who wish to know the meaning of each word may read the older commentary that I published in 1519. There, I demonstrated, according to my ability, the nature and strength of each*

---

[151] *species libidinis.*

word in the entire catalogue of all the works of the flesh and the fruit of the Spirit. Now as I expound on the Epistle to the Galatians, our main purpose has been to deliver to you as clearly as possible the article of justification.

Idolatry

The most exalted religions and the most pious and fervent devotions of all who reject Christ the Mediator and worship God without His word and command are nothing more than pure idolatry. In the papacy, there was a time when the monks were locked up in their cells pondering and meditating on God and His works. When they felt fired up by their most passionate devotions, they fell on their knees, prayed, and lay there in ecstasy contemplating heavenly things, tears of joy rolling down their cheeks. These were considered as the holiest and most spiritual deeds. They were not there thinking about women or about any other creature but on God alone the Creator and His marvelous works. However, this most spiritual work (as valued by reason) according to Paul is a work of the flesh and mere idolatry. The holier and more pious in appearances are so much more dangerous and pernicious. That is because it is the cause for people to separate from faith in Christ and for them to trust in their own strength, works, and righteousness. Such is the religion of the Anabaptists today, although daily they betray themselves demonstrating they are possessed by the devil and that they are seditious and vicious men.

Thus the fasts, dressing up in animal skins, holy works, strict regulations, and the entire life of the Carthusian monks and nuns, whose rule is the most strict and severe, are nothing else but the works of the flesh, yes, they are pure idolatry, for they imagine they are holy, that they will be saved not through Christ (who they serve out of fear as if He were a severe and cruel judge) but by serving their rules and orders. It is true that they think about God and in Christ and in heavenly things but according to their own reasoning and not according to God's word—that is, they think that due to their tunics and lifestyle that their entire life is holy and pleasing to Christ. They not only hope to placate Him through their life of austerity but also hope that He will reward them due to their good works and righteousness. Therefore, their most spiritual thoughts (according to their imagination) are not only almost entirely carnal but also extremely wicked. They would like to blot out their sins and obtain grace and eternal life trusting and holding on to their own righteousness, rejecting and despising the word, faith, and Christ. Thus all their acts of worship and service to God and all the religions without Christ are idolatry and worship to idols. Only in Christ is the Father well pleased. Anyone who hears Him and does what He has ordained is loved for the sake of the Beloved. He orders us to believe in His word and be baptized and not to invent some other modality of worshipping or serving God.

As I've said before, the works of the flesh are obvious, such as adultery, fornication, and others like them. But idolatry presents such a good theatrical performance, and is so spiritual that very few—that is, among the faithful—recognize it as a work of the flesh, for when the monk lives in celibacy, fasts, prays as required by his order, or says mass, he is far from being considered an idolater or satisfying any work of the flesh. Rather, he is completely persuaded and confident that he is led and governed by the Spirit, walking according to the Spirit, which thinks, speaks, and does nothing else except spiritual things. Further, he thinks that the service he renders to God is the most acceptable. No one today could persuade the Papists that their mass is a great blasphemy toward God and such horrible idolatry that has never been seen in the church since the time of the apostles. That is because they are blind and obstinate and have such a perverse notion of God and things pertaining to God, for they think that idolatry is a true service to God, and on the contrary, they believe faith is idolatry. But we who believe in Christ and know His mind are capable of judging and discerning all things in truth and no one can judge us before God.

Thus in this text it is perfectly clear that what Paul calls "flesh" is everything there is in man, extending to the three powers of the soul. These are a lustful will, the will that leans to anger, and reason. The works of the lustful will are adultery, fornication, impurity, and the like. The works of the will that leans to anger are feuds, disputes, murder, and others like these. The works of reason or the intellect are errors, false religions, superstitions, idolatry, heresies (these are the sects), and similar others. It is very necessary for us to know these things for this word *flesh* has been so obscured in the world of the Pope that they have understood the work of the flesh as nothing more than the satisfaction of carnal desire, or the act of lusting. Therefore, it has been impossible for them to understand Paul. But here we can clearly see that Paul counts idolatry and heresy as works of the flesh. However, reason values these two (as I've said before) as if they were the most exalted and excellent virtues, wisdom, religion, holiness, and righteousness. Paul calls them the religion of angels (Colossians 2). However, although to all appearances it boasts of being the holiest and spiritual, it is nothing more than a work of the flesh, an abominable idolatry against the Gospel, against faith, and against true service to God. The faithful are able to see this, for they have spiritual eyes. But the legalists judge to the contrary, for a monk could never convince himself that his vows are works of the flesh. In the same way, the Muslim could never believe that his Koran, his washings, and other ceremonies that he keeps are also works of the flesh.

Witchcraft

In chapter 3, I already spoke about witchcraft. Before the light and truth of the Gospel were revealed, this vice was so common in our day. When I was a boy, there were many witches and sorcerers that cast spells on cattle as well as people, especially children. Entire harvests were lost with hailstorms and tempests caused by spells. However, now in the light of the Gospel, you don't hear about these things as frequently, for the light of the Gospel has cast the devil out of his seat, together with all his deceitful illusions. But now, he has bewitched people with more terrible things—that is, with spiritual charms and spells.

Paul counts witchcraft among the works of the flesh, which nonetheless as everyone knows is not a work of carnal desire or lust but rather a type of idolatry, for witchcraft makes a deal with the devil. Superstition or idolatry swears an oath to god but not the true God but with a false god. Therefore, idolatry is truly spiritual witchcraft, for just as the sorcerers charm cattle and people so the idolaters—that is, all the legalists or those who justify themselves—strive to charm God or better said a god of their own invention. Well, then they come to imagine that such an imaginary god will justify them, not from his free grace and mercy and by faith in Christ but out of respect for their acts of worship born from their will and works of their own willpower, and will grant them eternal life as a reward. But while they attempt to charm God, they bewitch themselves; and if they continue in this wicked opinion they have conceived of God, they will die in their idolatry and will be condemned. Most of the works of the flesh are well known, thus it is not necessary to clarify them to greater extent.

Sects

By sects, Paul is not referring here to those arguments or squabbles that sometimes arise in the management of the home, in the local governments, or in mundane and worldly matters. Instead, he is talking about those that arise in the church regarding the doctrine, faith, and works. Heresies, in other words, sects, have always existed in the church in various places (as I've said before). However, the Pope is the supreme heretic and head of all heretics, for he has filled the world with an immense deluge of infinite sects and errors. What accord and unity could there be in such a great diversity of monks and other religious orders? There's no type of sect that could in any way agree with the others, for they measured their holiness by the severity of their orders. By way of example, that is how the Carthusians consider themselves more pious than the Franciscans and so on with the rest. Consequently, there's no unity of spirit or a meeting of the minds but the greatest discord![152] There's no conformity in their doctrine, faith, worship, religion, worship, and reason but all things are contrary to each other. On the other hand, Christians hold the same things in common: the word, faith, worship, religion, the Sacraments, Christ, God, the heart, feelings, the soul, the will, and the same spirit are common to all. Neither does it prevent diversity in status, external conditions, and life experiences, as I've frequently pointed out. Further, those who have this unity of spirit can certainly judge with respect to other sects; otherwise, no

---

[152] *sed summa discordia.*

one could understand this. Indeed, there was not one single theologian in all the papacy who understood Paul in this text, where he condemns all acts of worship, religions, prohibitions, showing off pious living, the pretend holy life of all the Papists, and sectarians. But all of them thought that he spoke of the gross idolatry of the Gentiles and the Muslims, who openly blaspheme the name of Christ.

Drunkenness and Gluttony

Paul doesn't say that eating and drinking are works of the flesh but rather, drunkenness and debauchery are, of all the vices, the most common today. All who have surrendered to this beast of debauchery and excess should know they are not spiritual, no matter all they boast that they are, since they follow the flesh and satisfy its desires. This horrible sentence is pronounced against them, that none of them will inherit the kingdom of God. Thus Paul longs for Christians to flee from drunkenness and dissipation; he wants them to live soberly and moderately, without excesses, for fear that in consenting to the flesh, they will be provoked to debauchery. Indeed, after dissipation and parties of gluttony, the flesh tends to excess and inflammation with shameful lust. However, it is not enough to bridle this shameful dissipation and lust of the flesh that follows drunkenness and debauchery or any other type of excess. Rather, the flesh as well, even when it is the most sober and moderate should be subdued and suppressed, fearing that it will satisfy its lusts and desires, for it happens that even the most sober of all are tempted. Jerome said that much about himself: "My face," he said, "was pale with fasting, but my mind was inflamed with carnal desires in my cold body; and although my flesh was already half dead, the flames of impure lust still raged within me." This was also my experience when I was a monk. Well then, the flame of impure desires is not only extinguished with fasting alone, but we should receive the aid of the Spirit—that is, as we meditate in God's word, faith and prayer. It is true that fasting suppresses the powerful attacks of carnal desire. But the desires of the flesh are overcome not in abstinence of food and drink but only through the mediation of God's word and calling upon Christ.

VERSE 21. And things like these [WEB].

For it is impossible to count all the deeds of the flesh.

VERSE 21. I warn you, as I did before, that those who live like this will not inherit the kingdom of God [NIV].

This is a powerful sentence but most necessary against the false Christians and careless hypocrites who boast in the Gospel, faith, and the Spirit yet nonetheless with all confidence satisfy the works of the flesh, for it is mainly the heretics, inflamed with their own opinions regarding spiritual matters (that they dream up in their imaginations), who are possessed by the devil and are entirely carnal. Thus they fulfill and satisfy the desires of the flesh, even with all the faculties of their soul. That is why it is extremely necessary for the apostle to pronounce such a horrifying and terrible sentence against these careless legalists and hardheaded hypocrites (that all who do such works of the flesh that Paul has listed will not inherit the kingdom of God). Consequently, some of them, horrified at this severe sentence begin to strive against the works of the flesh through the Spirit so that the flesh will not satisfy its desires.

VERSE 22. But the fruit of the Spirit is love, joy, peace, patience, kindness, goodness, faithfulness.

The apostle does not say the works of the Spirit, as he said the works of the flesh. Instead, he adorns these Christian virtues with a more honorable title calling them the fruit of the Spirit, for they bring with them the most useful and beneficial fruits, for all who have these render glory to God, and with these, they attract and provoke others to embrace the doctrine and faith in Christ.

Love

Just saying "love" and nothing else would have been enough, for love embraces all the fruits of the Spirit. Further, in 1 Corinthians 13, Paul attributes love to all the fruits that are done in the Spirit when he says, "Love is patient, kind, etc."

However, he finds a place for it all by itself, among the other fruits of the Spirit, and given first place. With this, he admonishes Christians that before all things, they should love one another, mutually honoring one another, and preferring one another, since Christ and the Holy Spirit dwell in them and they have the word, baptism, and other gifts from God that Christians possess.

Joy

This is the voice of the bride and the bridegroom. It refers to the sweet meditations upon Christ, useful exhortations, psalms and pleasant songs, praises and gifts of grace, with which the faithful instruct, encourage, and comfort each other. Thus God does not love a doubtful and downcast spirit. He hates the tedious doctrine and heavy and sad meditations, but He loves cheerful hearts. That is why He has sent His Son, not to oppress us with gloom and sadness, but to fill our souls with joy in Him. That is also why the prophets, apostles, and Christ Himself admonish us, yes, they command us to rejoice and be glad: "Rejoice greatly, Daughter Zion! Shout, Daughter Jerusalem! See, your king comes to you, righteous and victorious" (Zachariah 9:9). In the Psalms, we find the words "Rejoice in the Lord" frequently. Paul says, "Rejoice in the Lord always" (Philippians 4:4). And Christ says, "Rejoice that your names are written in heaven" (Luke 10:20). Whenever this Spirit is found there you will find a heart that rejoices through faith in Christ, fully assured that He is our Savior and High Priest. Externally, this joy is expressed with words and gestures. Also, the faithful rejoice as they see that the Gospel is spread to distant places so that many will be won to the faith and thus the kingdom of Christ will expand.

Peace

Toward God as well as toward men for the purpose is for Christians to be meek and gentle, not contentious or hateful toward each other, but bearing one another's burdens through patient tolerance. Without patience, peace cannot remain, and that is why Paul placed it following peace.

Long-Suffering[153]

Which I think is constant patience. With it, a person is able not only to tolerate adversities, offenses, injuries, and others like these but also to patiently wait for those who have harmed you to change their ways. When the devil cannot forcibly overcome the tempted, he sets the long-range plan in motion, for he knows that we are pots of clay, that we cannot resist and take many blows and violent hits. Thus when he extends his temptations, in the long run, he conquers many. To overcome these continuous attacks, we should use perseverance, which together with patience fixes its eyes on waiting not just for those who harm us to mend their ways but also for those temptations that the devil provokes against us to come to an end.

Kindness[154]

This is when people are good natured and charming as they relate to others with their whole life. Those who follow the Gospel will not be sharp and bitter but instead meek, human,[155] courteous, well-spoken, aiming to create harmony. They will overlook others' faults or at least interpret[156] them in the best light possible. They will be happily satisfied to yield their place to others, content to tolerate the impulsive and hard to deal with. Even the pagans say, "You should know the habits of your friend, but don't hate them." That's how Christ was as we can see throughout the Gospels. It is written about Peter, that he cried every time he remembered

---

[153] In this title, Luther uses the Greek μακροθυμια, which he proceeds to describe as *assiduitatem patientiae*.

[154] Here, Luther also uses the Greek χρηστότης.

[155] *humani.*

[156] *interpretentur.*

Christ's meekness, which He used in His daily life. It is an excellent virtue and most necessary in every aspect of life.

Goodness

This is a willingness to help others suffering poverty by being generous, lending to them, and other similar works.

Faith

Since Paul here counts faith among the fruits of the Spirit, it is obvious that he is not talking about the faith that is placed in Christ. Instead, he talks about faithfulness or honesty[157] from one person to another. That is why he says in 1 Corinthians 13:7 that love believes all things. Thus he says that this faith is not suspicious but kind and sees the best in everyone. If someone is betrayed and finds out he has been double crossed, even so, with patience and kindness, he overlooks the matter. In summary, he is willing to believe everyone, although he will not put his confidence in just anyone. On the other hand, when this virtue is lacking, people become suspicious, touchy, sullen, and stubborn so that no one believes anyone nor allows anyone to be heard; no one can tolerate anyone! No matter how well someone may speak or all the good he may do, his motives are questioned and slandered so that if he does not praise and root for them, he is then considered to be a hateful person. That is why it is impossible that they could ever love, have friendships, come to agreements, or be at peace with any other human being. But if these virtues are lacking, what else would be left in this life but to bite and devour one another? Therefore, the faith in this text is when one values another regarding those matters that apply to this present life, for what kind of life would we have in this world if we didn't believe in one another?

Gentleness

This is when the person is not annoyed or easily provoked to anger. In this life, there is an infinite number of situations that provoke to anger, but the faithful overcome them with gentleness.

Self-Control[158]

This is sobriety or careful moderation[159] in a person's entire life. It is a virtue that Paul sets opposite to the works of the flesh. He'd like for the Christian to live

---

[157] *candorem.*

[158] *continentia.*

[159] *sobrietas, temperantia seu moderatio.*

soberly and dignified, that the Christian will not be an adulterer or fornicator or out of control. And if they cannot live without sexual relations, then they should marry. Also, they should not be contentious or quarrelsome and they should not be given to drunkenness or debauchery but need to abstain from all these things. Purity or self-control includes it all. Jerome explains self-control only in relation to virginity, as if married people could not be pure or as if the apostle would have written these things only to those who never lost their virginity. In Titus, chapters 1 and 2, he also gives the same admonition to bishops, young people, married men and women, to be chaste and pure.

VERSE 23. Against such there is no law.

It is true that there is a law but not against these things. He said the same thing in another text: "The law is not made for a righteous person" (1 Timothy 1:9, NKJV). That is because the righteous live in such a way that they don't need any law at all, nor admonitions, nor bridles. However, they willingly fulfill all the things the law requires without the bridle of the law. Thus the law can neither accuse nor condemn those who believe in Christ. The law certainly accuses and perturbs our conscience, but Christ (whom we grasp by faith) conquers it with all its terrors and threats. Consequently, for them the law has been totally abolished, and does not have the power to accuse them, for they willingly fulfill all that the law requires. By faith, they have received the Holy Spirit who will not allow them to be idle. Although the flesh opposes them, they walk according to the Spirit. That is how a Christian fulfills the law inwardly by faith (for Christ is the perfection of the law for righteousness to all who believe) and outwardly by works and the remission of sins. However, the law accuses and condemns regarding civil law and matters of the Spirit in those who satisfy the works or desires of the flesh.

VERSE 24. And those who belong to Christ Jesus have crucified the flesh with its passions and desires.

This entire passage regarding works demonstrates that the true believers are not hypocrites. Thus don't let anyone fool himself, he says, for all who belong to Christ have crucified the flesh with all its vices and desires. That is because the saints have not yet completely shed their corrupt and sinful flesh, and they lean toward sin. Neither do they fear or love God as perfectly as they should. They are also provoked to anger, envy, impatience, impure desires and such emotions. However, they do not satisfy them. That is because—as Paul said before—they crucify the flesh with all its passions and desires not only when they restrain the unruly flesh with fasts and other exercises but also (as Paul said before) when they walk according to the Spirit—that is, when having been admonished by God's warnings through which He teaches that He will severely punish sin, they are afraid to sin; they also arm themselves with God's word, with faith, prayer, and do not satisfy the desires of the flesh.

When they resist the flesh in this manner, they crucify it to the cross, with all its passions and desires. Thus although the flesh still has life, it does not satisfy what it would like to do, since it has been tied hand and foot and has been firmly nailed to the cross. The faithful then, as long as they live, crucify the flesh—that is, they feel the desires of the flesh but do not satisfy them, for they are armed with God's armor—that is, with faith, hope, and the sword of the Spirit. Thus they resist the flesh and crucify it to the cross with those spiritual nails compelling it to obey the spirit. Thereafter, when they die, they shed it altogether, and when they rise again from death to life, they will have a pure and incorrupt flesh, without its fanciful desires and lusts.

LECTURE 39: Saturday, December 5

VERSE 25. If we live by the Spirit, let us also walk by the Spirit.[160]

Previously, the apostle included among the works of the flesh heresy and jealousy. He condemned the envious, the authors of sects, saying they would not inherit the kingdom of God. Now, as if he had forgotten what he had just said, he once again reproves those who are easily provoked and envy one another. Why does he repeat it? Was the first time not enough? Indeed, he did it on purpose, for here he takes advantage of the moment to denounce that repulsive habit of κενοδοξία (kenodoxia),[161] the cause of the many problems in all the churches of Galatia and which has always been most pernicious and damaging for Christ's entire church. Thus in his Epistle to Titus, he does not approve that someone conceited should be ordained as a bishop. Arrogance (as Augustine noted) is the mother of all heresies or better yet the source of all sin and confusion. History, both sacred and secular, has witnessed it throughout the years.

Κενοδοξία [arrogance or conceit] has always been a common poison in the world. Even the pagan poets and historians have reproved it in no uncertain terms. In every town, you will find a certain someone who wants to be considered more wise and worthy of respect than all the others. But they are infected with this disease, for they lean on the reputation given to them by their learning and wisdom. In this case, no one yields to the other; according to the proverb, "it's not easy to find someone who will praise someone else" due to their ingenuity and ability, for it's a good thing to see people point to someone else, saying, "That's the one."

---

[160] In Irmischer's Latin text, 5:25 begins chapter 6. The same versification is given in the Weimar Latin text.

[161] From Philippians 2:3, "empty conceit, self-importance, vain glory, arrogance." Luther used the Greek term during his lecture.

Nonetheless, arrogance is not as damaging in ordinary people, no, not even among any kind of magistrate as it is in those who have some position in the church. However (particularly when found in great personalities), it is the cause of great quarrels in which communities come to ruin; it has thrown entire kingdoms and empires into bewilderment and disarray. Both sacred and secular history testify about this in their writings.

However, when this poison slips into the church or within the spiritual kingdom, words are inadequate to describe the damage that it causes. At that point, there is no issue regarding scholarship, ingenuity, beauty, riches, kingdoms, empires, and similar things. Rather, it has to do with salvation or condemnation, eternal life or eternal death. That is why Paul so urgently calls on the ministers of the word to flee from this vice, saying, "If we live in the Spirit" etc. It's as if he had said, "If it's true that we live by the Spirit, then let us proceed to walk in an orderly manner in the Spirit, for wherever the Spirit is found, it renews people and works new motives within them—that is, before, they were arrogant, furious, and envious; now, they are humble, meek, and patient. They don't seek out their own glory but God's glory. They don't provoke one against the other, but yield their place to the other, and in honor they prefer one another. But instead, we have those who go rummaging around for glory and envy one another. They may boast that they have the Spirit and live in the Spirit, but they deceive themselves, for they go after the flesh and do its works and already have their well-deserved judgment, that they will not inherit the kingdom of God."

Well then, nothing is as dangerous a plague for the church as this horrendous vice and yet nothing is as common, for when God sends His workers for the harvest, immediately Satan also sends his ministers, who will not allow themselves to be considered inferior to the ministers duly called by God. At this moment, dissension immediately arises. The wicked don't yield by one hair to the faithful, for they imagine they surpass them in sagacity, scholarship, piety, spirit, and other virtues. Much less should the faithful yield to the wicked lest they endanger the doctrine of faith. Further, such is the nature of Satan's ministers that they put on a great theatrical performance, starring their love, covenants, humility, and other fruits of the Spirit. They also protest that they strive after nothing more than God's glory and salvation for the souls of men. Truth is, they are puffed up with pride, and all they do has no other goal in mind than to receive the κενόδοξοι[162] and endorsement of others. In brief, they think that a pious life is profitable (1 Timothy 6:5) and that the ministry of the word has been placed in their hands so that they will achieve fame and admiration. Thus they are nothing more than authors of dissensions and sects.

It follows then that the κενοδοξία of the false apostles caused the upheaval in the Galatian churches and their abandonment of Paul. In this chapter, Paul's

---

[162] Compliments and praise.

purpose was to suppress this despicable vice. Yes, and it was this evil that gave occasion for the apostle to write this entire epistle. Had he not done it, all his effort poured into the preaching of the Gospel would have been in vain, for in his absence, the false apostles who to all appearances flaunted great authority, reigned in Galatia. Further, they not only pretended to be seeking God's glory and the salvation of the Galatians but also boasted that they had been in very close contact with the apostles and had followed in their footsteps. They added that Paul had not even seen Christ in the flesh, nor had he kept company with the apostles. In this way, they discredited him, rejected his doctrine, and boasted that their own doctrine was true and sincere. That is how they had perturbed the Galatians and raised up sects among them so that they provoked and envied one another. All this was an unmistakable sign that neither the teachers nor the pupils lived and walked according to the Spirit but continued to follow the flesh satisfying its desires. Consequently, they lost the true doctrine, faith, Christ, and all the gifts of the Holy Spirit. They had become worse than the pagans.

Nonetheless, he not only blamed the false apostles that during his time had perturbed the Galatian churches, but he also foresaw in the Spirit that countless others like them would arise until the end of the world. These, having been infected with that pernicious vice, would burst into the church without a calling, boasting of the Spirit and having received a heavenly doctrine. With these pretexts, they would strive to overthrow the true doctrine and the faith. In our day, we have seen many like them who have welcomed themselves into the kingdom of the Spirit—that is, the ministry of the word. Utilizing this hypocrisy, they have garnered fame and approval presuming to be great teachers of the Gospel feigning that they live in the Spirit and are directed by the Spirit. *But once they conquered the minds of the people with their captivating words, they immediately went off course from the straight and narrow and began to teach some new idea. Thus they preached among the ordinary people to have been the first to unmask the errors of the church, removed and corrected the abuses, overthrown the papacy, and discovered some new doctrine. Thus they claimed to have earned their stripes as foremost scholars among the evangelicals.*[163] But since their glory was derived from the mouth of men and not from God, they could not be firm and stable. It was just as Paul had prophesied, for they ended up lost within their own confusion, and their end was destruction, for "the wicked are like the chaff blown about by the wind."

The same finding awaits all those who seek to preach the Gospel for self-profit and not for the glory of Jesus Christ, for the Gospel has not been placed in our hands for us to strive for self-glory and praise or for the people to honor and exalt us because we are its ministers. Rather, it has been given to us so that the benefit and glory of Christ is preached and published. Further, so that the Father is glorified in the mercy,

---

[163] *ideoque merito haberent primas inter evangelicos doctores.* Said tongue in cheek, of course.

He offers us in Christ His Son who gave Himself for us all and who has given all things to us. Thus the Gospel is a doctrine by which the last thing we should do is strive for our own glory, for the Gospel presents us with matters divine and celestial, which are not ours; neither is it about things we have done or deserve. Rather, it offers us, I say it again, what we don't deserve, which is God's pure kindness and grace. Then why should we look to find in it our own glory and praise? Thus whoever looks for his own glory in the Gospel is only talking about himself, and whoever talks about himself is a liar, and there is no righteousness in him. Instead, whoever seeks the glory of the One who sent Him is true, and there is no unrighteousness in Him (John 7:18).

Accordingly, Paul fervently charges all the ministers of the word, saying, "If we live in the Spirit, let us also walk in the Spirit—that is, let us remain in the truth that we have been taught, in brotherly love and spiritual accord. Let us preach Christ and God's glory in simplicity of heart. Let us confess that we have received all things from Him. Let us not think that we are more than others. Let us not organize sects, for these things are the same as not walking as we should but going astray from the path and establish a new but perverse way of walking."

By which, we may understand that God out of His special grace subjects the teachers of the Gospel to the cross and to all kinds of suffering, for the sake of their own salvation and of the people. Otherwise, they could neither repress nor slay this beast called κενοδοξία, for if persecution, the cross, and injuries of all kinds did not follow the doctrine of the Gospel, then its teachers would be infected and perish due to the poison of arrogance. Jerome said that he had seen many who could suffer great hardships with their bodies and lack of goods but none who could shrug off praise, for it is almost impossible for anyone not to get all puffed up when he hears someone else praise his virtues. Although Paul had the Spirit of Christ, he said a messenger from Satan was sent to slap him around[164] so that he would not get overly exalted due to the greatness of his revelations (2 Corinthians 12:7). Augustine said it well: "If a minister of the word is praised, he is in danger. If a brother despises or discredits him, he is also in danger. Whoever hears the preacher of the word should respect him because of the word, but if he gets all conceited, he is in danger. But on the other hand, if he is despised, he is out of danger but not so with the one who despised him."

Thus we should honor our great benefit, which is the preaching of the word and the partaking of the Sacraments. We should also have reverence one another, according to the text "In honor preferring one another" (Romans 12:10). But everywhere this is practiced, immediately, the flesh gets tickled with arrogance and puffs up with pride, for there is no one (no, not even among the faithful) who does not prefer to be praised rather than despised. Perhaps someone may be so settled on this matter that he would be the exception by permitting neither praise nor criticism to affect him. That is what David's wife said: "For even as an angel of God, so

---

[164] *colaphis* = blow with fist, box on the ear; *caederet* = strike down.

is my lord the king, that he is neither moved with blessing nor cursing" (2 Kings 14; 2 Samuel 14:17, DRA). Paul says the same: "In honor and dishonor, in ill repute and good repute" (2 Corinthians 6:8). Those who neither get puffed up with praise nor get knocked down by criticism but simply strive to establish Christ's benefit and seek the salvation of souls are those who walk in a dignified manner.

Therefore, let everyone stay vigilant walking with dignity and particularly those who boast of the Holy Spirit. If you are praised, be assured it is not you who is praised but Christ, to whom all honor is owed. As far as teaching the word correctly, living piously, these are not your own gifts but gifts from God. Be assured that you are not the one who is praised but God who has revealed Himself to you. When you admit to this, you will be walking in a straight line and not puffed up with conceit, for "what do you have that you didn't receive?" It is better that you confess what you have received from God and you will not be moved by personal hurts, rejections, or persecution as an excuse to abandon your calling.

That is why God, on account solely of His grace, today covers our glory with infamy, reproaches, mortal hate, cruel persecution, harassment, and the curse pronounced by the entire world against us. There is also the disdain and ingratitude of those who surround us, as well as the ordinary people, the citizens, the knights, the nobles (whose enmity, hate, and persecution is against the Gospel, for although it is private and discreet, it is even more dangerous than the external treatment of our declared enemies). All this is so that we will not brag about God's gifts in us. It is necessary for this millstone to be hung around our necks so that we will not be infected with that fatal poison of conceit. There are some on our side who love and reverence us for the ministry of the word. But for each one who respects us, on the other side, there are a hundred who hate and persecute us. Thus that spiteful treatment, these persecutions from our enemies, that great scorn and ingratitude, that cruel and private hate from those who form part of our circle become pleasant sceneries that bring us joy, for too easily we forget our pride.

Therefore, rejoicing in the Lord, our glory, let us keep on walking humbly in a straight line. The gifts we have we recognize as gifts from God; they are not ours. They are given to edify the body of Christ; that's why we will not brag about them, for we well know that more is required from those to whom much is given than from those who have received little (Luke 12:48). Further, we know that God does not discriminate between people. Thus the church caretaker who uses the gift that God has given him does not please God any less than the preacher of the word. He serves God with the same faith, and the same spirit. Accordingly, we should honor the most ordinary Christians with the same esteem that they confer upon us. This is how we will be safe from the poison of arrogance as we march along in the Spirit.

On the other hand, the fanatical heads strive after their own glory, the endorsement and applause of others, peace in the world, the comforts of the flesh—anything but the glory of Christ. Neither do they strive after the salvation of the souls of men (although they contend they want nothing more).

However, they cannot avoid exposing themselves by recommending their own doctrine and ingenuity while denigrating the others. Their purpose is to gather fame and praise. They say, "No one knew about this before I discovered it; I was the first to see it and teach it." Thus they are κενόδοξοι—that is, they don't rejoice and glory in the Lord. But when they do glory, they are strong and robust because they are inflated by the people whose hearts were won through their marvelous tricks and subtleties, for through their performance and the script they follow, they can fake and pretend anything! However, when they are not praised and highly commended by the people, then of all people in the world they are the most frightened because they hate and avoid the cross of Christ and persecution. But on the other hand, as I said, when they are praised and exalted, there is no one so daring and fit as they, no, not even strongmen Hector and Achilles!

Therefore, the flesh is such a cunning and sly beast that it abandons its function,[165] corrupts the true doctrine, and breaks up the harmony of the church, all because of this damned κενοδοξίαν. That is why there is just cause for Paul's harsh reproach, here as well as in other texts: "What they want is to alienate you from us, so that you may have zeal for them" (Galatians 4:17)—that is, they discredit me so that they themselves can become famous. They don't seek the glory of Christ and your salvation but rather their own glory, my disgrace, and your slavery.

VERSE 26. Let us not become conceited [NIV].

As I've said before, let us not become full of empty glory. This is nothing but holding back the glory that rightly belongs to God and to the truth. Instead, conceit glories in made-up stories, in the opinions, and in the compliments of all those willing to applaud who don't know any better. Here, there is no foundation for true glory but a counterfeit, and thus it is impossible for it to last. Whoever praises a man for being a man is a liar, for in him, there is nothing worthy of praise; rather, the only thing he deserves is condemnation. Thus as far as our person, our glory is this: all have sinned and deserve eternal death before the presence of God. But when our ministry is honored, that is another matter, for we should not only desire this honor but also do all we can so that people may magnify it, and grant it due respect, for it will turn into their salvation. Paul admonishes the Romans to offend no one; otherwise (he said), "what you know is good be spoken of as evil" (Romans 14:16). In another text, he says, "We put no obstacle in any one's way, so that no fault may be found with our ministry" (2 Corinthians 6:3). Thus when someone in our ministry is praised, we are not complimented on account of our own persons, but rather (as the Psalm says) we are praised in God, and in His holy name.

---

[165] *ordinem.*

VERSE 26. Provoking and envying each other [NIV].

Here, he describes the effect and fruit of hungering for glory. Whoever teaches any error, or is the author of any new doctrine, has not gained anything else than to provoke others. When they do not approve or receive their doctrine, immediately, they begin to hate them bitterly. Today, we see the mortal hatred with which the sectarians hate us because we do not pay attention to their errors. We do not provoke them nor spread throughout the world a bad opinion about them. Instead, we reprove certain abuses in the church and faithfully teach the article of justification; we have walked along the straight line. But they, abandoning this article, have taught many things contrary to the word of God. At this point, since we were not about to lose the truth of the Gospel, we opposed them and have condemned their errors. As a result, since they did not accept our teaching, not only did they offend us first without cause, but they still hate us with great resentment and for no other reason than conceit, for they more than happily would blot us out from existence, as long as they alone would reign and govern. They imagine that it brings such great glory to profess the Gospel. But it's just the opposite; before the watching world, we suffer no greater disgrace!

Galatians 6

VERSE 1. Brothers and sisters, if someone is caught in a sin, you who live by the Spirit should restore that person gently. But watch yourselves, or you also may be tempted [NIV].

This is another admirable moral precept and extremely necessary in our day. But the sectarians get a hold of this text and infer that we should, to some degree, overlook the blunders of our brothers.[1] We should cover up their error with love, which "believes all things, hopes all things, bears all things," especially since Paul teaches that so clearly in this text. Further, those who are spiritual should restore them with a forgiving spirit. "The issue is not all that important," they claim. "Just because of this one article we should not tear apart the Christian bond." They claim that nothing else is more dear and valuable for the church. Thus they carry on about the forgiveness of sins and accuse us of being hardheaded because we won't budge, not even by a hair. They allege that we will not tolerate their error (which they don't willingly admit) and even less gently dialogue with them in order to restore the relationship. That is how these suave fellows[2] adorn themselves and their cause, but they hate and falsely accuse us.

Nothing has so painfully aggrieved me (God is my witness) throughout all these years as the discord in this doctrine. The Sacramentarians know full well that I was not the author of this dispute if they admit to the truth. Because what I believed and taught at the beginning of this cause with respect to justification, the Sacraments, and all other articles of the Christian doctrine hasn't changed one bit to this day! However, I believe and profess them with greater confidence, for I have been strengthened through study, practice, and experience, as well as through great and frequent temptations. Daily, I plead with Christ that He might preserve and empower[3] me in this faith and confession until the day of His coming in glory. Amen.

Since we began, it is obvious that throughout all Germany no one challenged the doctrine of the Gospel, except the Papists. Among us who received the Gospel, we were in full agreement concerning all the articles of the Christian doctrine. This agreement lasted until the Sectarians came out of nowhere with new opinions regarding not only the Sacraments but also certain other beliefs. They were the first to perturb the churches and tear us apart. Since that time and beyond our control, more sects have gradually carved us up, increasing the feelings of hostility.

---

[1] *aliquid condonare lapsis fratribus.*
[2] *suaves homines.*
[3] *conservet et corroboret.*

Going against their own conscience, they have inflicted this great injury that has affected us much more than we deserve. They have ruined our reputation everywhere. It is much more painful than the innocent should suffer the penalty, especially when the other side is the guilty party.

However, we could easily forget this harm, receive and restore them with a spirit of meekness, if only they would return to the straight and narrow way and march in step with us—that is, if they believed and faithfully taught regarding the Lord's Supper and other articles of the Christian doctrine and in unanimous consent with what we preach and not their own opinions. We preach Christ alone so that the Son of God may be glorified through us and the Father through Him. However, seeing they magnify love and joint agreements but minimize the significance of the Sacrament, as if it mattered little what we think of the Eucharist established by our Lord, we will not join in. However, just as they preach so much about living in harmony, so we also preach harmony in doctrine and faith. Now, if they leave us alone and not put a finger on this article, then we together with them will also exalt the agreement on love, which is just not as important. But if you toss it, then you have thrown Christ away, and when Christ is gone, love is worthless to you. But if on the contrary you retain unity in the Spirit, and in Christ, you will not be at a loss if you dissent from those who corrupt the word and thus break the unity of the Spirit. Thus I prefer that they together with the entire world would cut ties with me and declare themselves to be my enemies than I should separate from Christ and have Him as my enemy. That's what would happen if I go astray from His simple and clear word to chase their empty dreams or twist around Christ's words to join in with them. For me, having one Christ is so much greater than an infinite number of accords based on love.

But when it comes to those who love Christ and faithfully teach and believe in His word, we offer not only to retain the peace and harmony but to bear their weaknesses and sins and restore them when they fall, according to Paul's instruction, with a spirit of meekness. That is how Paul took on the weakness and fall of the Galatians and others (who were led astray by the false apostles) as soon as they came to their senses. That is how that incestuous Corinthian received grace. Similarly, that is how Onesimus (that fugitive slave whom Paul conceived in the Lord) was reconciled to his master when Paul was in Rome and in chains for Christ. Thus what he teaches here about restoring the weak, Paul himself practiced but only with those who could be healed—that is, those who acknowledged their sin, their fall, their error, and came back to their senses. On the other hand, with the false apostles who obstinately defended their doctrine, saying they were not in error, he was very severe. "I wish," he said, "[that] those who unsettle you would mutilate themselves!" (Galatians 5:12) and "He who is troubling you will bear his judgment, whoever he is" (Galatians 5:10). Likewise, he said, "but even if we, or an angel from heaven, should preach to you a gospel contrary to that which we preached to you, let him be damned!" (Galatians 1:8).

Undoubtedly, there were many who defended the false apostles against Paul. They said they had the same measure of the Spirit; they were also ministers of Christ, who taught the Gospel just as Paul. Further, that although they did not consent with Paul in all his doctrine, he still should not pronounce such a horrible decree against them. His obstinacy was accomplishing nothing more than perturbing the churches and tearing apart their glorious harmony.

But Paul remained unmoved. He confidently cursed and condemned the false apostles, calling them troublers of the churches and subversive against the Gospel of Christ. On the other hand, he doubles down on his doctrine[4] so that simply everything would yield to it: the harmony of love, the apostles, an angel from heaven, and all else.

Thus we should not let this matter be minimized, for He to whom this cause belongs is great. Indeed, He was once an infant laying in the manger. Yet at the same time, He was so great that angels adored Him and proclaimed Him Lord of all. Accordingly, we will not permit for His word to be struck in any one article of faith. In these articles of faith, nothing should seem to us as insignificant, as if we could live without it, or that we should minimize it, for the remission of sins belongs to the weak in the faith and morality,[5] those who recognize their sin and seek forgiveness. It does not belong to those who overthrow the doctrine, who do not recognize their error and sin, but who stubbornly defend it as if it were truth and righteousness. In consequence, we lose the remission of sins because the word that preaches and announces the forgiveness of sins is depraved and denied. Therefore, let them first become one with us in Christ; that is, let them acknowledge their sin and correct their error. Then if we are still lacking in the spirit of gentleness, they could justly accuse us.

Whoever diligently weighs the apostle's words may see that he is not talking about heretical errors and offenses but about sins of minor consequence, in which anyone may fall not of his own free will or a firm purpose but out of weakness. That is why he uses such tender and fatherly words, for he does not call an error a sin but a fault. Again, intending to minimize and to even excuse the sin and remove any blame from the person, he adds, "If anyone is overtaken in a fault," as if saying, "If anyone were seduced by the devil or by the flesh." Yes, and this name or expression of "anyone" helps somewhat in reducing and qualifying the subject. It's as if he had said, "What is so common to people than to fall, be seduced, and err?" That is what Moses says in Leviticus 6: "Anything that someone might do and so sin."[6] Consequently, this statement is replete with heavenly comfort, which in a certain horrible conflict delivered me from death. Then the saints in this life

---

[4]   *doctrinam suam ita extollit*, literally "extols his doctrine." In twenty-first-century English, "doubling down" means insisting on the importance of an issue by repeating its value and highlighting its virtues.

[5]   *fide et moribus.*

[6]   *sicut homines solent peccare.* Translation is from Leviticus 6:3, CEB.

not only live in the flesh but also, occasionally, due to the devil's deceptions, satisfy the sins of the flesh. They fall into impatience, envy, anger, error, doubt, mistrust, and other similar things. Satan always besieges them on both fronts, in their purity as well as in their doctrine. He strives to take the doctrine apart through sects and dissensions, as well as in the integrity of their life, which he corrupts with daily faults. Thus Paul teaches how to deal with people who have fallen in this way—that is, those who are strong should lift them up and restore them with a spirit of meekness.

Those who are leading the church should be aware of these things, lest they be in such a hurry to kick people out that they forget the paternal and maternal affection that Paul requires from all who have souls in their care. He also gives an example of this teaching (2 Corinthians 2:6–8), saying that the one who was cast out of the church was excessively reproved and that they should now forgive and comfort him; otherwise, he could be consumed by grief. Therefore, "I plead," he says, "that you treat him with love." The pastors and ministers should certainly censure firmly those who have fallen but when they see that they are sorry for their offenses, then they should begin to lift them up, comfort and diminish their faults all they can. They should counter their sin with mercy, lest the fallen drown in an overwhelming despair. The Holy Spirit is just as timely keeping and defending the doctrine of faith so the Spirit is restrained and compassionate, bearing and overlooking the sins of everyone when they feel tormented by something they did.

However, in the synagogue of the Pope, as in everything else, the Pope has taught and done totally the contrary to Paul's mandate and example. On this matter, he has done totally the opposite. The Pope together with all his bishops have been only tyrants and butchers of people's conscience, for time and again they have burdened them with new traditions. For each trifle, they have harassed them with their excommunications. To get them to obey with less difficulty they have added these dictates of Pope Gregory: "Every sound mind has the duty and right to fear that there is some fault even where there is none." Further, "Our reproaches should be feared, even though they may be unjust and mistaken." Through these dictates (brought to the church by the devil), they established their excommunications, and this majesty of the papacy, which brings such great horrors to the world. There is no need for such humility and piety in people's minds that they should fear they have faults even where there are none. "Oh Roman Satan, who gave you this power to intimidate and condemn people's consciences who already suffered with the terror of your unjust and mistaken decrees? You should have lifted them up, freed them from false fears, and brought them back from following after lies and mistakes into the truth. You omitted this, and according to your title and name, 'the man of sin and the son of perdition,' you imagine there are faults where there are none." This is certainly the craftsmanship and deceit of the Antichrist with whom he has established his powerful excommunications and tyranny. That is why anyone who despised his unjust verdicts was held out to be the most obstinate and wicked. That's how they reacted toward some of the princes, even violating their conscience, for in those times of darkness, they did not understand that the Pope's curses were worthless.

Therefore, those who have the care of people's consciences learn Paul's mandate how to deal with those who have committed offenses. "Brothers and sisters," he says, "if anyone be taken in some fault, don't harass them or cause them greater shame. Don't deal with them with resentment neither reject nor condemn them. Instead, restore and lift them up again and, through a spirit of understanding and compassion, rehabilitate in them what has been corrupted by the devil's deceit or due to the weakness of the flesh, for the kingdom to which you have been called is not the kingdom of terror nor despair but that of confidence, joy, and happiness. Therefore, if you see some brother over burdened by the sin he has committed, run to him, reach out to him, and pick him up again. Comfort him with sweet words and embrace him with motherly arms. As far as those who continue obstinate and hard-hearted, those who without any fear continue carelessly in their sins, reprove them firmly." On the other hand (as I've said) are those who have been found in some fault and are grief stricken and troubled without measure for the fault they have committed. These should be lifted up and admonished by you who are spiritual and in the spirit of kindness, not with zeal and severe justice, as some have done. They should have quenched the thirst of fatigued consciences with some sweet and refreshing comfort. Instead, they gave vinegar and bile, as the Jews gave Christ to drink when he hung from the tree.

From these things, we understand more than enough that the strength of the forgiveness of sins is not because you can get someone to consent to the doctrine, as the Sacramentarians contend, but because of its efficacy in our life and works.[7] *Here, let no one condemn the other or harshly and angrily reprove the other.* Ezekiel talks about the shepherds of Israel, who govern God's flock with cruelty and harshness (Ezekiel 34). However, a brother should comfort his fallen brother with a meek and loving spirit. Once again, the fallen should hear the word of the One who lifts him up as stated in the Psalm, for God has given them much more than us—that is, He has given His own life and the blood. Therefore, we should also receive, aid, and comfort them with all kindness and affection. *That is why we won't withhold forgiveness from the Sacramentarians and other authors of wicked sects, but from our hearts, we forgive them for their insults and blasphemies against Christ. With respect to the harm they have done us, we'll erase it from our memory if only they repent, rid themselves of their wicked doctrine with which they have perturbed the churches, and walk on the straight and narrow together with us. But if they persevere*

---

[7]   The Latin here is unclear, but the context was helpful in providing the translation. How Luther said it, his gestures, were obviously helpful to the listeners in understanding what he said. We are disadvantaged by not having been there, but the context provides the translation I have rendered.

in their error and destroy the proper order, in vain do they require from us the for-giveness of sins.

VERSE 1. Looking to yourself so that you also aren't tempted [WEB].

This is a quite serious admonition: "You cannot harshly and cruelly crush those who have fallen." "There is no sin," said Augustine, "committed by anyone, that someone else cannot repeat." We are on this slippery spot where it's easy to spin around. Thus if we get puffed up with pride and abandon our duty, there is nothing easier than to slip and fall. A certain book, *The Lives of Our Fathers,* said it well with respect to someone. When he was told that one of his brothers had fallen with a prostitute, he responded, "Yesterday, he fell; today, that could happen to me." Thus Paul adds this passionate warning, that the pastors should not be severe and lacking in mercy toward those who have offended; neither should they measure their own holiness with the sins of other people. It could be that I, myself, could fall more dangerously and shamelessly than he. Further, if you are going to be so ready to judge and condemn others, you would do well to consider your own sin, for you will realize that the sins of the fallen are only straw compared with the beams in their own eyes.

"Therefore let anyone who thinks that he stands take heed lest he fall." David, such a pious man, full of faith and God's Spirit, with so many outstanding promises from God, fell so regrettably after having done so many great things for the Lord. If once he was up in years, he was taken down by the lust of youth after so many and different temptations to which he was subjected by God, why should we brag about our own faithfulness? And it is that God by means of these examples shows us in the first place our weakness so that we will not get puffed with pride. Instead, we should fear. Further, He also shows us His judgments that cannot tolerate the least amount of pride against Himself or against our brothers and sisters. Thus there is good reason for which Paul says, "Looking to yourself so that you also aren't tempted." Those who are fatigued by temptation know the great need for this commandment. On the other hand, those who do not experience these trials cannot understand Paul and thus they are not moved by any compassion toward the fallen. Such was the case in the papacy, where nothing else reigned except tyranny and cruelty.

VERSE 2. Bear one another's burdens, and so fulfill the law of Christ.

This is a very tender command, to which he adds a great commendation. Christ's law is the law of love. Once He redeemed us, Christ renewed us, made us His church, but did not give us any other law except the law of mutual love: "A new commandment I give to you, that you love one another; even as I have loved you, that you also love one another" (John 13:34–35). To love is not to wish someone well (as the papal scholars imagine) but bearing one another's burdens—that is, to bear the things that would annoy you, those things that you would not be willing to bear. Thus Christians should have strong backs and hard bones so that they can bear with the weakness of the flesh—that is, with the weakness of their brothers and sisters—for Paul says they carry burdens and hurts. Love then is tender, courteous, and patient, not when it receives but when it gives, for it has the obligation to overlook many things and bear with them. The faithful teachers may see that there are many errors and grievous things in the church that they have the obligation to bear. In the municipal communities, the subjects never obey their magistrates, as they should. Thus unless the magistrate is able to look the other way and let things pass with respect to times and places, he could never govern his territory. In matters regarding the home there are many things that are not pleasing to the man of the house. But if we can bear and look the other way when it comes to our own vices and offenses we commit daily, then let us also bear one another's burdens according to this statement: "Bear each other's burdens." Likewise, "You shall love your neighbor as yourself."

Then since there are vices in all aspects of life and in all people, Paul presents the law of Christ to the faithful by which he exhorts them to bear each other's burdens. Those who won't do this give ample testimony that they don't understand one jot of Christ's law, which is the law of love, for, as Paul says, love believes all things, hopes all things, bears all the burdens of their brothers and sisters (1 Corinthians 13:7). Nonetheless, the first commandment must not be injured. When this commandment is broken, the law of Christ is not transgressed—that is, the law of love. No, the transgressors of the first commandment don't injure their neighbor. They offend Christ and His kingdom, which He has bought with His own blood. This kingdom is not sustained through the law of love but by God's word, faith, and the Holy Spirit. Then this command to bear each other's burdens does not belong to those who deny Christ. It's not just that they don't recognize their sin but that they also defend it. Neither does it belong to those who stubbornly keep on practicing their sins (in this aspect, they also deny Christ). They must answer for themselves, but we should stop hanging around with them; otherwise, we'll end up doing the same evil stuff that they do.[8] On the other hand, there are those who willingly hear God's word and believe it and still fall into sin against their will. When these are admonished, they not only receive the reproof with joy but also detest their sin and correct their ways. These, I say, are those who when found in some fault and have the burdens that Paul orders us to bear. In this case, let us not be merciless and

---

[8] In translating, I could have changed the register to make these sentences sound more professorial, but here the English vernacular pointedly translates Luther's Latin: *sed relinquendi sunt, ne communicemus operibus ipsorum malis.*

severe. Instead, following the example of Christ, who bore and carried them, let us also bear and carry their burdens. If he does not punish them (for He has every right to do so), much less should we punish them.

VERSE 3. For if any one thinks he is something, when he is nothing, he deceives himself.

Once again, he reproves the authors of sects and paints them with all the right colors—that is, they are stubborn, without mercy and compassion. They despise the weak and make no commitment to bear their burdens. Instead, like husbands out of control[9] and severe teachers, they are harsh and strict. Nothing pleases them except what they like to do. They will be your worst enemies unless you praise them for everything they say and do and comply with their every whim.[10] Of all people, they are the proudest, and they boldly hoard everything for themselves. That is what Paul says here, that they think they are something, that they do have the Spirit, that they understand all the mysteries of Scripture, and that they cannot be mistaken. That is also the reason Paul adds with all certainty that they are nothing, for they fool themselves with the empty conclusions regarding their own wisdom and holiness. Thus they don't understand anything about Christ or the law of Christ. If they understood, they would say, "Brother, you are infected with a certain vice and I with another. Since God has forgiven me a thousand denarii, I will forgive your ten denarii" (Matthew 18). But when they demand that all things be done exactly as they say and to perfection and yet they refuse to bear the burdens of the weak, they offend with such harshness and narrowness of mind. That is why the people begin to despise, hate, and avoid them and neither seek them out for comfort nor pay attention to their teachings. On the contrary, the pastor should deal with those in their care; they are to be honored and admired not for who they are but for their office and Christian virtues, which should shine brightly in them.

Thus Paul here has correctly pointed to these harsh, heartless Holy Joes when he says, "They think they are something"—that is, they are puffed up with their own foolish opinions and starry-eyed dreams. They have an amazing conviction about their own knowledge and consecration, which really is nothing; they do nothing but fool themselves, for such a deceit is obvious, when someone is persuaded that he is indeed something when frankly they are nothing. Revelation 3:17 best describes these folk with these words: "You say, 'I am rich; I have acquired wealth and do not need a thing.' But you do not realize that you are wretched, pitiful, poor, blind and naked" (NIV).

---

9 *morosi.*
10 *moribus.*

LECTURE 40: Friday, December 11

VERSE 4. But let each one test his own work, and then his reason to boast will be in himself alone and not in his neighbor.

He continues to draw a picture of these arrogant and boastful fellows, for empty boasting is a hateful and accursed habit. It is the cause of all evils and perturbs governments and consciences. In spiritual matters, it is an evil of an incurable nature. Although this text may be understood as pertaining to the works performed during this life or in daily life, nonetheless, the apostle is talking about the work of the ministry and indicts those who are full of themselves,[11] for they perturb well-balanced consciences with their fancied opinions.

This is specific to them whose works are the result of κενοδοξία.[12] They are not interested if their works, let's say, if their ministry is pure, simple, and faithful. The only thing they strive for is to receive the people's praise. That is how the false apostles, when they saw that Paul preached to the Galatians the Gospel in its purity and they could not come along with a better doctrine, began to find faults in the things that he had taught piously and faithfully. Then they gave preference to their own doctrine instead of Paul's and through that trickery won over the favor of the Galatians and introduced Paul to them in such a hateful manner. Thus the proud and arrogant[13] have these three vices in common. First, they covet for glory. Second, they are amazingly astute and savvy to find faults in others' works and words; that way they buy the love, esteem, and the applause of others. Third, once they have made themselves famous (although at the cost of others' effort), they become so strong and their bellies so full, they dare mandate with respect to any issue. Therefore, these fellows are so pernicious and foul that I hate them with all my heart for they seek their own glory and not that glory that is found in Jesus Christ.

Here, Paul speaks against these types of fellows. It's as if he had said, "These arrogant spirits do their work. They teach the Gospel with the intention of winning over people's praise and esteem"—that is, so that they will be counted as great scholars of renown with whom not even Paul or others bear any comparison. Once they receive those accolades, they begin to slander in words and deeds the teachings of others while highly promoting their own. Through this trickery they bewitch people's minds. Their itching ears not only delight in new opinions but rejoice that their former teachers now have been denigrated and overpowered by these new professors of renown, who are only full of pride and vomit the word.

---

[11] Luther here uses the Greek term κενοδοξους.
[12] In the Latin text, Luther uses the Greek κενοδοξία, "vain glory, arrogance."
[13] In the Latin text, Luther uses the Greek κενοδοξοι.

This should not be, he says. Instead, each one should be faithful to their assigned function. Don't look for your own glory or depend on the unfounded praises of people who don't know any better. Instead, get busy only with fulfilling your own true duty—that is, teach the Gospel in all its purity. If your work is sincere and whole, then be assured that you will not lack for praise before God or the faithful. Meanwhile, don't be upset if you don't receive praise from this unthankful world, for you know all too well that the purpose of your ministry is not yourself but the glory of Christ through your ministry. Thus clothed with the armor of righteousness on left and right, you may say, "I don't teach the Gospel to receive the compliments of the world. Thus I will not go back one step from preaching the Gospel, no matter if the world honors me with its praise or slanders me into disgrace." Such a teacher instructs in the word and faithfully cares for his duty without wondering what the world thinks or caring about glory or gain. He will proceed without praise, glory, strength, or wisdom from anyone. He does not work for the complimentary endorsement that he receives from others, for he has it within himself.

Whoever properly and faithfully fulfills his task will not care whatever the world may say about him. He will not care if the world praises or criticizes him, for he has the praise within himself, which is the witness of his own conscience, and his praise and glory are in God. Thus he can say with Paul, "For our boasting is this: the testimony of our conscience, that in holiness and sincerity of God, not in fleshly wisdom but in the grace of God we behaved ourselves in the world" (2 Corinthians 1:12, WEB). This glory is lasting and incorruptible for it does not depend on people's judgments but on our own conscience. Its testimony is that we have taught the Gospel with purity, properly administering the Sacraments, and have done all things well. Thus no one can snatch it away from us or disfigure it. Further, the glory sought by these κενοδοξοι[14] is uncertain and extremely unstable, for they don't have it in themselves, but it consists in what comes from the mouths of other people. Thus their own conscience cannot testify that what they have done has been accomplished with simplicity and sincerity. Their conscience cannot assent that their efforts have been only for advancing God's cause and the salvation of souls. Their only goal is to be considered famous due to the work and effort of their preaching and receiving people's praises.

Thus they have a glory, an assurance, and a testimony but before men and not before themselves or God. The faithful don't wish to have this kind of glory. If Paul would have had his praise before men and not in himself, he would have lost heart when he saw many cities, nations, and all Asia sever ties with him. When Christ was alone—that is, when not only the Jews were looking to kill him, but he also had been abandoned by His disciples—He was not alone. The Father was with Him, for He had glory in Himself.

---

[14] Seekers of glory, praises, compliments, and the like.

If today our confidence and glory depended on people's good opinion and good graces toward us, we would shortly be greatly depressed, for the Papists, sectarians, and the entire world is far from judging us worth of any respect or praise. Instead, they hate and bitterly persecute us. Yes, it would give them great satisfaction to overthrow our ministry and uproot our doctrine forever! Thus all that people have for us is nothing but disdain, but we rejoice and glory in the Lord. That is why we go about our work with joy and faithfulness, and we know that is pleasing to Him. In this way, it does not matter to us if our work is pleasing or not pleasing to the devil, if the world loves us or hates us. Knowing that our work has been well done and having a good conscience before God, we march forward with honor or dishonor, famous or infamous. This, says Paul, is to rejoice or glory in one's self.

This admonition is very necessary to counter act that repugnant vice of arrogant boasting. The Gospel's nature brings on the devil's evil intentions and his fury. Thus Paul has the habit of calling it the word of the cross and the reason people feel offended.[15] It does not always have faithful and constant disciples. Today, there are many who profess and embrace it, but if tomorrow they are offended because of the cross, they let it go and deny it. Therefore, those who teach the Gospel with a view to obtain people's favor and praise need to perish and may their glory turn into shame when people stop applauding and bowing down to them. That is why all the pastors and ministers of the word should learn to have glory and rejoicing with themselves and not from the mouth of others. If there should be someone to praise them, as the faithful sometimes do ("for fame or lack of fame," says Paul in 2 Corinthians 6:8), then let them receive this glory as happenstance glory.[16] But the substance of the glory truly resides in the witness of their own conscience. Those who do this give evidence that they don't consider their own work but that their only objective is to faithfully fulfill their task—that is, to teach the Gospel with purity and demonstrate the proper use of the Sacraments. Once they have proven themselves in this manner, they have glory and rejoicing in themselves, which no one can take away. These things have certainly been sown in their hearts and are rooted there. They don't come from the mouth of other people who Satan can easily twist around and that same mouth that just a short while before was replete with blessings is now overflowing with curses.

Thus says Paul, if you desire praises, look for these where you can find them, not in the mouth of other people but in your own heart, as you truly and faithfully fulfill your task. In consequence, in addition to the glory you will have in yourselves, you will also have the praise and encouragement from others. We have seen this in certain fanatical heads who sought false credit for their work—that is, they not only failed to preach the Gospel in its purity and simplicity, but they

---

15   *scandali*, literally "stumbling stone, offense, scandal."
16   *accidens gloriae.*

used their work improperly. All they sought was to gain the praise of men and thus transgressed against the second commandment. Thus in addition to their internal confusion, an external confusion and shame was added to them according to the sentence "For the Lord will not hold anyone guiltless who misuses his name" (Exodus 20:7, NIV). Also, "Those who honor me I will honor, but those who despise me will be disdained" (1 Samuel 2:30, NIV).

But if we seek first God's glory through the ministry of the word, then our own glory will follow according to what has been said, "Those who honor me I will honor." In brief, let each one prove his work—that is, strive to be faithful to His ministry, for this is what is required above all from the ministers of the word (1 Corinthians 4:2). It's as if he had said, "Let everyone strive to teach the word with purity and faithfulness. Don't fix your gaze on anything else but in the glory of God and the salvation of souls. Then your work will be rendered faithful and whole then you will have glory and rejoicing in your own conscience so that you may boldly say, 'This, my doctrine and ministry, is pleasing to God.'" Indeed, this is an excellent glory.

This statement may also be related to the works of the faithful regardless of the situation in which they may find themselves. If the magistrate, the man of the house, the servant, the teacher, and the scholar remain in their vocation and faithfully perform their duty and have no concern over the works that have nothing to do with their vocation, then they may well glory and rejoice within themselves. They may well say, "I have done the works of my duty as God assigned them to me with all faithfulness and diligence within my reach. Therefore, I know that this work that is done with faith and obedience is pleasing to God. If others talk bad about it, I will not let it bother me," for there will always be someone who despises and slanders the doctrine and life of the faithful. However, God has threatened to destroy every lying lip and slanderous tongue. Therefore, while such people covet adulation, and with lies and slander disfigure the faithful, it will happen to them as Paul said, "They glory in their shame" (Philippians 3:19). Further, in another text, it says, "Their folly will be clear to everyone" (2 Timothy 3:9). By whom? By God the righteous judge for just as He will bring to light their false accusations and slander so he will let the light of the righteous shine as the midday sun, as it says in Psalm 37.

This phrase "in himself" (as to summarize) should be understood in such a way that God is not left out—that is, let each one be certain that regardless of his condition in life, his work is a divine work, for God has ordained the work of his vocation.

VERSE 5. For each one should carry their own load [NIV].

This is, as it were, the reason or confirmation for the previous statement, for otherwise, someone would then lean to other people's opinion once they have praised or complimented him. It's as if he had said, "It is extreme insanity to see glory in someone else and not in yourself. That's because in the agony of death or in the final judgment it will not help you at all if people have praised you. No one else will be there to carry your burden, for you will be all alone before the judgment of Christ. You will bear your burden alone. None of those who praised you will be there to help you, for when we die, these praises will come to their end. In that day, when the Lord will judge all the secrets of every heart, the testimony of your own conscience will either be in your favor or be against you. It will be against you if you have gloried in other people. It will be in your favor if you have it within yourself—that is, if your conscience testifies to you that you have met your duty in the ministry of the word or in any other way, according to your calling, sincerely and faithfully respecting only the glory of God and the salvation of souls." These words, "Each one will bear their own testimony," are very moving and should perturb us so that we will not aspire to praise seeking.

Further, it should be noted here that we are not dealing with the subject of justification, in which nothing is helpful except pure grace and the forgiveness of sins that are received by faith alone, wherein with all our works, yes, even our best works and everything that is done by God's calling, are in need of the forgiveness of sins, but this is another matter. Here, he is not dealing with the forgiveness of sins, but rather, he compares true and hypocritical works altogether. Thus these things need to be understood in this fashion. Although the work of a faithful pastor in his ministry may not be perfect and still need the forgiveness of sins, nonetheless, in itself, it is good and perfect when compared to the ministry of the praise seekers.

Accordingly, our ministry is good and sound when we seek the glory of God and the salvation of souls. But it is not so with the ministry of the fanatical heads, for they are after their own glory. However, since there is no work at all that is able to pacify the conscience before God, it is necessary that we are confident that he have done our work with integrity, in truth, and according to God's calling—that is, that we have not corrupted God's word but rather, we have taught it faithfully and according to its purity. We need this testimony from our conscience: we have fulfilled our duty to the high norm of our task and calling, and we have lived our lives in the same manner. Then we should glory in our works for we know God has ordained them, and they please Him, for in the final judgment, everyone will bear their own burden and thus the praise from others will be worthless and good for nothing!

Up to here, he has spoken of this extremely virulent vice, the love for praise. No one has been able to suppress or resist it, except by persistence in prayer, for even among the faithful, who could find someone who does not delight when he is praised? Only the Holy Spirit is able to preserve us that we may not be infected with this vice.

VERSE 6. Nevertheless, the one who receives instruction in the word should share all good things with their instructor [NIV].

Here, he preaches to the disciples or hearers of the word. He commands them to shower every good thing over those who have been their teachers and tutors in the word. At times, I have wondered at the reason the apostles so diligently commanded the churches to provide for the sustenance of their teachers, for in the papacy, I saw how all contributed abundantly to the construction and maintenance of wonderful temples. It was profitable for the income and well-being of those who had been assigned to the care of that idolatrous worship. That was the cause for the increase in the estate and wealth of the bishops and the clergy, for everywhere they possessed the best and most fruitful lands. That is why I thought that in this instance Paul's command was needless, seeing that all kinds of good things were not only abundantly offered to the clergy, but consequently they had a surplus of goods and wealth. That is why I thought it would be better to exhort to shut the hands of such excessive giving instead of giving more; for I saw how due to this excessive generosity, the clergy became more greedy. But now I know the reason they had such an abundance of goods to this day, which contrasts starkly with the lack and want suffered by the pastors and ministers of the word.

In the past, when everything the church taught was nothing but error and wicked doctrine, they owned many things in great abundance. They did not share at all in Peter's legacy, for he denied having silver and gold. Neither did they partake in the spiritual wealth (as they called it), since today the Pope has turned into an emperor and the cardinals and bishops in kings and princes of this world. But today, since the Gospel has begun to be taught and published, those who profess it have amassed wealth as Christ and the apostles never did. Judging from experience then, we realize how this commandment to nourish and provide for the pastors and ministers of God's word is going to be kept. However, Paul in this text and others commands it with great urgency, repeating it into the ears of his hearers. We know that today there is not one single city that adequately feeds and provides for its ministers. These places more than adequately provide for their own good comfort but give nothing to Christ. Everyone holds back from what they could give Him. Remember He was laid in a manger instead of a crib, for there was no room for Him in the inn. Thereafter, when he lived among the people, He didn't have a place to rest His head. Finally, He was stripped of His clothes and hung naked from a cross between two thieves, dying the most miserable death. But the pope has received large grants of land to perform his abominations, smother the Gospel by teaching human traditions, and carry on with his wicked worship ceremonies.

Every time, I read Paul's exhortations with which he persuades the churches to nourish their pastors or alleviate the poverty of the believers within Judaism, I am amazed and ashamed that the great apostle would be compelled to use so many words to obtain benefits for the congregations. When he writes to the Corinthians, he devotes two whole chapters to this topic (2 Corinthians 8 and 9). I would be circumspect in defaming Wittenberg, for it cannot be compared at all with Corinth, as he defamed the Corinthians when he pleaded with them to provide aid and minister to the poor. But this is the risk that comes with the preaching of the Gospel. No one is willing to give anything for the training of ministers and providing sustenance for its scholars. Instead, people begin to dispossess, rob, steal, and deceive each other with a variety of tricks. In brief, suddenly, people lose their bearings and transform into cruel beasts. By contrast, when the doctrine of devils was preached, people were incredibly generous and willingly offered all things to those who deceived them. The prophets reproved the same sin in the Jews, for they resisted to provide anything at all to the faithful priests and the Levites but gave abundantly from all things to the wicked.

But now, we begin to realize the importance of this command from Paul regarding the sustenance of the church's ministers. That is because the only thing that Satan cannot tolerate is the light of the Gospel. Thus when he sees that it has begun to shine, he becomes furious, and with all his might and perseverance, he persists in blowing it out. He attempts to accomplish this in two ways: first, through the lies of the heretics and the power of the tyrants and then, through poverty and famine. But since to this day he has not been able to suppress the Gospel in this country (praised be the Lord) through the heretics and tyrants, he has then attempted to suffocate it in another way—that is, by withdrawing the sustenance from the ministers of the word. Consequently, they will be forced to abandon the ministry due to poverty and want. Thus the people once again in their misery, lacking the word of God, with the passing of time become as furious as wild beasts. Satan then cooperates in furthering this horrible evil through wicked magistrates in the cities, as well as the nobles and lords in the farmlands, who keep the properties of the church that otherwise would be for the provision of the ministers of the Gospel. But they turn these over for the wicked to use "because she collected the wages of prostitution, and to the wages of prostitution they will return" (Micah 1:7, ISV).

Further, Satan also is successful at leading people astray from the Gospel when people have their bellies full, for when the Gospel is diligently preached daily, many get overstuffed and begin to despise it. Then, little by little, they become negligent and become careless in their disciplines of devotion. These days there's not a man who raises his children with good instruction, much less in the study of the Holy Scriptures. Instead, they put them to work doing handicrafts or in amassing wealth. Satan provides these practices with no other purpose than to oppress the Gospel in our country with the despotism of the tyrants or the subtle trickery of the heretics.

Thus there's good reason Paul admonishes the hearers of the Gospel to share every good gift with their pastors and teachers. Speaking to the Corinthians, he said, "If we have sown spiritual seed among you, is it too much if we reap a material harvest from you?" (1 Corinthians 9:11, NIV). Thus the hearers must administer material things to those who have ministered spiritual things to them. But both groups, citizens as well as nobles, to this day abuse our doctrine because they amass wealth under its shelter. But until recently, during the reign of the Pope, there was not one man who didn't have to make a yearly payment for his priests' anniversaries (as they called them) and for masses, vigils, and such. The mendicant Friars also received their cut. Likewise, the Roman merchants and the daily offerings also took part of the revenue. From these things and countless other taxations, our compatriots have been delivered by the Gospel. But do you think they are grateful to God for this freedom? Those who once were such generous donors now have turned into shameless thieves and robbers, and they refuse to contribute even though it were only a cent for the Gospel or its ministers; neither do they contribute one thing to alleviate and aid the saints in their lack of everything. This is indeed certain proof that they have lost the word of faith and that the spirit of kindness does not exist in them, for it is impossible that the true faithful will allow their pastors to live in need and want. They laugh and rejoice when their pastors suffer any adversity, they hold back their hand to provide for them, or don't give with the needed regularity. Thus they truly prove that they are worse than pagans.

However, before too much time goes by, they will feel the calamities that will follow their ingratitude, for they will lose their temporal as well as spiritual goods. This sin must be grievously punished. Indeed, I believe the churches in Galatia, Corinth, and other places were so perturbed by the false apostles for no other reason than they held their pastors and preachers in so little esteem, for there is no good reason someone who refuses to give once cent to God (He who gives all that is good and eternal life) will give the devil a bar of gold, the author of all evil and eternal death. Thus whoever does not serve God in the very least (which is to his great benefit) then let him be a servant of the devil in great plenty. Accordingly, he will receive extreme and total confusion. Thus now that the light of the Gospel has begun to shine, we can see who the devil really is and what his world looks like.

With respect to what he says, "In all his goods," it should not be understood that everyone is obligated to give all they have to their ministers but that they provide for them a generous sustenance to provide for their well-being. Anyone familiar with the Greek would know the meaning of the term κατηχούμενος (kateixoumenos).[17]

VERSE 7. Do not be deceived: God cannot be mocked. A man reaps what he sows.

In this text, the apostle fervently promotes the sustenance and nourishment of the ministers so that in addition to his previous reproach and admonition he now also

---

[17] The one who receives instruction. The English transliteration is *catechumen*.

adds a threat, saying, "God cannot be mocked." With this, he pierces to the core of our compatriots' perversity, since they proudly despise our ministry, for they think that it is only a game and a sport. Thus they are committed (particularly the nobles) to take the pastors as their subjects, as servants and slaves. If we didn't have such a pious prince who loves the truth, they would have long ago expelled us from the country. When the pastors asked for what is due to them or complain that they are going through economic difficulties, the princes are the ones who complain. They say, "The priests are greedy, they want to live in riches, no one can satisfy their insatiable greed. If they were true preachers of the Gospel, they would get rid of all their goods and follow Christ in His poverty and suffer all their difficulties."

So here Paul turns the tables on them and harshly threatens these tyrants and mockers of God who so carelessly and proudly make fun of the preachers' difficulties. Yet they want to be known as true evangelicals and not as mockers of God but as devoted worshippers. "Don't be deceived," he said. "God cannot be mocked"—that is, "He will not allow to be mocked in His ministers," for He says, "He who rejects me rejects him who sent me" (Luke 10:16). He also said to Samuel, "They have not rejected you, but they have rejected me" (1 Samuel 8:7). Therefore, oh mockers, although God may postpone His punishment for a time, it will come when it is timely, He will bring you to light and punish this rejection of His word and bitter hate toward His ministers. Thus it is not God who you fool but you yourselves. You will not laugh at God, but it is God who will be laughing at you (Psalm 2:4). But our proud gentry, citizens, and ordinary people don't move at all due to these warnings. However, they will indeed when death stalks them, if they have mocked themselves or if they have mocked us. But no! They would not have mocked us but God Himself, as Paul says here. Meanwhile, since they arrogantly despise our warnings with intolerable conceit, we say these things for our comfort so that we may know that it is better to suffer evil than to do evil, for patience is always innocent and meek. Further, God will not permit His ministers to die of hunger, for even when the affluent suffer want and hunger, He will feed them, and in the days of famine, they will be filled.

VERSE 7. For whatever a man sows, that he will also reap.

All these things were intended to obtain food and provisions for the ministers. As for me, it doesn't give me great pleasure to interpret these statements for it appears they are commands and indeed they are orders. Further, if they are frequently repeated to the hearers, then it takes on a certain form of greed. However, people must be admonished so that they may grant to their pastors not only respect but the provisions they need. In Luke 10, Christ taught the same thing: "And remain in the same house, eating and drinking what they provide, for the laborer deserves his wages" (Luke 10:7). In another text, Paul states, "Don't you know that those who serve in the temple get their food from the temple, and that those who serve at the altar share in what is offered on the altar? In the same way, the Lord has commanded that those who preach the gospel should receive their living from the gospel" (1 Corinthians 9:13–14).

It is well for us who are also in the ministry to know these things for fear that our conscience will accuse us because our compensation proceeds from the Pope's goods. Although such goods were hoarded by fraud and deceit, taking note that God plundered the Egyptians—that is, the Papists—of their goods, now, it is granted to us that these are put to a good and holy use. This is not because the nobles plunder and abuse them, but when they are offered to the glory of God, they are used to instruct the youth in virtues and for their sustenance, *for it is impossible for ministers to work day and night in ordinary labor to provide for themselves and at the same time devote themselves to the study of sacred matters as required by the office of the preacher.* Let us be assured then with a good conscience, for God so ordained and commanded, that those who preach the Gospel, live from the Gospel. We have been given the use of the goods offered to the church for our work to put them to a better use—that is, for the necessary provision of our lives so that we may better carry out our work. Here, let no one have scruples about it, as if it were not legitimate to use such goods.

VERSE 8. For he who sows to his own flesh will from the flesh reap corruption; but he who sows to the Spirit will from the Spirit reap eternal life.

Here, he adds a simile and an allegory. He relates this generalized statement regarding the harvest to the subject of the sustenance and provision for the ministers of the word. He says, "Whoever sows to the Spirit," meaning whoever values the teachers of God's word furthers a spiritual work and will reap eternal life. Here, the question arises, do we then earn eternal life because of our works? That is what Paul seems to affirm in this text. Regarding such statements that talk about works and their rewards, we have already dealt fully with this topic in chapter 5. But following Paul's example, it is very necessary to urge the faithful to do good works—that is, to exercise their faith through good works, for if they do not proceed from faith, it is obvious that it is not true faith. Thus the apostle says, "Whoever sows to the flesh" (some understand it as referring to their own flesh)—that is, they do not contribute at all to the ministers of God's word. Instead, they only feed and provide for their own flesh (for that is the advice from the flesh). Thus such person will reap corruption, not only in this current life but also in the life to come, for all the earthly goods of the wicked will pass away, and they themselves in time will shamefully perish. The apostle wishes to encourage his hearers to be generous and beneficial with their pastors and preachers. But it is such a disgrace that people can be so perverse and ungrateful that the churches would need this admonition.

The Encratites[18] abused this text to confirm their wicked opinion against marriage and explain it in the following way: "Whoever sows to the flesh will reap corruption"—that is, whoever marries a wife will be condemned. Thus a wife is a damnable thing, marriage is wicked, and if you are married, you are sowing to the flesh. These beasts are so destitute of all good judgment that they could not see where the apostle was going. I talk like this so you may see how easily the devil through his ministers can lead astray from the truth the hearts of simple people. Soon Germany will have an infinite number of such beasts (ministers of the devil), yes, and there are already aplenty! On the one hand, the devil persecutes and kills the faithful ministers, and on the other, he causes their neglect and rejection, compelling them to live in abject poverty. We must arm ourselves against these and similar errors and learn the true meaning of Scriptures, for here Paul is not talking about marriage but providing for the ministers of the church. Anyone gifted with reason's common sense[19] can see this. Although the nourishment is only for the body, he calls it sowing in the Spirit. But on the contrary, when people greedily hoard all they can and seek only their own gain, he calls it "sowing to the flesh." To those who sow in the Spirit, he pronounces a blessing in this life as in the life to come. But those who sow to the flesh, he declares under a curse in this life as in the life to come.

VERSE 9. Let us not become weary in doing good, for at the proper time we will reap a harvest if we do not give up [NIV].

The apostle, intending to conclude his epistle, now, goes from the particular to the general and exhorts all in general to good works. It's as if he had said, "Let us be liberal and generous, not only toward the ministers of the word but also to all people and without growing weary, for it is rather easy to do what is right once or twice but to persevere and not grow weary due to ingratitude or perversity from those to whom the good deed was done, that is very difficult." Thus he urges us to not only do the good but also not get tired doing what is good. And to persuade us even more, he adds, "For at the proper time we will reap a harvest if we don't grow weary." It's as if he had said, "Wait with your gaze fixed on the coming promise. At that time, there won't be any ingratitude or crooked dealings from people who could detour you from doing what is good. At harvest time, you will receive the most abundant increase in the fruit of your seed." Thus with the sweetest words he urges the faithful to carry on with their good works.

---

[18] Sectarian heresy that arose about two centuries after Christ. They professed a rigid and strict asceticism, prohibiting the eating of meat and the drinking of wine with meals, and were opposed to marriage.

[19] *communi sensu.*

VERSE 10. Therefore, as we have opportunity, let us do good to all people, especially to those who belong to the family of believers.

This is the sweet closing of his appeal to generously provide for the ministers of the word and give offerings to all the needy. It's as if he had said, "As long as it is day, we must do the works of him who sent me. Night is coming, when no one can work." It is true that people do many things when the light of the truth goes out but everything is worthless. They walk in darkness and don't know where they are going. Therefore, their entire life, all their suffering and death, is in vain. These are the words he addresses to the Galatians. It's as if he had said, "Unless you persevere in the sound doctrine you received from me, all the good you do, all the suffering in your trials, and other such things, are worthless to you." As he said before in Galatians 3:4, "Have you suffered so many things in vain?" He coins a new name to describe the community of faith;[20] within it, first, are the ministers of the word and then all the faithful.

LECTURE 41: Saturday, December 12

VERSE 11. See with what large letters I am writing to you with my own hand.

He closes his epistle with an appeal to the faithful and a strong reproach or invective against the false apostles.[21] He had cursed and damned the false apostles before. Now he repeats himself but with other words; he reluctantly but forcefully accuses them. He seeks to frighten and entice them away from their doctrine, regardless of how highly they regard their authority. You have such great teachers, he says, that in the first place, they do not put Christ on the highest pedestal and give Him all the glory for the salvation of your souls. Instead, they only look out for their own glory. Second, they run away from the cross. Third, they don't understand, much less practice, the things they teach. If anyone, especially the apostles, should endorse them as doctors of theology with these three virtues [in their résumé], then let everyone ignore such recommendations![22] But all the Galatians looked the other way and did not take Paul's advice. Paul's rough words did not make any impression on the false apostles. Thus based on his apostolic

---

[20] *qui sunt in nostra societate fidei.*

[21] In verses 11 and 12, I have followed the order of the 1538 edition as it appears in the Weimar text for the *CDE*. The Irmischer Latin text has a slightly different order for the text in these two verses, which is immaterial to the meaning of Luther's comments.

[22] Other English translations omit this phrase. Following Luther's own directives regarding translations, the translated material should read as if originally said or written in the target language, I have included the phrase in brackets since in twenty-first-century English, that is a common way of stating one's qualifications.

authority, he attacked them more forcefully. In the same way, if we call the Pope the "Antichrist" and damn the bishops and the fanatics,[23] we are not taking anything away from them, but through divine authority, we judge them as damned, just as Scripture says, "even if we, or an angel from heaven," and so on (Galatians 1:8). That's because they are persecuting and overthrowing the doctrine of Christ.

"See," he says, "with what large letters I am writing to you with my own hand." He says this to move them and show them his maternal affection toward them. It's as if he had said, "I never wrote such a long epistle to any other church with my own hand." Regarding his other epistles, others wrote while he dictated. Thereafter, he would inscribe his greeting and name with his own hand, as we can observe at the end of his epistles. With these words (I suppose), he points to the lengthiness of this epistle. Others have a different understanding. What follows is an accusation and condemnation.

VERSE 12. For whoever will please in the flesh, these constrain you to be circumcised, only that they suffer not the persecution of Christ's cross [WYC].

Here, he uses a highly meaningful word: εὐπροσωπῆσαι (euprosopeisai).[24] It is the same we say in German, wohl geberden, sich sein wissen zu stellen.[25] Their primary virtue (he said) is this: They praise the dignitaries and religious personalities. They do for them whatever they want in order to conserve and not lose any of their own glory, as long as they can get you circumcised. The Jewish rulers are unyielding in their opposition to the Gospel and defense of Moses. Accordingly, the false apostles study how to get into good graces with them and keep their egos propped up. Thus to this end, they teach that circumcision is necessary for salvation and thus avoid persecution on account of the cross. In the same way, today, we have those who astutely praise the Pope, the bishops, and the princes. These folks wickedly denounce and defame our writings but not out of their love to defend the truth. Against their own conscience, they impugn and blaspheme but to please their idols the Pope, the bishops, the kings and princes of this world and avoid suffering persecution for the cause of the cross of Christ. But if they could get the Gospel to give them the creature comforts they

---

[23] *phanatici homines.* Rörer's manuscript reads, *Oecolampadium, Karolstadium.*

[24] Remember Luther is addressing a group of seminarians, so he assumes they know their Greek. The meaning of the Greek term is "to put on a show in order to please."

[25] In Luther's Greek–German Lexicon, he renders the Greek term εὐπροσωπῆσαι (euprosopeisai) with the same German expression he has provided here: *wohl geberden / fich sein zu stellen wissen.* A precise translation of this old German proverb is difficult, but it may be rendered something like the following: to put on an act in order to get into good graces with someone.

seek granted by their idols or if by professing the Gospel they could get rich, indulge their pleasures, live in peace and quiet, then immediately they would unite with us.

Your doctors of theology (he said) have their heads full of pride. They are not concerned about the glory of Christ and your salvation; they only seek their own glory. Again, since they are afraid of the cross, they preach circumcision and the righteousness of the flesh, lest they provoke the Jews to hate and persecute them. Thus even though you listen to them with joy as you have never felt before and keep on listening to them, you will only be hearing those who have made a god out of their bellies, those who seek their own glory and avoid the cross. Here, you must note a certain passion in the word *constrain*, for circumcision in itself is nothing but to allow yourself to be circumcised and in having it done you trust it as righteousness and holiness but believing that you sin if you are not circumcised, then, you are offending Christ. I have talked about this before at quite some length.

VERSE 13. For even those who receive circumcision do not themselves keep the law, but they desire to have you circumcised that they may glory in your flesh.

Wouldn't you say this is enough to call Paul a heretic? He says that not only the false apostles but also the entire Jewish nation, which had been circumcised, did not keep the law. Thus the circumcised while keeping the law did not observe it. Is this not talking against Moses? He says that the circumcised keep the law; and uncircumcision is to make the covenant null and void (Genesis 17:14). The Jews were circumcised for no other reason than to observe the law, which commanded that every male child should be circumcised on the eighth day. We have already dealt with this previously, so it's not necessary to repeat ourselves. Well, these things serve to condemn the false apostles so that the Galatians would be fearful to pay them attention. It's as if he had said, "Look, I place before you the kind of teachers you have. First, they are arrogantly boastful and seek nothing but their own profit. They don't care about anything else but their own bellies. Second, they flee from the cross and don't faithfully teach the truth or anything else with any certainty. Rather, all they say and do are falsehoods full of hypocrisy. Thus even though to all appearances they keep the law, giving a great impression of their observance, they don't actually keep it, for without the Holy Spirit the law cannot be kept. But the Holy Spirit cannot be received without Christ, and where the Holy Spirit does not dwell is the dwelling place of an unclean spirit—that is, they despise God and seek self-gain and self-glory. Thus all they do with respect to the law is only hypocrisy and double sin, for an unclean heart does not keep the law but only puts on a theatrical performance of observances and thus confirms itself even more in its wickedness and hypocrisy."

This statement must be kept diligently in mind, that the circumcised don't keep the law—that is, that the circumcised are not circumcised. It may also be related to works. Whoever works, prays, or suffers without Christ, works, prays, and suffers in vain, "for whatever does not proceed from faith is sin." Therefore, there is no benefit at all that comes from circumcision or fasting or praying or any other external work if inwardly the person despises grace, forgiveness of sins, faith, and Christ. Further it is also to be all puffed up with the opinion and presumption of one's own righteousness, which are horrible sins against the first table of the law. Thereafter follow the other sins against the second table, such as disobedience, prostitution, fury, anger, hate, and such. That is why he has said it so well, that those who are circumcised don't keep the law but just pretend that they do. But this make-believe, or rather, hypocrisy, is double wickedness before God.

What do the false apostles pretend when they try to get you circumcised? It's not for you to become righteous, no matter how much attention they pay to you. Instead, it's that they want to brag about what they have done to your flesh. Well, who would not detest this horrible pestilent vice of desiring glory that attempts to put the souls of people at risk? These are (he said) deceiving spirits, shameless and vain, who serve their own bellies and hate the cross. Once again (and this is the worst), they compel you to get circumcised according to the law. However, all they've done is abuse your flesh so they can brag about it, putting your souls at peril of eternal destruction while they were at it! But what else have you gained before God except our eternal condemnation? And what else have you achieved before men, except that the false apostles boast that they were your teachers, and you were their disciples? However, they teach what they themselves don't keep. In this way, he reproaches the false apostles with great power.

These words, "glory in your flesh," are very effective. It's as if he had said, "You don't have the word of the Spirit. Thus it is impossible for you to receive the Spirit through what they preach. All they do is get you to offer up your flesh so that you will become your own judges because of what you have done to your flesh—in other words, justify yourselves. Externally they observe days, times, sacrifices, and other things according to the law, things that are entirely carnal." Consequently, all you reap is nothing more than work without gain and you're condemned just the same. On the other hand, what they get from all this is boasting that they were your teachers and that they have succeeded in getting you to leave behind Paul's doctrine, that heretic, and return to your mother, the synagogue. That is how today the Papists boast. They say they have been able to call back many to the holy mother church. On the contrary, we do not glory in your flesh, but we glory regarding your spirit because you have received the Spirit through our preaching (Galatians 3:2).

VERSE 14. But far be it from me to glory except in the cross of our Lord Jesus Christ.

The apostle concludes the matter with indignation. With great passionate spirit, he exclaims these words: "Far be it from me to glory." It's as if he had said, "The false apostles' glory and carnal ambition is such a dangerous poison that I wish it were buried in hell, for it causes the destruction of so many. But let them glory in the flesh all they want, and let them perish with their accursed glory. With respect to me, I don't desire any other glory but the one by which I rejoice in the cross of Christ." In the same way, he says, "We glory in our afflictions" (Romans 5). Also, in 2 Corinthians 12:9, "I will glory in my afflictions." Here, Paul teaches what is the meaning of the Christians' joy and glory—that is, to glory and boast in tribulations, reproaches, weaknesses, etc. The world not only judges Christians, saying they are the most deplorable and disgraceful of all people, but also, in the cruelest of ways and with great conviction, hates, persecutes, condemns, and kills them as if they were the most pernicious plague of the spiritual and earthly worlds, deeming them heretics and insurgents. But they don't suffer these things because they are murderers, robbers, and other wicked people. Instead, for the love of Christ, they suffer because they are devoted to proclaiming His benefit and glory. Thus they glory in tribulation and in the cross of Christ and with the apostles they rejoice in having been considered worthy to suffer indignities for the name of Christ. Similarly, today we glory when the Pope and the entire world persecute us with great cruelty and we are condemned and killed. But we suffer these things not because of our wicked works such as thievery, murder, and similar deeds but for Christ's sake, our Lord and Savior, whose Gospel we teach in truth.

Well, our glory increases and is confirmed mainly for two reasons: first, because we are certain that our doctrine is pure and divine and second, because our cross and suffering is Christ's. Thus when the world persecutes and kills us, that is no reason to complain or mourn, but rather, we should rejoice and consider ourselves joyful. Indeed, the entire world judges us as wretched and accursed. On the other hand, Christ, who is greater than the world and for whom we suffer, declares us blessed, and in His will, we rejoice. "Blessed are you when men revile you and persecute you and utter all kinds of evil against you falsely on my account. Rejoice and be glad, for your reward is great in heaven, for so men persecuted the prophets who were before you" (Matthew 5:11, 12). Then our glory is another kind of glory, different from the world's, which does not rejoice in tribulation, insults, persecution, death, etc. Instead, the world glories in power, wealth, honor, wisdom, and self-righteousness. But the end of that glory is regret and confusion.

Further, the cross of Christ does not mean that piece of wood that Christ carried on His shoulders to which he was nailed. Instead, it generally means all the trials of the faithful, whose sufferings are the sufferings of Christ: "We share abundantly in Christ's sufferings" (2 Corinthians 1:5) and also "In my flesh I complete what is lacking in Christ's afflictions for the sake of his body—that is, the church" (Colossians 1:24). Thus the cross of Christ generally means all the afflictions the church suffers for Christ, of which He, Himself, gave testimony when He said, "Saul, Saul, why do you persecute me?" (Acts 9:4). Saul did not violently lunge against Christ but against His church, for whoever touches it, touches the apple of His eye, for there is greater sensibility in the head than on any other member of the body. We know this from experience, for whenever the little toe or any other minor part of the body is injured, it is the head itself that displays the pain it feels due to the gestures it makes. That is how Christ our head assimilates all our afflictions as His very own and suffers when we suffer, for we are His body.

It is for our benefit to know these things, otherwise we would be consumed by pain or fall into despondency when we see how cruelly our adversaries persecute, excommunicate, and kill us. But let us think for ourselves, following Paul's example, that we should glory in the cross that we carry, not for our sins but for Christ's sake. If we only think of ourselves because of the sufferings we bear, they would be not only extremely painful but intolerable. However, when we say, "We share abundantly in Christ's sufferings," or as Psalm 44:22 says, "For your sake we face death all day long" (Psalm 44:22, NIV), then these sufferings are not only easy but sweet, according to what has been said: "My yoke is easy and my burden is light" (Matthew 11:30).

Well, today, it is well known that we suffer hate and persecution from our adversaries for no other reason than we faithfully preach with purity the Gospel of Christ. If we were to deny Him and consent to pernicious errors and a wicked religion, they would not only quit hating and persecuting us but also grant us honor, wealth, and many other good things. But because we suffer these things on account of Christ, we can truly rejoice with Paul in the cross of our Lord Jesus Christ—that is, not in riches, power, and good standing with people. Instead, we rejoice in trials, weaknesses, grief, struggles within our bodies, terrors of spirit, persecutions, and all other evils. Thus we trust that soon Christ will tell us what David said to Abiathar the priest, "I am responsible for the death of your whole family" (1 Kings 22; 1 Samuel 22:22) and "Whoever touches you touches the apple of his eye." It's as if he had said, "Whoever hurts you, hurts me, for if you did not preach my word and confess me, you would not suffer these things." John also said the same: "If you belonged to the world, it would love you as its own. As it is, you do not belong to the world, but I have chosen you out of the world. That is why the world hates you" (John 15:19, NIV). But we have already dealt with this topic.

VERSE 14. Through which the world has been crucified to me, and I to the world [NIV].

This is a typical expression from Paul: "The world has been crucified to me"—that is, "My verdict is that the world has already been condemned." "And I to the world"—that is, the world in turn concludes that I have been condemned. Thus we crucify and condemn each other. I despise the doctrine, righteousness, and works of the world as if it were the devil's poison. In turn, the world detests my doctrine and works and judges that I am seditious, pernicious, a plague, and a heretic. That is how the world today is crucified to us, and we to the world. We curse and condemn all the traditions regarding the mass, the orders, vows, will power, worship, and all the Pope's abominations and other heretics as the devil's dirt. They in turn persecute and kill us for destroying the religion and disturbing the peace among the people.

The monks had the illusion that once they entered their monasteries they were crucifying the world. But on the contrary, they crucify Christ and not the world. Yes, in this way, the world is not crucified at all. Instead, they promote themselves even more through that opinion regarding their holiness and confidence in their own righteousness, which they thought to gain through their religious order. Thus in the most headstrong and wicked way, this statement by the apostle was forced to support their voluntary recruitment into the monasteries. However, Paul is talking here about a subject of high and great importance—that is, everything that the faithful judges as wisdom, righteousness, and God's power is what the world condemns as the greatest foolishness, wickedness, and weakness. On the contrary, what the world judges as the most exalted religion and service to God, the faithful know it is nothing but the most despicable and horrible blasphemy before God. That is how the faithful condemn the world and, in turn, the world condemns the faithful. But the faithful on their part judge correctly, for the spiritual believer judges all things (1 Corinthians 2:15).

The world's judgment and the believers' faith regarding religion and righteousness before God oppose each other as God and the devil are opposite and contrary, for the devil crucifies God, and God crucifies the devil (for the Son of God appeared, as John says, to destroy the works of the devil, 1 John 3:8). In the same way, the devil condemns and overthrows the word and the works of God, for the devil is a murderer and father of lies. In such a way, the devil condemns the doctrine and life of the faithful, calling them the most pernicious heretics and disturbers of the peace among the people. But the faithful also call the world the son of the devil, which has followed in its father's footsteps, and thus for the same reason, the world is a murderer and a liar just as his father. This is Paul's message when he says, "Through which the world has been crucified to me, and I to the world." Now, in the Sacred Scriptures, the world refers not only to the wicked and evil but also to the very best, the wisest, and those who pass themselves off as the holiest saints in the entire world.

In passing, he covertly points to the false apostles. It's as if he had said, "I hate and totally detest as something accursed all the glory that is not through the cross of Christ. Yes, *I consider it not only as all dead but also as having died through such a horrible death as a crucifixion.* For the world, with all its glory, is crucified to me, and I to the world. Thus all who glory in their flesh and not in the cross of Christ, be accursed!" With these words, Paul testifies that he hates the world with the Holy Spirit's perfect hatred. In turn, the world hates him with the perfect hatred of an evil spirit. It's as if he had said, "It's impossible for me and the world to come to an agreement. Then what should I do? Should I yield my place and teach things that are pleasing to the world? No! Instead, with a courageous spirit, I will oppose it, despise, and crucify it in the same way that the world despises and crucifies me."

In conclusion, here, Paul teaches how we should fight against Satan. He not only torments our bodies with various afflictions, but he also continually wounds our hearts with his fiery darts. He wants to conquer us with his perseverance and overthrow our faith and drive us away from the truth and Christ. So just as we see how Paul so boldly despised the world, so we should also repudiate the world, its prince, and all his army, deceits, and infernal furies. Then trusting in Christ's help and aid, we should triumph against him in the following way: "Oh Satan, however much you try to wound and hurt me, so much more I boldly rise against you and laugh at you with disdain. However much you perturb me and attempt me to despair, I will become so much more bold and confident. I will glory in the middle of your furies and wickedness, not through any power in me but through the power of Christ, my Lord and Savior, whose power is perfected in my weakness. Thus when I am weak, then I am strong" (2 Corinthians 12:9, 10). However, when he realizes that his threats and terrors cause fear, he rejoices and terrifies even more those who he has already frightened.

VERSE 15. For in Christ Jesus neither circumcision nor uncircumcision avails anything, but a new creation [NKJV].

This is an amazing way to state the issue, when Paul says that "in Christ, neither circumcision or uncircumcision avails anything." It seems that instead it should have said, "It's either circumcision or uncircumcision, one of the two is of value," seeing that these two are in opposition. But now he denies that any of the two have any value at all. It's as if he would have said, "You should climb higher, for circumcision and uncircumcision are things of little importance, for with neither of these two things are you able to attain righteousness before God. It is true that they are contrary to each other, but they are nothing regarding Christian righteousness, for righteousness is heavenly and is not of this earth. Therefore, it does not consist in things of the body. Thus whether you have been circumcised or are uncircumcised, it's all the same, for in Christ Jesus neither one or the other has any value."

The Jews were greatly offended when they heard that circumcision had no value at all. They had no problem consenting to the argument that uncircumcision had no value but could not tolerate hearing the same regarding the law and circumcision, for they were even willing to spill their blood for defending the law and circumcision. Likewise, the Papists are fierce fighters when it comes to defending traditions regarding meats, celibacy, festivals, etc. They excommunicate and curse us for we teach that in Jesus Christ these things have no value at all. *And there are some among our own people no less stupid*[26] *than the Papists who think that freedom from the Pope's tradi-*

---

[26] *insulsi,* literally this word means "stupid."

tions is something so necessary that unless they immediately violate and annul them all, they fear they would be sinning. But Paul says that we should understand that to attain *righteousness before God there is something else much more excellent and precious that either circumcision or uncircumcision or the observance or violation of the Pope's traditions.* In Christ Jesus, he says, neither circumcision nor uncircumcision, nor celibacy, nor marriage, nor eating meat, nor fasts are worth anything at all. Meats do not make us acceptable before God; neither are we any better for abstaining, nor will we get any worse by eating. All these things, yes, even the whole world with its laws and righteousness amount to nothing for justification. *Yes, they should not even be dragged into the conversation when the passage is about justification.*

Neither reason nor the wisdom of the flesh understands this, for it "does not accept the things that come from the Spirit of God." Thus it is necessary that righteousness be founded on external things, for the word of God teaches us that there is nothing under heaven that can purchase righteousness before God but Christ alone, or as Paul says here, a new creature.[27] The civil and political laws, people's traditions, the ceremonies of the church, yes, even the law of Moses are things that exist without Christ; thus they have no righteousness value before God. In their proper place and time, we may use them as good and necessary things. But if we are talking about the subject of justification, they are worthless; instead, they are damaging. "For in Christ Jesus neither circumcision nor uncircumcision avails anything but the new creature."

Through these two things then, circumcision and uncircumcision, Paul absolutely rejects everything else and denies that in Jesus Christ they could have any value at all—that is, in the matter of faith and salvation, for here he takes a part to represent the whole—that is, by uncircumcision he represents all the Gentiles, and by circumcision, he represents all the Jews, with their power and glory. It's as if he had said, "All that the Gentiles could ever do with their wisdom, righteousness, laws, powers, kingdoms, and empires have no value at all in Christ Jesus. Further, all that the Jews could ever do with their Moses, law, their circumcision, worships, their temple, their kingdom and priesthood is worthless. Therefore, in Jesus Christ, or regarding the subject of justification, we should dispute neither the laws of the Gentiles nor those of the Jews but simply dictate this sentence: 'Neither circumcision nor uncircumcision avails anything.'"

So then, are laws bad? Not at all; categorically, no. They are good and profitable but in their time and place—that is, in matters pertaining to the body and regarding civil law, for these are matters that without laws there could be no government. Further, in our churches, we use certain ceremonies and laws, not that through them we attain righteousness but to keep everything orderly, give an example, provide calm and concord, according to what has been said, "But all things should be done decently and in order" (1 Corinthians 14:40). But if the laws are presented and urged

---

[27] *praeter unicum Christum, seu, ut hic dicit, "novam creaturam."*

as if by keeping them people can be justified or if by breaking them you are condemned, then they should be stripped away and abolished. Otherwise, Christ loses His office and glory, for He alone is who justifies us and gives us the Holy Spirit. Thus through these words, Paul affirms that neither circumcision nor uncircumcision avail to anything but the new creature etc. Well, since neither the laws of the Gentiles nor those of the Jews amount to anything, the Pope has worked in the most wicked manner, for he has compelled people to keep his laws with a view to attaining righteousness.

Well then, a new creation, made anew in the image of God,[28] cannot be created by painting it with colors or with a forgery of good works (for in Christ Jesus neither circumcision nor uncircumcision amount to anything). Instead, it is by Christ, who in Himself is the true creation according to God's image in righteousness and true holiness.[29] When works are done, they certainly convey the report of a new type of species.[30] The world and the flesh are highly captivated, but there is no new creature.[31] That is because the heart remains wicked, the same as before, full to the brim with its scorn for God and lacking faith. Therefore, a new creature is the work of the Holy Spirit[32] that through faith frees the heart from heavy loads; brings about the fear of God, love, modesty; etc. The Spirit also grants the courage to subdue the flesh and to flee from the righteousness and wisdom of the world. Here, we are not talking about watercolors or a new external species[33] but a fact so real you can carry with you.[34] Another thought pattern and way to judge things—namely, spiritual—is born. Whatever previously was praiseworthy is now detested.[35] For instance, the monastic life with its orders bewitched us to such an extent that we thought there was no other way to be saved. But now, we judge those very differently. Now we blush when we remember the saints we used to worship as supremely celestial and holy before we were reborn into this new creation.[36]

---

[28] *Nova autem creatura, qua reparatur imago Dei.*

[29] *sed per Christum ad imaginem Dei in justitia et sanctitate veritatis creaturam.* The Vulgate reads in Genesis 1:27, *ad imaginem suam ad imaginem Dei.* Luther emphasizes that Christ is the new creation in God's image, He is our new humanity, God's new creation on our behalf.

[30] *novam quidem speciem afferunt.*

[31] *sed non novam creaturam.*

[32] *Ideo nova creatura est opus Spiritus sancti.*

[33] *fucus aut tantum nova externa species.*

[34] *sed res ipsa geritur.*

[35] Note that up to this point, Luther has been describing Christ as the new creation. From here on, Luther describes what it means to be born into the incarnate Christ, who is the believer's righteousness.

[36] *Quae igitur ante hanc novam creaturam pro summe sanctis adoravius, de illis, cum redenunt in memoriam, jam erubescimus.*

Therefore, to change your garments and other external things (as the monks imagine) is not the same as a new creation. Instead, it is the renewal of the mind through the Holy Spirit from which proceeds a change in the body's members and emotions, for when the heart has been illumined by a new light, a new way to understand things, and by new emotions conceived by the Gospel, the external feelings are also renewed.[37] Now the ears desire to hear the word of God and not the traditions and the fantasies of men. The mouth and the tongue no longer boast of their own works, righteousness, and regulations. Now they ceaselessly and joyfully magnify God's mercy offered to us in Jesus Christ. These changes, so to speak, are not in mere words but are real.[38] They bring a new way of thinking,[39] a new will, new feelings; the flesh will feel new sensations and carry out new actions. Now the eyes, ears, mouth, and the tongue no longer see, hear, and talk as they did before. Rather, the mind approves and takes different stands than it did before.[40] Previously, blinded by the papal errors and such darkness, we imagined that God was a merchant, who was selling us His grace in exchange for our works and merits. But now in the light of the Gospel, we are given the assurance that we are counted as righteous by faith in Christ alone.[41] We praise and magnify God's mercy, rejoice and glory in the only assurance and guarantee that there is, which is God's mercy through Jesus Christ. If we are to suffer trials or affliction, we carry them with joy and gladness although the flesh moans and complains. This is what Paul calls being born into a new creation.[42]

VERSE 16. Peace and mercy be upon all who walk by this rule, upon the Israel of God.

This he adds by way of a summary.[43] This is the only and true rule by which we must walk—that is, the new creature. *The Franciscans wickedly twist this Pauline text and relate it to their own order. Thus there are many who have blasphemed and committed sacrilege declaring that their order is holier than the rest, since they claim it has been established and confirmed through the authority of the apostle. But Paul, no doubt, is*

---

[37] *ut externi quoque sensus innoventur.*

[38] *non verbales, sed reales.*

[39] *mentem.*

[40] *sed ut ipsa mens etiam aliud probet et sequatur.*

[41] *sola fide in Christum reputari justos.*

[42] *Hanc Paulus novam creaturam appellat.* The translation rendered in the text is indicated by the context, given that Luther (following Paul's lead) considers Christ "the true creation according to God's image in righteousness and true holiness," as cited in the previous paragraph (see previous footnote). Luther's thought would indicate that the believer is born anew into Christ, who in Himself is "the true creation according to God's image in righteousness and true holiness."

[43] *epiphonema.*

not talking here about cowls, tonsures,[44] *rope belts,*[45] *wooden shoes, bellowing in the shrines, and other similar inane trash they include in the regulations of their orders. Rather, he is talking about the new creature,* which is neither circumcision nor uncircumcision but the new being created to the image of God in righteousness and true holiness. This new creature is righteous in spirit and outwardly in the flesh is holy and clean. The monks have a righteousness and holiness, but it's hypocritical and wicked, for they don't aspire to be justified by faith alone in Christ but through the observance of their regulations. Further, although outwardly they falsify holiness and their eyes, hands, tongue and other members abstain from evil; their heart is impure, up to the brim of unclean lust, envy, anger, obscenity, disdain and hatred for God, and blasphemy against Christ, for they are the most bitter and cruel enemies of the truth.

Thus cursed be the Orders of Francis, Dominique, and all the monks, first, because they obscure and bury with their rules the benefit and the glory of Christ. Then they take the Gospel of grace and life and utterly crush it. Then they fill the whole world with endless idolatry, false worship, wicked religion, works of will power, and the like. But blessed be this one text from Paul by which we live in the faith of Christ and are made new creatures—that is, righteous and indeed holy through the Holy Spirit without color touch ups or falsifications. To those who walk according to this rule, peace be upon them—that is, God's favor, the forgiveness of sins, a peaceful conscience, and mercy—that is, help in afflictions and forgiveness for the remnants of sin that remains in our flesh. Yes, and although those who walk according to this rule may be overtaken by any sin, nonetheless, since they are already children of grace and peace, they are sustained by mercy so that their sin will not be counted[46] against them.

VERSE 16. Upon the Israel of God.

Here, he links together the false apostles and the Jews, who gloried in their ancestors, boasted that they were God's people, and had the law. It's as if he had said, "Those who are the Israel of God are those who together with Abraham the faithful believe in the promises of God already offered up in Christ, whether they are Jews or Gentiles, but not those who according to the flesh were conceived by Abraham, Isaac, and Jacob." We have already dealt with this topic previously in chapter 3.

---

[44] A small shaved circle at the crown of the monk's head.
[45] The Franciscan monks use a rope belt called a cincture.
[46] *non imputetur.*

VERSE 17. From now on, let no one cause me trouble, for I bear on my body the marks of Jesus [NIV].

He concludes his epistle with certain indignation. It's as if he had said, "I have faithfully taught the Gospel such as I received it through a revelation from Christ. Whoever doesn't wish to follow it, let him follow what he will so that thereafter no one will cause me any more trouble. In a word, this is my verdict, that Christ, about whom I have preached, is the only High Priest and Savior of the world. Thus let the world march forward along this norm, of which I have spoken here and throughout this entire epistle. Otherwise, let the world perish forever!"

VERSE 17. For I bear on my body the marks of Jesus [NIV].

Just as the Minorites interpret the previous sentence, "Peace and mercy be upon all who walk by this rule," as relating to their order, they also similarly interpret this statement, that its meaning is found within the marks found on their Francis, that's what they say on the subject. But I sustain that this is nothing but vain imagination and an empty game. For although Francis would have carried the mark on his body (such as they draw it), it was not pressed on his body because of Christ! Instead, Francis himself put it on himself due to a foolish devotion, or rather an empty arrogance, for then he could boast that he now was so beloved by Christ that He had drawn his wounds on his body.

This is the true meaning of this text: "That the marks I bear on my body thoroughly demonstrate whose servant I am. If I wished to please people requiring circumcision and the observance of the law as necessary for salvation and glory in your flesh as the false apostles have done, I would not necessarily bear these marks on my body. But because I am a servant of Jesus Christ and walk according to the norm of truth—that is, I openly teach and confess that no one is able to obtain God's favor, righteousness, and salvation except through Christ alone then I am obligated to bear the emblems of Christ my Lord. I did not strive to get these marks, but they were placed on me against my own will, by the world and the devil, for no other reason than for preaching that Jesus is the Christ!"

Thus he calls the wounds and sufferings he carried on his body "marks." Also included are the fiery darts from the devil, the anguish and terror of spirit. He also mentions these sufferings throughout all his epistles, just as Luke mentions them in Acts. "For I think," he said, "that God has exhibited us apostles as last of all, like men sentenced to death; because we have become a spectacle to the world, to angels and to men" (1 Corinthians 4:9, 11–13). Further, he said, "To this very hour we go hungry and thirsty, we are in rags, we are brutally treated, we are homeless. We work hard with our own hands. When we are cursed, we bless; when we are persecuted, we endure it; when we are slandered, we answer kindly. We have become the scum of the earth, the garbage of the world—right up to this moment." Also, in another text, he says, "Rather, as servants of God we commend ourselves in every way: in great endurance; in troubles, hardships and distresses; in beatings, imprisonments and riots; in hard work, sleepless nights and hunger; in purity, understanding, patience and kindness; in the Holy Spirit and in sincere love" (2 Corinthians 6:4-5, NIV). Once again, he states, "I have worked much harder, been in prison more frequently, been flogged more severely, and been exposed to death again and again. Five times I received from the Jews the forty lashes minus one. Three times I was beaten with rods, once I was pelted with stones, three times I was shipwrecked, I spent a night and a day in the open sea, I have been constantly on the move. I have been in danger from rivers, in danger from bandits, in danger from my fellow Jews, in danger from Gentiles; in danger in the city, in danger in the country, in danger at sea; and in danger from false believers" (2 Corinthians 11:23-26, NIV).

These are the true stamped marks and signs of which the apostle talks in this text. We ourselves today, by the grace of God, bear the same on our bodies because of Christ, for the world persecutes and kills us, false believers hate us with mortal hatred, internally Satan frightens us with his fiery darts, and for no other reason than we teach that Christ is our righteousness and life.[47] We did not choose to bear these marks just to fulfill a sweet devotion; neither did we commit to gladly suffer them. Rather, they have been pressed on us by the world and the devil because of Christ. We see ourselves compelled to suffer them, and we rejoice in the Spirit, together with Paul (who is always willing, he glories and rejoices) that we bear them in our body, for they are a seal and trusted witness of the true doctrine and faith. As I said before, Paul said these things with certain displeasure and indignation.

VERSE 18. The grace of our Lord Jesus Christ be with your spirit, brothers and sisters. Amen [NIV].

This is his last farewell. He concludes the epistle with the same words he used at the beginning. It's as if had said, "I have taught Christ to you with all purity, I have urged you, I have reproached you, I have not left anything undone that would be of benefit to you. There is nothing else I could have told you. But with all my heart I pray that our Lord Jesus Christ bless and multiply my effort and govern you by His Spirit throughout eternity."

This then is the exposition on the Epistle of Paul to the Galatians. The Lord Jesus Christ, our Justifier and Savior, has given me the grace and the faculties to expound on this epistle and similarly to you to have heard it. May He also preserve and establish me and you[48] (this is my heart's greatest desire). Thus we may grow

---

[47] *docemus Christum justitiam et vitam nostrum esse.*

[48] *idem conservet et confirmet me et vos.*

daily more and more in the knowledge of His grace and faith, and faking nothing,[49] may we be found without fault and guilt on the day of our redemption. To Him, together with the Father and the Holy Spirit, be the glory forever and ever without end. Amen.[50]

Luke 2

"Glory to God in the highest,
And on earth peace,
goodwill toward men!" (NKJV)

Isaiah 40

"The word of our God shall stand for ever." (KJV)[51]

---

[49] *non simulata.*
[50] *sacecula saeculoru, amen.*
[51] These two texts appear at the end of the early editions.

Bible Versions Used in the Translation[1]

BBE—Bible in Basic English

CEB—Common English Bible

CJB—Complete Jewish Bible

CEV—Contemporary English Version

DARBY—Darby Translation

DLNT—Disciples' Literal New Testament

DRA—Douay-Rheims 1899 American Edition

GNB—Good News Bible

GNT—Good News Translation

HCSB—Holman Christian Standard Bible

JUB—Jubilee Bible 2000

KJV—King James Version

KJ21—21st Century King James Version

LEB—Lexham English Bible

MEV—Modern English Version

NABRE—New American Bible (Revised Edition)

NASB—New American Standard Bible

NIRV—New International Reader's Version

NIV—New International Version

NKJV—New King James Version

NLV—New Life Version

NRSV—New Revised Standard Version Bible

RSV—Revised Standard Version

VULGATE (382 A.D.)—Eusebius Sophronius Hieronymus

WEB—World English Bible

WYC—Wycliffe Bible 2001

---

[1] Given Luther's penchant for innovation and breaking with tradition, were he to have dictated these lectures today, he most certainly would have used these modern versions and then some!

About the Latin Text

There are five early editions of the Latin text of Luther's *Lectures on Galatians*. In the Weimar Edition's introduction to Luther's *Commentary on Galatians,* these are listed as *A, B, C, D,* and *E.* Editions *A* and *B* correspond to the year 1535.[1] There are no differences in the Latin text between these two. Each just had a different publisher. Editions *C, D,* and *E* correspond to the years 1538 (*C*), 1543 (*D*), and 1546 (*E*).[2] The Latin text in all *CDE* editions is the same. However, there are differences between the Latin text of *AB* and *CDE* in nuances of syntax, word order, word choice, or additional phrases expanding and clarifying the content throughout the entire text.

The main Latin text in the Weimar Edition (WA[1] 40) is the *AB,* or the first publication text (1535). However, every change or revision made in *CDE* is referenced in the footnotes. There are hundreds of these minor changes. The Weimar editors of Luther's *Commentary on Galatians* do not reference anywhere in the *CDE* editions where there might be an explanation as to why and how the changes were made or who was responsible for the re-editing. Nor do the Weimar editors offer their own explanation. We can only speculate. We do know that George Rörer, Caspar Cruciger, and Veit Deitrich were involved in the note-taking, with Rörer foremost among them. The Weimar edition does provide Rörer's notes, interspersed with a few of the others. The Weimar edition conveniently has Rörer's notes at the top of the page, followed by the actual *AB* Latin text at the bottom half of the page, followed by the footnotes that reference the changes made in *CDE.* In fact, in the footnotes, every reference to a change is followed by the initials *CDE,* indicating those editions.[3] In looking at all three sections, a pattern begins to emerge, which only leads to an informed assumption with regard to the changes in *CDE.* Rörer's notes, of course, are concise. Obviously, these were taken as prompts to remember Luther's words. The *AB* Latin text represents the first transcript of lectures given by Luther as remembered by Rörer and his assistants. There is no reason to doubt or distrust their memory, as they re-created Luther's spoken lectures from their notes. However, the *AB* text tends to be more concise. I am of the impression that Rörer et al. sought to correct the all too concise *AB* text

---

[1]   WA 40[1], 13.

[2]   WA 40[1], 13, 14.

[3]   Rather than detracting from the text, the alterations include clarification and emphatic sentences, preference for other synonyms, and changes in sentence structure, which instead of amending the meaning, enhance and clarify the 1535 text.

in the following edition *C* (1538). *D* (1543) and *E* (1546) are copies of *C* and contain no further changes. When Rörer and assistants prepared edition *C*, it is not improbable that they re-read out loud the Latin text and remembered phrases and explanations they had not included in the *AB* editions. It is also not at all improbable that Luther, having an outstanding memory himself, helped them with further recall. In his "Preface to the Commentary," Luther himself says that he could not believe *tam verbossum fuisse me* with respect to the abundance of words he used during his lectures and reported in the text. The *CDE* versions, in my estimation, contain the more complete rendition of Luther's thought on Galatians.

Thus for the purposes of this translation into modern English, and assuming that the *CDE* versions represent Luther's most complete exposition on Galatians, I have used the *CDE* Latin text instead of the *AB* Latin text as the more accurate record of his lectures.

However, there is a more significant and decisive reason for my use of the *CDE*. This version, the more complete version of Luther's *Commentary on the Epistle to the Galatians,* has never been translated into modern English. Jarislav Pelikan, notwithstanding his landmark translation of 1963, translated the more concise version *AB*.[4] Thus this is the first time a readers' edition of Luther's complete *Commentary on the Epistle to the Galatians* is available to modern English readers (2017ff).

I have used the *CDE* text as it appears in Johann Konrad[5] Irmischer's 1843–44 edition of the Latin text, since it was more readily available to me both online and in hard copy. Irmischer's edition of Luther's lectures on Galatians is also referenced in the Weimar edition as one of the latter editions of the *CDE* text.[6] Irmischer's significant contribution to the collection of Luther's works is part of the heritage surrounding the history, collection, and custody of those works. Together with J. G. Plockmann, J. K. Irmischer co-edited *Dr. Martin Luther's sämmtliche Werke*[7] and also contributed to the supplementary *D. Martini Lutheri Exegetica Opera Latina,* 33 vols. (Erlangen: Heyder, 1829ff). These two were held as one single collection of Luther's works. The first held both English and Latin works, and the supplement held only Latin works. Irmischer's edition of Luther's *Commentary on Galatians* is volume 12 of the supplementary collection, commonly cited as *Lutheri Op. exegete,* vol. XII. Hurst in his *History of the Christian Church* considered

---

[4] Jaroslav Pelikan, "Introduction to Volume 26," in *Luther's Works, The American Edition,* 55 vols., ed. Jaroslav Pelikan and Helmut T. Lehmann (St. Louis: Concordia, 1955–86), 26:x.

[5] This name is sometimes spelled "Conrad" in the academic literature. Also found in the literature as T. K. Irmischer.

[6] WA 40¹, 14.

[7] *Dr. Martin Luther's sämmtliche Werke,* ed. J. G. Plochmann and J. K. Irmischer, 67 vols. (Erlangen: Heyder und Zimmer, 1826ff). For a digital catalog that includes a viewable edition of each volume, see https://catalog.hathitrust.org/Record/008627458.

the Irmischer/Plockmann collection as one of the three standard editions of his time and as a "complete and critical" edition of Luther's works.[8] Philip Schaff in his landmark *History of the Christian Church* cites the *Opera Latina* as one of his main references for Luther's works.[9]

These two collections of Luther's works preceded the Weimar edition and are occasionally referred to and cited as *EA* (Erlanger Ausgabe). Irmischer published not only Luther's *Commentary on Galatians* (1531/1535) but also the *Small Catechism*.[10] Both of these are also included in *Lutheri Exegetica Opera Latina*. It seems appropriate that on the 500th anniversary of the Reformation (1517), we pay tribute to these transitional collections of Luther's works and their editors. For many years, before the Weimar edition became the academic standard for Luther's works, these editions were used for the publication and republication of the Reformer's Latin texts. Their careful copying, editing, and publishing of Luther's works is also a significant and indispensable part of his legacy.[11] This contribution is enhanced, since Irmischer's Latin text is so far the only stand-alone text available online[12] and thus contributes to the transmission of the text to future generations.

The intended purpose of my translation is for a twenty-first-century English lay reader to hear Luther's lectures as a transcript of his spoken Latin and as a stand-alone historical event. Thus my translation in its critical apparatus mostly cross-references previous English translations (rather than German renditions),

---

[8]   John Fletcher Hurst, *History of the Christian Church*, vol. 5 (New York: Eaton & Mains, 1900), quoted in George R. Crooks and John F. Hurst, *Library of Biblical and Theological Literature*, vol. 8 (New York: Eaton & Mains, 1900). Although Hurst's judgment may be considered as dated (1900), none of the three standard editions he lists (Walch, Plockmann/Irmischer, and Weimar) have been superseded neither has any one of them nullified the others as invalid. All three are still considered standard and served a useful purpose in their time.

[9]   Cited in Philipp Schaff, bibliography of *History of the Christian Church*, vol. 7 (New York): "The Erlangen-Frankfurt ed. by Plochmann, Irmischer, and Enders, etc., Erlangen, and Frankfurt a. M., 1827 sqq., 2d ed., 1862–83, 101 vols. 8vo. (not yet finished). German writings, 67 vols.; Opera Latina, 25 vols.; Com. in Ep. and Gal., 3 vols."

[10]   Martin Luther, *Dr. Martin Luthers kleiner katechismus: Nebst der evangelischen glaubens-und sittenlehre, entworfen von d. Georg Friedrich Seiler, umgearb. von d. Johann Konrad Irmischer* (Leipzig: F. Fleischer, 1834).

[11]   For visual presentation of this edition which remained without major modifications see: https://play.google.com/books/reader?id=8LNFAAAAIAAJ&printsec= frontcover&output=reader&hl=en&pg=GBS.PR3. For the presentation of the Weimar edition, please see: https://archive.org/stream/werkekritischege40luthuoft#page/n7/mode/2up. The Irmischer edition retains the Latin frontispiece and the Roman type. The Irmischer edition retains the Latin text and font style of the *CDE* editions. The Weimar edition (WA 40) changes the font styles to Gothic type.

[12]   With the exception of the *ABCDE* texts found in the Weimar edition. However, this is not a stand-alone readers' edition, but a technical, academic edition with important introductions and critical notes in German.

such as Erasmus Middleton and Philip S. Watson's well-known English editions.[13] Watson's work is based on Middleton, and Middleton based his work on the republications of the earliest English translation of 1575.[14] It is noteworthy that Middleton's English edition of Luther's *Commentary on Galatians* (which he compared to the Latin texts available to him) predated the Weimar edition by at least half a century!

While translating, I dealt directly with the Latin text as a transcript of Luther's lectures and then rendered the text for a twenty-first-century English lay reader. The present modern English translation embraces Luther's Latin lectures on Galatians transmitted in the Irmischer text. Whenever I encountered a particularly difficult passage (which was often) I referenced the Weimar edition's Latin text for a cross check on accuracy of the text. However, I found consistent accuracy between the Irmischer text and the operative Latin texts used by the Weimar editors. Although my claim is that this is a modern English edition seeing light within North American spoken English and culture, it is offered as a continuation of the English translations begun in 1575; furthered by Middleton, Watson, and Pelikan[15]; and based on the Latin texts of 1535[16] and 1538, 1543, and 1546.[17] Soli Dei Glori.

Haroldo S. Camacho, PhD

November 16, 2017

---

[13] Erasmus Middleton, *A Commentary on Saint Paul's Epistle to the Galatians. To Which Is Prefixed, the Life of the Author, and a Complete and Impartial History of the Times in Which He Lived* (London: B. Blake, 1838). A bibliographic reference in this work contains this citation: "This translation first published in 1575." See: https://babel .hathitrust.org/cgi/pt?id=nnc1.50175181;view=1up;seq=7.

Watson, Philipp S. *A Commentary on St. Paul's Epistle to the Galatians* (London: James Clarke, 1953).

[14] However, Middleton does not provide any other introduction for his work except the one provided by Edwinus London for the first English translation, dated April 28, 1575. This was the first English translation. Thus Middleton sees his work as a republication of the earliest English translation. However, as stated by Watson, Middleton does not make any reference to which Latin text he used. He sees his work as a faithful republication of the first English translation.

Of the first English translators, Edwinus London says: "They refuse to be named, seeking neither their own gain nor glory, but thinking it their happiness, if by any means they may relieve afflicted minds, and do good to the church of Christ, yielding all glory to God, to whom all glory is due." As cited by Middleton in his introduction.

[15] Important abridgments and paraphrases of Luther's works are not considered in this listing.

[16] *AB* as per Weimar 40^1, 13.

[17] *CDE* as per Weimar 40^1, 14.

Translator's Notes

Although the claim of this translation is that it is a twenty-first-century, modern English version of Luther commenting on Galatians, it stands in the tradition of several English versions since the first English translation of 1575. In more recent times, Erasmus Middleton's 1807 popular English version (in Victorian English), signaled a renewed interest among English speakers in this commentary. However, due to no fault of his own, it is incomplete. The first Elizabethan translators of 1575, who chose to remain anonymous, left out important and significant sections of the Latin text when they translated into English. Their reasoning was that those portions would offend the Zwinglians, who differed from Luther's teaching on the Sacraments. These sections were later rescued by Phillip Watson in his watershed version of 1953. Watson also provided a compelling and masterful history of the commentary.[1] However, Watson retained the Victorian English found in Middleton and the previous versions, which is difficult to read for a twenty-first-century lay reader. The modern English version now in your hands also rescues and translates those sections, and they are noted in the text with italics. As the careful reader will observe, the Elizabethan translators also omitted portions that vigorously defend the article of justification. Their redactions were not limited to sections dealing only with the Sacramentarian controversy.

Commendable attempts have been made to have Luther speak modern English. Among these is J. P. Fallows's abridgment of 1939. A shorter paraphrase is that of Theodore Graebner of 1949. Although more readable, these versions give us the editors' paraphrases of Luther's thought but not Luther's own words. Sometimes they even take us down the wrong path. For instance, Graebner translates imputatio justitiae as "transfusion of righteousness." Luther would have winced at having "imputed righteousness" mean "transfusion of righteousness." That definition would have coincided with "infused righteousness," which is the very concept Luther opposed in Roman Catholic theology, which the Roman Catholic Church later defended by the Council of Trent. Luther rediscovered that "imputed righteousness" was "counted as righteous," or "declared righteous." Imputation means that the righteousness of Christ is credited to the sinner's behalf by faith alone and due to Christ's work alone.

Although it is not a "standalone" work, the greatest contribution in contemporary English is Jaroslav Pelikan's rendition of the commentary in volumes 26 and 27 of Luther's Works, The American Edition. His 1963 version unquestionably will

---

[1] Please see appendix "Translator's Bibliography."

stand as the landmark translation of Luther's commentary into post-Elizabethan English. Although certainly not his intention, Pelikan's masterful translation skills, his choice of paraphrase versus accuracy when clarity was the overriding norm,[2] and his fluid syntax and sentence structure incorporates his English translation of the commentary into the entire opus and literary style of his translations of Luther's works. Thus, Pelikan's virtuosity as a translator perhaps has mitigated against hearing, seeing, and reading Luther's 1531 Lectures on Galatians as a unique historical event at the Wittenberg seminary.

Throughout these forty-one lectures, Luther was now the experienced and Gospel-filled Reformer. He had successfully engaged the papacy on several fronts, particularly on the issues of law versus grace, faith versus works, imputed versus infused righteousness. He was at the pinnacle of his exegetical, hermeneutical, and expository skills. In my translation of the commentary, we can see and hear that Luther expounding on the Epistle to the Galatians. This translation does not smooth out the rough edges of Luther's speech and does not pretend to convert his spoken lectures into a literary work. Neither is it my intention to set aside or substitute any of the existing aforementioned and outstanding English translations.

My purpose is to recreate the 1531 event, from July 3 to December 12 of that year and, as much as possible, render those 41 lectures into twenty-first-century modern English.[3] I take it at face value that George Rörer's notes represent a transcript of Luther's lectures. At that time, he was one of Luther's student assistants and, aided by Veit Dietrich and Caspar Cruciger, took careful notes in a Latin shorthand of their own invention and later compiled them for publication. Luther proofread and approved them as well, adding some of his own notes and redactions. The final Latin edition represented his thoughts on Galatians as he declares in his preface.

However, the final Latin edition represented more than his thought on Galatians. It represented his actual exposition on Galatians in the Wittenberg seminary lecture hall, with Martin Luther, Doctor in Divinity, at the podium. Rörer's Latin edition, which has been preserved through several editions to the present, is as close as we have to a transcript of Luther's lectures. He thus accomplished, to a limited degree, what an eager student would have done today: captured Luther's lectures digitally or on videotape.

---

[2] In his general introduction to *Luther's Works, The American Edition*, Pelikan states, "Where literal accuracy and clarity have conflicted, it is clarity that we have preferred, so that sometimes paraphrase seemed more faithful than literal fidelity" (vol. 26, p. 5).

[3] I have placed within the text the approximate starting point of each lecture by lecture number, day and date when it was given. This organization of the text by lectures may be helpful for church groups, retreats, college and seminary classes in the study and reading of the lectures. To this end, I have followed Rörer's notes found in the Weimar edition of the Latin text.

The Latin spoken by Luther throughout the lectures is far from a classical Latin. Instead, it is a vernacular or Vulgar Latin, mixed with a smattering of Latin academic language reflecting the strong influence of Luther's training as an Augustinian monk and priest. For good measure, Luther also throws in a scattering of Hebrew and Greek terms that he assumed were familiar to his seminarians.[4]

One difficulty of the Latin text is Luther's seemingly bad habit of not knowing when to bring a paragraph to a close. One long paragraph may actually be one sentence punctuated by many commas. My assumption is that this was Rörer's way of indicating pauses in speech, after each comma, as Luther allowed for some time for his arguments to "sink in." Many times, each sentence fragment will stand on its own as a complete sentence. When I first began this translation, these endless sentences were too wordy, and it was easy to get lost within the paragraph. Thus I took the liberty to place a period rather than a comma because in English a period rather than a comma would indicate a pause in spoken speech. There are some difficult passages where a verb or the subject noun or an adjectival phrase may be missing. My assumption is that these are not difficulties at all, or grammatical lapses, but indicate pauses where Luther intended the young seminarians to finish filling the sentence with the appropriate verb or noun as indicated by the theological context of his lecture. I believe these seeming grammatical lapses are actual indications of Luther's spoken lecture and reflect an accurate transcript of each lecture.

Luther was always concluding, even several times within one paragraph. He would go from one "ideo" to "igitur" to "itaque" and other synonyms, building on each conclusion until he closed the entire section with one final and powerful "ergo." Again, these "therefores" point to the spoken word by which a good expositor will build an argument and close off the entire section with one powerful and persuasive argument.

The Bible texts used throughout this version are from the RSV unless otherwise noted. In some instances, the text from the NIV or other modern versions approximates Luther's biblical quotes. Luther knew many texts by memory. However, since at times he lectured extemporaneously and from memory, his quotes from the Latin Vulgate are not always precise. I have attempted to include as accurately as possible all the Biblical references given in the Latin text.[5] However, as I studied the way Luther quoted Scriptures, and cited Biblical references, I found that he practiced what many preachers and teachers do today

---

[4] "Most apparently, the latter commentary reads much less like a scholarly work of textual exegesis, and something more like a set of sermons or a polemical treatise." David C. Fink, "Martin Luther on Galatians," 7, https://www.academia.edu/7895640/Martin_Luther_on_Galatians.

[5] Rörer included many supporting references in the margin to his Latin text. I did not include these. In keeping with my assumption that the Latin text is a transcript of Luther's lectures, I only included the references within the text. There are a few

when quoting Scriptures. Sometimes Luther remembers a phrase, an entire text, or a few words from a Biblical text, and quotes these as he speaks. However, more often than not, he did not provide specific Biblical reference for the text he quoted. At other times he did. Sometimes Luther only provided the chapter and not the verse, as if he remembered just the chapter where the reference was found but not the specific verse. This also happens to the best of preachers and teachers today. It seems as if Luther's prepared class notes had a list of certain Biblical texts he wanted to reference with regards to the specific Galatians text he was expounding. Thus he quoted and referenced these throughout his lectures. However, he quoted many Biblical passages without giving the Biblical reference. In most instances, I have found published English translations that most closely follow Luther's quotes, or I have translated them directly from the Latin. I have noted these instances in the footnotes. The fact that neither Luther nor his assistants filled in the missing Biblical references when they republished the lectures in 1538, is further evidence to me that they intended for the 1531 lectures to be transmitted as a verbatim record of his spoken lectures. Luther's use of Biblical references when teaching and preaching opens an interesting and helpful area of study for anyone willing to pursue it. With regards to the critical apparatus, I have included many footnotes citing the Latin text so as to provide the flavor of the original for the more than casual student. Further, these Latin footnotes will help the reader understand the context for many of the Latin "sola" phrases that were in common usage in theological circles during and after the Reformation. Luther added some footnotes to the Latin text, and when I have included them, I have noted them as Luther's own footnotes. The reader must also remember that Luther was not addressing the average citizen during these lectures. He was addressing these lectures to seminarians well versed already in Latin, Greek, and philosophy, among other disciplines. At times, Luther used theological terms that I felt would lose their impact if I tried to find a modern English equivalent. Further, the historical context of the lectures and the issues at stake during the Reformation would be diminished by removing specific theological terminology. Thus, I let the terminology stand clarifying or explaining them in the footnotes.

The twenty-first-century English reader may ask, what about gender inclusive language? I struggled with this issue. The theological milieu of Luther's time was male dominated, and theological discussions had no second thought about how they would impact the other gender. Whenever the context addresses the theological establishment, I have left the male dominant language. However, whenever Luther is applying the Gospel to all in general I have attempted to make the language as gender inclusive as possible. Otherwise, I beg the readers' "bearing

---

exceptions where in my opinion the Biblical reference was a significant aid in understanding the translated passage.

that burden for me," for I confess this is a matter that could still be improved throughout this version.

I have attempted to follow Luther's main guideline for translating. The original language is translated to the target language as if one were speaking or writing originally in the target language. This is particularly true when Luther used idiomatic expressions known in his time, whether from the German or the Latin. Whenever these are found in the original Latin text, I chose corresponding modern English phrases or idiomatic expressions that most closely approximate the Latin original intent. Whether I have been successful in all these tasks, the reader will judge. But my greatest wish is that the reader will conclude that he or she has been justified by faith alone through the righteousness of Christ alone and to God's glory alone.

Haroldo S. Camacho, PhD (Claremont School of Theology, 1991)

Certified Court Interpreter, Judicial Council of California

Cathedral City, CA

November 16, 2017

Translator's Bibliography

Carson, D. A. "The Vindication of Imputation." In *Justification: What's at Stake in the Current Debate*, edited by M. Husbands and D. J. Treier, 46–78. Westmont: InterVarsity Press, 2004.

Pelikan, Jaroslav. "Introduction to Volume 26." Vol. 26 of *Luther's Works, The American Edition*. Edited by Jaroslav Pelikan and Helmut T. Lehmann, x. St. Louis: Concordia, 1955–86.

Luther, Martin. *Commentary on the Epistle to the Galatians*. Translated by Theodore Graebner. St. Louis: Project Wittenberg, Robert E. Smith Walther Library Concordia Theological Seminary, 2018.

———. *Dr. Martin Luther's sämmtliche Werke*. Edited by J. G. Plochmann and J. K. Irmischer. 67 vols. Erlangen: Heyder und Zimmer, 1826ff. For a digital catalog that includes a viewable edition of each volume, see https://catalog.hathitrust.org/Record/008627458.

Schaff, Philip. *History of the Christian Church*. Vol. 7. New York.

Luther, Martin. *Dr. Martin Luthers kleiner katechismus: Nebst der evangelischen glaubens-und sittenlehre, entworfen von D. Georg Friedrich Seiler, umgearbeitet von D. Johann Konrad Irmischer*. Leipzig: F. Fleischer, 1834.

Middleton, Erasmus. *A Commentary on Saint Paul's Epistle to the Galatians. To Which Is Prefixed, the Life of the Author, and a Complete and Impartial History of the Times in Which He Lived*. London: B. Blake, 1838.

Watson, Philipp S. *A Commentary on St. Paul's Epistle to the Galatians*. London: James Clarke, 1953.

Luther, Martin. *D. Martin Luthers Werke*. Kritische Gesamtausgabe. WA 40. Weimar: Hermann Böhlaus Nachfolger, 1911.

https://www.lutheranworld.org/sites/default/files/Joint%20Declaration%20on%20the%20Doctrine%20of%20Justification.pdf.

http://www.vatican.va/roman_curia/pontifical_councils/chrstuni/documents/rc_pc_chrstuni_doc_31101999_cath-luth-joint-declaration_en.html.

https://www.firstthings.com/blogs/firstthoughts/2010/03/a-betrayal-of-the-gospel-the-joint-declaration-on-the-doctrine-of-justification.

Index

225, 229, 234, 238, 240, 241, 244,
256, 261, 266, 267, 269, 274, 281,
282, 293, 302, 303, 305, 306, 312,
315, 316, 319, 349, 354, 357, 385,
390, 391, 415, 417, 418, 420, 421,
423, 425, 426, 428, 429, 430, 450,
457, 458, 459, 461, 463, 467, 469,
470, 475, 478, 522
justified by Christ, 119, 123, 247, 306
justified by faith, 44, 62, 68, 70, 114, 116,
117, 129, 131, 176, 177, 179, 191,
204, 206, 208, 210, 215, 225, 226,
240, 241, 249, 251, 305, 320, 325,
387, 390, 421, 424, 425, 524, 538
justified by the law, 64, 100, 119, 120, 123,
133, 144, 157, 171, 173, 180, 203,
208, 218, 219, 240, 262, 281, 286,
299, 303, 306, 353, 354, 355, 356,
358, 390, 412, 415, 416, 417, 459
justified in Christ, 119, 120, 124
Justifier and Redeemer, 120
justify, xx, 52, 54, 70, 71, 87, 96, 98, 99,
100, 101, 104, 106, 112, 114, 116,
119, 120, 121, 124, 125, 127, 131,
134, 136, 139, 144, 145, 148, 154,
155, 156, 158, 159, 171, 173, 176,
179, 182, 183, 187, 200, 205, 206,
207, 212, 215, 219, 221, 222, 223,
228, 231, 233, 234, 239, 261, 263,
265, 266, 267, 268, 269, 270, 275,
276, 280, 281, 282, 286, 287, 290,
291, 293, 302, 305, 306, 319, 327,
348, 349, 352, 355, 358, 383, 388,
401, 409, 415, 417, 419, 420, 428,
459, 481, 516

K

kenodoxia, 487
Kraus de Halle, 168

L

Lamb of God, 19, 115, 121, 124, 128,
185, 243, 244, 250
last will and testament, 257, 259, 260
law and grace, 121, 122, 129, 390
law is good, holy, and just, 123, 216
law of God, xxiii, 38, 56, 62, 116, 117,
118, 119, 121, 159, 171, 290, 307,
352, 470
law of Moses, 19, 34, 52, 61, 64, 89, 122,
129, 132, 151, 160, 175, 178, 182,
191, 242, 244, 252, 253, 257, 319,
322, 351, 359, 393, 419, 521
lawgiver, 305, 310, 323, 434
leaven, xx, 308, 434, 436, 437, 443
Lebanon, 314
legalists, 14, 196, 216, 219, 260, 273,
293, 303, 349, 354, 401, 449, 456,
478, 480, 481, 483
legislator, 56, 92, 125, 127, 153, 154,
227, 322, 323, 326, 413
Life of Caesar, 165
Lives of Our Fathers, 499
Lives of the Fathers, 126, 165, 474
Lord's Supper, 31, 195, 371, 474, 495
love as an instrument of faith, 429

M

Macarius, 165, 166, 168
Macedonians, 18
Madame Law, 264
Manicheans, 454
Martha, 185
Mary, 29, 130, 185, 195, 229, 230, 242,
251, 322, 369, 403, 473
mass, 19, 53, 101, 107, 113, 117, 131,
155, 172, 192, 308, 429, 435, 476,
480, 518

R

reason, xv, xvi, xxiv, 1, 8, 13, 14, 17, 21,
25, 26, 28, 29, 35, 38, 42, 44, 45, 48,
49, 50, 52, 57, 58, 59, 60, 67, 69, 70,
71, 72, 75, 88, 90, 91, 92, 93, 95,
101, 104, 111, 117, 125, 126, 127,
133, 134, 138, 139, 143, 149, 150,
153, 155, 159, 167, 172, 173, 178,
181, 184, 186, 191, 193, 195, 196,
197, 198, 200, 201, 202, 203, 205,
207, 208, 213, 215, 226, 227, 230,
231, 232, 233, 236, 239, 249, 250,
251, 254, 261, 265, 266, 267, 268,
276, 277, 281, 282, 283, 284, 288,
290, 298, 300, 301, 302, 303, 305,
306, 308, 313, 318, 321, 323, 324,
326, 328, 330, 335, 338, 342, 346,
347, 351, 355, 356, 359, 362, 367,
368, 370, 392, 394, 397, 399, 400,
404, 408, 409, 415, 416, 425, 426,
427, 428, 435, 438, 443, 444, 449,
451, 452, 453, 466, 468, 472, 479,
480, 481, 493, 499, 501, 502, 504,
505, 507, 508, 509, 512, 515, 517,
518, 519, 521, 525, 526, 530, 531
Rechabites, 258
redemption, xvi, xxvii, 56, 110, 131,
153, 232, 233, 234, 247, 251, 316,
320, 324, 328, 433, 474, 527
religious order, 74, 103, 117, 119, 130,
173, 519
religious philosophers, 99, 147, 198,
231, 232, 233, 234, 235, 241, 243,
251
remission of sins, 13, 14, 19, 66, 88, 94,
97, 101, 104, 108, 111, 112, 128,
135, 155, 173, 193, 205, 227, 239,
257, 271, 291, 295, 297, 310, 330,
383, 393, 455, 471, 474, 477, 486,
496

remnants of sin, 225, 241, 316, 329, 407,
450, 466, 470, 524
residues of sin, 197, 199, 308
resurrection, 8, 9, 10, 11, 72, 133, 134,
135, 140, 160, 193, 313, 323, 343,
373, 411, 420, 474
rhetoric, 74, 160, 161, 188, 351, 361,
424
righteousness cannot be seen or felt,
422
righteousness is imputed, 112, 197
righteousness of Christ, xi, xxv, xxix,
2, 9, 26, 120, 126, 141, 144, 154,
155, 163, 220, 291, 310, 448, 534,
538
righteousness of faith, xxiii, xxiv, xxx, 1,
57, 79, 83, 92, 100, 113, 122, 174,
195, 198, 202, 207, 210, 214, 218,
219, 233, 237, 239, 254, 264, 268,
303, 347, 382, 390, 393, 402, 408,
440, 467
righteousness of God, 8, 135, 153, 175,
219, 243, 247, 252, 353
righteousness of grace, xxv, xxviii, 39,
134
righteousness of the flesh, 30, 39, 187,
214, 264, 318, 451, 515
righteousness of the Gospel, 93
righteousness of the law, xix, xxiii, xxvi,
xxvii, xxviii, xxix, 37, 39, 51, 52,
57, 66, 92, 93, 94, 97, 98, 100, 119,
133, 134, 147, 150, 152, 154, 155,
156, 158, 159, 164, 170, 171, 173,
174, 175, 178, 186, 187, 188, 191,
209, 216, 218, 219, 221, 224, 226,
237, 239, 245, 253, 254, 265, 267,
269, 271, 286, 303, 307, 310, 312,
318, 319, 352, 353, 387, 390, 392,
393, 394, 401, 404, 408, 416, 418,
457, 538

seed (*continued*)
256, 259, 260, 261, 265, 266, 292,
314, 316, 327, 328, 346, 349, 380,
381, 383, 394, 403, 419, 508, 512
self-righteousness, xv, xix, 66, 159, 164,
170, 174, 271, 275, 282, 295, 418,
464, 517
serpent, xviii, 135, 142, 164, 166, 205,
212, 251, 269, 292, 313, 407, 412
serve one another in love, 451, 456
Sin remains in the flesh, 344
Sisyphus, 356
slavery, xx, xxviii, 2, 34, 97, 126, 188,
193, 307, 312, 316, 317, 318, 323,
324, 341, 345, 358, 359, 382, 384,
385, 386, 388, 389, 391, 394, 404,
405, 407, 408, 409, 410, 412, 446,
447, 492
Slay reason and believe in Christ, 200
Sodom and Gomorrah, 11, 113, 434
Solomon, 87, 337, 338, 339
sorcery, 164, 478
sound doctrine, xxx, 6, 32, 59, 191, 361,
362, 374, 376, 432, 454, 513
spade a spade, 124
Staupitz, 49, 92, 466
stimulus carnis, 368
stumbling block of the cross, 441
Suetonius, 165
supererogation, 172
supererogatory works, 148, 290, 403
sweeper woman, 267
synecdoche, 82, 430

T

Ten Commandments, xviii, xxiii, 99,
100, 116, 138, 156, 157, 172, 175,
257, 290, 319, 373, 388, 392, 447
testator, 259

Theology of the Scholastics, 105
Throne of Grace, 168
time of the law, 275, 299, 300, 301, 302,
316, 321
tonsure, 73, 151, 171, 205, 233, 431
transcript, xii, xii, 19, 67, 137, 237, 239,
282, 315, 530, 532, 533, 535, 536
true church, 388
True repentance, 109
tutor, 77, 266, 267, 291, 297, 304, 305,
306, 311, 315, 316, 452, 455

U

uncircumcised, 62, 64, 66, 68, 71, 84,
176, 177, 181, 208, 288, 520
uncircumcision, 77, 80, 81, 82, 84, 428,
429, 515, 520, 521, 522, 524

V

veil, 76, 77, 210, 283, 284, 285, 469
victory, xi, 9, 15, 17, 18, 68, 115, 123,
138, 142, 144, 160, 167, 188, 192,
196, 245, 246, 247, 249, 274, 278,
301, 313, 323, 324, 325, 368, 411,
423, 464, 474, 475, 478
victory of Christ, 9, 102
Vulgate, xxvi, 76, 114, 117, 128, 197,
246, 278, 298, 420, 522, 536

W

we are not justified through love, 461
Weimar Edition, xii, 530
When He died for my sins, I was
granted His righteousness, 433
willpower, 115, 150, 481
wisdom, xiv, xvii, xxv, xxvii, 1, 8, 9, 13,
15, 16, 17, 22, 23, 26, 27, 28, 39, 43,